D0793238

Selwyn Goldsmith studied at Cambridge University and
University College London, becoming a member of the
Royal Institute of British Architects in 1960. He was
appointed in 1961 to undertake the research project leading
to the publication in 1963 of the first edition of *Designing
for the disabled*, followed by a further research programme
in Norwich and the publication of the second edition in 1967.
He was an assistant editor with the *Architects' Journal* for
three years, and since 1972 has been adviser in the
Department of the Environment on housing services for
disabled people.

Designing for the disabled

Designing for the disabled

Third edition, fully revised

Selwyn Goldsmith MA(Cantab), RIBA

First edition published 1963
Second revised edition published 1967
Third revised edition published 1976

© RIBA Publications Limited 1976

ISBN 0 900630 50 7

Diagrams by Louis Dezart
Design and production by Michael Stribbling
and Gordon Burrows
Printed by Jolly & Barber Ltd, Rugby

Published by RIBA Publications Limited
66 Portland Place, London W1N 4AD, England

This publication is copyright under the Berne Convention and
the International Copyright Convention. All rights reserved.
Apart from any fair dealing under the UK Copyright Act 1956,
part 1, section 7, whereby a single copy of an article may be
supplied, under certain conditions, for the purposes of research
or private study, by a library of a class prescribed by the UK
Board of Trade Regulations (Statutory Instruments 1957,
No. 868), no part of this publication may be reproduced, stored in
a retrieval system or transmitted in any form or by any means
without the prior permission of the copyright owners. Multiple
copying of the contents of the publication without permission is
always illegal.

Contents

Arch.
N A
2545
P5
G6
1976

Preface

The first edition of *Designing for the disabled*, published in 1963, was subtitled 'A manual of technical information'. It was a straightforward catalogue of design recommendations for architects. The second edition in 1967, with its introductory commentary exploring underlying psychological, economic and practical issues, saw a shift of emphasis. The process is continued in this third edition, so that while the focus is still primarily on practising architects, there is an orientation also towards the managers who shape the world of handicapped people by administering services and formulating the briefs from which buildings emerge.

In the main, it is as a practical aid that this book will be used. In physical terms, the problems of disabled people are much the same the world over. But while problems may coincide, the ways by which they ought to be resolved may not. Appropriate solutions are governed by the way that services are organized, along with social, economic and cultural influences. In this edition there is an extended examination of enabling legislation in Britain and the machinery of government against which practical decisions are made. For architects and others working outside Britain there will be some circumstances where similar design solutions will be proper, and others where they will not be.

My standpoint as author as this book needs to be made clear. I am employed by the Department of the Environment in London to advise on housing services for disabled people, and it might be supposed that the views I express are in line with current government and departmental policies. On some issues they are, on others not. Where there are differences, they are ones of emphasis. Government policies must respond to broader considerations than the aspirations of disabled people. The business of government, subjected all the time to competing pressures, is to determine priorities; inevitably, conflicts occur, and decisions are made that strike balances. These balances will not give to disabled people all that in an ideal world they might like to have. In respect of building design, what might be desirable for disabled people may have to be subordinated to other controls, such as the maintenance of public safety and the constraints of building budgets.

While the views expressed are mine and not necessarily those of government departments, I have been greatly aided in that I have worked on this book with the encouragement of the senior administrators to whom in my official capacity I am responsible. Many colleagues in a variety of divisions within the Department of the Environment have advised and commented on drafts, often more than once. Valuable advice has come also from officials in the Department of Health and Social Security, the Department of Education and Science, the Department of Employment and the Home Office. In respect of areas where there has not been mutual accord, the generous view of government colleagues has been that the book is mine and it is right that it should reflect my own opinions. Thus any biases apparent in the commentary are an expression of personal views, and, as with any errors of fact that have inadvertently been made, are my responsibility only.

Although the structure of this book is similar to the second edition, the text has been entirely rewritten. In part, this is because there was much that needed revising for practical reasons, in part because I did not like what I had written before, but most because of the large amount of new evidence that has been generated over the past nine years. It is a cause for astonishment that a field virtually untrodden in 1961 when I was first sent in to cultivate it has today become a topic of international concern. There is now a broad public awareness of the obstacles facing disabled people who set about using the buildings which an able-bodied world has fashioned to its own undemanding purposes. It is because of this awareness that so many people are concerned to make buildings fitter places for people with disabilities to use, and there is a continuing job for this book to perform.

There are many people who have contributed in one way or another to the creation of this book. In a category of his own at the head of the list is Louis Dezart, who drew all the diagrams, and did so with phenomenal professionalism, patience and good humour. Next, my special thanks go to Sarah Lomas, information officer with the Disabled Living Foundation, who did valuable work on the preparation of the cost notes and the list of disability-associated organizations. Advice on the glossary and related medical information was helpfully given by Shona Hodgson, John Goodwill and Gil Wenley, on the material on fire protection by Alan Parnell, and on prices for the cost notes by Cedric Crawley.

My thanks are recorded to those who capably and conscientiously tackled the enormous quantity of typing, in particular Georgie, Maggie and Felicity. After that, I am obliged to friends who were supportive and criticized constructively. I have in mind not only professional friends and colleagues, but more especially those who were themselves disabled, and who had a legitimately selfish interest in what I was doing. Above all, I am indebted to Rosalie Wilkins, who kept a check on my uncharitable inclinations, and encouraged me to make this a nicer book than it might otherwise have been.

The notion of a fourth edition is not one that I can for the moment regard with relish. But one day I expect I shall have to start again the mammoth job of taking the book apart and putting it together again. I have learned from experience that appeals for feedback of information will get little response. If there happens, however, to be any architect – or anyone else – who feels prompted to offer observations, corrections or criticism, I shall be delighted to hear from them.

Selwyn Goldsmith
London, May 1976

How the book is arranged

This book is structured in a similar way to the second edition, in nine principal parts.

The commentary in part 1 begins with a brief preamble (section 10). To put the problems of disabled people and buildings into perspective there is first (section 11) an examination of parameters and conflicts, followed by evidence regarding the use of buildings by disabled people (section 12) and a discussion of the psychological issues involved (section 13). From this material, guidelines for architectural action are formulated (section 14). On living arrangements for disabled people there is an analysis of institutions (section 15), an examination of possible housing alternatives (section 16) and a discussion of housing provision for disabled people who are in families or are able to manage independently (section 17).

Anthropometric data and information on wheelchair users and wheelchairs are contained in part 2. The practical data sections which follow are arranged broadly on the pattern of the 1961 SfB classification of building elements (part 3), services installations (part 4) and general spaces (part 5). Parts 6 and 7 deal with buildings other than housing, part 6 covering general requirements for public buildings and part 7 recommendations for individual building types. Housing is the subject of part 8 and part 9 comprises appendices. Principal recommendations are summarized in section 81 for housing and sections 62–64 for public buildings.

The commentary in part 1 is concerned with the development of strategies. Recommendations for tactical implementation for housing are in sections 82–86 and for public buildings in sections 60–61, the latter supplemented where appropriate by comment on individual building types in sections 70–79. The distinction between strategy and tactics is not always a simple one, and nor is that between tactics and detail provision; in consequence there is occasional overlapping between the various parts of the book.

Referencing
To aid cross-referencing and the location of information via the index, a system of decimal subdivision is employed to identify main sections, subsections and individual paragraphs. The first two digits of the reference indicate the main section in which the information is to be found, and these two digits are also used to identify diagrams and tables in the text. In most sections paragraphs are individually numbered; where there are two paragraphs to one number the subparagraph is explanatory comment or supplementary data. Paragraphs are not numbered in part 1: instead there is sequential numbering of crossheadings within each main section.

References to sources of evidence are dealt with by a footnote such as 'Bib 93350', meaning that the source is item 93350, in section 93 which is the bibliography. Items in the bibliography are grouped under subject headings; there is a contents list at the start of section 93.

Dimensional data
Dimensional information is given in metric units only. In the main data sections (20–90) linear dimensions are cited in the style 0·500, meaning 500mm. For designers working in feet and inches, equivalents are to be found in section 95, as also are Imperial conversions for other metric measures.

Commentary

1

1000 The woman who went to church

She was a woman a little over 60, crippled for 25 years by arthritis. When she went out she was pushed in a wheelchair. Yes, she said in answer to my question about the buildings she used, she liked to go to church each Sunday. Yes, there were steps. Might it not be easier, I suggested, if it was all on the level or there was a ramp instead? She thought for a minute. She wasn't sure. What she liked about going to church was having two strong young men to pull her up the steps, and being the centre of attention. If there were no steps perhaps she wouldn't go to church.

The story of the woman who went to church because there were steps is one example of the relationship between buildings and disabled people. It is not typical. If it were, the message of this book would be to leave buildings as they are, because disabled people like them that way. It bears telling because it is challenging. The woman was not behaving in the way that the stereotypes would have her do. According to the rules she ought to have wanted to be independent. She ought not to have enjoyed being helped. She ought to have been disguising her disability. And the message of the steps ought to have been 'keep out' not 'come in'.

What this woman actually did was odd, but not inexplicable. The psychology of disability, as it relates to the use of buildings, is explored later in this commentary, and with the benefit of foresight the woman's behaviour is comprehensible. For the moment it is simplest just to say that she was odd.

1001 Making the most of living

This book is about the interactions between buildings which architects design and the people with disabilities who use them. It is concerned with all sorts of buildings and with all sorts of disabled people. Its theme is that people who are disabled are people who need help from architects, help in the planning of the houses they live in and the design and organization of the buildings they use for work, education, recreation and so on. They need opportunities to participate in the busy life of the world, to be involved, to do the same sort of things that other people do. They need to be able to get the most out of life and they need architects to help them.

The underlying precept of this book is a simple one: the purpose of living is to make the most of being alive. It means realizing one's potential; making use of the talents one is born with and the opportunities and challenges that life affords, to achieve in some measure personal fulfilment. In the action of life the person with a disability is doubly handicapped. First, he is handicapped simply because he does not physically have the capabilities that others have. This can have a variety of effects, causing social, financial and emotional deprivations. Second, he is handicapped because he is perceived by others as handicapped, because there is a social doctrine which says that to have a disability is to be blighted and im-poverished. His better endowed colleagues tend to manage the situation for him so that his opportunities actually are limited, and his performance matches their expectations.

The first kind of handicap can be alleviated by props, usually of a physical character. The second kind is more damaging, in that its cause is culturally entrenched. It cannot be modified by physical remedies. The extreme position postulates that the disabled person is handicapped not on account of his disability at all, but because the cultural mores say so[1]. It is the fault of our society and its competitive value system. To rectify the situation demands a social revolution and a rejection of the prevailing ethos. No amount of tinkering with superficial physical causes can assist. Indeed, the conventional strategy of modification and amelioration by compensation, in essence the strategy endorsed in this book, serves only to exacerbate the position, by reinforcing the already established evaluation of disabled people as deprived and disadvantaged.

While in theory this position may be tenable, it does not in practice afford a viable platform for action. The evidence of history does not indicate that any cultural revolution can be anticipated which, among other things, will radically affect prevailing attitudes to disablement. The policy advocated in this book is therefore one of pragmatism; we need to develop stagies on the basis that our society is as it is, and that, little by little, we must endeavour to reshape it.

There are still problems. The commitment is to the enhancing of opportunities for people with disabilities, and to the enlarging of possibilities for them to participate and be involved in the ordinary busy world. This means channelling resources and utilizing them to best effect. Gloomy prognostications on the state of the universe are not a cause for capitulation. Along with other societies, Britain does not always use available resources either fairly or wisely. A bigger slice of the bounty might be switched in the direction of handicapped people. The slice that there is could in any event be doled out more profitably. Too often the subventions of central and local government and of charitable agencies are employed to perpetuate among handicapped people isolation, lack of opportunity and the maintenance of inferior status. They go to support segregated institutional living, or employment and educational services detached from the mainstream of social advancement. The manifest effect is to stifle opportunity among handicapped people rather than to enhance it.

There are dangers here for architects and others who use this book. In the structuring of buildings aiming to support handicapped people there has to be caution that the results do not serve, by consolidating misguided systems, actually to diminish the lives of handicapped people. The balance may be delicate because policies of segregation are not always unwholesome and polices of normalization, independence and challenge have pitfalls. Not all disabled people have the physical or emotional resources to cope with the challenges of normal living, and some prefer to opt out. Opportunities for opting out

---

[1] For an example see Bib 93314.

there should be; for living in a special community or for employment in a special workshop. But opportunities for opting in are more important, and this is the recurring theme of this book. Having said that, a quick caveat is necessary. I do not advocate the lavishing on handicapped people of unlimited goodies; the opportunities that are offered must be opportunities for them to give, and not always to take.

1002 The economic fallacy

Few of the recommendations for practical action made in this book are supportable on straight economic grounds. Staunch accessibility campaigners may claim that it makes good business sense to plan buildings so that disabled people are able to use them independently; that without usable buildings disabled people cannot work and become productive tax-paying members of the community[2]. They may similarly claim that without suitable housing the community may have to spend heavily to support a disabled person in a hospital or institution.

It does of course make sound economic sense to rehabilitate to tax-paying status a person disabled by disease or injury, and to see that he has an environment in which he can operate efficiently. But it is naive to suppose that there is a simple deterministic relationship between the structure of buildings and the material productiveness of disabled people. And for each person with a severe disability who does have the potential to become financially independent there are many others who do not. Incontestably it costs the community far more to support its chronically disabled members than it can hope to recover from them in return

1003 Antecedents

The first edition of this book, published in 1963, was uncomplicated. There was at the time little relevant published evidence on which to draw, and the result was a catalogue of generally self-evident physical recommendations presented without comment.

With continued support from the Polio Research Fund[3] I subsequently spent four and a half years in Norwich, mostly on fieldwork finding out from handicapped people themselves what their problems actually were, how they managed in their homes and how they coped when they used buildings outside. The second edition was published in 1967 and it reflected in its introductory commentary some of the disillusion provoked by my early inquiries at Norwich. The substance was that disabled people by and large were not as critically handicapped by buildings as I had supposed, that independence, normality and access-ibility were not all-important goals and that there were good reasons why architects had not done all that they might to help.

This third edition has a more positive philosophy. It benefits from a more considered appreciation of the practical difficulties which people with severe disabilities

encounter when they use ordinary buildings and, also, as suggested by the preceding comments, from a more profitable evaluation of the contribution that buildings can make to the scheme of human living. It is not without its personal viewpoints, relating for example to normal able-bodied people, to the medical profession, to disability organizations, to 'special' establishments for disabled people, to 'disabled representatives' and to prevailing disability terminology. These are elaborated on in the discussion which follows, and at this stage brief comment is needed only on consumer representation and disability terminology.

1004 Consumer representation

It is right that people with disabilities should involve themselves in the political processes which affect their lives. But it is important that those who do have empathy with others who are disabled. In the past it has been predominantly capable middle-class people, frequently those with polio, who have been appointed to committees to represent the interests of 'the disabled'. Among people with disabilities there is an understandable tendency to generalize from personal and specific experiences, and to imagine that others respond similarly. The importance of the disability per se as a determining factor in behaviour is exaggerated. It ought instead to be recognized that, according to their resources, individuals who are disabled respond in different ways to the same situation.

Arising from the promotion of the 'disabled representative'[4] is the increasingly widespread notion that it is only disabled people 'who know what it is like to be disabled' and who are qualified to speak on behalf of 'the disabled'. In respect of political activities there is much merit in initiatives coming from involved consumers: in respect of the provision of services the notion is, to say the least, debatable.

1005 Disability terminology

Prevailing attitudes to people with disability are reflected in the vocabulary we use. Most revealing, and irritating, is the indiscriminate use of the term 'the disabled'. It is bald, it is stereotyping, and it categorizes as homogeneous a diverse group of people with no behavioural commonalities on which it is proper to generalize. This book is still called *Designing for the Disabled* because that is how it has always been: in extenuation the generic term 'the disabled' does in this context have some validity, in

---

[2] An illuminating example of this kind of attitude is cited subsequently in 1320.

[3] The Polio Research Fund, as it was then known, initiated *Designing for the Disabled*, in that it financed the project which resulted in the publication of the first edition. The fund now operates (1976) under the slogan 'Action research for the crippled child'.

[4] There are seven sections of the Chronically Sick and Disabled Persons Act 1970 which encourage the appointment of people who are disabled to national advisory committees and local authority committees.

that the book's terms of reference cover all people with physical disabilities in all physical environmental situations.

Because it is offensive the term 'the disabled' is not used at all in this commentary. Instead the expressions are 'people with disabilities', 'people who have disabilities', 'people who are disabled', and 'disabled people'. The last is a phrase which ought wherever possible to be avoided. It is patently contradictory and absurd to talk, as we commonly do, of 'disabled students', 'disabled housewives', 'disabled professionals' or 'disabled drivers'. No one after all, unless he is entirely paralyzed, blind, deaf and irretrievably brain damaged, is totally disabled. It is the negative prefix *dis*abled which is damaging. The hazard is that by emphasizing the absence of desirable attributes in terms of physique, judgements of quite unrelated personality traits may be affected, provoking an evaluation of the individual as being generally inferior. Other terms which we use to describe people with disabilities have the same built-in attitudinal biases: *in*firm, *de*formed, *in*valid and *im*paired.

The vocabulary which people who are disabled attract is often socially devaluing and personally demeaning. Among the words used frequently and unthinkingly are 'victim', 'sufferer' and 'unfortunate'. They betray on the part of those who apply them an attitude of 'Thank goodness I am not like that' and they are words which, along with others of their kind, could helpfully be proscribed.

The term 'cripple' deserves rehabilitation. It has the advantage that it is explicit; the *Shorter Oxford English Dictionary* says: 'One who is disabled (either from birth or by accident or injury) from the use of his limbs; a lame person'. This definition is, for the purposes of this book, wholly appropriate.

The word cripple is pejorative. Any polite person knows that we do not call a person a cripple any more than we call him a bastard. So until the status of cripples improves it cannot be used indiscriminately, as disabled presently is. For the moment the continuing capability of the term cripple to shock is one of its merits; so also is the way it particularizes. Encouragingly, it is becoming more familiarly used among people with disabilities, in part perhaps because of its honesty.

11   Buildings and disabled people: Parameters and conflicts

1100   The determinants of building design

Buildings always have been, are, and always will be, geared to suit two-legged able-bodied people and not people propped on sticks or rolling about in chairs on wheels. This is not an encouraging fashion by which to open a debate calling for buildings to be made accessible to disabled people, but it is reality. It is so because able-bodied people are by definition normal and disabled people are abnormal.

The counter proposition for the disability defence can be anticipated. It argues that nearly all of us will eventually become old and doddery, that nearly all of us will at some stage in life have a temporarily crippling accident or disease, that all of us were at the start clumsy toddlers, and that approaching half of us have had or will have our mobility restrained by pregnancy; all of us therefore can claim handicappedness and will benefit from having buildings suitably organized for wheelchair users and others who are disabled. Mothers who push prams, workers who propel trolleys or remove furniture, undertakers who handle coffins; all these will also gain. The population concerned is not therefore a minority group. It will be convenient for all if there are no steps at building entrances, no awkward threshold sills to trip over, if doors are wider, if window openers are lower, if electric sockets are higher, if doorsprings are lighter, if lifts are bigger, if door handles are more grippable, and if floors are not so slippable on.

To which the comprehensive and simple answer is yes, everyone would benefit. These are all good reasons why buildings ought to be designed to suit people who are disabled. But they do not, however morally beguiling, determine how in actuality buildings are designed.

The way that a building is designed depends on a variety of factors. Most obviously it depends on technical factors; the structure must be sound, and materials efficient. It depends next on geographical and climatic factors, for example topography, altitude, orientation, warmth, cold and humidity. Rain and snow must be kept out, so there is a barrier between inside and outside. Heat has to be kept out or kept in.

There are social factors, meaning the kind of people who can be expected to use the building and the sort of activities they will perform in it, whether they want to be together or apart. Overlapping here are cultural factors, associated with the style of living of the building's users; there are differences for example between the living arrangements of eastern and western cultures, reflected in buildings designed for domestic, religious and recreational purposes. The culture may demand a monumental building or it may want a self-effacing one. Political issues can also intrude; public buildings such as the offices of multi-national corporations are political statements, reflecting the ethic and morality of the organization. Efforts may be made to see that such buildings are visually powerful, technologically efficient or seem welcoming to visitors. Aesthetic factors also have an important role, affected by the architect's ideas of what might be attractive or impressive to look at.

Then there are regulations and legislation. In Britain, for reasons of health and safety, buildings have to conform to the national building regulations, and also to a variety of requirements for protection against fire hazards. They are also subject to planning control, and demands may be made for example regarding siting, density, volume and height. Last, the way that a building is built will depend as much as anything on the matter of cost. The client has a budget, and what he usually wants is a building which serves its purpose without being more expensive than it has to be.

1101   Conflicts and reconciliations

The significance of each of these determinants varies between one building and another, and so does the facility with which they can be reconciled with the criterion of accessibility for disabled people. Each factor competes for attention and inevitably there are conflicts. Political considerations generally favour disabled people, and so commonly do social ones. Cultural considerations are not always sympathetic, in that culture is primarily a function of the behaviour of normal people. Climatic and geographical (particularly topographical) factors, technical considerations and aesthetic influences are generally antagonistic. There is invariably a straight conflict with fire protection requirements.

Financial considerations are also as a rule in direct opposition. The inadmissibility of employing economic criteria to justify the general provision of services for disabled people has already been exposed, and the rule applies equally to special provisions in buildings. By providing facilities supplementary to those which cater adequately for the normal able-bodied population the client can anticipate few if any commercial bonuses.

Without political influences the outlook would be bleak. Since the last edition of this book was written in 1967 there has been an encouraging growth of public awareness and concern about the accessibility of buildings to disabled people, crystallized by legislation in sections 4–8 of the Chronically Sick and Disabled Persons Act 1970. Since 1970 there has been a trail of questions in Parliament relating to the implementation of the Act. There has been constant pressure on local authorities from individuals and voluntary organizations to ensure that they do their duty under the Act. There is therefore more cause for optimism now than there was in 1967 that buildings of the future will generally be manageable by people with disabilities

1102   The principles of anthropometrics

Working at his drawing board the architect does not ordinarily give any searching attention to the physical characteristics of the people who will use his building. Only in particular cases, such as an old people's home, a primary school and occasionally a hospital, does he deliberately think about the attributes of his building users and the possibility that there could be something special about them. In other circumstances he takes it for granted that they will be 'normal' people.

For the typical architect the application of the principles of anthropometrics to the design of his buildings is not an affair of science. He has a rough idea of how tall an average person is, how high he can reach and what sort of steps he can manage comfortably. He also knows that people come in different shapes and sizes, so that it is a good thing to add on a few inches here and take away a few there. If he were a bit more scientific he would enquire about the structure of his population. He would say, for example, that he would like at least 90 per cent of the people using his building to be able to do so comfortably, and he would therefore want to know the operational limits of these 90 per cent. The basis of his calculations would be that his population conforms to what is known statistically as a normal distribution; this assumes that people average out, there are an equal number who are short and tall, and the distribution of their measures is symmetrical. With sufficient statistical evidence to hand in respect of a particular dimension he would be able to predict with some confidence what the measure would be for a person towards the bottom of the range (the 5th percentile) and a person towards the top (the 95th percentile).

Although generally acceptable, the commonly adopted 5 to 95 condition can cause compromise solutions not ideal for anyone. The provision of universal satisfaction is recognized as an unattainable goal, and the requirements of people in the middle become the criterion. The needs of the deviant people who are found in the 5 per cent sectors at the extremities are by common consent ignored. In practice, however, because there is a cut-off in one direction only, it is a matter of critical limits rather than middle ranges, meaning as a rule that either the top 95 per cent or the bottom 95 per cent are accommodated. Examples of design application are the width of doors, the gradient of stairs, the height of window controls and the size of lifts.

It is disabled people who are left out. They are by definition people who are not normal. In at least one crucial respect, such as ability to climb stairs, reach high level window controls, negotiate narrow openings, handle heavy doors or use normal size wc compartments, and frequently in a combination of respects, the disabled person is not to be found among the favoured 95 per cent. If he were he would not be handicapped. This is not to suggest that all disabled people are in all respects abnormal; the completely abnormal person no more exists than the completely average person.

There are two good practical reasons for basing design criteria on the characteristics of people in the normal range. The first is functional. The more a facility is designed for specific purposes the more probable it is that it will be functionally successful; the more universal it attempts to be the more inevitable it is that there will be opposing criteria and hence that a poor compromise will result. An example is the height of a wash basin; the lower it is made for the benefit of short people the more

unsatisfactory it becomes for people of normal height who are the majority of users.

The second reason is economic. The accommodation of people at the extremities will cause additional expense. Consider for example staircases and lifts. Some 98.5 per cent of people other than tiny children can climb stairs without discomfort [1]. In a small building of two or three floors a staircase is, because of its economy, the obvious answer. If the architect is asked to cover the total population, including the odd person in 100 who cannot cope with stairs, a lift has to be installed which adds enormously to the cost of the building.

Where criteria for normal people and disabled people are in conflict there is the difficult problem of deciding what to do about the disabled people. If criteria are just about compatible a little stretching may be in order, but it has to be decided how far it is tolerable to compromise the position of able-bodied people in order to include those with disabilities. If criteria are not reconcilable people with disabilities have to be regarded as a subgroup whose needs should be considered secondarily, though not necessarily secondary, to those of normal people. Conflicts occur only rarely between ambulant disabled people and able-bodied people, and it is therefore generally reasonable for the architect to treat ambulant disabled people as an extension of the normal population. People in wheelchairs on the other hand comprise a distinct population. Because of the abnormal way in which they move around and perform routine activities they pose special problems to the architect. These problems are considered in greater detail later, but at this stage it is helpful to clarify exactly who the disabled people are that this book is concerned about.

1103 Disability and handicap

'Disability' and 'handicap' are not synonymous. A disabled person is not automatically a handicapped person; whether or not there is handicap depends on the nature of the individual's impairment and the circumstances in which he is placed. A blind person for example is not handicapped when he is doing work for which it is not necessary to be able to see. A chairbound person is not handicapped if what he wishes to do can be managed from a wheelchair without difficulty. On the other hand there can be handicap where there is no medically identifiable impairment. A person whose ambition it is to be an international athlete is handicapped if his physical capacities are no more than average. The precept needs to be emphasized: a physical disability is a handicap only where it constitutes a barrier to the achievement of specific goals.

---

[1] This estimate is derived from statistical data in Bib 93730, p98, and in Bib 93270. The same data indicate that approximately 99.5 per cent of people of working age can climb stairs. The number of people who have some difficulty climbing stairs is considerably higher; Bib 93730 estimates that they include some 45 per cent of people aged over 65.

In practice, as is made clear in the pages which follow, it is impossible to attach any neat operational definitions to the concepts of disability and handicap. It is none the less essential to have statistical information if services are to be properly formulated, and attempts to define and measure must be made. In 1967 when the second edition of this book was being prepared there were no comprehensive disability statistics available in Britain and reference was made to a survey carried out in Denmark during 1961 and 1962[2]. A large-scale British equivalent was then being planned; it has since been published in three volumes under the title *Handicapped and impaired in Great Britain*, the first two in 1971 and the third in 1972[3].

1104   The OPCS survey

The survey of handicapped people in Britain, directed by Amelia Harris of the Social Survey Division of the Office of Population Censuses and Surveys (OPCS), was a study 'designed to give reliable estimates of the number of handicapped people aged 16 and over, living in private households in Great Britain, and to examine what local authority health and welfare services were being made available to the handicapped aged 16 and over living in private households to assist them to overcome their disablement as far as possible[4].

The following definitions were used for the survey:

Impairment: (1) lacking part or all of a limb or having a defective limb, or (2) having a defective organ or mechanism of the body which stops or limits getting about, working or self-care.

Disablement: the loss or reduction of functional ability.

Handicap: the disadvantage or restriction of activity caused by disability.

The scale of the survey was massive. A stratified random sample of 249 259 households was approached by post, yielding 13 451 households with one or more persons claiming to be impaired. All identified impaired persons aged under 65 were interviewed, and one in four of those aged 65 or over; the total number interviewed in the sample was 8538, with a successful response rate of 89 per cent. Interviewing was carried out between October 1968 and February 1969.

To establish whether those interviewed were handicapped or impaired, a series of questions was put regarding people's capacity to care for themselves. Each item was scored according to whether it could be managed without difficulty, with difficulty, or only with help. Certain items were deemed more important for the overall assessment than others, and were given double weight.

The major items were:
1. Getting to and using the wc.
2. Eating and drinking.
3. Doing up buttons and zips.
The last was included so that one major item would reflect fine hand movements.

The minor items were:
1. Getting in and out of bed.
2. Having a bath or all-over wash.
3. Washing hands and face.
4. Putting on shoes and stockings.
5. Dressing, other than buttons and shoes.
6. Combing and brushing hair (for women only) or shaving (for men only).

According to his score each respondent was categorized as either (1) having a very severe handicap, (2) having a severe handicap, (3) having an appreciable handicap or (4) having a minor handicap or no handicap. Any person who needed help or had difficulty performing even one of the self-care items was automatically categorized as, at the least, having an appreciable handicap. People who by definition had an impairment but who were not at all handicapped in terms of physically caring for themselves were placed in the fourth category of minor or no handicap. This last group is distinguished as 'the impaired' as against people in the first three groups who are 'handicapped'. The number of adult people in Britain estimated to be handicapped or impaired at the time the study was made was 3 071 000, or 7.80 per cent of the total population. The total number estimated to be handicapped was 1 329 000 or 2.89 per cent.

1105   Information from OPCS survey data

Table 11.1 is an attempt to extract from the OPCS data information of practical relevance, in the expectation that what the architect, housing manager or planner of social services wants is some idea of the extent and pattern of handicap in a population whose overall size is known. By a process of extrapolation from the OPCS tables, in conjunction with official population figures, estimates for a typical population in Britain at the present time (mid-1975) can be made. These figures can only be properly applied to a local population known to have the same age structure as that found nationally, and in practice this is unlikely to occur. Even if this were to obtain, the estimates could still be unreliable owing to the influence of other important variables affecting the prevalence of handicap such as the presence of heavy industry.

It is hazardous therefore to draw inferences in respect of any given locality from the OPCS data, but the table gives some impression of how the incidence of handicap may vary in different kinds of community. Numbers are estimated for two extremes, one a new town population where young people predominate, the other a south coast town population where ageing people predominate; proportionately the latter has approaching three times as many handicapped people as the former. Expressed in terms of the adult population only, the percentage for the new town is 5.56, compared with 11.80 for the south coast

[2] Bib 93212–4
[3] Bib 93210–1, 93250
[4] Bib 93210, p1

Table 11.1 Incidence of handicap

The figures in this table of estimated numbers of handicapped people in different populations in Britain are derived from data in the OPCS survey *Handicapped and impaired in Great Britain* (Bib 93210), official population projections (Bib 93780) and 1971 county census reports (Bib 93782, 93783).

age	per cent population	estimated number by degree of handicap per 100 000 population				
		very severe	severe	appreciable	minor or no handicap	all handicapped or impaired
Great Britain, mid-1975						
0–15	24·7	*	*	*	*	*
16–29	20·0	10	8	21	141	180
30–49	23·6	22	54	99	484	659
50–64	17·7	47	167	288	980	1482
65–74	9·0	80	221	462	1229	1992
75+	5·0	177	271	380	1054	1882
total	100·0	336	721	1250	3888	6195
Great Britain, mid-1985						
0–15	22·2	*	*	*	*	*
16–29	21·6	11	9	22	150	192
30–49	25·4	24	58	106	521	709
50–64	16·3	44	156	269	915	1384
65–74	8·5	76	209	437	1163	1885
75+	5·9	211	323	454	1258	2246
total	100·0	366	755	1288	4007	6416
New town in south-east England, 1971						
0–15	33·2	*	*	*	*	*
16–29	21·7	11	9	22	151	193
30–49	26·7	25	61	112	548	746
50–64	11·8	32	113	194	661	1000
65–74	4·2	37	102	214	570	923
75+	2·4	85	131	183	508	907
total	100·0	190	416	725	2438	3769
South coast town, 1971						
0–15	17·1	*	*	*	*	*
16–29	15·9	8	7	16	110	141
30–49	19·7	19	45	83	404	551
50–64	21·9	60	211	361	1232	1864
65–74	15·0	132	366	765	2036	3299
75+	10·4	369	566	794	2201	3930
total	100·0	588	1195	2019	5983	9785

* no estimates made

town. The estimated percentage for Britain as a whole in mid-1975 is 8.23, compared with 7.80 when the OPCS survey was made in 1968–69. The predicted percentage for the year 1985, based on official population projections, is 8.25.

The table shows that the handicapped population is very largely an elderly population. Of people classified as handicapped, 90 per cent are aged 50 or over, 65 per cent are aged 65 or over and 34 per cent are aged 75 or over. These findings are illustrated with more force in diagram 11.1, which is derived from the table in the OPCS report estimating the proportion of men and women in different age groups with some impairment. This indicates that a man aged 75 or over is more than 30 times as likely to be impaired or handicapped as a man aged between 16 and 29; for women the comparable likelihood is 50 times as great.

For the record, the main causes of impairment among adults in Britain as estimated by the OPCS survey are listed in table 11.2. This gives a brief indication of the principal diseases but its relevance to the practical material contained in this book is limited. Additional statistical information on specific disability conditions is given in the glossary (section 91), together with comments on their physical environmental implications.

1106 Definitions

The findings of the OPCS survey are reported here as a guide for action, and there are further references to them in the course of this book. It is however necessary to make reservations both about their validity and their reliability. The basic problem is the insoluble one of definitions.

Harris's definition of disablement as 'the loss or reduction of functional ability' is confusing. The cause of confusion is that to measure function in terms of loss or reduction of ability is simply to measure handicappedness; the point being that disability can *only* meaningfully be measured in terms of handicappedness. In the same way, impairment can only be measured in terms of handicappedness; this is made explicit by Harris when she defines impairment as having a defective organ or mechanism of the body 'which stops or limits getting about, working or self-care'.

Although disability is only measurable in terms of handicappedness, it needs to be appreciated that handicap is never, or hardly ever, simply a function of disability. Handicap is determined by the degree of disability, in terms of bodily defectiveness, along with the whole spectrum of environmental influences. Thus, with reference to Harris's measures of handicap by capacity for self-care, a person who lives on his own is more handicapped by not being able to do up buttons and zips or feed himself than a person who has a wife who administers these tasks for him. Handicap is therefore a very variable phenomenon whose significance varies among people with the same degree of disability, and in respect of a particular person varies according to environmental circumstances. A person with a changeable disability condition is handicapped one day by not being able to do up zips but not the next, when he can. Similarly a person with a stable disability condition may be handicapped when he goes out one day because it is raining, and not the next when the sun is shining.

One further proviso needs to be made about the OPCS data. This is that reliance simply on a criterion of self-care (as described earlier) is inevitably distorting. It means that

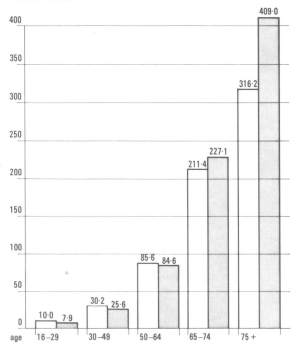

11.1 Impaired people in Great Britain per 1000 total population by age, 1968–9. Untinted columns are men, tinted columns are women. Source: Bib 93210, p5.

Table 11.2 Main cause of impairment, estimated numbers in Great Britain, 1969

Diseases of bones and organs of movement Osteo and rheumatoid arthritis, osteomyelitis, slipped discs, lumbago, fractures, muscular dystrophy etc.	1 187 000
Diseases of circulatory system Heart diseases, arteriosclerosis, high blood pressure etc.	492 000
Diseases of central nervous system Cerebral haemorrhage, strokes, paraplegia, multiple sclerosis, poliomyelitis, cerebral palsy, epilepsy, Parkinson's disease	360 000
Diseases of respiratory system Bronchitis, emphysema, asthma etc.	284 000
Diseases of sense organs Blindness, deafness	277 000

Source: Bib 93210, p 7

the components of handicap are narrowly based, in that all are in the domestic sphere, unaffected by the disabled person's performance when he goes outside his home. There are no items in Harris's inventory relating to mobility, about whether for example the individual can move about the house or go outside on his own, or can cope with steps. There is the interesting theoretical possibility that a paraplegic housewife who is incontinent and dependent for mobility on a wheelchair can score zeros throughout, and be categorized as not handicapped. It is questionable therefore that Harris's self-care criterion should be used as a yardstick for transport or employment services for people with disabilities, or in respect of the use of public buildings.

1107 'Handicapped by buildings'

The people with whom this book is concerned can be described as 'people who on account of disability are handicapped in the use of buildings'. Instead of relating this description to Harris's definitions it is helpful to refer instead to Beatrice Wright. In her *Physical disability – a psychological approach* she defines a disability as 'a condition of impairment having an objective aspect that can usually be described by a physician'. She defines a handicap as 'the cumulative result of the obstacles which disability interposes between the individual and his maximum functional level'[5].

In the context of the use of buildings a paraphrase of Wright's definition of handicap is that it is 'the cumulative result of the obstacles which the lack of suitable facilities in buildings interposes between the individual and his maximum functional level'. To offer some examples, 'lack of suitable facilities' could mean that light switches are too high, that socket outlets are too low, that there is no rail beside the wc or that the walking distance from car park to building entrance is too much to be managed. In the application of the definition the important variable is the characteristics of the building against which the disabled person is measured. The only buildings which matter are those which he uses or wishes to use. A person who is totally incapacitated and bedfast is not as a rule greatly handicapped by buildings. Similarly, a person may be defined as handicapped because the building against which he is measured lacks modern amenities such as an indoor wc; in a building conforming to contemporary standards he would not be handicapped.

This heterogeneity of the disabled population bedevils architectural answers; what may be convenient for one set of disabled people can be anathema to another, and what for the majority is execrable can be indispensable for the few. In the arena of architectural villains there is one besetting feature of buildings which can be relied upon to handicap disabled people: steps. More than any other component of buildings it is steps which, for the mass of disabled people, mean trouble. The simple remedy is to design buildings so that there is no need for steps to be used. For reinforcement of this policy the convenience-for-all argument can be brought into action. Lifts, it can be

maintained, ought always to be installed as an alternative to stair-climbing. Although technologically advanced societies have made some progress towards this comfortable utopia, the need to put steps in buildings (and the need to use them) will never be entirely eliminated. While the architect should recognize that provision for disabled people will as a rule make his buildings safer and easier for all to use, it is important that he does not confuse the population which is genuinely handicapped by steps with the population which is not handicapped and would merely find it more relaxing not to have to use them.

1108 Human adaptability

The human being is an extraordinarily flexible animal, able to adapt successfully to even the most demanding conditions imposed by his environment. Over the centuries the designers of buildings have taken advantage of his apparently unlimited ability to tolerate discomfort, inconvenience and danger. The idea of fitting buildings or equipment so that they actually suit people is relatively new, and so is the concept – ergonomics – by which it is known.

The majority of buildings around us, including many designed by architects, are poor examples of efficient planning, safety or common sense. The complaint applies most of all to ordinary housing: unreachable window openers, inaccessible storage shelves, tortuous staircases, unfindable light switches, ill-situated socket outlets, ungrippable door handles and energy wasting kitchens – all these are features commonplace in contemporary houses. For young and active people they may be a nuisance but they are manageable. For elderly or disabled people they are the cause of frustration and a threat to safety; in Britain more people are injured or killed each year by accidents in the home than on the road.

Apart from those in wheelchairs, people with disabilities do not pose new problems to the architect but only acute cases of existing ones. The able-bodied person is liable to go thump on a polished floor, topple over in the bath, trip over a sill or walk into a glass door. Ways of countering dangers do not alter if consideration is given to disabled people, they simply become more significant. What might be a useful bonus becomes a prerequisite; non-slip floors for example, low level shelves, manageable window openers, intelligently ordered kitchens and rails for support by the bath[6].

Given that the needs of disabled people are, by comparison with those of able-bodied people, simply a matter of degree, the only reasonable excuse for not taking account of them is often simply finance. It is cheaper to put in a staircase than a lift. Cost controls are of course unavoidable but they ought not to be so constraining that they encourage a lack of regard for handicapped or old people. It is pertinent to enquire whether we are not

[5] Bib 93300, p9
[6] In this connection see the check list for prevention of accidents in the home, section 892.

perpetuating values which may may have been reasonable fifty years ago but which are now disreputable.

Between ambulant handicapped people and able-bodied people there can be conflicting physical criteria for a particular design problem, and it is not always the same factor which is of greatest significance to each side. A specific example is the height of the wc seat. A consideration for all users is that it should not be too difficult to revert from a seated to a standing position, indicating a relatively high seat. But for the majority of able-bodied users this factor is subordinated to the more important criterion of efficient physiological functioning, indicating a low seat. The standard wc seat is therefore relatively low, though not perhaps as low as it should be [7]. For ambulant handicapped people the demand for efficient physiological functioning has to a greater degree to yield to ease of rising. Arguably the problem is again a conflict between physical and financial criteria, in that it could be resolved if the height and angle of the seat were mechanically adjustable, or if alternative appliances were available. If neither of these solutions is a possibility the likelihood is that the statistically greater strength of the able-bodied lobby will prevail, resulting in a low rather than a high seat.

1109   Steps

In the field of discrimination against disabled people, low level wc seats are of minor account compared with the proliferation of steps in and around buildings. The simple explanation here is financial and technical. It is necessary to keep out snow, rain and damp, and the obvious answer is to put the ground floor some inches above earth level, with one or two steps to get up to the plateau.

Looking across the spectrum of public buildings it is apparent there is a tendency for some varieties of buildings to have steps at entrances whereas others have not. Along the High Street of any typical British town the department stores, supermarkets and most other shops have unobstructed access – there are no steps. In some cases the customer does not even have to work the door; it opens itself when he puts a foot on a mat, or crosses a light beam. Such service is welcome for old, handicapped or chairbound people, but it is unlikely to be there for altruistic reasons. A more probable explanation is that, for commercial reasons, the shopkeeper is anxious that nothing should discourage the customer from entering.

The other buildings in the same High Street more probably have steps. There are steps at the post office, the bank, the town hall, the public library, the tax office, the public lavatory, the church, the cinema, and quite possibly the restaurant and public house. By analogy, the people who manage these establishments are not so obsessed with commercial constraints, and they can therefore afford a step or two. An alternative explanation is that architects and clients, if they thought about the matter at all, came to the convenient conclusion that people who were going to use these buildings would

already be sufficiently motivated to do so whether or not they were going to be hindered in the process, and that human beings, being tolerant and adaptable creatures, could cope well enough with a few steps.

1110   Barrier versus free movement buildings

There is a third possibility. This is that the presence or not of steps at building entrances is a matter which is rooted historically in the culture and psychology of our society. Some buildings are arranged so that people can move freely in and out, others so that there is a barrier between inside and outside. In the one, the aim is to minimize any distinction between internal territory and external territory, and to encourage people to behave anonymously, coming in as isolated individuals to conduct their business and going out without exposing their identity. In the other, the individual uses the building as a member of a group having mutual interests. Where the group is formally structured he need to display the fact that he belongs before he can come in. Alternatively the building serves the general population, but, because the nature of transactions conducted there demands that the individual exposes his identity, there is a need for some privacy. Such buildings can also serve purposes where, although there is no need to expose identity, privacy is still required. In all these barrier kinds of buildings it is desirable that there is a clear demarcation line between the private territory of the building in which these special operations are conducted, and the public territory outside. A physical barrier may need to be constructed.

The great majority of building types are of the barrier kind, and only a few are of the free movement kind. Clearly on the barrier side are, for example, private houses, banks, police stations, doctors' surgeries, churches, clubs, town halls, public lavatories and public libraries. Clearly on the free movement side are only shops and amusement arcades. Superficially the thesis sounds neat but there is the hazard with this kind of theorizing that rules are bent by selectivity to validate the hypothesis. Railway stations, air terminals, and zoos for example are primarily free movement buildings, but in each case a token of entitlement to enter is needed, requiring some form of barrier. Buildings which tend in the barrier direction but have some free movement component include restaurants, hotels and pubs, theatres, concert halls and cinemas, schools and education buildings, museums and exhibition buildings, swimming pools, sports centres and recreation buildings, and hospitals and post offices. In these cases the demarcation line between private and public territory may not be displayed by a flight of steps but may be marked for example by a checkpoint through which users have to pass and reveal their identity, or pay to come in.

In these terms the presence of steps at the entrances to the majority of traditionally planned public buildings is explicable. It is interesting to note however, quite independent it would seem of any access-for-disabled influences, that in recent years some buildings which were once firmly on the barrier side have been developing free

[7] See 5425, 5426

movement characteristics. Thus for example new public libraries, banks, churches, town halls and police stations tend to be more welcoming than their predecessors 20 or even 10 years ago. This is no doubt in part attributable to the change in social values, whereby those who administer authority are making practical efforts to achieve greater empathy and communication with those whom they serve, but, whatever the causes, these buildings are significantly more accessible to handicapped people than they used to be.

1111 The multiple handicap of wheelchair users

The handicap of an ambulant disabled person who uses buildings is simply that he has a disability, that his body is defective. The person in a wheelchair is by comparison handicapped three times over. First, he has a disability, which invariably, because it has put him into a wheelchair, is severely handicapping. Second, he is obliged to operate at a lower level than normal standing people (and always at the same level), which is constraining both physically and psychologically. Third, he rolls around in a cumbersome, awkward, space-consuming, distinctive and inelegant vehicle.

It is diverting to speculate how we might manage if we were all dependent on wheelchairs for mobility. Our dwellings would be all on one level, with ceilings at about half the height they are now. We should have wider doors, and often do without them entirely. We should have different kitchens and bathroom equipment. Private and public transport would be radically redesigned. One can continue to speculate, but the whole notion is bizarre. It does however serve to reemphasize that the physical environment is, and always will be, designed essentially for people who walk on two legs.

Much of the access campaigning literature published elsewhere, particularly in the United States, disregards this basic tenet. The official *American national standard specifications for making buildings and facilities accessible to, and usable by, the physically handicapped*[8] and the official report of the National Commission on Architectural Barriers *Design for ALL Americans*[9] are two examples. The philosophy is that the entire physical environment can and should be designed to cater for all people indiscriminately, and that people in wheelchairs should have the same opportunities and be treated in the same way as able-bodied people. It would be convenient for all, so the argument goes, if the physical world were planned for wheelchair users, and in consequence it ought to be. Some of the fallacies behind this reasoning have been exposed earlier, but an extended examination is warranted to illustrate some of the conflicts between design criteria for wheelchair users and ambulant people.

1112 Mobility

Design criteria for personal mobility are determined by the way that people move from one place to another. The able-bodied person walks on two feet. He can walk on the level, up and down inclines, and up and down steps. The person in a wheelchair on the other hand moves on wheels. If he can manage a self-propelled chair he can get himself along on the level and up or down inclines which are very gently graded. He may be able to get himself down a single low step and if he is agile he can also get up a low step. If he is a wheelchair gymnast he can cope with moving escalators and can balance his chair on the rear wheels to go down four or five steps. But this kind of athleticism among wheelchair users is rare; for vertical circulation the person in a wheelchair needs a lift, and if there is no lift he has to be carted up or down steps by helpers.

Ramps are of crucial importance to wheelchair users. If one works from the premise that whatever is good for wheelchair users is good for all it is necessary to claim that ramps are good for all, and this has been done before now [10]. But for many ambulant handicapped people, collectively a much bigger population than wheelchair users, a flight of normally graded steps with a handrail is much easier to manage than a ramp[11]. The typical hemiplegic or amputee for example has to be very careful when descending a ramp not to lose his balance; it is also the case that ramps can be more difficult for women with high-heeled shoes, and for all users they are generally more hazardous in wet or frosty conditions.

On the assumption that there has to be a right answer for any design problem, studies have been made to determine the right gradient for a ramp for wheelchair users[12]. But there are many wheelchair users who can cope only with the shallowest of ramps, and if the aim is to accommodate all of them the only satisfactory answer is level surfaces, in association with lifts. There cannot be a *right* gradient for ramps for wheelchair users.

A second problem is floor surfaces. For the able-bodied person floor texture is not usually critical, though from the safety angle it should not be slippery. For the ambulant disabled person the most important condition is a non-slip finish, indicating a roughened and somewhat resilient surface. For the wheelchair user what is needed is a smooth, non-resilient and hard finish.

For the floor surface problem a compromise solution is acceptable, since there is no question of a disabled person being absolutely unable to cope. For the vertical circulation problem there is no acceptable compromise, given that it is not practicable to put lifts into every building wherever there happens to be a change of level. There are also insoluble problems in the case of concert

---

[8] Bib 93020
[9] Two of the 'facts' presented in this report without substantiating evidence are 'The greatest single obstacle to employment for the handicapped is the physical design of the buildings and facilities they must use' and 'One out of ten persons has some disability which prevents him from using buildings and facilities designed only for the physically fit' (Bib 93030, p3).
[10] See for example Bib 93021, p59
[11] For discussion see 1224.
[12] A common recommendation, cited for example in Bib 93000, 93020 and 93072, is a maximum gradient of 1:12. For related discussion see 320, 321.

halls, theatres, sports stadia and similar auditoria buildings. The important condition here is that people in the audience can see without obstruction, meaning that seats are arranged in tiers. Such buildings cannot be organized so that chairbound people can use them on the same basis as others, and the only answer is special accessible areas.

1113 Space

A person sitting in a wheelchair occupies about five times as much space as a standing person. To turn about he needs about nine times as much space. The effect on design criteria is substantial. For example, an able-bodied person can get through a door having an opening of some 500mm, whereas a wheelchair user needs an opening approaching 800mm. The positioning of the door and the amount of clear space on either side are not usually critical to the able- bodied person, but can be an absolute obstacle to the wheelchair user. Similarly the space needed by the wheelchair user at, for example, a dining table or in a theatre audience is much greater than the able-bodied person needs.

Although it sometimes occurs, as in an auditorium or public cloakroom, that small spaces are more efficient for able-bodied people than large spaces, it generally happens that space which is supplementary to basic requirements can be put to good use. This means that space criteria for wheelchair users and for able-bodied people are not usually irreconcilable. Problems are more often caused by conflicting physical and financial criteria, explaining why, particularly in ordinary housing, it is rare that there is enough space for wheelchair users. Where there happens to be enough money to provide lavish spaces it does not always happen that surpluses are distributed in areas critical to wheelchair users. As a rule however wheelchair users can expect to cope relatively well in big buildings such as department stores, hospitals and large office complexes, where the scale of traffic has already dictated the provision of level access, large lifts and generous circulation spaces.

Whereas space criteria for wheelchair users and able-bodied people are not usually incompatible, those of wheelchair users and ambulant disabled people sometimes are. An example is the wc compartment. The wheelchair user needs space to manoeuvre and to transfer to the wc from either a frontal or lateral position, indicating a wide and spacious compartment. The ambulant disabled person on the other hand may require a narrow compartment with rails securely fixed at either hand, and side walls he can lean against for support.

1114 Posture

There are certain activities which able-bodied people prefer to stand to do, for example working at the kitchen sink and washing hands or shaving at the wash basin. The wheelchair user has to sit for these activities and design criteria are therefore different. As a matter of basic ergonomics, the more that a piece of equipment is geared to be usable from a seated position the less convenient it is

going to be if used standing. It happens fortuitously that wash basins are commonly fixed at a level (about 800mm) which is reasonably satisfactory for wheelchair users. This is because the wash basin is conventionally installed at a level which is uncomfortably low for standing people; if it were at a more manageable height it would be impossibly high for wheelchair users.

The posture of the wheelchair user also affects the fixing height of mirrors, the position of glazing to doorways and the height of window sills. Except where statutory regulations are incompatible with wheelchair criteria these problems are generally capable of resolution without inconvenience to either able-bodied people or wheelchair users, for example by installing larger mirrors, additional door glazing and lower window sills.

1115 Reach

In the design of buildings people's range of reach governs (or should govern) the location of a variety of fixtures such as window and ventilator openers, alarm controls, storage shelves, light switches and socket outlets. The able-bodied person can typically reach comfortably anything from floor level to a height of about 2000mm; architects, taking advantage of this, scatter fixed equipment in a somewhat arbitrary fashion. The wheelchair user by contrast has a narrow range of reach. A person with fairly good arms can comfortably manage fixtures between 600 and 1200mm high, but others can only reach a narrow range about 1000mm above floor level directly beside the chair.

In the case of door handles and light switches both populations can conveniently be accommodated. Kitchen shelves, and book shelves in for instance public libraries, are a different matter. It would be unrealistic, both for practical and financial reasons, to insist that the reach criteria of wheelchair users should determine the positioning of shelves. In such cases requirements for the two populations are not compatible.

Control panels in automatic lift cars pose similar problems. The reach limitations of chairbound people suggest a horizontal arrangement of lift buttons, conflicting with the commonsense factor that lift buttons are arranged vertically so that there is a direct functional correspondence with the direction of travel of the lift. The optimum position of vertically arranged buttons is determined first by the range of reach of lift users and second by their line of vision. In the case of able-bodied people the second factor is as important a determinant as the first. Unless the panel is related to eye level the lift user may find it difficult to check information, relating for example to departments or offices served. It is also important that where a lift is crowded the lift panel is not completely obscured by those standing beside it. Given a span of 400mm, the most convenient level for lift controls for able-bodied people is from say 1250 to 1650mm above floor level. For the chairbound person the same factors apply, except that the reach criterion warrants greater attention than the visual criterion owing to the difficulty of positioning the wheelchair conveniently to reach the controls. For chairbound people control buttons are probably best located between 750 and 1150mm above floor level.

In the case of lift controls the requirements of able-bodied people and chairbound people conflict. Where there is only one panel its location should be governed by the needs of normal standing people. A compromise solution, for example placing controls between 1000 and 1400mm above floor level, would not be ideal for either group. A possibility is to have two panels at different levels; even this may not be acceptable where it is necessary that controls are at a level where they are not misused by small children.

In practice, aided by pressure from handicapped organizations, it may happen that criteria of reachability for wheelchair users prevail over criteria of common sense. In Sweden, where in new buildings provision for handicapped people is more general than in Britain, standard lifts are now manufactured with controls arranged horizontally at low level.

1116 Strength

Heavy spring-loaded doors are often a nuisance for able-bodied people but they are much more irritating for disabled people. The problem is most critical among wheelchair users, who find that the layout of the door commonly prevents them from manoeuvring into a position where only minimum effort is needed to open the door. A heavy door which has to be pushed open can be even more difficult.

The problem is that requirements for closers to keep the door closed as protection against fire conflict with the needs of disabled people. This can be resolved by installing automatic opening doors or motorized door closers, or by having doors held open by magnetic catches activated by fire detectors. Once again, both physical and financial factors militate against the wheelchair user.

1117 Guidelines for action

Two basic guidelines for architectural action emerge. The first is that the differences between able-bodied people and ambulant disabled people are a matter of degree, and physical criteria are only rarely incompatible. The second is that the differences between able-bodied people and chairbound people are basic. Whereas ambulant disabled people can, in the context of physical requirements, be regarded as deviants within the normal population, chairbound people are so atypical that they have to be regarded as a quite separate and distinct population. It is for this reason that so much of the material in this book focuses on the needs of wheelchair users, and why a more careful look at the wheelchair population is needed; who people who use wheelchairs are, what sort of buildings they use, what sort of problems they encounter and how their problems can be resolved.

12 Buildings and disabled people: Evidence

1200 The Norwich inquiry

The discussion which follows on the use of buildings by disabled people draws extensively on the study of wheelchair users in Norwich which I made during the years 1964-8. Although it is now (1976) over seven years since the inquiry was completed, its findings are of more relevance to the theme of this commentary than any others available and there is no indication that they will be superseded in the immediate future by more authoritative evidence.

The purpose of the Norwich inquiry was to find out something about severely disabled people in a typical urban community in Britain, who they were, what the age distribution was, what kind of households they lived in, how they managed in their homes, what sort of work they did, what transport they had available and how they coped when they went outside their homes and used public buildings. The survey of wheelchair users was always envisaged as the principal component of the study. Other work was done, particularly among disabled drivers and on the signposting of facilities in buildings, but the greater part of the evidence documented in this book and drawn from Norwich relates to the wheelchair population.

To avoid terminological confusion it is helpful at the start to record the definitions employed:

Wheelchair population: people supplied with a wheelchair by the (then) Ministry of Health or who had obtained a wheelchair privately.

Wheelchair users: people who regularly or occasionally used a wheelchair as a mobility aid.

Chairbound: people who were unable to walk, either with or without assistance, and who depended on a wheelchair for mobility.

These definitions appear straightforward but in practice it was not always a simple matter to allocate people into one slot rather than another. The wheelchair population was defined as comprising people who used chairs regularly, who used them infrequently, or who did not use them but retained them in case they might one day be wanted. People who had wheelchairs but had no intention of ever using them were excluded. Because the study was concerned with housing arrangements and the use of public buildings it excluded wheelchair users who were permanently in hospital.

Wheelchair users were defined as people who regularly or occasionally used their wheelchairs, the line being drawn at people who had not used their wheelchair at least once during the previous twelve months. In the event a sizable minority, 14 per cent, of people who had wheelchairs were not wheelchair users. Determining which wheelchair users were chairbound was difficult, and discussion of the operational definition of this term is postponed until later in the commentary.

The aim was to identify and interview as many as possible of the people in Norwich who had been supplied with wheelchairs through the National Health Service or who had obtained chairs privately. There is no foolproof means of locating people who simply walk into a shop and buy a wheelchair, and inevitably there must have been some wheelchair users in Norwich who were not discovered. But it can be reasonably claimed, on the basis of evidence about the 45 people with private wheelchairs who were located, that the omission of an unknown number of people with private chairs did not seriously affect the validity of the study's findings about the use of buildings by disabled people.

1201 The wheelchair population in Norwich

From a total population of 120 000, the names and addresses of 442 people in Norwich who might be wheelchair users were assembled. The number with whom or for whom interviews were obtained, and for which data analyses have been made, was 284. Of the other 158, 101 were dead before visits were made, 15 were permanently resident in hospital, nine had moved out of Norwich, six could not be located, 25 said that wheelchairs had been returned or that they had no need of them, and two refused interviews.

Of the 284 people studied (table 12.1), 99 (35 per cent) were male and 185 (65 per cent) were female. These figures represented one person per 410 of the total population, 1:562 for males and 1:330 for females. The high proportion of females is attributable first to the preponderance of women among the very old (where the prevalence of wheelchair users is highest) and second to the higher incidence of females in the two major diagnostic categories of arthritis and hemiplegia. Among those aged less than 55, males and females were evenly distributed (37 against 35), whereas among those aged 75 or more females outnumbered males by more than four to one. The clear association between wheelchair issue and age is shown in diagram 22.1. Distributions by age and sex for the Norwich wheelchair population were similar to those found in the national survey of wheelchair users made in 1973 by the Office of Population Censuses and Surveys.

One of the assumptions on which the survey was based was that wheelchair users are dependent on their chairs for mobility, and use them both inside and outside their homes. In practice it was found that 80 per cent regularly used a chair when they went outside, but only 38 per cent used a wheelchair inside the home. Less than one person in three routinely used his wheelchair both inside and outside. One in seven did not regularly use a wheelchair either when at home or when out. Of the 18 people who used wheelchairs inside but not out (table 12.2) 14 never went out at all. The 39 who did not regularly use their chairs either inside or out comprised people who used their chairs only in special circumstances (such as when on holiday, at their place of work or at the swimming pool) or who kept them against the contingency that they might one day be needed, for example if their health deteriorated. People who did not regularly use a chair when they went out were classified as 'chair not used'. People who always used a chair when they went out, even if it happened to be only once or twice a year, were deemed

Table 12.1 The wheelchair population in Norwich: Age and sex

age	male	female	all	NHS issued chairs	private chairs only
5–9	4	4	8	8	—
10–14	2	2	4	4	—
15–19	4	1	5	5	—
20–24	4	4	8	8	—
25–29	2	4	6	6	—
30–34	3	1	4	4	—
35–39	4	6	10	9	1
40–44	4	4	8	8	—
45–49	10	9	19	18	1
50–54	3	16	19	17	2
55–59	9	17	26	22	4
60–64	9	19	28	25	3
65–69	16	17	33	28	5
70–74	10	16	26	18	8
75–79	9	25	34	23	11
80–84	4	27	31	27	4
85–89	2	9	11	7	4
90+	—	4	4	2	2
total	99	185	284	239	45
mean age	54·6	63·6	60·4	58·3	72·1

regular wheelchair users. In some instances it was not easy to determine whether an individual deserved to be regular, but in cases of doubt people were recorded as chair users rather than non-chair users.

The causes of disablement of people in the study are listed in table 12.3. An early expectation was that a substantial number of people would be found who were paraplegic as a consequence of road accidents, and that as a group they would have an important influence on findings and recommendations. In the event only one such person was discovered, a result at variance with common belief that the rising incidence of road accidents, itself a proposition of arguable validity, means a steady increase in the numbers of disabled people in the community[1].

1202   Cars and transport

One in nine of people in the study were able to drive, using either a car or an invalid tricycle supplied by the (then) Ministry of Health. Two people had private cars in addition to a ministry tricycle. Of people living in private households 12 per cent drove their own vehicles or, as ex-service disabled people, had a nominated driver for their car. Those who did not have a car of their own, but were living in a household where there was a car, comprised 18 per cent. For the remaining 70 per cent there was no vehicle in the household. Whether people with ministry tricycles should be labelled car-owning is debatable; even if they are there were still only 30 per cent in the study

[1] In this connection see footnote to 1305.

Table 12.2 The wheelchair population in Norwich: Summary of wheelchair use

	no.	%
chair used inside and outside	90	32
chair used outside, not inside	137	48
chair used inside, not outside	18	6
chair not used outside or inside	39	14

Table 12.3 The wheelchair population in Norwich: Cause of disability

	male	female	all	%
osteo or rheumatoid arthritis	12	69	81	28·5
hemiplegia	10	31	41	14·4
multiple sclerosis	15	18	33	11·6
single lower limb amputation	15	12	27	9·5
cerebral palsy	6	11	17	6·0
polio	4	7	11	3·9
paraplegia	6	5	11	3·9
congenital disabilities involving only physical impairment	5	5	10	3·5
double lower limb amputation	4	5	9	3·2
cardiac and respiratory diseases, including tuberculosis	4	5	9	3·2
muscular dystrophy	6	3	9	3·2
fractures	1	4	5	1·8
Parkinson's disease	1	2	3	1·1
other causes	10	8	18	6·3

Table 12.4 The wheelchair population in Norwich: Means of transport

	no.	%
not dependent on others for transport		
drives own car	4	1
drives own petrol or electric invalid tricycle	28	10
uses hand-propelled tricycle	1	0·3
uses public transport (buses)	3	1
dependent on others for transport		
taken out regularly by car (1× week or more often)	63	22
taken out by car less frequently	124	44
personal transport not used		
never taken out by car, or only by ambulance to hospital etc.	56	20

Table 12.5 The wheelchair population in Norwich: Buildings and facilities used.

	yes	no	% yes	if yes ambulant without wheelchair	semi-ambulant with wheelchair	accompanied in wheelchair non-ambulant	alone in wheelchair non-ambulant
public parks	166	113	60	19	59	71	5
cafes/restaurants	112	167	40	30	32	46	4
hospitals	111	168	40	27	11	31	—
department stores	105	174	39	21	34	46	4
local shops	100	179	36	31	21	43	5
public lavatories	82	197	29	34	26	16	3
clothes shops	73	206	26	24	17	29	3
hairdressers	70	209	25	33	15	20	2
supermarkets	68	211	24	17	18	31	2
churches, chapels	65	214	23	20	15	29	1
clubs	57	222	20	25	11	19	2
hotels	46	232	17	10	17	19	—
chemists shops	36	243	13	23	6	3	4
post offices	35	244	13	25	5	1	4
public houses	34	245	12	10	8	11	5
shoe shops	34	245	12	17	6	10	1
cinemas	27	252	10	12	3	11	1
railway stations	26	253	9	4	5	17	—
doctor's surgery	24	255	9	18	4	2	—
dentist's surgery	21	258	8	10	2	9	—
theatres	21	258	8	9	3	8	1
banks	11	268	4	8	2	—	1
public libraries	10	269	4	7	—	1	2
swimming pools	10	269	4	5	1	3	1
health clinics	9	270	3	6	2	1	—
football matches	9	270	3	3	3	1	—
concert halls	7	272	3	3	—	4	—
museums etc	5	274	2	1	1	3	—
air transport	2	277	1	—	1	1	—

who were members of car owning households, compared with 41 per cent for all people in Norwich in 1966.

Two out of three people did not have anyone on whom they could depend to take them out regularly by car (table 12.4). Among the 124 people who were reported as being taken out less frequently than once each week there were many who had been out only two or three times during the previous year. Ten had been out only on expeditions with the special coach for handicapped people.

In reporting these findings, and those which follow regarding the use of public buildings, on the general inactivity of people with wheelchairs the question occurs whether in practice able-bodied people perform any better. To be able responsibly to say that wheelchair users are underprivileged, lack opportunities, are generally inactive and so on, it is proper to provide comparative evidence from a control group of able-bodied people. In theory this is right but in practice it cannot be done. In respect of the performance of disabled people it is not possible to isolate the effect of the disability per se, because performance is associated with other factors, particularly cash resources, household circumstances and

transport, which may themselves have been directly influenced by the fact of disability.

1203 Record of building use

The public buildings and facilities used by people in the study are listed in table 12.5, in rank order of the number using each type. The usage of buildings is of course affected by cultural and other factors, and the figures are not always neatly comparable. As an example, children were not users of public houses, and nor were people whose disability conditions meant a non-alcoholic diet. Each person was asked which buildings or facilities he had used at least once during the previous twelve months, but the results need to be treated with caution. Respondents were often unable to recall with confidence exactly which buildings they had used, and the probability is that the figures in table 12.5 under-record the actual incidence of building use.

For people who actually had used buildings a record was made of the manner in which this was done, by classifying into one or other of four categories (table 12.6). The first was 'ambulant without wheelchair', meaning that the

Table 12.6 The wheelchair population in Norwich: Mobility classification of building users

	no.	%
ambulant without wheelchair	32	11
semi-ambulant with wheelchair	93	33
accompanied in wheelchair, non-ambulant	71	25
alone in wheelchair, non-ambulant	6	2
all building users	202	72
non-building users	77	28

Table 12.7 The wheelchair population in Norwich: Number of building types used

number of different building types used	number of respondents	number of different building types used	number of respondents
0	77	11	3
1	43	12	7
2	28	13	3
3	26	14	2
4	18	15	6
5	15	16	4
6	15	17	3
7	7	18	—
8	10	19	—
9	6	20	1
10	5		

person concerned did not take his wheelchair with him when he used the building. The second was 'semi-ambulant with wheelchair', meaning that he normally went out in his wheelchair, but was able to transfer out of it to get into the building, or to use facilities such as cloakrooms inside it. The third was 'accompanied in wheelchair, non-ambulant', meaning that he was chairbound or, having difficulty transferring to his feet, preferred always to remain in the chair. Chairbound people who were always accompanied by someone else when they used the building asked about were placed in this category whether or not they were potentially able to manage independently. The fourth category was 'alone in wheelchair, non-ambulant', meaning chairbound people who used buildings independently or without the help of a personal escort. Admission to this category was stringently controlled: people who pushed themselves out independently in their wheelchairs but who could if they wished use their feet (for example to manage one or two steps or to get inside wc compartments) were classified as semi-ambulant with wheelchair.

Between building types the same person could be placed in different categories. For example a person able to go out on his own in his wheelchair could be classed as independent chairbound in respect of local shops, but as accompanied in wheelchair for the use of cinemas. Similarly, people able to walk might use the local post office without having their wheelchair with them but would take the chair when they went to department stores in the city. Where in respect of the same building type alternative classifications were possible 'alone in wheelchair' took priority over 'accompanied in wheel-chair' and 'semi-ambulant with wheelchair' priority over 'ambulant without wheelchair', meaning always that the allocation was to the category requiring the more demanding architectural conditions.

1204   The characteristics of building users

Before looking at particular types of building and the reasons why they were used or not, it is helpful to look generally at the characteristics of people who used buildings a good deal by contrast with those who did not.

The measure of intensity of building use was simply the number of different types of building used by each person during the twelve months prior to interview. In calculating individual scores public parks were discounted, and hospitals if the person concerned had been either only a ward patient or else when he had been to hospital had always travelled by ambulance. Clubs were discounted in respect of people who had used only the club in Norwich for physically handicapped people, and hotels were discounted if 'hotel use' meant only attending holiday camps for parties of elderly or handicapped people. Excluding public parks, the total number of building types listed on the questionnaire was 28, and this was therefore the maximum score obtainable.

The results, showing how many people used how many buildings, are listed in table 12.7. No fewer than 77 out of the 284 people in the sample, representing 28 per cent, had used no buildings at all. A further 43 (15 per cent) had used one only, and 54 (19 per cent) had used two or three. There were 55 people (20 per cent) who had used between four and seven, and 24 (9 per cent) who had used between eight and eleven. There were 26 (9 per cent) who had used 12 or more building types. Thus approaching half of the people in the sample had used no public buildings at all, or had used one type of building only. It would be generous to describe a person using 12 types of building out of a possible 28 as an intensive user of buildings, but if this is allowable it still means that less than one in ten of all people having wheelchairs in Norwich were intensive users of buildings.

Predictably, the extent to which people in the sample used buildings was associated with variables such as their age, the kind of disability they were affected by, the length of time they had used a wheelchair for, and the size of household they lived in. The more important of these variables are analyzed by intensity of building use in table 12.8. For each subgroup under the main headings a 'building use rating' is given, calculated as described in the footnote to the table.

1205 The age factor

The use of buildings by people with wheelchairs is very much associated with age. In general, people aged below 60 scored higher ratings than the mean, whereas after the age of 60 there was a marked and consistent decline in the level of building usage. The association between age and the use of buildings is reflected in the associations between building use and other variables, and it is relevant therefore to look first at the association between age and other characteristics.

Men in the study (mean age 54.6 years) were generally younger than women (63.6), and people with wheelchairs prescribed through the National Health Service (58.3) were younger than those who obtained chairs privately (72.1). Of causes of disability, three comprised predominantly young people, namely cerebral palsy (22.2), congenital disabilities without mental impairment (28.0) and muscular dystrophy (30.8). Two categories comprised chiefly middle-aged people, namely polio (43.9) and multiple sclerosis (49.8). The mean age of people in the other six categories recorded in table 12.8 was 60 years or over; this included paraplegia where, as reported earlier (1201) the Norwich population was probably atypical. There was an association between age and size of household, the people who were members of 1 or 2 person households generally being older than those who were members of larger households. There was also an association between age and the length of time people had been using wheelchairs; in general people who had had wheelchairs for ten years or more were younger than those who had had them for only a short time.

1206 Variables associated with use of buildings

Table 12.8 shows that among the wheelchair population in Norwich men tended to use buildings more intensively than women. This may not be entirely attributable to the age factor, since the analysis of building use by employment shows that housewives in the sample were on average less intensive users of buildings than people below retirement age who were either in employment or not employed.

The table also shows that there are important associations between the cause of disability and the use of buildings. The person disabled by either polio or a congenital condition involving physical impairment only was much more likely to be an intensive user of buildings than a person in any other diagnostic category. Although reservations need to be made on account of the smallness of the sample the evidence here supports the thesis developed later in this commentary (1305) regarding the hierarchy of disability conditions.

Among the other findings, it is notable that people who had been wheelchair users for 20 years or more used buildings very much more intensively than those who had had their chairs five years or less. People with wheelchairs obtained privately used buildings very little (42 per cent of them not at all) confirming that this study of the importance of building accessibility to wheelchair

users was not gravely handicapped by the impossibility of locating all of the population.

Not surprisingly, people who were able to drive their own cars used buildings a great deal more frequently than those who had no transport available. Of the 23 people in private households who had used 12 or more buildings, 17 owned cars or invalid tricycles. In respect of mobility classifications people at the two extremes, those able to walk who went out without wheelchairs and those not able to walk who went out independently, used buildings more intensively than those who were semi-ambulant, or who were chairbound and needed to be pushed when they went out.

Later in this commentary these findings regarding the characteristics of people with wheelchairs who tend to use buildings frequently are discussed in relation to the characteristics and behaviour of disabled people in general. To be able to draw broad conclusions, and also to aid the developing of practical design criteria, it is helpful at this stage to look in some detail at the usage by people in the Norwich study of particular kinds of buildings and facilities.

1207 Shops and stores

Department stores, supermarkets and local shops were together the service most frequently used by people in the study. In all, 129 people (46 per cent) had used shops or stores. Some people who said they had been to shops were always pushed out by someone else, remained in their chairs outside the shop, and did not go in; as a rule these were recorded as not using shops. On the other hand people who drove invalid tricycles and relied on shopkeepers to come out to ask what they wanted were recorded as being users of shops.

Among the 129 shop users, 14 (12 women and 2 men) were people who regularly did their own shopping, including collecting their own groceries. All except 3 of these 14 were ambulant, and could use local shops without taking a chair with them. One person who was chairbound and another who was semi-ambulant were regularly pushed to the shops by someone in the family. The fourteenth person, a resident in an old people's home, used his hand-propelled tricycle to get to the shops, and did not as a rule get out of it.

Among people who could go out independently in their wheelchairs, and also those who were ambulant and could cope without wheelchairs, local shops were used more frequently than either supermarkets or department stores. Of local shop users 31 per cent were ambulant, compared with 20 per cent of department store users and 25 per cent of supermarket users. A factor here was the greater amount of walking necessary when using department stores or supermarkets; some of the people able to use local shops without their wheelchairs were pushed out in their chairs when they visited stores or supermarkets in the city.

Table 12.8 The wheelchair population in Norwich: Analysis of characteristics associated with intensity of building use

	Number of different building types used during 12 months previous to interview						building use rating
	0	1	2–3	4–7	8–11	12+	
all	77	43	54	55	24	26	3·1
sex							
male	22	12	23	19	7	14	3·7
female	55	31	31	36	17	12	2·8
age							
0–9	—	1	1	1	3	—	5·2
10–19	2	1	1	2	1	2	4·8
20–29	—	1	1	3	3	5	7·6
30–39	3	1	1	6	—	3	4·5
40–49	5	1	5	7	4	5	4·8
50–59	7	4	9	10	6	9	4·8
60–69	15	11	13	16	5	1	2·5
70–79	23	10	16	8	1	1	1·6
80 +	22	13	7	2	1	—	0·9
cause of disability							
congenital	—	—	1	—	1	7	9·4
polio	—	—	—	5	2	4	7·6
muscular dystrophy	—	—	3	3	3	—	4·7
multiple sclerosis	8	1	9	6	3	6	4·2
double lower limb amputation	2	3	2	—	—	2	3·4
paraplegia	2	3	1	4	—	1	3·0
cerebral palsy	3	4	1	7	2	—	3·0
single lower limb amputation	7	4	8	4	3	1	2·7
hemiplegia	13	7	8	6	3	3	2·7
osteo or rheumatoid arthritis	31	19	15	11	4	1	1·7
cardiac, respiratory	4	—	2	2	—	—	1·5
period of wheelchair use							
more than 20 years	2	1	3	6	1	6	5·8
11–20 years	2	1	5	8	4	4	5·1
5–10 years	18	8	7	13	4	7	3·3
less than 5 years	55	33	39	28	15	9	2·5
NHS or private wheelchair							
NHS issue	59	34	47	49	22	25	3·4
privately obtained	18	9	7	6	2	1	1·7
transport availability (private households only)							
drives own vehicle, or nominated driver for ministry car	4	1	2	2	2	17	8·3
car in household, not driven by wheelchair user	7	7	8	9	8	2	3·6
no car in household	60	31	33	29	8	4	2·0
mobility classification							
independent chairbound	—	—	—	3	1	2	7·3
ambulant non-wheelchair user	—	7	2	5	6	12	7·0
ambulant wheelchair user	—	23	26	27	8	9	3·8
accompanied chairbound	—	13	26	20	9	3	3·6
non-building user	77	—	—	—	—	—	0·0

In each category, people scored 0, 1, 2, 4, 8 or 12, according to whether they had used 0, 1, 2–3, 4–7, 8–11 or 12 or more buildings. The building use rating is in each case the aggregate score divided by the number of people concerned.

The availability of car parking was an influence on the use of shops and stores. The finding of a convenient parking place was generally more critical among chairbound people who were taken out by car than it was among those who drove their own vehicles and had parking badges entitling them to leave their cars on streets where parking by other drivers was prohibited. The impression was that police and traffic wardens were less tolerant of passengers who were disabled than they were of disabled drivers. The relative ease of parking alongside local shops by comparison with department stores or supermarkets was a factor which encouraged greater dependence on them.

Two further factors contributed to the use of local shops. The first, in conjunction with the lack of anyone to take them out by car, was the inability of many disabled people to use public transport. The second was that some people found it impossible, for example because they could not sit comfortably in their chairs for long or because they were incontinent, to leave their homes for more than a short period. For many of all these people who had to rely on local shops the additional expense (compared with cheaper supermarkets) was a frequent cause of complaint.

Among people who took wheelchairs into supermarkets it was commonly discovered that gangways by cashdesks were too narrow; the normal solution was to leave by the entrance door. In two of the multiple stores in the city there was a goods lift serving the departments of the upper floor, but no passenger lift. On days when the stores were not overcrowded staff would volunteer to take people in wheelchairs up in the goods lift, although strictly it was not permitted. When the signposting programme was put into operation signs were put in each of these stores with the legend 'Wheelchair users: for access to upper floor please ask staff' [2].

Because shopping is a basic necessity the reasons (among those who did not use them) why shops were not used tended to be disability-affected; there were not for example, as with other types of building, cultural reasons. In the circumstances it could be anticipated that physical accessibility might be a matter of critical concern. There were however no instances of people prevented from using shops they wished to use simply on account of physical barriers; in this connection the discussion earlier on barrier and free movement buildings (1110) is relevant.

1208 Clothes shops, chemists and hairdressers

Questions were asked about the use of specialist shops, though in some cases where positive replies were recorded people were using the same places they had previously mentioned under department stores. Those who said they had used clothes shops comprised 73, representing 26 per cent of people in the study. Of the people who said they had not used clothes shops, the majority relied on a member of the family to shop for them, a few relied on a home help or neighbour, and others asked shops to send goods on approval.

[2] For an account of this programme see Bib 93082.

Shoes had been bought by 34 people. Among others the normal practice was for a member of the family or a neighbour to get shoes for them. There were 20 people who were double amputees or had shoes specially made and fitted for them at the hospital or a surgical appliance store. Because many people spent their time sitting in wheelchairs or else went out only infrequently, the impression was that shoes were given relatively little wear by comparison with able-bodied people's footwear.

Only 36 people (13 per cent of the total) had used chemists' shops. Regarding accessibility, no problems were recorded and, for reasons discussed later about the practicability of delegating to another person functions relating to the use of chemists' shops (1221), the impression was that access was not as a rule a matter of crucial concern. Of the 243 people who had not used chemists' shops, 195 (78 per cent) said they had had prescriptions which had to be taken to a chemist; of these 173 relied on a member of the family (inside or outside the household) to collect goods for them, and 22 on a home help or neighbour.

Hairdressers' salons or barbers' shops had been used by 70 people (25 per cent) in the study. The majority of local hairdressers' shops appeared to be accessible, and only 7 of the 70 reported that their choice was restricted on account of accessibility. Among the 70, the two independent wheelchair users both went to places which had steps, and each had to be lifted in; they did not find it bothering or embarrassing. Of the 209 people who did not go out to a hairdresser, 91 (44 per cent) had their hair cut at home by a friend or member of the family. There were 64 (31 per cent) who arranged for a hairdresser to visit them at home; many of these were people who in the past had used a particular hairdresser, who was willing to make special visits when they had become so severely handicapped that they were not easily able to get out themselves.

Since the survey was made a purpose-designed day centre for physically handicapped people has opened in Norwich, incorporating hairdressing facilities. This service is evidently most valuable to many handicapped people, and its importance in the planning of new day centres is referred to again later in this commentary.

1209 Cafes and restaurants

Cafes and restaurants had been used by 112 people in the study, representing 40 per cent of the total. Those who used them regularly tended to be selective, going only to establishments which they knew to be easily accessible. When they had used the same place more than once they were often recognized by the staff, given special consideration (for example a table by the door) and made to feel welcome.

People who went on day outings by car to local seaside resorts said they made a practice of noting which cafes were easily accessible, so that they would know where to go on their next visit. Among those severely handicapped who were taken out by car for afternoon outings, it was a common routine for a cup of tea to be brought out to the car from a snack bar or cafe having parking facilities. People who did this said it was easier than getting an elderly handicapped person out of the car, into a wheelchair, into the cafe and back again, and however physically accessible the cafe might be it was still simpler not to take the wheelchair in.

Two people who were not able to feed themselves said they were embarrassed in public cafes and restaurants if other people saw them being fed. For this reason they did not like to go to cafes, and one of the two, who had on one occasion stayed at a hotel, had arranged to have his meals brought to him in his bedroom in order to avoid being exposed in the public restaurant. His behaviour was not typical – others who had to be fed by someone else said they had no inhibitions about using cafes or restaurants. Overt discrimination against people in cafes or rest-aurants was unusual. One person had been told at a cafe (on a visit to Cornwall) that she would have to use the room at the back because her wheelchair tyres would damage the carpet; she decided to go elsewhere.

1210   Post offices and banks

Of the people in the study 35 had used post offices and 11 reported they had visited banks. None of the people unable to get to a post office on their own felt that their self-sufficiency was greatly compromised by having to ask someone to go for them. None of the three main post offices in the centre of Norwich at that time was accessible to wheelchair users, and three of the four people who used post offices independently went to local branches; the other accosted people outside one of the major post offices and asked them to go in for him.

The limited usage of banks by people in the study was probably primarily a cultural matter, and it could be that among handicapped people habits have changed in recent years. One of the people who did use banks had moved her account to one of the three banks in Norwich at that time accessible to wheelchair users, on account of its convenience and ease of parking. In her case accessibility had clearly determined her choice, since the bank was nearly two miles from her home.

1211   Churches and chapels

The odd case of the lady who went to church because there were steps was reported at the start of this commentary. There was one other case where accessibility had been a direct influence on churchgoing. A woman had always attended the principal Congregational church in the city, but the steps had become unmanageable and she had switched to an accessible Church of England church. By the time she was interviewed she was too handicapped to continue to go there either, and a clergyman was visiting her regularly. There were in all 65 people (23 per cent) who said they had been to church or chapel at least once during the previous twelve months, but these included many who had been to attend family marriages or christenings. One person no longer went to church because she said it was too draughty, another did not go

because she had become deaf, and another (a chairbound woman aged 75) said she no longer enjoyed going to church because she did not like displaying herself there in a wheelchair. A number of people said that the unreliability of wheelchair pushers arranged by church people was a disincentive; in this situation – as in others – it was vitally important for disabled people who had been promised that someone would collect them that they were not let down.

1212   Hotels

Of the 46 people reported as having used hotels, 27 had been to one of the holiday camps at local seaside resorts where special arrangements were made for parties of elderly or physically handicapped people. The number of people who had stayed in a hotel or boarding house during the previous year, and had made private arrangements, was therefore 19, representing 7 per cent of the total.

One person who could manage independently in his wheelchair (he did not travel on his own, and is therefore included in the analysis as an accompanied wheelchair user) said that he never made prior arrangements before visiting hotels. On a variety of occasions he had been carried up and down stairs, but this was not a serious inconvenience. On one occasion a hotel manager had insisted he could not cope, and had made excuses about inaccessible toilet facilities. Protestations by the wheelchair user that he could manage perfectly well were unavailing, and he had been obliged to go elsewhere.

1213   Public houses

Among the 34 people who had used pubs was an active man of 88 who complained that it was difficult to get a drink because of the steps at the pub. One other person reported that his choice of pubs was restricted by steps and two who went to local pubs where there were steps usually stayed outside in their wheelchairs while someone else got a drink for them. Incontinence, particularly among people with multiple sclerosis, restrained pub-going; so also did medical instructions to avoid drinking (for example by diabetics) and the incompatability of alcohol and the drugs prescribed to disabled people.

1214   Cinemas and theatres

Had it not been that 'The Sound of Music' was showing in Norwich during the course of the survey there would probably have been fewer cinema visitors than 27; one wheelchair user who was able to transfer to an ordinary seat reported that she had seen the film ten times. At the time there were no special arrangements for wheelchair users at local cinemas in Norwich (they have since been made) but all except one of the five cinemas was accessible without too much difficulty. As a rule people in wheelchairs were asked to transfer to ordinary seats, and because of this one person who was chairbound did not go to cinemas. The people who were able to cope independently in their wheelchairs did in fact transfer to ordinary seats; they reported that cinema seats were more comfortable than wheelchair seats, and they would not use places set aside for wheelchairs if they were available. On the other hand three people mentioned that because of their disability they were not able to sit comfortably for more than a few minutes in an ordinary seat, and did not visit cinemas for that reason.

Most wheelchair users reported that cinema managers and staff were helpful. A teenager with a severe walking handicap said that he regularly asked for tickets for the cheapest seats in the front few rows. When he staggered into the auditorium the immediate reaction of the attendant was to say 'Oh you mustn't walk all the way to the front – sit at the back'. No one who had turned up at a cinema in Norwich in a wheelchair reported that they had been refused admission, except on one occasion when six chair users had gone in a party without making arrangements beforehand. Two people reported that at cinemas outside Norwich they had been refused admission because they were in wheelchairs.

The experience of people who had been to theatres was comparable to that of cinema users. The majority of the 21 (8 per cent) recorded as theatre users were people who had been to shows at the Theatre Royal in Norwich, at that time used more frequently for cinema shows. One person with multiple sclerosis reported that she always asked for a seat near the lavatories and close to the exit. In the smaller Maddermarket Theatre in Norwich arrangements were made for wheelchair users to remain in their chairs and this was appreciated.

1215 Libraries

The central library in Norwich has its public entrance on the far side of an internal courtyard approached only by a flight of steps. There is, however, a staff entrance at the rear of the building which gives access without steps, and when the signposting programme was implemented this facility was advertised by three signs around the outside of the building. Only ten people in the study had used public libraries in the city, but two people, who did not know of the alternative access at the rear, had been deterred by the flight of steps at the central library. One person who had been to a branch library claimed that the staff were unhelpful; because she used shoulder crutches she was not able to reach books herself, and none of the staff, she said, had offered to help.

1216 Health services

A relatively large number of people – 111, representing 40 per cent of the total – had used hospitals. Of these, 42 (38 per cent) had been ward patients only; of the other 69, one person had been to hospital to visit a friend and the remainder had been to the outpatients' department, to have physiotherapy treatment or for other clinical reasons. There were no complaints about the accessibility of local hospitals.

The majority of people in the study (68 per cent) reported that their general practitioner always visited them at home when he was needed, and among these many said that he called at regular and frequent intervals. One woman said she had changed her doctor because his surgery was at first floor level and, as her condition steadily deteriorated, she found it impossible to get there. When the doctor found out that she was no longer his patient he said that he would of course have been happy to visit her in her home whenever she wished. Ten people said that they never had cause to call on their doctor, and two did not know who their doctor was. Of the 24 people in the sample who had in fact visited their doctor at his surgery three out of four were people who were ambulant and did not take their chairs with them.

There were 21 people (8 per cent of the total) who had been to see their dentist at his surgery. No record was made, but it was clear that the principal reason why the other 92 per cent had not been to a dentist was that they did not have teeth of their own. Among those who did have genuine teeth, the tendency among dentists to have their consulting rooms at first floor level was a cause of inconvenience. Occasionally dentists could make alternative arrangements, for example (where there was a partnership) for the downstairs room of a colleague to be borrowed temporarily.

Where physical problems made visits to the dentist's surgery extremely difficult it was sometimes possible for patients to attend the dental clinic at the hospital.

1217 Transport services

There were 26 people in the study who had travelled by train during the previous 12 months. Seventeen were chairbound, and of these ten travelled always in the guard's van. A further 20 people reported that they had also used railways since they became disabled, though not in the previous 12 months. The normal practice was for the handicapped person to be lifted out of his wheelchair by a porter, the chair then lifted into the guard's van, and the person then placed in it. None of the people transferred in and out of trains in this fashion was exceptionally heavy, and there had been no accidents. Some railway stations have portable ramps for moving loaded wheelchairs in and out of guards' vans; on account of the steepness of ramps this is more hazardous than manual lifting, and on one occasion a chair had overbalanced and tipped its occupant out. Apart from this misadventure the experience of train travellers was that railway staff were exceptionally helpful, and took great trouble to ensure that handicapped people were well looked after. A service which a number of people had found helpful was the availability at Norwich station of a wheelchair for use by ambulant handicapped people[3]. Predictably, the principal difficulty experienced by wheelchair travellers

---

[3] This was a standard wheelchair pushed by an attendant. At certain stations British Rail have available a narrow wheelchair, able to negotiate train doors and corridors, which can be used to transfer a disabled person direct from his own wheelchair to a seat on the train.

was the inaccessibility of wc compartments; the normal practice was dehydration before travelling.

It was not expected that people with wheelchairs would be travellers on local buses, and questions about buses were not put. But it transpired that ten or more people had in fact used local buses, often at some peril. Two people had attempted to take their wheelchairs with them by bus, but on each occasion the conductor (this was at the time when there were conductors on buses) had objected. Bus conductors were criticized for their lack of patience by the same people who applauded the helpfulness of railway staff, without giving proper due to the different circumstances. Apart from users of public buses, two people made regular coach trips during the summer season. One was not able to walk at all; he travelled with a friend, his wheelchair was left behind at the bus station, he was lifted into the coach and stayed in his seat all day. He had the good fortune not to need to take a urine bottle with him.

Only two people had travelled by air during the previous 12 months, and it is unreasonable, on account of the changing pattern of air travel and the likelihood that any survey made today would give different results, to draw conclusions from their experiences. It is also perhaps unreasonable to generalize from reports of habitual air travellers with wheelchairs I have talked to on other occasions. The impression is that they deprecate the cosseting treatment they are subjected to by British airlines, with the paraphernalia of ambulances, special hoists, attentive nurses, medical surveillance and the routine of health-centre processing. Rather than being caressed as fragile invalids in danger of expiry they would prefer to be treated as ordinary customers who happen to have wheelchairs. The reactions of disabled people unaccustomed to air travel may be different; the two people in Norwich who had travelled by air that year and the six who said they had done so at one time or another since they had become disabled all relished the special treatment.

1218 Swimming and football

The public indoor swimming pool in Norwich is used by handicapped people for a club session each Sunday morning. Ten people in the study had been to these sessions, and although four were chairbound none had any problems of coping. Most people who went were ferried there by voluntary helpers, and there were also helpers for those not able to undress or dress themselves. The club had invested in a hydraulic hoist to transfer severely handicapped people in and out of the pool, but after a short while it had been discarded. It was much easier for two able-bodied people to help a handicapped person in or out than to transfer him from chair to hoist and then from hoist to pool. There were no special changing cubicles large enough for wheelchair users but this was not a serious inconvenience, and other rooms in the building could be used. Among people in the sample who did not go swimming but said they would like to have done so a common reason was fear of inadvertently polluting the water. Others did not go because the water

was too cold; an effort was made each Sunday to boost the temperature but it rarely got above 25°C, which for some handicapped people was uncomfortable.

Norwich City Football Club issued each year 30 free passes to handicapped people, entitling them to sit behind the touch line at one end of the ground, either on a bench, in their wheelchairs or in invalid tricycles. These passes were used by nine people in the study. The arrangements made by the club were welcomed, but because the special area was exposed to wind and rain only the most hardy wheelchair users were able to go regularly. There had been discussions with the club secretary as to how the facility might be improved, but no practicable alternative could at that time be developed.

1219 Public lavatories

Among people in the Norwich study, 82 (29 per cent) had used public lavatories, defined as facilities provided by local authorities, and excluding public cloakrooms in buildings such as department stores and restaurants.

At the mention of public lavatories people who, while being interviewed, had been cursory suddenly became eloquent. There were vivid descriptions of encounters with public lavatories, and of the embarrassing incidents incurred by inadequate access provision. In respect of other public buildings a few steps were merely a hindrance; at public lavatories they could provoke a crisis.

For women in wheelchairs the conventional public lavatory is more blighting than it is for men. There are three factors here. The first is that a man who is disabled can, when he goes out by car or invalid tricycle, take with him a urine bottle which he can use with relative facility; analagous receptacles for women are often unmanageable. The second is that among those who actually use sanitary equipment it is much simpler for a typical disabled man to use a urinal (or if in a wheelchair to use a wc as a urinal) than it is for a disabled woman to use a wc. The third is that male incontinence appliances are much easier to wear, conceal and employ than female appliances. To compound these problems it happens that multiple sclerosis, the disability condition which in this context is most aggravating, is more prevalent among women than it is among men.

Among people interviewed in Norwich whose bladder control was poor a recurring theme was the critical necessity of dehydration – the avoidance of having anything to drink for some hours beforehand – whenever they made trips away from home. Apart from any metabolical ill effects, many found this difficult to achieve, but unless it was done it was impossible to go out with confidence. For a Saturday evening social outing the routine for some was a cutback on drinking from as early as Friday afternoon. Because of the need for prior dehydration people were not able to go out on impulse. On a sunny day friends might turn up unannounced with a pleasant car outing planned, and they would be obliged to refuse. If they were pressed they might go, decide after a few minutes it was vital to get home fast, the outing would be abandoned and the friendship threatened with termination.

Even among those careful about their drinking habits there was often a limit on the amount of time that could be spent away from home. Three people said that they had previously been able to go out all day, but now had to confine themselves to half-day outings. Some women took a commode with them in the back of the car, but it was awkward and unsavoury to use, and it was disconcerting having to ask others in the family to assist. In all the circumstances it was not surprising that a suggestion was made that the best solution would be to buy a caravan. There was not in Norwich anyone who had in fact bought a caravan simply to be able to manage an afternoon outing, but some three years later I met near Birmingham a middle-aged woman with multiple sclerosis whose husband had done so for just this purpose. She said it had given a big boost to their family life; instead of having to stop at home every weekend they were able to go on all-day trips to the Cotswolds or into Wales.

This evidence suggests that if it were a routine event for there to be provision for wheelchair users in public lavatories the lives of severely handicapped people could be much enhanced. If it were the case, for example, that every petrol station with toilet facilities incorporated suitable provision, many more handicapped people might be able to travel away from home with confidence. It would also be valuable if any new hotel building could be relied upon to have accessible lavatories. Although some disabled people would be greatly helped by these arrangements it needs to be recognized that they would not be a panacea for all; no physical provision could in practice be sufficiently comprehensive to cater for disabled people with severely malfunctioning bladders.

In Norwich one public lavatory had been adapted to cater for wheelchair users but only one person in the study had ever attempted to use it. Wheelchair users in Norwich who went into the city preferred to use accessible cloakrooms in department stores, hotels or restaurants because they were considerably more convenient, comfortable and private than the public lavatory. It is predictable that where local authorities provide lavatories catering for wheelchair users they will be of benefit to visitors from other places, and it is essential that their availability is known and their location advertised. In this connection the guidebook published in 1973 by the Central Council for the Disabled on accessible public conveniences in Britain is a useful aid[4].

Among people who had used public lavatories a common complaint was the lack of adjacent parking to facilities which appeared to be manageable. People who did visit places unfamiliar to them said that their first job when they arrived was to scout around by car to identify public lavatories they would be able to use. Three people reported that when they had been to London they had found it impossible to find accessible public lavatories. One family who had been on a Sunday said that all the lavatories they found were below ground level and that eventually the husband had had to carry his wife down a flight of steps and help her into the ladies' wc.

Among severely handicapped people a regular lament was that the cultural scheme of segregated compartments in public lavatories for men and women meant that in any normal situation it was impossible for a husband to help his wife (or vice versa) to transfer from the wheelchair to the wc seat and back again. This was a job which many husbands did at home, and which they would readily have done in public lavatories had there been a unisex compartment. One extremely handicapped woman was always pushed out in her wheelchair and did not as a rule get out of it. Because of the conventional structure of wc compartments in public lavatories she was obliged when she went on outings from Norwich to take a stick and a tripod walking aid with her (in addition to her wheelchair) in order that she could be assisted into wc compartments on her feet. When her husband had taken his holiday earlier in the year they had made a series of day trips by train to Yarmouth, Lowestoft and Cromer. Because she could not cope independently and her husband could not help her into women's wc compartments they had to arrange for a friend (female) to take her holiday at the same time as themselves in order that she could be helped into public lavatories.

1220 Public buildings: Accessibility priorities

In an attempt to determine priorities for accessibility the question was put to people in the Norwich study: 'From a personal point of view which buildings would you like to see made easy for people in wheelchairs to use, in order of preference?'

Table 12.9 The wheelchair population in Norwich: Accessibility preferences

Responses to question 'Which types of building would you like to see made easier for wheelchair users to use?'; each respondent was offered four choices.

public lavatories	64	dentists' surgeries	3
cinemas	17	public houses	3
restaurants	16	city hall	2
local shops	15	employment buildings	2
churches	12	sports stadia	2
department stores	10	art galleries	1
hotels	9	car park buildings	1
hairdressers	7	concert halls	1
theatres	7	doctors' surgeries	1
public libraries	5	museums	1
post offices	4		

The number of people giving no preferences and who were not concerned about the accessibility of buildings was 180, representing 64 per cent of the sample.

[4] Bib 93092

People who did not go out at all were not concerned whether buildings were accessible, and of those who did go out many were not in practice actually handicapped by buildings, and the question had no personal relevance. Among the others, there were some who could think of no building type that it was important for them to be easy to use. Thus of the 279 people for whom data was obtained 180 (64 per cent) were recorded as 'not concerned'. There were 49 people (18 per cent) who could think of one building type only they would like to see made more accessible, 25 (9 per cent) who mentioned two, 16 (6 per cent) three, and 9 (3 per cent) four.

The number of times that individual building types were mentioned for access desirability are listed in table 12.9. This, it can be claimed, is a rough measure of the relative importance of accessibility among different types of building. Unsurprisingly, public lavatories got the biggest vote; of the 99 people who stated any preferences 64 said public lavatories, this being 35 per cent of the 183 individual preferences which were given. The number of times that other building types were mentioned was small; only cinemas, restaurants, churches and shops were mentioned ten or more times.

1221 Priorities of accompanied chairbound people

An alternative measure of accessibility importance is simply the frequency (in terms of the number of people reported) of the use of buildings. Looking at the rank order of building types in table 12.5, this is evidently a crude instrument, but it can be refined by isolating building usage among people who are most severely handicapped. In terms of the mobility classifications employed for the survey (table 12.6) people in the 'accompanied chairbound' group are by definition the most severely handicapped. (Although building design criteria for independent wheelchair users are in certain practical respects more demanding than those for accompanied chairbound people, the superior physical abilities of people who can use their wheelchairs independently mean that they are as a rule less handicapped by the physical characteristics of buildings than chairbound people who are not independent.) Looking at the usage of buildings among all members of the wheelchair population, it can be hypothesized that where accompanied chairbound people represent a relatively high proportion of the users of a particular building or facility, there is a powerful motivation among those who are most severely handicapped to use that particular building, and a correspondingly high requirement that it should be as accessible as possible.

Table 12.10 lists principal buildings and facilities in the schedule, ranked according to the percentage of users who were categorized as accompanied chairbound. Among all people in the sample the incidence of building usage was 1376, of which the number contributed by accompanied chairbound users was 486, representing 35 per cent. This means that where the percentage scores for accompanied chairbound people are above the 35 per cent line the usage was higher than average; where it is below the line usage was lower than average.

Table 12.10 The wheelchair population in Norwich: Usage of buildings and facilities ranked by proportion of accompanied chairbound users

	all users	accompanied chairbound users	%
railway stations	26	17	65
supermarkets	68	31	46
churches	65	29	45
department stores	105	46	44
local shops	100	43	43
dentists' surgeries	21	9	43
public parks	166	71	43
cafes/restaurants	112	46	41
cinemas	27	11	41
clothes shops	73	29	40
theatres	21	8	38
all buildings	1376	486	35
public houses	34	11	32
shoe shops	34	10	29
hairdressers	70	20	29
public lavatories	82	16	20
chemists	36	3	8
doctors' surgeries	24	2	8
post offices	35	1	3

There is a discernible pattern in the ranking. Broadly, buildings which afford a service which can be delegated by the handicapped person to someone else feature low on the list, whereas those where the service cannot be delegated feature high. On this basis it is explicable that railway stations, churches and dentists' surgeries come towards the top. It is also understandable that everyday shopping facilities, given that where possible people prefer to exercise their own choice rather than rely on others, are high on the list. In that public parks offer an amenity which can only be enjoyed by the individual in person, their relatively high position is also explicable.

Buildings providing a service which, though its procurement cannot be delegated by a handicapped person to someone else, is not critical for the maintenance of basic needs feature lower on the list; in this category come cinemas, restaurants, theatres and public houses. At about the same level, though marginally lower, come buildings giving a service which, while a handicapped person might prefer to obtain it personally, can if necessary be delegated to someone else or otherwise circumvented; examples are clothes shops, hairdressers and shoe shops. At the bottom of the list come the buildings where the service can without difficulty be achieved by an agent, or which can be translated to the home of the handicapped person. On this basis the low ranking of chemists, doctors' surgeries and post offices is explicable.

The building type whose usage by accompanied chairbound people appears to contradict the thesis is public lavatories, where the score was only 20 per cent. The tentative inference which can be drawn from the data here is that in the case of public lavatories (unlike other building types, where physical obstacles are not such a deterrent as to markedly affect usage by chairbound people) problems of accessibility are so acute that they are a major determinant of usage by chairbound people.

1222 Priorities of independent chairbound people

The small number of chairbound people in Norwich who used buildings independently in their wheelchairs makes it hazardous to draw from the evidence inferences about accessibility priorities. Of the six people in this group, five had used local shops and pubs, four had used department stores, chemists, post offices and cafes or restaurants, and three had used public lavatories and clothes shops or tailors. The higher rating (by comparison with the accompanied chairbound group) received by chemists and post offices is perhaps significant. From my discussions over the years with chairbound people who travel about independently the impression is that accessibility priorities are food shops, clothes shops, chemists, hairdressers and post offices – not buildings which rate so importantly with other wheelchair users. Apart from this, priorities depend on individual interests or work; for those who are academics or students the accessibility of public libraries is vital, for those who travel frequently hotels and banks are important, for those who are interested in the arts, cinemas, theatres and concert halls are a primary concern, and for those who are religious it is churches that matter. For chairbound people who manage their own homes it can be important that self-service launderettes (not included in the Norwich questionnaire) are accessible; in any community the launderette is a valuable social meeting place but for disabled people it has often a greater significance, in that, perhaps more than any other, it is a place where they can feel that they are integrated with the goings-on of the ordinary world.

1223 Employment

One of the unrealized expectations of the Norwich study was that a substantial proportion of the wheelchair population would be in employment. Only 11 out of the 284 people, representing 4 per cent, were working in open employment, and a further five were employed in workshops for handicapped people. Two people had part-time work at home, and one person was temporarily out of work at the time of interview. Of the 50 men in the sample of working age, 39 were not employed. Of the 63 women of working age 21 were classified as housewives, and there were 35 who were not housewives and not in employment.

The people in open employment comprised seven men and four women. Three of these people were chairbound and eight were able to walk. Of the latter group one was a haemophiliac who could when he was able to go to work cope as a normal person, and travelled by public transport. Of those in employment having locomotory disabilities five were people disabled by polio, four had congenital disabilities causing only physical impairment,

and one was a double amputee. The man who was temporarily unemployed (and who shortly after the interview obtained employment) was also a double amputee. Two of the people who were able to walk used a wheelchair at their place of work, but travelled without it. Of the three who were chairbound one was able to manage independently, one was partially independent, and the other needed regular assistance, for example to transfer from his invalid tricycle to his wheelchair, and from his wheelchair to the wc. Two of these three were doing office work, one of whom worked at first floor level involving his being carried up and down stairs in his wheelchair. The third person (a woman) had trained for secretarial work but had found it difficult, principally she said because of problems of steps and stairs, to find suitable office work, and instead was doing manual work in a local factory. The ambulant people in employment included one telephonist, two office workers, one tailor, one printer and two people doing semi-skilled work in industry, one in the shoe trade and the other in an electrical components factory. Of the five employed in special workshops four were working at the local Remploy factory (the agency which administers sheltered workshops for handicapped people with support from the Department of Employment) and one was working at the adult training centre for mentally handicapped people administered at the time by the health department of Norwich Corporation. Since the survey was made the social services department in Norwich has built a purpose-designed day centre and work centre, where people who are too handicapped to manage at the Remploy factory can work when they are able and earn a small income.

In the national survey made by the Office of Population Censuses and Surveys in late 1973[5], only 5 per cent of the 978 adult wheelchair users in the sample were in employment, indicating that the Norwich population may be typical. In the national sample the disablement categories with the highest proportion of people in employment were polio (28 per cent), paraplegics and tetraplegics (19 per cent), and cerebral palsy (16 per cent). In the study of wheelchair users made in Hull 4 out of 71 were in employment[6], and in Taunton 4 out of 49[7]. In the postal questionnaire survey made in Leicestershire, 58 out of the wheelchair population of 448 answered yes to the question 'Do you go out to work away from your home?'[8].

While there was no evidence from the Norwich study that anyone looking for employment had actually been prevented from obtaining it because of the physical difficulties of coping with awkward buildings, there did appear to be a tendency among employers to under-estimate the capacity of severely disabled people to cope with physical obstacles. They assumed (it was alleged) that because a disabled person could not get about the office independently or manage the wc on his own he would not be able to do the work for which he was being considered, even though the individual might be

[5] Bib 93512
[6] Bib 93234
[7] Bib 93233
[8] Bib 93232, p10

physically quite capable of doing the actual job. The two employed people in the sample who for mobility relied always on others showed that it was not essential to be able to get about independently.

Given that physical environmental problems were not a major determinant, there is still the question why it was that so few people were employed. Although no attempt was made to explore this area thoroughly there is no doubt that the reason among most people was that, simply on account of the degree of their disability, they did not have the resources to manage a day's work, or if they did were not always able to do it with regularity. Compared with the effect of personal physical handicap other contributory causes – a shortage of opportunities for example, lack of transport or inadequate vocational training – were of little account.

Among people interviewed in the parallel study of disabled drivers (reported in the following pages) there were 75 people out of 162 who were in open employment. Here again, physical barriers in buildings were not as a rule a cause of major concern. In two cases disabled people said that employers had been most anxious to help, and had adapted buildings to make it easier for them to cope. A schoolteacher said that a school where she had applied for a job had wanted to entirely reorganize school schedules in order to accommodate her, avoiding the necessity for her to get up and down stairs to attend classes.

1224   Kerbs and ramps

In discussions with wheelchair users in Norwich about how they actually got from their homes to the buildings that they used, 68 people in the sample said that street kerbs were a major problem. Many people said they would be able to manage more comfortably and might go out more frequently if it were a regular practice for kerbs to be ramped at street intersections. It was not uncommon for alternative travel routes, for example from home to shops in the city, to have been carefully analyzed, with the selected route being not always the most direct but the one with fewest awkward kerbs to negotiate. Because kerbs were such obstacles it was a regular practice for wheelchairs to be pushed along the roadway, so causing a hazard to other road users. One couple said that they preferred to go round the city on Sundays, when the wheelchair could be pushed along the road without being a nuisance.

Arising from all this it was arranged with the city engineer's department that some 15 kerbs at strategic points in the central shopping area of the city should be ramped to assist wheelchair users; when the programme was implemented there were appreciative comments from people who had previously complained. As a direct response to pressure from disability organizations, many local authorities in Britain have in recent years undertaken extensive programmes of kerb ramping at street corners, and make it a rule in new constructions that stepped kerbs can be avoided. For many wheelchair users these programmes have probably been of greater practical benefit than concentrated campaigning for accessibility to public buildings in general.

The preferred gradient of ramps for wheelchair users was not a question which the Norwich study aimed to answer. It was apparent however, particularly among people pushed out by an elderly husband or wife, that even the gentlest gradient could be an obstacle. One husband, citing a local street having a gradient of the order of 1 in 20, said that he and his wife were obliged to limit their expeditions to journeys around the block from their home, where streets were level. On the question of steps versus ramps, specific questions were included in the study of disabled drivers, and it is appropriate to record the evidence here.

Of the 162 people in the disabled driver study there were 118 people who did not use wheelchairs. These people were asked whether they had a distinct preference for ramps (the term 'slopes' was used during interviews) or steps, and 32 said that they had. There was a marked preference for steps; 20 people preferred them as against 8 in favour of slopes, and among those who were amputees there was only one who said he found it easier to cope with slopes rather than steps. Four people said that when going down they preferred to use steps, and when going up to use slopes. The point here is that for ambulant disabled people there is a greater hazard of overbalancing when descending ramps, and in the case of long leg amputees there is the additional danger that the action of descending a ramp can cause the knee lock to disengage. Short steep ramps are the biggest threat; one woman in the wheelchair study reported that the only time she had had a bad accident, causing a fractured leg, was when she overbalanced on a portable ramp installed to avoid the use of a single high step.

Regarding steps and staircases in and around public buildings there were frequent complaints from people in both samples regarding the lack of handrails. Severely handicapped ambulant people said that steps were usually manageable if a handrail was available, but if not they had to rely on someone else for support. Among people in the disabled driver group steps to buildings were not insuperable obstacles. One man who went out independently said that he regularly had to accost passers by to help him up steps, and did not have any inhibitions about doing so.

1225   Doors and lifts

Among people in the wheelchair study there were few complaints regarding doors. The six people who went out independently in their wheelchairs reported that other people were always willing to open doors when asked, and to help them through. One person said that when she went into the city she had two people to accompany her, one to push the chair, and the other to hold doors open; when she went to the bank she needed two people to hold the doors open. Apart from comments from two people about the heaviness of the lift doors at the city hall there were no reports of inability to manage lifts, either on account of their being too small or controls being inaccessible.

1226 Disabled drivers in Norwich

To complement the study of wheelchair users in Norwich, a related study was made of disabled drivers. Apart from findings already reported relating to employment buildings, steps and ramps, it provided information regarding car parking, pedestrian precincts, shopping habits and the general effects of obstacles in and around buildings. In the context of the need for special provisions in buildings, it was also designed to evaluate the responses of disabled people to special equipment and facilities, such as invalid tricycles, parking badges and reserved parking places, which drew attention to their status as people with disabilities in the community.

Of the 162 people in the study the great majority – 84 per cent – were male. To account for this, there are three subpopulations where men predominate: (1) the normal driver population; (2) the disabled population in employment and needing personal transport to get to and from work, and (3) those with disabilities associated with war service. Of the people in the study, 35 per cent were aged 60 or over, and 64 per cent were 50 or over.

Compared with people in the wheelchair study the disabled drivers were active; 137 (85 per cent) went out every day or nearly every day, six went out two or three times each week, and 19 went out only about once each week or less frequently. Two out of three travelled regularly into the city.

The expectation was that these people would be severely restricted in their mobility, and able to walk a short distance only. The external criteria for membership of the study appeared to guarantee this. Either a person had to have been issued with a parking badge saying 'the driver of this vehicle suffers from severe physical disability which impairs mobility', or had been issued with a vehicle on health grounds, among which the most important consideration was the degree to which independent mobility was affected. Each person was asked how far he was able to walk (with personal assistance if need be) without discomfort. Where walking ability varied from day to day, the least distance which could commonly be walked was recorded. Surprisingly, 44 people (27 per cent) claimed that they were able to walk at least a quarter of a mile. A further 69 (43 per cent) said they could walk between 50 yards and a quarter of a mile. Only 49 (30 per cent) were severely limited.

1227 Parking places

At the time the study was made there were three special parking bays in Norwich reserved for disabled drivers. They were all in one place, away from the shops at the top of the hill alongside the central library. It was known from the survey of wheelchair users that not many disabled people used the library, and it was a surprise therefore to find that no less than 45 people in the study, representing 28 per cent, had in fact used them. It seemed that disabled drivers regarded these places as their own

special property. They made a point of using them, even if it seemed irrational that they should. Complaints against ordinary drivers trespassing were a recurring theme at interviews, and there were five drivers who said that, when they arrived to find all places occupied by ordinary cars, they made a point of parking their own car so that it obstructed the motorist who was poaching on their territory. On a number of occasions there had been angry scenes.

It was apparent from discussions with disabled drivers during the survey that the abuse by normal drivers of special parking places was not unique to Norwich. Control was ineffective elsewhere, and there was no sure technique for deterring trespassers. The possibility of employing special symbols on signs was discussed, and two people suggested that the floor surface of reserved bays should be marked by special lines or other indicators.

A purpose of the survey was to determine whether there was a demand for reserved parking places in other parts of the city, particularly in the central shopping area. Of people in the study 100 favoured additional reserved places, 21 were not in favour or said they could manage satisfactorily without, and 41, mainly people who rarely came into the city, said they were not concerned. When people were asked where they would like to have reserved parking places, 22 different locations were suggested. Clearly it was impossible to satisfy everyone.

It was pointed out by many of the most severely handicapped people that reserved parking places would be virtually useless for them unless they were immediately adjacent to the building they were visiting. In this connection it was clear that the reserved places at the library were of benefit only to people who had relatively little impairment; this was confirmed by the record of occupancy, showing that on only 5 out of 98 occasions were they ever used by the most handicapped group, those with invalid tricycles. It is not practicable for reserved parking places for disabled drivers to be made available every few yards along principal shopping streets; in the circumstances it is clear that the privilege for parking on restricted streets (and in other towns unlimited time at meters) is more beneficial than having special parking bays. The people who were most pressing in their advocacy of reserved parking bays were those not severely limited in their walking ability, and who did not appreciate that having what they wanted would not be in the interest of people more handicapped than themselves or of other road users.

1228 The orange badge scheme

The practical procedures which this evidence suggests might be of most benefit to disabled drivers are now endorsed by official regulations. The Disabled Persons (Badges for Motor Vehicles) Regulations 1975 allow for a disabled driver or passenger holding the official orange badge to park at meter bays for an unlimited period or, by showing an official disc, for a period of up to two hours on streets where there are yellow lines. Paragraph 8 of the accompanying Department of the Environment Circular[9] says:

'Many measures introduced in town centres for traffic safety or environmental reasons – parking restrictions, pedestrianization, provision of footbridges etc – while of great value to the public at large, may present problems to disabled people. The orange badge scheme goes some way to overcome these, but local authorities are asked to have regard to their needs wherever measures of this kind are introduced, and in particular to consider providing parking space for use by orange badge holders as close as possible to their work, restaurants, shops, theatres, churches and other places they may need to visit. These may be reserved for their exclusive use by orders made under the Road Traffic Regulation Act 1967. Whether to allow badge holders' vehicles to enter pedestrianized areas can only be decided in the light of local circumstances. Where this is done it is suggested that all types of vehicles displaying an orange badge should be free to enter.'

1229 Pedestrian precincts

The long term development plan for the central area of Norwich allows for the whole of the central shopping district to be restricted to pedestrian use, with special access arrangements for essential vehicles. As a start one of the main shopping streets, London Street, was made a foot street in July 1967. One of the purposes of the survey was to ascertain to what extent the shopping habits of disabled people had altered because of this, and to predict the effects of further pedestrianization.

When the closing to traffic of London Street was planned concern was expressed about the problems of disabled people, and it was arranged that they should be permitted to take their cars into the prohibited zone. Drivers who had done so had had no difficulty obtaining permission from the police to park, and many used the area regularly. Others had however been deterred by the prohibitory signs, they did not want to trouble policemen or traffic wardens for permission to enter, and they preferred to go elsewhere. There were 14 who said that they tended not to visit shops in London Street they had formerly used; they did not consider this a major inconvenience.

Regarding general shopping habits, the preference for local shopping centres found among wheelchair users was repeated among disabled drivers. It is also confirmed in the evidence from a selected sample of disabled people reported in the Edinburgh University study *Planning for disabled people in the urban environment*[10]. Among reasons from disabled drivers for not using the centre of Norwich were that it was too crowded for comfort and safety, that there was too much traffic, that the one-way street system was complicated, and that there were too many hills.

1230 The effect of architectural obstacles

Based on the evidence which disabled drivers gave of their coping difficulties, it was estimated that about one person in three would benefit significantly if steps to buildings and other 'architectural barriers' were avoidable. For many of these, modifications to buildings would in practice only be advantageous if at the same time the route to the building, particularly in respect of accessible parking, could be facilitated.

The people whom it was estimated would not benefit significantly were in the main those who were not handicapped by the way that buildings are conveniently designed; they could use steps and staircases without difficulty, and were not inconvenienced by the lack of facilities such as special wcs. Of the others, seven did not use public buildings at all, and a further seven were so severely disabled that no modification of the physical environment could aid them. A final group – comprising 24 people – were those with limited energy resources, such as people with severe bronchitis and heart complaints. For them the problems posed by the topography of Norwich meant that the accessibility of buildings was often irrelevant.

1231 Camouflage versus exposure

In many situations people with disabilities cannot easily use buildings if they are treated in the same way as able-bodied people. In some situations they cannot cope at all. If, either in the planning of new buildings or the adaptation of existing ones, these difficulties are recognized and special arrangements made, what ought to be the tactics? If practical policies of helping disabled people to opt into the ordinary busy world are to be applied, ought the implications of disablement to be suppressed in order to minimize differences and achieve normalization goals? Should the tactics employed be those of disguise or euphemy? Or ought the differences to be explicitly expressed, using tactics of acknowledgement and advertisement?

The strategy advocated in this book is, with qualifications according to circumstances, one of explicit exposure. Before examining *why* this strategy is preferred it is important to know something of *how* disabled people respond to provisions which reflect their situation as people who have disabilities; if the response is generally hostile the strategy will fail. Reference has already been made to parking places reserved exclusively for disabled drivers, the evidence being that they were generally welcomed rather than being shunned. In respect of disability reflecting devices the study of disabled drivers in Norwich examined also attitudes to invalid tricycles, 'disabled driver' car plates, parking badges on cars and symbols identifying special services for disabled people[11].

[9] Bib 93542
[10] Bib 93006, p18
[11] For a more comprehensive examination of this topic than the report which follows see Bib 93082.

1232 Invalid tricycles

Of the 162 disabled drivers in the Norwich study, 100 had had personal experience of using an invalid tricycle. The general impression was that it served as a badge rather than a brand of disability, with positive rather than negative associations. Typical responses were 'I couldn't have managed without it', 'I was only too glad to have it' and, in respect of its supposed stigmatizing characteristics, 'I don't take no notice of that'. People who had previously not been able to leave their homes by themselves said that they were so pleased to get out and about that they were not bothered what other people might think of their vehicles. They did not mind what sort of vehicle it was, and the initial exhilaration of independence had persisted.

It is not the business of this book to engage in the long-running controversy over whether disabled people in Britain currently issued with invalid tricycles should have small cars instead. The fact that disabled drivers in Norwich were generally well disposed to invalid tricycles is no basis for claiming that they are better than small cars. It simply confirms that it is better to have a tricycle than not to have a vehicle at all. No one who had graduated to being a car user wanted to revert to being a tricycle user.

1233 Disabled driver plates

There were some 20 people in the study who displayed plates saying for example: 'Disabled driver, No hand signals'. They were in the main drivers of ordinary cars, since invalid tricycle drivers considered additional advertisement superfluous.

Two drivers had reservations about proclaiming their disablement, and said they only did so because they had been told driving test examiners would require it. Five people thought it was advantageous to display plates, the consequence being more consideration from other drivers. A man employed at a local printing works had had enormous 'Disabled driver' notices printed; he displayed them prominently at both ends of his car and had passed copies on to other disabled drivers. Three people felt that the fact they were disabled drivers ought to be advertised more effectively. One suggested that disabled drivers should be issued with special registration marks, incorporating for example the letters MOH for Ministry of Health.

1234 Parking badges

Of the 162 disabled drivers in the Norwich study, 131 had been issued with concessionary parking badges, and of these 104 (79 per cent) had no criticisms or reservations about them. Of the 27 people who did have reservations, two refused to display their badges. Four more did not display them because they felt their invalid tricycles were sufficient identity of their status. There were 17 people who put their badges on show only when parked in places where badges were needed; of these the majority did not display their badges because they did not consider the inscription on the badges applied to themselves.

1235 Special symbols on signs

One of the purposes of the study of disabled drivers was to discover reactions to a proposal that distinctive notices incorporating special symbols should be used to identify facilities suitable for disabled people in and around buildings. The significance of special symbols on signs is discussed later in this commentary.

At the time of the study it was anticipated that the symbol employed on signs and notices in Norwich would depict a figure in a wheelchair only, comparable to the design subsequently adopted internationally (diagram 14.1). The purpose was to discover whether, if this course were adopted, handicapped people other than wheelchair users would regard themselves as included, or excluded because they did not in fact use wheelchairs. The questions put were hypothetical but the impression was that most people would welcome distinctive symbols they could relate to. Of the 120 people in the study who expressed opinions, 101 (84 per cent) did not have reservations about the proposed wheelchair symbol. Of these people 31 were wheelchair users, but the great majority were ambulant disabled people; they said they would not be deterred by a wheelchair symbol, and if it were apparent that the facility was intended for handicapped people in general (for example parking bays) they would have no reservations about using it. Of the 19 who expressed reservations, 10 wished always to be treated as normal people. The other nine expressed reservations about how the programme might be implemented or whether it would have any relevance. One person only was opposed.

1236 Rejection of disability status

An analysis was made among people in the disabled driver study to ascertain whether those who appeared to reject membership of the disabled group were among those relatively severely disabled or not. The criteria used to identify people as 'group rejects' were (1) those concerned about the 'stigma' of invalid tricycles, (2) those refusing to display parking badges, or displaying them only when in use, (3) those refusing to obtain parking badges, and (4) those who disapproved of the proposal for distinctive symbols on signs. On this basis, 32 people (20 per cent) were classed as 'rejects'. If it were the case that there was no association between degree of disability (measured in terms of wheelchair use) and rejection of disability status there would be about 9 wheelchair users among these 32. In fact there were only five, which, while not being statistically significant, suggests there may be a tendency among people who are most severely disabled to have fewer inhibitions about perceiving themselves as disabled than those who are less handicapped. The great majority of wheelchair users, 89 per cent, did not indicate any inclination to deny their situation as disabled people.

13 The behaviour of disabled people

1300 The handicapping effects of disability

Among people with physical disabilities there is no direct cause and effect relationship between the degree of disability and the usage of buildings. Apart from the disability itself, there are a whole range of contributory influences which determine how actively a disabled person involves himself in the life of the ordinary world. Personality, in terms of attitudes, motivations and goals, is a crucial factor. On a practical level, the disabled person who is supported by a capable spouse or family is at an advantage. It helps if there is someone in the family with a car, and the disabled person able to drive himself is even better situated. Given that transport is available, income and cash resources are likely to determine the extent to which a disabled person uses buildings, particularly those such as pubs, restaurants, theatres, cinemas and hotels. The number of buildings which a disabled person uses is admittedly a crude index of achievement, but it is a permissible measure and table 12.8 confirms that among wheelchair users in Norwich the availability of transport was strongly associated with building usage.

It is very rare that a disease or injury which causes a physical disability has no related handicapping effects. Among these may be damage to mental faculties, incontinence, loss of speech, blindness, pain, loss of sensation, faulty coordination and impotence. The ways in which these and other handicapping effects tend to be associated with particular kinds of disablement are shown in table 13.1. The table lists conditions which are overtly disabling and excludes those such as epilepsy, haemophilia, cardiac disease and chronic bronchitis which, while they can be severely physically handicapping, do not necessarily involve locomotory impairment.

The values given in the table need to be interpreted with caution. Actual handicapping effects vary widely between individuals having the same disabling condition, for example among hemiplegics and people with multiple sclerosis. The values assigned are based on the known aetiology of disabling conditions, on observations of disabled people and on guidance from medical and paramedical advisers; no quantifiable evidence is available by which they can be substantiated or not.

Handicapping effects are ranked across the table, in estimated order of the significance of their influence on the use of buildings. The disabling conditions are ranked from top to bottom, roughly according to the aggregate score of handicapping effects. While practising clinicians may not concur with the values assigned and may be critical of the definitive structure of the table, the concept of a hierarchy of disability is commonly implicit in the writings of rehabilitation specialists, and in particular those of P J R Nichols[1].

The hierarchy has multiple sclerosis at one extreme and polio at the other. The ranking does not purport to be a reliable indicator of achievement in terms of building usage. It does however support the hypothesis, confirmed by reference to table 12.8, that, other factors being equal,

people with some kinds of disability are better equipped than others to tackle the trials of life.

1301 Physical disability and mental impairment

The most damaging handicapping effect that can be associated with physical disablement is impairment of mental faculties. To state the obvious, a physical disability is physically handicapping. It is only handicapping where, to meet particular goals, effort is needed from the damaged parts of the body. Thus professional people such as accountants, solicitors and civil servants are barely handicapped by lower limb disability, or even by being confined to a wheelchair. Other professional people, such as doctors, engineers, teachers, architects and journalists, may not be able to undertake all the duties they might otherwise have handled, but they can often find alternative means of successfully exploiting the special professional skills and expertise they have acquired.

By contrast bus drivers, construction workers, restaurant waiters, coal miners, industrial assembly line workers, farm workers and others whose capacity to earn a livelihood is dependent on physical attributes are utterly handicapped if they become disabled. Housewives, in that their work is almost wholly physical, are in the same situation, with the further complication that no alternative role is open; the consequence may be that the wage earner has to abandon his job to look after the family, with financial dependence on state benefits.

In respect of the associations shown in table 13.1 between disabling conditions and impairment of mental faculties, qualifications are needed. There are important variations in the handicapping effects of different forms of mental impairment. There can be intellectual impairment or emotional disturbance, or a combination of the two. Loss of memory may occur as a consequence of the impairment. As an example birth trauma (aside from causing physical disability) may also mean impairment of appreciation of space and number; this will be a permanent defect, capable to some extent of being mitigated by training. On the other hand emotional instability, of the kind which may occur with hemiplegia or multiple sclerosis, can seriously interfere with a person's ability to achieve his potential in areas where he appears to be relatively normal.

There is a high incidence of mental impairment among people disabled from birth by spina bifida. When in the early 1960s valve surgery on spina bifida babies was pioneered, there were expectations that these children would have capabilities comparable to those of polio children ten years previously. Now that careful studies of actual performance have been made, particularly those by Michael Laurence[2], there is disillusion. A high proportion of children were, it is clear, already

---

[1] For example, Bib 93410, 93412, 93430, 93431. For further notes on the effects of specific conditions reference should be made to the glossary, section 91.
[2] For example Bib 93282

irretrievably brain damaged when the operation was performed[3]. Had it been the case that spina bifida did not generally cause brain damage, affected children would still, because of the problems imposed by incontinence and sensory paralysis, have been less well equipped to cope with competitive living than those with polio.

In the case of people handicapped from birth by cerebral palsy, those with spastic cerebral palsy (the most common variety) are invariably handicapped mentally, whereas those with athetoid cerebral palsy are not. Despite the handicaps of gross deformity, uncontrollable movements and inability to communicate by speech, there are some severe athetoid people who have been able to realize remarkable intellectual talents.

1302 Incontinence

The problems which beset people who are incontinent have already been discussed in relation to the use of buildings and the need for suitable lavatory facilities. Incontinence is not an attribute which disabled people customarily flaunt in public. In the lay mind it is associated with elderly confused people, and not with capable-looking young people in wheelchairs. Ignorance about the ramifications of incontinence can provoke unwarranted criticism of particular people who have disabilities. It is unfair, for example, to expect a traumatic paraplegic to manage as smoothly as a polio paraplegic with superficially identical physical impairment, or a person with multiple sclerosis and little outward sign of disability to do as well as an apparently similar person with Friedrich's ataxia.

1303 Other handicapping effects

The third important disability-associated handicapping effect which can influence the use of buildings is the uncertainty of knowing from one day to the next how well one is going to be able to manage physically. This unpredictability is most acute among people with multiple sclerosis; capabilities can fluctuate spectacularly from day to day, making it impossible to plan programmes ahead with any confidence that they can be fulfilled. Among people with rheumatoid arthritis, pain and joint stiffness may vary from one day to the next, and among amputees pain can at times be debilitating; drugs may relieve pain but they can also make the disabled person less mentally alert and affect his ability to work to a predetermined programme.

In the context of the use of buildings other handicapping effects associated with disability are relatively of lesser significance. The impairment of speech can be more handicapping than impairment of vision, for reasons discussed below with reference to deafness, communication and blindness[4]. Bodily deformity can also be handicapping. Among normal people, attitudes of revulsion, intolerance and impatience are perhaps most prevalent in the case of disabilities involving severe bodily deformity, along with deafness or an inability to speak coherently. Such attitudes can be reflected in a

denial of opportunities for employment and other activities involving the use of buildings. Equally the disabled person himself may, because of the negative reactions which his disability evokes, concur in the evaluation of his inferior status, and be discouraged from participating in normal activities.

The remaining handicapping effects listed in table 13.1, namely physical deterioration, loss of sensation, lack of coordination and impairment of sex function, have little association with the use of buildings; they serve to give a more comprehensive indication of the relative status of different conditions. In the lay mind, steady physical deterioration, such as commonly occurs with muscular dystrophy, is imagined to be particularly damaging and disturbing. In practice it very rarely is; in his study of people with muscular dystrophy Surridge found, despite severe physical disability, a complete lack of neuroticism[5].

1304 Congenital versus acquired conditions

There is an important distinction to be made between congenitally disabling conditions – those present at birth – and acquired disability conditions caused by injury or disease. Of the conditions listed in table 13.1 only cerebral palsy and spina bifida are present at birth, although muscular dystrophy, brittle bones (Fragilitas ossium) and Friedrich's ataxia are genetically determined, and tend to become manifest during childhood. The advantage that people with acquired disabilities have is that they have a fund of normal experience on which they can draw, making them more competent in social and other situations. It is valuable if a particular skill, trade or profession has been learned which can continue to be employed subsequently. This issue is discussed again with regard to education, where there is a marked difference between the performance of congenitally handicapped students and those with acquired disabilities.

In his relations with others, affecting for example employment opportunities, the person with an acquired disability has more prestige than a person with a congenital or inherited disability. In a study among employees in the New York area reported by Yuker and others[6], orthopaedically disabled people were found to be most acceptable, followed closely by cardiacs. Epileptics, people with cerebral palsy and blind or partially sighted people were much less acceptable. The physical disability caused by an accident has no social stigma. Paraplegics are considered unfortunate because their handicap is known to be purely physical; the person with cerebral palsy on the other hand has always to prove that he is not stupid. The child congenitally disabled because of thalidomide is socially relatively advantaged;

[3] Anderson (Bib 93380, p180) reports a review of surveys of children with spina bifida and hydrocephalus suggesting that the majority in this group fall into the IQ range 70–90.
[4] See 1307. The evidence of table 12.8, while being based on small numbers, is also supportive.
[5] Bib 93302, p89, see also 9162
[6] Bib 93301, p75

Table 13.1 Hierarchy of disabling conditions

	impairment of mental faculties	incontinence	day-to-day condition unpredictable	communication difficulties	impairment of vision	bodily deformity	pain	progressive deterioration	sensory impairment	lack of coordination	impairment of sex functions
poliomyelitis	○	○	○	○	○	◔	○	○	○	○	○
lower limb amputation	○	○	○	○	○	◔	◔	○	◔	○	○
brittle bones	○	○	○	○	○	◑	◔	○	○	○	○
muscular dystrophy	○	○	○	○	○	◕	○	◕	○	○	○
motor neurone disease	○	◔	○	○	○	◑	○	●	○	○	○
syringomyelia	○	○	○	○	○	◑	○	◕	◑	○	○
osteoarthritis	○	○	◔	○	○	◔	◑	◑	○	○	◔
Parkinson's disease	○	○	○	◑	○	◔	○	◑	◔	◔	◔
Friedrich's ataxia	○	○	○	◔	○	◔	○	●	○	●	○
paraplegia and tetraplegia	○	●	○	○	○	◔	○	○	●	○	◑
hemiplegia	◑	◔	○	◑	◔	◑	◔	◔	◑	◔	◔
rheumatoid arthritis	○	○	◕	○	○	●	●	◕	○	○	◔
spina bifida	◕	●	○	○	○	◔	○	○	●	○	◑
cerebral palsy	◕	◔	○	●	○	◕	○	○	◑	◑	◔
multiple sclerosis	◕	●	●	◔	◑	◑	○	●	◔	◕	◑

The values signified by the circles are as follows

○ No directly associated effects.

◔ Directly associated effects in some cases, or slight associated effects in general.

◑ Commonly associated effects, particularly prevalent where the disability is severe.

◕ Associated effects in the majority of cases, general where the disability is severe.

● Associated effects in all cases, with exceptions only where the disability is minimal.

his disability is known to have been caused by the drug manufacturer, and is not attributable to any genetic defects[7].

Bearing in mind that the data in table 12.8 on the usage of buildings by people with different disability conditions do not discount the important age variable there are, in the light of the preceding discussion, comments to be made. Of the diagnostic categories where the mean age of people in the Norwich study was below 50, there was no one with polio, muscular dystrophy or a congenital disability not causing mental impairment who had used no buildings at all or only one. By contrast 9 of the 33 people with multiple sclerosis and 7 of the 17 people with cerebral palsy had used no buildings or one only. These data are not conclusive but they do support the contention that people with privileged disability conditions are more likely to be frequent users of buildings than those with non-privileged conditions.

1305   The hierarchy of disability

In the hierarchy of disability conditions poliomyelitis is unique in that, apart from causing bodily deformity in severe cases, it has none of the inhibiting effects associated with other disabilities. Polio, when it flourished in the late 1940s and early 1950s, was a disease of civilization, tending disproportionately to disable people in the middle and upper social groups[8]. During the past 20 years or so people with polio have been particularly prominent in disability-interest groups, often serving on committees as representatives of 'the disabled', a role (as mentioned earlier) they are ill-qualified to perform on account of their unrepresentativeness.

With the disappearance of polio and war injury disabled people (a large proportion of the latter being in the privileged amputation group) it is likely that an increasingly dominant role in disablement politics will be assumed by traumatic paraplegics, despite their small numbers and the variety of disability-associated problems they contend with. There is at present (1976) a valuable and vocal contingent of paraplegics in the British House of Lords, a happening related to the propensity of the upper classes to fall off horses.

An effect of continuing advances in medical technology is that the calibre of the disabled population is deteriorating. First, the number of people with simple disabilities caused by injury or disease is declining; in this connection there is in Britain no marked continuing increase in the incidence of traffic injuries[9], and those that are severe are often multiple injuries involving brain injury. Second, the diseases not yet defeated by medical science, such as multiple sclerosis, hemiplegia and rheumatoid arthritis, tend to be among the more intractably handicapping. Third, there is among the residue of the population a higher proportion of congenitally disabled people who are often multiply handicapped. Fourth, by benefit of medical intervention, larger numbers of people, who in the past would not have stayed alive, are surviving from birth with multiple handicaps. Fifth, medical capabilities and the

development of life-sustaining drugs mean that old people are living longer, and as they live longer they are prone to the multiple handicapping conditions associated with old age.

In the political arena of working for improved services for handicapped people there is a crucial role for those who are themselves handicapped. In view of the deteriorating calibre of the population as a whole an enhanced responsibility falls on those disabled people who are high up in the hierarchy; their duty as consumers should be to expand their area of social and political concern, rather than retracting it by establishing defensive elitist groups.

1306   Employment statistics

An issue related to this discussion is the actual as well as the relative decline in recent years in the numbers of employable disabled people. The register of disabled persons maintained by the Department of Employment is arguably a valid index, but the proposition is supported by statistics. In 1951 there were 906 008 disabled people on the register, 666 454 in 1961 and 574 640 in 1974[10]. The register is allied to the quota scheme, whereby all firms of 20 or more people are required to employ 3 per cent who are disabled. In 1972 nearly 60 per cent of firms were failing to comply, and, owing to the shortage of numbers of people registering, the 3 per cent rate had become a practical impossibility, however the distribution of disabled employees might be made[11]. With reference to the calibre of disabled people seeking employment a recent report from the Department of Employment says:

'The Department's recent detailed analysis of the characteristics of its unemployed disabled clients indicates that many of those who have been unemployed for any length of time would find it hard to get jobs on account of their age, lack of education or skill, or the presence of some social disadvantage, whether or not they were disabled.'[12]

1307   Blind and deaf people

In the hierarchy of disabling conditions blindness is relatively privileged, and deafness is very underprivileged. Among normal outsiders blindness, because it is much easier to imagine how distressing it

---

[7] These issues are discussed by F Schoenberger in Bib 93302, p44.
[8] For relevant evidence see Bib 93236, p12.
[9] Statistics of road casualties issued by the Department of the Environment (Bib 93794) show that in Great Britain the casualty rate per vehicle mile has been declining for many years. Compared with 1973, road deaths in 1974 decreased by 7 per cent to their lowest figure since 1969, and serious casualties decreased by 8 per cent to their lowest figure since 1959. There was a fall of 8 per cent in the number of slight casualties.
[10] Bib 93481, p11, supplemented by information from the Department of Employment.
[11] Bib 93481, p13
[12] Bib 93481, p12

might be, is regarded as a tragedy[13]; deafness by contrast is a music hall joke. There are many examples of blind people who manage well in the community, and have achieved notable careers in administration, journalism, politics, the professions, teaching and other fields. There are few examples of equal success among deaf people[14]. Deafness is isolating and socially destructive in a way that blindness is not.

In respect of modifications to buildings there is relatively little that architects can do to enhance the potential for living of blind and deaf people, although possibilities for mitigating the effect of physical obstacles and hazards are discussed later in this commentary[15]. In respect of the wider arena of environmental services there is much that can be done. Society's expectations of the competitive performance of blind people are low, and by sustaining a network of special schools, workshops and residential institutions for the blind, it helps to ensure that in actuality achievement matches expectations. As with special services for the physically handicapped, not all of these special solutions ought to be condemned, but with imaginative initiative blind people could be helped to take their place among sighted people in the busy world.

For deaf people the problems of communication are greater, and it is more difficult for example to assimilate deaf children into ordinary schools. People with severe speech disabilities have comparable problems. Christy Brown, the athetoid spastic who learned to communicate by typing with the big toe of his left foot, has written:

'Speech has always been one of the biggest obstacles in my endeavour to make ordinary contact with people. It has been the one aspect of my handicap that has caused me the bitterest pain, for without speech one is practically lost, curtained off from other people, left wishing to say a million things and not able to say one.'[16]

1308 Mental handicap

In the lay mind 'mental patients' are a vague assembly of people with mental troubles of an indeterminate kind. The basic distinction between mental handicap, meaning people of low intelligence or a low level of performance owing to brain damage, and mental illness, meaning people whose behaviour is abnormal or disturbed, is not widely understood.

Because mentally handicapped people are not ill it is arguable that they should be looked after in hospitals under medical direction. This is however the traditional practice in Britain, where large numbers of mentally handicapped people are cared for in subnormality institutions administered by hospital authorities. In recent years, fostered by increasing political concern about the social and moral propriety of perpetuating large institutions, efforts have been made to establish alternatives. Among the more publicized achievements have been those of the Wessex Regional Health Authority which has pioneered the development of community hostels. Placed, as most of them are, on hospital campuses with the inhibiting paraphernalia of medical

administration, they do not appear to be a radical alternative[17].

The Department of Health has also been doing its best to encourage the transfer of responsibility for mentally handicapped people from hospital authorities to the social services departments of local authorities[18]. An official building note on the planning of local authority hostels for adult mentally handicapped people has been issued[19], its recommendations being a prescription for the establishment of small institutions.

In terms of the integration of mentally handicapped people into the community, a preferred strategy might be that local housing authorities should become more actively involved. Little so far has been done in this direction by housing authorities, but some of the more progressive social services authorities have schemes for renting ordinary housing from local authorities or other landlords for the accommodation of small groups of mentally handicapped people, usually with a resident warden. Some encouraging developments are reported by Sandra Francklin[20].

In the field of employment services for mentally handicapped people there have in recent years been improvements. What formerly were known as adult training centres and administered by health departments of local authorities have since April 1971 been the responsibility of social services departments. In some areas these are supplemented by work centres managed by voluntary agencies, in particular the Spastics Society.

Schools for mentally handicapped children are commonly referred to as ESN and SSN, meaning Educationally Subnormal and Severely Subnormal[21]. ESN schools, sometimes known as schools for slow learners, cater for children who are roughly in the IQ range of 50 to 70. In this group there are probably significantly more physically handicapped children than among a normal school population, due in part to the prevalence of mental handicap among children affected by spina bifida. For the most severely handicapped children, broadly those having

---

[13] Yuker and others (Bib 93301, p76) report a study among high school students rating blindness as the worst handicap 'to face', followed by loss of a leg, deafness, loss of an arm and facial burns. Two other studies reported blindness as being thought worse than deafness.
[14] The most notable example in contemporary public life is Jack Ashley, whose traumatic experience of deafness is described in his autobiography, Bib 93324.
[15] See 1423, 1424
[16] Bib 93323, p137
[17] For an account of the Wessex policy see Bib 93363. For a report of a comparable project in Wales of institutionalized housing on a hospital campus see Bib 93369.
[18] Bib 93340, p35
[19] Bib 93360. For a criticism of DHSS policy see Ann Shearer's report in Bib 93367.
[20] Bib 93361
[21] The preferred official usage is to drop the term SSN, and to refer to schools for mentally handicapped children as ESN (Moderate) or ESN (Severe). Design recommendations for these schools are in sections 727 and 728.

an IQ of less than 50, there are SSN schools. These were formerly administered by health departments of local authorities and known as junior training centres; they were transferred to education authorities in April 1971. Because the congenital brain damage which causes severe mental impairment frequently also causes severe physical impairment, for example children with spastic cerebral palsy, a substantial proportion of children in these schools are physically handicapped and many are non-ambulant.

1309 Mental illness

Among people who are categorized as mentally ill the incidence of physical impairment is probably no more than among the mentally normal population. There can be no operational definition of what constitutes mental illness, nor can a demarcation line be defined between mental normality or mental healthiness on one hand and mental abnormality or mental illness on the other.

Mental illnesses comprise neuroses and psychoses. In over-simplified terms, neurotics are people who worry unduly, psychotics are people whose behaviour is pathologically peculiar. A broadly valid distinction is that neurotics are those whose behaviour is peculiar but comprehensible, whereas psychotics are those whose behaviour is peculiar and incomprehensible. Psychotics are often completely irrational and disorganised; this dissociation between intellect and behaviour is most extreme in the case of paranoid schizophrenics. The majority of people who are labelled mentally ill are neurotics, and the label is misleading. With understanding of the cause of their worries and intelligent guidance, people who are neurotic can be rehabilitated successfully so that they can manage again at work or at home. All people behave at times in an irrational or peculiar way, they have their fears, hang-ups and worries. It is only when worries become intolerably bothering that professional help is needed; there is nothing pathologically wrong with neurotics which requires, as is the case with psychotics, skilled medical treatment and care in a psychiatric hospital.

In this connection, the official policy of transferring responsibility for mentally ill people needing long term care from hospital authorities to social services authorities is, whatever the immediate logistic problems, right and proper. But there is the hazard that purpose-designed hostels for these people may too often be small replicas of the institutions they are replacing. More promising have been the efforts of some local housing authorities and housing associations who have cooperated with psychiatric hospitals in moving rehabilitated people into ordinary housing[22].

1310 The psychology of disability

The axiom put at the start of this commentary, that the purpose of living is to make the most of being alive, warrants repeating. Accessibility for disabled people to public buildings is not an end in itself, but a means to an end. It is a means to enable people who would otherwise be excluded to opt in and to participate, on the same basis as able-bodied colleagues, in the action of human living.

The practising architect needs to understand in what ways the buildings he designs will aid disabled people to opt in, rather than perpetuating the custom that they are separated out. Practical implementation is not always uncomplicated, because opting-in strategies may necessitate the employment of special treatment devices. The crucial issue is how these special treatment devices are expressed. To achieve appropriate solutions demands first some appreciation of the psychology of disability.

In their efforts to find their way in the world disabled people encounter the obstacles of prejudice and myth which normal people put across their path. On prejudice the common contention nowadays is that, with education and the propagation of tolerant liberal attitudes, there is less punitive discrimination against physically disabled people than there used to be. There is however no firm evidence to support this, or that young people are generally less prejudiced against disabled people. Studies in North America reported by Yuker and others showed that there was no discernible association between age and attitudes to disablement[23].

1311 Discrimination

The possibility that discrimination against disabled people is inherent in our culture and will never be eradicated is disturbing for people on the comfortable outside oppressed by guilt, and painful for people on the inside courageous enough to examine impartially their predicament. With force, Louis Battye confirms that it is more than a possibility:

'Somewhere deep inside us is the almost unbearable knowledge that the way the able-bodied world regards us is as much as we have the right to expect. We are not full members of that world, and the vast majority of us can never hope to be. If we think otherwise we are deluding ourselves. Like children and the insane, we inhabit a special sub-world, a world with its own unique set of referents. Although it has correspondence and communications with that greater world within which it is encapsulated, it is not the same world nor even co-extensive with it: it is within – lesser, weaker, poorer.'[24]

There are, Beatrice Wright suggests, well-meaning people who do not accept that people with disabilities are generally looked upon as inferior, perhaps because they believe that to recognize the existence of inferiority as an attitude would be to grant that such inferiority actually exists. Socially derogatory attitudes towards disabled people are displayed in many ways. Most commonly they are observed in devaluing expressions of pity of the kind which say (or imply) 'Thank God I am healthy and not like you.'

[22] For an account of an active housing association in this field see Bib 93365.
[23] Bib 93301, p44
[24] Bib 93320, p8

Studies have been made which show that negative attitudes towards physically handicapped people are highly correlated with anti-minority, anti-Negro and pro-authoritarian attitudes[25]. The person who seeks for the sake of his own security to identify himself always with the majority commonly has intolerant attitudes towards minority groups. He views physically handicapped people in the same light as Negroes and Jews – they are a threat to his status and a challenge to his values. Because of the importance which normal physique has for him, a disability is something which frightens and is best ignored. As Paul Hunt says:

'For the able-bodied, normal world we are representatives of many of the things they most fear – tragedy, loss, dark and the unknown. Involuntarily we walk – or more often sit – in the valley of the shadow of death. Contact with us throws up in people's faces the fact of sickness and death in the world. No one likes to think of such things, which in themselves are an affront to all our aspirations and hopes. A deformed and paralyzed body attacks everyone's sense of well-being and invincibility. People do not want to acknowledge what disability affirms – that life is tragic and we shall all soon be dead.'[26]

1312　Myths and stereotypes

In addition to prejudice, the disabled person who tackles the ordinary world is plagued by myths and stereotypes. Normal people, attempting to empathize with disabled people, make assumptions about how people with disabilities behave or ought to behave, which do not at all correspond with how they actually do behave. These assumptions are probably at least as prevalent among architects as they are anywhere else, and since the consequences of acting upon them can be damaging it is instructive to examine them carefully.

An assumption commonly made by architects is that disabled people want always to be treated in the same way as normal people. Another is that they want always to be independent. Both these propositions are based on the presumption that disablement has negative effects, so that the proper course is to fight against it until it is beaten. The underlying expectation is that people who are disabled are neurotic about their disabilities. The empirical evidence cited in the course of this commentary indicates clearly that, on the contrary, disabled people tend to be very unneurotic about their disabilities.

A sounder generalization is that it is normal able-bodied people who are neurotic about disablement. They tend to put great emphasis on the value of good health and normal physique. Athleticism and physical beauty are greatly prized. The communications media, along with powerful advertising conditioning, encourage the belief that these attributes are vitally important, and that success in life is dependent on them. By inference (if these values are endorsed) the disabled person, because he lacks the crucial property of normal physique, has suffered a misfortune which has damaged his whole life. There is a tendency to suppose that because a person is inferior in this all-important area of physique he is inevitably inferior in other respects also. The effects of disability are exaggerated; because of the power of physique to evoke a variety of stereotyped impressions about people, there is a proneness among able-bodied people to regard the disability itself as the dominant factor determining the behaviour and personality of someone who is disabled[27].

As has already been made clear in this commentary, the degree of disability does not itself determine how capably a disabled person performs, reflected for example in the way that he uses buildings. Adherence to the basic fallacy, followed by action on it, is not unique to architects. The guiding doctrine of the medical profession is that the reduction of disability will automatically yield rewards. In the clinical treatment of disabled people, exemplified in the recommendations of the Tunbridge and Mair reports on rehabilitation[28], the focus is on medical and physical rehabilitation. Little attention is given to social or psychological rehabilitation.

1313　The hazards of normal treatment

On the assumption (on the part of able-bodied people) that disabled people aspire to be normal, the implication is that they are best helped by pretending that the loss of normality has never occurred. In the context of public buildings this means that special facilities ought not to be incorporated, since they would explicitly admit that disabled people do not measure up to normal modes of behaviour. But it is important, as emphasized earlier, to appreciate that people *are* different from each other. Wherever the line is drawn between physical normality and physical abnormality there are people who are normal and people who are abnormal. In consequence it is a mistake to treat all people in an identical way. Identity of treatment can draw attention to differences which would not be noticed if special treatment had been allowed. By treating everyone as normal, abnormal people will be excluded. Special treatment does not mean stigmatizing treatment. It does not debase a deaf person to make sure he has adequate light for lip-reading, nor does it debase a person in a wheelchair to make sure that he has access to suitable wc compartments. In the past architects have perhaps been too ready to accept at face value requests from clients planning buildings for elderly or disabled people, and from disabled and elderly people themselves, that treatment 'as normal' is what is wanted. In the circumstances, along with the competing and often conflicting demands on the architect's attention discussed earlier, it is not surprising that there are today so few buildings which are convenient for elderly or disabled people to use.

People with disabilities are handicapped not only by being treated in the same way as non-disabled people, but also by the fact that they are not applauded if they behave in a

[25] Bib 93300, p15. Yuker and others (Bib 93301, p80) report three studies showing that favourable attitudes towards disability were related to a lack of authoritarian attitudes.
[26] Bib 93320, p155
[27] This phenomenon is discussed by Wright, Bib 93300, p118
[28] Bib 93400, 93401

way which unambiguously reflects their disablement. The typical advice to a disabled person is that he should attempt to appear as much like an able-bodied person as he can. His success in 'adjusting' to his disability is measured in terms of his ability to behave as if he were not disabled, in other words on his skill as an actor[29]. But the disabled person who tries continually to act as if he were not disabled is not well-adjusted. Examples are the elderly person who will not use a stick, the partially sighted person who pretends he can see without difficulty, and the hard of hearing person who refuses to wear a hearing aid. The price of trying neurotically to hide and forget disablement is high, because the effort will be wasted. Trying always to forget is the most certain way to remember. By trying to forget, the disability cannot be forgotten, for if it were it might not be adequately concealed. If the disabled person is successfully to come to terms with his situation the first thing he has to do is to recognize that the disability exists.

Beatrice Wright suggests that the person with the most wholesome attitude to disablement is one who views physical normality not as a comparative value but as an asset value[30]. This means for example that the person with only one good arm does not think 'I am worse off than a normal person who has two good arms' or 'I am better off than someone who has no arms at all' but 'I am well off because I have one good arm.' This reassessment of the value of physical attributes has wide implications. It means that the possession of normal physique is no longer important, and that the disabled person has no cause to regard himself as intrinsically inferior to people who physically are better endowed. It also means that normality goals become irrelevant.

1314 The deposition of normality goals

In *Stigma*, a collection of autobiographical essays by disabled people, Paul Hunt writes:

'Normality is so often put forward as *the* goal for people with special handicaps, that we have come to accept its desirability as a dogma. But even if one takes a commonsense meaning for the word – being like most people in our society – it is doubtful if this is what we should really fix our sights on. For one thing it is impossible of achievement, at certain levels anyway. Obviously we cannot be physically normal, are doomed to be deviants in this sense at least. Also we must be affected psychologically by our disabilities, and to some extent be moulded into a distinct class by our experiences. But more important, what *kind* of goal is this elusive normality? If it does mean simply trying to be like the majority, then it is hardly a good enough ideal at which to aim. Whether they are physically handicapped or not, people need something more than this to work towards if they are to contribute their best to society and grow to maturity.'[31]

The proposition that, for disabled people, normality goals are not proper goals to strive for is tendentious. It does not for example accord with conventional medical approaches to disability problems. The answer to this is perhaps, as

already suggested, that it is time medical approaches looked in new directions.

A second objection to the deposition of normality goals is that the admittance of lesser goals will, where normality goals are theoretically attainable, divert disabled people from achieving the successes which might have been theirs. The objection is answered by Beatrice Wright:

'Arbitrarily holding up "normal" performance as the model of behaviour unnecessarily commits many persons with a disability to repeated feelings of failure and inferiority. Careful experimental work has demonstrated that the experience of success and failure is largely independent of the person's performance per se but is determined by his goals, expectations and aspirations. Usually people set their aspirations near the top of their abilities. After success, goals are usually raised; after failure, they are usually lowered. In other words, the level of aspiration operates as a protective mechanism so that most persons, whatever their abilities, experience success much of the time. Where normal performance is unattainable, the person who idolizes this as the standard must suffer the ignominy of repeated failure[32].

Confronted by the example of the severely disabled person who, spurred on by feelings of shame, embarrassment and inferiority about his condition, has finally 'overcome' his disability and achieved a degree of normality which on a rational appraisal of his initial condition was out of the question, Wright counters: 'So what? Reducing the disability in no way assures a better adjustment . . . Was the gain worth the price of self-debasement?'[33]

1315 Inspiration and example

The notion that the person who has 'overcome' his disability serves as an inspiration and example to others similarly disabled is widely endorsed, as shown by the popularity of biographies and films recording the fighting-against-odds of handicapped people. On a practical level disabled people can benefit from observing others with comparable physical handicaps, and can learn from successful examples how they also can cope. This is not however the same thing as being emotionally inspired with an urge to emulate and surpass. In the study of disabled drivers in Norwich questions on this were put, citing the example of a widely known disabled person whose achievements have been extensively acclaimed. Among the 36 people whose disabilities were comparable to the exemplar, there were two who expressed admiration. The others were unanimously and often vehemently hostile. Some of the antipathy may have been motivated by envy, but irritation was more apparent. As one man said, they did not like to have the example of a man whose circumstances they knew were very different

[29] In this connection see Bib 93300, p20–24, and Bib 93751, p122.
[30] Bib 93300, p303
[31] Bib 93320, p150
[32] Bib 93300, p25
[33] Bib 93300, p30

from their own 'shoved at us all the time'. For disabled people who see themselves as exemplars it may be boosting to struggle on crutches the length of the land, to swim the channel with a broken back, or to do, minus legs, clever things with mountains or aeroplanes. For most other disabled people it is irrelevant.

Associated with the 'inspiration by example' stereotype is the one which goes 'it helps to see others worse off than yourself'. As a measure of successful adjustment, this has already been dented by the discussion on comparative versus asset values, but it could be unwise to assume that as an attitude of mind it is of no consequence. The impression from the study of disabled drivers in Norwich was that the more intellectual, capable and active people in the sample tended not to gain satisfaction from seeing people less well placed than themselves, but that people with fewer resources commonly found it a source of encouragement. Some of those who benefited from seeing people worse than themselves were fortified by their contacts with handicapped people at the special handicap club. Many of the more independent people appeared on the other hand to be satisfied by their contacts with ordinary people, and tended to reject, sometimes emphatically, the suggestion that they could usefully associate with others who were handicapped. One said aggressively that if he had his way he would have all clubs for the handicapped closed 'They're the invention of the Devil'. This is too harsh: if, as is no doubt the case, the motivation of handicapped people for joining handicapped people's clubs is to seek sympathetic company there is no cause for condemnation. Desiring sympathetic company is, as Beatrice Wright points out, a healthy and honourable motive and need not imply segregation[34].

1316   The process of adjustment

The process of adjusting to disablement is a process of coming to terms with limitations. It means accepting that, because there are things one cannot do, there are areas where it is not possible to compete on equal terms with able-bodied people. The process is identical to that of able-bodied people who have to come to terms with *their* limitations; to operate according to the constraints determined by individual material, physical and intellectual endowments. If these constraints are not observed the consequence will always be failure. For a disabled person the degree of physical disability determines where the physical threshold is, and for some it may be a low one. The paralyzed person in a wheelchair cannot for example hope to be a bus driver, a steeplechase jockey, a naval captain, an airline pilot or an opera singer.

This is not to advocate opting out whenever the course becomes uncomfortable. Life is a process of trial and adjustment, of mutual accommodation between the individual and his environment. For the disabled person there are often frustrations, but frustrations can be valuable, in that it is only in the solving of problems that

insights are attained. For the disabled person the job of tackling difficult challenges can be more rewarding than for the able-bodied person, where achievement is routine.

Disablement can reduce opportunities for accomplishment in many areas of endeavour, but its limiting effects must never be overestimated. If too much credence is given to the apparent insuperability of obstacles, whether physical barriers or other handicapping circumstances, the potential of people with severe disabilities will be underrated. There are numerous demanding occupations which can be successfully undertaken without the benefit of normal physique. Among people confined to wheelchairs who have led active and profitable lives have been writers, scientists, administrators, teachers, lawyers, actors, politicians, musicians and social workers; like people without physical handicaps who have achieved success, they have done so by subordinating their disabilities and concentrating instead on developing their abilities.

1317   Employment buildings and discrimination

By the way that he designs buildings the architect cannot directly counter the prejudices and myths which impede the lives of disabled people. He can however assist by structuring environments in which prejudice and myth can less obtrusively flourish.

The person who is prejudiced tends to camouflage his attitudes and rationalize his behaviour by ostensibly plausible excuses. The bigoted employer may not mind employing a handicapped person where the stigma is not evident, but he will draw the line at say an athetoid spastic in a wheelchair, however well-equipped he may be for the job. Not so long ago a plausible excuse used to be 'It would be upsetting for the rest of the staff to have a person like that around'. Nowadays, encouraged by greater awareness of physical barrier problems, a more respectable excuse is 'He would not be able to manage the steps' or 'He would not be able to get himself around the office on his own'. Sometimes the fire officer comes to his aid by refusing to allow the employment of wheelchair users in buildings where means of escape might be hazardous.

Excuses based on physical difficulties occasionally are justified; if the office is up two flights of stairs the employment of a person in a wheelchair may be out of the question. On the other hand a determined disabled person, even if severely handicapped and in a wheelchair, is, as has been indicated already, a very adaptable animal. Encouraged by a sympathetic and reasonable employer he can be catered for in almost any situation, however unpromising it at first appears.

There are differences, though perhaps only of degree, between the prejudiced attitude of the employer who says 'There are steps' meaning 'I have no intention of employing you', and the embarrassed attitude of the employer who says 'There are steps' meaning 'Someone else better qualified and more competent has been selected for the job'. The latter is under the impression that it is

[34] Bib 93300, p44

kinder to the poor cripple not to tell him that it was only because his qualifications did not measure up that he did not get the job. If there were no physical barriers in employment buildings there would be no reason for either excuse to be made.

Although, as reported earlier, examples of negative discrimination are to be found in buildings other than employment buildings, the example of the prejudiced employer is discussed here because it is the area where discrimination can have the most damaging consequences on a disabled person anxious to make his way in the world. It needs only one or two such experiences for a not very resilient or resourceful person to feel that he is rejected. In the circumstances he may begin to suppose that society's assessment of his worth really is correct, and that he actually is an inferior person.

An important reason why public buildings in general, and employment and education buildings in particular, should be easily accessible is that the simple business of social contact on an equal basis between able-bodied and disabled people helps to foster more tolerant attitudes to disablement. The closer that social and personal contacts are, the greater the acceptance of disabled people in general. Such contacts are instrumental in combating the discrimination which favours the continued segregation by society of people with disabilities. Yuker and others report studies in employment situations showing that tolerant attitudes are positively related to the amount of contact[35]. In education settings the amount of contact was even more significantly related. Contact in medical settings was, by contrast, less positively effective, because it tended to provide information about the inabilities of disabled people rather than about their capabilities.

Apart from the importance of ensuring that employment buildings are accessible in order to combat prejudices against handicapped people there are four other reasons why they are emphasized. The first is that it is a waste of human resources for potentially productive people to be unnecessarily idle. The second is that no charity or state handouts are so lavish that they afford to disabled people all the material goodies they might hanker after. The third is that there is a fellowship in working with others. The fourth and most important is that by working the disabled person is contributing to his community; he becomes a giver and not merely a taker.

1318 'Put the architect in a wheelchair'

A purpose of this discussion is to put across to practising architects some appreciation of how it is to be a disabled person. To counter ineptitude among architects a remedy commonly counselled is 'Put the architect in a wheelchair for a week, then he'll understand'. While, on a strictly practical level, this medicine is therapeutic, in that the architect, physically suppressed, is obliged to confront steps, narrow doors and unreachable wcs, it does nothing to give him any real psychological insight. The architect is a guinea pig, he knows that his performance is a charade, and that it is not something he has to face permanently. It will also be misleading in that, owing to

his lack of practice with a wheelchair, he makes an unduly burdensome job of coping with it. Most importantly, and hazardously, it helps to reinforce any preconception he may have that it is physical problems which are the most troublesome thing about being disabled. As an antidote he will do well to bear in mind what Louis Battye has to say:

'The cripple is an object of Christian charity, a socio-medical problem, a stumbling nuisance, and an embarrassment to the girls he falls in love with. He is a vocation for saints, a livelihood for the manufacturers of wheelchairs, a target for busybodies, and a means by which prosperous citizens assuage their consciences. He is at the mercy of overworked doctors and nurses and underworked bureaucrats and social investigators. He is pitied and ignored, helped and patronized, understood and stared at. But he is hardly ever taken seriously as a *man*.'[36]

1319   Independence

The belief that the only laudable way for a disabled person to operate is by being aggressively and determinedly independent is one which is widely endorsed. Its questionable validity has already been hinted at; it is one more stereotype which needs to be examined critically..

No man is an island. All human societies, if they are to flourish, must be based on cooperation; any which opt for unrestrained competition will perish. The human being is an essentially cooperative species. He has learned that, for his own benefit, he needs to give as well as to take, and in all communities, with varying degrees of egalitarianism, a complex network of mutual support has been established. A measure of a civilized society is the way that it treats its disadvantaged members; whether it requires them, for the material prosperity of the fittest and most powerful, to be inert parasites on the economic body or whether it affords to them opportunities, however meagre their talents, to contribute.

The competitive ethic of industrialized society is at odds with the advancement of disabled people. To be accepted and valued the disabled person has to demonstrate that he can compete on the same terms as his able-bodied colleagues; if he has the resources to do so he can join the establishment club, if he does not he can be left to languish outside. In contemporary western society independence is highly valued as an ideal. It is associated with strength, masculinity and leadership. Dependence on the other hand is associated with weakness, femininity, indecision and helplessness. Independence for disabled people has an emotive appeal for another reason. Non-disabled people are anxious to ascribe to people with disabilities a desire to be independent, because it is the way they like to suppose they themselves would react in similar circumstances. To think otherwise would be to deny the overriding importance of the values that they hold in high esteem. In this cultural scheme the role of the

[35] Bib 93301, p85
[36] Bib 93320, p16

medical practitioner is seen primarily as one of restoring the disabled person to a state of independent functioning. If medical techniques fail the individual is discarded, to live out his life (if there is no family he can look to for support) in an institution along with other socially rejected people. If on the other hand he is rehabilitated to independence and tax-paying status he is given powerful support, with, in some communities, additional bonuses such as transport and housing privileges.

1320 Independence criteria: Buildings and transport

It was a vision of the worthiness of disabled people operating independently and paying their own taxes which, in the United States in the early 1960s, powered the crusade to make buildings accessible to disabled people. The practical objectives of the campaign were crystallized in a brief document, the *American national standard specifications for making buildings and facilities accessible to, and usable by, the physically handicapped*[37].

The specifications in these standards are geared to a criterion of independence, in particular the accommodation of independent wheelchair users. This criterion is not all-accommodating. If minimal standards for the independent chair user are observed the person who needs assistance is not necessarily catered for. A critical matter is the planning of wc compartments, whose importance has already been emphasized. The exclusion of the segment of the population which is most handicapped means that the adoption of the independence criterion here is discriminatory – it implies that some people are valuable and deserve to be accommodated, whereas others are less valuable and may be ignored. Publications relating to these standards indicate that they are pre-eminently designed to accommodate people able to contribute materially to the wealth of society[38].

The same ethic has motivated campaigns in the United States to make new systems of public transport accessible to and usable by physically handicapped people. In his evidence to the United States Senate Special Committee on Aging, 'A barrier-free environment for the elderly and handicapped', Harold L Willson, the paraplegic chairman of the Architectural Barriers Committee of the Easter Seal Society for Crippled Children and Adults said, in explanation of why up to $10million of state finance was to be spent on facilities for the elderly and handicapped for the San Francisco Bay Area Rapid Transit system:

'In my opinion, it is an individual's right to have public transportation available and accessible, and if you deny him transportation, he has to go on welfare. If he goes on welfare, you are violating the rights of the population, through higher taxes, especially if the handicapped individual is willing and able to work, but has only to have a way to transport to and from work.'[39]

1321 The balance between independence and dependence

Judgements of the worthiness of handicapped people by criteria of their potential material productiveness are on moral grounds an arguable basis for action. If instead a philosophy is substituted that all people are valuable, whether capable of operating independently or not, the consequences in terms of practical environmental provision are extensive. The fact that, throughout this book, so much attention is given to the needs of disabled people not able to function independently is not to devalue the practical and psychological benefits of self-sufficiency. Independence ought not to be despised. If a disabled person is to learn to manage his disability he needs to reject help if he is to discover how to do things for himself. He finds for example that routine household and other tasks can be tackled by novel and unsuspected techniques. Having satisfied himself that, with some effort, he can manage on his own, he can more readily and courteously accept help when it is offered.

There are hazards if independence becomes an obsession. By attaching excessive significance to physical independence the handicapped person can jeopardize the crucial process of coming to terms with his disability and with himself as an individual. The person with a progressive disability condition, whose independence is only temporary, will not respond easily to limitations imposed by deteriorating physical capacity if he regards independent management as the only tolerable goal. For all people, whether disabled or not, independence is only a transient state. In old age absolute independence becomes a practical impossibility. Even among able-bodied people it is illusory, for the conditions imposed by modern technology in a mechanized society increasingly mean that human beings must be interdependent rather than independent. The essence of rehabilitation is to teach the disabled individual to come to terms with his problems so that he recognizes that neither absolute independence nor absolute dependence is an acceptable objective to strive for, and that there needs to be a healthy balance between the two.

In her contribution to *Stigma*, Audrey Shepherd, a schoolteacher disabled by polio at the age of 30, discusses the value of independence: 'But I think too much emphasis on independence can breed fanaticism. If I am in the wheelchair at school, it bothers me not at all if somebody pushes it along for a bit, making a joke of having something to lean on.'[40] Because her views do not conform to customary stereotypes she then goes on to acknowledge apologetically that her philosophy will be considered sacrilege by many.

Thus dependence has a value, and in personal relationships is often essential. A disabled person, or an able-bodied person for that matter, ought to be able to rely on others, to ask for help when it is needed, and to know

[37] Bib 93020
[38] See particularly Bib 93021, also Bib 93022, 93024, 93025, 93027.
[39] Bib 93031, part 3, p144
[40] Bib 93320, p61

when to accept it, even when it is not needed. Erving Goffman reports an author disabled by polio:

'When my neighbours ring the bell on a snowy day to inquire if I need something from the store, even though I am prepared for bad weather I try to think up some item rather than reject a generous offer. It is kinder to accept help than refuse it in an effort to prove independence[41].

There was a similar comment from one of the disabled drivers in Norwich. He found when he went out in his invalid tricycle to the centre of the city that people came up to offer to do his shopping for him. He liked to give people the pleasure of helping him, and although he could post his own letters he made a regular practice of asking other people to put them in the letterbox for him.

1322 Help

For the able-bodied person, giving or receiving help is not a problem. Help is a good thing, reflecting mutual concern and interdependence. For the disabled person it can be a threat. It is not simply an act which may be useful or not, but an expression of social relationships which is likely to be disparaging, the disabled person being perceived as inferior. If the help offered is not necessary, the interpretation is that the helper judges the disabled person to be more helpless than he is, so devaluing his status. On other occasions the help appears to be offered by a person who merely wishes to boost his own ego. And on further occasions, for the handicapped person most unpleasantly, the help offered is motivated by pity.

The act of helping is not always helpful. Probably nearly everyone in a wheelchair has undergone the frightening experience of being lurched up or down steps by a belligerently well-meaning helper anxious to display his solicitude and gain prestige among the people he is with. There is no pause to ask how the chair ought to be handled; the consequences can be decomposing, with fury and distress on the part of the helpee.

Apart from its being useless or interfering, help may be unwanted because the disabled person would rather try to do for himself. To achieve the immediate goal it may well be more economical to be helped, but the long-range goal of learning how to cope capably on one's own is hazarded. Thus disabled people tend to restrict acceptance of help to situations where it is absolutely necessary. Their criteria of necessity are commonly stringent, and the degree of inconvenience tolerated by a disabled person before he considers help necessary frequently exceeds that tolerated by an able-bodied person[42].

Restricting help to situations where help is needed, and then accepting it willingly, is a wholesome reaction to disablement but not by any means a universal one. The extent to which many disabled people effectively trade on their disabilities (where there is no cause) is not commonly recognized by others. In discussing the exploitation of help by disabled people Beatrice Wright comments 'There is ample clinical evidence to show that certain individuals revel in their disability, demanding all kinds of unnessary help, as a way of ruling the roost or satisfying their need for dependency or perversely reassuring themselves that they are loved.'[43] In this connection, it is pertinent to draw attention again to the example cited at the start of this commentary, of the woman who went to church because there were steps.

Many disabled people, along with many able-bodied people, find that life is more comfortable if tedious routine chores are done for them by others. It is an aspect of human behaviour which has much encouraged the development of a whole range of mechanical aids, electric gadgetry and labour-saving devices. With or without these aids, people who can afford to do so employ others to carry out their household chores. Not many people are positively exhilarated by doing the washing up or scrubbing the floors. The great advantage of people with disabilities is that they have a ready-made excuse – their physical handicap – for not doing the washing up or scrubbing the floors. It is unreasonable to malign them for behaving in ways which, if they had the opportunity, others would do also.

---

[41] Bib 93751, p119
[42] Wright's discussion of help is useful here, Bib 93300, p225.
[43] Bib 93300, p225

14 Buildings and disabled people: Architectural directions

1400 The argument so far

Before exploring architectural directions it is helpful to summarize the argument so far.

Buildings are designed essentially for normal able-bodied people, and they are not always convenient for people who happen to be disabled. The human being is an exceptionally adaptable animal, who contrives to cope successfully in an awkward and uncomfortable environment. The problems of the ambulant disabled person, because in important respects he is not very different from the able-bodied person, are commonly not insuperable. By contrast the problems of the wheelchair user, because of the characteristics of wheelchairs and the conflicts of design criteria, are not so easily resolved.

Although people in wheelchairs are commonly infrequent users of buildings, they will invariably, if they are determined to do so, find ways of managing. They are not as a rule deterred by physical barriers, and will if necessary enlist the help of others to reach their goals. They are not in general neurotic about their wheelchairs or their disability. Along with other people who are severely disabled, they give ready endorsement to aids and services which reflect their status as disabled people, such as special vehicles, car badges, parking bays and wc compartments.

Successful adjustment to disability involves a reorientation of the prevailing value system, whereby attributes are perceived in asset terms rather than comparative terms. This means a reassessment of normality and physique values, so that they become unimportant. There needs to be a balance between dependence and independence. While independence is important, there are occasions where help is needed and should be asked for.

1401 Architectural criteria

The outcome, in terms of architectural design criteria, is that any strategy of uncompromising independence and adherence to normality goals is inappropriate. An alternative strategy needs to be formulated.

The strategy proposed, applicable to public buildings, and not to housing and living arrangements which are discussed later in the commentary, is that in place of the independence goal there should be one of usability, and in place of the normality goal one of matter of fact recognition of differences and allowance for them.

The degree of independence which the wheelchair user has to have to be able to use buildings ought not to be overestimated. Except in the case of his own home, where practical considerations mean more stringent conditions, all that he has to be able to do is to gain access and use internal facilities and equipment whose operation cannot conveniently be delegated to others. This means, most importantly, that he has to be able to approach the building without effort, move his wheelchair around inside without being obstructed by steps, and manage

cloakroom facilities independently. It is on the basis of affording usability by these criteria that the practical recommendations for public buildings in parts 6 and 7 are determined. Where failure to cope might otherwise occur, ie where a disabled person might be physically prevented from using a building because of architectural features, the relevant specifications incorporate the word 'must'.

There are supplementary arrangements which can be incorporated to enhance the independence of chairbound people without in any way comprising the convenience of normal people. They concern for example the gradient of ramps, the location of light switches and the weight of doors. There are also refinements, relating for example to the specification of handrails and door ironmongery, which can benefit all handicapped people, and particular provisions, such as raised digits for lift controls as an aid for blind people, which benefit particular groups.

1402 The 'ease-of-help' criterion

The incorporation of these additional arrangements, the specifications for which are identified in parts 6 and 7 by the word 'should', will satisfy what can be termed an 'ease-of-help' criterion. It can be objected, given no practical constraints, that the compromise is unwarranted, and that observance of the ease-of-help criterion ought to be demanded as a matter of course. The reason is that in many situations observance of 'should' as well as 'must' specifications will involve substantial additional expenditure; if the budget does not allow for comprehensive provision it is better that the basic requirements are met rather than none at all.

Even in buildings where the ease-of-help criterion is carefully observed there are likely in practice to be occasions when the independent wheelchair user will need to ask help, for example when negotiating long ramps, dealing with an awkward or heavy door, operating lift controls when they are obstructed by other users, or getting a window opened to give extra ventilation. These are all situations where help can be offered in a matter of fact way in response to the needs of a person who has difficulty in particular situations. There is no reason why there should be any loss of self respect, or why the relationship between the helper and the helped should be devaluing.

Because of the different purposes for which buildings are used there are some situations where a more generous interpretation of the recommendations is appropriate, to afford greater independence to disabled people. The most important example is employment buildings. If people in wheelchairs are to be employed, it is proper for the sake of efficiency, apart from any psychological bonuses, that they are able to manage independently. Doors should be openable without difficulty and light switches, window openers and lift controls should be at low level. Ramps ought to be virtually non-existent; if a person in a wheelchair wishes to work late at the office he ought not to be obliged to cause inconvenience by having someone else stop on to assist him, merely because there is a ramp up to the place where his car is parked.

Despite all the potent arguments assembled in favour of a modified rather than an absolute independence criterion, there may still be some who, dedicated to the maintenance of independence at any cost, are still unconvinced. It needs to be emphasized again that the compromise is of academic rather than practical significance. By every measure the usability criterion, extended where appropriate to meet the ease-of-help criterion, is tactically right. It is helpful to refer again to Beatrice Wright:

'Excessive independence . . . may wear a person out. Being goaded by independence, he may insist on doing for himself only to be depleted of energy and emotional resources that might well have been spent more usefully. Glorification of independence must give way to an appreciation that independence and interdependence go hand in hand.'[1]

1403   The treatment of special facilities

The normalization strategy, which argues that, to avoid the stigmatizing exposure of differences, people with disabilities must in all situations be treated as normal, is epitomized by the American Standards. The policy is reported by Tim Nugent (secretary to the standards committee) whose contention is that 'severely disabled people can be accommodated in all buildings and facilities for public use independently and without distinction'[2], and who has written of the research undertaken for the programme 'At no time was this project dedicated to "special" buildings and facilities for the physically disabled'[3]. By contrast the thesis developed in this commentary recognizes that normalization tactics are neither physically practicable nor psychologically responsible, and that the proper course is a policy of recognition and exposure. For disabled people to use buildings without difficulty special facilities have to be provided and suitably identified. Such facilities include reserved parking bays for disabled drivers, accessible side entrances where the main entrance to a building has a flight of steps, larger wc compartments equipped for use by people in wheelchairs, and special seating arrangements in cinemas, theatres and auditoria buildings.

If special facilities are incorporated in buildings it is important that potential users know that they are there, and where they are to be found. In line with the thesis so far developed, the proposal is that there should be signs incorporating a symbol relating specifically to disabled people. An international symbol (diagram 14.1) has been devised for the purpose and has been widely promoted. While reservations need to be expressed about the design of this symbol, and of its fitness for its purpose, there is no question of suggesting that it ought not to be used. It is however relevant to the theme of this commentary to record its history.

The practical and psychological issues associated with the use of a special symbol are discussed at greater length in the report *A symbol for disabled people* which I helped to prepare[4]. Over the years a variety of different solutions have been proposed, and some of them are illustrated here. The first four (diagrams 14.2–14.5) appear to have no

associations with handicapped people. They are based on the now discredited camouflage doctrine – that any symbol employed ought not explicitly to express its purpose, for fear of stigmatizing still further the people to whom it refers. Also now of curiosity value is the ugly device promoted in the second edition of this book (diagram 14.6) which fortunately was never much used.

As part of the study I made in Norwich a project was promoted at the local college of art. The students were asked to devise a symbol which would meet a variety of criteria, among them that it should be explicit and unambiguous, it should display clearly recognition and acceptance of the disablement situation and that, while a representation of a person seated in a wheelchair should be an essential component, it should indicate that in appropriate situations other handicapped people are also accommodated[5]. The resulting device, put forward by Phil Bush, is shown in diagram 14.7.

1404   The international symbol

During 1969 ICTA (the International Society for Rehabilitation of the Disabled subcommittee on technical aids, housing and transportation) conducted an inquiry to find a device suitable for international use. The desirability of having a universal symbol had for some years been discussed, and clearly it had practical advantages. On the other hand it could be that, owing to cultural differences reflected in varied treatment of disabled people, a symbol suitable in one part of the world might be inappropriate elsewhere. Cultural differences were not of concern to ICTA and six symbols were selected for an international opinion poll. The six were the Norwich symbol, the Canadian symbol (diagram 14.2), the New York State symbol (diagram 14.4), the symbol used for Expo 67 at Montreal (diagram 14.8), a symbol produced for an American organisation 'Open doors for the handi-capped' (diagram 14.9) and a symbol designed by a Danish student, Susanne Kofoed, for a Scandinavian design seminar (diagram 14.10). Of the last symbol I had written in the Norwich report:

'The Scandinavian symbol is the most successful of the concept-related symbols. Once the cue of disability is given the concept of a wheelchair is readily appreciated. Aesthetically it is admirable, and it makes a more powerful and dynamic impact than the comparable Expo symbol. The reservation that has to be made is that it is ambiguous – it is not apparent whether the upper component of the device implies a person or whether, as seems more probable on account of the lack of a 'head' it represents the frame of a wheelchair.'[6]

[1] Bib 93300, p310
[2] Bib 93021, p59
[3] Bib 93022, p9
[4] Bib 93082
[5] For full specifications see Bib 93082, p24.
[6] Bib 93082, p10

14.1

14.2

14.3

14.4

14.5

14.6

14.7

14.8

14.9

14.10

14.11

The outcome of the jury voting organized by ICTA was a clear majority for the Scandinavian symbol. The report on the voting read:

'The following characteristics have been ascribed to the symbol: – it is outstanding and expressive – it is simple but yet has an aesthetic form – it is easily identifiable both at a short and at a long distance – it cannot be mixed up with any other symbol – it is easily remembered – it is easy to reproduce and to manufacture in all sizes, materials and colours. Thus this symbol meets all the desirable criteria which were previously mentioned. A slight inconvenience with the symbol is the equally thick lines which may give an impression of monogram of letters. With a "head" on the symbol this inconvenience would disappear and as two members of the jury independent of each other have suggested to equip the symbol with such a "head" we have had this done.'[7]

The decision of the chairman of the committee on his own initiative to add a 'head', without reference to the original designer, was reprehensible. It converted what had been a graphically successful design on a square tile into a poor device on an awkward rectangular tile. No detailed instructions have been issued by ICTA on how the device is to be used in practice. What has unfortunately happened is that ICTA, Rehabilitation International in New York, the Central Council for the Disabled in London and other organizations serving handicapped people have been issuing for official reproduction a weak and ineptly modified version of the original (diagram 14.11). While it may be difficult to prevent the continued employment of this faulty design, efforts should be made to replace it with the version shown in diagram 14.1, in line with the recommendations detailed in section 65.

Although the international symbol has been adopted extensively, there is no evidence that it is being used with sufficient intensity to make any substantial impact on ordinary people. This failure of communication on a large scale might have occurred with any device, but the Norwich report read:

'One of the principal objectives of the programme is to make an impression on normal able-bodied people. The intention is that normal people should, by being confronted by unambiguous signs, be encouraged to think about the nature and implications of disablement, and should develop a more realistic appreciation of the circumstances of disabled people.'[8]

To achieve these objectives it is necessary that the international symbol is employed in a variety of everyday situations. The impression is that this is nowhere being done. Its potential for communication is not being realized; too often it appears that it is being used simply as a stick-on badge on buildings and signposts, with no explanation of what it means.

[7] Bib 93080, p3
[8] Bib 93082, p28

1405   Guidebooks

The issuing of guidebooks listing the availability and whereabouts of suitable facilities for disabled people is complementary to advertising by means of special signs. Most large towns in Britain, and many elsewhere, have such guides, cataloguing access arrangements to shops, restaurants, cinemas, theatres, sports facilities, hotels, churches, post offices and so on[9]. There is also a valuable national guide issued by the Automobile Association listing accessible hotels[10], a guide to public conveniences issued by the Central Council for the Disabled[11], and a guide to British Rail stations and facilities[12]. Another very valuable aid is that one of the principal restaurant guides, the *Good Food Guide*, now incorporates the access symbol against restaurants which are easily manageable. It is to be hoped that it will soon be a regular practice for tourist guides listing hotels, restaurants, entertainment and recreation facilities to include as a matter of course notes on the suitability for disabled people of the buildings concerned.

1406   Access legislation

The Chronically Sick and Disabled Persons Act 1970 is the only piece of legislation on the British statute book devoted exclusively to services for handicapped people. Initiated as a private member's bill by Alfred Morris, it includes sections on the duties of social services authorities to identify the needs of handicapped people in their area, the provision of a range of welfare services and on the duties of housing authorities to provide suitable housing for people with disabilities. It also, most importantly for architects, includes sections on access to buildings. The critical section is section 4 which requires that when new buildings for public use are planned or existing buildings are adapted, suitable access arrangements are made for disabled people where practicable, along with suitable internal planning, cloakroom accommodation and parking facilities[13].

The legal effectiveness of section 4 is dissipated by the words 'in so far as it is in the circumstances both practicable and reasonable'; when the Bill was drafted it was found not to be possible to eliminate this escape clause. Thus developers who, for one reason or another, decide not to implement the Act can afford to do so without threat of penalty. There has been only one case to date where a local authority, attempting to realize the intentions of section 4, has applied to the courts for a decision against a developer who planned an inaccessible building.

1407   The Liverpool case

The case was that of Tesco Stores Ltd and Classic Cinemas Ltd versus the Liverpool Corporation[14]. In 1971 the old Classic cinema at Allerton in Liverpool was demolished, the developers' intention being to replace it with a supermarket at ground level and a new smaller cinema above. Building plans deposited in accordance with the Public Health Act 1936 showed that no provision

had been made for disabled people to gain access to the cinema. Liverpool Corporation's view was that section 4 could not be used to obtain appropriate action because there were no penal or enforcing provisions in the Act. Nor did they consider that access for disabled people was strictly a matter on which planning permission could be refused. They were therefore thrown back on the provisions of the Public Health Act, and rejected the plans on two grounds: first that pursuant to section 43 of the Act the plans did not show that satisfactory sanitary accommodation would be provided for disabled people, and second, that pursuant to section 59 of the Act the plans did not show that satisfactory means of ingress and egress, and in particular a lift, were to be provided.

The initial reaction of the developers was to agree to incorporate the required provisions. But they were subsequently advised by the Cinematograph Exhibitors' Association that the lift would not be admissible as means of escape, and chairbound people would not therefore be allowed into the cinema. They therefore appealed to the magistrates' court against the rejection of the plans, an appeal which was dismissed by the stipendiary magistrates in November 1972.

The developers then appealed to the crown court and the case was heard in May 1973. They claimed that to admit disabled people, particularly those in wheelchairs, would be risky. In an emergency there would be panic; the lift would not be in action and the stairs would be dangerous. On the corporation's side it was reported that the fire risk was minimal, and that all potential hazards had been taken into account. But the court upheld the developers' appeal. The consequence is that the cinema as built is not accessible to people who cannot climb stairs.

The Liverpool case demonstrates that the Chronically Sick Act is weak. There have been demands that section 4 must be stiffened and made mandatory. If this were to be done it is predictable that the requisite standards would, for practical and economic reasons, be so undemanding as to be of little avail. The matter is hypothetical but it is probable that more successful results are achieved by having permissive rather than mandatory legislation.

1408   Buildings and fire regulations

For access provision to be legally enforceable in Britain there needs to be appropriate covering legislation, regulations and standards. In respect both of new construction and conversions of existing buildings there are possibilities here under the Health and Safety at Work etc Act 1974. Under section 61 in part III of this Act the

[9] Information on guides currently available may be obtained from the Central Council for the Disabled, see 94.
[10] Bib 93093
[11] Bib 93092
[12] Bib 93094
[13] For full text of section 4 and guidance on interpretation see 6010.
[14] I am indebted to the Liverpool City Solicitor for information here.

Secretary of State for the Environment has broad powers to make new building regulations which take account of health, safety, welfare and convenience, rather than, as was the case prior to 1974 when building regulations were made under the powers of Public Health Acts, of health and safety only. Under the 1974 Act there is the opportunity for regulations relating to accessibility and the use of buildings by disabled people to be introduced.

The British Standard Code of Practice *Access for the disabled to buildings*, issued in 1967 and customarily referred to as CP96, sets down general recommendations for provisions for disabled people in buildings, and has potential as an instrument for statutory enforcement. As it stands at present it does not have the ability: it is outdated, it is imprecise and it is incomplete[15]. With intelligent redrafting it could however be updated, made precise and comprehensive; it could then qualify for reference in building regulations.

Fire regulations directly affect the way that disabled people are able to use buildings[16]. In the Liverpool case it was fire requirements which were in conflict with the needs of disabled people, and which preventented a suitable compromise being found. In the planning of buildings it occurs often that fire protection criteria are not easy to reconcile with criteria for helping disabled people. Examples are regulations involving heavy self-closing doors which interfere with the easy movement of disabled people, regulations prohibiting the use of lifts as a means of escape, and regulations imposed by licensing authorities curtailing the freedom of disabled people to use all areas of entertainment or assembly buildings.

The complex structure of fire regulations and their administration is examined in detail in section 60, along with suggestions as to how inhibiting effects can be mitigated. Behind the practicalities of regulations there are moral issues, discussed in the paragraphs which follow. In considering these issues it needs to be recognized that fire regulations are geared to one overriding objective – that no human lives are lost. What happens to buildings and their contents is a matter of more concern to insurance companies than it is to fire authorities.

1409 Living and dying

The thesis of this book relies on the premise that human lives are valuable, and that the lives of disabled humans are as valuable as any. On this basis there appears to be no objection to the fire authorities' principle, but important moral issues are raised. It is relevant to quote yet again the maxim put forward at the start of this commentary 'The purpose of living is to make the most of being alive'. What matters is the quality of life, more than its quantity. It is also relevant to relate the fire issue to the discussion on the psychology of disability. Because of their circumstances those who are severely handicapped tend, if they are inquiring people, to probe basic questions, asking about their role in the world, their reason for being alive, and the morality of the values by which contemporary society operates. In the process of

accepting and adjusting to their situation they find themselves obliged to reject or modify important values, relating for example to normality, physique and material success, which pass unchallenged through the lives of others. They are also, commonly, obliged to face the reality of death.

There has not, to my knowledge, been any study made of comparative attitudes to death among disabled and able-bodied people. It could therefore be that this analysis is at fault. The impression is, however, that people with severe disabilities are in general not at all as neurotic about dying as able-bodied people are. For all people there is the possibility that death is imminent, but it is a possibility which is generally ignored. Among many disabled people, either because of poor prognosis or proneness to injury, it is a possibility which cannot be ignored. The response is to make the most of the days that remain. It is important to be able to carry on doing the things that are fulfilling, to go to work, to carry on studying, to see shows at the theatre, to hear music at the concert hall, to keep up with the latest films at the cinema. Given this philosophy of living, the possibility that the local cinema may one day burn down, leaving one stranded in a fixed seat (fire officers insisting, for the sake of not blocking gangways, that people in wheelchairs transfer out of them) is not a threat to worry about unduly. In the circumstances the disabled person is entitled to ask of the fire officer 'What moral right have you to say "You cannot come in here because you might die"'.

The hazard is that other people's lives may be put at risk. It is not enough for the disabled person to make an arrangement with, for example, his workmates to leave him alone when the building starts to burn; they know they would not leave and he knows they would not. They would face the wrath of the press if they did so: 'Cripple left to die in blazing building'. So it can happen that, gradually, fire regulations serve to circumscribe the lives of disabled people. Each time a building fire occurs with extensive loss of life, pressures on the administrators of fire regulations are intensified, with the possible consequence that opportunities for disabled people to carry on being a part of the busy world are diminished.

In their search for hazards in buildings which might threaten human lives, fire officers have focused on wheelchairs. The person in a wheelchair has the disadvantage that, on account of the distinction of his wheelchair, he can be easily identified, categorized and discriminated against. Thus in the course of using buildings he encounters administrative obstacles, for example at cinemas, exhibition buildings and concert halls.

---

[15] For discussion on the shortcomings of CP96 see 6122.
[16] In this section the term 'fire regulations' is used to describe the range of regulations and requirements to do with buildings and fire, ie building regulations to do with means of escape or structural fire protection, fire certification requirements, and licensing requirements to do with the prevention of fire hazards. Similarly the term 'fire officer' is used to describe the inspectors of fire authorities and other agents employed to administer fire regulations.

It would be improper to advocate that the lives of the majority of people who are fit and able should be hazarded to satisfy the aspirations of the few who are disabled. And the fire officers' rules seem reasonable. A wheelchair in a building might appear to be quite a real hazard. But what evidence is there that it is? It could be claimed in fact that a person in a wheelchair can move or be moved out of a building with more alacrity than people in many other groups. Is he for example more of a risk than confused old people, than people with weak hearts, than blind people, than hypochondriacs, than mentally handicapped people, than neurotic people, or than people with dogs?

From time to time it has been suggested that to accompany the code of practice *Access for the disabled to buildings* there should be a complementary code 'Egress for the disabled from buildings'[17]. Given that the underlying objective of the accessibility campaign is to get disabled people into buildings, the consequences of an egress code would be counter-productive. Standards would need to be stringent to achieve approval, and would serve to further circumscribe opportunities for living. There are, I suspect, disabled people – usefully employed for example on the upper floors of buildings – whose lives are fulfilling only because they have avoided confrontation with fire officers, or else have settled for an arrangement which bends the interpretation of the rules. Given strict enforcement of regulations on egress the alternative would be fruitless survival in a little room at home or a little room in an institution; in either respect a life sentence.

The prospect is not encouraging. Every time that old or handicapped people are the victims of a building fire there is massive publicity. There are demands for yet more stringent controls. For those who administer fire regulations the easy way out is always to say 'Yes, we must impose more controls because we are bothered about people dying'. The more difficult alternative is to say 'No, we shall not, because we are concerned about people living'.

1410 Transportation

The extent to which public transport systems cater for disabled people has implications for access provision in transport buildings. Conventional public transport equipment, the train, the bus and the aircraft, are examples of economic design solutions geared for normal able-bodied people rather than for those who are disabled. The dynamics of orthodox railway equipment means that access to passenger coaches has to be by way of high steps. Remedial artefacts such as the provision of wider doors can be introduced, but there are no simple prescriptions for making conventional rail travel convenient for people in wheelchairs[18]. Evidence from the Norwich study confirms that if wheelchair users need to travel by train they are given special treatment and contrive to manage. But it is not a comfortable business.

Similarly there is no simple way of redesigning conventional buses so that they are easy for disabled people to use. There are not only economic, but practical and technical problems involved, for example of lowering the floor level of buses, and ensuring close approach to kerbs. When efforts were made by General Motors in North America to design a bus convenient for handicapped people, commercial operators showed no interest[19].

An official circular from the Department of the Environment *The disabled traveller on public transport*[20] was issued in August 1973. It discusses the problems encountered by disabled travellers, particularly when using trains and buses, and suggests practical ways by which they can be alleviated. These include, for example, asking bus operators to see that buses draw up close to kerbs at bus stops, designing bus steps so that they are as low as possible, placing grab rails and bells within easy reach, issuing prepaid tickets to disabled bus passengers to avoid the difficulties of automatic fare collection, allocating selected seats for disabled and elderly people in buses where few seats are provided, and giving consideration to storage space in buses for folding wheelchairs. In respect of London underground trains the circular notes that the Greater London Council and the London Transport Executive are giving consideration to the problem of the effective exclusion of disabled travellers to trains where there is no convenient access to platforms.

1411 Rapid transit systems

Although it is not feasible to adapt conventional urban public transport equipment to suit handicapped people, there are opportunities when radically new transit systems are developed. Elaborate practical applications have been made in the United States where, for both the San Francisco and Washington rapid transit systems, the aim has been to secure '100 per cent ridership'[21]. In San Francisco, where facilities for handicapped people were not in the original brief for the Bay Area Rapid Transit system, an additional $10million has been spent, principally on the building of special elevators. In Washington, designers aimed from the start to cater for handicapped people, so that escalators are installed to carry travellers direct from platform to street level without having to negotiate steps. It was claimed that this, in conjunction with special acoustical, visual and other aids, would make the system 'easily accessible to all but approximately one tenth of one per cent of the physically handicapped persons who are not confined to

---

[17] For an example see Bib 93018.
[18] New Inter City rolling stock currently being developed by British Rail will have a space to take a standard wheelchair within the carriage. In some existing Inter City second class coaches tables are omitted from certain positions to help ambulant handicapped people.
[19] Bib 93031 (part 3), p165. The same report has interesting evidence regarding the intractable problems of making bus travel convenient for handicapped people. For an analysis of British bus design with reference to handicapped people see Bib 93563.
[20] Bib 93560
[21] Bib 93031, part 3, p140

the home'[22]. People in wheelchairs would however still be excluded – the estimate was that in Washington there would be 427 people in wheelchairs who might otherwise use the system[23]. To cater for this small number of disabled people, and so achieve 100 per cent ridership, two possibilities were considered; inclined elevators in association with escalators, or conventional vertical elevators. The cost of this one special provision was estimated in 1971 at between 44 and $60million.

The motives for spending these large quantities of public money for a small number of handicapped people are laudable, but it is arguable that, if resources of this order are available for handicapped people, this is the best way to employ them. In the first place the goal of 100 per cent ridership can never be achieved. There will inevitably be physically handicapped people who cannot manage rail services designed essentially for normal people. The contention made by the design chief of the San Francisco system regarding the seating, that 'there are 72 seats available on each car of the regular type which we feel are suitable for everyone to sit down'[24] is not, for reasons discussed earlier in relation to the anthropometric characteristics of handicapped people, admissible.

The second point is the awkward question of how handicapped people cope at the terminal points of an accessible public transport system. The fallacious basis of the San Francisco programme was exposed by the paraplegic chairman of the architectural barriers committee, when he said 'I am going to use BART if I can talk AC Transit (presumably his employers) into hauling me about five blocks to my office in the Ordway building. I think I would be laughed out of town if I did not use BART, after all the work I have done on the BART system'[25].

1412 Individual transport

However extravagantly conceived, no public transport system can cater for all disabled people. The only answer, if disabled people are to be enabled to use urban amenities easily reached by able-bodied people, is that special by-passing arrangements are made. The only convenient way for the severely handicapped person to move about is by individually tailored transport, in a car driven by himself, or by another person if he is too handicapped. To travel into zones where access is restricted for ordinary car users concessionary arrangements have to be made. It is not, again referring back to the discussion on disability psychology, devaluing or stigmatizing to introduce these special arrangements, and disabled people are unlikely to be neurotic because they are not being treated as normal.

The important strategic matter is that, instead of tampering at great expense with individual components of community services, such as public transport (the job of which is not after all a goal in itself, but a means to achieving goals), the whole network of services needs to be re-evaluated, taking into account the needs of disabled users as well as those of able-bodied people. An evaluation such as this might demonstrate that, in terms of cost benefits, it would be desirable to channel resources in

directions other than massive capital expenditure on the adaptation of buildings or the development of suitable public transport. It could for example be more economical, and advantageous to consumers, to administer a taxi service subsidized by public funds; a service of this kind is operated by many local authorities in Sweden, where handicapped people may summon special minibuses, travelling free or paying only a fare equivalent to the cost of public transport. Facilities such as this ought not however to be thought of as a substitute for making buildings accessible or transport usable; they ought instead to be viewed as part of the broad spectrum of supporting services which help to minimize the handicapping effects of disablement.

1413 Education and special schools

The education of physically handicapped children, and in particular the role of special schools, is an arena into which the lay person ventures at some hazard. It is one where there is no firm strategic consensus among educationists and administrators, and one where the kind of goals that are looked for demand substantial resources in terms of finance, staffing, buildings and equipment.

In England and Wales the policy of the Department of Education is that no handicapped child should attend a special school if his needs can be met by an ordinary school[26]. The debate in recent years has been not about the principle, but about its application. The department's view is that some physically handicapped children need the more sheltered environment of a special school with smaller classes, intensive medical and nursing care and a full range of therapeutic support within the school. Local education authorities have many hundreds of children on their waiting lists for special schools, and the 1973 white paper from the Department of Education *Education: a framework for expansion*[27] proposed an acceleration of the special school building programme. At the same time, a DES report *Special education: a fresh look*[28] encouraged local education authorities to plan and carry out experiments in the integration of more handicapped children in ordinary schools.

[22] Bib 93031, part 3, p156. This estimate was based on statistics published by the US National Health Survey 'Chronic conditions causing limitation of activity.' and subjected to the same analysis as that for estimating usage of the transit system by the general public.
[23] Bib 93031, part 3, p160
[24] Bib 93031, part 3, p162
[25] Bib 93031, part 3, p145
[26] Comments on educational policy in this section relate to England and Wales only. For the purposes of this discussion no special inquiry has been made in respect of Scotland, where education is administered independently.
[27] Bib 93791
[28] Bib 93385. It is expected that the integration of handicapped children in ordinary schools will be a major topic to be reported on by the Warnock committee of inquiry into the education of handicapped children and young people, appointed by the Secretary of State for Education in July 1974.

In simple terms, integration may take one of two forms. First, handicapped children may be placed in special classes and units attached to ordinary schools, mixing socially with non-handicapped children in the playground for example, and at meal times. Second, handicapped children may be placed in regular classes where they are taught alongside non-handicapped children, with the use of special teaching methods and aids. In Scandinavia, most actively in Sweden, the educational policy is that physically handicapped children are placed in ordinary classes, a policy which Elizabeth Anderson's reports *The disabled school child, a study of integration in primary schools*[29] and *Making ordinary schools special*[30] show can be made to work. But even in Sweden there are some physically handicapped children in special schools, and the majority of those in ordinary schools are in special classes and units, mixing socially with other children to varying degrees.

On the question of preferences for special versus ordinary schooling, Elizabeth Anderson writes:

'There is a striking similarity between the wishes in this matter of parents in Scandinavia and in England, and also in the problems they have to meet. No doubts can exist about the strength and generality of the desire that their children should go to ordinary schools, however varied their reasons for wishing this may be. The difference lies in the extent to which such a desire can be realized, with the Scandinavian parents, on the whole, in a much stronger position'.[31]

It does none the less happen that there are in England and Wales more physically handicapped children in ordinary schools than there are in special schools. A survey undertaken in 1969–70 by the Department of Education by means of questionnaires sent to school medical officers, to which 147 of the 163 education authorities responded, found 10 200 children identified as physically handicapped in ordinary schools, compared with 8545 in special schools[32]. Among the findings were that in the ordinary schools surveyed there were 789 children with spina bifida, 637 who were incontinent (473 of them wearing appliances), 393 using wheelchairs and 1482 using walking aids.

1414 The need for special schools

In respect of children who are physically disabled, physical factors alone are not a cause of the provision of special schools. First, the important processes of education do not demand of the child any exceptional physical capacities. Second, while it is the case that few schools are designed to be convenient for children in wheelchairs, there is no evidence that children are obliged to attend special schools simply because buildings are unmanageable. Anderson reports of ordinary primary schools that head teachers often went to considerable trouble to make special arrangements to suit handicapped children, for example reorganizing the location of classes so that the physically handicapped child's room was accessible to a wheelchair[33].

Twenty or so years ago, children handicapped as a result of polio, some with considerable academic potential, constituted a sizeable proportion of the physically handicapped school population. With the disappearance of polio and the eradication of disabling diseases caused by poor environmental conditions, the balance has shifted so that today physically handicapped schools are comprised almost exclusively of children who are congenitally handicapped[34]. These are commonly children with multiple handicaps, often with mental as well as physical impairment. A consequence has been a deterioration of intellectual calibre among pupils in physically handicapped schools[35]. Apart from the lack of stimulus from competition with peers, it may happen that children with latent potential have been handicapped by the impossibility of providing in a small all-age special school a full range of educational opportunities for expanding individual aptitudes and talents.

For children who are mentally as well as physically handicapped, placement in a special school is more often indicated than for children who are simply physically handicapped, although evidence from Scandinavia suggests that the case is not overwhelming, given appropriate resources[36]. For blind children, again given adequate resources, assimilation into ordinary schools might often be practicable; for deaf children communication problems make integration much less feasible.

1415 Architectural directions: Special schools

The architect with a brief from a local educational authority for a special physically handicapped school has rather more latitude, particularly in terms of space, than when he is designing an ordinary primary or secondary school. There will also be opportunities for design initiatives which may have a significant bearing on how handicapped children respond to their school environment and learn from it. In this connection, the architect should look to specialists such as the medical officer and the educational psychologist for guidance. In the same way that the education of children in special schools requires a harmony of contributing skills from teachers, psychologists, doctors, therapists and others, so the design of the building ought to express a harmony of approach. It may be a mistake for example to afford too much prominence to any one particular aspect. One school I visited in 1971, by a local authority with an outstanding record for imaginative school design, was on

[29] Bib 93380
[30] Bib 93381
[31] Bib 93381, p54
[32] Bib 93260, p46
[33] Bib 93380, p236. In connection with this discussion Bib 93262 provides useful material.
[34] Relevant statistical evidence is given in Bib 93260, p42.
[35] Anderson (Bib 93380, p82) reports a study made of a typical day school for physically handicapped children, where about 66 per cent of pupils were 'clearly ESN (educationally sub-normal) in addition to their physical handicaps'.
[36] Bib 93381. Special schools for mentally handicapped children are discussed briefly elsewhere in this commentary, see 1308.

a hospital campus (to facilitate clinical work), with wide dull corridors (for wheelchair circulation) and conventional cellular classrooms. The architect felt that in a school for physically handicapped children it was proper to apply quite different criteria from those which governed the planning of other school buildings.

There is no cause in special schools, any more than there is in ordinary schools, for not using space economically and productively, and avoiding wasteful circulation areas. The teaching areas need to be planned to afford flexibility in use, with appropriate facilities (such as cloakrooms) geared to cater for the special individual needs of disabled children[37]. It may be wise to keep the overt expression of disability requirements to a minimum; the case for buffer rails to protect against wheelchair damage is for example arguable. While an intelligently designed building can aid the educational process and provide a stimulus for learning, the architect ought not to presume that the way he designs his building will determine how children behave. The incorporation or not of elaborate disability-orientated aids, such as special door or window ironmongery, is unlikely to be significant. Nor need there be too much concern over whether equipment, for example in domestic science teaching spaces, is specially geared for use from a wheelchair, or whether it is of the sort found in everyday situations outside. On the basis that children are learning to cope with the world as it is rather than with a sub-world of disabled people, it may be wiser that equipment is non-special, with relatively few concessions. There needs to be suitable provision for children in wheelchairs, but the architect ought not to expect that all the children will be in wheelchairs. A report of a recently built physically handicapped school in London found that only 7 out of 90 children were in wheelchairs[38].

1416 Architectural directions: Ordinary schools

The absorption of physically handicapped children into ordinary schools is relatively easily undertaken in primary schools, with their small communities, intimate relationships between staff and pupils, and generally amenable architectural organization. In secondary schools there are bigger problems, but developments in Sweden indicate that they can be resolved. The regulations for school buildings in Sweden require that in each 'headmaster area' (an area having some 1000–2000 school-age children) at least one school building must be suitable for children who are disabled. This means for example the provision of lifts, ramps and special cloakroom facilities. In the case of existing schools, appropriate adaptations have also to be made, even where there is only one child who is disabled[39]. The practice in these ordinary schools is to place handicapped children in a special class or to assimilate them in an ordinary class, taking them out for special remedial work.

Comparable tactics could perhaps be employed in England, assuming that financial resources were available. Each local education authority might designate one or two of its comprehensive schools as suitable for children with disabilities, with special units attached to them for therapy and remedial classes. The buildings would of course need to be made accessible to wheelchair users, with lifts for vertical circulation. This would be in contrast to the invariable practice in contemporary school building in Britain, where no allowance is made for lifts. In this connection it needs to be pointed out that section 8 of the Chronically Sick Act requires that any person undertaking the provision of a school building must make provision, so far as it is practicable and reasonable, for disabled users. In respect of new buildings, it rests with local education authorities to decide that at new primary or secondary schools special provision is made for handicapped pupils, such as providing lifts, ramps and suitable wcs; if this is done there are no formal cost limits for the work but the cost has to be met within the authority's lump sum allocation. In respect of existing buildings, the DES agrees in its special education building programme to allow the provision of lifts in ordinary schools which cater for physically handicapped children. In addition, local education authorities may put lifts into school buildings using their minor works allocation.

An advantage of having in each local authority area at least one secondary school catering for children who are disabled would be to facilitate the employment of teaching staff who are disabled. The impression at present is that where a teacher who is chairbound is employed in an ordinary school, ad hoc arrangements of a more or less satisfactory character are made. These may mean rescheduling or relocation of teaching periods to suit the disabled member of staff. Complete flexibility is out of the question; with a school designed throughout to be accessible there will be no problems.

If physically handicapped children from a large area are concentrated in one school, daily commuting will be impossible for all. The alternatives are either a purpose-designed hostel or arranging for children to be boarded out with local families on a four day a week basis. If the decision is in favour of a hostel, there are probably economic advantages in locating it on the school campus. On the other hand, in terms of community involvement and separation of education and living functions, a hostel away from the campus is preferred.

1417 Further education and universities

The question of special further education facilities is analogous to that of special schools. There are some severely disabled students who need special equipment and facilities, along with residential provision and supporting services such as can only be provided in a suitable building. In this connection, the recently established Hereward College at Coventry performs a valuable role, by offering to physically handicapped students whose schooling may have been limited the opportunity to develop their academic potential at a special further education college. But in terms of the

---

[37] Detailed design guidance on schools and other educational buildings is given in section 72.
[38] Bib 93391, p507. This example is probably atypical.
[39] Bib 93381, p17

educational resources which can be incorporated, special further education colleges are likely to have the same drawbacks as special schools; the preferred policy, which is being followed by DES to the extent that financial resources allow, is that further education buildings are convenient for disabled students, with ad hoc arrangements made to meet individual needs.

The axiom that universities should cater for students who are disabled is nowhere contested. The University Grants Committee issued in 1972 a short report *Provision for the disabled at universities*[40] setting down architectural guidelines, and a survey published in the same year by the Central Council for the Disabled on access to university and polytechnic buildings[41] showed that the great majority of colleges in Britain were making suitable provision for disabled students, including those in wheelchairs. In recent years nearly all buildings at new universities, and new buildings at existing universities, have been designed so that they are usable by students in wheelchairs and others who are disabled; only one college in the CCD survey reported that cost limits administered by the University Grants Committee had precluded suitable arrangements.

A report by the National Innovations Centre published in 1974 of a comprehensive survey of disabled students at universities and polytechnics found it rare that any student had difficulty obtaining admission simply on account of his disability[42]. Registrars and admissions officers were invariably sympathetic to students with disabilities; some made it a rule that provided a student was otherwise acceptable he would automatically be given a place, and his needs for special assistance would be tackled as they arose. While in principle such policies are laudable they may not always in practice be in the best interests of the student. At one university a student at the start of her second year had had to withdraw from her science course on account of inaccessible laboratories; she had subsequently moved to another university to take an arts course. Another student in a wheelchair had found when he arrived at his polytechnic that many of the facilities were unmanageable; he had given up his place and transferred elsewhere. At the same polytechnic a further student had abandoned his course because he could not use the buildings.

1418   Provision for disabled students and staff

Many universities and colleges make a special effort on behalf of individual students, for example rearranging the venue and timing of lectures. One of the problems reported by disabled students in the NIC survey was the physical strain of attending consecutive lectures; in relation to the design of buildings, problems cited were ramps which were too steep, heavy swing doors and buildings which as planned by the architect allowed for independent functioning but in practice, owing to locked doors to private areas, could be used only with assistance. Reference was also made to the need for a soundproof room for blind students in libraries, and for induction loops in lecture halls to aid students who are hard of hearing. The report suggests that where the welfare of a

disabled student requires extra expenditure, costs should be paid by the Department of Education, to meet for example the provision of suitable accommodation, including equipment in living areas, cloakrooms and lecture halls.

To cater for students who are severely disabled special hostel accommodation may be considered necessary. Sussex University has recently built a unit for four disabled students, staffed through the university health service to give twenty four hours clinical support[43]. It will be interesting to observe in practice how much demand there is for this kind of special provision. It may be small, but it is valuable none the less that the possibility is tested. Twenty or so years ago, the preponderance of disabled students at university were people affected by polio. No statistics are available but, with the disappearance of polio, the probability is that the actual number of students with severe physical disabilities at universities has declined.

In at least one important respect the disabled student population does not reflect the general disabled population of the same age. This is that a relatively small number of congenitally disabled people achieve university entrance, whereas a substantially higher proportion do so among those who have acquired disabilities during their school careers or subsequently. There is no conclusive statistical information to back this proposition, but the evidence from the NIC survey supports it. It reports that only 16 per cent of disabled students at universities and polytechnics had spent all their school time at special schools, and that among students using wheelchairs 41 per cent became disabled after leaving school[44]. The report also found that students with disabilities numbered only some 2 per 1000 of the university and polytechnic population, compared with an estimated figure of 9 per 1000 of the general population of the same age[45]. An unexpected finding was that the relative number of disabled students at polytechnics outnumbered those at universities by some three to one; one of the reasons for this may be that the education received by disabled young people, either because of its poor quality or liability to frequent interruption, could be enough to get a capable student to a polytechnic but not to a university. The conclusion to be drawn from the evidence discussed here is that, while it is crucially important that there are no architectural barriers in higher education buildings, it is more likely to be other kinds of barriers which prevent disabled students making the most of their potential, and which more urgently need to be tackled.

Apart from the question of accessibility to disabled students it is important that university buildings can cater for staff who are disabled. In a number of disciplines, for example medicine, engineering, and the sciences

[40] Bib 93378
[41] Bib 93370
[42] Bib 93371. The findings reported here are drawn from paras 62, 75, 76, 98, 129, 130, 135, 103 and 307.
[43] Bib 93373
[44] Bib 93371, paras 42, 39 and 55.
[45] This estimate was drawn from the OPCS survey, Bib 93210.

generally, graduates who have employed their vocational skills in commerce, industry, the professions or public administration may find, if they become disabled, that they can use their experience most effectively by moving into the academic sphere. In the past, people with polio tended to predominate among severely disabled people in teaching and research fields but their places are now being taken by others, in particular by paraplegics.

1419   Recreation

If the strategy put forward in this commentary is applied consistently, provision for disabled people who want to participate in sports and recreation activities will be made in ordinary buildings for general use. The provision of special-for-disabled facilities is not a real alternative. There is at Stoke Mandeville Hospital a lavish but under-used purpose-designed sports centre for paraplegic games[46]; while this is valued by those disabled people who favour the ethic of rehabilitation through sporting competitions with other disabled people, it is an enterprise which doubtfully warrants repetition elsewhere. The emphasis might instead be on community provision, whereby disabled people can take part, either as members of disability groups or alongside able-bodied people, in leisure and sporting activities which are part of the broad spectrum of community services.

In recent years in Britain there has been a trend away from competition-oriented sports centres to recreation centres catering for all kinds of leisure pursuits[47]. There has also been a surge of joint education and recreation complexes whereby in the developing of new secondary schools cooperation between various local and central government agencies affords more comprehensive and lavish amenities than could be devised by agencies operating independently. The most notable example is the Abraham Moss Centre in the Cheetham Crumpsall area of Manchester[48]. It comprises a comprehensive secondary school, a further education college, a short stay residential unit for pupils and staff, a youth centre, a public library, a sports and recreation centre, some shops and a social club for elderly and handicapped people. All parts of the centre are accessible to wheelchair users, with full facilities for disabled people to use the recreation services. The result is a complex which offers to disabled people a real opportunity to be assimilated into the community. The implications of this type of development for the integration of disabled people into the life of the community are extensive. Under one roof, with, on account of the scale, no problems of physical accessibility, a whole range of coordinated services can be developed.

1420   Day centres for handicapped people

The all-purpose local authority day centre for physically handicapped people is a relatively recent development in Britain, and an encouraging one. It is not a straightforward matter to describe exactly what a day centre is, for two good reasons. First, because its make-up varies from place to place according to circumstances; to the size of the locality, to the availability of related support facilities and to the prevailing needs of handicapped people in the area. Second it does not serve to plug any single specific hole in the fabric of disablement aid, but to tackle a variety of patches where the cover is thin.

The day centre has evolved from an assortment of services traditionally managed by voluntary agencies: the old people's club, the institute for the blind and the social club for the physically handicapped. By incorporating training facilities for the activities of daily living it has links with medical rehabilitation, by catering for arts, crafts and vocational activities it links with education, and by having workshop facilities modelled on open industry it has links with employment. Its role is primarily supportive, in that it helps people to live with disablement. It is also occupational, in that it gives them a job to do with the possibility of supplementing their income. It is also rehabilitative, in that it can teach people how to manage everyday household activities, and can aid people on their way to open employment.

It is customary for day centres to be client group orientated. In a district where there are already, for example, centres for old people and a training centre for mentally handicapped people, it may be fitting to extend the pattern by providing a centre for physically handicapped people. But in a small community it will not be practicable to have separate facilities for each client group, in which case there might be a single day centre which would be activity oriented, providing a base for people with a variety of limitations.

In view of the multi-faceted and diverse role of day centres there can be no standard prescriptions for them, and no common architectural specifications. Any practical recommendations which may be made will commonly need to be qualified by saying that in certain circumstances they will not be appropriate.

Other than activity oriented centres in small communities, the general rule should be that centres for physically handicapped people are separate from centres for old people. The reason is basically cultural. The social centre for old people caters for those who have already made their important contribution to the community, by a busy working life in the factory or office, or by managing a home and family. They seek in their retirement congenial social company among people with similar experiences and interests, together with an opportunity of passing the time in a useful but undemanding fashion. These needs can best be met by a local centre for old people, within walking distance of homes, in a small building comprising perhaps a hall with two or three other rooms. There are hazards if an attempt is made to mix handicapped and

[46] Bib 93582
[47] An example of this type of centre is reported in Bib 93743.
[48] A DES bulletin has been published on this centre, Bib 93744.

elderly people in the same building, as reported by Alan Lipman of a well-intentioned example in South Wales; he found that despite the planning of the building to encourage social movement, contact between handicapped and elderly was minimal or non-existent, the division between the two sides had become entrenched, and his conclusion was that the way the building was used by those who were handicapped reinforced their social segregation and highlighted their socially distinctive identity as people set apart because of their disabilities[49].

1421 Occupational services in day centres

The occupational role of the day centre is determined by the structure of related employment services. In Britain, the ruling that in sheltered workshops for handicapped people employees must be capable of managing a full five-day week means that many relatively capable people with fluctuating disability conditions may look to the day centre for diversionary employment. Among them may be young people, who, but for their physical handicap, would be working in offices or factories, or managing home and family. Their need is not merely for activities which pass the time of day, but to be doing something meaningful, productive and cash-earning. Disabled people using day centres are commonly dependent financially on social security, and the amount they can earn without their benefit being affected is limited. While this may be a disincentive to productivity it is not a good cause for constraining employment opportunities. Although the resources of people attending day centres, in terms of physical ability, energy and concentration, may be limited, they ought not to be underestimated. Relatively demanding work may be practicable, for which the necessary services need to be incorporated.

It may be inappropriate to mix mentally and physically handicapped people in a day centre workshop, on the grounds that it could be damaging to the esteem of the physically handicapped workers. On the other hand, a relatively structured organization of work of the type found in adult training centres for mentally handicapped people might prove a stimulus to people with physical disabilities[50].

Similar issues are raised in respect of people who are being rehabilitated following a period of mental illness. For mentally ill people the goal is a return to open employment, and relatively disciplined work conditions may be required. Apart from this it may happen that the overtly normal mentally ill people resent being mixed among the physically handicapped whom they regard as inferior to themselves.

[49] Bib 93471, p490
[50] Services for mentally handicapped people are discussed in 1308. Guidance on the design of adult training centres is in section 708.

1422 Day centres: Planning and strategy

Guidance on the planning and design of day centres, set down in section 704 of this book, is summarized here in relation to the overall strategy of services. First, the workshop area should be kept relatively self-contained; other areas will be used outside working hours and it is important that they can be closed off from the workshop. Second, the facilities provided for carpentry and metalwork should be planned so that they can be used for making practical aids for handicapped people in the locality, such as bath seats, tap turners and cleaning and kitchen trolleys. Third, individual clubrooms may be provided for local associations, but if the aim is to avoid segregative or elitist groups it is preferable that rooms are included which can be hired out to individual organizations. Fourth, there should be a shop, preferably managed by a handicapped person, which can be a general store for the housebound people attending the centre. Fifth, there should be a hairdressing salon serving both men and women, again for the benefit of those who are housebound. Sixth, there should be a room for a visiting chiropodist. Seventh, there should be baths, showers and washing facilities so that people who are unable to have a bath at home because they cannot manage the stairs to get there, or who need an attendant for bathing and would otherwise rely on a home help or district nurse, can have a bath when they visit the centre. Eighth, there should be a training kitchen and a training bathroom where handicapped people can be helped to learn how to do things for themselves at home.

While having a rehabilitative role, the extent to which day centres should incorporate medical rehabilitation facilities is a matter for the health authority to decide in cooperation with the social services authority. Where comprehensive medical therapy is undertaken in a local hospital there will not be a case for including in the local authority centre a gymnasium, a physiotherapy room or a hydrotherapy pool. The rehabilitative role of the local authority centre will be on a broader level, in terms of expanding the potential of disabled people for living. The centre is thus an important component of the spectrum of rehabilitation services and medical consultants should, if not actively associated with its administration, be well acquainted with the services it affords, so that patients can be referred through medical social workers.

Practical advice on the management of daily living activities is clearly part of the centre's role; there should be a training kitchen and bathroom, and a display of disability aids. These services may be duplicated in a hospital rehabilitation unit, where the emphasis may be more on assessment and the determination of suitable clinical equipment, such as wheelchairs and walking aids. It may be helpful if there is a link between the two departments, the local authority training facilities being under the supervision of an occupational therapist who knows when it is appropriate to refer a client to the hospital for specialist advice.

The resulting complex is more than a simple social centre, a work centre or a recreation centre, and it is more than an aggregation of the three. It is a community centre for handicapped people, a centre where there are opportunities for constructive social interactions and for learning about living. Having broadened its role this far, ought the centre still to be exclusively the domain of handicapped people? If the goal is to help disabled people to be active members of the ordinary community the proper course is for the facilities of the centre to overlap with provision for the general public. The assembly hall and social rooms might be places where events can be arranged by handicapped people to which friends and others can be invited. The craft rooms may be used for evening classes in association with the local education authority. The library could be an integral part of the local public library service. There will be even bigger opportunities if the centre for the handicapped is part of a large education and amenity centre, of the kind discussed earlier under education services. If for example the complex includes a swimming pool there might be possibilities to include a small recreational pool geared particularly to meet the needs of handicapped people. The conclusion is that there ought to be no standard or formula solutions: if the purpose is to help disabled people to become active citizens it is wrong to stop at buildings which say 'This is special for disabled – others keep out'.

1423   Blind people

The traditional stereotype of the blind man with a white stick, tapping uncertainly along the edge of the pavement as he goes, persists. Where it has been modified, the substitute may be of the blind person moving more confidently with the aid of a guide dog. There are some blind people who are able to get about, including in places with which they are unfamiliar, without the help of either a stick or a dog. They do this by facial vision, sensing the pressure of nearby objects against the skin. This pressure is a combination of feeling and hearing, felt by the pores around the ears. In a recent study of the mobility of blind people, 87 per cent of people who were totally blind claimed they were able to sense when walking along a pavement the presence of a lorry with the engine off, and a similar number claimed they could sense the location of lamp-posts[51]. In his autobiography Ved Mehta tells how as a blind boy he went from his home in India to a school for the blind in America, where his instructor sent him out on an independence test:

'I found that the noise of the cane made me very self-conscious and was quite distracting, so I flung it into the gutter at the end of the driveway in front of the school, and having made a mental note of the spot so that I might pick up the cane on my return, I started walking rapidly towards the bus stop, with my hands thrust into my pockets. Rather than wait at the nearest bus stop, I decided I would walk three or four blocks to the next one. Just to test my facial vision, I counted the lamp-posts and tried to guess the distance from which I first perceived them.'[52]

In another survey of the mobility of blind people in Britain the question was asked 'Amongst the common obstacles to be met with outdoors, which do you find to be the greatest menace, and why?'[53] The obstacles most frequently mentioned were bicycles 40, roadworks 32, thin posts 24, prams 21, toys 19, ladders 16, scaffolding 14, overhanging branches, awnings etc 11, tricycles 10, children 8, dogs 7, dustbins 6, and jutting steps 5. The emphasis is predominantly on temporary, insubstantial, movable and unpredictable obstacles. Features of any size could be perceptually sensed – some people in the survey claimed (perhaps exaggeratedly) that they could detect walls at 20m, buildings at 15m and trees at 10m. It is apparent from this evidence that there is relatively little that the architect can do to mitigate the extent to which blind people are handicapped by their physical environment.

The blind person not having a dog or whose perceptual senses are not acute, will, when using an unfamiliar building for the first time, have someone to guide him. After one or two visits he is sufficiently well-acquainted with the geography of the building to move about without difficulty. Aids such as raised letters on doorways, braille labels to identify room functions, knurled doorhandles and studs on handrails are all superfluous.

In respect of external environmental arrangements for blind people, it has been suggested that the ramping of kerbs at pedestrian crossings to suit wheelchair users might be a positive hazard[54]. This is questionable. The blind person using a street with which he is familiar will know exactly where the pavement surface gives way to the road surface. If he is unfamiliar with the street but using a dog there will be no hazard. If he is using a long cane he will locate where the pavement surface dips before stepping into the street[55]. If he relies on facial vision he will not perceive the kerb itself, but will as a rule be able to predict its position from his awareness of the location of adjoining buildings and vehicles. Rather than being a hazard, the probability is that raised kerbs will be advantageous, in that there will be a lesser risk of tripping.

There are significant differences between the environmental requirements of people who are totally blind and those who have some residual vision. People with some vision rely on it to detect obstacles, rather than on hearing and feeling. The mobility study reported earlier found that people with poor vision were much less easily able to perceive lamp-posts for example than those who were totally blind[56]. Whereas those with some vision found it difficult to walk safely where pavements were crowded, those who were blind did not[57]. For people who were blind but independently mobile the most difficult problem was managing when there was deep snow on the ground.

[51] Bib 93330, p51
[52] Bib 93322, p223
[53] Bib 93331, p147
[54] See for example Bib 93020, p8
[55] The principle of the long cane technique is that the cane senses the area just ahead of where the blind traveller is about to step.
[56] Bib 93330, p51
[57] Bib 93330, p49

For blind people one of the more helpful things that architects can do is to specify noisy and resonant floor surfaces – something unlikely to be appreciated by other building users. Apart from this, and the matter of raised digits for lift controls, there are not many positive prescriptions, but a number of useful things that architects, engineers and designers can avoid doing. They can avoid, for example, having doors opening out on to circulation routes, having litter bins fixed to posts at chest height, having street furniture which obstructs pavements, and having passageways below the sloping underside of staircases.

1424   Deaf people

For reasons discussed earlier in this commentary, deafness is as a rule a more handicapping disability than blindness[58]. Measured by the criterion of the handicap caused by buildings, deaf people may be relatively more affected than blind people. This is because there is frequently no visual indication inside buildings of the whereabouts of cloakroom facilities, particular departments or specific offices. Normal people are expected to ask if they do not know their way around; deaf people cannot do this, and it is of importance to them that adequate notices are displayed.

People who are hard of hearing may inflict agony on neighbours or other building users by operating television sets, radios or record players at full blast. The remedy is effective sound insulation, particularly of partition walls between dwelling units. While such provision is likely to be welcomed by all there are cost penalties. For the majority of householders or building users it could be that financial resources might with more advantage be deployed elsewhere. The incidence of severe hearing disability across the community as a whole is not such as to warrant acoustically impenetrable conditions in all buildings. A provision which is valuable for people who use certain types of hearing aid is the incorporation in buildings such as churches, concert halls or lecture theatres of an induction loop into which attachments can be plugged.

1425   Short people

It is too facile to say simply that short people are handicapped because they are short. Apart from being disadvantaged by shortness, being a dwarf means that one is an object of curiosity and astonishment, pointed out and stared at wherever one goes. 'A dwarf' has associations of ridicule, Snow White and circuses, and for lack of a suitable euphemism the preferred term is now 'persons of restricted growth'.

There is the apocryphal story of the dwarf who lived on the twelfth floor of a block of flats, took the lift down to the bottom when he went out to work, walking up from the fifth floor when he returned; apocryphal because he could well enough have carried a stick to poke at out-of-reach

controls. There is also the point that he would not, had he been severely handicapped, have been able to walk up seven flights of steps; not being able to manage high steps is a disability among dwarfs which is not always appreciated.

There are other problems in buildings, such as not being able to reach high shelves, not being able to use standard-height sinks or basins, or cope with wall-hung urinals. The most bizarre situation was one pointed out to me when I visited in 1972 the home of a boy aged about 15. He was very short and the house had been adapted to give him a downstairs bedroom because he was not able to climb the stairs. The big problem, his mother said, was the bed. To get on to it each night he had to run the length of the room to gather sufficient momentum to bounce on top of it. It did not seem to have occurred to either of them that the legs of the bed might have been cut down.

It needs to be emphasized that the problems which dwarfs encounter when using buildings are not unique; they are often exactly the same as those of small children, and in many situations, because they also operate at low level, of wheelchair users. Thus, both in public buildings and in housing, provision made for wheelchair users will generally be advantageous. The additional space allowed for wheelchair circulation will be superfluous, but not as a rule handicapping.

1426   Non-overt disabilities

People with physical disabilities which are not visually apparent – such as those with bronchitis or heart complaints – are frequently handicapped by buildings.

They are in an ambiguous position. They do not carry with them a stick, chair or other banner which proclaims their status and differentness, and they do not therefore customarily receive from other people the patience and consideration accorded to people with obvious problems. On the other hand they may, because the consequences of exceeding their physical threshold can be fatal, behave more rationally than people with locomotory disabilities anxious to convince themselves that they can operate 'as normal'. The severe cardiac person is constrained by the threat of mortality – he will not labour up a flight of steps until he is blue in the face simply to prove that he is the same as everyone else. Similarly the severe bronchitic or person with pulmonary tuberculosis will not struggle to achieve an objective which he well knows is beyond the limits of his capacity.

Once again, the recommendation is that no specific provision in buildings is made for people in this group. In general, facilities incorporated for people with locomotory disabilities will be welcomed. If it is advantageous for a cardiac or bronchitic person to use services identified as special for disabled people he is unlikely to be deterred because he is anxious not to expose his problems.

[58] See 1307

1427 Epileptics

Among people with severe epilepsy there is the constant hazard of falls and injuries. Dangers are most acute among children and adolescents liable without warning to drop falls; to guard against head damage, and also cuts, bruises and broken teeth, protective headgear has to be worn permanently. The headgear cannot always guarantee security and the question arises whether modified environmental conditions can alleviate threats.

In respect of the home environment there are a number of useful precautions which can be taken, for example regarding the selection of furniture, the specification of floor finishes and the avoidance of equipment with sharp edges; these and other possibilities are discussed elsewhere[59]. In respect of the external environment nothing very effective can be done – it is unrealistic to suppose that floor surfaces, furniture and equipment can all be modified or protected to minimize the risk to epileptics. For the person with severe epilepsy, as for others with disabilities, the proper course is to recognize and accept the circumstances of his disability, and to adapt himself to his environment rather than expecting it to be adapted for him. Having to wear a peculiar helmet may be necessary but the mature person will not be neurotic about it, any more than is the typical paraplegic about the wheelchair which he has to use.

[59] See 9138

15 Institutions for disabled people

1500 Accommodation options

For people who are disabled, living in institutions is a bad thing. Living in ordinary housing is a good thing. There are qualifications to be made to this blanket judgement but the essence of the discussion which follows is that, by and large, it is admissible.

No evaluation of accommodation possibilities for disabled people ought to examine in isolation particular options, such as hospital units, residential homes, serviced housing or independent housing. There is a continuum, and each of these options is one piece, interacting and overlapping with the next. The properness of any accommodation prescription for an individual person who is disabled depends on a congregation of factors: on degree of physical disability, on intellectual and emotional resources, and on the availability of social support from family, friends or relatives. And in practice it is often none of these things, but simply cash – how much money a disabled person or his family can muster – which determines what happens. Even if the inequalities of opportunities to determine how, as a disabled person, one lives were not so gross, there would still be no cause for laying down rules for allocating handicapped people to one kind of accommodation rather than another.

For reasons of history, economics and political expediency there has in Britain been a tendency (probably no more marked than in many other communities) to categorize disabled people into administrative slots and to pack them into parcels whose makeup is determined more by what the system happens to offer than by what people actually need. So there are disabled people who find themselves in hospital units because residential services cannot cope with them, and others who find themselves in residential homes because housing services cannot cope.

The first principle is options. For people who are disabled, the aim of the agencies which administer accommodation services must be to see that each disabled person has a choice to determine for himself, within the bounds of what is physically practicable, how he lives. The second principle, inherent in the first, is that there must be possibilities for him to remain part of the ordinary busy world, rather than being forcibly, for lack of choice, separated from it. He must be able to take part in everyday social and community events, to go shopping for instance, to have a drink with friends or to attend the local church. By implication he must have the choice of carrying on living in ordinary housing, with the physical assistance which he needs being brought in from outside if it cannot be provided inside. Only if this option is open will the person who elects for communal living in a residential home be making a real choice. Similarly only if there is the option of the residential home which, while providing comprehensive physical care, gives the disabled person a chance to manage his own affairs and to participate in the management of the community, will the person who elects to live in a hospital unit be making a real choice.

A third principle, safeguarded if the first two are observed, is that the disabled person is treated as a human being and not as a case. Too often the living arrangements of

disabled people are determined by what doctors decide are for medical reasons appropriate, rather than by what for the disabled person is socially desirable. It needs to be emphasized, and re-emphasized, that the decision about how to live must be a social matter and not a medical matter. Only in circumstances where other people's health may be affected, and not always then, does the doctor morally have the right to control how a disabled person lives.

1501 The structure of services in Britain

Two central government departments are concerned with the administration of accommodation for disabled people in England and Wales, the Department of the Environment and the Department of Health and Social Security. The notes which follow relate specifically to the structure of services in England, but the structure in Wales – channelled through the Welsh office – is similar, and is comparable in Scotland, where services are administered by the Scottish Development Department and the Scottish Home and Health Department.

The Department of the Environment works through local housing authorities, and the Department of Health and Social Security on the one part through local social services authorities and on the other through regional and area health authorities (diagram 15.1). On the DoE side the housing authorities are the 32 London borough councils, the 36 metropolitan district councils and the 296 district councils. On the DHSS side the social services authorities are the 32 London boroughs, the 36 metropolitan districts and the 39 non-metropolitan county councils. There are thus 68 authorities where the same council is responsible for the administration of both housing services and social services. The health authorities are the 14 regional authorities and the 90 area authorities, the majority of area authorities having the same territorial boundaries as the non-metropolitan counties and metropolitan districts.

1502 The role of housing authorities

On the housing front the relevant pieces of legislation are the Housing Act 1957 and the Chronically Sick and Disabled Persons Act 1970. Section 91 of the 1957 Act requires that, in discharging their responsibilities under the Act, housing authorities should consider the housing needs in their area in relation to existing housing conditions and the provision of further housing accommodation.

Section 3 of the 1970 Act says 'every local authority . . . in discharging their duty under section 91 (of the Housing Act 1957) . . . shall have regard to the special needs of chronically sick or disabled persons'. The Chronically Sick Act does not therefore give housing authorities any new powers, it simply draws attention to and emphasizes their existing responsibilities.

In 1969 the Cullingworth report *Council housing: purposes, procedures and priorities* said that local housing

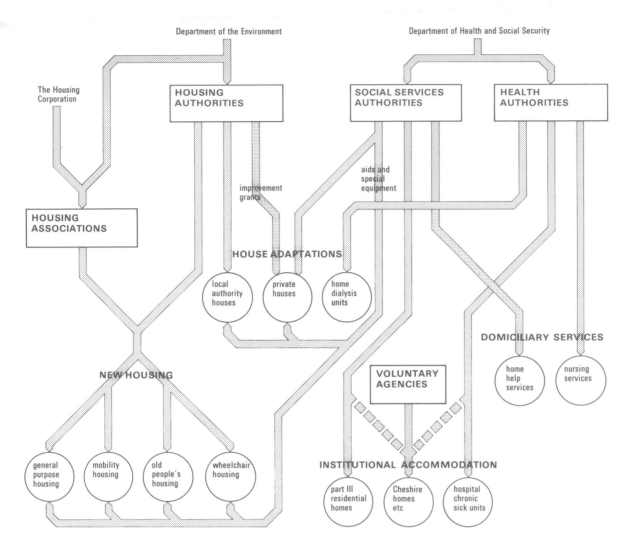

15.1 Administration of housing services for disabled people in England and Wales.

authorities ought to give special consideration to people with special needs[1]. This theme is repeated in the 1973 Government White Paper *Widening the choice: the next steps in housing* which says 'In the Government's view, local authorities have a special responsibility for ensuring that adequate and suitable accommodation to rent is available to those who have special needs or suffer from special disadvantages.' The report goes on to say that particular consideration needs to be given to the needs of elderly and physically handicapped people 'for whom the provision so far made is often inadequate.'[2]

Regarding the provision of what is known as sheltered housing the 1973 white paper says:

'In many cases the needs of the elderly or handicapped can best be met by small houses or flatlets grouped under the supervision of a warden. The provision of accommodation of this kind brings several advantages. To the old or handicapped person it brings an extended possibility of independent living combined with the assurance of security and the opportunity of social life. This can lead to the relief of hospital and other services. Grouped flatlets can also enable the elderly or handicapped to leave under-occupied accommodation and thus to release other

dwellings for family occupation. Much has been done already to provide supervised group housing both by local authorities and by housing associations, but both will need to do more.'[3]

The most recent official guidance on housing for disabled people is in the Department of the Environment's Circular 74/74 *Housing for people who are physically handicapped*[4]. The value of adaptations is emphasized:

'For many handicapped people, it is better to adapt their existing home, if suitable for adaptation, than to rehouse them in purpose-built accommodation. This means, above all, that they do not have to move away from the house and area they are used to living in and can continue to rely on established links with relatives and friends nearby.'

[1] Bib 93721, p37
[2] Bib 93722, p11. This paper expresses the policy views of the then Conservative government; similar policies are endorsed by the current (1976) administration.
[3] Bib 93722, p11–12
[4] Bib 93110

The circular also introduces the concept of 'mobility' housing, meaning ordinary new housing to prevailing space and cost standards, with certain features so designed that it is suitable for many handicapped people; the important role of this kind of housing is discussed later in the commentary [5]. The circular suggests that specially designed housing is needed for people who are totally dependent on wheelchairs, and for housewives who, although they may not use wheelchairs at all times, use them inside the home and need suitably designed kitchens.

Of the special housing built for disabled people in recent years a substantial proportion is family accommodation, where even a person who is totally dependent can manage if there is someone else in the household to help him, for example with dressing, washing and using the lavatory. By contrast there are probably very few single people who are severely disabled living in purpose-designed housing units [6].

1503   The bridge between housing and institutions

The practicability of making housing provision for single severely disabled people or couples both of whom are handicapped is discussed later in this commentary. In this connection, circular 74/74 says:

'For some severely handicapped people, provision will continue to be required in hospitals and local authority residential accommodation. To enable those who wish, and would be able, to live in housing in the community, efforts are increasingly being made by local authorities and voluntary bodies to strengthen the necessary social services and to encourage support from local communities. The process of collaboration between health and local authorities should ensure availability of services of the primary health care team (including community nursing). Suitably designed and equipped housing, for which these supporting services are available, has an important part to play in providing disabled people with some freedom of choice [7].

A recent modification of legislation may assist the process of bridging the gap between conventional housing arrangements and institutional provision. This is that under section 33 and related powers of the Housing Act 1974, housing authorities and housing associations can obtain government subsidy for hostel provision; hostels were not previously entitled to special subsidy and housing authorities had no particular incentive to build them.

These trends indicate that the traditional housing ethic is being modified. Historically, the line has been that families or individuals who can manage independently, and earn enough to pay their rent, deserve to be in homes of their own, whereas those who cannot may be rejected and placed in institutions. It is not only physically disabled people who have been subject to this rule; among others affected by it are the mentally ill, the mentally handicapped and impoverished single people.

The distinction between physically disabled people on the one hand and the mentally ill and mentally handicapped on the other is that, whereas mentally ill and mentally handicapped people need more to manage independently than simple physical props, there are disabled people for whom convenient physical provision can make a critical difference between dependence and independence. Thus housing authorities are ready to extend their social responsibility to the physically disabled, and generous subsidies for capital expenditure are available to help them. They do not yet regard those who are mentally ill or mentally handicapped in the same fashion, and relatively little has been done in the ordinary housing field to help these people [8].

1504   Administration of institutions

Under the DHSS umbrella, institutions for disabled people can be provided either by social services authorities or by area health authorities. On the social services side, section 21 of the National Assistance Act 1948 says:

'It shall be the duty of every local authority . . . to provide residential accommodation for persons who by reason of age, infirmity or any other circumstances are in need of care and attention which is not otherwise available to them.' [9]

Section 21 is in part III of the 1948 Act and hence accommodation provided under this power, in the main old people's homes, is known generically as part III homes. From time to time the Department of Health has tried to discourage, because of its associations, the use of the term part III in favour of, for example, 'residential accommodation' but the usage has persisted and, by benefit of its definitiveness, is continued here.

Historically there is a powerful tradition in Britain of institutional provision for indigent people by charitable agencies. Recognizing this, the 1948 Act did not require that local authorities always themselves provide part III accommodation but permitted them, if they wished, to delegate their authority to approved agencies. In respect of institutions for physically handicapped people a large number of national and local agencies are concerned, the major agency being the Leonard Cheshire Foundation, which, from its beginnings in 1948, now has a network of 61 Cheshire homes throughout Britain.

[5] See 1702–1709
[6] This is an impression based on observations of recent housing schemes. In a survey of purpose-designed wheelchair housing undertaken by the Department of the Environment in 1972 dwelling units approved in 1968 were studied; 71 of 249 (29 per cent) were 3 bedroom units.
[7] Bib 93110, para 5
[8] In respect of housing accommodation for mentally handicapped people some encouraging developments are reported by Sandra Francklin (Bib 93361); the majority of these have been initiated by local social services authorities rather than housing authorities.
[9] Section 21 of the 1948 Act has been amended by section 195 of the Local Government Act 1972; although the word 'may' is substituted for 'shall' the statutory duty remains.

a First floor plan

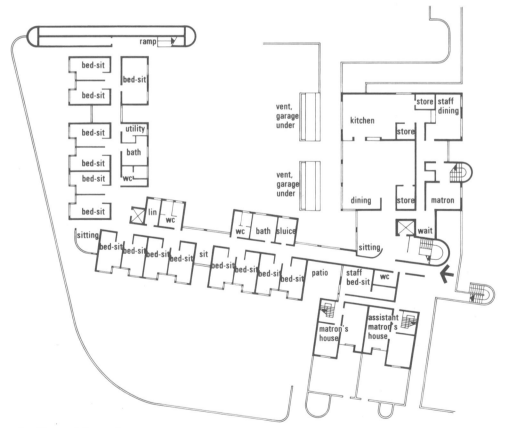

b Ground floor plan

15.2 Proposed Stockwell home for younger physically handicapped people (1:500).
Edward Hollamby, director of development to London Borough of Lambeth.

1505 Local authority homes and Cheshire homes

Although they operate to the same piece of legislation there are often notable differences between residential homes administered directly by local authorities and those managed by voluntary agencies. The notes which follow discuss some of the differences, a theorized typical Cheshire home being used as representative of the voluntary agency side. They are based on the documented evidence referred to, and also from impressions in the course of visits I have made to 10 local authority homes and 18 Cheshire homes. The actual characteristics of residents, in terms for example of age, sex, diagnostic conditions and effects of disability, do not differ markedly, and consideration of these factors is postponed to the discussion later in the commentary about the sort of architectural arrangements needed in new homes.

The typical local authority home accommodates about 30 residents. The building is purpose-designed to afford residents as much personal independence as possible, and is located in an urban setting alongside ordinary housing and close to shops and other amenities. The majority of the residents have single rooms, equipped with tastefully selected modern furniture and fabrics. Administration is by a subcommittee of the council's social services committee, who appoint the person who is to have day to day charge, known variously as the superintendent, warden, manager or matron. Residents of the home are not represented on the management committee and are not directly involved in the selection of new residents for admission. Diagram 15.2 is an example of a recently designed home for the London Borough of Lambeth.

The typical Cheshire home also accommodates about 30 residents, though some homes are large institutions having more than 100 residents. The building is a converted country house, with purpose-designed additions. It is in a rural setting with a long private drive isolating it from the neighbouring community. Some of the bedrooms are large, and few of the residents have rooms of their own. An axiom of the Cheshire Foundation is that local management committees should be autonomous. Government is by a self-perpetuating committee of local people, predominantly middle class professionals. The policy of the foundation is to encourage the appointment of residents as full members of management committees, and this has so far happened in a small number of cases.

In all Cheshire homes there is a tradition of local fund raising activities to finance new buildings and provide such things as special buses for outings. Most of the income of homes comes from the local authorities who sponsor residents, and pay for each an agreed amount. In practice this rarely covers all necessary day to day expenditure and the homes expect to have to supplement it by additional fund raising. A beneficial effect of the fund raising is that, by contrast with the typical local authority home, there is much more involvement on the part of the residents with the local community outside and more involvement of local people in the day to day running of the home. One other characteristic of the typical Cheshire home is that it has a lovely view. But, as one resident put

it to me: 'You can't eat the grass and you can't talk to the cows'.

The majority of Cheshire homes are registered as disabled persons' homes under section 37 of the National Assistance Act 1948, though a few are registered as nursing homes under section 187 of the Public Health Act 1936, as amended by section 41 of the National Health Service Reorganisation Act 1973. Registration as a nursing home means that the home can take residents who are hospital-sponsored rather than local authority sponsored, the arrangement being that a certain number of beds in the home are contracted to the local area health authority and are available for their patients. There is thus in some Cheshire homes, unlike local authority homes, an overlap between the two sides of the DHSS structure, as shown in diagram 15.1.

1506 Hospital units

Parallel with the provision by social services authorities of accommodation for chronically handicapped people, health authorities, working to powers given them in section 12 of the Health Services and Public Health Act 1968 and section 2 of the National Health Service Reorganisation Act 1973, provide accommodation in hospital units for people known collectively as 'the younger chronic sick'.

In 1968 the then Ministry of Health issued a memorandum offering guidance to hospital authorities on the care of these patients[10]. With the assistance of hospital authorities throughout the country a survey had been made which showed that in April 1967 there were 4233 chronic sick patients aged between 15 and 59 in non-psychiatric hospitals. Half of these were accommodated in wards of geriatric departments or in chronic sick wards. In an accompanying enclosure to the memorandum giving statistical information the definition by which these younger chronic sick people had been identified was quoted 'Patients aged 15 to 59 who are receiving long-term care for chronic disabilities or illnesses other than those with long-term mental illness or subnormality but including those with brain damage due to injury'[11]. This, it needs to be noted, was not a definition of chronic sick people who *needed* to be in hospital but of those who *happened* to be in hospital.

The memorandum says:

'The working group which studied the problem in the field found generally that the medical and nursing conditions precipitating admission of younger chronic sick patients to hospitals were (a) incontinence, (b) the need for nursing care at night, (c) paralysis, particularly of the upper limbs, and (d) the need for frequent and continuous basic nursing care such as feeding, bathing, care of pressure areas and frequent change of position. There were also social reasons precipitating demand such as the inability of the family to continue providing care at home.'

[10] Bib 93150
[11] Bib 93151

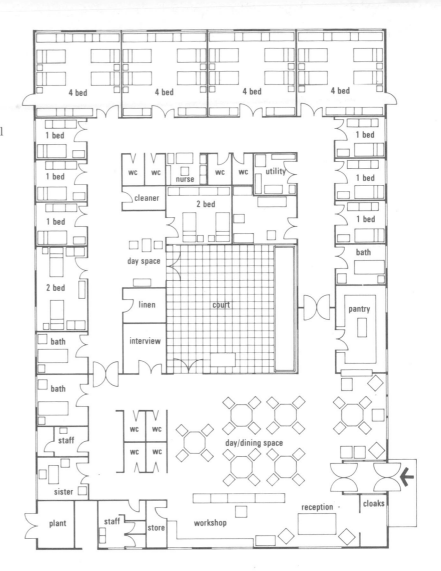

15.3 South East Metropolitan Regional Hospital Board (now South East Thames Regional Health Authority) 26 bed standard younger chronic sick unit (1:250). Charles Scott, regional architect

Some question marks are appropriate here. Why do the 'medical and nursing conditions' itemized need care in a hospital rather than elsewhere? Are feeding and bathing matters for 'continuous basic nursing care'? Why are social reasons a cause for admission to hospital?

The memorandum goes on to make recommendations on the planning of these units. It says:

'Units of from 25 to 50 beds are considered to provide the best environment; smaller units are difficult to staff and tend to be isolated'.

'The nursing requirements and problems are such that they alone are a strong reason for siting units in the environment of general hospitals.'

'The aim should be to provide as relaxed and permissive an atmosphere as possible within a hospital setting.'

'The ward should be subdivided into small units, with at least 25 per cent of single rooms.'

The memorandum suggested that it might be necessary to provide units by adapting existing buildings, but that where they could be associated with new building or major redevelopment purpose-built units should be provided. To help architects a model plan was drawn up by the Department of Health, showing how units of 26 beds each might be grouped in threes, giving a concentration of 78 patients[12]. This model plan has been followed closely for example by the South East Metropolitan Regional

Hospital Board (now the South East Thames Regional Health Authority); its standard unit is shown in diagram 15.3.

1507 The hospital unit building programme

The first purpose-designed younger chronic sick unit, for 12 patients, was opened in 1968 by the Wessex Regional Hospital Board at Ashurst hospital in Hampshire. The programme of building new units was accelerated by the passing of the Chronically Sick and Disabled Persons Act in 1970, which in section 17 requires that 'in any hospital a person who is suffering from a condition of chronic illness or disability is not cared for in the hospital as an in-patient in any part of the hospital which is normally used wholly or mainly for the care of elderly persons, unless he is himself an elderly person'.

In August 1970 when the Act came into effect, a memorandum was sent by the Department of Health to hospital authorities[13]. It said:

'The attention of hospital authorities is drawn especially to section 17 . . . The underlying purpose of this provision is that despite their illness or disability many chronically sick or disabled people have active intellects and especially for such people when they must spend long

---

[12] Bib 93160
[13] Bib 93152

periods in hospital it can be particularly hard if they are placed in an environment where there are few patients of their own age and where the regime is orientated towards meeting the needs of mainly senile patients'.

The programme received sympathetic treatment from the Treasury and in consequence a specifically reserved sum of £5million was added to the hospital building budget (since increased to £7million to cover rising costs), which it was expected would increase the total of beds to 1800 in 70 units[14]. At the same time, in response to the same political pressures, there has been a surge of building activity by social services authorities. There are currently (May 1976) 30 purposely-built homes for younger physically disabled people administered by local authorities; of these 20 have opened since 1970. There are 18 further homes being built[15].

1508 A hospital or local authority responsibility?

There is no clear demarcation line at which a handicapped person becomes a hospital rather than a local authority responsibility, and no firm guidelines are set down by the Department of Health. For lack of any such guidance attention is drawn to the memorandum for local authorities and hospital authorities *Care of the elderly in hospitals and residential homes* issued in 1965[16]. This says that categories of patient, apart from the acutely ill, likely to require hospital geriatric care include patients with long term illness 'requiring continuous medical or nursing care of a kind which could not adequately be provided in their own homes'.

The critical phrase is 'continuous medical or nursing care', and since part III homes are not statutorily obliged to have qualified nurses on the staff the interpretation is that when a patient needs continuous nursing care he must be transferred to a nursing home or hospital unit. But in practice it is invariable that part III homes employ nurses on their staff. It is also invariable, both in local authority and voluntary homes, that residents are sustained until they die and are not transferred to a long-stay hospital unit on account of medical needs. There is thus no clear distinction between hospital sponsored residents and local authority residents, demonstrated by the Cheshire homes which cater for both categories (where residents commonly do not know who is on which side) and confirmed by the evidence documented in *A Life Apart* by Miller and Gwynne[17].

The escape clause of 'continuous nursing care' is often used by local authorities and Cheshire homes to reject potential residents they regard as unsuitable and pass them on to hospital authorities as a last refuge. The excuse often made is incontinence, but among residents in part III homes there is commonly a sizable proportion who *are* incontinent. More often the rejection is on social grounds, the institution suspecting that the potential resident would not fit in or would be a disturbance to the community. Voluntary homes can afford to be more selective than local authority homes and the point is made by Miller and Gwynne in respect of local authority homes:

'There is a higher incidence of emotional disorders, often the outcome of severe deprivation. It seems probable that acute or long-standing social and domestic problems attract the attention of local welfare officers, who then see the institution on their own doorstep as offering a ready solution.'[18]

On the well tried premise that if institutions are established people can, by one means or another, be found to fill them, hospital units and residential homes will no doubt be filled. At the same time it is pertinent to record that local authorities and Cheshire homes are finding it increasingly difficult, and sometimes impossible, to find for their institutions the sort of young severely disabled but mentally capable people for whom they were intended. Miller and Gwynne say about the local authority institution they studied:

'Although it had been expected that the new purpose-built institution would attract people out of squalid home environments, it failed to do so in in sufficient numbers. Beds remained empty and the contributing authority felt under pressure to fill them in order to justify the cost of building the establishment.'[19]

Regarding the overall institutional scene they then go on to comment:

'Thus, either through having failed to establish in the first instance a realistic policy about an acceptable range of age and incapacity or else through having failed to enforce such a policy, a number of institutions are finding themselves with a population markedly older, more static, and more heavily handicapped than they originally envisaged . . . The upshot is that a young newcomer to such an institution may find that it does not differ greatly from the type of geriatric unit it was designed to replace.'[20]

The suspicion occurs that there has been less coordination than there could have been between the different agencies providing care for the same sort of people. The basic questions 'why hospital units rather than other sorts of institutions?' and 'why institutions at all?' do not seem to have been probed. These issues are returned to subsequently, but at this stage it is worth looking more carefully at the general complaint which

[14] Symons (Bib 93130, p12) reports that at October 1973 a total of 91 purpose-built units were proposed by (the then) Regional Hospital Boards in England and Wales, of which 9 had been completed and 11 were under construction, with 6 interim units being erected. With two exceptions only all the units planned or proposed were to be on existing hospital sites.
[15] Information supplied by DHSS.
[16] Bib 93643
[17] Bib 93131, p71. Relevant confirmatory evidence is provided in Bib 93280. Among a special group of 14 people living at home dependent on respiratory machines, 7 were the responsibility of hospital services and 7 of local authority services; on a measure of degree of disability those who were a local authority responsibility were marginally more severely handicapped.
[18] Bib 93131, p97
[19] Bib 93131, p97
[20] Bib 93131, p103

has already been raised: that institutions in general, and hospital institutions in particular, are a bad thing.

1509   The nature of institutions

Hospital units for the younger chronic sick, local authority homes and Cheshire homes are institutions. They are institutions in the classic sense described by Erving Goffman: 'A total institution may be defined as a place of residence and work where a large number of like-situated individuals, cut off from the wider society for an appreciable period of time, together lead an enclosed, formally administered round of life'[21]. This Goffman contrasts with the basic social arrangement in modern society whereby individuals tend to sleep, play and work in different places, with different co-participants under different authorities, and without an overall rational plan.

Goffman's analysis concentrates on mental hospitals, but looks also at prisons, concentration camps, army barracks, boarding schools, monasteries and old people's homes. He discusses the regulation of the lives of inmates by the management, the requirement of inmates that they conform, the tendency to treat them as all alike, and the scheduling of their days to a pre-arranged pattern. He discusses the basic split between the staff and the group of people who are managed, and how each sees the other in terms of stereotypes; staff seeing inmates as bitter and inmates seeing staff as condescending. There are tendencies among staff to feel superior and righteous, and among inmates to feel inferior and weak[22].

Louis Battye, crippled since birth and resident for many years in a Cheshire home, has written of the situation of a young patient in the chronic ward of a long-stay hospital:

'But the atmosphere of the workhouse, like the smell of disease, defaecation and death, still tends to hang around these places, and if he remains there he will in time succumb to it and become dull and apathetic, his life circumscribed by the petty, tedious, sordid routine of a place designed for a quite different type of patient: he will become, in a word, institutionalized.'[23]

He goes on to say of the residential home alternative:

'But unless he fights a constant battle to retain his intellectual integrity and sense of purpose, as the years go by he will gradually feel the atmosphere of the place closing in on him, as it did in the chronic ward, shrinking his horizons to the limits of the house and grounds, a condition in which trivial details of the home's day-to-day routine assume a disproportionate importance. In spite of efforts to arouse or retain his interest in life, he will feel boredom and apathy creeping over him like a slow paralysis, eroding his will, dulling his critical wits, dousing his spirit, killing his independence. The temptation to sit day after day, year after year, with the same little clique in the same corner of the same room, doing the same things, thinking the same thoughts, making and listening to the same banal remarks, becomes almost irresistible. In a subtler, more civilized way than in

the chronic ward, he will have become institutionalized. The difference between a residential home, however comfortable, and a chronic ward is really only one of degree, not of kind: at the bottom they are both places where one simply whiles away the time until death – dead ends in an all too literal sense; and no amount of benevolent idealism, skilled care, home-like surroundings, good food, entertainments, outings, Christmas parties and occupational therapy can disguise this melancholy fact.'[24]

Eric Miller and Geraldine Gwynne's report *A Life Apart*, subtitled 'A pilot study of residential institutions for the physically handicapped and the young chronic sick' was published in 1972. It was sponsored by the Ministry of Health but was provoked by two residents in a Cheshire home concerned about the quality of their own institution. The authors argue that the essential characteristic of handicapped people taken into the institutions is not simply that they are crippled and in need of physical care, but that they have been written off by society. Comparing institutions for the physically handicapped with other institutions they say:

'A physical handicap by itself is not the discriminating factor; nor is the experience of personal rejection. More critical is the fact that when people cross the boundary into such an institution they are displaying that they have failed to occupy or retain any role which, according to the norms of society, confers social status on the individual. Even in this respect, however, the crippled inmate is comparable with the convict committed to prison or the patient committed to a psychiatric hospital. What is significantly different is that the prison and, nowadays, the psychiatric hospital sooner or later discharge almost all their inmates and have grounds for hoping that some will be reformed or cured and take up socially valued roles in the outside world. By contrast the boundary of the kind of institution we are discussing is, by and large, a point of no return. It is exceptional indeed for an inmate to be restored to some semblance of a normal role in a wider society. Usually he will remain in the institution, or in another of the same category, until he dies.'[25]

1510   Warehousing and horticulture

Describing the treatment of physically handicapped people in institutions, Miller and Gwynne suggest that there are basically two models of care, which they label 'warehousing' and 'horticultural'. The warehousing institution expresses the humanitarian or medical value that prolongation of life is a good thing and that although when residents are admitted to institutions the social death sentence has been passed, it is important to keep the interval between social and physical death as long as possible. The question is not asked to what purpose life is prolonged. The emphasis is on physical care, and to

---

[21] Bib 93750, p11
[22] Bib 93750, p18
[23] Bib 93320, p14
[24] Bib 93320, p15
[25] Bib 93131, p80

facilitate this inmates are required to be dependent and depersonalized; any attempts to assert themselves or display individuality are discouraged.

The horticultural model by contrast emphasizes the individuality of each inmate, his ability to operate independently and 'as normal' and his potential to realize unfulfilled capacities and ambitions. In horticultural institutions the individual is encouraged to exert as much control as he can over his environment; a useful indicator of a horticultural institution is, for example, the presence of numbers of electrically powered wheelchairs.

The conventional approach to residential care is the warehousing model, still found in a barely damaged fashion in many hospital units. The horticultural model is a recent development, unlikely to be found in a pure form. In some institutions the two are uncomfortably mixed.

Miller and Gwynne cite examples of the inhumanity of warehousing institutions, with one report of a woman who, left in the lavatory for two or three hours and deprived of her solace of cigarettes, managed to commit suicide. In my own meetings with physically handicapped people in residential homes there have been reports of a pregnant girl who was obliged to have an abortion, of a couple dragged forcibly from the register office where they were to have been married back to the 'home' they came from, and of an elderly man who had to pay five shillings each time he wanted to get out of the bath.

One institution I visited in 1972 was a Victorian mansion virtually unaltered since built nearly one hundred years before. It was insulated from the busy city which surrounded it by a fine garden and at the bottom of the drive a gate kept permanently locked to keep out the local vandals. Inside there was a marble monument to the founder and an ornate chapel kept scrupulously clean. 'Yes' I was told 'they all attend at least once a week, because it's in the rules'. Upstairs the dormitories had rows of tidily ranked beds to either side, each with an identical locker and no personal artefact in sight. In the dining room the matron introduced me to a man aged about 60, who had had a severe stroke: 'This is George. George tried to run away last week, but you're not going to run away again, are you George?' I met some of the professional people who managed the institution. They realized it was outdated and ought to be replaced but they believed they were doing a commendable job, and were concerned as to what might happen if the matron were not able to carry on.

Following their analysis of horticultural versus warehousing institutions Miller and Gwynne have reservations to make about the horticultural ethic. They suggest that the over-valuing of independence can lead to distortions, to denial of disability and to the setting of goals of performance that individuals do not have the capacity to attain. Dependency, even when it is appropriate, may become unacceptable. The horticultural ideology is a defence mechanism which prevents staff from relating to inmates as they really are, and can be almost as misleading as the more patronizing warehousing attitude[26].

1511 'Parasite people'

Paul Hunt, who has spent much of his life in institutions for the physically handicapped, has written critically of Miller and Gwynne's study under the title *Parasite people*[27]. What he has to say has a pertinence for architects and others who may find themselves involved in sustaining the British institutional tradition. He does not challenge the contention that the task of institutions is to cater for the period residents have between social and physical death. He does however challenge the judgements of Miller and Gwynne on warehousing and horticulture:

'They have not placed half enough emphasis on two basic truths. The first is that the warehousing approach has nothing whatever to recommend it and causes untold misery amongst residents. The second is that the liberal 'growth' approach, whatever criticisms may be made of some of its theories and assumptions, represents a genuine advance towards securing the rights and freedoms of a civilized life for many severely handicapped people.'

He also criticizes Miller and Gwynne for not looking at alternatives to institutional care as it is at present provided:

'They are not interested in the question of what numbers of people with comparable or more severe handicaps manage to live out in the community, how this is made possible, or what kind of life they lead . . . Instead they take it for granted that residential accommodation in virtually its present form is an unpleasant necessity for many of the severely physically handicapped until some (mythical) future state of universal kindness and generosity is reached.'

He says finally:

'In order for their study to have produced a more helpful conclusion, the authors would have had to abandon their conventional assumptions about the parasitical severely disabled. It would have been necessary for them to substitute an alternative philosophy which emphasized the rights and dignity of the residents as fully human adults . . . Dr Miller and Miss Gwynne have not risen to this challenge. They have instead done a hatchet job for the competitive society.'

In the face of this indictment of institutions, it may seem inconsistent to continue by suggesting how new institutions might best be organized. But the strategy determined at the start of this commentary was not one of revolution, it was one of achieving gradual improvement by modifying and making more humane the system that we have. Tentatively, therefore, practical guidelines are put forward.

[26] Bib 93131, p135–136
[27] Bib 93132

1512   The residents of institutions

The architect who sets out to build a residential home for disabled people needs first to know something of the characteristics of the people his building will serve. He needs to know what sort of age they are likely to be, what sort of practical problems are caused by their disabilities and in what sort of ways they will want to use their time.

For the planning of a new local authority home or hospital unit there are three particular sources of data which can help. These are first, Miller and Gwynne's study of institutions[28]; second, a survey made for the Cheshire Foundation[29] and third, the inquiry made by the Ministry of Health among young disabled people in hospitals[30]. Qualifications need to be made about the data drawn from all three. The inquiries were made some years ago (the most recent being the Cheshire Foundation survey in 1971) and overall the current picture is doubtless different. It is also the case that each inquiry looked at the situation as it was, and not as how desirably it might be.

Miller and Gwynne looked carefully at only five institutions, and do not claim that they are representative of their kind. They comprised two Cheshire homes, one local authority home and two younger chronic sick units, chosen on grounds of practical interest and convenience rather than typicality. The survey of Cheshire homes (which was not a survey of residents' views) was made by one of the Foundation's trustees, and the statistical information was not scientifically assembled. The report is also a very personal document, displaying the values and attitudes of the author, though it is none the worse for that. The Ministry of Health inquiry limited itself to the compilation of bare statistical information, published without comment or interpretation.

In respect of sex the data (tables 15.1, 15.4) suggest that numbers are almost equally divided, with rather more women than men. Without the male-only establishment, however, the Miller and Gwynne figures would be somewhat different, giving ratio of 57–43. A factor causing a greater demand for places for women in institutions is the preponderance of women among people with multiple sclerosis, the condition most prevalent in all types of institution. When planning new institutions architects may reasonably expect the ratio of women to men will not be less than 55–45.

Regarding age, the hospital figures (table 15.4) clearly show the concentration of need among people aged 50 or over. These figures may be affected by the selection procedures of part III homes, which commonly reject middle-aged people, particularly those with multiple sclerosis (though if hospital patients are excluded from table 15.1 there are still 69 per cent of residents who are aged 36 or over). The problem that institutions planned for young people have in finding young people to fill their places will almost certainly become more rather than less

[28] Bib 93131
[29] Bib 93134
[30] Bib 93151

Table 15.1 Age and sex of residents in institutions for disabled people

This table and table 15.2 summarize data recorded by Miller and Gwynne (Bib 93131, p64, 65, 71, 113, 114) about 147 residents in 5 institutions. The 147 comprised 60 in two Cheshire homes, 47 in one local authority home and 40 in two hospital units.

Age		%
–20	7	5
21–35	34	23
36–50	77	52
50+	29	20
Sex		
men	72	49
women	75	51
Impairment of movement		
both upper and lower limbs affected	116	79
lower limbs only	25	17
upper limbs only	2	1
limbs not affected	4	3

Table 15.2 Daily living activities in institutions for disabled people

	Full assistance	%	Some assistance	%	No assistance	%
dressing	67	46	46	31	34	23
washing	39	27	18	12	90	61
bathing	103	70	34	23	10	7
feeding	43	29	33	22	71	48
using wc	48	33	24	16	75	51

difficult. There is therefore a case when new institutions are planned for them to be geared to serving people aged (say) 45 or over, leaving any younger people in existing institutions which strive to cater for as young a population as possible. There is also the point that the needs of middle-aged people, in terms for example of active social gatherings, noise-making and other cultural activities, do not always coincide with those of younger people and there is therefore some social validity for division by age.

On the matter of marital status Miller and Gwynne found that only 12 per cent of inmates in their five institutions were married, and in practice many of these marriages had effectively disintegrated. While traditionally institutions have catered for single, divorced or widowed people there is clearly nowadays a growing tendency, particularly in Cheshire homes, for residents to get married, a procedure which no longer encounters implacable disapprobation from the management and expulsion from the institution. Increasingly therefore Cheshire homes, and local authority homes also, are adapting their accommodation so that married couples may live together. In the traditional warehousing institution such behaviour would of course have been inconceivable, and if it had been considered would have been viewed as nasty and perverted. Proper warehouses have in fact always been single-sex establishments. The willingness, though often reluctant, of managements to tolerate marriage and sex among their inmates is indeed as good an indicator as any that the warehousing regime is faltering.

Table 15.3 Residents in Cheshire homes

Disabling conditions		%
Multiple sclerosis	441	30·3
Cerebral palsy	192	13·4
Paraplegia (cause unspecified)	121	8·3
Arthritis (including osteo and rheumatoid arthritis, Still's disease and ankylosing spondylitis)	120	8·2
Muscular dystrophy	84	5·8
Parkinson's disease	82	5·6
Hemiplegia (cause unspecified), cerebrovascular accident	54	3·7
Polio	35	2·4
Friedrich's Ataxia	24	1·6
Congenital disorders of spine	16	1·1
Head injury	15	1·0
Hydrocephalus	15	1·0
Syringomyelia	10	0·7
Other causes, including amputation, tuberculosis, epilepsy, chronic bronchitis, motor neurone disease, tetraplegia (cause unspecified), haemophilia. Also unspecified conditions	247	16·9

Mobility		
users of wheelchairs	1073	73·7
users of powered wheelchairs	182	12·5
users of invalid motor vehicles	81	5·6
ambulant, users of walking aids	143	9·9
Total	1456	100·0

The data in this table are drawn from an analysis made in 1971 of 1456 residents in 50 Cheshire homes (Bib 93134). The subgroups under the Mobility heading are not mutually exclusive.

1513 Causes of institutionalization

Looking at the disabling conditions which are the basic cause of people being institutionalized (tables 15.3 and 15.4) multiple sclerosis comes at the top of the league for both Cheshire home residents and hospital patients. The potentially damaging effects of multiple sclerosis are reported elsewhere (table 13.1, 9162) and in institutions these effects can pervade the whole community. The tendency of people with multiple sclerosis to be, without themselves realizing it, inconsiderate, disgruntled and at the same time apathetic, can affect the morale of an institution. Many local authority homes and Cheshire homes attempt to avoid having too large a proportion of residents with multiple sclerosis, though the prevalence of the disease and the fact that institutionalization is often the only answer mean that they cannot win.

The cause of multiple sclerosis is unknown but the suspicion among medical scientists is that it is provoked by a virus infection. If this is the case and the virus can be identified there is a possibility that a vaccine can be developed to prevent it. In that event mass immunization could make multiple sclerosis as obsolete as polio. The consequences for institutions for disabled people would be enormous, making superfluous a large part of the building programme now under way. The eradication of multiple sclerosis would alter radically, and entirely beneficially, the whole institutional scene.

Table 15.4 Analysis of younger chronic sick patients in non-psychiatric hospitals in England and Wales, April 1967

Sex		%
men	2026	48
women	2197	52

Age		
15–34	502	12
35–49	1302	31
50–59	2361	56
age breakdown not available	58	1

Type of illness or disability		
multiple sclerosis	984	23·3
cerebro-vascular disease	803	19·0
rheumatoid arthritis	261	6·2
paraplegia and tetraplegia due to injury	224	5·3
post-head injury	167	4·0
muscular dystrophy	131	3·1
poliomyelitis	78	1·8
others	1575	37·3
Total	4223	100·0

Source: Bib 93151.

In the Cheshire home disability table paraplegia comes high up the list, with 8.3 per cent. It should not be supposed that these are all people who have had accidents causing paralysis; the term paraplegia is descriptive, implying people with paralyzed lower limbs. The classification is likely therefore to cover a number of people with congenital impairments causing paralysis, and others where the causation of the condition has not been reliably diagnosed. It is a mistake for architects to imagine that in the institutions they plan there will be quantities of alert, independent and capable paraplegics propelling themselves around in their chairs; such people can, by and large, cope successfully outside in the normal community.

In the future it may be anticipated that a larger proportion of the residents in part III homes will be young people with spina bifida, classified as congenital disorders of spine or hydrocephalus in the Cheshire home table. Many of these may be people with considerable physical and emotional problems, and it is unlikely that they will go far to counter the prevailing tendency for residents in part III homes to become decreasingly busy and active.

A feature of the hospital list, by comparison with the Cheshire home list, is the high proportion of people with cerebro-vascular disease. These are in the main people with severe hemiplegias; as a consequence of associated brain damage it might be supposed that many of these people have impossible communication problems, along with little capacity for independent mobility or self-care. On the other hand effective rehabilitation services can make it possible for people with severe hemiplegia to achieve much in terms of mobility and self-care, and with proper speech therapy communication problems can be overcome.

The comprehensiveness of locomotor disability among residents in institutions is shown by the analysis drawn from Miller and Gwynne (table 15.1), indicating that four out of five people were affected in both upper and lower limbs. The residents in the hospital units were rather more severely disabled than others. In respect of impairment of other faculties among people in each of the five institutions, speech defects ranged from 25 to 75 per cent, hearing defects from none to 11 per cent, sight impairments from 13 to 30 per cent and incontinence from 5 to 67 per cent[31]. Relatively there was a higher incidence of speech defects and incontinence among the hospital patients than among the others, but no significant differences for hearing and sight.

1514 Capacity for self-care

The analysis made by Miller and Gwynne of the capacity for self-care of residents in institutions (table 15.2) is based on a functional classification which I used for an appraisal in the Architects' Journal of the local authority home in Norwich[32]. In the context of architectural design the important activities are bathing, where the table shows that more than two in three of residents need full assistance, and 'going to the lavatory' where one

resident out of two cannot manage independently. In respect of washing, which means limited washing of face and hands in a basin, three out of five people could manage independently.

The figures for the five institutions have been aggregated; on a scale of dependence obtained by ranking each resident from 5 to 0 according to the number of activities where he needed some or full assistance, the mean for residents in the local authority home was 2.2, for residents in the Cheshire homes 3.2 and 3.5 respectively and for patients in the two hospital units 3.7 and 3.8. While the residents in the local authority home are generally less handicapped than the others, there is little difference between those in the Cheshire homes and the hospital units.

As Miller and Gwynne point out, independence is a function not only of the capacities of the individual but also of the relationship between him and his environment in terms of the resources that are available and the way in which they are used. This is where the architect can make a useful contribution, and where the independence ethic of the institution is also important. One can speculate for example, whether the hospital patients, if placed in one of the Cheshire homes, might be found to be capable of operating without so much assistance.

1515 The planning of new institutions

For any public authority or voluntary organization preparing the brief for a new institution for disabled people, and for the architect charged with the job of implementing the brief, the course to take is clear; buildings must be structured to promote a regime of achievement, growth and independence for residents. There is no case for the perpetuation of systems breeding apathy, withdrawal and dependency. It is on this principle that the recommendations which follow, and those detailed in section 700, are based. They relate to institutions for younger people: while modifications are proposed for homes for old people the principle is not affected. If evidence of the inhumanity which can afflict old people in warehousing institutions is needed, it can be found in quantity in Peter Townsend's study of residential homes *The Last Refuge*[33] and Barbara Robb's report on mental hospitals *Sans Everything*[34].

How large ought new institutions to be? The advice from DHSS is that not more than 30 places should be provided[35]. The preferred limit appears to be based not on sound evidence of the social desirability of this degree of concentration, but on a belief that larger homes threaten to be institutional, and that smaller homes are uneconomic, both in terms of finance and the deployment of care staff. Very probably there is a threat that there will be tendencies for larger homes to become too

[31] Bib 93131, p71
[32] Bib 93144
[33] Bib 93640
[34] Bib 93605
[35] Bib 93140

regimented, with hazards of the depersonalization of residents and a lack of tolerance of eccentricity and deviance. On the other hand there is not sufficient evidence that smaller homes are in practice uneconomic, and in any event it is questionable that administrative economy should be a more important determinant than social criteria. Thus the general rule that the smaller the home the better, down to say a community of 16, is sound.

1516 Siting and location

New residential homes for younger disabled people ought always to be located in urban areas. As a precept this is challengeable, in that there are undeniably people who would prefer a rural rather than an urban scene. But, equally undeniably, there are more than enough existing rural institutions to cater for those who opt for them.

The urban location is important if residents are to be able to keep continually in touch with the busy ordinary world, to go shopping, to visit the local pub, and to take advantage of local cultural and recreational amenities. The accessibility of shops is particularly important if residents are to have the self-sufficiency that comes from spending their own money as they choose rather than as someone else decides for them; some shops at least must be reachable from the home by electric wheelchair.

There are advantages if the home is in among an estate of family housing. There will be constant activity on view – the passing traffic, the children returning from school, the coming and going of milkmen, postmen and window cleaners. By contrast the view of fields and trees, however pretty, soon palls. It may be hoped that location among family housing will assist spontaneous contact with ordinary people round about, even if acquaintanceships are nodding ones only. Friendships with local children can be particularly rewarding. For small children wheelchairs are contrivances of mechanical fascination and the occupants people of absorbing curiosity; behaviour which is ill-regarded by parents embarrassed by cripples, but which to people in wheelchairs can be refreshing.

It may also be that staff for the institution can be drawn from the surrounding estate, helping to break down the barriers to involvement. There is the possibility that arrangements can be made with the housing authority for conveniently placed accommodation to be reserved for the superintendent of the home, the matron, or others on the staff who need to live close by but not inside the institution. For staff who travel from further away it is desirable that there is a local bus route within easy reach; this facility is valuable also for friends and relatives who come to visit residents.

The common topographical prescription is a level site, but there can be advantages in having a sloping site, provided that immediate access from the roadway and parking areas is level. A sloping site generally offers more variety of outlook, and also aids the planning of the building on more than one level. (On a flat site, given the size of home advocated here, there is virtually no possibility that it will be sensible to plan the home on more than one level, for reasons of capital expenditure, problems of circulation and means of escape in case of fire.)

1517 Single rooms

The days when people who decide how new residential homes are to be planned used successfully to advocate the sharing of bedrooms by residents, on grounds of mutual support and companionship, are it seems over. In existing institutions there is however a great deal of dormitory accommodation still in use which needs to be put out of use as soon as possible; the survey of Cheshire homes made in 1970 and 1971 found that only 202 of 1456 residents (14 per cent) had single rooms[36].

The case in favour of single rooms ought not to need repeating. But for doubters the points put by Paul Hunt are convincing:

'In a single room residents can entertain their friends and relatives in privacy. They can express their personalities by having their own things around them and deciding on fittings and colour schemes. They can listen to the radio when they like, have the window or door open or shut, turn the heating on or off, go to bed early or late, all without upsetting anyone else – and without the nervous strain of constantly adjusting to their companions' conflicting habits, tastes and wishes. They can pursue a wide range of activities and interests without distraction. They have far more privacy both physically and in personal affairs – things that are highly valued in our society but sadly lacking in the average institution, especially where the residents are dependent on staff for intimate daily needs. Perhaps the most important gain of all is having a personal piece of territory to which boundaries can be drawn. There seems to be a fundamental animal and human need to possess an area which is in effect an extension of oneself: without it the adult human being tends to be too insecure to form a constructive and stable network of personal relationships.'[37]

From the administrative angle there are also advantages. It is easier to cater for people, the incontinent and noisy snorers for example, who can make life unpleasant for others if they have to share a bedroom. It also permits more flexibility of admission between men and women, given that it is not any longer considered necessary to enforce separation of the sexes by putting males on one side of the building, females on the other.

Not all rooms should be single rooms. Friends may wish to share, and they should have the opportunity to do so. Provision may also be wanted for married couples where both partners are handicapped. For married couples the first option that ought to be available is self-contained housing, with adequate domiciliary support. The tendency among people living in institutions to develop mature relationships leading to marriage is however likely to

[36] Bib 93134, p10
[37] Bib 93143, p19

increase, and among them there are those who may prefer to retain the security which the institution affords rather than meet the bigger challenge of independent living. The putting into effect of the policy that, as near as can be, handicapped residents in an institution have the same personal freedom as those living in the world outside means that, in time, managements – and, more importantly, other residents – may tolerate shared living arrangements between couples who are not married.

There is no sound basis on which the proportion of double versus single rooms needed can be predicted. Perhaps in a unit for 20 people the distribution could be 14 single rooms and 3 doubles, giving a ratio of just over two to one. As an insurance, it can be helpful to plan single rooms so that they can be converted by means of a connecting door into a double set, but such a solution would not be ideal and at least some of the shared accommodation should be purpose planned from the start.

1518   The planning of living units

The quality of living implied by these proposals, giving a life-style matching so far as is possible that of able-bodied people elsewhere, requires a re-evaluation of prevailing accommodation standards. For a start, it is time to abandon reliance on multi-purpose bed-sitting rooms with external common sanitary facilities. The wash basin should be moved out of the sitting room, and each resident should have his own wc. On physical, social and health grounds there is no good case for requiring that when a resident needs to use the wc he must get dressed and trail down the public passageway to sit on an appliance which may have been contaminated by the previous visitor. The basic accommodation for each resident ought therefore to comprise at least a decent sized bed-sitting room and a separate washroom behind a front door, to the sort of space standards provided for residents of the Dutch village Het Dorp (diagram 16.1). By contrast with current institutional standards in Britain this looks lavish, but with savings elsewhere and intelligent allocation of space by the architect the additional expenditure ought not to be out of court.

The bed-sitting room should be planned so that there is a choice of position for the bed. There is no justification for the traditional doctrine that in institutions for handicapped people beds must be freestanding to facilitate nursing from either side. Nor should there be fixed bedhead services which commit the bed to the middle of the room; where in the past this has been done there have been efforts to rearrange beds, with consequential problems of inaccessible services[38].

The case against the freestanding bed is psychological and functional. For psychological reasons which have to do with security, sheltering and warmth, people prefer to have single beds in the corner of rooms. By contrast the freestanding bed is uncomfortably exposed, and in a residential home for handicapped people has hospital connotations. Functionally, it sterilizes valuable floor space; in a room of limited dimensions the likelihood is that there will be space for convenient wheelchair

manoeuvre only if the bed is placed against a wall. In the case of some residents, for example tetraplegics who need to be turned during the night, it can be helpful if there is space both sides of the bed, but the need will not be critical. There is always the possibility of simply pushing the bed out on its castors to gain access. Freestanding beds are not ruled out, it is simply that, where they are allowed for, there must be against-the-wall alternatives.

Space in bed-sitting rooms should be sufficiently generous for residents to install their own pieces of furniture, such as desk, comfortable chairs and chest of drawers. There ought to be a part of the room where residents can pursue hobbies such as writing, stamp collecting or using recording or hi-fi equipment. It ought also to be expected that residents will have their own television set. An occupation likely to appeal to some residents is tending flowering plants; provision should be made for a window box at wheelchair level.

Residents should be able to plan their own colour scheme, hang pictures and select wall coverings and curtain fabrics. The architect should allow for this in his specification of equipment, and the management might set aside the sum which might have been included in the contract for residents to dispose as they prefer.

Allowance ought also to be made for tea making and the preparation of light snacks. It is important in terms of the quality of relationships that the resident is able to play the role of host, offering his visitors simple hospitality. The complaint that it can be hazardous for severely handicapped people to handle boiling kettles or use electric hotplates should be overruled; if the individual is himself too disabled there is no reason why his guests should not be able to act for him. Storage provision ought therefore to be made for kettles and pans, crockery and cutlery, and a small amount of food. While desirable, the incorporation of a small refrigerator may not be feasible, in which case a communal refrigerator for residents' use is suggested.

1519   Wcs and wash basins

The washroom to each living unit should contain a wc and a wash basin. It may with advantage incorporate a shower also, but few handicapped people can manage a shower independently and among those who need assistance the majority (at least in Britain) prefer to have a bath. The range of bathing provision needed to cater for residents in a home means that, apart from any economic factors, it is not reasonable to advocate baths to individual living units. The wc should be planned so that it can be approached frontally or from one side. Owing to the variability of disabling conditions found in residential homes it may be impossible to meet all contingencies, and it is helpful if the plumbing allows sufficient flexibility for the wc to be positioned to meet optimum individual needs. Some residents may only be able to manage independently if an appliance such as the Clos o mat is installed[39].

[38] For an example see Bib 93144, p998
[39] See 5423

It is not possible to standardize the height of the wash basin so that it caters for all individual requirements. Anthropometric characteristics among severely disabled people, ranging from a small person in a low wheelchair to a tall person who stands to use the basin, are such that the only solution is for the height of basins to be adjustable. In this connection a cautionary tale is relevant. I visited in 1972 a purpose-designed residential home. The architect, relying extensively on the second edition of this book, had made every effort to get things right and his building was attractive. The matron, on the basis I gathered of much hospital experience of managing handicapped people, knew that she knew better than the architect and was dissatisfied with his performance. She had told him that all the wash basins were much too high, and admittedly they were. The architect's inadequate defence had been 'it's what it says in the book'. 'The book' was in matron's view a thing of derision; the architect had been fired and there was now another architect, regarded with equal disaffection, working on a new extension with instructions from matron on how to do his job.

1520   Doors, floors and walls

The entrance door to each living unit should indicate access to private territory; it should be lockable and, to prevent abuse of privacy by staff, it should not be controllable by a master key. For access when necessary a duplicate set of keys to all rooms should be kept by the warden. For residents who are severely handicapped it is advantageous if the opening of the door can be controlled remotely from a wheelchair. To confirm the resident's room-ownership status a plate may be fixed to the door in which a card with the occupant's name can be placed.

Any request from the local fire officer that doors to individual living units should be sufficiently wide to permit a bed to be moved through should be challenged. In the national building regulations residential homes for handicapped people are, for structural fire precaution purposes, in the same category as hospitals; because of this the fire officer may suggest that double-leaf doors, of the order of 1.6m wide overall, are necessary. The incorporation of such doors will compromise beyond repair the proposition that the environment being created is akin to a normal living scene rather than a hospital scene. It can be pointed out to the fire officer that there will be no circumstances when a resident needs to be rescued from fire complete with bed, it being always much simpler to use a wheelchair if the person concerned cannot walk, or to carry him out. For an alternative escape route it is desirable that there is a door from the bedroom giving direct access to the outside.

If these units in residential homes are to have a semblance of normal living it is essential that the floor in the bed-sitting area is carpeted. To assist independent wheelchair manoeuvring it is desirable that the carpet does not have a deep pile. Any claim on the management side that carpeting will be unsuitable because residents may be incontinent should be refuted; synthetic sheet carpeting now available is not difficult to clean.

Partition walls between one resident's room and the next should give acoustic insulation comparable to that of party walls between dwelling units on an ordinary housing estate. Some residents will like noisy music and parties, whereas their neighbours may prefer peace and going to bed early. Tensions between groups of culturally dissimilar residents can be exacerbated by lightweight partitions, with damaging effects on community morale. The solution in one recently planned home has been a special soundproof room for hi-fi enthusiasts, but it is preferable that the expense of such a facility should be employed instead on partitions having better sound reduction properties.

1521   Bathrooms and clinical services

Detailed guidance on bathing provision in residential homes is given elsewhere in this book[40]. It is important that baths fixed against walls are available, since some who might manage independently will not be able to do so if a freestanding bath only is installed.

The number of special service rooms should be limited. A linen room will be needed, a sluice room, and an all-purpose staff room serving both as duty room for care staff on call and as an office for the superintendent (or whoever it is who has day-to-day responsibility for the running of the home). Inside the office there should be a lockable drugs cupboard, though drugs used regularly by individual residents will normally be kept by them in their own rooms. There is no need for a sick room for residents needing special supervision; the practice will be that residents are cared for in their own rooms. In cases where residents temporarily need special medical care they will be transferred to hospital in the same fashion as people living in the community. Nor is there a need for a medical examination room, the practice being that residents are seen by their own general practitioners in their own rooms[41].

There should be no special physiotherapy room. The notion that residential homes for disabled people are medical rehabilitation units is one which has been favoured in warehousing institutions, with their emphasis on the treatment of people as patients. The concept of rehabilitation in a unit for chronically disabled people for whom the traditional curative objectives of medicine have failed is questionable, and it is always pertinent to ask 'rehabilitation for what?' In horticulturally oriented homes, where the emphasis is on managing independently and as normally as possible without medical supervision, any residents who require clinical physiotherapy will attend the local hospital unit, in the same fashion as other patients living in the community.

[40] See 7025, 5459
[41] When this was drafted the advice from DHSS in Circular 22/65 (Bib 93145) was that a medical treatment room of about 9·0–11·0m^2 should be provided. Updated advice in Circular LASSL (75)19 (Bib 93140) is that a visitors/student room of about 11·0m^2 should replace the medical room.

1522 Communal provisions

An institution based on horticultural values aims to give to each of its residents opportunities for self-determined living with independence and dignity. This is reflected in the enhanced quality (by contrast with conventional practice) of individual living units, the corollary being that there is a lesser demand for lavish communal rooms. The successful planning of communal spaces requires an understanding of their role, and a brief diversion to consider the matter in the context of relationships in old people's homes is appropriate.

Social relationships of the kind which communal spaces can help to foster are of two kinds. First, there are the arranged, formal, structured, contractual associations geared to the common enterprise – bingo, whist-drives, amateur entertainments, religious services and other approved group activities. Second, there are the spontaneous, informal, unstructured, interpersonal relationships among individual residents. By and large the traditional large-scale sitting room in an old people's home (an expression of the warehousing ethic) caters well for the arranged rituals and not at all for spontaneous interactions; the typical sitting room, with each chair tenaciously guarded by its 'owner', is disconcertingly inhospitable to the apprehensive old person who comes in hesitantly looking for someone to talk to. If (as may well happen) he is unsuccessful he is obliged to retreat, having in the process embarrassingly exposed his intentions. If his motives could be masked his predicament would not be so frightening; with the sitting room planned not as a cul-de-sac but with an escape route available he could pretend that he had some other purpose in view.

Devices to aid spontaneous relationship can be incorporated into homes without it being recognized or admitted that they are being exploited as such. Examples are loitering spaces overlooking scenes of activity, notice boards and illuminated tropical fish tanks. Spaces where there can be a view of activity, particularly passing traffic or playgrounds, ought to be used to good advantage. A related possibility is a place where residents can watch meals being prepared in the kitchen.

Facilities of these kinds may be in greater demand in homes for old people than in those for physically handicapped people, but they have a relevance, with implications for the architect. While there is the need for some group socializing provision the emphasis ought primarily to be on spaces for informal meetings.

If the dining room in a residential home for physically handicapped people is sufficiently large for all residents to have a meal together it will also be capable of coping with other group activities, such as the occasional party or organized meetings. Additional formal communal rooms may not be needed. Bays of circulation spaces can serve for small gatherings, or for residents to talk to people from outside whom they do not wish to invite to their rooms. There may be no requirement for special television rooms, games rooms, clubrooms, quiet rooms or similar spaces. In respect of television, the expectation is that residents will have their own sets; if, as may happen, a benefactor

presents a television set, a place for it can no doubt be found in the dining room or one of the sitting areas.

The exception to the rule of no arranged communal provision is that a hobbies room is valuable, which residents can use for activities not easily undertaken in bed-sitting rooms, such as painting, woodwork, model making and other hobbies, and cash-making occupations such as jewellery making and watch repairs. A hobbies room can also serve as a general social meeting place for residents.

A shop may or may not be required. In existing homes the practice has developed of one of the residents managing a shop which keeps tobacco, confectionery, bathroom and cosmetic needs, and other general provisions, the proceeds from the shop going to the residents' amenities fund. In a new home where local shops are not easily reached by residents a small room to serve as a shop inside the home is recommended. But an important point made earlier about location was that new homes should be established only where shops can be easily reached by residents, including those using electric chairs. Where this is the case the majority of residents will probably prefer to do their shopping along with normal people in the ordinary shops outside, and it is better to do without the institutional shop.

A bar may also be inappropriate in a residential home; if the home is suitably located it ought to be possible for residents who wish to go to a local pub for their social drinking. On the other hand a bar can encourage informal meetings of groups of residents; this may be particularly valuable in a building where the emphasis is on individual living units and occasions for communal interactions are limited.

1523 Staff accommodation

Living-in accommodation for staff is not necessary. Residents will benefit from relationships with staff who are living outside in ordinary housing, coming in each day fresh to their duties and refreshing the residents by their contact with the normal world. There is also the advantage that stressful emotional relationships between residents and staff are less likely to develop where staff have other roles and commitments outside. Apart from these factors there is the simple practical matter that it becomes increasingly difficult for institutions to find people who are willing to be full-time living-in employees. There is a growing reliance on part-time and voluntary staff, and in terms of variety of relationships this is beneficial to residents.

The long-held view that the matron at least must live in, to be on hand to cope with unforeseen emergencies, is losing currency. If the matron lives in an ordinary house in the vicinity she can in the event of trouble be called on by phone, and can be on the spot almost as quickly as if she were living on the premises. Now that the regime of spinster matrons is ended, a common arrangement being the employment of someone with husband and family, it becomes virtually impossible for residential staff accommodation to be planned with any confidence that it will be wanted, and if it is that it will be a living unit of the required size. All in all, it is preferable that arrangements are made with the local housing authority for houses in the area to be allocated for key staff working in the institution.

While living-in accommodation may not be warranted for permanent staff it may be valuable to have one or two bed-sitting rooms available for students who take a job at the home during the course of their training.

1524   Garaging

The need for garages for residents who have vehicles of their own will be minimal. In the past there has been an optimistic expectancy among authorities planning new residential homes that they would be catering for numbers of active disabled people able to go out and do a job of work, and in consequence generous garage provision has sometimes been made. In practice, however, few if any residents of a newly established home will have the resources to work outside; the likelihood is that if someone is capable of working he will also, however severely disabled, be capable of managing a home of his own outside. In a new home for 20 or fewer people the most likely happening is that no resident will have a vehicle. In some cases there will be one person with a vehicle, less frequently two people, and rarely if ever more than two.

1525   Short-stay accommodation

This discussion of the planning of new residential homes for disabled people has been based on the principle of a horticultural style institution with a small number of permanent residents, each of whom has his own private territory in a situation as near as possible like ordinary living in the world outside. Local authorities do however have a duty, under section 2 of the 1970 Chronically Sick Act, to provide short-stay and holiday accommodation for handicapped people, and residential homes are commonly used for this purpose. The common practice is that either a small number of rooms in a home is set aside for short-stay residents, or that when permanent residents are away on holiday their rooms are used temporarily by outsiders. Sometimes these latter arrangements are reciprocal between residents of different homes, but commonly the outsiders are severely handicapped people living in ordinary housing, where the husband, wife or parent has a 168 hour a week job of caring and supporting, and for the sake of health and sanity needs an occasional break.

If the principle is that each resident's accommodation is his personal and private territory, on the same basis as ordinary living, it is improper to insist that when he is away it should be made available by the agency who supports him to someone else nominated by them. Equally, it is arguable that if the people living permanently in the home are as a group to regard it as their place, it should at the same time be catering for peripatetic people whom they do not select to live with them. On the other hand residents in some homes where short stay accommodation

is incorporated benefit from having new faces around them and appreciate new relationships and contacts.

1526   The future of hospital units

There is no evidence that the quality of accommodation in the new younger chronic sick units being built by regional health authorities in Britain will be passable by the criteria outlined in this commentary. The standardized package unit developed by the South East Thames Regional Health Authority[42] (diagram 15.3) is illustrated not because it is a particularly good or bad example of its kind, but because it has been the first standard unit to go into operation and has been widely publicized[43]. In essence the unit is a conventional hospital ward, with modifications incorporated to give it some attractiveness. As a place for long-stay living for people of sensitivity it is a non-starter. With variations, such as the incorporation of a greater number of single rooms, rather more day space or rather fewer clinical rooms, this is the kind of provision being developed elsewhere in Britain. Given that these units are being built, what ought to be done with them?

Dependent on their location and local circumstances there are a number of possibilities. First, they could be used for long-stay 'vegetable' patients, meaning people with severe brain damage from head injuries. Second, they could be used for terminal patients, in the main people with cancer. Third, they could be used as weekly boarding hospitals, where patients would arrive on a Monday morning, spend a week and return home on a Friday evening. Fourth, they could be used for short-stay patients, in the main people coming in for two or three weeks to give their families a break, or those needing clinical assessment.

There are reservations to be made about each of these possibilities and it is doubtful whether the units being planned will be well structured to cater for any of them. With the exception of long-stay brain-damaged patients, it is arguable that the conventional hospital ward unit is appropriate, the preference being for more liberal and flexible arrangements. In respect of terminal cancer or multiple sclerosis patients it is desirable, for example, that provision is made for husbands or wives to live in. The same requirement would apply if the unit were to be a weekly boarding establishment, catering principally for patients with multiple sclerosis. A weekly boarding arrangement might however help alleviate the stresses encountered by families, and avoid or postpone the breakdowns of relationships that multiple sclerosis can cause. The difficult and all too common situation is a wife crippled by multiple sclerosis and a husband who has to give up his work to be always at home to nurse here. If during the week he were able to carry on working, with the family together at weekends, the pain and guilt associated with breakdowns precipitated by multiple

[42] Until the reorganization in 1974 the South East Metropolitan Regional Hospital Board.
[43] For example in Bib 93161, 93162.

sclerosis might be avoided. Equally, this arrangement might be beneficial where there has been a severe stroke in the family.

The use of these units for short-stay patients needing assessment would be practicable only where full supporting clinical services were available. For most holiday patients the probability is that a residential home would generally suit better than a hospital unit.

As a footnote to this discussion, confirmation of the indefensibility of the programme of hospital care for disabled people is provided by Douglas Lillie, physician in charge of the young chronic sick at Ashurst mentioned earlier. In a letter to *The Guardian* commenting on Ann Shearer's article 'Housing to fit the handicapped'[44] he says:

'Like the disabled themselves, we, working in this hospital, realise that hospital care is no solution to the problem of long standing disablement. It is authoritarian and uncongenial to patients, it is highly expensive to the community at large but its worst aspect is that it conceals from local authorities the very large need which calls urgently for a massive expansion of provision for the disabled in their own homes.'[45]

1527   Holiday hotels for disabled people

Monks in a monastery, soldiers in barracks, guests in a hotel, students in a residential hall: none of these is properly analogous to the situation of a resident in a home for disabled people; each has parallels but also divergencies. By contrast for holiday homes there is a good and simple analogy, which is of guests in a hotel. In a holiday home the disabled visitors are there to enjoy their stay and gain refreshment from it, and it is the job of the management to see that they do. If the contention made earlier is granted, that in residential homes the proper course, on the basis of treatment comparable to living arrangements elsewhere, is that each resident has a semi self-contained unit with his own bed-sitting room, washroom and front door, it follows that in holiday homes prevailing hotel standards, meaning personal washing and wc facilities, should apply. It may not be practicable, because of the impossibility of devising specific solutions to meet varying needs, to incorporate a private bath or shower, but it is important that each guest has his own wc.

No less than able-bodied people, people with disabilities customarily prefer to spend their holiday with a friend or member of the family. By contrast with residential homes there is therefore a bigger requirement for double rooms as against single rooms. There is no reliable evidence for a recommendation here but a suggested ratio is two double rooms to each single room. Alternatively all rooms may be planned to serve one or two guests as the need occurs.

Accommodation for staff living in may be limited, bearing in mind that the majority of staff are likely to be people living locally. Where provision is made for living-in staff

the preference is for small flatlets rather than bed-sitting rooms. These rooms should be accessible to wheelchair users, allowing them to be used by holiday visitors if they are not needed for staff.

1528   Residential accommodation for old people

Local authority old people's homes in Britain have evolved historically from Victorian Poor Law institutions. In the early 1960s the state of old people's institutions was thoroughly examined and analyzed by Peter Townsend, and reported in *The last refuge*[46] published in 1962. His conclusion was that the concept was outdated and should be abandoned; that old people in need of care should be looked after in sheltered housing schemes with the support of domiciliary services, and that for those needing intensive nursing suitable provision administered by hospital authorities should be available. His carefully argued thesis has been a topic of controversy and debate over the years, but it has not been endorsed by the Department of Health; short of restructuring the administrative system there is no possibility that it could be.

Building standards for old people's homes were set down by the then Ministry of Health in an official building note in 1962, reissued with minor variations in 1973. The 1973 note says 'The style of a home for elderly people, both externally and internally, should be "domestic" as befits its function, and an institutional appearance is to be avoided'[47]. While sympathetic architectural treatment may alleviate an institutional appearance, the apparatus of institutionalism will inevitably be perpetuated by adherence to the building note's recommendations. Bed-sitting rooms (including wash basins) of 10m² for single rooms, 15.5m² for double rooms, are suggested. Baths or showers are to be provided in the ratio of one to each 15 residents, and wcs in the ratio of one to four[48]. Suggested ancillary provision includes an office, a medical room, a chiropody/hairdressing room, a sluice room, a dirty linen room, a domestic laundry room, a sewing room, a store for linen and blankets, a general purpose room, a general store, cleaners rooms and general ancillary rooms for 'storage, utility, day care, etc.'

In that architects designing local authority old people's homes will be obliged to work to constraints imposed by the space standards and cost allowances prescribed by the Department of Health, the advocacy of reasonable standards in Britain is for the time being a matter of academic interest. Ideally however standards should

[44] Bib 93100
[45] *The Guardian*, 12 July 1973, p12
[46] Bib 93640
[47] Bib 93650, p5
[48] In January 1974 an official interdepartmental government circular advising local authorities about cuts in public expenditure specifically drew attention to the standards cited here. It read 'Ways in which these reductions of expenditure might be sought are . . . by restricting proposed improvements in standards in residential accommodation and adult training centres' (Bib 93792, para 20).

accord with those suggested earlier for residential homes for physically handicapped people: each resident should have a living unit comprising bed-sitting room and separate washroom with basin and wc, and baths or showers should be provided in the ratio of say one to six rather than of one to fifteen.

There is a case for relatively more generous provision for communal sitting areas in old people's homes than in homes for physically handicapped people. Whereas intellectually lively physically handicapped people may be expected to exploit the opportunity which private rooms afford for pursuing personal interests and activities, and thus have limited call on communal spaces, typical residents of an old people's home may have fewer resources and may rely more frequently for their social needs on communal spaces. The role of these spaces in the fostering of social relationships among residents in an old people's home has already been discussed; apart from being arranged to cater for group socializing activities it is important that spaces are planned to foster spontaneous meetings and small gatherings.

1529   Residential accommodation for blind people

There are in Britain a large number of residential institutions, administered invariably by voluntary agencies, catering exclusively for blind people. New ones, often lavishly equipped by contrast with local authority standards, continue to be built[49]. It is a policy of arguable merit. If the thesis developed in the course of this commentary has a validity there is no place for segregative residential institutions for blind people. It is probable that, given the choice between one institution and another, the majority of elderly people who are blind would prefer to be in a home for old people rather than one for blind people. For those who prefer to be with others who are blind there are without doubt enough existing institutions, and there is no cause for adding to their number.

[49] For an example see Bib 93335

16 Housing alternatives to institutions

1600 The distinction between housing and institutions

If institutions, whether hospital units, local authority homes, Cheshire homes or any other residential homes managed by statutory or voluntary organizations, are not suitable places for intellectually lively people with disabilities to live in and die in, what are the housing alternatives? What, first of all, is it which distinguishes housing from institutions?

It is a matter of the style of living. The important thing is that the disabled person is the householder. If he does not actually own the property he is personally responsible for paying the rent; the structure is not just made available to him. He comes and goes as he wishes; he does not have to tell someone in authority where he is going and what he will do when he gets there. What he does with his time is constrained by the law of the land rather than by a private oligarchy. In short, he manages his own affairs rather than having someone else manage them for him.

The self-management condition does not mean that the disabled person in housing is out on his own. He can be, but equally he can be among a group of others like himself. At one extreme are individual disabled people scattered about in their own houses among ordinary people, with no organized connection with each other. At the other extreme is the self-contained community exclusively for disabled people. The polarities are not however the only options. In between there are degrees of concentration, and degrees of overlapping between disabled groups and normal people.

1601 Het Dorp

At one end of the spectrum of accommodation for disabled people is the colony. As cripples' colonies go, Het Dorp at Arnhem in Holland is attractive. Het Dorp means the village. In this case it is a community of 400 severely disabled people, nearly all of whom get about independently in electrically-powered wheelchairs. The aim of Dr Klapwijk, the medical administrator who launched the project, and of Professor Bakema, the architect who translated the ideal into reality, was to make Het Dorp a microcosm of a typical urban community. In addition to the housing it has its supermarket, post office, hairdresser's salon, travel agency, petrol station, church, library, restaurant, sports hall and clinic. It has its own workshops for people in the village able to work, with additional clinical and therapy services available in the rehabilitation centre alongside.

Of the 387 residents of Het Dorp at March 1971 just over four in five were single people, the remainder being married couples, most of whom were both handicapped. Women outnumbered men in the ratio of 7 to 5, the average age of women being 41 years and of men 38 years. The most common causes of disability were cerebral palsy, accounting for 25 per cent, multiple sclerosis (13 per cent) and muscular dystrophy (12 per cent). More than 90 per cent of residents used a wheelchair, and of these only a small minority were able to transfer in and out of their chairs or dress themselves independently[1].

Each resident has a self-contained flat of some 25m² comprising a bed-sitting room and a washroom containing shower, wash basin and wc (diagram 16.1). Each flat has its own lockable front door and doorbell; the more severely handicapped residents can open the door by remote control from their wheelchairs. Housing clusters are of 30 units, divided into three groups of ten. In each group of ten there are nine flats for handicapped people and one for the attendant who serves the group. At the centre is a social and dining room for the group, main meals being delivered by trolley from a central kitchen.

16.1 Het Dorp, Arnhem, Holland. Typical flat (1:200). J B Bakema, architect.

It is demonstrated at Het Dorp that it is possible for care staff to cater successfully for severely handicapped people living in flats, among them many who need frequent attention, often at short notice. There is no need for visual supervision, no need for concentrating particularly demanding handicapped people together, and no need for separating off in an intensive care zone those who need special oversight.

The merit of Het Dorp is the independence which it affords to handicapped residents. Despite the unusual topography – a mini-ravine runs through the site – people in wheelchairs can get in and out of their homes on their own, can buy groceries and food for their supper which they can cook themselves, can have their hair attended to, can borrow books from the public library, can join friends for a cup of coffee at the restaurant or take part in a church service. All this they can do without needing someone to go with them to help.

In one respect – the integration of villagers with ordinary people living nearby – Het Dorp has not, it seems, lived up to its ideals. The hope was that by locating the village in an urban setting with ordinary housing estates to either side, by introducing public amenities such as library, church and supermarket, and by retaining a well-used public footpath across the site, people living in the village would get to know those who came in from outside. In practice social interaction seems to be minimal; people do come from outside to use the restaurant and supermarket but they tend to avoid becoming involved with villagers. Even the church does not appear to have fostered many friendships.

[1] Bib 93310, p65. For a detailed report on Het Dorp see Bib 93180.

There has been an increasing tendency among the inhabitants of Het Dorp to marry or live together; the small number of double units initially provided in the village has proved inadequate, and adaptations, by knocking down partition walls, have been made to single person units to cater for couples. Whether these married couples would prefer, given the opportunity, to be living in the ordinary community with domiciliary support is problematical. The services currently available in Holland do not cover handicapped people living together and needing support on a 24 hour basis. Nor are there transport facilities which can be called on by handicapped people wishing to go into town to do their own shopping or visit the cinema. The impression is, however, that even if these services existed outside many of the married couples at Het Dorp would prefer to stay in the village. That they might do so is not to imply, because it works here, that the village solution should be applied universally; it ought to be one only of the variety of housing options open to handicapped people.

In Britain there is no community analogous to Het Dorp, and, given the powerful prevailing pressures against segregation, there is little possibility that there ever will be. The nearest equivalents are the Thistle Foundation village in Edinburgh for ex-service paraplegics and the colonies for disabled people at Papworth in Cambridgeshire and Enham Alamein in Hampshire. They offer a sort of option, but it is not one, regrettably, which comes anywhere near the Het Dorp model.

1602   Danish Collective Houses

Moving down the scale from the cripples' colony is a concept which can be termed diluted concentration. It is best demonstrated by the series of Collective Houses established in Denmark over the past 15 years. The first and biggest is the block in Copenhagen, comprising 170 flats in 13 storeys. Although there is a concentration of handicapped people the aim was to avoid an institutional atmosphere, and two-thirds of the flats were intended for ordinary households. The majority of flats are small, for one, two or three people. On the thirteenth floor is a nursing unit for 17 people severely disabled by polio and dependent on respiratory machines; it was the polio epidemics in Denmark in the early 1950s which provided the impetus for large-scale special housing developments for disabled people. The Copenhagen block contains a hostel for single younger disabled people, workshops for handicapped people and a communal restaurant.

In 1971 nine collective houses, containing 1100 flats, were established in different places in Denmark. Eight more, with 900 flats, were being planned, and negotiations were in progress for five more buildings with 700 flats[2]. The Danish strategy is to concentrate in collective houses all people with severe physical disabilities who need clinical support and who are not managing in family housing.

The collective house ethic is different from the Het Dorp ethic. Both admit that normal society fails to cope with severely disabled people on their own. Both work from the premise that to achieve efficient clinical servicing

disabled people have to be concentrated in quantity. But where Het Dorp opts for total separation the collective houses attempt integration with normals. The impression is that, despite questions about the social propriety of the exercise, the Danish authorities have become wholly committed to the collective house programme. No careful sociological inquiry has been made and there is no substantiating evidence, but it does seem that in practice integration barely happens. At a 1 to 3 ratio of dwelling units there is too large a concentration of handicapped people in a single housing block, too many to be discreetly assimilated and comfortably absorbed. So inevitably there are social divisions, of inferior disabled versus superior normals. It also happens that because of their character the blocks are regarded outside as peculiar cripple institutions. The social bonuses that might have been gained on both sides by scattering handicapped people more thinly are lost by hiving them off in quantity.

1603   British housing associations

The assembling of disabled people in groups detached from normals is not exclusively a British phenomenon, but it is a peculiarly British sort of compromise. It is demonstrated in the main by housing association schemes where the association specializes in housing for disabled people. Examples are Friendship House at Poole by the Inskip Housing Association, St Giles Court at Ealing by the St Giles Housing Association[3] and Princess Crescent at Finsbury Park by John Grooms Housing Association.

16.2   Princess Crescent, Finsbury Park, London. Typical flat plan (1:200). C Wycliffe Noble, architect.

These are assemblies of between 12 and 25 flats grouped together to form a mini-colony, with a warden or caretaker to oversee the residents. The underlying doctrine is that too many disabled units together would be institutional, and institutions are bad, whereas a smaller group placed in a typical urban scene can pretend to achieve normality and integration. In accord with the established housing ethic these schemes cater for people who can cope independently and who desirably go out to work. They do not cater for people who are unable to manage independently.

[2] Bib 93310, p50
[3] Since these schemes were built the Inskip and St Giles associations amalgamated as the Inskip St Giles Housing Association, now the Raglan Housing Association.

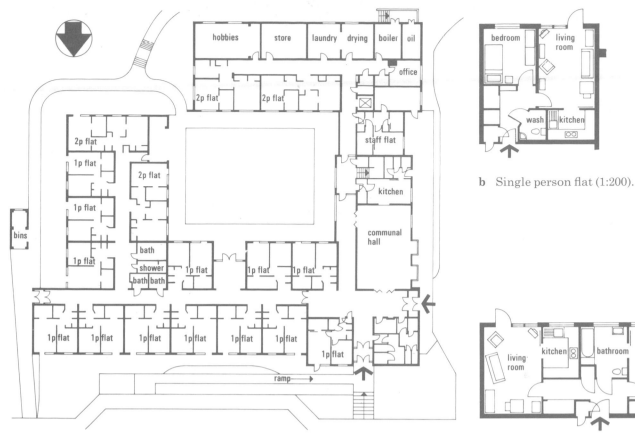

a Ground floor plan (1:500). Upper floor has flats and staff accommodation over south and west wings

b Single person flat (1:200).

c Two person flat (1:200).

16.3 Friendship House, Poole. Wyvern Design Group, architects.

St Giles Court at Ealing is a three storey block comprising 15 flats, 4 bed-sitting room units, 8 one bedroom units and 3 two bedroom units. In that the caretaker's role is supervisory rather than giving clinical support and the tenants are all expected to cope without outside assistance, this scheme falls somewhat outside the scope of this discussion which focuses on housing accommodation for severely handicapped people. The situation is similar with the Finsbury Park scheme (diagram 16.2), comprising 9 one person flats, 2 two person flats and a flat for the warden and his family.

Friendship House (diagram 16.3) goes further by employing full-time care staff who live in the block. There are 25 units, comprising 16 one person units (diagram 16.3b) and 9 two person units (diagram 16.3c). With the help of sophisticated aids and gadgetry, and intelligent planning by a sensitive architect, Friendship House caters successfully for people with very severe disabilities[4]. Among the tenants are for example a spastic couple formerly living in an institution, individually both dependent, but with mutual support able to cope independently together.

Undeniably housing schemes such as these are, for disabled people with the independence wherewithal, more congenial than any institution. But by normalization precepts they fail. The residents who live in them are placed among others of their kind effectively insulated from the world of ordinary people outside. Protected by their sympathetically organized physical environment the disabled residents are left to get on with their own affairs.

1604 Housing linked to institutions

A variant of the assembly concept is the practice of linking a group of disabled housing units to an existing institution. An example is the close of 12 bungalows associated with Heatherley Cheshire Home, some five miles outside Crawley in Sussex. The semi-detached bungalows are all one bedroom units designed to cater for a married couple one of whom is disabled, allowing for example a handicapped wife to make use of the services in the institution while her husband is out at work.

The concept sounds attractive, in that independence can be retained with the bonus of security, but there are hazards. They are the same hazards that affect old people's schemes where flats are linked to residential homes. Some local authorities claim that these linked old people's schemes are successful, but there is inherent in them a fungus of discontent[5]. On the one side, among the privileged house tenants is the apprehension that if something goes wrong they will be transferred to the institution, and on the other side, among the disadvantaged institution residents, there is jealousy

[4] For a detailed report on Friendship House see Bib 93125.
[5] Cheshire County Council has for example adopted and widely implemented this policy. Doubts are expressed by Jameson (Bib 93646) about its merits. For a report on a scheme where there was a breakdown of social relationships between the two sides see Bib 93652. In its official building note (Bib 93650, p4) the Department of Health expresses reservations about the concept of linked schemes, but gives guidance on how they can be implemented.

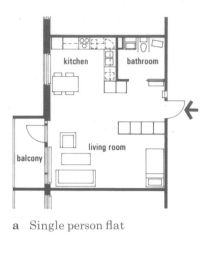

a   Single person flat

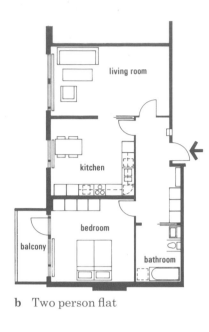

b   Two person flat

c   Three person flat

16.4   Fokus Housing Society, Sweden. Typical flat plans (1:200).

because the people in the houses are much better provided for than they are.

A visit to Heatherley confirms that these hazards are not illusory. It is not an institution well equipped for this kind of experiment, being handicapped by its rural isolation, and it is among the more paternalistic of Cheshire homes. Residents are collectively known as 'the family' and their daily routine is rather more carefully arranged for them by the management than in most homes[6]. Given a more horticulturally orientated institution the linked housing formula might succeed, but it would require exceptional tolerance on all sides. It might perhaps be wise to promote no more experiments of this kind[7].

1605   Fokus Housing Society schemes in Sweden

Group integration – the placing of groups of disabled people alongside normal people in ordinary housing – is demonstrated by the housing schemes of the Fokus Society in Sweden. Reports from the society suggest that here for the first time is a proper answer, where severely disabled people supported by domiciliary services can live in their own flats, integrated in an ordinary housing block containing ordinary families[8].

Under the direction of Sven-Olof Brattgård, who is qualified both medically and by being a paraplegic in a wheelchair, the Fokus Society started work in 1964 and its first block of flats was opened at Kalmar in 1968. By the end of 1973, when the administration of projects put into operation by the Fokus Society was transferred to local authorities, there were 13 schemes across Sweden providing flats for some 280 handicapped people. Brattgård estimates that there are throughout Sweden some 2000 handicapped people such as Fokus schemes are designed for, and his aim, working now through local housing authorities, is to establish a group of flats in each

large town. They are as a rule located close to the centre of towns to aid those handicapped people who can go out to work or make use of education services. The policy of the Fokus Society has been always to employ local architects, to ensure that Fokus houses look just the same as those among which they are set.

The Fokus Society does not build the flats, but rents them from house building companies who obtain from the government a substantial subsidy for each flat specially adapted for a disabled person. Each tenant has the same rights and obligations as a tenant in an ordinary flat; as Brattgård says, Fokus is a philosophy of living and not just an architectural solution[9]. The concept of the bed-sitting room with communal services outside is abandoned. Standard house plans, of a quality superior to that of normal housing in Sweden, have been developed.

From a survey made in 1971 of the 168 flats in the first eight Fokus schemes, 55 per cent were single person units, 28 per cent were two person units and 17 per cent were three person units. Single person units have a large general-purpose room serving as living room, kitchen and bedroom (diagram 16.4a). The area of single person units ranges from 42m² to 50m², compared with the minimum space standard of 30m² for one person flats in public authority housing in Britain. The two person units (diagram 16.4b) have a separate bedroom, with areas

[6] In this connection it is relevant to record that while a resident at Heatherley Peter Marshall wrote *The Raging Moon* (Bib 93313) a melodramatic but harrowing novel of personal relationships in a cripples' institution.
[7] A housing scheme comparable to Heatherley was opened in 1974 in association with the Cheshire home at Hitchin; the committee managing it has had difficulty in attracting suitable tenants to it, and eight months after opening (May 1975) only three of eight flats had been let.
[8] Bib 93170, 93171
[9] Bib 93171, p2

ranging from 64m² to 75m², compared with the British minimum standard for ordinary housing of 44.5m². The three person units (diagram 16.4c) range from 80m² to 95m², compared with the minimum British standard of 57m². A high proportion of two and three person units makes it possible for tenants to marry or live together; in 1971 36 per cent of the tenants were married or were cohabiting.

In the equipping of Fokus flats any aid which can help personal independence is incorporated. Bathrooms and kitchens have flexible height fittings adjustable to suit people with varying disabilities. For severely handicapped people there are remote control devices attached to wheelchairs to open doors, turn lights on and off, summon help and so on.

1606   Services in Fokus flats

Supported initially by charitable funds, the Fokus Society was able to work across the administrative boundaries of Swedish housing, welfare and hospital authorities. A range of communal provision, of a kind that housing authorities could not themselves provide, was associated with each group of flats, including a communal dining room and kitchen, a sitting room, gymnasium, hobbies room and sauna bath. The cost of this communal provision added some 30 per cent to the rental, met initially by the Fokus Society and now carried by the local housing authority. Administratively the society was also able to coordinate within its schemes the services provided by housing authorities, meaning a home help coming in for a prescribed period each morning to clean the flat, help with the clothes washing, prepare meals and do essential shopping, and the services of welfare authorities, meaning domiciliary staff coming in for help with dressing or undressing, personal washing and help with the wc. The normal arrangement is that each tenant has an individual home help coming in each morning for routine services, relying for his needs at other times of the day on the care staff on duty in the building.

Among the 168 tenants of the first eight Fokus schemes, 77 per cent were at the time of the 1971 survey dependent on a wheelchair for mobility and 14 per cent used crutches. The proportion needing help with dressing was 52 per cent, and with managing the wc 36 per cent. Those needing turning in bed during the night were 18 per cent. The cost of keeping each tenant, taking into account both capital expenditure and services, was in 1971 about half the cost of keeping a patient in a modern nursing home[10].

In September 1973 I spent ten days in Sweden, visiting 8 of the 13 Fokus schemes, and gaining first-hand information on a ninth. Before I went I was sceptical on three scores: first that Fokus was not catering for people who were very severely handicapped, second that owing to the administrative and physical structure they were in effect benign institutions, and third that there was little integration between handicapped tenants and ordinary people around them.

On the first score scepticism was unwarranted. Observations of tenants, discussions with them and an analysis of evidence on needs and services, confirmed that disabled people living in Fokus schemes are typically equally as handicapped as those in residential homes or young chronic sick units in Britain. On the second score of institutional tendencies my scepticism was not allayed. Given communities of upwards of 25 handicapped tenants, the simple logistics of care and support mean that some of the apparatus of institutionalism is inevitable[11]. When 25 handicapped people are concentrated together and supplied with communal sitting room, kitchen, dining room, gymnasium, hobbies room, sauna bath and other services, along with duty staff on call in a duty room, it is unrealistic to expect to find them managing as self-sufficiently as non-disabled tenants of flats alongside. A consequence of the substantial communal facilities, not as a rule open for use by outsiders, is that tenants do stick together, regarding themselves as members of the Fokus community rather than of the overall housing community.

It is arguable whether in Fokus schemes the goal of integration is achieved, the concept being neither simply definable nor quantifiable. If it means working together and doing things together Fokus schemes fail; it is rare that any of the people in ordinary flats alongside help either voluntarily or by being members of the care staff. If it means nodding hello and stopping for an occasional chat Fokus scores better; in one scheme only was there no contact at all, in others there was apparently extensive social mixing. It was also clear that tenants regarded their living place as ordinary housing, even though people living nearby imagined it was some sort of hospital. Although only a minority of tenants (some 14 per cent of those visited) were able to go out to work, a substantial proportion went out regularly to classes in local colleges or universities. By whatever criteria integration is measured there is no doubt that Fokus housing schemes in Sweden score more highly than Het Dorp in Holland, collective houses in Denmark or Cheshire homes in Britain.

1607   The Habinteg Housing Association

In Britain the only housing development to date (1976) along Fokus lines is the Habinteg housing association scheme at Haringey in North London (diagram 16.5) opened in 1973[12]. It is an estate comprising 58 dwelling units, 41 being for ordinary families. The other 17 are purpose-designed for severely disabled people, 5 being one person units, 5 two person units (diagram 16.5a), 5 three person units and 2 four person units. It is a cooperative venture between the Habinteg housing association, an offshoot of the Spastics Society which has been shifting its orientation from institutions to housing, and Haringey London Borough Council. Haringey housing department has a share in the allocation of tenancies, nearly all the

[10] Bib 93170, p36
[11] Of the eight schemes visited four had respectively 26, 29, 29 and 32 handicapped tenants.
[12] The Habinteg housing association is currently planning a number of comparable schemes, though none has yet been opened. For a report on the Haringey scheme see Bib 93102.

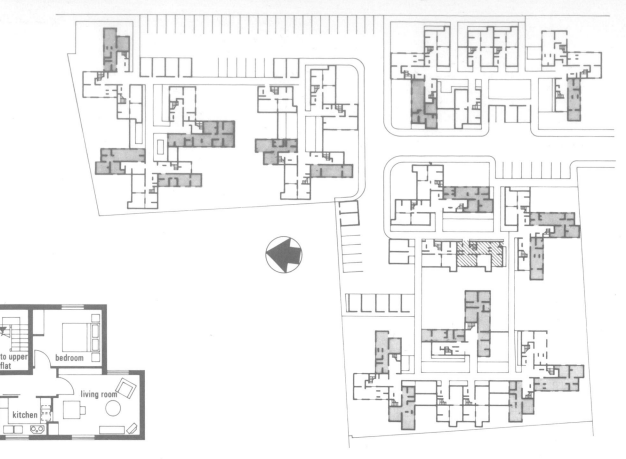

a Typical two person flat (1:200).

b Ground floor plan (1:1000). Flats for disabled tenants are shown tinted. Warden's flat is hatched.

16.5 Moira Close, Haringey, London.
Roman Halter and Associates, architects.

disabled tenants receive domiciliary help from the social services department, and the housing association employs a 'community assistant' to give support for tenants who need special help. Among the 19 disabled people living there when I visited in November 1973 there were two handicapped couples who had been able to move out of institutions.

In philosophy, organization, planning and equipping, Habinteg at Haringey owes much to the Fokus Society originals. But in one important respect it falls short. The tenants, while being severely disabled (all are wheelchair users) are not severely handicapped. Nearly all are able to go out to work, and can drive their own vehicles. None of them (in November 1973) needed help from outside for dressing, feeding or managing the wc. There was an opportunity at Haringey to demonstrate that people equally as handicapped as those in Cheshire homes or hospital units could be supported in ordinary housing, but it has not been realized.

1608 Scattering

The great majority of severely disabled people are scattered in ordinary housing. There is invariably a family to give support, and if resources are sufficient the tactic is both practicable and preferred. But often where family resources are limited and the handicapped person demands a great deal of attention the situation becomes unmanageable. To alleviate the strain the local authority may send in domiciliary services but defences are often intolerably stretched. In the case of severely disabled

people who are on their own, or of couples where both are handicapped, the dispersal tactic is not as a rule a practicable proposition. For some it is a question of not having the necessary intellectual or emotional resources to manage independently, for many more it is a matter of not having the financial resources to cope or to supplement the inadequate support services offered by the local authority.

There are however exceptions. Among them are some of the small number of people in Britain paralyzed by polio and who keep breathing only with the aid of respiratory machines. In 1969, on the personal intervention of the then Secretary of State for Health, it was arranged that 18 of these patients who were being expensively maintained in hospital should instead have if they wished whatever support they needed to live on their own[13]. Diana Staples, for example, has a full-time paid attendant living with her, who dresses her, prepares meals and hoists her on and off the wc and in and out of the respirator tank which she uses every night. With this backing she manages her home and goes out to work. As a way of living it is more attractive than the Cheshire homes and hospital wards she has known, but it makes its own problems. A peculiar one is that the intimate one to one relationship, based not, as in marriage, on personal compatibility but on the contractual basis of employer and employee, places the dependent disabled person in an invidious position. She cannot get angry, she cannot walk out, and to hang on to sanity the relationship has to be delicately sustained. The practical assistance she needs is

[13] Bib 93280 is a report on this programme.

concentrated at particular hours of the day, with large chunks of time in between when the attendant has nothing to do; this also has psychological hazards.

Jack and Margaret Wymer are a rare example, possibly unique in Britain, of very severely disabled partners where the dispersal tactic operates successfully. Both are handicapped by muscular dystrophy, both move about the house in electric wheelchairs, both are completely dependent for dressing, washing and managing the wc. Before they married Margaret lived with her family, Jack in an institution. A local authority flat under construction in Norwich was adapted for their use, with electric hoist, special telephone and an alarm communicating with the warden of a sheltered housing scheme nearby. With financial help from social security and the social services department Margaret organizes a fleet of eight helpers who come in at regular intervals 23 times each week. So far the system has not failed, and Margaret says that despite the risks they would not change; life is more fulfilling than ever it was before. But she says that in practice there is little latitude for self-determined home management, she is dependent for assistance on those helpers she can find. She and Jack tell them exactly what the procedures are for example for dressing, preparing meals or using the wc. She reports that the only failure has been a trained nurse who already knew what should be done and did not want to learn.

The common factor of these two examples, and parallels can be found among people less severely handicapped, is the enforced limitation of activity options imposed by the ties of dependency on attendants. If these ties could be loosened, for example by spreading the load among a group of handicapped people and introducing timetable flexibility, keeping going might be less stressful.

1609   Boarding out

Before looking at liberating techniques one tactic needs to be discarded. This is the notion of 'boarding out', advocated in the Economist Intelligence Unit report *Care with dignity*. A parallel is drawn between physically handicapped adults and children in need of fostering: 'One possible alternative to institutional care, in some instances at least, is boarding out. This of course has been done extensively with children in care, and is widely regarded as psychologically advantageous, and has also been shown to be cheaper.'[14] The report goes on 'We believe that there is scope for an experimental project to see whether potential 'foster' families could be found for at least some of the physically handicapped, if adequate incentives were available. We believe that there may be a pool of potentially willing families, especially those where the wife is a trained nurse, with older children.'

This is cloud-cuckoo land; the idea that there are lots of nice devoted people around ready to spend 168 hours each week at the beck and call of someone who needs to be dressed, washed and fed and is incontinent, is unrealistic. Even if the idea were practicable there is no doubt that in terms of personal relationships the situation would be, to say the least, stressful.

1610   The cost of home care

The *Care with dignity* report, whatever its shortcomings, makes a commendable effort to quantify the cost of maintaining severely disabled people in ordinary housing versus maintaining them in long-stay hospitals or residential homes. The cost assumptions made in the report are open to a variety of objections but the message is clear. It costs substantially less, of the order of £10 each week at 1973 prices, to support people at home rather than in institutions. Taking into account running costs, capital costs and other expenditure the estimated weekly cost of hospital care was £40·70 per week, and of care in a modern residential home £32·50. The comparable cost for a disabled person in a family, with the support of what the report terms a moderate package including two home nurse visits, five hours of home help time and five meals on wheels each week, was estimated at £20·77. The cost of supporting a single disabled person living at home, with an intensive package including seven home nurse visits, ten hours of home help time and five meals on wheels, was £28·46[15].

Because, in respect of home care, the basis for calculations in the report is typical existing conditions rather than the more sophisticated arrangements proposed in the discussion which follows it is hazardous to claim that, given ideal physical provisions and supporting services, costs of maintaining a disabled person at home will always be less than institutional alternatives. But even if it could be demonstrated that institutional care were more economical it would be irresponsible to reject the living-at-home alternatives. Social benefit should be as important a consideration as financial expediency.

1611   Guidelines for action

There can be no general prescription for housing people with severe disabilities which is universally beneficial. But from the preceding discussions guidelines can be formulated, and it is on the concept of group integration that the most palatable and practical remedies to institutionalization can be structured[16].

It is the quality of living which matters, and four fundamental precepts are offered. These are (not in any particular order of priority) self-management, security, social freedom and physical independence.

Self-management: tenants must have opportunities wherever practicable to manage their own housing affairs, without interference from the bureaucracy of statutory agencies or the paternalism of voluntary agencies.

[14] Bib 93251, p56
[15] Bib 93251, p34. For a single person the actual figure given on p34 is £29·76 but there are two errors of calculation.
[16] For an interim report on work undertaken in this field by the Department of the Environment see Bib 93112.

Security: tenants must be as secure in the occupancy of their dwellings as other local authority tenants, without the threat of removal to an institution if they do not behave; they should be moved to hospital only when acute clinical care is needed.

Social freedom: tenants are entitled to privacy in their own homes, with the same freedoms of social intercourse that others have.

Physical independence: with the aid of intelligent architectural design, suitable equipment and special aids, tenants must be able to operate as independently as is physically possible.

A prerequisite to independent living of this quality is finance. In respect of the proposals which follow it therefore needs to be underlined at this stage that for the disabled person in Britain who has no income of his own, adequate provision *can* be made. Provision of suitable housing, payment of rent and rates, payments for heating, payments for clothing, provision of meals, provision of a telephone, provision of domiciliary health and welfare services, allowances for constant attendance, and finance for everyday personal needs: all these can be provided by one means or another through the various agencies of the Supplementary Benefits Commission (social security), housing authorities, social services authorities and health authorities. Exactly how the empowering legislation is interpreted is often at the discretion of an officer of the dispensing agency. But the legislation is not per se limiting.

In essence the four precepts constitute a bill of rights for disabled people to live like other people, in a normal home in a normal community. Obviously there are going to be some practical constraints, but to establish guidelines for the implementation of these rights it is helpful to develop hypothetical solutions on the group integration model, looking first at the framework of physical and environmental provision, at location and architectural organization.

1612   The location of special units

Housing schemes in which units for disabled people are incorporated ought to be in a town or city. It is not practicable to provide the range of essential supporting services in a rural setting, and people with severe disabilities who want trees, fields, cows and birds will have to fall back on one or other of the country mansion institutions which are likely to be around for some time yet. There ought in any catchment area to be towns of sufficient size – a population of say 20 000 or more – to meet two important conditions. The first is that there is access to buildings and facilities offering opportunities for education, culture, recreation and so on. Employment opportunities are also a factor, but owing to the likelihood that few if any of the tenants will be able to go out to work it is more important that there is an occupational day centre for handicapped people within commuting distance. The second condition is that the local

population is large enough to provide the numerous daily helpers who will support the group.

Convenient access to one or two general provision shops is important. There should also be an accessible pub and a launderette. Tenants are not likely to drive cars of their own and will rely for mobility on electric wheelchairs. For immediate local outings it should not be necessary to transfer to a wheelchair pushed by an attendant. Standard electric wheelchairs are not designed for use outside and can cope only with gentle ramps; ideally therefore the housing scheme should be part of a traffic-free development with pedestrian access to shops and services. If this is not possible it is desirable that shops can be reached without crossing roads.

The accessibility of local shops is important for the reasons discussed earlier in respect of residential homes, that disabled people ought for example to be able to go out and decide for themselves what sort of toothpaste they buy. The local shop is also valuable as a social meeting ground where disabled people can make contact with ordinary people living in the neighbourhood. Equally, an accessible pub is important to break down communication barriers. A launderette is useful for the same reason, apart from the preference many disabled people may have to do their own clothes washing. Ideally there ought also to be an accessible public library, so that disabled people who have limited physical resources have the opportunity to develop and use to their advantage their intellectual potential. For recreation it is helpful if there is a nearby park which can be reached by wheelchair.

1613   Support services

Design guidelines for housing for severely disabled people are detailed in section 84. While design standards are important it needs to be emphasized that it is not the scale of architectural provision which determines the sort of disabled people these schemes will accommodate, but the nature of support services. It is also the nature of support services which affects the incorporation of communal facilities, the general rule being that, to avoid institutional associations, communal facilities ought to be at a minimum.

The kind of support which severely disabled people will need can be categorized on three levels. These are first, routine help; second, emergency help; and third, for lack of a better description, extra-mural help. The last category means, in the main, help with activities outside the home, for example accompanying on shopping expeditions or doing the shopping where the tenant is not able to get out, escorting to cinemas, clubs, meetings and so on, and assistance with clothes washing at the launderette. It may be that tenants will have friends or relatives who can help with these things; if not voluntary associations in the locality may be able to assist. These voluntary helpers ought also to be able to do odd jobs and repairs around the house, such as hanging curtains and changing lightbulbs.

The extra-mural support services do not directly affect the issue of institutional trappings. It is the scale of routine help and emergency support which will determine whether it is necessary to have staff always available in the building, and hence in a significant way how affected by the apparatus of institutionalism the scheme becomes. Similarly, the immediacy with which help is available determines what degree of handicap can be catered for among tenants. The list of services in table 16.1 is an attempt to clarify the issues involved.

Table 16.1 Domiciliary services for severely disabled people

Routine help: non-timetable controlled services
1 floor cleaning
2 house cleaning, including refuse disposal
3 manicure and pedicure

Routine help: timetable controlled services
4 getting in and out of bed
5 transfer to and from the wheelchair
6 putting on or taking off prostheses
7 dressing and undressing
8 shaving
9 washing
10 bathing or showering
11 preparation of meals
12 feeding
13 administration of medicines, injections and surgical dressings
14 using the wc at pre-arranged times
15 changing incontinence appliances
16 turning in bed during the night

Emergency help
17 using the wc other than at pre-arranged times
18 help with respiratory aids, or other clinical non-routine needs
19 help in the event of falls or other accidents

From the management angle the awkward services to cater for are 16, 17, 18 and 19. If it were the case that severely disabled people did not need these services or could generally manage without them, housing schemes could be organized without any full-time living-in staff, with no communal facilities and no institutional trappings. There are of course many severely disabled people who must have these services, but it may be that they are not so high a proportion as might be supposed.

The critical service is 17, help with using the wc other than at pre-arranged times. In this context it is important to make clear that schemes are catering for people who have the intellectual and emotional resources to manage their own affairs. Excluding for the moment people with multiple sclerosis, they are commonly people who can regulate a bowel and bladder routine and schedule their visits to the wc. This does not automatically exclude all people who are incontinent.

The scheduled wc visiting routine is generally more manageable for men than for women, meaning that severely disabled men are often more easily able to manage in housing schemes which do not have emergency support than are severely disabled women. It is a question of urinary appliances: the basic point is that the male anatomy lends itself more readily than does the female anatomy to the wearing of appliances which avoid the need for unscheduled wc visits[17]. In respect of a defecation many severely disabled men and women operate a regular schedule, subject to temporary stomach upsets.

1614 External versus internal support

Having established that there may be a significant number of severely disabled people who, while needing a considerable amount of routine or scheduled support, do not often need emergency support, two housing concepts can be developed. These are external support schemes which rely only on helpers coming in from outside, and internal support schemes which rely on care staff on the premises as well as those coming in from outside. The suggestion is that external support schemes can theoretically cater for people needing help for items 1 to 15 on the list, but do not need help with turning in bed, and do not frequently need help other than at pre-arranged times with the wc, or help with unscheduled clinical needs. The possibility of including within external support schemes people who need turning in bed at night ought not to be ruled out; some health and social services authorities in Britain already administer schemes whereby domiciliary staff are on duty through the night, and visit people who regularly need turning in bed.

The significance of providing cover for turning in bed during the night is shown by the fact that no less than 18 per cent of the 168 tenants in Fokus flats surveyed in 1971 needed help for turning at night[18]. If bed-turning is needed by tetraplegics the likelihood is that help will also be needed to deal with catheters and manual evacuation of the bowels. In view of the clinical problems associated with these tasks at least one nurse will regularly need to come in from outside. It could be however that with the development of an efficient routine the amount of help needed from a qualified nurse could be reduced; with training under the guidance of a district nurse capable unqualified helpers could take over the business of bed-turning and manual evacuation.

External support schemes will not in practice be operable without any emergency cover at all, but the suggestion is that this cover can be provided on an ad hoc basis (discussed again later) rather than by means of full-time living-in staff. At this point comes the question 'Is it worth it; why risk the hazards of a breakdown, why not have living-in staff anyway?' There are five answers.

Normality. The underlying purpose is to enable severely disabled people to live in normal housing, as near like other people as possible, without institutional trappings.

[17] For amplification of this topic see 9152.
[18] Bib 93170, p32

Hazards of authoritarianism. The presence of living-in staff is a hazard, in that they may, perhaps unwittingly, adopt an authoritarian role in their relationships with tenants. This hazard is accentuated when, as is likely, any staff are employed by an agency (such as a local authority, voluntary organization or housing association) acting on behalf of tenants, rather than being employed direct by the tenants themselves.

Self-management. Intelligent adult people should have opportunities to exercise their common sense and maturity, being likely to welcome for example the challenge of responsibly managing their own affairs. If things go right they themselves will have the satisfaction. If however someone on the staff lives in, the likelihood is that responsibility will be delegated to her (or him) and that day to day management will be removed from the tenants.

Social stimulation. As discussed earlier in respect of residential homes, it is socially more stimulating for tenants if helpers come from various outside situations, rather than from inside with a narrower repertoire of daily experiences.

Logistics. Given the capabilities of the type of tenant under consideration, the small number of them, the peak-period character of their routine needs and the infrequency of their requests for emergency help, it is improbable that there will be sufficient work to keep a full-time person on the staff employed. It is also unrealistic to expect to get by with one attendant only, who has time off and should be asked to be on duty for the customary 38 hours or so each week. If full-time staff are employed at all there ought logically to be $4\frac{1}{2}$ staff, being the number needed to cover 168 hours.

1615   Management of external support schemes

To avoid any impression of a distinctive colony the size of any group where support comes from outside must be kept low, to say not more than six dwelling units. To afford mutual help and emotional support the group ought not to be less than four; a group of five, comprising two single units and three double units, is suggested (see table 84.1). If it happens that one of the double units is occupied by one person only the number of disabled people accommodated by such a group will be seven. Although the practicability of one of the tenants taking over the job of organizing and administering support services might be examined, the more likely arrangement is that the management of domiciliary staff will be handled direct by the local office of the social services authority. The peak early morning and late evening demands for services will require a more flexible organization than conventional home help services. A larger number of people may be employed for short periods, some perhaps only for three or four hours each week. The viability of this ad hoc organization will depend on the availability in the locality of people willing to help, and doing so without compromising the efficiency of existing and perhaps already stretched statutory services.

The list of routine services given earlier shows that what is needed from helpers is common sense and a readiness to learn from individual disabled people how best jobs should be done, rather than professional nursing skills. A check on the need for nursing help will be kept by the district nurse calling on a regular basis. Tenants will normally administer their own drugs, including injections. It will be valuable if there is an incontinence laundry service available, administered by the health or social services authority under section 13 of the Health Services and Public Health Act 1968.

1616   Emergency cover

Behind the network of routine support there has to be emergency cover. The proposal is that tenants will summon aid by telephone, calling to a permanently manned control point run by the social services authority, from which peripatetic domiciliary staff can be contacted. The speed with which helpers can reach handicapped tenants will determine the range of disabled people who can be accommodated; if help can be made available within say five minutes virtually no one will be excluded. If it can only be guaranteed within say 20 or 30 minutes the range will be reduced.

In theory it might seem essential that help is forthcoming almost instantly. In practice a 20 minute wait is not likely to be critical; in a pilot enquiry made among eight severely handicapped Cheshire home residents to whom a questionnaire on hypothesized housing alternatives was administered, none said that they would anticipate needing emergency help at less than 20 minutes notice[19].

A relevant practical factor is the reliability of the telephone as a means of summoning aid. There may be tenants who cannot cope with the mechanics, and they may have falls which put them out of reach of a telephone. The point has to be made that no emergency call system can ever give 100 per cent security – in any housing situation there will always be some risk. Available evidence, discussed in sections 893–897, indicates firmly that the telephone is more reliable than any alternative yet devised, and has vitally important side benefits.

There need to be contingency plans for occasions when first-stop helpers cannot be reached. One possibility is a link with a nearby old people's sheltered housing scheme, where the warden could be called upon if need be. It may also happen that contingency plans can be made by the group of handicapped tenants themselves, for example that in the event of immediate assistance being needed one of the tenants can summon an able-bodied friend living in an ordinary flat alongside. It could be that on account of the character of the scheme, aided by its physical organization, interactions between tenants will

[19] This inquiry was made as part of the DoE study of housing for disabled people. A check was made of the amount of care staff time each handicapped person might require; this ranged from 15 minutes to 5 hours 50 minutes each day, with a mean of 2 hours 40 minutes.

be more supportive than in typical contemporary housing estates. While this may seem optimistic, an encouraging phenomenon in recent years has been the evolution of effective volunteer agencies to back up the work of statutory authorities.

The normality ethic of external support schemes, along with the comprehensiveness of physical provision in individual flats, means that there is no case for the sort of communal facilities provided in residential homes. There is no case for communal eating arrangements, or for communal sitting rooms; if tenants wish to get together they can do so in each other's flats.

1617 The scope of external support schemes

From this description of the apparatus of hypothesized external support schemes it is possible to draw up a list of the disability conditions of people who might be catered for. They include:
 1 athetoid cerebral palsy
 2 spina bifida where there is no mental impairment
 3 other congenitally disabling conditions not involving brain damage
 4 muscular dystrophy
 5 rheumatoid arthritis
 6 polio, including those with respiratory aids provided that failure of the machinery is not immediately lethal
 7 paraplegia and tetraplegia excluding very high lesions
 8 syringomyelia
 9 multiple sclerosis, excluding those needing to use the wc frequently and at short notice
10 hemiplegia not involving brain damage.

1618 Internal support schemes: Scope and services

The distinguishing feature of internal support schemes is that emergency support is available at short notice on the premises for 24 hours each day. This means that people with more severely handicapping conditions can be catered for than in external support schemes. Degree of physical disability ought not to be a determining factor, it being possible to support even people who are totally dependent. The criterion is that they are people who wish to live independently in their own housing, and have the intellectual and emotional resources to do so. This means that people who can be catered for include:
1 people with severe hemiplegia not involving brain damage
2 people with polio dependent on respiratory machines
3 people with multiple sclerosis.

To ensure continuous cover to internal support schemes at least three care staff would need to be employed on a permanent basis, and perhaps four. On this account it would be administratively uneconomic to limit the number of units in a scheme to the five or six suggested for external support schemes. The suggestion is that a scheme might comprise two or three groups placed around an ordinary housing estate, each group to be served by one full-time helper. Each helper might take on the major share of the routine duties for people in her group, with an

arrangement when she was not on duty for routine help to come from outside domiciliary staff. With three associated groups it might be practicable to have a shift system of standby duty, with handicapped tenants in one group being able to call on the helper attached to another when their own helper was not on duty.

Although these schemes are described as internal support, it is not essential that the care staff serving them are actually living within the groups. Instead they could be in specially allocated housing units alongside, where they could be called either by telephone or intercom. In terms of the urgency of answering calls for aid, the marginally longer time needed to travel from one house to another rather than simply along a passage would be unlikely to be a critical disadvantage.

In these schemes it may be appropriate to have a general purpose room to serve as office, focal point for meetings between tenants, care staff and social workers, and as a bed-sitting room for a helper on duty when a regular helper happens to be away.

On the basis of these suggestions guidelines for the distribution of units in internal support schemes are detailed in table 84.1. No firm evidence is available which allows reliable predictions to be made as to the relative number of units required for single people, for couples who are married and for two or three people who need separate bedroom provision. In internal support schemes it may be that there is a lesser requirement for accommodation for married couples, the point being that couples who are both handicapped tend to look to themselves for mutual emotional support rather than, as may happen in the case of single people, to other disabled people in dwelling units alongside. It is also likely to be the case that couples who are both handicapped, or couples where one partner only is handicapped, may in terms of essential physical support be more readily placed in scattered housing units elsewhere. On the other hand for some couples, for example a husband going out to work whose wife has multiple sclerosis, living in a group scheme can be advantageous.

The distributions detailed in table 84.1 are made on the assumption that the requirement for units for single people as against couples will be of the order of three to two, and that, to afford flexibility of tenancy allocations, between 60 and 70 per cent of dwellings should be 2 person units. Relevant practical issues are discussed on section 841.

1619 Internal support schemes: Accommodation, potential tenants

Space standards for housing units for severely disabled people are discussed in section 84 and summarized in table 81.3. On the principle that these are *housing* solutions there is no cause for a communal kitchen and dining room; such provision should be reserved for residential homes. Where there may not be an accessible launderette in the locality the incorporation of a communal laundry room to serve a group of units might be considered. Dependent on the availability of local community and day centre services, a hobbies room might be provided to serve a group of units.

A day centre on the site is not advocated. To do an effective job a day centre needs to cater for a large population, serving a variety of needs and offering a range of occupational options. As with residents in part III homes, it is better that disabled tenants in housing schemes who can benefit from a day centre are taken there in transport arranged by the local authority. They will thus be treated on the same basis as handicapped people living elsewhere, with corresponding social benefits.

Regarding accommodation for care staff, there should be a variety of provision in the overall housing scheme, allowing flexibility for the placement of staff. It ought to be possible to employ a single person, one part of a married couple or a member of a family. The physical planning of the estate should afford opportunities for mutual support and cooperation between disabled tenants and others. Support need not be entirely one sided; disabled tenants may help for example by taking in parcels or messages, and perhaps by doing occasional baby-sitting. So far as is practicable, ordinary housing in the scheme should be accessible to visitors who are disabled.

No studies have been made in Britain which allow reliable estimates to be made of the number of severely disabled people who might take advantage of these kind of housing schemes. On the basis of an investigation made in Sweden by the Fokus Society[20] and on the evidence of Fokus schemes now in operation a reasonable guess is that the number will be between 5 and 10 per 100 000 of the total population. Where these people will come from is a matter for conjecture, but it is possible that the majority – perhaps about 75 per cent – will come from family homes, 20–25 per cent from existing local authority residential homes or voluntary homes, and not more than 5 per cent from existing hospital units. These proportions may not vary significantly between people needing internal support schemes and those needing external support schemes. Local authorities considering the establishment of these housing schemes ought however to make their own inquiries; it should be possible for social services departments to check among their social workers regarding disabled people living at home, and through their records of handicapped residents sponsored in part III institutions. Hospital authorities will probably readily allow inquiries to be made among their long-term patients.

Among potential tenants for these schemes a significant group will be single severely disabled people aged between say 20 and 40, handicapped from birth and supported by ageing parents. There will often be a determination on both sides that the handicapped person does not go into an institution or hospital, but against this the physical process of managing may be increasingly difficult. An advantage of the sort of schemes proposed here is that it may be possible to place the disabled person in a flat of his own, with his parents continuing to live nearby.

[20] Bib 93171, p2

17 Independent housing

1700 The parameters of ordinary housing

This final section of the commentary is concerned with independent housing, meaning housing for disabled people who can manage with the help of their family or on their own if their accommodation is convenient. The emphasis is on housing which, by being purpose-designed or suitably planned, enables disabled people to cope independently. The thesis is developed that, with minor qualifications, it is only people who are confined to wheelchairs who need special purpose-designed housing. People who are less severely disabled can be satisfactorily accommodated in conveniently planned ordinary housing. Special housing is termed 'wheelchair housing' and convenient ordinary housing is termed 'mobility housing', the latter title being related to Lady Sharp's report *Mobility of physically disabled people*[1] which recommended, among other things, that ordinary housing should be made more suitable for handicapped people. To understand the role of mobility housing, and, beyond that, of wheelchair housing, it is helpful to look first at the determinants of ordinary housing designed, by and large, to cater for able-bodied people.

The building of public authority housing in Britain is affected by the twin controls of minimum space standards and the cost yardstick. The space standards are derived from the recommendations of the Parker Morris report *Homes for today and tomorrow* issued in 1961[2]. They are minimum overall areas, prescribed according to size of household and form of dwelling (for example flats or terrace housing). The report also sets out amenity standards, relating for example to storage space, kitchen equipment, wc provision and heating.

The administration of the housing cost yardstick is described in Ministry of Housing and Local Government Circular 36/67[3]. To finance their housing developments local authorities apply for loan sanction and subsidy from central government. Within the permitted yardstick, determined by the number of bed spaces proposed in relation to the area of the site, local authorities have latitude to design as they wish, provided that they satisfy the minimum space and amenity standards. To take account of variations in building costs in different localities the basic yardstick is augmented by a percentage increase known as the regional variation, which is updated from time to time by the Department of the Environment.

In the private housebuilding sector there is no obligation to observe space or amenity standards other than those of the national building regulations, and quality is determined by what people will pay. The consequence is that in low cost speculative developments standards are commonly inferior to local authority housing, meaning that contemporary private housing is often less convenient for disabled people. Housing associations, who as a rule obtain their finance through the agency of the Housing Corporation, have to build to the same standards as local authorities, with the additional constraint that, unlike local authorities, there are often no funds they can call on to finance desirable but unsubsidized facilities.

If the question is put 'What can be done to make ordinary housing more suitable for wheelchair users and other disabled people?' the facile response is likely to be 'Just make it a little bit larger.' The fact has to be faced however that, at a time of restraint on spending by local authorities, it is unrealistic to expect that space standards for ordinary housing will in the immediate future be generally enhanced. The next question is 'If overall standards cannot be raised is it possible to reallocate spaces within dwellings to make them more convenient?' The answering of this question requires an appreciation of the practical considerations which govern the detailed planning of housing, and it is from this that the concept of mobility housing emerges.

1701 The effects of dimensional coordination

In recent years, pressures for greater efficiency and economy have generated increasing standardization and prefabrication of components, along with coordination of dimensions for planning. In Britain the switch from feet and inches to metric design has served to give these processes a boost. All public authority housing is now designed to a basic planning grid of 300mm (a fraction under 1ft) within which are increments for components of 100mm. Thus passageways are generally 900mm wide, doorsets (the controlling dimension being the structural opening) are 900mm, 800mm or 700mm wide, windows are made in widths which are multiples of 300mm, and the width and depth of standard kitchen units is 600mm. With standard sizes comes standard detailing; the standard external door for example has a standard frame and a standard threshold sill.

The discipline is pervasive. The architect cannot easily stretch a space a bit here, retract it a bit there; the mathematics will not permit it. Constrained by the yardstick, minimum space standards are in practice maximum standards also. The lay person's notion that all that is needed for people in wheelchairs to manage is to make doors and passageways just a little bit wider sounds attractive but it is not in practice a viable proposition. The only alternative is to work within the system; to ascertain how far disabled people can in practice be accommodated by it.

In the course of the Norwich inquiry it was not feasible to gather accurate dimensional data on the space requirements, in terms of passage and door widths, of wheelchair users living in ordinary housing. In local authority houses the typical condition was 3ft (914mm) passages and 2ft 6in doors giving a clear opening of 2ft 4in (711mm). Surprisingly, this was manageable by people

---

[1] Bib 93540
[2] Bib 93720. The standards as they are currently applied are set down in MHLG Circular 27/70 (Bib 93712). Amenity standards are detailed in section 804 of this book, space standards in table 81.3.
[3] Bib 93710. This was updated for metric practice by MHLG Circular 56/69 (Bib 93711). During the period between the preparation and publication of this book the cost control system administered by the Department of the Environment may be revised.

using standard wheelchairs; studies of the circulation requirements of wheelchair users had indicated that more generous provision was essential[4]. In only one case, that of an obese polio lady, had structural alterations been necessary because the 3ft–2ft 6in condition was impossible.

The normal provision in public authority housing is 900mm passageways, 900mm doorsets to principal rooms, 800mm doorsets to bathrooms and 700mm or 800mm doorsets to wc compartments. Space and financial considerations mean that it is not practicable to incorporate 1000mm doorsets, or generally to increase passage widths to 1000mm. The consequence is that the only people with wheelchairs who can be expected to manage in ordinary housing are those with a chair which can be propelled through a 775mm opening (the clear dimension given by a 900mm doorset) from a 900mm passageway.

1702   Ergonomic and planning evidence

To obtain evidence on the potential of ordinary housing to cater for wheelchair users a special study was made by the Institute for Consumer Ergonomics at Loughborough University for the Department of the Environment[5]. A test rig was set up to ascertain whether the standard wheelchairs issued by the Department of Health could pass through a 775mm opening from a 900mm passageway, or vice versa. The manoeuvre was manageable in respect of all standard self-propelled chairs (though with difficulty by the general purpose model 8L chair[6]), standard electric wheelchairs and standard chairs pushed by attendants. Most unexpectedly, the cumbersome model 13 chair[7] could be got through, although with some shunting. The chairs which could not manage the manoeuvre were the largest of the electric indoor wheelchairs and those having extended legrests.

This evidence does not prove that all wheelchair users can manage satisfactorily in ordinary housing, but it does suggest that for many there is a genuine possibility. The next question to resolve was how far the 900mm passage/900mm doorset provision could be generally applied to flats or single storey houses designed to current standards and, as a supplementary, whether it would be practicable to substitute a ramped approach with flush threshold for a standard stepped entrance door detail. To gather relevant evidence an inquiry was made by the Department of the Environment among some 100 architects engaged on metric house planning. It was pointed out that the intention was to cater first for ambulant handicapped people using sticks, crutches or walking aids, and second for people who, while not being chairbound, might regularly or occasionally use a wheelchair when at home. It was assumed that people in the latter group would be able to stand to transfer from a wheelchair and might be able to take a few short steps, perhaps using furniture, support rails, other aids or another person for support.

Responses were encouraging. The consensus was that there would be no difficulty providing 900mm doorsets to

the front entrance and to principal rooms such as sitting room, dining room and kitchen; this would not mean additional space or expenditure, it would simply confirm existing practice. For bedrooms at entrance level the provision might not be so readily obtainable, owing to the disposition of circulation spaces, but in general it was felt to be achievable. It was considered that the use of 800mm doorsets to bedrooms was in any event ill-advised, given the need to move large double beds and bulky furniture.

1703   Ramping of entrances

Regarding the substitution of a ramped for a stepped approach at the front door, there were reservations from architects. It was pointed out that the elimination of the normal step to the front door is contrary to good building practice, calling for an expensive detail to avoid complications of water penetration. Aside from the question of dampproofing, two variations from normal practice are required; first, the modification of the doorset to incorporate a flush or near-flush threshold, for example a flexible insert in an extruded strip, and second, a ramped approach in place of steps.

Some local authorities (predominantly those in rural areas) felt that the extra expense, perhaps of the order of £40 at 1972 prices, could be absorbed within the basic yardstick allowance. Others were firm that it could not be: standards had already been compromised more than enough by cost controls and there was no latitude left. The conclusion was that if housing authorities were to be encouraged to develop on a substantial scale the kind of housing proposed, extra cost allowances would need to be granted. This was confirmed in DoE Circular 74/74, which, while suggesting that any extra cost involved in achieving mobility standards should be minimal, advised that applications could be submitted for small ad hoc additions to the normal cost allowance[8]. With the issuing in 1975 of DoE Circular 92/75 *Wheelchair and mobility housing: Standards and costs*, administrative procedures have been simplified: the current arrangement is that an additional allowance of £50 per dwelling (exclusive of regional variation) may be claimed for each dwelling designated as mobility housing[9].

1704   Bathrooms and wcs

There was the further issue of whether in flats and single storey houses, bathrooms and wcs could, by the use of 900mm doorsets, be made accessible to people in wheelchairs, so substantially increasing the scope of mobility housing. Here the response by the architects was firmly negative.

[4] See for example Felix Walter's report, Bib 93501, p10
[5] This study is reported in Bib 93506. A summary is incorporated in the DoE report on mobility housing (Bib 93111).
[6] See diagrams 23.1–23.2
[7] See diagram 23.13
[8] Bib 93110, para 13
[9] Bib 93121. The design standards to be observed are set down in the DoE report *Mobility housing* (Bib 93111); see 8710.

For a bathroom containing a wc the normal provision is an 800mm doorset. In respect of some plan arrangements it is possible to substitute a 900mm doorset; in others, owing to lack of wall space, particularly where a warm air home heating unit is installed, it is not. Even where a 900mm doorset can be incorporated the matter is not entirely resolved, since it is not always practicable to afford wheelchair manoeuvring space inside the bathroom.

1705 Other features of mobility housing

Apart from the basic requirements of accessibility there are other features which can be incorporated in mobility housing to enhance its suitability for handicapped people. They relate for example to the positioning and hanging of doors to facilitate wheelchair manoeuvre, the specification of easily manipulated door and window ironmongery, the convenient placing of light switches and socket outlets, the disposition of kitchen equipment and storage, the location of garages or carports, the provision of a conveniently accessible bath, the specification of wcs, wash basins and sanitary equipment generally, and the selection of suitable floor finishes. How far all these things can be done will depend on individual circumstances, and in particular cost considerations.

Wherever practicable, flats and single storey houses should be built to mobility standards. The possibility will depend on local conditions, most importantly topography. In the case of sloping sites there could be considerable additional expenditure on extended approach paths to avoid the need for steps; in practice the application of mobility standards will be limited to level or near-level sites, for example where a path gradient not exceeding 1 in 12 is practicable.

1706 Two storey housing

With the general abandonment for social and economic reasons of high-rise housing by local authorities in Britain a large proportion of current public authority house building (about 50 per cent) is two storey terraced housing. Such housing is suited for mobility treatment if the bathroom and one bedroom are at entrance level, but the invariable condition is that both bathroom and bedrooms are upstairs. The consequence, with qualifications discussed below, is housing which is not satisfactory for living in by disabled people but which can be made accessible for visiting. If access arrangements are made which facilitate visiting it is also advantageous that the downstairs wc, where provided, is accessible.

This issue is of concern only for 5 and 6 person units; in 4 person two storey units there is usually only one wc, which is upstairs; this is not a common type of housing in England but is used regularly in Scotland. In the DoE inquiry the question was put whether in wc compartments at entrance level sufficient space could be provided for wheelchairs. The response was definite, it could not be. There are three related influences: first, the wc compartment is small in area to give as much living space as possible elsewhere in the house; second, where the door

opens inwards the tight space does not permit a large door, and third, the general practice that the door is parallel with the wc rather than facing it, making it impossible for a person in a chair to manoeuvre, even if he can get through the door.

Given the impossibility of arranging wheelchair access to wc compartments in two storey housing it is arguable that the provision of an accessible entrance is warranted. There is however good cause on social grounds for making housing convenient for wheelchair visitors where possible, enabling a person in a wheelchair to call to see friends and relatives. The answer perhaps is not to insist on a flush threshold but to permit a standard threshold still or single step; in terms of obstacles to wheelchairs a single step is only a minor hindrance, whereas a pair of steps can be unmanageable[10]. With single step treatment there is no need for modifying the entrance door specification.

a First floor plan

b Ground floor plan

17.1 Six person house (1:200). R H Fogg, chief architect, Bedford Borough Council.

Having set down the reasons why the mobility housing concept is not achievable in respect of two storey housing to prevailing space and yardstick controls, it needs to be pointed out that there can be exceptions. Diagram 17.1 shows an example from Bedford District Council of how a typical two storey 5 person unit can be modified to become a 6 person mobility unit; dwellings of this type have been built without special cost allowances being claimed.

---

[10] For further discussion on this see 3114.

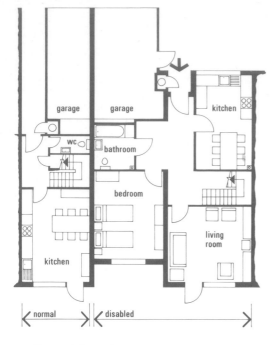

a Ground floor plan

b First floor plan

17.2 Two storey housing for London Borough of Croydon (1:200).
Hugh Lea, director of development. M Dolman, head of architecture.

There is also the possibility that interlocking housing units of the type shown in diagram 17.2 can be designed to give family housing to mobility standards; although the example shown is of a unit to wheelchair standards the principle is the same.

In respect of typical two storey terraced housing a further qualification can be made. This is that where a straight flight staircase is incorporated there is the possibility (subject to undemanding design constraints discussed in 827) that, should there be a disabled person in the household, a mechanical stairlift can be installed. This will give access to rooms at first floor level, and, since some stairlifts can carry wheelchairs, it is desirable that doors to upstairs rooms have 900mm doorsets, including the bathroom if practicable.

1707 Mobility housing: Summary

To summarize, mobility housing is potentially suitable for (1) all ambulant disabled people and (2) people who use wheelchairs but are able to stand to transfer and move a few steps, if need be with something to hang on to. It is not convenient for chairbound people, or, among those not chairbound, housewives who use a wheelchair when working in the kitchen or people with very large chairs. The proportion of the wheelchair population that it could cater for is high; analysis of data from the Norwich survey suggests that 59 per cent would, given their circumstances at the time of interview, have been comfortably accommodated by mobility housing; taking possible physical deterioration into account 33 per cent would have been satisfied. Using the Norwich data in conjunction with information from the OPCS survey[11] it can be estimated that 96.1 per cent of those categorized as handicapped could conveniently be catered for in mobility housing, and 98.3 per cent of those categorized as impaired.

This is not to propose that all people who are handicapped or impaired need or ought to be placed in mobility housing; a large proportion have no problems affecting mobility. In this connection the OPCS survey, since it did not include questions on ability to manage steps or stairs, gives no immediately relevant evidence. Regarding general mobility, its findings were that 13.3 per cent of impaired people were housebound or able to get out only if accompanied[12]; it is predictable that people in this group, apart from those requiring wheelchair housing, would benefit from being in mobility housing.

The OPCS figures on handicapped people with a reasonable demand for rehousing are also relevant here; these comprised one in four of the impaired population, and of these three in five wishes to move to accommodation without stairs[13]. Thus the indications are that of all people categorized as impaired some 2 per cent need to be in wheelchair housing and a further 15 per cent in mobility housing. Among people in the OPCS survey who were housebound or able to go out only if accompanied, more than 60 per cent were aged 65 or over[14]; the primary mobility housing need is therefore for small dwelling units. Among impaired people in the OPCS survey with a demand for rehousing, 72 per cent were members of one or two person households, 21 per cent of three or four person households, and 7 per cent of households having five or more members[15]. The suggested application of these data in terms of the distribution of housing units is detailed in 8203.

[11] Bib 93210
[12] Bib 93210, p26
[13] Bib 93210, p117
[14] Bib 93210, p26, 27
[15] Bib 93210, p116

1708 Purpose-designed housing for wheelchair users

The number of people who need special wheelchair housing is small. It is also a very variable population, making it impossible for there to be formula solutions which will be universally appropriate. The architect's dilemma is illustrated by two examples, the first of a paraplegic housewife, the second of an elderly hemiplegic widower.

The paraplegic housewife lives with her husband and two school-age children. She is paralyzed from the waist down, meaning that there is loss of sensation, incontinence and an inability to stand at all. She is able to get about independently in her wheelchair and can drive a car. Her husband is out at work during the day. The list of special provisions which she needs to be able to manage without difficulty is extensive:

1. Wheelchair access to all rooms in the home, including all bedrooms.
2. Space in all bedrooms for bedmaking to be done from a wheelchair.
3. A kitchen designed so that the preparation and management of meals can be done entirely from a wheelchair, with wheelchair access to sink, split-level cooking unit, wheelchair access to preparation area and adequate storage accommodation within reach.
4. A bathroom with bath, basin and wc, the bath to have a platform at the head end for seated transfer, the basin to be at a level convenient for wheelchair use.
5. A wc compartment separate from the bathroom allowing space for lateral transfer from wheelchair to wc.
6. A garage or carport with space for wheelchair transfer to and from the car, direct undercover access to the dwelling, and (if a garage) an automatic opening door.
7. All window openers, socket outlets, switches and other controls to be reachable from a wheelchair.
8. Undercover access to refuse disposal area, or installation of waste disposal unit in kitchen.

The elderly hemiplegic man is disabled from a stroke, meaning that he is paralyzed on one side, has to be pushed in a wheelchair when he moves about but can with support stand to transfer, is partly incontinent and tends to be mentally confused. For overall washing he needs to have a blanket bath. He lives with his daughter and son-in-law who have two children of their own. His daughter spends much of her time in the house with him, his son-in-law has a car and goes out to work. The special provision which he needs is limited:

1. Wheelchair access to sitting room, kitchen, bathroom and one bedroom.
2. Space for wheelchair approach to wc and wash basin.

The list of special provisions he does not need is extensive. He does not need access to all bedrooms in the house, nor does he need space for bedmaking from a wheelchair. He does not need any special provision in the kitchen for working from a wheelchair. He does not need to have all window openers and switches where they can be reached from a wheelchair. He does not need space for lateral transfer from his wheelchair to the wc or bath. The family

does not need a garage which has space for wheelchair transfer to the car, the garage does not have to be within the curtilage of the dwelling, and nor does it need to have an automatic opening door.

In respect of special provisions needed there are other disabled people similar to the hemiplegic widower; the child with spina bifida for example, the elderly relative who is arthritic, or the adolescent son who is mentally as well as physically handicapped as a consequence of cerebral palsy.

If the majority of people who need wheelchair housing are like the hemiplegic widower rather than the paraplegic housewife it is arguable that it is sensible to design all wheelchair housing to cater for paraplegic housewives. The preferred strategy might be to design generally for a norm between the two, leaving people with requirements for substantial special provision to be covered by ad hoc solutions. Alternatively it might be tactically sound to have more than one norm for wheelchair housing. To resolve these issues it is helpful at this stage to examine evidence regarding the characteristics of people identified as needing wheelchair housing.

1709 Evidence on the need for special housing

The national survey of handicapped people carried out by the Office of Population Censuses and Surveys did not attempt to estimate numbers in need of purpose-designed special housing. Of local surveys undertaken in response to the Chronically Sick Act, one of those to do so was that in Kensington and Chelsea, which studied a random sample of 7541 households and identified five wheelchair users who appeared to need purpose-built accommodation[16]. This suggests that, for reasons of statistical reliability, a survey of a relatively small sample of the total population is not a satisfactory means of assessing the special housing needs of disabled people.

On the premise that it is only chairbound people, not all who use wheelchairs, who need purpose-designed housing, it is more fruitful to look to evidence on wheelchair populations, and in this connection the findings of the Norwich inquiry are relevant[17].

Of the 284 wheelchair users in Norwich located and interviewed, 40 were not living in private housing; 28 were in the residential home for physically handicapped people, 11 were in old people's homes and one was living in a hotel. Of the 244, full information was obtained for 233; of these, 121 (52 per cent) were in local authority housing, 69 (30 per cent) were in owner-occupied housing and 43 (18 per cent) were in privately rented housing. In the houses in which they were living 78 of these people (one-third of the total) used their wheelchairs inside their homes and 155 did not. In some cases people did not use their chairs

[16] Bib 93223
[17] At the time of preparing this material (May 1976) the OPCS report of the survey of people issued with DHSS wheelchairs had not been published; it can be expected that its findings will add appreciably to the evidence.

at home because of inconvenient physical arrangements; it was estimated that a further 27 people might have used their wheelchairs in their homes had conditions been more suitable.

A picture of overall accommodation requirements was built up by recording each individual's particular needs against a checklist itemizing, for example, wheelchair access, room for chair use in the kitchen, sink and cooker provision, transfer space from wheelchair to bath or wc, space in bedrooms and garage requirements. It was then possible to classify people according to whether in theory they could be accommodated in housing incorporating wheelchair access to sitting room, kitchen and one bedroom but not bathroom or wc (mobility housing) or chairbound housing incorporating comprehensive provision for wheelchair users (wheelchair housing). On analysis three people were found not to need any disability-associated arrangements, 134 (58 per cent) would be catered for by mobility housing and 96 (41 per cent) would need wheelchair housing.

It is a mistake to suppose that for individual disabled people housing requirements will be unchanging. People with disabilities tend to deteriorate physically and while in the short term mobility housing may be adequate, in the long term they will be catered for only by wheelchair housing. Strategically therefore it can help to accommodate ambulant disabled people in wheelchair housing. In the analysis of the Norwich wheelchair population an attempt was made, on the basis of observation along with information from interviewing and some knowledge of diagnoses and prognoses, to predict which people who at the time of interview needed mobility housing might in time need wheelchair housing. The findings which emerged are summarized in table 17.1.

Table 17.1 Wheelchair users in Norwich, analysis of housing requirements

	current requirements %		contingency requirements %	
no special arrangements	3	1	3	1
mobility housing	134	58	75	32
wheelchair housing	96	41	155	67

1710   Wheelchair housing: Household size

Table 17.2 gives a breakdown by size of household of the 155 people in the Norwich survey assessed as needing wheelchair housing or having a potential need for it. For purposes of comparison data are also given from the survey of purpose-designed wheelchair housing undertaken by the Department of the Environment in 1972[18]. The two populations are not strictly comparable. The DoE survey comprises people who happened to have been placed in special housing; had there been suitable mobility housing available in their area it is possible that a significant proportion would not have needed to be in wheelchair housing.

Table 17.2 Wheelchair housing: Evidence on household size

household size	Norwich study of 155 people estimated as needing or potentially needing wheelchair housing		DoE study of 249 disabled people accommodated in purpose-designed wheelchair housing	
		%		%
1 (disabled person only)	19	12	48	19
2	77	50	113	45
3	30	19	38	15
4	14	9	31	13
5	12	8	9	4
6	1	1	6	2
7	2	1	3	1
8	–	–	1	0·3

Some caution is needed regarding the practical interpretation of the data in table 17.2. Although in percentage distributions by household size there is comparability between the Norwich and DoE results, both studies exclude the severely handicapped people living in institutions for whom housing alternatives might be practicable with the aid of a full range of domiciliary services. It is not easy to estimate from the data the extent to which single severely handicapped people are underrepresented. In the case of the DoE survey, Amelia Harris's measure of capacity for self-care was administered[19]; only 3 of the 48 people living alone were identified as very severely handicapped, representing 6 per cent, compared with 54 of the 201 people living in two person or larger households, representing 27 per cent.

In the case of the Norwich survey no comparable measures of handicappedness were applied. There were however rough measures of degree of disability; if the hypothesis is that single people with severe disability might be underrepresented among wheelchair users in ordinary housing, the expectation would be that among those living alone there would be relatively few chairbound people. The Norwich findings show that of the 155 people in the sample there were among the 19 people living alone 6 who were chairbound, representing 31 per cent. Among the 136 people in two person or larger households there were 52 who were chairbound, representing 36 per cent. There is not thus a significant relationship. The inference to be made tentatively from the slight shortfall of chairbound people in single person households is that people who were severely handicapped (as distinct from those who were simply severely disabled[20]) were in institutions; severely handicapped chairbound people could, if members of families, be supported in ordinary housing.

[18] Bib 93122
[19] See 1104
[20] For discussion on the distinction between disability and handicap see 1103, 1106.

Table 17.3 Households with disabled member, estimates of household composition by degree of handicap in typical population of 100 000 in Great Britain, mid-1975

	estimated numbers by degree of handicap			
Disabled person living	very severe	severe	appreciable	total
alone	18	171	295	484
with husband or wife only	99	232	398	729
with husband or wife and married children, or unmarried children some over 15 years	44	94	150	288
with husband or wife and children aged under 15 years	6	22	51	79
without husband or wife, with married children, or unmarried children some over 15 years	110	119	191	420
without husband or wife, with children aged under 15 years	–	2	4	6
with one or both parents	21	16	30	67
with brother or sister	18	21	66	105
with husband or wife and others (not children), others	20	44	65	129
total	336	721	1250	2307

Source: Bib 93210, p24, Bib 93780

The OPCS survey of the housing circumstances of handicapped people excluded those living in institutions.

As an aid for predicting appropriate distributions by household size of new housing for disabled people its findings are of limited value; the most relevant data, updated to show estimated figures for mid-1975, are given in table 17.3.

1711 The suitability of two storey housing units

For the purpose of establishing if it ought to be advocated that all wheelchair housing units are on one level only, or whether, with people such as the hemiplegic widower in mind, a proportion might be two storey accommodation, an analysis of family households in Norwich is relevant.

Of the 155 people identified as potentially needing wheelchair housing, there were 29 living in households comprising four or more people, of whom 9 were housewives and 20 were not. The disabled housewives ought in any event to be in single storey accommodation, and a similar claim can be made on behalf of the fathers of families (of whom there were five), on the grounds that fathers as well as mothers should have access to all family rooms. There was also one mother who was too severely handicapped to do any work in the home.

This leaves 14 candidates for two storey housing, comprising seven children aged under 16 (for whom a case might also be made for single storey accommodation), two adults (both in their 20s) living with parents, and five elderly relatives. If in two storey housing garaging is not within the curtilage the one person of these 14 who was a vehicle driver would not be conveniently catered for.

Although on social grounds the provision of two storey wheelchair units can be argued, the economic advantages might be significant and practical advice is given in 8308. The proposal is that the downstairs bedroom is planned to accommodate two single beds; a potential advantage of this kind of accommodation is that it is well suited for use by kidney patients dependent on home dialysis.

Diagram 17.2 is an example of how two storey wheelchair housing can, by means of interlocking units, be incorporated in a typical low-rise housing scheme; although in this case the garage is within the curtilage it could equally well have been planned outside.

1712 Wheelchair housing for old people

This discussion of wheelchair housing has focused primarily on family accommodation. The handicapped population as a whole is however predominantly an elderly population and a reasonable inference is that a correspondingly large proportion of wheelchair housing should be planned for elderly people. In practice however the association is not necessarily direct. A reason is that there are important differences between the aetiology of disablement among the elderly by comparison with younger people. Among younger people the principal causes of disability are first, congenital or inherited conditions such as cerebral palsy, spina bifida and muscular dystrophy; second, accidents causing paraplegia and tetraplegia, and third, crippling diseases such as multiple sclerosis, rheumatoid arthritis and polio – the last extinct, but with a substantial residue of disabled people remaining. Among old people the principal causes of severe disability are osteo-arthritis, hemiplegia and arteriosclerosis.

A characteristic of the disabling conditions prevalent among younger people which are allied with wheelchair prescription is that there is a relatively high likelihood of the people affected being not able to walk at all. In the case of the conditions prevalent among old people it is more likely that people affected will not be chairbound and will be able to walk a short distance, or at least stand to transfer to and from the wheelchair. It is more frequently the case that old people who use wheelchairs are able to manage satisfactorily in mobility housing.

In support of these predictions, analysis of the Norwich data shows that 35 per cent of people aged 60 or over were assessed as being capable of managing in mobility housing, compared with 28 per cent of those aged 59 or under. The discrepancy would be more marked if account were taken of wheelchair users living in institutions but capable, if given the option, of managing in special housing. Data from the OPCS survey (as extrapolated in table 11.1) can also be compared with findings from the Norwich study of need for wheelchair housing. Of people in the total population categorized as impaired, those in the 16–64 age range comprise 38 per cent, against 62 per cent aged 65 or over; of people in the Norwich wheelchair housing study 49 per cent were in the 16–64 age range, against 51 per cent aged 65 or over.

There are cultural differences between young and old people which can properly be reflected in planning arrangements for wheelchair housing. Among young people who are disabled and can live independently there is as a rule no urgent desire for their accommodation to be concentrated in a colony of special housing; they generally have no particular wish to share their lives with other disabled people and would prefer to be integrated among ordinary families. The houses they live in should be perceived as normal rather than as distinctive.

On the same basis, wheelchair housing for old people may be regarded first as old people's housing, and only incidentally as disabled people's housing. Some old people prefer, on account of shared interests, experiences and attitudes, to be among people of their own generation. When a sheltered housing scheme is planned for old people it can be valuable, because the purpose is to cater for elderly people who need support, that a sizable proportion of units are suitable for old people who use wheelchairs. On social grounds it can be a mistake to introduce younger disabled people, say below the age of 60, into a community of old people. For younger disabled people who need supporting services to hand, special provisions of the kind discussed earlier can be made, with units mixed in among ordinary housing.

1713 Contingencies and flexibility

The aim of housing authorities should be to establish a fund of wheelchair housing so that there can be flexibility of tenancy allocation. It may seem sensible, when the disabled person in a specially planned house dies, to transfer the other members of the family to different accommodation so as to bring in a new household with a disabled member. In practice the family may be reluctant to move and they ought if they wish to be enabled to stay; if there is other accommocation for wheelchair users available in the area there will be less disturbance. On these grounds also it is wise, when wheelchair housing is first commissioned, to avoid incorporating equipment which may be superfluous.

Ideally when wheelchair housing is planned there are prospective tenants whose particular requirements can be established in advance. In practice this rarely occurs. The period from gestation to occupation is frequently so prolonged that prior booking is not feasible. There is also the possibility that the chosen tenant late in the day changes his mind about moving.

Pragmatic procedures are preferred. Dwelling units should be planned with latitude for adjustments, the final fitting to be delayed as long as practicable. The building contract should cover the essentials; convenient access, internal circulation which eases wheelchair manoeuvre, and a functional organization of spaces to achieve efficiency and economy. At a relatively early stage it will need to be decided whether to have an enclosed garage rather than a carport, and it may also be difficult to delay too long the decision between bath and shower. Other matters, such as the fixing height of kitchen units, the height of the basin, the height of the wc, the installation of track for electric hoist, the provision of remote control window or door openers and the fitting of an automatic garage door opener, can wait until later.

In theory it sounds attractive. In actuality there will be problems. The logistics, mechanics and financing of housebuilding make it advantageous if everything can be determined and detailed before work begins. It is expensive to make variations and if they involve unscheduled organization of building labour, particularly in the specialist trades, there can be big cost penalties. Another factor is that both local and central government like to know in advance exactly what any housing project will cost, so that the financial arrangements can be approved. While tight budgetary procedures may be appropriate in the context of large-scale public authority housing it is arguable that they should be so rigidly applied in respect of housing for disabled people.

The typical local housing authority has little experience of catering for disabled people; it is accustomed to producing standard housing articles for standard customers and there is the hazard that it treats housing for disabled people in the same fashion. There may be a tendency to attempt standard solutions where variety is more appropriate, and to standardize the incorporation of special provisions where there is a need for flexibility. What has commonly happened, in the past, in an effort to take account of all contingencies, has been comprehensive coverage, meaning for example the general prescription of extra-large garages, automatic garage door openers, special tap fittings and sanitary equipment, remote control window openers and kitchens organized for wheelchair housewives. The consequence has been that resources have not always been used either efficiently or economically.

With the publication in July 1975 of the Department of the Environment's Housing Development Directorate Occasional Paper *Wheelchair housing*[21] and the issuing in October 1975 of the accompanying Circular 92/75 *Wheelchair and Mobility housing: Standards and costs*[22] a new and more flexible procedure has been introduced. The arrangement is that provisions of a general housing character, or incorporated as general for disabled people as a group, are covered by the housing contract, and that bespoke provisions geared to the particular requirements of disabled tenants are introduced by means of variations to the contract. These provisions should be determined by the housing authority in cooperation with the social services authority; they may include items such as special kitchen equipment, special support rails to bath and wc, remote control window openers where needed, the provision of a shower and special fixtures such as a Clos o mat wc.

1714 Planning principles

Architectural tactics for wheelchair housing are discussed in some detail in section 83 of this book. At this point a short comment only is needed to help define the strategy. Basically, planning principles for wheelchair housing are the same as for ordinary housing. The aim, given that the budget determines approximately what can be achieved, should be to maximize usable living space and to minimize sterile circulation space. The limitation of circulation space is important for two reasons. First, space is expensive and it is a waste of resources if what is provided is functionally superfluous. Second, exaggerated circulation spaces will mean exaggerated heating costs, and in housing for people whose financial resources may be already inadequate the necessity for heating wasteful circulation spaces is an unwanted burden.

A planning tactic commonly used for wheelchair housing is a central hall giving access to peripheral rooms[23]. This may be appropriate in the case of units planned individually in places where building land is not scarce. But more often it is important for financial reasons that sites are used economically, indicating narrow frontage

dwelling units. A related factor is that where the aim is to integrate dwellings for disabled people with ordinary housing, it is advantageous if the overall development is compact. The possibilities of single storey patio units, of the kind shown in diagram 17.3, may be examined.

17.3 Patio housing for Southwark London Borough Council (1:200). Neylan and Ungless, architects.

By comparison with ordinary housing, generous spaces are needed in wheelchair housing to allow for comfortable manoeuvre. Because the extra space tends to be concentrated in specific areas common to all dwellings (such as the bathroom) the proportionate increase required to give equivalent convenience is higher for small units than it is for larger ones. In single person units the appropriate increase may be of the order of 20 per cent, in larger units 10 per cent may be sufficient. Areas which it is suggested architects should aim for are set out in table 81.3, with proposals for distribution by household size in table 81.1.

The amount of purpose-designed wheelchair housing which it is appropriate that local housing authorities should plan to provide in their areas depends on a variety of factors. One is the prevalence of severe disability in the area – in places where there is a high incidence of industrial injury there may be a higher than average need for wheelchair housing. Equally the age distribution of the local population has an effect, meaning for example that where there are large concentrations of old people there may be a bigger demand for special housing. An

[21] Bib 93120
[22] Bib 93121
[23] For examples of wheelchair housing units with comments on planning see Bib 93120.

important factor will be the amount of mobility housing available to the authority; as programmes in this sphere develop the need for special wheelchair housing may be alleviated. A further significant factor will be the policy of the local social services authority regarding adaptations to existing housing for handicapped people.

1715 Adaptations to existing housing

It is a sound principle that it is better, by carrying out adaptation work, to maintain disabled people in their existing homes rather than moving them into newly built wheelchair housing. The crucial benefits are social ones. The disabled person concerned may have developed over the years a network of local support. She (or he) may have neighbours and friends who have known her as one of themselves, who understand her difficulties, appreciate what kind of help she needs, and know when it is wanted. If she is housebound they may look in regularly to exchange local gossip, to check that she is coping and to undertake errands for her. They do not intrude, they know they will be welcome. Local tradespeople may put themselves out on her behalf, delivering goods if they know she cannot get out to do her own shopping.

If the disabled person moves to a new house she has to face the upheaval of leaving the home to which she is emotionally attached. She may lose the support of her friends and neighbours. On the new estate other newcomers may prefer to keep to themselves. They may hesitate to offer help to a neighbour who is handicapped because they suppose they might be thought interfering, or fear that if any aid is given more will be requested and they will find themselves exploited. For the disabled person in a new place there is the possibility of social isolation and loneliness, a loss of human support which no physical arrangements can compensate for.

While these hazards are real ones, it should be recognized that in practice they will not invariably occur. The survey made by the Department of the Environment of people living in purpose-designed wheelchair housing found that in general people were well satisfied with their new homes by comparison with their former dwellings, both on practical and social grounds[24].

In some circumstances adaptation may be out of the question, for example because the climbing of stairs is unavoidable, because structural alterations are technically impossible, because the area is being redeveloped, or because the accommodation is rented and the landlord is unhelpful. In such cases the only satisfactory solution is a move to more suitable housing.

1716 Measuring the need for adaptations

Social factors apart, the need for adaptations or rehousing is governed by two factors. The first is the physical character of the existing accommodation, the second the nature of the disability of the handicapped person. In the course of the Norwich study an attempt was made to measure the convenience of the homes in which people who used wheelchairs were living, in order to find out which kinds of people were most in need of rehousing or extensive adaptations. The measuring was done by identifying various components of the dwelling, such as approach, internal circulation, heating, kitchen arrangements, wc and bath facilities, each of which was given a weighting within which an inconvenience score was calculated. The score was related to the nature of the individual's disability; for example entrance steps rated a maximum on the inconvenience score for chairbound people, less for those able to cope with steps. The typical poorly equipped kitchen scored highly if the disabled person was a housewife in a wheelchair, and scored nil if the disabled person did not use the kitchen and had no wish to do so. An aggregate inconvenience score was then calculated; the theoretical maximum was 10.0 but ratings tended to cluster around the 4 mark.

Table 17.4 shows the mean ratings by some of the more significant variables of the dwellings and the disabled people living in them. The mean overall rating for dwelling convenience was 4.6, meaning that lower scores elsewhere on the diagram indicate a better-than-average condition, higher scores a poorer-than-average condition.

Women in the sample tended to be more inconvenienced than men by their housing arrangements, having an average rating of 4.8 compared with 4.2; the main reason for this was the difficulties caused by inadequate kitchens. Predictably therefore housewives (rating 5.1) were significantly more handicapped by their dwellings than non-housewives (4.4). In terms of tenure, local authority housing, because it was generally more recently built and better provided with standard amenities, was at 4.1 more convenient than owner-occupied accommodation, at 5.0 reflecting a predominance of sub-standard property, and very significantly better than privately rented accommodation at 5.8. Flats in multi-storey blocks having lift access were modern and well equipped, achieving the exceptionally good rating of 1.3. Bungalows (including prefabricated houses whose design was well suited to people in wheelchairs) were also very convenient at 2.4 whereas, not unexpectedly, two or three storey houses were generally not satisfactory at 5.2. Housing dating from before the first war was predictably very poor at 5.8, whereas housing built between the wars was rather better than average at 4.4. Post second war housing was relatively convenient at 3.6; that it did not score better was attributable to inadequate heating and poor kitchen and bathroom facilities in housing of pre Parker Morris vintage.

There was no clear association between the age of wheelchair users and the convenience of their houses. People in the youngest age range were least handicapped, because for example they tended not to be kitchen users and were not usually handicapped by wc, bath or internal circulation arrangements. Between middle-aged and older people there was nothing to choose; the problems which housewives had with poor kitchens were countered by the predominantly elderly accommodation in which old people were living. On mobility classification people who

[24] Bib 93120, paras 7.06–7.10

Table 17.4 Wheelchair population in Norwich: Dwelling convenience ratings

```
        0 . . . 1 . . . 2 . . . 3 . . . 4 . . . 5 . . . 6 . . .
```

sex	men **4.2**
	women **4.8**
housewives	non-housewives **4.4**
	housewives **5.1**
tenancy	local authority **4.1**
	owner-occupied **5.0**
	privately rented **5.8**
dwelling type	flat with lift **1.3**
	bungalow **2.4**
	2 or 3 storey house **5.2**
age of dwelling	post 1945 **3.6**
	1914–1945 **4.4**
	pre 1914 **5.8**
age of wheelchair person	0–19 **3.3**
	20–39 **4.4**
	40–59 **4.8**
	60–69 **4.6**
	70 + **4.7**
mobility	bedfast **3.7**
	ambulant **4.2**
	chair user/ambulant **5.3**
	chairbound **5.3**

were bedfast were least handicapped, it being a matter of little concern to them whether for example the kitchen or bathroom were well equipped. Ambulant disabled people were also relatively little handicapped by comparison with people who were chairbound or chair users. Size of household (a variable not recorded on the diagram) was not associated with dwelling convenience.

From these findings a composite picture of the kind of person most likely to need rehousing emerges. She is a housewife, chairbound, living in a pre first war privately rented house. By contrast the person least likely to need rehousing is a young man, ambulant, living in a local authority post-war flat with lift access.

1717 Adaptation requirements

'Work and housing of impaired persons in Great Britain' the second volume of the Office of Population Censuses and Surveys report *Handicapped and impaired in Great Britain* contains statistical data on the housing circumstances of impaired people. The information is difficult to interpret meaningfully or to relate to practical housing programmes; the following notes are a summary of the findings relevant to house adaptations.

Regarding the availability of basic household amenities the report found that handicapped people were in general slightly worse off than the population as a whole[25]. More people in the survey sample than in the 1966 national census were without a hot water tap (11.3 per cent against 10.3 per cent); more were without a fixed bath (14.9 per cent against 13.1 per cent) and more had an outside wc only (17.4 per cent against 15.0 per cent). About one in ten of all impaired people were not able to use all of the rooms in their house, the principal reason, mentioned by 93 per cent, being inability to climb stairs[26]. Among very severely handicapped people, 53 per cent were not able to use all the rooms in the house, and 20 per cent used the living room as a bedroom[27].

One in four of the people in the survey sample had had adaptations made to their homes. The most common was the replacement of coal fires by an easier form of heating, followed by the provision of handrails to staircases and the fitting of support rails to baths. Ramps had been made or pathways altered for one in five of wheelchair users[28]. Overall, the degree of handicap of impaired persons was not markedly associated with the carrying out of adaptations. The inference here is that as a rule it was the physical shortcomings of the dwelling rather than the degree of the disability of the individual which had caused adaptations to be undertaken.

When people in the sample were asked whether they would like adaptations made, or further ones carried out, one in five said that they would. Among people who were very severely handicapped the most frequent responses

[25] Bib 93211, table 70
[26] Bib 93211, p73
[27] Bib 93211, p74

were 'install or change position of wc' (29 per cent), 'install ramps or pathways' (21 per cent), 'handrails to bath' (16 per cent), 'install or change position of bathroom' (14 per cent), 'bannister rails' (12 per cent) and 'handrails to wc' (11 per cent)[29]. Of all impaired people, about one in four said they would like to move to a flat or bungalow which did not have stairs[30].

The report does not give any reliable indicators of the numbers or proportion of handicapped people needing special housing on account of disability. Crude measures were applied of need for rehousing, which is not the same as need for special housing, based on certain criteria. It was estimated that 18.6 per cent of all impaired people in Britain needed rehousing or substantial improvements to their homes because they had no inside wc, 4.9 per cent because the position of the wc was inconvenient, 4.5 per cent because some rooms were inaccessible and 3.1 per cent because they had to sleep in the living room[31].

1718 Local authority responsibilities for house adaptations

Under current legislation, detailed in sections 801–803, social services authorities have a responsibility for helping handicapped people whose homes need to be adapted. Section 2 of the Chronically Sick and Disabled Persons Act 1970 requires (to paraphrase) that where someone living in the area of the authority who is handicapped has a demonstrable need for adaptations which will make things easier for him to manage, the social services authority has a duty to assist him and see that the work is carried out. The authority can if it wishes ask the handicapped tenant (if he owns his house) or the landlord to contribute towards the expenditure; the way that this is done and the extent to which personal means-tests are applied vary among authorities.

In the case of local authority housing, housing authorities have concurrent powers with social services authorities to undertake adaptations. Section 3 of the Chronically Sick Act requires that housing authorities when carrying out their general duties under housing legislation (specifically section 91 of the Housing Act 1957) shall 'have regard to the special need of chronically sick or disabled persons'. Section 92 of the 1957 Act prescribes how housing authorities may provide accommodation; they may do it by building, acquisition, conversion or alteration, and they may also alter or improve any dwellings which they own.

Housing authorities do not have powers under the Chronically Sick Act to adapt owner-occupied or privately rented accommodation. Under section 56 of the Housing Act 1974 improvement grant legislation (which is administered by housing authorities) can however be employed to adapt housing for disabled people; this

legislation is detailed in 8017–8 and its administration is discussed in 864.

In respect of private sector housing it is in the interests of social services authorities to divert executive responsibility for house adaptations from their own budgets to housing authorities to deal with under improvement grant legislation. In the case of London borough councils and metropolitan district councils this can be arranged internally. In view of this involvement of housing authorities in private sector adaptation work it would seem sensible if under new legislation housing authorities were to take over from social services authorities the primary responsibility for house adaptations for disabled people throughout the private sector. This course would appear to have advantages, for example in terms of concentrating housing functions on the housing authority, resolving the confused position regarding adaptations to local authority housing, aiding the work of housing associations and enabling housing programmes for disabled people to be planned on a coherent comprehensive basis. This matter is currently under consideration by the Department of the Environment and the Department of Health and Social Security, and a consultative document was issued for comment in February 1976.

If new legislation were to be enacted transferring responsibility for house adaptations to housing authorities it would not at the same time be necessary to amend social services legislation. Social services authorities would continue, along with their other duties, to provide aids for handicapped people; there is no simple demarcation line between aids on the one hand and adaptations on the other, and it would in any event be administratively unwise to attempt to set down rigid rules. The suggestion is that broadly, work involving alterations to the structure of houses should be carried out by the housing authority, and work not affecting the structure by the social services authority.

If housing authorities are to take on responsibility for adaptation work as well as new construction they will need, if disabled people are to be capably served, to rely extensively on guidance from their local social services authority. In this connection the role of occupational therapists is crucial. In social services authorities it is becoming general for domiciliary occupational therapists to work alongside teams of social workers and advise about aids, equipment and related house adaptation work. Administratively it will be advantageous for area offices of social services authorities to have territories corresponding to those of housing authorities, for there to be an occupational therapist in each area, and for the occupational therapist to be kept in touch through contact with social workers with the needs of handicapped people in the area. The therapist can then arrange to visit clients where adaptations are wanted, and advise the technical department of the housing authority about the work that needs to be done. Ideally in each housing authority there should be an architect who has special responsibility for house adaptation work for disabled people, and who will have a close working relationship with the area occupational therapist.

[28] Bib 93211, p88
[29] Bib 93211, p99
[30] Bib 93211, p109
[31] Bib 93211, p123

While it might be argued that special provisions in new housing for disabled people should be treated as adaptations and paid for by social services authorities, it is an established practice that the entire cost of new construction is met by housing authorities. As a rule any special provisions incorporated are admissible for subsidy under the Housing Rents and Subsidies Act 1975; administrative arrangements are discussed in 8613.

1719 House adaptation for renal dialysis patients

The position of the patient dependent on home dialysing to keep his kidneys working, and who has to have a room in his house adapted for the necessary equipment, is in an important way different from the disabled person requiring house adaptations. The kidney patient is receiving a medical rather than a housing or social service, and administrative responsibility is therefore with the patient's health authority rather than his social services authority.

Among medical consultants home dialysis is favoured rather than hospital dialysis because it minimizes the hazards of hepatitis infection and helps reduce the hospital work load. The installation of a home dialysis unit means in effect that the hospital ward is transferred to the patient's home, with the patient looking after his own treatment. The room which is adapted is suitable only for dialysing and must not be used for any other purpose. Its provision does not enhance the functional or social value of the home as a place for living.

According to figures issued by the Department of Health in June 1973 there were 964 patients on home dialysis in England and Wales. The numbers are currently (1976) increasing at the rate of about 200 each year but it is expected that this increase will level out and the numbers stabilize in about ten years time at about 3000, depending on the number of successful transplants achieved[32]. Given a population of 3000 spread over 401 housing authorities the mean will be seven or eight each, although large authorities may expect to have some 20 or 30 patients in their areas. Logistically therefore, and bearing in mind the ad hoc fashion in which the service has to be provided, it is arguable that there is a case for housing authorities to include in their building programme dwelling units purpose-designed for dialysis patients. It is however relevant that the kind of wheelchair housing discussed earlier, whereby a two storey family unit has an extra bedroom at ground level, is ideally suited for home dialysis purposes. Where these units are planned it could be advantageous to take account of their potential dual role, perhaps building in the necessary infrastructure of services for a dialysis unit.

1720 Conclusion

It is fitting that this commentary, which has ranged across the entire arena of the built environment of disabled people, happens to close with a note on home dialysis units. They are for people who in conventional terms do not qualify for the description 'disabled', but who, because of their total dependence on their dialysis machine, may be as severely constrained as any of the overtly disabled people on whom this book is focused. Although their need for special building provision is determined by medical rather than physically handicapping factors the goals are identical. If the purpose of living is to make the most of being alive, and the purpose of buildings is to help people to get the most out of life, then home dialysis units epitomize what buildings are for. Buildings can be instruments by which we put apart people with disabilities, ostracizing them from a world they want to know but which too often does not want to know them. On the other hand they can be instruments of involvement and participation, of communication and understanding, of mutual support and mutual regard; instruments which illuminate, both for the people whom they serve who are disabled and for those alongside them who are not, the essence of humanity.

[32] Information supplied by DHSS

Ancillary data

2

20 Anthropometrics

200 Anthropometrics: General considerations

2000 The formulation of design criteria for buildings depends to a considerable extent on the dimensional characteristics of people at rest and moving, and on their range of physical capabilities in terms of strength and flexibility. In the case of disabled people these criteria may be modified by the use of aids such as sticks, artificial limbs and wheelchairs.

2001 No special anthropometric study has been made for the purposes of this book. Data on the general population have been derived principally from the comprehensive study made by Dreyfuss[1], and for elderly people from the more limited study made by Roberts[2]. Data on chairbound people are drawn from the study made by W F Floyd and others[3] supplemented by sources discussed in 202. The Department of Health's Health Service Design Note 3[4] has provided supporting evidence.

Women, old people
2002 Housing criteria are generally based on the physical characteristics of women rather than men. There are three principal reasons for this:

1. The physical performance of women, particularly in respect of reaching ability, is more constraining than that of men.
2. Many recommendations concern domestic activities customarily performed by a housewife.
3. Among elderly people, where disability is most prevalent, there is a preponderance of women.

2003 Distinctions are frequently made between requirements for elderly people and requirements for the general population. The differences are significant because among elderly people there is a greater incidence of disabling conditions which restrict the range of joint movement, and also because normal physical changes occur which affect agility, posture, stance and reach.

Ambulant disabled people
2004 As a group, ambulant disabled people are not, in anthropometric terms, distinguishable from able-bodied people. The recommendations relating to ambulant disabled people have therefore been derived in the main from studies made by Dreyfuss and Roberts, with in some cases adjustments to cater for people outside normal statistical limits. In practice many ambulant disabled people have severe limitations, particularly in respect of reaching ability, and design recommendations based on normal parameters must therefore be treated with caution.

[1] Bib 93760
[2] Bib 93691
[3] Bib 93500
[4] Bib 93761

Uses of data
2005 The wide application of anthropometric data is indicated in the measurement data forms in section 21. These forms are for use when the architect is designing for a specific disabled person whose physical characteristics can be individually measured. The application of data for general purposes is discussed in the commentary (1111–1117) with particular reference to the contrasts between ambulant disabled people and wheelchair users.

201 Statistical principles of anthropometrics

2010 It is hazardous to make design decisions on the basis of catering for the average man or woman. In a representative sample of a population, 50 per cent of measures will be greater than the average and 50 per cent will be less. Dimensions based on the average will therefore at best satisfy only 50 per cent of potential users.

Percentiles
2011 To determine appropriate limits for the range of the population to be accommodated, the statistical technique of percentile distribution is used. The expressing of population parameters in terms of percentiles is illustrated by the example of head height for ambulant men (diagram 20.1). The value of 1·650 for the 5th percentile means that 5 per cent of ambulant men are 1·650 high, or shorter. The value of 1·860 for the 95th percentile means that 95 per cent are 1·860 high, or shorter.

2012 Among anthropometric measures, height is often the controlling variable and has special significance. But other measures such as shoulder width and length of limbs have their own percentile ranges, and may have a significant application depending on the design situation.

2013 In the graph of percentile distribution where the population follows the pattern of a normal distribution, ie where there is an equal number of people either side of the mean and fewer towards the extremes, values rise steeply over the first 5 per cent, there is then a flatter gradient from 5 to 95 per cent, following which there is a steeper rise from 95 to 100 per cent (diagram 20.1).

2014 The pattern of the percentile curve means that it is generally reasonable to design for the 90 per cent of the population between the 5th and the 95th percentile; the 5 per cent at each of the extremities are disregarded because to include them would extend disproportionately the range of dimensions having to be considered. In practice, parameters are usually critical in one direction only. As an example, the observance of the 5th percentile value for the placing of window controls will ensure that 95 per cent of the population, rather than 90 per cent, are accommodated.

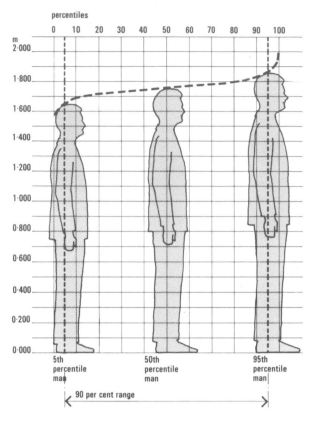

20.1 Graph of percentile distribution

Clothing

2015 Dimensional values in diagrams 20.2–20.12 take account of the wearing of clothing and shoes. In special situations where shoes or clothing are not worn, minor adjustments may be appropriate, but these are not likely to be of significance. Sources of the data are studies made in Britain and the United States; for communities where human body characteristics vary significantly from those of western countries adjustments may also have to be made.

202   Anthropometric studies of wheelchair users

2020 Dimensional recommendations for wheelchair users throughout this book are based largely on a study of paraplegics made by Floyd and others in 1964[5]. In respect of many applications the Floyd data must be treated with caution, for reasons discussed below.

Lack of reliable data

2021 No authoritative anthropometric study of the total wheelchair population has yet been made, and none has been attempted. One cause is the heterogeneity of the population, making it very difficult to determine realistic operational parameters of the population to be measured. First, it is inappropriate to include all people who have wheelchairs, since many do not regularly use them. Second, of those who do, many can stand for most functional activities and it would be difficult to define in operational terms which wheelchair users are properly describable as chairbound, and which not. Third, the characteristics of the wheelchair population vary much more markedly than do those of the normal able-bodied population in respect of the usage of different buildings and facilities; there could therefore be no confidence that a sample representative of the population in one set of circumstances would be equally representative in others.

2022 The impossibility of obtaining reliable anthropometric information on wheelchair users is admitted from the start. The alternative is to use such information as is available, which, though it is unreliable, may in some circumstances have validity. Apart from Floyd's study two other studies are noted here: neither of these was a sample selected by scientifically reliable means.

Paraplegic populations

2023 In the case of Floyd's study the sample was of paraplegics who happened to be available in the course of a study made at Stoke Mandeville hospital in 1965. Stoke Mandeville is a special hospital, treating patients having a particular type of injury; it would be unwise to claim that these patients are representative of any wider population, not even of a general population of paraplegics. Of the 127 subjects who took part in the Floyd study, only 38 could be regarded as possibly representative of paraplegics in typical external environmental conditions, these being people who were ex-patients and were returning to the hospital for check-ups. Of the other 89, 53 were patients whose rehabilitation was not completed and 36 were sports participants at the Stoke Mandeville Games[6].

2024 Apart from the bias of including a large proportion of athletic paraplegics, the sample was biased in that it had a 5:2 ratio of men to women compared with a ratio of nearly 1:2 in the general population. It also consisted predominantly of young people; people aged 45 or less accounted for 85 per cent of the sample, compared with less than 30 per cent in the general population[7].

2025 Paraplegics are people who generally have good upper limbs, corresponding to the stereotype of the wheelchair user who can use buildings independently. In Floyd's study reach measures for the 23 tetraplegics in the sample, ie those with poor upper limbs, were not recorded[8].

[5] Bib 93500. Data from the same study are documented by Noble, Bib 93502.
[6] Bib 93502, p100
[7] Bib 93502, p102. For related data on the general wheelchair population see table 22.3.
[8] Bib 93502, p101

Table 20.1 Anthropometric data from surveys of chairbound people

		Floyd: paraplegics			Knight: multiple sclerotics			Knight: rheumatoid arthritics		
		5th %ile	mean	95th %ile	5th %ile	mean	95th %ile	5th %ile	mean	95th %ile
head height	men	1·247	1·331	1·415	1·153	1·245	1·337	*	1·257	*
	women	1·192	1·280	1·368	1·085	1·189	1·293	1·156	1·214	1·272
shoulder height	men	0·973	1·036	1·099	0·880	0·947	1·014	*	0·970	*
	women	0·923	0·998	1·073	0·837	0·925	1·013	0·883	0·925	0·967
elbow level	men	0·630	0·693	0·756	0·579	0·650	0·721	*	0·678	*
	women	0·590	0·678	0·766	0·557	0·645	0·733	0·606	0·660	0·714
comfortable vertical reach	men	1·569	1·661	1·753	1·425	1·521	1·617	*	1·509	*
	women	1·479	1·588	1·697	1·312	1·458	1·604	1·344	1·478	1·612
mean age	men		34·7 years			51·9 years			50·1 years	
	women		32·1 years			49·4 years			52·0 years	

* For male rheumatoid arthritics in Knight's sample numbers were too small for percentile values to be reliable.

Multiple sclerotics and rheumatoid arthritics

2026 Apart from Floyd's study, two small-scale studies, one of multiple sclerotics and one of rheumatoid arthritics, were made by K L Knight and published in 1965[9]. For comparison with Floyd's data Knight's findings are noted in table 20.1. There is a closer correspondence between the multiple sclerotics and the rheumatoid arthritics than there is between either the multiple sclerotics and the paraplegics or the rheumatoid arthritics and the paraplegics. The generally diminished values found among the multiple sclerotics and rheumatoid arthritics are perhaps attributable to a higher incidence of general bodily impairment, and also to the greater incidence of old people; in both these respects people with multiple sclerosis and rheumatoid arthritis are more typical of the general wheelchair population than are paraplegics.

203 Wheelchair users: Application of anthropometric data

2030 Despite the objections already discussed, Floyd's findings are incorporated in diagrams 20.7–20.10 and are the basis for recommendations in this book. On scientific grounds they should be rejected, but they are the only usable data; Knight's figures are too limited to be admissible. The alternative, which was the procedure used in the first and second editions of this book, is to calculate the theoretical body and reach dimensions of wheelchair users on the evidence of measures of normal ambulant people as they might be if seated in wheelchairs. On balance it is more reasonable to apply actual recorded data rather than theoretical data. In a number of instances the values given in diagrams 20.7–20.10 are estimated; these are measures which were not recorded by Floyd.

2031 The second point in favour of using Floyd's data is that paraplegics are a relatively homogeneous group for whom it is meaningful to apply conventional anthropometric principles of percentile ranges.

An unresolvable problem

2032 Any attempt to apply anthropometric principles for the general chairbound population, assuming it could be isolated, would be unmanageable in practice. A high proportion of the population would be found to have severe arm limitations, meaning that functional parameters based on a 90 per cent range would be intolerably constraining in terms of architectural design. The assumed use of flexible fittings would not resolve the problem; nowhere approaching 90 per cent of chairbound people have the potential to operate independently, irrespective of the environment in which they are placed.

2033 Inevitably there has to be compromise, for example that the coverage is limited to people who have the potential to function successfully in a sympathetically planned environment. In this connection, reliance on data from a paraplegic population does have some justification, particularly where arrangements are made specifically for independent wheelchair users.

2034 Owing to the difficulties of defining a wheelchair population for anthropometric study, of obtaining a passably representative sample and of assembling subjects so that body and reach characteristics can be adequately recorded, there is little likelihood that the data reported here will be superseded by any other having more validity.

[9] Bib 93505

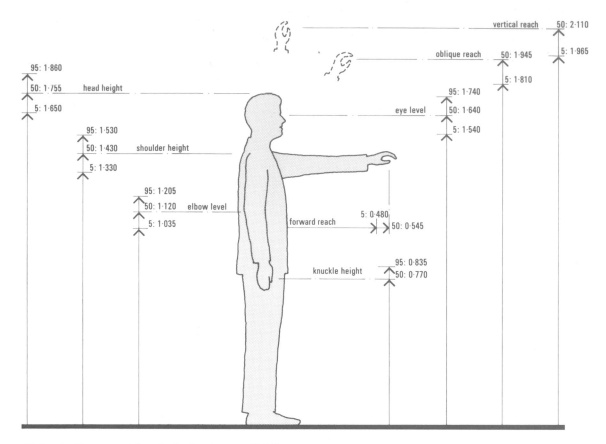

95: 1·860
50: 1·755 head height
5: 1·650

95: 1·530
50: 1·430 shoulder height
5: 1·330

95: 1·205
50: 1·120 elbow level
5: 1·035

forward reach

knuckle height

vertical reach 50: 2·110
5: 1·965

oblique reach 50: 1·945
5: 1·810

95: 1·740
eye level 50: 1·640
5: 1·540

5: 0·480
50: 0·545

95: 0·835
50: 0·770

20.2 Anthropometrics: Ambulant men   (1:20)

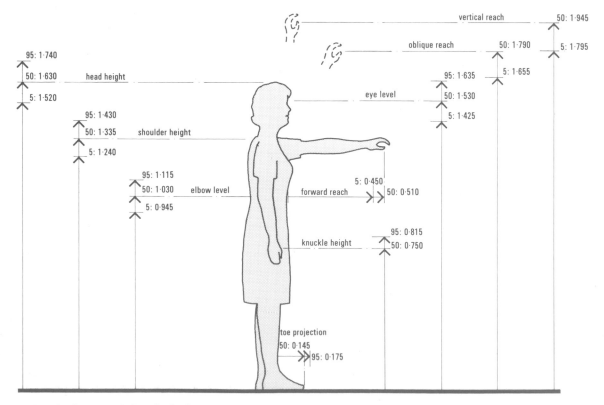

95: 1·740
50: 1·630 head height
5: 1·520

95: 1·430
50: 1·335 shoulder height
5: 1·240

95: 1·115
50: 1·030 elbow level
5: 0·945

forward reach

knuckle height

toe projection
50: 0·145
95: 0·175

vertical reach 50: 1·945
5: 1·795

oblique reach 50: 1·790
5: 1·655

95: 1·635
eye level 50: 1·530
5: 1·425

5: 0·450
50: 0·510

95: 0·815
50: 0·750

20.3 Anthropometrics: Ambulant women aged 18–60   (1:20)

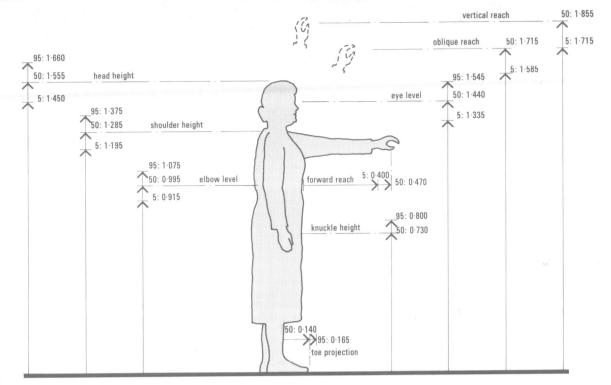

20.4 Anthropometrics: Ambulant women aged 60+ (1:20)

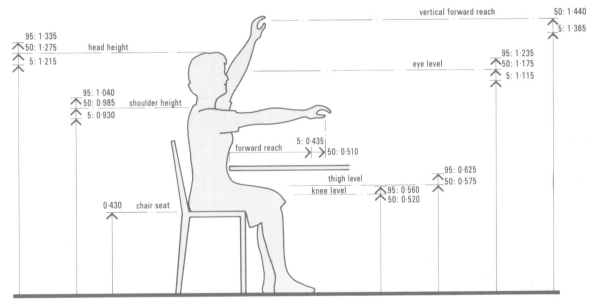

20.5 Anthropometrics: Seated women aged 18–60 (1:20)

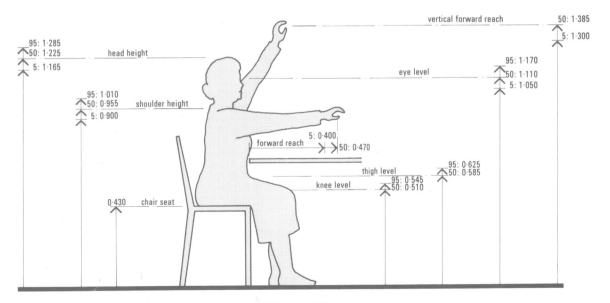

20.6 Anthropometrics: Seated women aged 60+ (1:20)

204 Reach dimensions of chairbound people

2040 The reach dimensions given in diagram 20.7–20.10 are of comfortable reaches of wheelchair users in static body positions. Owing to the flexibility of the human body, with joints permitting a great range of movements, the effective or maximum range of reach is substantially greater than the comfortable reach.

2041 The area which can be covered with a sweep of the forearm is the comfortable reach, and materials or equipment to be handled on a workspace ought desirably to be inside it. For handicapped people, storage accommodation ought also to be within comfortable reach, but this ideal is not as a rule attainable. For related discussion see 5131.

Forward, downwards and upwards reach

2042 For chairbound people reaching forward, as for example over a worktop, the range of comfortable reach is only approximately as far as the line of the wheelchair footrest (diagrams 20.7, 20.9). To reach articles outside this range the chairbound person has to utilize his effective range of reach by leaning forward with his trunk flexed from the hips. In Floyd's sample of paraplegics the mean maximum forward reach at a level 1·070 above floor for males was 0·340 more than the comfortable reach, and for females 0·265 more.

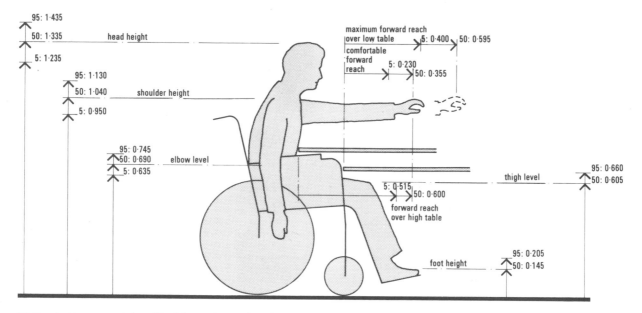

20.7 Anthropometrics: Chairbound men (1:20)

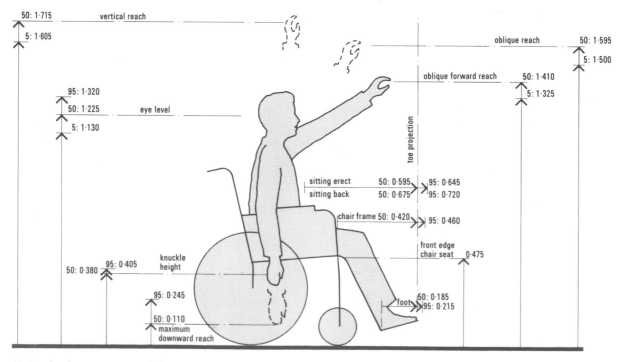

20.8 Anthropometrics: Chairbound men (1:20)

2043 For downwards reach the mean comfortable dimension approximates, as shown in diagrams 20.8 and 20.10, to knuckle height. With the body flexed to extend the area within reach, the increases for the mean maximum dimension found in Floyd's study were 0·310 for males and 0·270 for females.

2044 For upwards reach the increase of maximum over comfortable reach is proportionately less, since gains are obtainable by arm and shoulder movements only, and not by trunk movements. In Floyd's study the mean maximum vertical reach of males was 0·075 greater than the mean comfortable reach, and for females 0·060 greater.

Application of reach dimensions

2045 In housing for chairbound people, controls for fixtures such as light switches, socket outlets, heaters, meters and window openers should be within the comfortable reach of a person seated in a wheelchair. Exceptions may be made in family housing where there will generally be someone other than the wheelchair user available to manipulate controls, for example in respect of some window openers. In public buildings, controls which may need to be operated by chairbound people should be within the effective reach of a person seated in a wheelchair.

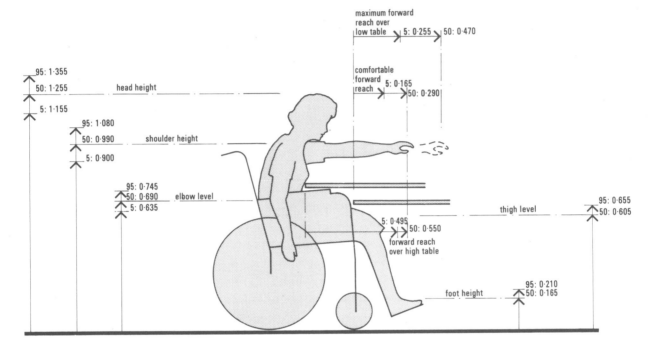

20.9 Anthropometrics: Chairbound women (1:20)

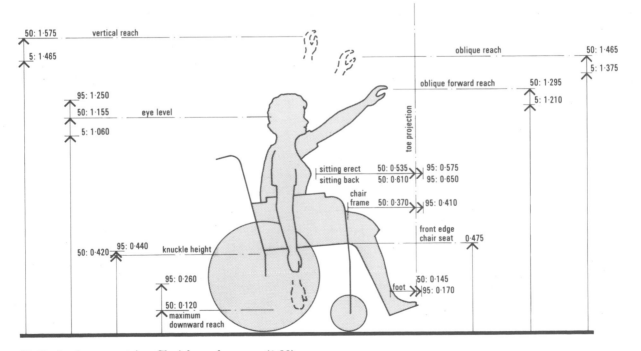

20.10 Anthropometrics: Chairbound women (1:20)

Lift controls

2046 It is not always essential, for reasons discussed in 1115, that lift controls in public buildings are within the comfortable reach of chairbound people. The suggested maximum height is 1·600 above floor level (45311); for further discussion see 6170.

2047 Analysis of the data for paraplegics in Floyd's study indicates that among chairbound people who have little or no upper limb impairment, about 95 per cent of men and 55 per cent of women are able to reach a lift control at 1·600 above floor level, provided it is immediately to the side of the chair. With a wheelchair placed so that a 45° oblique reach is necessary about 80 per cent of men and 71 per cent of women without upper limb impairments can reach a lift control at 1·600 above floor level. From a similar position with the side of the chair about 0·200 away from the wall, some 95 per cent of paraplegic men can reach a lift control not higher than about 1·550 above floor level, and 95 per cent of women can reach a lift control not higher than about 1·420 above floor level.

Height of chair seat

2048 The area within comfortable reach is affected by the height of the chair seat. Data given above and elsewhere in this book generally assume the use of a standard wheelchair as described in 2301, with a mean seat height of 0·475 above floor level.

205 Handicapped children

2050 The dimensions for children in wheelchairs given in diagrams 20.11 and 20.12 are estimated mean measures for boys and girls aged four, eight and twelve. They are derived from data given by Dreyfuss (Bib 93760); in that the figures represent non-disabled children seated in chairs, the same reservations need to be made as for adult wheelchair users. In practice, the variability of physical characteristics among handicapped children using wheelchairs is at least as substantial as among adults in wheelchairs; in consequence the data must be treated with caution.

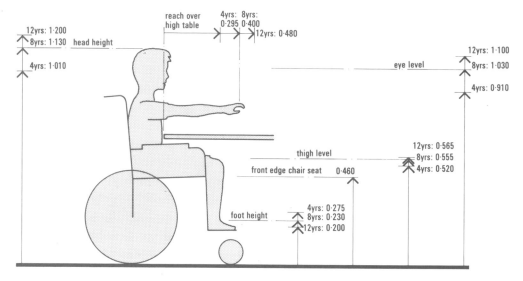

20.11 Anthropometrics: Chairbound boys aged 4, 8 and 12 (1:20)

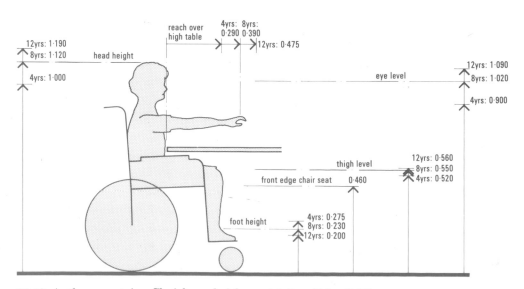

20.12 Anthropometrics: Chairbound girls aged 4, 8 and 12 (1:20)

This section has been prepared to assist the architect when planning facilities for a specific disabled person. The convenient positioning of fittings and equipment is governed by body and reach dimensions; while it may not be essential, for example in a family home, that the advice given here is followed rigorously, the general application of the recommendations should ensure that fittings and equipment are suitably located.

210 Ambulant people

Measurements of standing person (diagram 21.1a)

A Comfortable vertical reach
A *minus* 0·070: maximum height of storage shelves, allowing access to front of shelf.
A *minus* 0·150: maximum height of 0·300 deep storage shelves over 0·600 floor units, allowing access to front of shelf.

B Oblique vertical reach
B: maximum height of window and blind controls.
B *minus* 0·060: maximum height of 0·200 deep storage shelves over 0·600 floor units, allowing access to front of shelf.
B *minus* 0·080: maximum height of unobstructed storage shelves, allowing reach to back of shelf.

C Head height
C: relate to fixed mirror heights and position of shower fittings.

D Eye level
D: avoid window transomes at this level.
D: relate to fixed mirror heights (see diagrams 54.39, 54.40).

E Shoulder level
E: preferred maximum height of switches and controls.

F Elbow level
F *minus* 0·130: preferred level of kitchen surfaces where sink rim and general work surfaces are at the same height. (For discussion on conflicting criteria for work surfaces see 51102.)
F *minus* 0·100: preferred level of sink rim.
F *minus* 0·150: preferred level of general work surfaces.
F *minus* 0·100: preferred level of wash basin rim.
F *minus* 0·250: preferred level of fixed ironing board.

G Knuckle height (comfortable downward reach)
G: lower level of preferred zone for most-used articles stored in kitchens.
G: preferred minimum height of socket outlets and other controls.
G: preferred height of letter basket and delivery shelves adjacent to entrance door.

H Effective downward reach
H: minimum height of storage shelves, socket outlets, heater controls, and oven floor.

J Comfortable forward reach
J *plus* 0·100: maximum depth of kitchen work surfaces.
J: preferred maximum dimension, sink fascia to sink taps.

K Toe projection
K: preferred minimum depth, toe recesses to kitchen units.

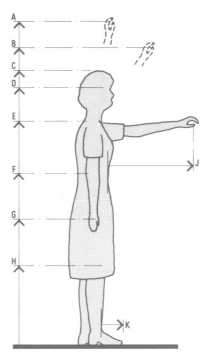

21.1a   Measurement data: Standing person.

Measurements of seated person (diagram 21.1b)

L Comfortable forward vertical reach
L *plus* seat dimension: maximum height of shelves to be reached from seated position.

M Head height
M: relate to height of shower fittings.

N Eye level
N *plus* seat dimension: avoid window transomes at this level: relate to sill heights.

O Thigh level
O: minimum unobstructed height at face of knee recesses to tables, desks, kitchen sink etc.

P Knee level
P: preferred minimum unobstructed height at rear of knee recesses.

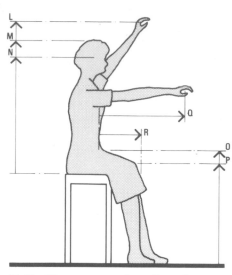

21.1b Measurement data: Seated person.

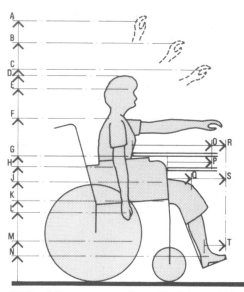

22.2 Measurement data: Chairbound person.

Q Forward reach
Q: comfortable reach over table tops etc.

R Knee projection
R: minimum depth knee recesses.

211 Wheelchair users

Measurements of chairbound person (diagram 21.2)

A Comfortable vertical reach
A *minus* 0·070: maximum height of unobstructed storage shelves with lateral approach, reach to front of shelf.

B Oblique vertical reach
B: maximum height of window and blind controls.
B *minus* 0·120: maximum height of 0·300 deep storage shelves over 0·600 floor units, allowing reach to front of shelf.
B *minus* 0·160: maximum height of unobstructed storage shelves with frontal approach, allowing reach to back of shelves.

C Comfortable forward vertical reach
C: preferred maximum height of window and other controls.
C: maximum height of electric switches.

D Head height
D: relate to height of shower fittings.

E Eye level
E: avoid window transomes at this level; relate to sill heights.
E: relate to fixed mirror heights.

F Shoulder level
F *plus* 0·100: upper level of preferred zone for most-used articles stored in kitchen.
F: preferred maximum height of electric switches.

G Chair armrest level
G: minimum unobstructed dimension below work surfaces or tables to permit close approach.

H Elbow level
H *plus* 0·020: preferred height of letter basket and delivery shelves adjacent to entrance door.
H *minus* 0·030: preferred height of pull-out for food preparation.
H *minus* 0·040: preferred height of fixed ironing board.

J Thigh level
J: minimum unobstructed vertical dimension for knee recesses to tables, desks, kitchen sink, preparation centre and wash hand basin.
J *plus* 0·160: preferred height of kitchen work surfaces at consistent level, assuming 0·150 deep sink bowl.

K Chair seat level, centre front edge (with cushion if used)
K: preferred level of wc seat, platform at head end of bath and shower seat.

L Knuckle height
L *plus* 0·100: minimum height of heater controls.
L *plus* 0·050 lower level of preferred zone for most-used articles stored in kitchen.
L: minimum level of oven floor.

M Comfortable downward reach
M: minimum height of storage shelves.

N Foot height
N: minimum height of toe recesses to kitchen units.

O Effective forward reach
O: maximum depth of kitchen work surfaces.

P Forward reach beyond face of chair arm
P: comfortable reach over low level tables etc.
P: preferred maximum dimension, sink fascia to
sink taps.

Q Knee projection beyond face of chair arm
Q: minimum dimension sink fascia to waste pipe,
and wash basin fascia to waste pipe.

R Toe projection from front of waist
R: preferred minimum depth of tables and knee
recesses to permit close approach.

S Toe projection beyond face of chair arm
S: minimum depth of knee recesses to kitchen sink,
preparation centre, wash basins etc.

T Toe projection at lower leg level
T: minimum depth of toe recesses to kitchen units.

220 The size of the wheelchair population

2200 It is not easy to estimate reliably the size of the wheelchair population in Britain. The national survey *Handicapped and impaired in Great Britain* indicated that in early 1969 the number of people in Britain having wheelchairs was of the order of 128 000, representing about one person in 400 of the total population[1].

2201 Data regarding Department of Health wheelchair issues, in conjunction with information from sources discussed below, suggests that the current (1976) figure is much higher. At the end of 1975 the total number of nonpowered and powered wheelchairs on issue from DHSS in England was 182 000 (table 22.1)[2]. Taking into account that a proportion of these wheelchairs (between 15 and 20 per cent) are issued to people who have more than one chair, and adding also the people who have wheelchairs which they have obtained privately without having a DHSS wheelchair, the number of people in England with wheelchairs is probably (mid-1976) about 185 000. This means that about 1 in 250 of the total population has a wheelchair.

2202 The most authoritative source for data on the wheelchair population in England and Wales is the report of the survey made in 1973–4 by the Social Survey Division of the Office of Population Censuses and Surveys on behalf of the Department of Health and Social Security. It is to be published in 1976 or 1977 under the title *Wheelchairs and their users*. Selected findings have generously been made available by the Department of Health for the purposes of preparing this book.

Table 22.1 Wheelchairs supplied by DHSS 1968–1975, England

	Non-powered wheelchairs		Powered indoor wheelchairs	
	supplied during year	total on issue at 31 December	supplied during year	total on issue at 31 December
1968	36 040	101 064	498	1162
1969	36 809	106 534	605	1510
1970	37 225	112 734	631	1770
1971	39 239	120 354	975	2200
1972	40 774	134 463	1019	2853
1973	45 449	152 911	1390	3657
1974	46 703	168 819	1659	4546
1975	56 858	182 000	1744	5274

Source: DHSS annual reports and data supplied by DHSS

221 DHSS wheelchair issues

2210 In Britain, wheelchairs are available free of charge on National Health Service recommendation to people who in the opinion of their hospital specialist or general practitioner are in need of one because of some permanent disability which affects their ability to walk. The advice given to doctors regarding the supply of wheelchairs says:

'A wheelchair or spinal carriage may be provided for a patient if the doctor considers one necessary and the need permanent. An indoor and/or transit chair can, where necessary, be supplied as well as a powered vehicle or hand propelled tricycle. When the use of a transit chair will not meet a patient's needs at work a second chair may be supplied.'[3].

2211 Regarding the supply of electric wheelchairs the advice is:

'Electrically propelled indoor chairs may be provided for patients who are not only unable to walk but who are also unable to propel themselves in a wheelchair if, but only if, this will help them to achieve some measure of independence in the home.'[4]

2212 Statistics of the number of wheelchairs on issue are published annually by DHSS. The latest available figures, relating to England only, are given in table 22.1. A breakdown by the types of wheelchair on issue in 1975 is given in table 23.1.

222 Privately obtained wheelchairs

2220 People with private wheelchairs are those who buy one themselves, who obtained one from a friend or relative or who have one on loan from an agency such as the Red Cross. No reliable estimate is possible of privately owned wheelchairs, principally because no records are available of people who simply go out and buy one, and nor can there be any practicable means of identifying those who do. Even if figures were available it would still not be known how many were obtained by people who already had a DHSS wheelchair, and nor can it be known how often a DHSS chair is issued to

[1] Bib 93210, p26
[2] Data in table 22.1 on the number of non-powered wheelchairs on issue at 31 December for the years 1968–74 are inaccurate. DHSS report that from a 1967 base the record was updated each year by adding the difference between new issues and withdrawals; this gave a 1975 figure of 192 147. In practice, withdrawal information was unreliable and a special check showed that at 31 December 1975 the actual number on issue was about 182 000.
[3] Bib 93511, para 3
[4] Bib 93511, para 13

someone who already has a private wheelchair[5]. In the course of the inquiry among wheelchair users in Norwich an attempt was made to locate as many people with privately owned wheelchairs as possible, and 45 were discovered who did not also have a DHSS wheelchair. These 45 represented 16 per cent of wheelchair users found in the city.

2221   It appears that there are important differences between the two sub-groups of the wheelchair population, ie between DHSS and non-DHSS wheelchair users. Virtually all people who have at any time been under the case of a medical specialist either inside or outside a hospital will, if the specialist considered it necessary, have been prescribed a DHSS wheelchair. The consequence is that the DHSS lists contain virtually all severely disabled and all young disabled people. As a corollary, people who have only private wheelchairs tend to be elderly; of the 45 people concerned in Norwich only two were aged below 50.

223   Sources of information

2230   The general findings of the OPCS report *Handicapped and impaired in Great Britain* are discussed in the commentary (1209). In respect of wheelchair users the report is not very helpful. From the 250 000 households who were approached by post late in 1968 and early in 1969 there were found to be 535 people with wheelchairs. No special analysis of these wheelchair users was made in respect of age, sex or cause of disability.

2231   The 1973 OPCS survey was of a random sample of 978 wheelchair users aged 18 or over, drawn from the records of eight representative DHSS appliance centres in England and Wales. Interviewing was carried out towards the end of 1973.

2232   The survey of wheelchair users in Norwich, made between 1964 and 1968, covered 284 people; its findings in relation to the use of buildings by disabled people are discussed in the commentary, principally in section 12, and elsewhere in this book. The survey in Leicestershire was made by Elizabeth Platts between 1966 and 1968; by means of a postal questionnaire and interview questionnaire it covered 448 wheelchair users, drawn from the records of the Ministry of Health and of Leicestershire county welfare department[6].

2233   In 1961 the then Ministry of Health made a desk analysis of a sample of 2000 records of people issued with wheelchairs. The findings are now outdated as a reliable basis for action, but are recorded in tables 22.2 and 22.3 for purposes of comparison with data from the Norwich, Leicestershire and OPCS surveys. The proviso is made that the MoH sample was not strictly comparable, in that it excluded people with wheelchairs who were in addition issued with MoH cars or invalid tricycles.

2234   Local surveys of wheelchair users were made in 1966 in Taunton and Hull[7]. The number of people surveyed (49 and 71) was too small for valid comparison with the other inquiries; data in respect of employment are reported in 1223.

224   Causes of disablement

2240   Table 22.2 lists the principal causes of disablement among wheelchair users in the OPCS, Norwich and Leicestershire surveys, and in the 1961 MoH analysis.

Diagnostic classifications
2241   This table needs to be interpreted with caution. Its classifications follow the pattern employed by the Department of Health to categorize people with physical handicaps. The principal shortcoming is that some of the classifications, for example amputations and paraplegia, describe the consequences and not the primary cause of disablement. It would have been more consistent to classify amputees under (for example) arteriosclerosis, trauma or diabetic gangrene, and paraplegics under spinal lesions, tumours, other diseases, effects of operations and so on. A further shortcoming is the unreliability of diagnostic evidence given at interviews by people with wheelchairs.

2242   In respect of the percentage figures detailed in table 22.2, the proviso is made that the classifications used for the four inquiries were not identical, and in the case of the 1973 OPCS survey were not always mutually exclusive. On the basis of the more detailed information given in the reports of the inquiries, percentage figures for certain diagnostic subgroups have been reallocated to achieve comparability.

Variations among wheelchair populations
2243   The figures in table 22.2 indicate a general consistency among the populations surveyed. Some of the more marked variations are not easily explained, for example the low proportion of hemiplegics in Leicestershire, and the higher proportions of amputees in both Norwich and Leicestershire compared with the national samples. The high figure for people with polio in Leicestershire is presumably the consequence of an epidemic in the county.

---

[5] In this connection, the 1973 OPCS survey found that among the NHS wheelchair population, 4 per cent of chairs being used had been obtained privately.
[6] Bib 93232
[7] Bib 93233, 93234

2244 The omission from the 1973 OPCS survey of people aged less than 18 may not have had a marked effect on relative percentages overall. Two exceptions may be that there are lower percentages in the cerebral palsy and muscular dystrophy categories than would otherwise have been the case. A curiosity is that the percentage figure for polio is higher in 1973 than in 1961; this may in part be attributable to the exclusion from the 1961 sample of people issued with road vehicles, among whom there could have been a disproportionate number of polio people with wheelchairs.

Changing pattern of wheelchair prescription

2245 There appear to be few significant changes between 1961 and 1973 in the pattern of causation of wheelchair prescription. The decrease in the percentage of amputees may be in part attributable to mortality among ex-first war servicemen, and the increase in cardiac and respiratory diseases to less stringent criteria for wheelchair prescription.

2246 Account should be taken of the exclusion of people with private wheelchairs from the Ministry samples. As previously mentioned, the 45 people in the Norwich sample with private wheelchairs were predominantly elderly. A further point is that the increasing number of new wheelchair issues each year is attributable principally to the rising number of elderly people who have physical disabilities associated with old age. In the circumstances it is probable that the figures given in the table underestimate for example the proportion of the wheelchair population who are arthritics or hemiplegics.

Table 22.2 Wheelchair users: Causes of disablement

	OPCS survey	Norwich survey	Leicestershire survey	Ministry of Health analysis
	1973	1964–68	1966–68	1961
	%	%	%	%
arthritis osteoarthritis, rheumatoid arthritis, spondylitis	29·0	28·5	21·8	28·3
organic nervous diseases principally multiple sclerosis	15·8	12·0	17·2	14·0
cerebro-vascular disease principally people described as hemiplegic	14·0	14·4	6·0	12·8
lower limb amputations	6·8	12·7	12·2	8·7
cerebral palsy principally people described as spastic	6·1	6·3	7·3	7·8
paraplegia and tetraplegia	5·5	4·6	7·3	7·0
poliomyelitis	3·7	3·9	12·7	3·5
cardiac and respiratory diseases	4·9	3·2	3·1	2·7
neuro-muscular disease principally muscular dystrophy	1·4	3·5	3·6	3·4
miscellaneous disabilities for example Parkinson's disease, bone injuries and deformities, Friedrich's ataxia, epilepsy, spina bifida, haemophilia	12·8	10·9	8·8	11·8
total	100·0	100·0	100·0	100·0
number of respondents	978 adults	284	448	2000

225 Sex and age distribution

2250 Table 22.3 records the sex and age distribution of people with wheelchairs in the three studies covering all age groups. It indicates that the ratio of women to men in the wheelchair population is approaching two to one. In the 1973 OPCS survey of adult wheelchair users the ratio of women to men was 65:35. The consensus suggests that the Leicestershire population is atypical.

2251 The preponderance of women is attributable to two main factors. The first is the much higher proportion of women among the very old, where the prevalence of wheelchair issue is highest. The second, which is related to the age factor, is the preponderance of women in the three major diagnostic categories of arthritis, multiple sclerosis and hemiplegia.

Age distribution

2252 The wheelchair population is predominantly an elderly population. The relationship between age and wheelchair use is most marked among women; as shown in table 22.3 about three women out of four who use wheelchairs are aged 50 or over.

2253 The ratio of wheelchair users to total population rises consistently with age. The histogram in diagram 22.1 relates the number of wheelchair users in each age group in the Norwich sample to the total population in the city of people in the same age group. It indicates that a person aged 75 or more is 25 times more likely to be a wheelchair user than a person aged 20 or less. Expressed in another way, one person in 70 who is aged over 75 uses a wheelchair, against one person in 2000 aged less than 20.

Table 22.3 Wheelchair users: Distribution by sex and age

	Norwich survey	Leicestershire survey	Ministry of Health analysis
	%	%	%
men	35	44	34
women	65	56	66
men under 50	38	47	36
men over 50	62	53	64
women under 50	21	33	26
women over 50	79	67	74

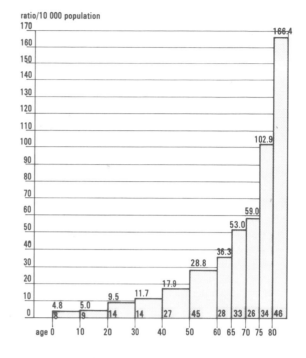

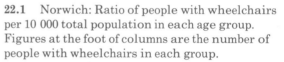

22.1 Norwich: Ratio of people with wheelchairs per 10 000 total population in each age group. Figures at the foot of columns are the number of people with wheelchairs in each group.

2254 The 1973 OPCS survey (which excluded people aged less than 18) confirms these indications. Of the men in the sample, 73 per cent were aged 50 or over. Of the women, 85 per cent were aged 50 or over, and 50 per cent aged 70 or over.

226 Use of wheelchairs

2260 Among people with wheelchairs a sizable proportion do not use them at all. In the Norwich study 14 per cent did not use their wheelchairs either inside or outside the home. Of the 978 people in the 1973 OPCS survey, 6 per cent said their wheelchairs were permanently out of use, and a further 6 per cent said they were temporarily out of use. There were 46 per cent who said they did not use their wheelchairs in their home.

2261 Of people in the Leicestershire study, 32 per cent said they did not use their wheelchairs inside the home, and 5 per cent said they did not use them at all outside. Of the 535 people with wheelchairs identified in the 1968–9 national survey *Handicapped and impaired in Great Britain*, 23 per cent used their wheelchairs both inside and outside, 56 per cent outside only, 13 per cent inside only, and 8 per cent did not use them at all[8].

[8] Bib 93210

Non-users of wheelchairs

2262 People who do not use their wheelchairs at all include those who have recovered from the disabling condition for which the wheelchair was prescribed, for example some polios and hemiplegics, those who have trained themselves to manage without using a wheelchair, those whose condition has deteriorated so that they are bedfast and those who might use a wheelchair but are unable to do so because for example their home has narrow doors or passageways.

2263 Of the 57 people in the 1973 OPCS survey who said their wheelchairs were permanently out of use, 37 per cent said they were bedridden or housebound because their condition had deteriorated, 32 per cent said there was nobody to do the pushing, and 26 per cent said it was because their condition had improved. Other reasons were that the wheelchair was too large for indoor use, that it was kept for emergencies only, that it was too heavy or uncomfortable, and that there were too many steps or stairs around the house.

Use of more than one wheelchair

2264 Among the 978 people in the 1973 OPCS survey of adult wheelchair users, 81 per cent had one chair, 17 per cent had two and 2 per cent had three. Of those aged below 50, 37 per cent had two or more chairs, whereas of those aged 50 or over, only 15 per cent did. People with paraplegia, polio or multiple sclerosis were more likely than others to have two or more chairs.

227 Wheelchair manoeuvre

2270 The information which follows is drawn from the report of the Leicestershire survey [9].

Wheelchair propulsion

2271 The ability of people with wheelchairs to propel their own chairs and the means by which they do so are determined first, by whether they have a chair which can be self propelled, and second, whether they have hand or arm impairments. The conventional means of propelling a wheelchair – by using the handrims to propel the main wheels – is, owing to the high incidence of hand or arm impairment, not as general as might be supposed.

2272 In the Leicestershire survey, in answer to the question 'Are your arms very weak or frail?', 52 per cent said there was some arm impairment; 60 per cent of these said that both arms were weak and 40 per cent said that one arm was weak. In answer to questions relating to hand disabilities, 28 per cent said they had hand disabilities, the principal problems being deformed hands and weakness of grip.

2273 The Leicestershire answers to the question 'How is your wheelchair moved?' are summarized in table 22.4. Of the respondents, 30 per cent said that they did not usually use a wheelchair in the home, and 34 per cent said that someone else usually pushed them. Owing to multiple answers to the question, the figures are difficult to interpret. It appears that among all people with wheelchairs some 70 per cent used a wheelchair in the home, and, among those who did so, about three in four were able to propel themselves. Of those who did propel themselves about three in four did so by using hands on handrims. Thus out of the total wheelchair population, less than one person in two propels himself around the home in the conventional manner.

Wheelchair use outside

2274 In answer to the question 'How much do you push yourself about in your wheelchair outside over level ground?', 48 per cent said they were always pushed, and 5 per cent said they never went outside. Among those who did push themselves, 12 per cent (of the total response) said that they always did so, 9 per cent said they often did so, 11 per cent said they sometimes did so and 7 per cent said they did so when there was no one to push them.

Table 22.4 Leicestershire survey: Wheelchair movement

Answers to question 'How is your wheelchair moved around your home?

	%
Non wheelchair users	
wheelchair not usually used in home	30
Wheelchair users, non self-propelling	
by someone else pushing	34
Wheelchair users, self-propelling	
by using hands on handrims	38
by using hands on tyres	7
by using feet to push	5
by using two handrims on same side	3
by using one handrim, one foot on floor	2
by driving electric chair	1
by using knobs on handrim	1
by other methods	2

The number of respondents was 406. The answers listed are not necessarily mutually exclusive, and therefore sum to more than 100 per cent. Source: Bib 93232, p52.

Table 22.5 Leicestershire survey: Ability of wheelchair users to stand

Answers to question 'Can you stand up from a sitting position?'

	%
without help	21
with help of someone else	24
with help of appliance, eg rail or piece of furniture	17
with help both of appliance and someone else	6
not at all	32
total	**100**

The number of respondents was 384. Source: Bib 93232, p111.

Table 22.6 Leicestershire survey: Getting out of wheelchair

Answers to question 'How do you normally get out of your wheelchair?'

	%
Transfer by myself (242 respondents)	
by lifting myself up on my arms and swinging body round	44
by removing an armrest and sliding over side	15
by removing an armrest and sliding over front edge	9
by removing an armrest and sliding out on sliding board	0·5
by standing up without help	19
by standing up with the help of sticks, crutches or futniture	42
Transfer with help of another person (165 respondents)	
by lifting me out forwards	76
by removing armrest and lifting me out over the side	22
by lifting me out over the side without removing armrest	10

Answers listed are not necessarily mutually exclusive, and therefore sum to more than 100 per cent. Source: Bib 93232, p128.

228 **Transfer in and out of wheelchairs**

2280 The way that disabled people transfer in and out of their wheelchairs is determined in the main by their ability to use their legs to stand.

2281 In the Leicestershire survey (table 22.5) nearly one person in three was not able to stand at all, and of those who were able to stand up from a sitting position, only one in three could do so without help.

2282 The answers to the slightly different question 'How do you normally get out of your wheelchair?' are summarized in table 22.6, analyzed for the 242 respondents who said they transferred by themselves (59 per cent of all respondents) and the 165 people who said they transferred with the help of another person (41 per cent of all respondents). Responses to a similar question relating to transfer to and from the wc seat are discussed in 5411.

23 Wheelchairs

230 Wheelchairs: General

2300 DHSS wheelchair issues

23000 In Britain the Department of Health and Social Security issues wheelchairs on National Health Service prescriptions from medical consultants or general practitioners. Information on wheelchairs is given in DHSS's *Handbook of wheel chairs and hand propelled tricycles* [1]. This handbook, officially known as MHM 408, is regularly updated. A smaller version, the MHM 408 GP, is issued to general practitioners.

23001 Wheelchairs are manufactured under contract to DHSS by firms who tender on the basis of manufacturing drawings or detailed specifications.

23002 The types of wheelchair most commonly issued are listed in table 23.1. The dimensions of DHSS-supplied wheelchairs, together with those of electric wheelchairs and some not available through DHSS, are detailed in table 23.2. Where medical needs can only be met by the provision of a type of chair not listed in the handbook, the recommendation is accepted if those needs are satisfied, except that wheelchairs considered by DHSS to be unsafe are not issued.

Powered wheelchairs

23003 Electric indoor wheelchairs can be issued to people with a locomotory disability or a severe lung or heart condition, so that to all intents and purposes they are unable to walk; who are unable to propel themselves in an ordinary wheelchair; are not permanently bedfast, and are able to derive some measure of independence in the home from using a powered indoor chair.

23004 A power-assisted chair controlled and operated by an attendant may be issued to a person who needs to be pushed in a wheelchair when out of doors, provided that the attendant who would normally push is unable to do so because (1) the local topography makes the use of an ordinary wheelchair extremely arduous; or (2) the weight of the chairbound person is excessive; or (3) the attendant is elderly; or (4) the attendant is physically disabled.

2301 'Standard' wheelchairs

23010 In recommendations in this book reference is made to 'standard' wheelchairs. The term standard wheelchair does not imply any specific wheelchair but relates to self-propelling wheelchairs (ie wheelchairs propelled through the handrim by the user) which are in common use, such as DHSS model 8 or the Everest and Jennings Premier wheelchair. Chairs having similar characteristics are included in the general description 'standard wheelchairs'.

23011 The majority of design specifications are based on the performance and space requirements of the DHSS model 8 chair. Diagrams illustrating these specifications are generally based on the model 8L (diagrams 23.1, 23.2).

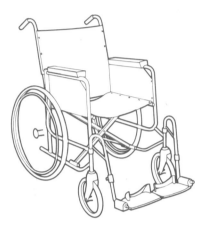

23.1   DHSS model 8L wheelchair

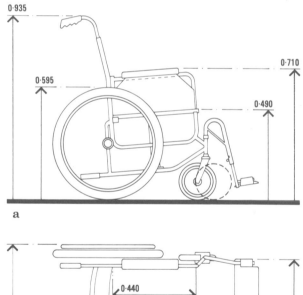

a

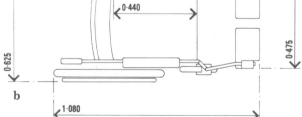

b

23.2   DHSS model 8L wheelchair (1:20)

[1] Bib 93510

Table 23.1 DHSS non-powered wheelchairs on issue, 1975

	number on issue at 31 December 1975		number supplied during 1975	
		%		%
Folding self-propelling chairs for indoor and outdoor use, principally model 8s	118 024	61·4	30 717	54·0
Folding car chairs for outdoor use, for pushing by attendant, principally model 9s	42 011	21·9	16 764	29·5
Collapsible lightweight chairs for outdoor use, for pushing by attendant, prescribed mainly for children, models 21 and 21C	12 637	6·6	4 426	7·8
Folding upholstered chairs for outdoor use, for pushing by attendant, model 13	8 093	4·2	1 356	2·4
Rigid self-propelling chairs for indoor use, principally model 1s	4 749	2·5	978	1·7
Other non-powered wheelchairs	6 633	3·4	2 617	4·6
Total	192 147	100·0	56 858	100·0

Source: Information supplied by DHSS; for qualifying note regarding the total number of wheelchairs on issue at 31 December 1975 see footnote [2] to 2201.

2302 Wheelchair seats

23020 For the purpose of relevant design recommendations throughout this book, the seat height of standard wheelchairs is taken to be 0·475. Data in table 23.2 indicate that seat heights for the more commonly used general purpose wheelchairs range from 0·450 to 0·490. The sag of the seat canvas when a person is seated in the chair reduces the effective height at the centre front edge of the seat by approx 0·015. The use of a typical seat cushion raises the effective height by approx 0·025.

Cushions

23021 A cushion is used by most wheelchair users, and not only by paraplegics for whom sensory impairment means that it is essential.
Even where there is no loss of sensation a cushion is needed because the standard folding wheelchair is not sprung and the seat canvas tends to sag with use.

23022 Of Leicestershire wheelchair users who answered the question 'Do you usually sit on a cushion?', 71 per cent said yes. Of those who answered the question 'Do you get pressures sores?', 28 per cent said yes [2].
The 1973 OPCS survey included questions on aches, pains and general comfort rather than specifically on pressure sores. There was no suggestion that pressure sores were commonly the result of wheelchair use.

[2] Bib 93232, p140

23023 Standard cushions for DHSS wheelchairs can be supplied which are 0·050, 0·075 or 0·100 thick.

23024 For paraplegics and others a cushion can be provided with a cut-out at the centre of the front in which a urinal can be accommodated.

231 Self-propelling folding wheelchairs

2310 DHSS model 8 wheelchairs: Variants

23100 The DHSS model 8 wheelchair is the standard self-propelling wheelchair for general purpose indoor and outdoor use. It can be carried in the invalid tricycle issued by DHSS (diagram 27.1) and normally has propelling wheels at the rear.

23101 There are three basic variants of the model 8, namely the 8G, the 8L and the 8BL; for dimensions see table 23.2.
The 8G (diagrams 23.3, 23.4) is a heavier chair than the 8L and has fixed rather than swinging detachable footrests. The 8BL (diagram 23.5) has smaller castor wheels than the 8G or the 8L and has a smaller seat. A junior version of the model 8G, known as the 8GJ, is issued and a junior version of the 8L is planned.

Materials

23102 The frame of the model 8 is of tubular steel, finished blue or silver grey stove enamelled. Seat and backrest are pvc coated canvas.

Folding

23103 The folding mechanism of model 8 chairs is a single or double cross-brace. The width when folded is approx 0·260.

23104 For chairs with detachable footrests the overall length when folded is reduced by approx 0·220, and for chairs with folding backrests the overall height when folded is reduced by approx 0·220.

Brakes

23105 Lever push-on brakes are fitted to each wheel. On all models a single parking brake lever can be fitted for either left or right hand operation to brake both wheels.

2311 DHSS model 8 wheelchairs: Seats

23110 The width and depth of standard wheelchair seats are detailed in table 23.2. The width dimension is between frame tubes.

Backrests

23111 For model 8L and 8G chairs the angle of the backrest is 15°. For model BL chairs the angle is 10°. Fully and semi-reclining backrests are available with model 8L chairs.
As a rule a near-vertical backrest is more satisfactory for users who propel their own chairs, allowing more effective thrust to be exerted on the hardrims. A more angled backrest may be more comfortable for normal sitting and relaxing, and may be preferred by people who are pushed by someone else. An effect of an angled backrest is that, to avoid the hazard of tipping over backwards, the axis of the main wheels has to be set back, increasing the wheelbase dimension and in consequence increasing the amount of space needed for wheelchair manoeuvre.

23112 A folding backrest is an alternative item on models 8BL and 8L.

23113 Zip backs are available for Everest and Jennings chairs but not for DHSS model 8 chairs. See 23173.

2312 Armrests

23120 Some 98 per cent of DHSS model 8 wheelchairs are fitted with padded detachable armrests, the majority having armrest locks [3].
The purpose of a detachable armrest is to facilitate lateral transfer, for example to or from a bed or wc seat. Some chairbound disabled people with good upper limbs are commonly able to transfer without difficulty from chairs with fixed armrests, and some E and J chairs (2317) have fixed armrests.

[3] This information and comparable data reported subsequently has been communicated by DHSS.

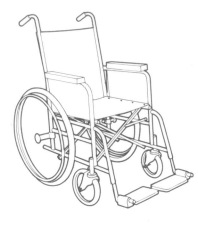

23.3 DHSS model 8G wheelchair

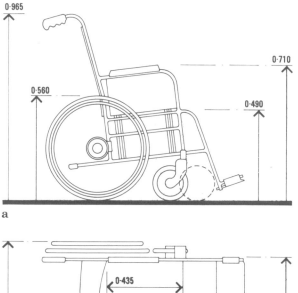

a

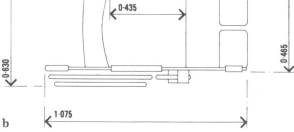

b

23.4 DHSS model 8G wheelchair (1:20)

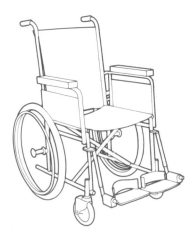

23.5 DHSS model 8BL wheelchair

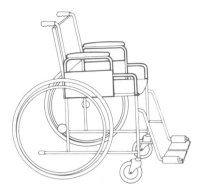

23.6 Domestic armrests

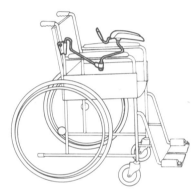

23.7 Ball bearing arm support

Domestic armrests

23121 Detachable domestic armrests are available for all DHSS model 8 wheelchairs.
These armrests are similar to the desk armrest available for E and J wheelchairs (diagram 23.6).

23122 The advantage of a domestic armrest is that it enables the user to approach some 0·150 closer to a sink, wash basin, dining table etc. A disadvantage is that it makes it more difficult for a person to push himself up to a standing position.

23123 Only a small number of DHSS wheelchairs are issued with domestic armrests. They can be discounted for the purposes of determining design standards, for example in respect of clearance below wash basins, kitchen sinks or tables.

23124 Some wheelchair users, for example low-level paraplegics able to maintain a stable posture, commonly use their wheelchair around the home without armrests, so permitting closer approach to fittings.

Ball bearing arm supports

23125 Ball bearing arm supports can be fitted to most standard wheelchairs (diagram 23.7).
The function of ball bearing arm supports (also known as mobile arm supports or balanced forearm orthoses) is to support weak arms in a working position, increasing the horizontal working area which can be reached. They also give some vertical

movement of the forearm over the pivot and assist supination of the forearm when needed. They are provided only for a very small number of users.

23126 Ball bearing arm supports are not helpful unless there is some residual function in the hands. People for whom they may be useful include those with residual paralysis of the shoulder and upper arm, for example some people affected by polio; those who have general weakness but retain use in their hands, for example some people with muscular dystrophy, and people who have painful and limited movement against gravity, for example some rheumatoid arthritics. People for whom they may not be helpful are those with spasticity or tremor.

23127 Arm supports project beyond the side of the chair. With the trough armrest in the normal relaxed position close to the chest, the projection is approx 0·330 beyond the side of the chair seat, or 0·240 beyond the wheel rims.

23128 For most users with ball bearing arm supports the armrests can be drawn in over the side of the chair, avoiding the need for additional circulation space.

2313   DHSS model 8 wheelchairs: Wheels

23130 Some 98 per cent of DHSS model 8 wheelchairs have propelling wheels at the rear. The following are reasons why a rear wheel chair may be preferred:

1. For people with good upper limbs it is easier to propel outside the home.
2. For people not able to stand at all it is easier to transfer to or from the chair; detachable armrests are unhelpful if the large wheels are at the front.
3. For people with lower limb disabilities only it is possible to tip the chair and balance it to mount kerbs; this cannot be done where main wheels are at the front.
4. It is easier to descend kerbs or single steps. The normal practice is to reverse the chair and allow the main wheels to drop down the step, or, among people with strong upper limbs, to tip the chair and balance it so that it rides down; neither of these techniques is possible with main wheels at the front, where there is a hazard of tipping out forward.
5. It is preferred by wheelchair pushers, since the foot tipping lever (see diagram 23.8) allows an attendant to tip the chair without difficulty to negotiate kerbs or single steps; it is difficult to negotiate kerbs where main wheels are at the front, whether or not the user has an attendant.
6. Better directional stability is obtained with rear propelling wheels; with front propelling wheels the rear of the chair tends to swing round.
7. Closer approach to desks and tables may be possible.
8. It is easier to load in or out of a car.

Front propelling wheels

23131 For a person with weak upper limbs a wheelchair with main wheels at the front is easier to propel independently.

23132 Chairs with main wheels at the front are sometimes specified for double lower limb amputees owing to the lesser risk of over balancing.
Where a chair with main wheels is prescribed for a double above-knee amputee not wearing prostheses the usual practice is to set the propelling wheels back about 0·080.

23133 The effect of placing propelling wheels at the front of a standard chair is to reduce marginally the overall length of the chair. This means that slightly less room is required for wheelchair manoeuvre.

Diameter of propelling wheels

23134 The majority of DHSS model 8 wheelchairs have propelling wheels with a nominal diameter of 0·560, giving an overall diameter of 0·595 when pneumatic tyres are fitted.
Model 8L chairs all have 0·560 wheels, and also standard 8G chairs. Model 8BL chairs have 0·510 wheels. Alternative wheel diameters of 0·510 or 0·610 are available for model 8G and 8GJ wheelchairs.

23135 People with strength in their arms can more easily propel chairs with large wheels. Smaller wheels are more suitable for people unable, or able only with difficulty, to propel their wheelchairs independently.
A disadvantage of large wheels can be that it is less easy to transfer laterally.

Tyres

23136 Almost all DHSS model 8 chairs have pneumatic tyres.
Pneumatic tyres are preferred where the wheelchair is used regularly outside; they also give a more comfortable ride for people liable to spasms.

23137 Solid tyres are available as an alternative on model 8BL, 8G and 8GJ chairs.
Chairs with solid tyres can be easier to control over smooth surfaces and inside the home. An advantage is that tyres cannot puncture.

Handrims

23138 Standard model 8 wheelchairs have pvc coated metal handrims, diameter approx 0·015.
For people who have a limited grip these handrims (and similar handrims on E and J chairs) can be difficult to manipulate. Alternatives are laminated wood oval section handrims, available on 8G and 8GJ chairs, or capstan handrims. Capstan hamdrims are available for all model 8 chairs, and may be helpful for some people, for example arthritics, who cannot use standard handrims.

Table 23.2: Explanatory comment

Dimensions listed in this table were measured directly on examples of currently available wheelchairs in a collection kept for demonstration purposes by the Department of Health. In many instances they differ from dimensions quoted in handbooks or manufacturers' catalogues, owing for example to varying criteria for endpoints, variations in examples of the same model, and conversions approximated from Imperial measurements. Some of the standard DHSS models are contracted to more than one manufacturer: although the same specifications have to be observed there can be variations in the design of components such as handrims and footrests, and overall dimensions can show significant differences. As an example, the model 8L is noted in the table as having overall dimensions 1·080 × 0·625; two other standard 8L chairs measured subsequently were 1·050 × 0·655 and 1·075 × 0·630.

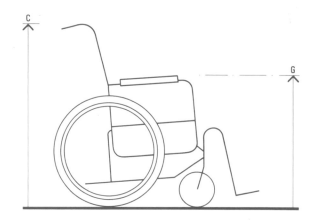

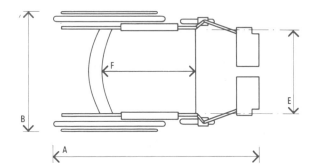

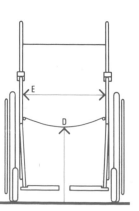

Diagrams showing endpoints for measures recorded in table 23.2

Table 23.2 Wheelchair dimensions

	A overall length	B overall width	C overall height	D height ground to seat	E seat width between frames	F seat depth	G height ground to armrest
Self-propelled wheelchairs							
Everest and Jennings Premier chair, adult style, 8AU200, pneumatic tyres	1·060	0·605	0·920	0·480	0·400	0·440	0·755
Everest and Jennings Premier chair, junior style, 8JU200, pneumatic tyres	1·050	0·565	0·845	0·460	0·350	0·440	0·685
DHSS lightweight general purpose, model 8L	1·080	0·625	0·935	0·490	0·435	0·440	0·710
DHSS general purpose model 8BL	0·915	0·560	0·945	0·470	0·400	0·430	0·710
DHSS general purpose model 8G	1·075	0·630	0·965	0·490	0·440	0·435	0·710
DHSS general purpose children's chair, model 8C	0·840	0·500	0·895	0·460	0·305	0·375	0·620
DHSS indoor chair model 1	0·970	0·640	1·015	0·545	0·450	0·460	0·745
Attendant-propelled wheelchairs							
Everest and Jennings Airglide	1·025	0·570	0·930	0·470	0·400	0·440	0·755
DHSS car chair, model 9	1·030	0·645	0·970	0·475	0·440	0·455	0·705
DHSS standard model 13	1·445	0·645	1·090	0·590	0·485	0·475	0·770
Major Buggy pushchair (DHSS model 21)	0·840	0·520	0·985	0·470	0·400	0·305	no armrest
Electrically powered wheelchairs							
Everest and Jennings Powerdrive	1·150	0·675	0·965	0·495	0·465	0·430	0·795
Everest and Jennings Sleyride	0·955	0·570	0·910	0·535	0·465	0·410	0·755
DHSS EPIC, model 102	0·945	0·550	0·935	0·550	0·435	0·465	0·740
BEC, model 103	0·855	0·625	0·925	0·475	0·430	0·400	0·735
DHSS attendant-controlled chair, model 28B	1·080	0·610	1·025	0·615	0·455	0·425	0·725

Castor wheels

23139 Model 8G and 8GJ chairs have solid castors
diameter 0·180. Model 8L chairs have spoked castor
wheels diameter 0·190. Model 8BL chairs have solid
castors diameter 0·125.

Large castors make it easier to propel the
wheelchair over obstacles, such as kerbs, gravel,
cobble stones and thresholds. Small castors have no
advantages.

2314 DHSS model 8 wheelchairs: Footrests

23140 Standard footrests are divided, hinged horizontally
at the outer side.

The division and hinging of footrests is needed for
folding the wheelchair, and also for people who can
push up to a standing position.

23141 Standard footrests are adjustable vertically over a
range of about 0·100. This gives a seat to footrest
dimension of between 0·330 and 0·430.

The typical user has his footrests about 0·380 from
the seat, so that they are about 0·100 above ground
level. This relatively high clearance is desirable for
negotiating kerbs or thresholds, but it does mean
that for the typical user the standard wheelchair
cannot be used to relax comfortably with feet flat
on the floor. The position of the lower leg and feet is
determined by the angle of the legrests, normally
about 15° to give clearance for rotating castor
wheels.

Swinging detachable footrests

23142 Models 8L and 8BL have swinging detachable
footrests as standard which can be locked in
position at 180° when required.

Detachable or swinging footrests permit close
approach for transfer, for example to cars. They
also prevent the feet from becoming entangled
while transferring or standing up. If footrests are
detached the overall length of the chair is reduced
by approx 0·230, which can be critical in restricted
spaces. Wheelchair users able to paddle with their
feet while sitting in the chair commonly remove
footrests permanently.

23143 As discussed in the commentary with reference to
mobility housing (1702), the 8L chair is not easy to
manoeuvre through a 0·775 door opening from a
0·900 wide passageway; forward movement can be
impracticable, and the manoeuvre may be
manageable only if the chair is reversed through
the opening.

A critical factor is that the swinging detachable
footrests fitted to the 8L increase the overall length
of the chair by some 0·050 compared with other
chairs in the group (table 23.2). To improve the
manoeuvrability of the 8L chair, the Department of
Health reports that a modified footrest design with
external corners rounded is under consideration.

Heel and leg rests

23144 Model 8L and 8BL chairs have heel loops on
footrests to hold feet in position.

Other models are supplied with a leg strap,
normally secured by buckle fastening.

23145 Detachable elevating legrests are available for 8G
and 8GJ chairs. Elevating legrests may be needed
by people with little or no flexion in their knees, for
example rheumatoid arthritics and some
osteoarthritics. The use of an elevated legrest,
particularly in a near-horizontal position, will
increase the overall length of the chair by up to
0·350. For people using elevated legrests, design
provision based on standard wheelchairs may be
inadequate and more generous circulation spaces
are needed.

Footrest extension

23146 A clip-on single piece footrest extension, front to
back dimension 0·125 or 0·230, is available for all
model 8 chairs.

2315 DHSS model 8 wheelchairs: Accessories

23150 A detachable tray, which can be useful for working,
writing or feeding, can be fitted to all model 8
chairs.

Such a tray may be helpful for people with
extremely limited arm reach, for example some
rheumatoid arthritics and people with muscular
dystrophy, to enable them to feed themselves.

23151 A detachable gantry to carry an armsling can be
fitted. The purpose is to support the user's arm, but
the gantry can be cumbersome and awkward, for
example when passing through doors, and ball
bearing arm supports are preferred (diagram 23.7).

2316 DHSS model 8C wheelchair

23160 The model 8C chair is a variant of the model 8
issued to children. The basic version has rear
propelling wheels, diameter 0·510. For dimensions
see table 23.2.

23161 Adaptations designed for spastic children include
box footrests, ankle straps, pummels for scissors
gait, adjustable shaped backrests, and harness and
groin straps.

23162 A footrest extension with adjustable legrest can be
fitted.

Some children, because of the nature of their
disability, may sit with legs projecting horizontally.
With a seat height at approx 0·450 and footrests at
high level, protection of wall surfaces at high level
may be necessary (373).

2317 Everest and Jennings Premier wheelchair

23170 The American Everest and Jennings Premier wheelchair (diagram 23.8) has similar characteristics to the DHSS model 8L, the most notable difference being the chromium plated finish. The standard model has rear propelling wheels, diameter 0·610, but a front main wheel version is available. For dimensions see table 23.2.

23171 E and J chairs are manufactured under licence in Britain by Zimmer Orthopaedic Ltd. They are occasionally supplied by DHSS in response to special recommendations from hospital consultants, particularly where one-arm drive and reclining chairs are needed.

Seat
23172 The seat width of the standard E and J chair is 0·410. The backrest is angled at 5°.
As noted in 23112, a near-vertical backrest is preferable for users who regularly propel their own chairs.

Zip back
23173 The E and J chair can be provided with a zip back for users who prefer to transfer through the back of the chair, for example to the wc seat (diagram 54.5d).
For many tetraplegics, where paralysis may be almost complete below shoulder level, pushing through the back of the chair is the only manageable means of independent transfer, for example to wc seat, bed or other chair. Sliding through the back may also be necessary for other users, for example when using narrow wc compartments.

Wheelchair narrower
23174 A device for making the wheelchair narrower, useful where confined doorways have to be negotiated, can be fitted to standard E and J chairs. It is operated by turning a handle which controls the disposition of the cross brace, decreasing the width of the chair by up to 0·100 while the individual remains seated. The chair is automatically locked at the required width and can be propelled in the normal way.

2318 One-arm drive wheelchairs

23180 A one-arm drive wheelchair (diagram 23.9) may be used by disabled people such as hemiplegics who have strong function in one arm only.
The DHSS model 8L is scheduled to be available with one-arm drive; at present where a folding one-arm chair is required on NHS prescription an E and J chair is issued.

23181 Two handrims are fitted on the same side, one attached to the adjacent wheel in the normal way, the other effective by means of a folding axle to the wheel on the other side.
When both handrims are gripped the chair is propelled in a straight line. To turn the chair the appropriate handrim is operated independently.

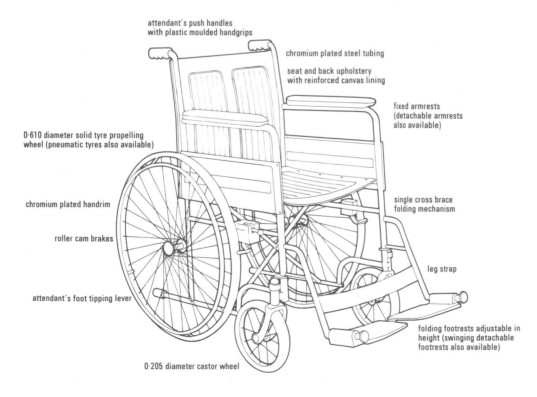

attendant's push handles with plastic moulded handgrips

chromium plated steel tubing

seat and back upholstery with reinforced canvas lining

fixed armrests (detachable armrests also available)

0·610 diameter solid tyre propelling wheel (pneumatic tyres also available)

chromium plated handrim

roller cam brakes

single cross brace folding mechanism

leg strap

attendant's foot tipping lever

folding footrests adjustable in height (swinging detachable footrests also available)

0·205 diameter castor wheel

23.8 Everest and Jennings Premier wheelchair

Use by hemiplegics

23182 It is only rarely that a one-arm drive wheelchair is manageable by a hemiplegic person whose disability is the result of a cerebrovascular accident.

This is because a hemiplegia which is so severe as to necessitate a one-arm drive wheelchair frequently involves brain damage affecting the memory span, meaning that the user tends to be confused about how to manipulate the chair.

23183 The hemiplegic person with relatively little involvement can as a rule manage a standard wheelchair by using his good hand and arm in the normal way, and pedalling with his good foot to do the steering. The DHSS can provide models 8L and 8BL with the steering controlled through either the right or left footrest.

232 Self-propelled non-folding wheelchairs

2320 DHSS model 1 wheelchair

23200 The DHSS model 1 wheelchair (diagrams 23.10, 23.11) is a tubular steel frame upholstered chair. For dimensions see table 23.2.

23201 Model 1 chairs are prescribed almost exclusively to old people. They are particularly convenient for users who are partly ambulant, as the retractable sliding footrest allows the chair to be easily pedalled along if preferred. The sliding footrest is also much easier to move out of the way when the user wants to push up to a standing position than the hinged footrests on the model 8 chair.

23202 The model 1 chair is generally more convenient for use inside the home than the model 8. It can be manoeuvred within a more confined space, and is more comfortable. Compared with the model 8, the front propelling wheels do not interfere with approach to tables, wash basins, sinks etc, as they are not appreciably more obstructive than the lower limb of a normal person seated on a rear wheel model 8 chair (compare diagrams 20.7 and 23.11). The model 1 chair is not suitable for use outside the home, owing to its low ground clearance.

Wheels

23203 The standard model 1 chair has front propelling wheels diameter 0·560, with a single rear castor wheel, diameter 0·180.

For outsize model 1 chairs, twin castors are available to give extra stability, but where space is restricted the single castor gives a smaller turning circle.

23204 The model 1 chair is normally supplied with solid tyres, which are preferred for indoor use. Push-on parking brakes operate on each wheel. The chair can be supplied with fixed or detachable armrests.

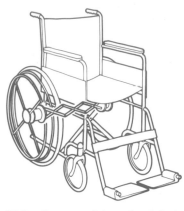

23.9 One-arm drive wheelchair, showing folding axle

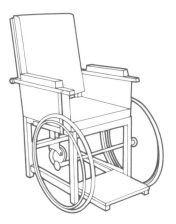

23.10 DHSS model 1 wheelchair

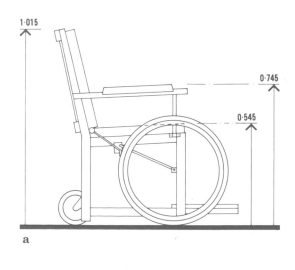

a

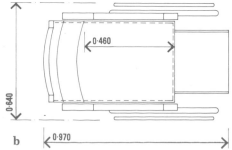

b

23.11 DHSS model 1 wheelchair (1:20)

Commode

23205 The model 1 chair can be fitted with a commode. Two types are available: a plywood base with aperture, covered with removable latex cushion, or latex cushion with exposed aperture. In this connection the model 1 is more suitable for elderly incontinent people than the model 8, which cannot be fitted with a commode.

233 Attendant-propelled wheelchairs

2330 DHSS model 9 wheelchair

23300 The DHSS model 9 chair, commonly known as the car chair, is a small folding chair. It is being increasingly prescribed, (accounting for about 30 per cent of current issues), replacing the model 13 as the general attendant-propelled outdoor chair. For dimensions see table 23.2.

23301 The version now issued as standard is the lightweight model 9L (diagram 23.12), which has pneumatic tyred rear wheels diameter 0·300 and spoked castor wheels diameter 0·190. Swinging detachable footrests and hinged backrest are standard. Fixed armrests are standard but alternative detachable armrests are available.

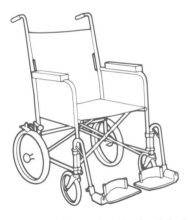

23.12 DHSS model 9L wheelchair

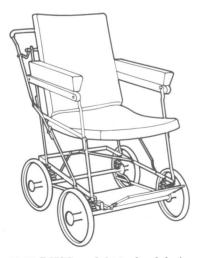

23.13 DHSS model 13 wheelchair

23302 To assist stowage in car boots the backrest can be folded; when this is done the height is reduced to 0·710.

23303 The backrest is pvc coated canvas, angled at 15°. Alternative angles are 20° and 5°.

2331 DHSS model 13 wheelchairs

23310 The DHSS model 13 wheelchair (diagram 23.13) is a large upholstered chair designed for pushing by an attendant. For dimensions see table 23.2.

23311 The model 13 was formerly widely prescribed to elderly handicapped people not able to propel themselves and needing a comfortable chair for occasions when they were taken out to the shops, round the park or on other trips. It is a cumbersome and awkward chair, difficult to take out by car, and with increasing car ownership it has been gradually replaced by the model 9 chair. Although DHSS reports that with the introduction in Britain of general practitioner prescriptions there was some revival of the model 13 chair – issues going perhaps to old people who had not previously known they could have a wheelchair – it is not expected that model 13 chairs will continue to be issued in quantity. DHSS now estimate that only about 4 per cent of wheelchairs on issue are model 13 chairs, compared with 15 per cent in 1967.

23312 The chair has a steel frame on helical springs. The backrest is adjustable. The footboard is a hinged toe ramp which can be folded under the chair.

Building design criteria

23313 For purposes of determining design standards in buildings it is not as a rule necessary to take account of the characteristics of the model 13 chair.

23314 In the previous edition of this book the model 13 chair determined design criteria for large wheelchairs. For reasons discussed above the model 13 does not warrant special attention. There are however situations when people who use chairs which are larger than standard need to be accommodated, for example in residential homes for old or handicapped people, and design standards should then be applied which cater generally for users of model 13 and similarly sized wheelchairs.

23315 For people who are extremely severely handicapped, for example rheumatoid arthritics unable to sit or bend at all, the overall length of a model 13 or similar chair can range up to 1·830.

2332 Other DHSS attendant-propelled wheelchairs

23320 The DHSS model 17 wheelchair is a folding chair for attendant control, having two small 0·075 castor wheels at the front and 0·280 diameter wheels at the rear, designed to negotiate stairways and narrow passages. It is not commonly prescribed.

23321 The DHSS model 21 chair is a lightweight folding push chair known as the Buggy Major, made by the manufacturer of the Baby Buggy pushchair for small children. The Buggy Major is suitable for people weighing up to 50kg; for dimensions see table 23.2.

23322 For further information on these and other chairs issued by DHSS reference should be made to MHM408 [4] or to the wheelchair supplement of *Equipment for the disabled* [5].

2333 Everest and Jennings attendant-propelled wheelchairs

23330 The E and J Airglide wheelchair (diagram 23.14) has four pneumatic tyres diameter 0·320. The chair has long lever handles to give additional leverage for an attendant negotiating kerbs or steps.

23331 The E and J Glideabout wheelchair (diagram 23.15) has four 0·125 castor wheels. It can be useful for some people, for example rheumatoid arthritics, who because of pain or deformity cannot use their hands on normal chair handrims but whose feet are less affected.

234 Powered indoor chairs

2340 DHSS issues

23400 Powered indoor wheelchairs are supplied by DHSS in special circumstances, as discussed in 23003. They were first made available in 1964 when 7 chairs were issued; in 1965 72 were issued and in 1975 the number was 5274.

2341 DHSS EPIC

23410 The DHSS EPIC (Electrically Powered Indoor Chair) (diagram 23.16) is the standard powered indoor chair manufactured under contract to DHSS, and is known as the model 102. For dimensions see table 23.2.
About 500 of these chairs are issued annually. They are suitable for some elderly handicapped people, some people with muscular dystrophy, some

[4] Bib 93510
[5] Bib 93514

23.14 Everest and Jennings Airglide wheelchair

23.15 Everest and Jennings Glideabout wheelchair

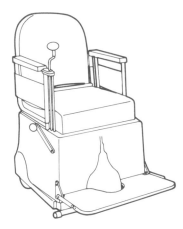

23.16 DHSS electrically powered indoor chair

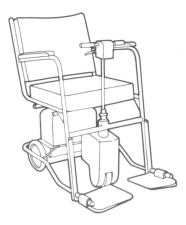

23.17 Sleyride chair

multiple sclerotics and others. They are not as a rule suitable for people with severe arthritis (who cannot sit comfortably in a conventionally styled chair with a deep seat) or for people subject to spasms.

23411 Motor and steering are powered by a 12 volt battery. A battery charger (240 volt AC supply) is concealed with the battery in the glass fibre casing beneath the seat. The chair has 0·205 solid rear wheels and a 0·180 solid tyre traction/steering wheel in front. For safety when entering or leaving there are stabilizers at the front.

Operating controls
23412 Fingertip control is by a short horizontal lever on the end of the right armrest; this can have a knob fitted to convert it to a short rotary handle. Steering and drive are carried out simultaneously. Current models have a motor giving a top speed of about 0·7mph.

23413 The chair is manoeuvrable in confined spaces but cannot cope with uneven surfaces. It is not suitable for outdoor use except on smooth and level garden paths. It can cope only with very shallow gradients; the DHSS performance specification requires an ability of 1:8 but in practice this is not always manageable.

23414 Lever brakes of the push-on type act simultaneously on both rear wheels.

Commode
23415 The EPIC can be supplied with a commode and aperture in the seat. Some 2 per cent of chairs are fitted with commodes. The left armrest is detachable.

2342 Sleyride chair

23420 The E and J Sleyride (diagram 23.17) is a compact electric chair, accounting for about 8 per cent of current DHSS issues of powered indoor chairs. For dimensions see table 23.2.

Operating controls
23421 The Sleyride has two 0·205 solid tyre rear wheels and a 0·205 solid tyre traction/steering wheel mounted in a unit at the front which also carries the motor. The 12 volt battery is carried in a tray under the seat.

23422 The user sits astride the removable T-shaped steering column which can be detached when getting in or out. A pull-up lever below the handle bar gives brake, freewheel, slow speed or fast speed. A second push-down lever gives reverse.
The top speed of the chair is approx 3mph and it can climb a slope approx 1:10. It can be used on smooth paths, but is not suitable on roads.

23423 The chair is extremely manoeuvrable and can turn in more confined spaces than the EPIC.

Seat
23424 The chair has a padded seat and padded armrests, one of which is removable. A disadvantage of the chair is that the steering column prevents close access to tables etc.

2343 Everest and Jennings Monodrive

23430 The E and J Monodrive conversion is the motor unit and control column of the Sleyride adapted for attachment to a standard E and J wheelchair. About 6 per cent of powered indoor chairs issued by DHSS are Monodrives.

23431 With the unit in position the chair is tilted slightly backwards and the front castors lifted clear of the ground; these are left in position to act as stabilizers.

23432 If required the battery and motor unit can be disconnected, leaving a basic wheelchair which can be used in the normal way.

2344 Everest and Jennings Powerdrive

23440 The Powerdrive (diagram 23.18) is basically an Everest and Jennings standard wheelchair with motors incorporated. The chair has all the normal features of the E and J wheelchair (2317). About 22 per cent of powered indoor chairs on DHSS issue are Powerdrives; the majority of these are issued to disabled people in residential homes. For dimensions see table 23.2.

23441 The rear wheels diameter 0·510 are set back 0·115 for stability; owing to the extra length the Powerdrive requires more room for manoeuvre than normal E and J chairs.

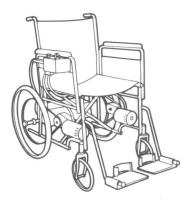

23.18 Everest and Jennings Powerdrive chair

Operating controls

23442 Each rear wheel is belt-driven from its own motor. Two 6 volt batteries are carried between the rear wheels. Front castor wheels have 0·205 air cushion tyres.

23443 The control box mounted on either armrest has a fingertip joystick. Alternatively motor and steering can be operated by remote control, for example by mouth or foot control.

23444 The top speed is approx 2½mph. The chair can manage ramp gradients of 1:10 and can cope with gravel, cobbles or grass. It is not suitable for use on roads.

2345 BEC chairs

23450 The BEC portable powered chair (diagram 23.19) has a tubular aluminium alloy frame, with detachable footplates and armrests. About 8 per cent of powered chairs issued by DHSS are BECs. For dimensions see table 23.2.

23451 The chair has four 0·205 solid tyres, with traction wheels, each driven by a separate motor, at the front. The chair is extremely manoeuvrable.

23452 The joystick on the control box on either armrest has a knob end operated either by fingers or palm.

23453 Maximum speed is 1½mph. The chair can cope with ramp gradients of about 1:10.

BEC mark 10

23454 The BEC mark 10 is similar to the portable but more robust. The chair measures 0·890 × 0·635, and can turn in a space approx 1·000 wide. The chair's claimed maximum speed is 4mph, with an ability to manage a 1:6 ramp. It is not available from the DHSS.

2346 Chairmobile

23460 The Chairmobile (diagram 23.20) is a three-wheeled powered platform with motorized traction/steering wheel in front. It is provided with either a fixed office chair or adjustable swivel chair, but can carry other types of chair if preferred.

23461 The Chairmobile is not on the approved DHSS list and is not obtainable on NHS prescription.

23462 Dimensions are 0·610 wide × 0·710 long. The chair is very manoeuvrable.

Operating controls

23463 A control knob on the removable steering tiller gives forward, reverse or brake positions. Battery and motor are housed in a box below the tiller.

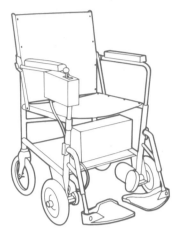

23.19 BEC powered chair

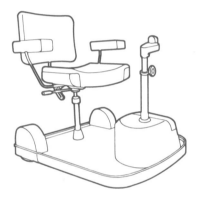

23.20 Chairmobile

23464 Maximum speed is 1mph. The chair is suitable only for indoor use, and can manage ramp gradients of 1:12.

23465 The Chairmobile is suitable for some elderly handicapped and ambulant handicapped people. Because it is supported on three wheels the wide platform can be unstable. For severely handicapped people the large box between the user's feet makes access difficult. The Chairmobile may be preferred by people who dislike conventional wheelchairs simply because they are wheelchairs.

2347 DHSS model 109 chair

23470 The DHSS model 109 chair is a powered version of the model 9L. It has two 0·205 rear solid tyres, each driven by a separate motor, and 0·190 solid front castors. Two 12v batteries are carried beneath the seat.

23471 The joystick control may be fitted on either armrest. Top speed is 1½mph and the chair can manage a ramp gradient of 1:10, but is suitable for hard surfaces only.

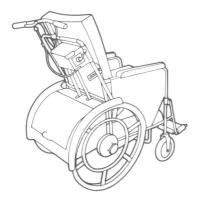

23.21 DHSS model 28B pedestrian-controlled powered chair

23.22 Permobil powered chair

23.23 Cavendish chair for responauts

235 Powered outdoor chairs

2350 DHSS model 28B

23500 The DHSS model 28B (diagram 23.21) is a powered attendant-controlled chair issued in special circumstances where a standard attendant-propelled chair is unsuitable (see 23004). The model 28B accounts for some 50 per cent of powered chairs currently issued by DHSS. For dimensions see table 23.2.

23501 Steering is by cycle type handle bars attached to the chair. Two motors giving two forward and two reverse speeds drive the rear wheels.

23502 On account of its weight and inability to cope on hills under its own power unless there is supplementary thrust from the attendant, the 28B chair is not easily managed by an attendant with limited strength.
It is a fairly common experience for the kind of person to whom it is issued, for example a handicapped woman whose husband is elderly, to have to return it because the attendant is unable to get it up inclines.

2351 Permobil

23510 The Permobil (diagram 23.22) is a powered chair for indoor and outdoor use designed and manufactured in Sweden.

23511 The length and height of the chair are variable. Typical dimensions are 0·660 wide × 1·200 high × 1·300 long.

236 Special chairs

2360 Cavendish chair

23600 The Cavendish chair (diagram 23.23) is purpose designed for responauts, ie people (predominantly post-polio) who are dependent on continuous breathing machinery.

23601 The length of the chair is 1·040 with the footrest retracted, and up to 1·500 with the footrest extended. The width is 0·660.

23602 The chair incorporates a battery so that the breathing machine can be operated independently of the main electricity supply for several hours when required. The battery does not power the chair, which is attendant-propelled.

23603 A respirator pump worked by mains electricity, battery or hand is carried on a tray beneath the chair seat.

24 Circulation spaces: Wheelchairs

240   Wheelchair criteria

2400   The majority of recommendations in this book regarding wheelchair circulation spaces are determined by the functioning of standard wheelchairs, with, where appropriate, allowance for large wheelchairs.

Studies made of wheelchair users indicate that there is greater variability of space requirements among the wheelchair population than is found among the ambulant population[1]. Some chairbound people use their wheelchairs economically and can manoeuvre within a comparatively confined space, others with less agility or dexterity need much more space in order to function at all. Varying recommendations are warranted because dependence on criteria for the most inefficient users in the largest chairs will involve extremely expensive solutions and, for the majority of wheelchair users, needlessly exaggerated space provision. The wide doorways and additional space needed by people in large wheelchairs are not, for reasons discussed in 3614, always advantageous for people in small wheelchairs.

Standard wheelchairs

2401   Standard wheelchairs are variants of the DHSS model 8 (diagrams 23.1, 23.3 and 23.5), and comparable chairs such as the E and J chair (diagram 23.8).

In the context of circulation spaces, chairs having similar characteristics, such as the attendant-propelled car chair (diagram 23.12), the indoor model 1 chair (diagram 23.10) and small electric wheelchairs such as the Epic (diagram 23.16), the Sleyride (diagram 23.17), the Bec (diagram 23.19), the E and J Monodrive and the Chairmobile (23.20) can also be regarded as standard wheelchairs.

Large wheelchairs

2402   Large wheelchairs are those whose dimensional or operational characteristics mean that they cannot be manoeuvred in spaces adequate for small wheelchairs. They include the attendant-propelled DHSS model 13 wheelchair (diagram 23.13), model 8 wheelchairs where the user needs an extended legrest or inclined backrest, and large electric wheelchairs such as the E and J Powerdrive (diagram 23.18).

Wheelchair housing

2403   For wheelchair housing (section 83) the circulation areas recommended are adequate for all standard chairs and, apart from exceptional cases, for users of large wheelchairs also.

For exceptional people, adaptations or ad hoc solutions may be required. In the case of housing for severely disabled people (section 84) where the amount of housing built is likely to be small and tenants may commonly have large wheelchairs, the recommendation is that circulation spaces are slightly more generous.

2404   In the case of mobility housing, meaning ordinary housing planned to be as suitable as possible for handicapped people to live in (section 82), circulation spaces are determined by the constraints of standard doors and passage widths. As discussed in 1702, this means that the majority of users with standard wheelchairs can be accommodated, though space for manoeuvring is inevitably tight.

Public buildings

2405   Circulation spaces recommended for public buildings cater for all people using small wheelchairs, and in most circumstances for people using large wheelchairs also. Where appropriate, reference is made in part 7 to the desirability of enhancing space standards to cater for people with exceptionally large chairs.

Special buildings for disabled people

2406   In the case of special buildings for disabled people, such as residential homes and day centres, the circulation spaces recommended cover people using large as well as standard wheelchairs.

241   Wheelchair circulation spaces: General considerations

2410   No special user study has been made for the purpose of establishing wheelchair circulation space recommendations in this book.

In practice it is virtually impossible for empirical studies of wheelchair users to give reliable data on circulation space requirements; this is because of the difficulty of establishing parameters for varying conditions and populations, and setting up test conditions which reliably simulate actuality. The Loughborough study of door widths and wheelchairs[2] is methodologically the most satisfactory, but on account of its confined scope has limited application. In the case of other reports it is often unclear whether findings are based on scientific evidence or surmise, and interpretation is often difficult[3].

Space constraints

2411   In both housing and public buildings in general, the most common wheelchair manoeuvring situation is passing from a circulation space through a door to a room space, or vice versa. The primary constraint is therefore the clear opening width of the door, in conjunction with dimensions of spaces to either side.

---

[1] See for example Bib 93504.
[2] Bib 93506
[3] Sources to which reference has been made for the purposes of determining circulation space recommendations are Bib 93502, 93501, 93170, 93500, 93761 and 93044.

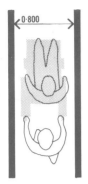

24.1 Straight line movement: Wheelchair with attendant (1:50)

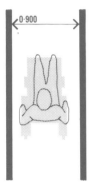

24.2 Straight line movement: Self-propelled wheelchair (1:50)

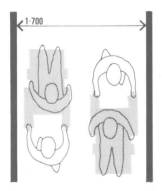

24.3 Passing space: Two wheelchairs with attendant (1:50)

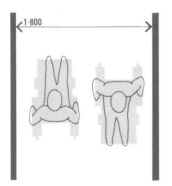

24.4 Passing space: Two self-propelled wheelchairs (1:50)

2412 Regarding wheelchair manoeuvre, the interaction of door widths and circulation spaces is discussed at length in 361. The door size recommended for general use in buildings catering for disabled people is the 0·900 doorset, having a door leaf 0·826 wide and giving a clear opening width of 0·775 (diagram 36.2). The 0·775 clear width is therefore the basic determinant of circulation space provision, meaning that the variable factor is the dimension of the adjoining passage or circulation space.

Tolerances

2413 The circulation arrangements suggested in diagrams in this section and elsewhere in this book are generally designed to afford a tolerance of not less than 0·050 between the face of any obstruction and the nearest position of the wheelchair during the course of manoeuvre.
Experienced wheelchair users are able with confidence to manoeuvre their chairs through tolerances of the order of 0·010.

2414 Situations where there is an obstruction directly in front of the wheelchair user, for example a knee recess below the kitchen sink, require space for the projection of feet beyond the leading edge of footrests; the allowance generally assumed is 0·100. A 0·100 tolerance is needed only when the chair is facing directly forward. During wheelchair manoeuvre, assuming that feet are positioned about the middle of footrests, the critical projection is the outer corner of the footrest structure. Where a wheelchair is facing an obstruction obliquely a tolerance of 0·050 is therefore sufficient.

Toe space

2415 Clear dimensions of circulation spaces may be reduced where recesses are provided at low level for feet and footrests.
The effective space for manoeuvre may be increased by up to 0·100 with the provision of toe recesses.

2416 The depth of toe recesses on plan should be not less than 0·150, assuming a height of not less than 0·200. For some users with small feet, a depth of 0·100 may be all that is needed; a depth of 0·150 is recommended to take account of people with large feet and the inclined angle of the lower leg.

242 Wheelchair circulation spaces: Movement in straight line

2420 For standard wheelchairs pushed by an attendant the minimum clear width needed for movement in a straight line is 0·800 (diagram 24.1).
For large wheelchairs the minimum clear width needs to be 0·850.

2421 For self-propelled standard wheelchairs the minimum clear width needs to be 0·900 (diagram 24.2).
More space is needed than for attendant-propelled chairs to cater for (1) clearance to either side for projecting elbows, and (2) the tendency among severely handicapped people to follow an erratic course.

2422 Although for all wheelchairs a passage width of 0·900 is theoretically sufficient for movement in a straight line, planning requirements mean that passage widths need to be not less than 1·200, as shown in diagrams 24.9a-f.

Space for wheelchairs to pass
2423 To allow for two attendant-propelled wheelchairs to pass, the minimum clear width needs to be 1·700 (diagram 24.3).

2424 To allow for two self-propelled wheelchairs to pass comfortably the clear width needs to be 1·800 (diagram 24.4).
A width of 1·800 is suggested for main circulation routes in residential homes and other special buildings for handicapped people.

243 Wheelchairs: Turning spaces

2430 The space required to turn a self-propelling wheelchair is dependent on the size of the chair, the capabilities of the user and the position of the main wheels.

2431 The most economical use of space is obtained when the chair user applies an equal but opposing thrust to each handrim, so that the perimeter of the chair swings on an arc centred on the mid-point of the axis of the main wheels.
The space required for this manoeuvre is affected by the position of the mid-point of the axis of the main wheels. The nearer this point is to the centre of gravity on plan of the wheelchair the less space is needed for manoeuvre.

Front main wheels
2432 Wheelchairs with main wheels at the front require less manoeuvring space than wheelchairs with main wheels at the rear.
Because buildings will not be used only by wheelchairs with main wheels at the front the recommendations which follow are based on wheelchairs with main wheels at the rear.

Turning in enclosed space
2433 For a standard wheelchair to turn through 90° in an enclosed space, for example within a room, the clear space on plan needs to be not less than 1·400 × 1·400 (diagram 24.5).
Small electric wheelchairs can be turned in confined spaces; a space having dimensions 0·200 wider than the length of the chair is adequate.

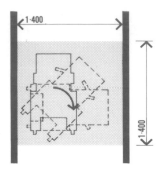

24.5   Space for wheelchair turn through 90° (1:50)

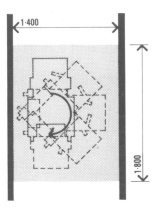

24.6   Space for wheelchair turn through 180° (1:50)

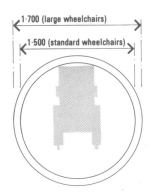

24.7   Planning rule for unobstructed space for wheelchair turning (1:50)

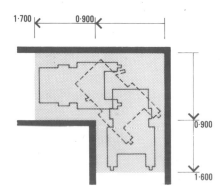

24.8   Wheelchair turn through 90° in circulation route (1:50)

2434   For large wheelchairs a space 1·600 × 1·600 is usually adequate for turning.
In the case of wheelchairs with extended legrests the turning space required will be greater.

180° turns

2435   For standard wheelchairs to turn through 180° the clear space should be not less than 1·800 × 1·400 (diagram 24.6).

2436   In practice, spaces within buildings are not enclosed on all four sides. There is always one open end, even if it is only a door opening. It is therefore commonly more economical to carry out a 3 point turn (forwards, backwards, forwards) rather than to turn through 180° in a single sweep as shown in diagram 24.6.

Turning circle

2437   A relatively crude but reliable planning rule where turning space may be needed within rooms, is to check, by superimposing circles on plan drawings, that an unobstructed space of either 1·500 or 1·700 diameter is available (diagram 24·7).

2438   In housing and public buildings catering for general use by disabled people, spaces allowing for wheelchair turning should be not less than 1·500 diameter.
In residential homes and other special buildings for disabled people, the space for wheelchair turning should be not less than 1·700 diameter.

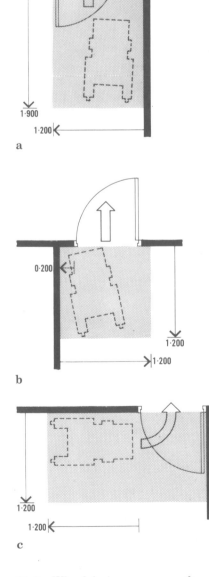

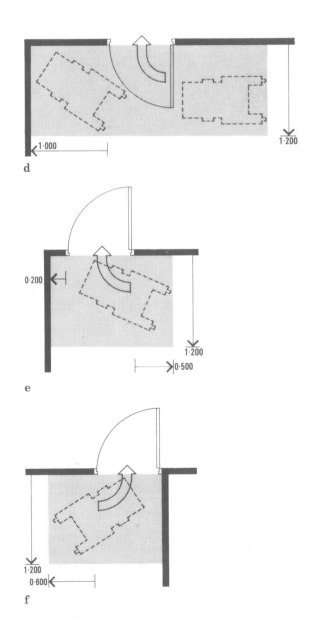

24.9   Wheelchair manoeuvre through door from passage: Examples of preferred conditions for wheelchair housing and public buildings (1:50)

360° turns

2439 If allowance is made for a turn through 180° it is not normally necessary to require space for the continuation of the turn to complete a 360° circle; the necessary manoeuvre can be obtained by reversing the chair back through 180°.

244 Wheelchairs: Turns in circulation routes

2440 A larger overall space is recommended for turning in circulation routes than for enclosed spaces. This is because when the chair is moving in a forward direction a turning thrust is applied to the handrim on the inner side of the turn, the outer rim being guided only.

2441 Standard wheelchairs can be turned through 90° in circulation routes where each arm is 0·900 wide (diagram 24.8).
In most situations there will be doors opening off circulation routes, and, as shown in diagrams 24.9a-f, the passage width will need to be 1·200.

2442 For users of large wheelchairs, circulation routes allowing for a right-angled turn should be not less than 1·000 wide.

245 Wheelchairs: Turns through doors

2450 The passage width needed to turn a wheelchair through a door opening is governed by the width of the door. For reasons discussed in 3614, the use of 0·900 doorsets, giving a clear opening width of 0·775, is generally assumed where provision is made for wheelchair users.

Mobility housing

2451 In mobility housing (1702, 823) the use of 0·900 doorsets in combination with 0·900 wide passages means that turning for standard wheelchairs is practicable, but extremely tight (diagram 24.10).

Preferred design conditions

2452 To allow for comfortable turning through a door giving an opening of 0·775 the passage should be 1·200 wide, as shown in diagrams 24.9a-f.

2453 The utilization space required for wheelchair approach and turning varies according to the location of the door handle and whether the door opens in or out.
Diagrams 24.9a-f illustrate the minimum clear dimensions which should be allowed.

2454 For associated recommendations regarding lobby spaces see diagrams 50.3 – 50.7.

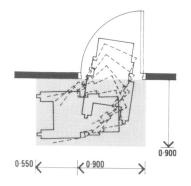

0·900
0·550   0·900

24.10 Wheelchair turn through door: Mobility housing requirement (1:50)

25 Circulation spaces: Ambulant disabled people

250 General provision

2500 For ambulant disabled people passageways in housing should not be less than 0·900 wide. In public buildings they should not be less than 1·200 wide.

2501 The dimensional data on ambulant disabled people illustrated in diagrams 25.1a-g are derived from material in DHSS Health Service Design Note 3[1]. In each case the criterion is the performance of a large man, representing the upper limit of the user range.

2502 Where provision is made only for small women or for children, spaces approx 0·100 narrower will generally be satisfactory.

251 Circulation spaces: Stick users

2510 For stick users, passage widths of 0·800 are adequate but are not recommended.
Buildings will not in practice be designed for stick users only, and the preferred minimum for passage widths of 0·900 should be observed.

2511 A large man using one stick occupies a space approx 0·600 wide, and needs a utilization space 0·750 wide (diagram 25.1a).

2512 A large man using two sticks occupies a space approx 0·650 wide, and needs a utilization space 0·800 wide (diagram 25.1b).

252 Circulation spaces: Crutch users

2520 For crutch users it is preferable that passage widths are 1·000 wide.
It is only rarely that a crutch user in ordinary housing will be inconvenienced by a passage width of 0·900 and it is not advocated that to cater for crutch users the minimum width should be 1·000 rather than 0·900.

2521 A large man using two elbow crutches occupies a space approx 0·780 wide and needs a utilization space 0·900 wide (diagram 25.1c).

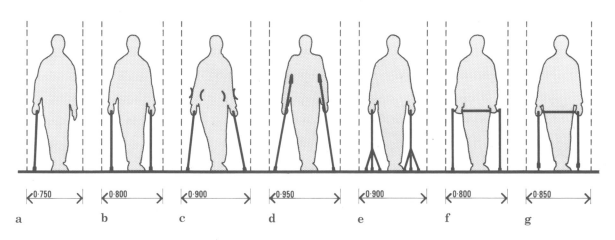

0·750	0·800	0·900	0·950	0·900	0·800	0·850
a	b	c	d	e	f	g

25.1 Ambulant disabled people: Circulation utilization spaces (1:50)

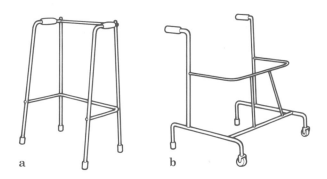

a   b

25.2 Walking aids

[1] Bib 93761

2522   A large man using two shoulder crutches occupies a space approx 0·820 wide, and needs a utilization space 0·950 wide (diagram 25.1d).

A large man using two shoulder crutches in a passageway 0·900 wide may find it necessary to use his crutches in a more vertical position than he would if space were more generous and he could swing them freely.

a

253   Circulation spaces: People with walking aids

2530   For some people with walking aids passage widths of 1·000 are advantageous, but for general purposes widths of 0·900 are adequate.

2531   A large man using two tripod walking aids occupies a space approx 0·740 wide, and needs a utilization space 0·900 wide (diagram 25.1e).

2532   A large man using a framed walking aid with ferrule tips occupies a space approx 0·650 wide, and needs a utilization space 0·800 wide (diagram 25.1f). An example of this type of walking aid is shown in diagram 25.2a.

b

2533   A large man using a wheeled walking aid occupies a space approx 0·660 wide, and needs a utilization space 0·850 wide (diagram 25.1g).

An example of a walking aid with front castor wheels is shown in diagram 25.2b.

Stair climbing frame

2534   A versatile walking frame which is capable of being used to go up and down steps with confidence is shown in diagram 25.3. The frame has sliding brake castors at the front, which travel across the floor until pressure is imposed on the frame to activate rubber brakes.

For stair climbing the frame is turned about, then tilted and slid forward with the leading legs on the second step (diagram 25.3b). When stepping up the user grips the top of the frame where it is parallel with the stair tread; the process is repeated to the head of the stairs. A similar technique is used for descending stairs (diagram 25.3c). Cost notes: 90003.

2535   Further information on walking aids for handicapped people may be obtained from the Disabled Living Foundation, see 94.

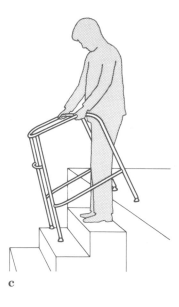

c

25.3   Stair climbing frame

26 Lifting aids

260 Manual lifting aids

2600 A suspended stirrup grip or similar manual lifting aid can assist a disabled person with impaired lower limbs to lift himself from the wheelchair seat to transfer, for example into a bath.

2601 Allowance for the fixing of manual lifting aids may be made in housing and residential accommodation for disabled people, but installation is not recommended as a matter of course; the fixing of aids should be deferred until a specific need is established.

2602 The value of manual lifting aids can be exaggerated. They are of use only to people with paralyzed lower limbs and relatively unimpaired upper limbs, for example traumatic paraplegics and some people with spina bifida or residual polio. It is commonly the case that where upper limbs are sufficiently strong for pulling up they are also capable of aiding transfer by more conventional means, for example by gripping the wc seat, bath rim or support rail; any overhead aid is therefore superfluous.

Ceiling eye bolts

2603 In new housing for wheelchair users allowance may be made for the fixing of eye bolts to ceilings in the bathroom (54730) and wc (54282), and if required in the bedroom (5361), garage (5783) and shower compartment.

2604 A detachable chain and stirrup grip are suspended from the eye bolt; diagram 26.1 shows a suggested method of fixing the bolt where the ceiling construction is of timber joists.

2605 The eye bolt should be designed to carry an applied point load of approx 140kg, ie a person weighing 110kg plus a 25 per cent impact factor. The beam sizes detailed in table 26.1 have been calculated assuming an applied load of 160kg at any point along the length of the beam.

Table 26.1 Timber beams for lifting aids

span	beam depth × width
less than 1·800	0·100 × 0·100
1·800 – 3·000	0·150 × 0·100
3·000 – 3·600	0·175 × 0·100 or 0·150 × 0·150
3·600 – 4·200	0·200 × 0·100 or 0·150 × 0·150

2606 To allow for deflection and avoid cracking of ceiling plaster the depth of the beam should be not less than 0·025 less than the depth of adjacent joists. No partition walls should be carried on the beam, nor should it be used as a trimmer to joists at right angles, except where special allowance is made. Adequate bearing should be provided at each end of the beam.

Adaptations

2607 In an existing dwelling it may not be possible to obtain an adequate ceiling fixing. An alternative is to span a piece of galvanized barrel diameter approx 0·040 across the room, securing it to the wall at either end. A chain and stirrup grip can then be suspended, giving a range of possible lifting positions.

2608 The proprietary aid shown in diagram 26.2 comprises a steel plate with four coach screws for fixing to ceiling rafters at approx 0·470 centres. The steel chain is 1·500 long, permitting adjustment of height of the stirrup grip. Costs are noted in 90000.

26.2 Chain and stirrup grip

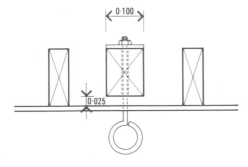

26.1 Ceiling eye bolt

261 Electric hoists

2610 Diagram 26.3 shows an electric hoist which assists severely disabled people, either with or without an attendant, to transfer on and off beds, wc seats etc. Costs are noted in 90001.

2611 The hoist is operated by a light pull on the control cord. The unit is designed for 230/250v AC mains systems, and may be used in bathrooms if a transformer is incorporated.

2612 The track may be fixed either to ceiling joists or to wall fixing plates. It should be aligned so that the disabled person can be raised or lowered directly over bed, bath or wc; diagrams 54.34 and 54.49 show suggested positions for tracks for wcs and baths. Where space is restricted the track may be turned through 90°. The hoist is designed to lift a weight of 100kg.

262 Contingency provision in new buildings

2620 In new housing or residential homes for disabled people it may not be possible to predict in advance the exact position where beam reinforcement will be needed for lifting aids or ceiling tracks. At the same time it may be difficult, owing to the character of the ceiling or roof structure, to put timber beams for carrying hoists into place after the building is completed.

2621 A possible solution is to lay a loose length of beam across the ceiling joists which can, should the need arise, be manoeuvred into the required position and then fixed.

2622 Where ceilings are of hollow pot construction a possibility is for selected pots to have a concrete fill, encasing timber plugs to which fixings for lifting aids may subsequently be made.

263 Portable hoists

2630 Diagram 26.4a shows a portable hydraulic hoist, lever-operated by an attendant. It has a lifting range of 1·200. The base is adjustable in width, permitting the hoist to pass through a 0·600 opening or round a 0·850 wide chair.

2631 Where floor construction permits, the hoist may be fixed into a floor socket, for example in the bathroom (diagram 26.4b). When required the hoist may be lifted out of the socket and used on the adjustable base for other purposes.

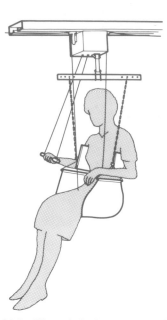

26.3 Electric hoist suspended from ceiling track

a Hoist with trolley base

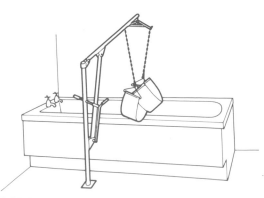

b Hoist in floor socket

26.4 Hydraulic hoist

2632 Diagram 26.5 shows a hoist which can also be used for moving a handicapped person from one room to another. It can be manoeuvred by an attendant to lift a handicapped person from or to an easy chair, bed, a bath, a wc or a shower seat. The spade seat is adjustable in height from 0·420 to 0·750, and is controlled by a pump. A person using the device as shown in the diagram sits facing left, with his back supported by the belt between the parallel rails.

2633 The proprietary lifting aid for bathing, toileting and sling lifting shown in diagram 26.6 incorporates a self-sustaining winding mechanism connected to a looped chain, enabling an attendant to lift and transfer a person weighing up to 160kg. Slings where used are mounted on a rigid spreader bar. A commode attachment is available.

2634 Costs of portable hoists are noted in 90002.

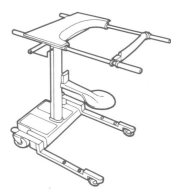

26.5 Portable hoist with spade seat

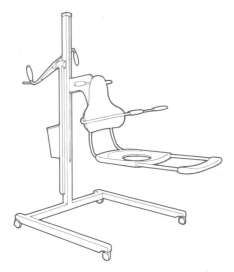

26.6 Portable hoist for bathing, toileting etc

27 Road vehicles for disabled people

270 Mobility services

2700 Some severely disabled people are supplied through the National Health Service with three-wheel road vehicles commonly known as invalid tricycles. Until January 1976 there were specific categories of disabled people, for example ex-service disabled people, haemophiliacs and disabled mothers with young children, who could elect if they wished to have a car (usually a Mini) instead of an invalid tricycle.

Mobility allowance

2701 With the introduction by DHSS in January 1976 of the mobility allowance, the car option has been removed. The mobility allowance is a taxable cash benefit, currently (1976) £5 per week, available to - eople who are unable or virtually unable to walk. A purpose of the scheme is to help severely disabled people not able to drive; this group, known as 'disabled passengers', had previously been neglected. Qualifying ages for the mobility allowance are 5–64 for men and 5–59 for women.

2702 People aged 16 or over who qualify for the allowance may opt instead for the supply of an invalid tricycle.

27.1 Model 70 invalid tricycle

271 Invalid tricycles

2710 Three-wheelers issued by DHSS are either petrol-driven or electrically powered. Numbers on issue at the end of 1975 are noted in table 27.1.
Electric vehicles are issued to handicapped people who for medical reasons may have difficulty controlling a petrol vehicle, but who can manage the slower and simpler electric version.

Petrol version

2711 The current petrol version is the model 70 (diagram 27.1), which has overall dimensions 2.970×1.370. The vehicle has a single seat, space to stow a folded wheelchair and sliding doors to both sides. Alternative features are available, most of which relate to the layout and operation of the controls.

Table 27.1 Powered three-wheel vehicles (invalid tricycles) issued by DHSS 1975, England

	supplied during year 1975	total on issue at 31 December 1975
model 70 petrol-engined	3326	9862
other petrol-engined models	164	7771
electrically powered models	134	1089

Source: Information supplied by DHSS

2712 Other petrol invalid tricycles still in use but no longer in production are the model 59 (Tippen), model 66 (Invacar) and 67 (Acedes); for building design purposes these can be disregarded.

Electric version

2713 The current electric version of the invalid tricycle is the model 69E, which is similar in design to the petrol model 59 (Tippen). Overall dimensions are 2.770×0.990.

Turning circles

2714 The turning circle of the model 70 is 7.010. The model 69E has a turning circle of 7.670 anti-clockwise and 7.520 clockwise.

2715 In addition to the 18 722 DHSS three-wheelers on issue at the end of 1975 (table 27.2) there were some 2000 petrol engined vehicles of various types and 300 electric vehicles kept in reserve for temporary loan purposes when a client's own vehicle is off the road for repairs[1].

2716 For notes on garages for invalid tricycles see section 57.

[1] Information supplied by DHSS

272 Cars

2720 For guidance relating to the planning of garages for cars see 571–575. The dimensions of selected cars currently in production (1976) are detailed in table 27.2.

Table 27.2 Car dimensions

	length	width
Austin Allegro	3·850	1·615
British Leyland Mini	3·055	1·415
Chrysler 180	4·525	1·725
Citroen GS	4·120	1·610
Fiat 128	3·840	1·590
Ford Cortina	4·260	1·700
Ford Escort	3·975	1·590
Morris Marina	4·120	1·645
Opel Rekord	4·570	1·730
Renault 12 estate	4·395	1·615
Saab 99	4·420	1·690
Volkswagen 1300	4·075	1·585
Volkswagen Golf	3·700	1·610
Volvo 66	3·875	1·540
Volvo 244	4·900	1·710

Building elements and finishes

3

30 External elements

300 Footways: Dimensional data

3000 To allow for wheelchair users, footways, pavements and so on should be not less than 1·200 wide (diagram 30.1a).

3001 To allow wheelchairs to pass each other, or wheelchairs to pass attendants with prams, footways should be not less than 2·000 wide (diagram 30.1b).

3002 Pavement gradients ought not to exceed 1:12 (8·3 per cent).
1:12 is the preferred maximum gradient for ambulant disabled and assisted chairbound people (table 32.1). Topographical conditions may necessitate steeper gradients, but the need for such gradients may be avoided by careful landscaping.

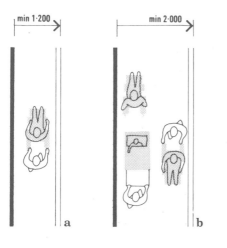

30.1 Footways (1:100).

Independent wheelchair users

3003 For independent wheelchair users, pavements should have a gradient not exceeding 1:20 (5 per cent).

301 Footways: Surfaces

3010 For external pedestrian surfaces the primary requirement is a non-slip surface which will minimize hazards to ambulant disabled people, rather than a smooth in situ surface which might be preferred by wheelchair users.
For discussion on floor surfaces see 1112; for notes on garden paths see 5813.

3011 Pavements, footways and footpaths should be of fixed and firm materials.
Suitable surfacings are bitumen macadam, tarmacadam and asphalt. Unsealed gravel surfaces must be avoided.

3012 Where precast paving slabs or comparable block materials are used, slabs must be carefully laid with flush joints.

For ambulant disabled people liable to trip and fall, uneven paved surfaces are a constant hazard. For chairbound people they can disturb the travel of wheelchair castors and cause the chair to shift direction.

3013 Paving slabs where used should have a carborundum or slightly corrugated finish to give a non-slip surface. Quartzite slabs are recommended. An inset pattern can give an attractive non-slip surface (diagram 30.2).

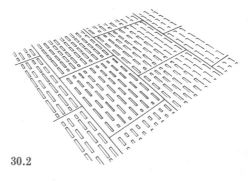

30.2

3014 Patented rubber treaded paving flags may be used where ordinary concrete or stone flags could be dangerous or slippery.
Rubber sections, moulded integrally with the concrete and fastened by reinforcing rods, protrude from the surface of the concrete slab, similar to that shown in diagram 30.2. Cost notes: 90100.

Brick setts

3015 Brick setts are permissible where surfaces and joints are flush.
A rough or porous brick is preferred to a smooth engineering brick; the latter can be extremely slippery in wet or icy conditions.

3016 Granite setts are not recommended, but are permissible if joints are flush or near flush with sett surfaces.

Surface dressings

3017 A self-adhesive slip-resistant surface dressing may be suitable for pavings. Cost notes: 90100.

302 Ramping of kerbs

3020 At pedestrian crossings, traffic signal junctions, street corners, junctions with vehicle parking areas and other crossing points, kerbs should be ramped. For discussion on difficulties and hazards where kerbs are not ramped see 1224.

3021 Ramped kerbs are essential for people who propel their own wheelchairs and are not able to mount or descend high kerbs independently, and for people who push wheelchairs and have difficulty getting a loaded wheelchair on or off a high kerb.
Wheelchair pushers are frequently elderly people who may themselves be frail or handicapped.

3022 Ramped kerbs can also be advantageous for handicapped ambulant people who have difficulty negotiating high steps, and for mothers with prams.

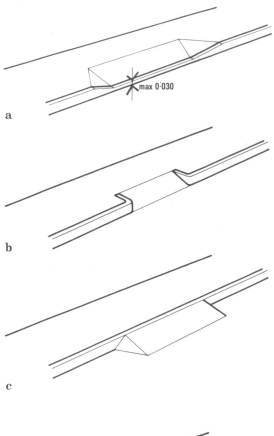

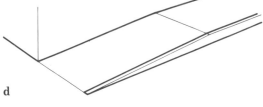

30.3 Ramping of kerbs

3023 Four methods for ramping kerbs are shown in diagram 30.3. They are:

1. Dropping the kerb to a level not higher than 0·030 above the adjacent channel, and ramping the pavement surface (diagram 30.3a).
This method is preferred at major intersections and where there is considerable traffic. It should be used where the kerb needs to be retained for safety purposes as a demarcation line between pedestrian and vehicular surfaces. For surface water drainage purposes it is preferred to the other three methods. The gradient of the pavement surface should preferably not exceed 1:10.

2. Turning the kerb in to either side of the ramp (diagram 30.3b).
This method has the advantage that the ramp merges with pavement and road surfaces; it is a satisfactory alternative to method 1.

3. Continuing the line of the kerb and building out a small ramp (diagram 30.3c).
Since the ramp here encroaches on the road surface this method is acceptable only where there is a minimal amount of vehicular road traffic. It also has the disadvantage that the ramp will be steep.

4. Inclining the pavement gradually to the level of the road surface (diagram 30.3d).
This method has the disadvantage that there is no clear indication to mark the point where the protection of the pavement area gives way to the hazards of the road.

Blind people

3024 For reasons discussed in the commentary (1423) the ramping of kerbs does not normally cause problems for blind people.
The change of floor plane will be a sufficient cue and, though desirable, it is not essential that the ramp has a distinguishing texture.

Ramp surfaces

3025 To give a secure foothold to ambulant disabled people, ramped kerbs should have a patterned surface or coarse aggregate finish.

3026 The colouring of the ramp surface to facilitate recognition of the hazard is not likely to be helpful.

Reconstruction of existing kerbs

3027 Where existing pavement kerbs are reconstructed to form a ramp, paving slabs which are cut and relaid must have flush joints.

303 **Gratings etc**

3030 Gratings can be a hazard to stick, crutch and wheelchair users.

3031 Parallel bar gratings should be avoided; where installed, bars should run at right angles to the direction of travel. Cast iron and similar gratings should have apertures not larger than 0·020 square, with bars minimum 0·013 wide (diagram 30.4).

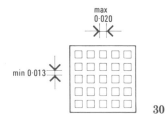

30.4 Gratings

Manholes

3032 Manhole covers and access covers must be flush with the adjacent pavement or road surface.

Bollards

3033 The minimum width between the base of bollards to allow for wheelchairs to pass should be 0·900.

31 Staircases, steps

310 Vertical circulation: General considerations

3100 In buildings where allowance is made for disabled people, the general rule is that suitable ramps and/or lifts must be provided in addition to or in place of steps and staircases.
For general discussion on steps versus ramps see 1112. For notes on the preferability of steps for ambulant disabled people see 1224. For staircases in public buildings see 6312, 6323.

Building regulations

3101 Specific building regulations requirements for stairways relevant to recommendations in this section are noted in table 31.1. These are abbreviated; for fuller instructions reference should be made to the table to Regulation H3 of the Building Regulations [1].
Under the Building Regulations a stairway is defined as 'any part of a building which provides a route of travel and is formed by a combination of two or more flights and one or more intervening landings'.

311 Variations in level

3110 Small changes in level should be avoided; where they are not avoidable suitably graded ramps are preferred to steps.

Single steps

3111 Single steps, because they are often overlooked, are hazardous and ought not to be used.

3112 Where single steps are used as thresholds at entrance doors it is desirable for handicapped people and wheelchair users that they are as low as possible. Where they have to be used elsewhere they ought not to be so low that they are easily overlooked, and the riser should therefore not be less than 0·100.

Wheelchair users

3113 Where steps are incorporated which may be used by wheelchair users a single high step is preferred to a pair of low steps.

3114 For wheelchair users, a pair of steps is much more handicapping than a single step. A capable independent wheelchair user can commonly negotiate a single step either up or down. To get up a single step he tips the wheelchair on approach, causing the leading castor wheels to rise clear of the step, and then thrusts the main wheels over as they strike the step. To get down a step he either approaches forward, tips the chair and balances it on the main wheels so that it rides down the step, or reverses the chair, approaches backwards, allows the main wheels to drop down the step and the castor wheels to follow.
In the case of the wheelchair user who is not independent it is not normally difficult for the pusher to cope with a single step, by using the foot tipping lever (see diagram 23.8) and then pushing the chair forward with the weight of the wheelchair and occupant on the step nosing.

3115 It is not possible even for a very capable independent wheelchair user to mount two consecutive steps. For the non-independent chair user, two steps are a considerable obstacle as the pusher cannot use the foot tipping lever to take the chair forward up more than one step; the normal routine is for the chair to be pulled up backwards. Similarly, two or more consecutive steps are much more difficult to negotiate when going down than a single step. It is only exceptional independent wheelchair users who are able to balance their chair on the rear wheels and let it ride down two or three steps.

---

[1] This and other references in this section to building regulations are to Part H in Schedule 1 of the Third Amendment (Bib 93802)

Table 31.1 Building Regulations: Requirements for stairways

	width of stairway	gradient	number of risers per flight	height of risers	going of steps
stairways within dwellings or serving one dwelling only	min 0·800	max 42°	min 2 max 16	min 0·075 max 0·220	min 0·220
common stairways serving two or more dwellings	min 0·900	max 38°	min 2 max 16	min 0·075 max 0·190	min 0·240
stairways in institutional buildings and large buildings used for assembly purposes	min 1·000	—	min 3 max 16	min 0·075 max 0·180	min 0·280
stairways in offices, shops, factories etc and small buildings used for assembly purposes	min 1·000	—	min 3 max 16	min 0·075 max 0·190	min 0·250

Source: Bib 93802, Table to Regulation H3

312   Staircase hazards, lighting

3120   Open riser staircases must be avoided.
Stairs with open risers can be hazardous to elderly
people and others prone to dizziness. They are also
unsatisfactory for ambulant disabled people, in that
it can be helpful for people who are unsteady on
their feet to be able to wedge the shoe against risers
when climbing a staircase.

3121   Winders and splayed steps should be avoided.
Where they are necessary they should be at the
bottom and not at the top of a flight of steps.

3122   Doors must not open directly on to the top of a
staircase or swing so as to obstruct the top or
bottom step.

External staircases
3123   External staircases are dangerous in wet or frosty
weather. They ought not to be installed as a means
of escape in buildings where occupants are
commonly elderly or disabled.

Illumination of stairs
3124   Windows and artificial lights should throw light
towards and not down staircases.

3125   Artificial lighting should give an average
illumination level on stair treads of 100 lux.

3126   For people with impaired vision, it can be helpful if
the colour of the treads contrasts with the colour of
risers.

313   Stair risers and treads

3130   Stair rise (from top of tread to top of tread) and
going (from face of riser to face of riser) must be the
same for all steps in any flight.

3131   The nosing of the top step of a staircase should
desirably be not closer than 0·300 on plan to the
point where an adjacent wall returns (diagram
31.1).
This is suggested for safety reasons, and to allow
the handrail to be extended horizontally at the head
of the staircase (3322). It is not always achievable
for staircases in public authority housing (315).

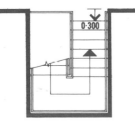

31.1   Staircase planning

Treads
3132   Tread surfaces must be non-slip.
Solid wood treads should have non-slip nosings.
Carpets where fitted must be securely fixed.

3133   A splayed riser with chamfered nosing (diagram
31.2a) is preferred to a square nosing.

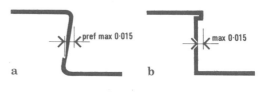

31.2   Step nosings

3134   Nosings ought not to project more than 0·015
(diagram 31.2b).
Where the tread is comparatively shallow, a person
descending the stairs tends to place the ball of the
foot (carrying the weight of the body) so that it
overlaps the nosing. Where the nosing is sharp
there is relatively little frictional resistance
between the ball of the foot and the edge of the
tread, with a greater risk of falling than where the
nosing is rounded. On deep treads where the going
is greater than 0·300 the ball of the foot usually falls
inside the nosing edge and the risk of accident is
lessened.

Open risers
3135   Where stairs have open risers the nosing of any
tread must overlap the back edge of the tread below
by not less than 0·015, as required by regulation
H3(4)(f) of the Building Regulations.
As noted in 3120, open risers are not recommended;
where they do occur it will not benefit disabled
users significantly for the overlap to be more than
0·015.

**314   Internal staircases: Ambulant disabled and
elderly people**

3140   In special buildings for ambulant disabled or
elderly handicapped people stairs must be designed
so that they are usable with minimum energy
expenditure.
Although some ambulant disabled people cannot
manage stairs at all, the majority will be catered for
by the following recommendations. In buildings of
more than one storey planned particularly for
ambulant disabled or elderly people a lift will
normally be available as an alternative.

Gradients
3141   Internal staircases should have a gradient not
exceeding 40°, preferred maximum 35°.
The suggested maximum height of risers is 0·190,
preferred maximum 0·170. The preferred minimum
length of goings is 0·250 (diagram 31.3).

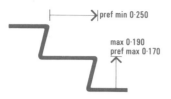

31.3   Internal stairs

3142   These recommendations are drawn from Ministry of Housing Design Bulletin 1 *Some aspects of designing for old people*[2]. It gives as a guide a study suggesting a going of 0·290 and a rise of 0·168, giving a gradient of 30°; if these figures cannot be observed it is better to reduce the going than to increase the rise. A report from the Dutch Bouwcentrum says 'efficient stairs should have a gradient of between 30° and 40°. Within this margin a satisfactory stair (is one where steps have) a rise of 0·175, a tread of 0·250 and thus a gradient of 35°'[3].

Vertical rise

3143   The vertical rise of a flight of steps ought not to exceed 1·800, except where a straight flight staircase is installed, as advised for two storey mobility housing (8274).

3144   A landing midway between floor levels can give a safe stopping place for people prone to dizziness or breathlessness, and also for cardiacs and others who need to conserve energy.

315   Internal staircases: Public authority housing

3150   In public authority housing in Britain designed to minimum space standards (see 8043, 811) the recommendations made in 314 are not achievable.

3151   The design of standard domestic staircases follows the recommendations of Ministry of Housing Design Bulletin 16 *Co-ordination of components in housing* which suggests that openings in floors for staircases should be 2·700 × 0·900 for a straight flight, and 2·100 × 1·800 for a dogleg[4]. With a standard floor to floor height of 2·600, these give 12 or 13 risers, with riser dimensions of 0·200 or 0·217, goings ranging from 0·205 to 0·258, and gradients ranging from 41° to 44°[5]. On the basis of an ergonomic study reported in 1970 staircases having 12 risers rather than 13 are recommended for normal domestic purposes[6].

Old people

3152   In housing designed for old people it is impossible to incorporate suitable staircases within floor openings of 2·700 × 0·900 or 2·100 × 1·800. Sizes of floor openings must be substantially increased, with consequential effects on overall costs.

3153   On the basis of an ergonomic study made in 1967 of the use of staircases by old people, it is recommended that for housing purposes, given a floor to floor height of 2·600, staircases should have 14 risers, each 0·186[7].
This indicates floor openings of 3·600 × 0·900 in the case of straight staircases, and 3·000 × 1·800 for dogleg stairs, the length of goings to be approx 0·270[8].

3154   If staircases are installed having 16 risers floor openings will need to be 3·900 × 0·900 for a straight flight and 3·300 × 1·800 for a dogleg.

3155   This evidence indicates that, by comparison with standard staircases for normal purposes, suitable domestic staircases for old people will be very expensive. Rather than have this expense and still not cater for all users, it is preferred that a lift is installed, in association if need be with an economic 12 riser staircase.

316   External steps

3160   For steps not under cover or otherwise protected from the weather, gradients should be shallower than those recommended for internal stairs.

3161   The step rise should be not more than 0·165, preferred maximum 0·150. The going should be not less than 0·280 (diagram 31.4). See also 6312.

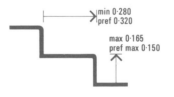

31.4   External steps

3162   The vertical rise of a flight of consecutive steps ought not to be more than 1·200.
Regulation H3(3)(c) of the Building Regulations requires that the total rise of a stairway exposed to the weather does not exceed 6·000.

[2] Bib 93610, p7. The study cited is Bib 93823
[3] Bib 93732, section 3.2, p4
[4] Bib 93725
[5] Bib 93821, p517
[6] Bib 93821, p520
[7] Bib 93820
[8] Bib 93821, p516

32 Ramps

320 Ramps: General considerations

3200 For wheelchair users the entrance to any building must be level or ramped.
A level or ramped access is also advantageous to elderly people, mothers with prams, furniture removers and undertakers.

Steps v ramps

3201 In many situations able-bodied and ambulant handicapped people, in particular amputees and hemiplegics, can more easily, safely and comfortably manage steps rather than ramps.
For ambulant handicapped people ramps can be particularly hazardous when descending; when ascending there is more control of body stability. In wet or icy conditions ramps can be more dangerous than steps. For related discussion see 1112 and 1224.

Alternative steps

3202 In the recommendations for public buildings in sections 63 and 64, the requirement is that where a ramp has a gradient of more than 1:12 an alternative stepped approach must be provided.

Public buildings

3203 For requirements for ramps to public buildings reference should be made to 6311 for ambulant disabled people and 6411 for chairbound disabled people.

Sources of data

3204 The dimensional data on ramps for handicapped people in this section and elsewhere in this book are based on an unpublished American study made in 1957[1] and Felix Walter's study of ramp gradients published in 1971[2].
Although the recommendations made by Walter on the basis of his findings are generally repeated here, three points need to be made regarding the reliability of the evidence. First, the tests were made inside a building, and were not subject to normal external climatic influences. Second, the 62 ambulant handicapped and 46 wheelchair subjects who took part in the study were selected by local authority welfare departments on rough medical and functional criteria and on willingness to participate; they were not necessarily representative of any wider population. Third, participants were supervised by an occupational therapist in conditions probably tending to encourage maximal achievement, and their behaviour, in terms of motivation to manage independently and display their ability, may not have corresponded to their behaviour in situations encountered externally in the normal course of events.

[1] Bib 93824
[2] Bib 93501
[3] This and other references in this section to building regulations are to part H of the third amendment (Bib 93802). A guidance note on part H is to be issued by the Department of the Environment

Building regulations

3205 Specific requirements for ramps under the Building Regulations are prescribed in the table to Regulation H4[3]. For a ramp within a dwelling the minimum width is 0·800; for a common ramp serving two or more dwellings the minimum is 0·900; for ramps in institutional and other buildings the minimum is 1·000. The maximum gradient is 1:12.
A ramp is defined as 'any part of a building which provides a route of travel for pedestrians or wheelchair users and has an inclined surface'. Guidance is not given as to the point at which a shallow gradient ceases to be an inclined surface and becomes a level surface rather than a ramp. Nor is guidance given as to when an approach ramp to a building is part of a building and when not.

3206 The Building Regulations require that handrails are provided to ramps, except where the side is formed by fixed seating.
The requirements in the table to regulation H4 state:

'Irrespective of the purpose group or compartment–
(a) any ramp with a total rise of more than 0·600 shall be provided with a handrail
(i) on each side if the width of the ramp is 1·000 or more; and
(ii) on at least one side in any other case; and
(b) any such handrail shall
(i) be so designed as to afford adequate means of support to persons using the ramp;
(ii) be continuous for the length of the ramp;
(iii) be securely fixed at a height of not less than 0·840 nor more than 1·000 (measured vertically above the top surface of the ramp); and
(iv) be terminated by a scroll or other suitable means.'

321 Ramps: Gradients

3210 Recommended ramp gradients are detailed in table 32.1.

Table 32.1 Recommended ramp gradients

	length of ramp	up to 3·000	3·000– 6·000	over 6·000
ambulant disabled people		1:9	1:12	1:12
independent wheelchair users		1:10	1:16	1:20
wheelchairs pushed by attendant		1:9	1:12	1:20
electric wheelchair users		1:16	1:16	1:20
all users, preferred maximum gradient		1:8	1:12	1:12

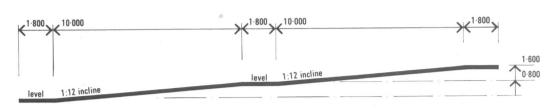

32.1 Long ramps (1:200)

3211 Although a maximum gradient of 1:12 for general purpose ramps is preferred, it should be recognized that there is no such thing as the 'right' gradient for a ramp for wheelchair users. For reasons discussed in 1112, the only 'right' gradient would be no gradient at all. Equally, although 1:12 is the preferred maximum, no absolute maximum is given.

3212 Practical constraints, for example the modification of an existing building entrance to make it accessible, may necessitate a ramp gradient of 1:8 or even 1:6. It is preferable, if circumstances demand it, that a very steep ramp is incorporated rather than no ramp at all, provided that steps are available for the use of people who would be hazarded by a ramp.

1:12 – For and against
3213 For general purposes a maximum ramp gradient of 1:12 is suggested, for the following reasons:

1. Some independent wheelchair users, including probably the majority of those who use buildings intensively, can climb a 1:12 ramp over a limited distance.

2. A 1:12 gradient is as steep as an independent wheelchair user can descend without the fear of tipping over forwards, and without having to balance the chair on its rear wheels. With a steeper ramp there is also the hazard of the chair running away, owing to the difficulty of braking by holding the hands on the handrims.

3. People who push loaded wheelchairs can as a rule negotiate a 1:12 gradient without difficulty, but may find a steeper ramp is exhausting or impossible to manage.

4. Ambulant handicapped people can as a rule walk up or down a 1:12 gradient without difficulty, but may find a steeper gradient is hazardous.

3214 Although a 1:12 ramp is generally permissible, a less steep ramp may be preferred because 1:12 can be too steep for:

1. Some electric wheelchairs to manage.

2. Independent wheelchairs to manage over an extended distance.

3. Wheelchair pushers who are not strong enough to manage without discomfort over any distance.

Independent wheelchair housing
3215 In the case of wheelchair housing, where it is essential that tenants who are chairbound are able to manage as independently as possible, a 1:12 ramp gradient ought not to be considered permissible. The preferred maximum gradient is 1:20.

Escape ramps
3216 In buildings where ramps are specifically incorporated as a means of escape and the requirement is that the gradient is not steeper than 1:10, it is not essential that a lesser incline of 1:12 is substituted to cater for disabled people. The additional cost penalty of having a shallower ramp may be so substantial as, on balance, to make it appropriate to compromise the preferred provision. The Greater London Council requires that escape ramps have a gradient of not more than 1:10[4].

3217 In cases where an escape ramp is used also for day-to-day purposes the gradient ought not to be steeper than 1:12.

322 Ramps: Dimensional data

Widths
3220 For general purpose ramps which allow wheelchairs to pass other wheelchairs, prams or pedestrians, the preferred minimum width is 1·500.

3221 For short ramps where there are alternative steps and no passing traffic, the width should be not less than 1·200.

Rest platforms
3222 In long ramps for use by disabled people, for example storey-height ramps, rest platforms may be incorporated.

3223 A suggested guideline is that a rest platform is provided for each 10·000 length of ramp or each 0·800 vertical rise (diagram 32·1).

3224 The length of rest platforms should be not less than 1·800.

3225 Variations in the plane of a ramp can be misleading to blind people or those with impaired sight, and rest platforms ought preferably to be incorporated only where ramps turn.

---

[4] Bib 93806, regulation 6.03

3226 A level platform having a length not less than 1·800 should be provided at the top of any general purpose ramp.

Area at foot of ramp

3227 At the foot of any ramp having a gradient of more than 1:12 there should where possible be a level area not less than 1·800 long.

3228 There should be adequate visibility and manoeuvring space at the foot of any ramp. A ramp falling to a point immediately at or behind a blind corner can be a hazard, particularly for wheelchair users.

323 Ramps: Handrails

3230 As a general rule, handrails to ramps are not needed as an aid for disabled people. This advice is debatable: it assumes the relaxation of building regulations (3206, 6005), and is at variance with advice given in the previous edition of this book [5], in CP96 [6], in the American national specifications [7] and in most other relevant publications. The reason is that handrails will commonly be superfluous if other recommendations are observed. Where a ramp has a gradient of more than 1:12, an alternative stepped approach, as recommended in 3202 and detailed in 63114, must be provided. This stepped approach will have rails to either side and will be preferred to the ramp by handicapped people, such as hemiplegics and old people generally, who would need rails to the ramp if an alternative were not available.
People who do use the ramp will be able-bodied people, wheelchair users or handicapped people who do not need rails for support. For some wheelchair users when climbing a ramp, a rail at the side can be useful to hang on to if the ramp is long; if the ramp is long the gradient, assuming observance of recommendations in table 32.1, will be sufficiently shallow to permit wheelchair brakes to hold the chair securely. This consideration is relevant only to independent wheelchair users climbing ramps: rails at either side are not of help to wheelchair users who are descending.

3231 A reason for not insisting on rails or balustrades to ramps is that they can be visually unattractive. This factor ought not to be a determining consideration where the primary criterion is the accommodation of disabled people. For many architects it is however an issue of real importance, and ought not to be disregarded.

[5] Bib 93002
[6] Bib 93000
[7] Bib 93020

Situations where handrails are necessary

3232 Where the gradient of a ramp is more than 1:12 and there is no alternative stepped approach, a handrail should be provided to both sides.

3233 Where the gradient of a ramp is between 1:12 and 1:20, and where there is no alternative stepped approach, a handrail should be provided to at least one side.

3234 Where there is an alternative stepped approach and a ramp, having a gradient steeper than 1:20, is likely to be used by ambulant handicapped people, a handrail should be provided to at least one side. This may occur where for example a ramp gives direct access to a building from parking places reserved for disabled drivers.

3235 Where there is a drop to the side of a ramp a balustrade must be provided.
Regulation H6 of the Building Regulations requires that the balustrade must be not less then 0·900 high where in a dwelling, and 1·100 where in other buildings.

3236 Where the gradient of a ramp is 1:20 or less no handrails need be installed.

Position of rails

3237 Handrails where provided should be at approx 1·000 above ramp level (diagram 32.2).
Ramp rails at levels rather higher than are suitable for some ambulant people are suggested, to aid ambulant handicapped people who put weight on the lower arm or elbow rather than only on the hand.

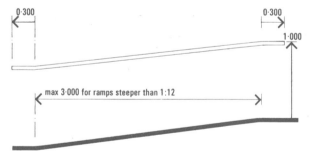

32.2   Short ramps (1:50)

3238 It is not recommended that parallel rails to ramps should be sufficiently close for both hands to be used on handrails simultaneously.
If this is to be done the width between rails needs to be approx 0·900, which means that the ramp will be too narrow for satisfactory use either by wheelchair users or for general purposes.

3239 Where handrails are installed to ramps it may be helpful if they extend horizontally not less than 0·300 at each end (diagram 32·2).

324 Ramps: Kerbs

3240 A kerb should be provided to the exposed side of any ramp, ie where there is a drop at the edge whether or not a handrail is installed.
A kerb is essential to check wheelchair wheels.

3241 To give adequate protection kerbs should be not less than 0·075 high, or 0·050 where there is a handrail.

3242 It is not recommended that a similar kerb is provided to the unexposed side of a ramp, for example where there is a side wall.
An auxiliary kerb may be suggested, on the basis that it could be useful to avoid the scuffing of wheel hubs or footrests against side walls[8]. Its value as a damage preventer is arguable, and it is likely in any event to be a hazard to ambulant handicapped people.

325 Ramps: Finishes, protection

3250 All ramps must have non-slip surfaces.
The provision of a smooth ramp surface for the benefit of wheelchair users is not in any circumstances recommended. Although a smooth surface may help reduce friction for the wheelchair user and allow him to climb the ramp with minimal effort, the hazards to other users are more significant. Only a very small number of wheelchair users might be less convenienced by having to use a rough rather than a smooth ramp surface.

3251 A textured finish with coarse aggregate not finer than 0·010 is recommended. A coarse aggregate bitumen or tarmacadam surface is satisfactory. If asphalt is used a roughened surface should be specified in preference to a sandpaper finish.

Concrete surfaces
3252 Polished concrete surfaces are dangerous; the surface should be treated with carborundum to prevent slipping when wet.

3253 A herringbone pattern may be incorporated to concrete ramps laid in situ (diagram 32.3).

Improving existing ramps
3254 Where existing ramp surfaces are slippery, non-slip surface dressing of hard wearing chippings may be applied. Where a non-abrasive material is required surfacing may be of cork granules.

Internal ramps
3255 Surfaces to internal ramps must be non-slip. A grooved rubber tile or sheet is suitable.
Corrugations should run at right angles to the direction of travel.

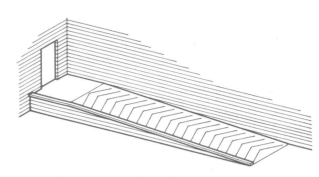

32.3   Ramps with side walls

Exposed ramps
3256 External ramps liable to be affected by frost or snow may be protected by built-in electric heating.

3257 A suitable method is by means of special duty cables laid directly on a concrete base, covered with 0·050 fine concrete screed and finished with a layer of asphalt to give a smooth wearing surface.

3258 For ramps to public buildings, controls are recommended which are sensitive to ice. For domestic ramps, control may be a manual switch or an air thermostat enclosed in a weatherproof box. An air thermostat may activate the heating during conditions of cold but dry weather when it is not necessarily required.

3259 Notes on the cost of ramp heating are in 90101.

326 Portable ramps

3260 Where the need is temporary or intermittent, the use of a portable ramp may prevent the necessity for expensive structural alteration to an entrance to a building or to internal areas where there are changes of levels.

3261 A portable ramp may also be used to facilitate access for wheelchair users in existing buildings where there are two or three steps, and where a permanent ramp is out of the question for reasons of space.

Proprietary portable ramps
3262 A number of proprietary portable ramps are now marketed in Britain. Most commonly they are made of mild steel channels, a pair being used in combination as tracks for wheelchair wheels. Long-section channel ramps are available which can be folded at the centre when not in use.

[8] See for example Bib 93002, para 3241

3263 An alternative is a broad ramp platform of expanded metal mesh, with low kerb pieces at either side (diagram 32.4). It is suitable for use on step heights of 0·110–0·240, with gradient not exceeding 1:8. The hinged angle support at the head end can be bolted to the step. The ramp can carry a load of up to 180kg. Cost notes: 90102.

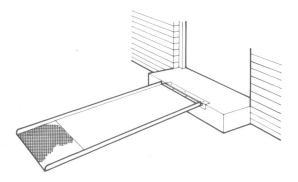

32.4　Portable ramp

Portable ramps: Rise

3264 The maximum rise that a portable ramp should be expected to cope with is about 0·600, which means not more than three high steps, or four low steps. A portable ramp will not be negotiable by wheelchair users independently, except in rare cases where the user has strong upper limbs and there is one low step only. For reasons discussed in 3114 the substitution of a portable ramp for a single step will not as a rule be an aid for a wheelchair pusher. Where there are two or more steps the ramp gradient will be steep. In the case of a rise of 0·600 and a ramp length of 2·000 the gradient will be nearly 1:3, which is too steep for all but the most capable wheelchair pusher to manage.

3265 When specifying a portable ramp which is to be removable, a check should be made to ensure that the hinged angle piece or pieces at the head of the ramp will grip the nosing of the top step securely.

33 Handrails

330   Handrails: General considerations

3300   Handrails and balustrades must be securely fixed. For notes on loadbearing requirements of internal walls and partitions see 370.

3301   Handrails should be provided to each side of any staircase or steep ramp.
Hemiplegics and others with weakness on one side may find it difficult to manage a staircase or ramp in both directions where a rail is on one side only. Among able-bodied people, right handed people may prefer a rail on the right and left handed people on the left. It can therefore be generally advantageous if there are rails to both sides.

3302   Handrails should be continuous and not broken at landings.

Corridor rails
3303   In residential homes or institutions for old or handicapped people, handrails may be provided to each side of any corridor.
The fixing of handrails to walls should be made with discretion. Not all walls will be on routes used by residents passing from one area to another, and the general fixing of rails is not necessary.

Metal handrails
3304   To avoid discomfort, metal handrails should be suitably protected, for example with a pvc or thermoplastic covering.

Blind people
3305   The fixing of studs or similar cues to the underside of handrails to indicate landings is sometimes advocated as an aid for blind people.
Such devices are of little or no value. In a familiar building, blind people know exactly how staircases are arranged. In an unfamiliar building blind people are invariably accompanied: if not they will be accustomed to coping with ordinary staircases. It is also probable they will not understand the intended meaning of the cue.

Handrails as hazard indicators
3306   Handrails should be provided to wall surfaces by short ramps and short flights of steps.
Short ramps and flights of one or two steps are hazardous because they can be overlooked. A handrail within the immediate line of vision can indicate the hazard more effectively than contrasting colours at floor level.

331   Handrails: Design data

3310   Handrails must be easy to grip. A circular section having a diameter of 0·045 or 0·050 is most satisfactory.
Rails with sharp edges or which are more than 0·055 wide or 0·050 deep are difficult for people with weak or arthritic hands to grip.

Wide handrails
3311   Where for structural reasons a handrail wider than 0·070 is necessary, a section of the type shown in diagram 33.1d should be provided, or there should be an additional narrow-section rail.

Deep handrails
3312   Where handrails are deeper than 0·050 a section should be provided which allows the hand to grip the rail securely.
The examples shown in diagrams 33.1a–d are suitable. The plain rectangular section shown in diagram 33.1e does not give a secure comfortable grip, and should be avoided. In diagrams 33.1a–d the thumb side is to the right.

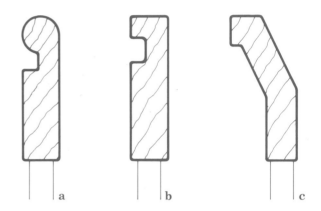

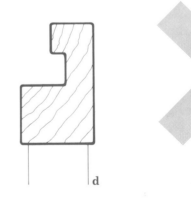

33.1   Handrail sections (1:5)

Wall-fixed handrails
3313   The preferred clear dimension between the inner edge of a handrail and the vertical wall surface alongside is 0·045, minimum 0·030 (diagram 33.2).

3314   In public buildings where a handrail projecting clear of the wall surface may be undesirable for safety reasons the wall should be chased and the handrail recessed, as shown in diagram 33.3.

3315   Brackets to wall handrails, whether recessed or projecting, should be fixed to the underside of rails, as shown in diagrams 33.2 and 33.3.

3316 The dimension from the surface of a handrail to the upper edge of a horizontal bracket or face of the sill below the rail should be not less than 0·070, preferred dimension 0·100 (diagrams 33.2 and 33.3). This is recommended to prevent discomfort to arthritics and others with hand disabilities, among whom a common practice is to trail the hand along the rail without flexing it.

3317 For data on handrails to ramps see 323.

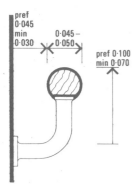

33.2   Wall-fixed handrails (1:5)

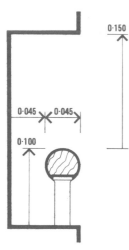

33.3   Recessed handrails (1:5)

332   Handrails: Staircases

3320 The vertical dimension from staircase nosings to the top of stair handrails should be approx 0·850 (diagram 33.4).
The optimum height for the rail for a person climbing the stairs is lower than when going down; 0·850 is a suitable compromise height.

3321 A dimension of 0·900 between parallel handrails is recommended to help handicapped people who need to hold a rail on both sides to pull themselves up.

3322 Where circumstances allow, handrails should extend horizontally not less than 0·300 at the top and bottom of any staircase (diagram 33.4).

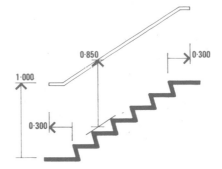

33.4   Handrails to stairs (1:50)

Falls on staircases occur most frequently when people are going down. Of these a large proportion, particularly among old people, occur because the bottom step is overlooked. If the handrail is extended horizontally beyond the bottom step there is a sensory cue at the point where the rail bends; the hand reaches this point when the leading foot is being transferred to floor level. A handrail extension at the top of the stair is an aid to blind people, particularly when descending.

3323 For cost notes on handrails to staircases see 9011.

333   **Support rails for baths and wcs**

3330 The notes below detail general requirements for support rails to baths and wcs. Specific requirements for wcs are detailed in section 5427, and for baths in sections 5470–5472. Costs are noted in 90324.

Uses of support rails
3331 Support rails are used basically either for (1) pushing the body up, (2) pulling the body up, (3) steadying the body when it is being lowered, or (4) steadying the body when transferring from one position to another.
Horizontal rails are generally indicated for lowering the body and for pushing up to a standing position, and vertical rails for pulling up to a standing position. For transferring position horizontal or vertical rails may be appropriate according to individual circumstances. Rails fixed diagonally at 45° are a poor compromise which serve well neither for pushing nor pulling; they ought not to be used.

3332 For the majority of disabled people it is much easier to push up to a standing position than to pull up, and the primary need is therefore for horizontal or near-horizontal support rails for pushing.

3333 Where a pushing rail is fixed to a side wall it can be helpful if it is slightly inclined (diagram 33.5) to support the arm, allowing the arm from elbow to hand, and not merely hand only, to carry weight when the body is being pushed up.

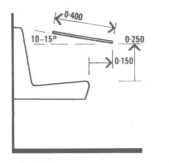

a (1:25)   b (1:5)

33.5   Support rails

Dimensions

3334   Support rails should have a diameter between 0·030 and 0·045, with a preferred diameter of 0·035 (diagram 33.5b).

3335   The clearance between support rails and the adjacent wall surface should be between 0·040 and 0·065, with a preferred dimension of 0·050 (diagram 33.5b).
A dimension less than 0·040 may not give adequate clearance for knuckles when rails are gripped by people with large hands. While a dimension of 0·065 is convenient for pulling rails, rails used for pushing or steadying should have a clearance not more than 0·050; there is otherwise the hazard that the lower arm will become wedged between wall and rail.

Materials and fixing

3336   Plastic-covered rails are preferred to chromium plated rails to give a secure grip when hands are wet. A slightly corrugated plastic surface is suggested.

3337   Support rails must be securely fixed to wall surfaces.
Horizontal or inclined support rails should be capable of carrying a static load of 150kg. See also 3703.

34 Thresholds

340 Thresholds: General considerations

3400 At entrances to buildings where special provision is made for wheelchair users, raised threshold sills should be avoided.

Raised thresholds can be hazardous to ambulant disabled and elderly people, and are an obstacle to wheelchairs. For disabled people using walking aids, or using trolleys for carrying purposes, even a small projection is an obstruction.

3401 Where provision is made for disabled people and for reasons of containing rain water it is necessary to have a low sill, the height of the sill should be not more than 0·025.

In certain circumstances (for example mobility housing, see 8221) it is admissible to incorporate a standard threshold sill, provided that, if required, the floor level to either side can be inclined to minimize the obstruction. The incline to either side should be not greater than 1:12.

3402 For housing for independent wheelchair users the height of any threshold sill ought not to exceed 0·015.

3403 The position of raised thresholds must be clearly defined. A high level of illumination is required. Raised thresholds may be coloured to contrast with adjacent floor surfaces.

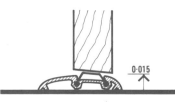

34.1 Flexible threshold

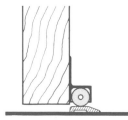

34.2 Threshold with neoprene seal insert

Flexible thresholds

3404 A permissible compromise in place of a raised threshold is a pvc or vinyl strip which serves as a draught excluder and water bar for either internal or external doors.

A strip of flexible pvc is arched into a base of extruded aluminium and is effective by means of spring action against the bottom of the door (diagram 34.1). Cost notes: 90120.

3405 An alternative which may avoid a raised threshold is shown in diagram 34.2.

An aluminium alloy threshold strip is screwed to the sill, fitted flat to make contact with the neoprene sealing insert which is fixed on the external face of the door. Cost notes: 90121.

341 External thresholds, water bars

3410 To prevent water penetrating across the threshold a gutter with a grating over may be provided in front of the threshold (diagram 34.3).

3411 Care should be taken to ensure that the grating does not inconvenience stick users (3030).

To dispose of condensation and water which crosses the threshold an internal channel with weep holes may be provided.

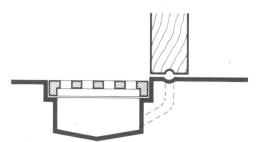

34.3 Threshold grating over gutter

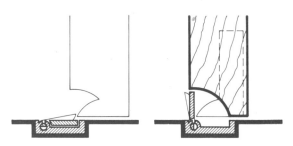

34.4 Hinged water bar

Hinged water bar

3412 A hinged water bar activated by an automatic catch may be used in place of a raised threshold. The water bar projects vertically when the door is closed, and falls flush with the floor surface when the door is opened (diagram 34.4).

This device is not suitable for use adjacent to gravel paths where loose particles may interfere with its functioning. Cost notes: 90122.

342   Thresholds: Internal doors

Standard doorsets

3420   Internal doorsets should be ordered without thresholds.

Internal doorsets to BS4787[1] are manufactured with a 0·015 high threshold, the purpose of which is to permit doors to clear carpets. Such a threshold is a hazard for disabled people where no carpet is fitted. In place of the threshold, doorsets may be ordered with a 0·015 batten tacked to the bottom of the frame, which can be simply removed when necessary.

Internal draught excluders

3421   To allow internal doors to clear carpets etc while maintaining an unobstructed threshold and avoiding the use of rising butt hinges, a retractable seal is suggested.

A vertical movable seal, for example of hard felt, is attached to the bottom of the door. The seal, which is activated by a striker plate on the hinge side of the jamb, rises when the door is open and drops when the door is closed (diagram 34.5). Cost notes: 90123.

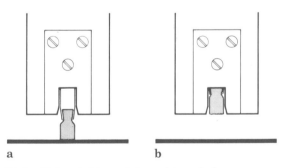

a   b

34.5   Retractable seal draught excluder

343   Thresholds: Sliding doors

3430   Upstanding door guides across the width of sliding door openings must be avoided.

3431   A channel recessed into the bottom rail and sliding over a guide fixed to one side of the door permits an unobstructed threshold (diagram 36.10).

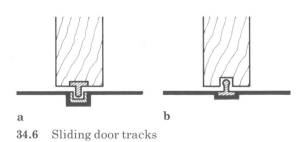

a   b

34.6   Sliding door tracks

3432   Where the door needs to be draughtproof, a tee and channel detail (diagram 34.6a) is preferred to a projecting bottom track (diagram 34.6b).

3433   Where insufficient headroom or an unsuitable lintel preclude the use of a top-hung track, a ball-bearing trolley fitting on a vee section bottom track is suggested.

The vee track should be maximum 0·015 deep to minimize floor obstruction.

[1] Bib 93831

35 Windows

350 Windows: General considerations

3500 Large windows should be carefully planned, particularly where glazed to low level.
Apart from factors of exposure and insecurity, windows at low level can aggravate draughts unless there is double glazing.

3501 Conditions causing draughts must be prevented. Cross draughts may be exacerbated by ill-fitting window casements and any consequent coldness may be keenly felt by a handicapped person. Even where the draught is minimal the psychological effect may be uncomfortable.

Bay windows
3502 Bay windows afford a wide range of view and are often appreciated by chairbound people.

Hazards
3503 Where side-hung casement or horizontally pivoted windows project externally the area outside should be landscaped so that paths are clear of any obstruction.

Double glazing
3504 Double glazing eliminates down draughts which can cause discomfort to disabled people.

3505 To minimize draughts and maintain warmth, windows to principal living rooms in housing for disabled people may with advantage be double glazed.

Cleaning
3506 To allow for cleaning, windows must not be placed in inaccessible positions.
In housing units for disabled people it may be assumed that external window cleaning will be done by an able-bodied member of the family or helper.

351 Windows: Sill heights

3510 In buildings for disabled people windows should allow for seated people to see the view outside (diagram 35.1).
The mean height of an elderly woman seated on a relatively high (0·430) chair is approx 1·110 (diagram 20·6). The eye level of a short woman seated on a relatively low (0·390) chair is approx 0·940. The eye height of a typical woman in a wheelchair is approx 1·160 (diagram 20.10).

Transomes
3511 In all living areas of housing for disabled people window transomes should not be installed inside the zone between 0·900 and 1·200 above floor level.

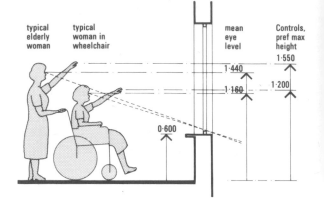

35.1 Window data (1:50)

Upper floors
3512 For windows at first floor level and above, sills should be low to allow seated people to look down to see the view; where regulations permit a level not higher than 0·600 above floor level is suggested.

3513 For safety reasons no opening part of an upper level window in family housing should be below 0·850 above floor level.

352 Daylighting

3520 In areas of buildings where illumination is by natural light it is important for safety reasons that windows are suitably placed; this applies to all users but is particularly relevant for people handicapped by failing eyesight.

3521 Higher illumination levels cannot fully compensate for failing eyesight.
Where daylight factors are increased it may be that sky glare is uncomfortable, and the advantages of more light are thereby lost.

3522 For people whose vision is seriously impaired special measures are suggested, such as supplementary local artificial lighting and the use of contrast and colour to identify danger areas.

3523 Curtain blinds or louvres may be used to reduce glare.

353 Ventilation: Height of window controls

3530 Where buildings are to be used independently by disabled people it should be borne in mind that ventilation may be provided other than by opening window lights.
Ventilation may be achieved by extractor fans or non-glazed ventilator panels associated with windows.

3531 Window opening and ventilator controls must be accessible and easy to manipulate.
The need to climb on a stool or chair to reach controls must be avoided.

Elderly people

3532 In housing for elderly people, controls ought not to be higher than 1·550 above floor level.

Chairbound people

3533 In housing to be used independently by chairbound people, controls ought not to be higher than 1·350 above floor level.
Although wheelchair users may be able to reach to a height of 1·450 obstructions are often placed in front of windows and a maximum height of 1·350 is recommended; the preferred maximum is 1·200.

3534 For practical and cost reasons it may be difficult to satisfy the suggested criteria for chairbound people. Where it is probable that an able-bodied person will be available to assist when required, the recommendations need not be strictly applied. Alternatively, controls to selected windows only may be located within the reach of chairbound people.

Out-opening side-hung casements

3535 To allow for reaching out, casement fasteners to out-opening side-hung windows should preferably be not higher than 0·075 below the maximum heights suggested.

354 Window ironmongery

3540 Special attention is needed for window openers to high level lights or where there is a fixed obstruction such as the kitchen sink.

3541 A louvre panel light controlled by a drop rod (diagram 35.2) is an alternative to the conventional fanlight with peg stay. Cost notes: 90130.

3542 Where remote control gear is installed a winding gear (diagram 35.3) is preferred to a sliding ring handle. A cord control gear is an alternative. Cost notes: 90131, 90132.

Hydraulic remote control

3543 Window lights beyond easy reach may be controlled by a hydraulic circuit either electrically or manually operated.
A transmitter can be mounted at a convenient point with a receiver actuator in a position to open and close the window. A series of windows may be operated by a single control.

Espagnolette bolt

3544 For tall windows a lever-operated espagnolette (or cremone) bolt with integral locking device is a possible alternative.

Stays

3545 A captive sliding stay locked in position with a lever arm (diagram 35.4) is preferred to a standard peg stay.
With a peg stay there is a danger of the window blowing open and out of reach.

35.2 Louvre panel light with drop rod

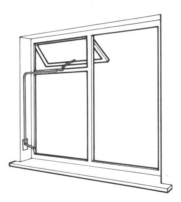

35.3 Window winding gear control

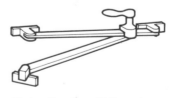

35.4 Captive sliding stay

3546 Friction stays may be suitable.
They may be preferred for people with hand impairments because they avoid the necessity for a double movement (ie operation of casement fastener and casement stay). The amount of friction should be adjustable. Cost notes: 90133.

Casement turns

3547 A lever-operated casement turn used in conjunction with a captive stay may be satisfactory.
A turn which can be engaged in a ventilating position, affording security from outside interference, may avoid the use of fanlights.

35.5   Cam stay control

Cam stay control

3548 For people with hand disabilities, a cam stay control for top-hung or horizontally pivoted lights is easy to manipulate (diagram 35.5).
This device is not suitable for large windows. A disadvantage is that the ventilation afforded by the window when open is restricted by the very limited throw of the stay. Cost notes: 90134.

355   Side-hung, louvre and sliding sash windows

Side-hung windows

3550 For people with reach limitations, in-opening side-hung windows may be preferred.
The casement fastener of an out-opening window in the open position may be beyond comfortable reach.

3551 Window cleaning is easier where casements open in.
The disadvantages of in-opening casements is that they may obstruct curtains or blinds when the window is open.

Louvre windows

3552 Louvre windows may be controlled by a single action lever handle or drop rod, permitting a variety of ventilating conditions.

3553 Because they are difficult to clean, louvre windows ought not to be used indiscriminately.

3554 To allow for cleaning, blades must open through at least 90°.

Sliding sash windows

3555 Vertical sliding sash windows are not recommended.
They are difficult to manipulate without the simultaneous use of both hands unless operation is by means of a geared handle. The locking device over the lower sash is often beyond the comfortable reach of disabled people.

3556 Horizontal sliding windows are permissible where draughts can be controlled.
They can usually be more conveniently operated using one hand than vertical sliding windows. The frame must be immune to warping.

356   Pivoted windows

3560 Horizontally pivoted windows with a friction pivot and single lever stay at sill level may be suitable for disabled people.
Controls to these windows can usually be located so that they are reachable by chairbound people.

3561 Where cleaning has to be from inside, horizontally pivoted windows are advantageous.

3562 Horizontal and vertical pivoted windows can be a hazard externally at ground level and are awkward to curtain internally.

Sliding projecting windows

3563 The curtain difficulty can be resolved if there is a sliding pivot.
The window opens as the pivot slides down, and is held in place by a captive stay at the sill. These windows are more difficult to close than simple horizontally pivoted windows, and may be unsuitable for people with upper limb impairments.

357   Blinds and curtains

3570 Blinds and curtains must be easy to operate.
Blind controls requiring the simultaneous use of both hands should be avoided.

3571 Curtains should be easy to remove and refix.

3572 Cord-operated curtain and blind controls are recommended.
Curtains attached to rollers or gliders running on a track and drawn across by hand may be unsuitable for disabled people with impaired coordination. Curtains and fittings can be damaged when weight is applied.

3573 Blinds and curtains may be electrically remote-controlled.

36 Doods

360   Doors: General.

3600   Doors: General planning considerations

36000   Where provision is made for disabled people,
careful attention must be given to the placing and
specification of doors.
For non-disabled people matters such as the width
and weight of doors, whether they open in or out,
and whether they are hinged in the corner or away
from the corner are not of significant account. For
disabled people, particularly wheelchair users,
these matters can be critical.

Corner positions

36001   Doors in corner positions should permit easy
approach.
There should be an unobstructed space adjacent to
the door handle on the leading face of any side-
hung door, see 36043.

36002   Where a side-hung door is placed in a corner
position, the conventional plan arrangement
whereby the door is hinged at the side further from
the corner should be reversed (diagram 36.1).

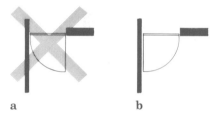

a   b

36.1   Doors in corner positions

Small rooms

36003   Doors to small rooms should slide or open out
instead of opening in.

36004   In-opening doors to bathrooms and wcs are not
recommended.
There is a danger that if an individual falls inside,
the door will be blocked; this is particularly
important with regard to epileptics.

Planning hazards

36005   In public buildings doors opening out into
circulation areas may be a hazard.
Where a wc compartment or changing cubicle is
planned for disabled people it should be in a
position where an out-opening door is not a hazard
to other users. See diagram 63.1.

36006   Doors opening out into passageways may be
recessed to avoid accident hazards.

36007   Doors should not be planned in such a way that
door swings conflict.

36008   Doors should not be positioned over the riser of the
top step of a flight of stairs.

3601   Standard doorsets

36010   In this section and elsewhere, recommendations
relating to side-hung doors are based on the use of
standard doorsets as specified in BS4787[1].

36011   The use of standard doorsets means in practice
that, where disabled people are to be catered for,
only three doorset sizes are possible, namely 1·000,
0·900 and 0·800.
The 1·000 doorset gives a doorleaf of 0·926 and a
clear opening width of 0·875; the 0·900 doorset gives
a doorleaf of 0·826 and an opening width of 0·775
(diagram 36.2), and the 0·800 doorset gives a
doorleaf of 0·726 and an opening width of 0·675.

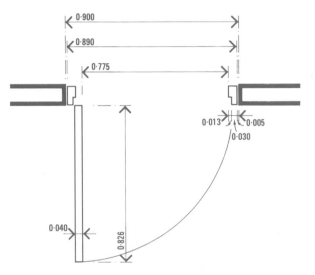

36.2   Plan of standard 0·900 internal doorset (1:20)

36012   Except for cupboard doors the 0·700 doorset should
not be used.
The 0·700 doorset, which is used occasionally in
general housing for wc compartments, gives an
opening width of only 0·575 which is too narrow for
disabled people to pass through comfortably.

Non-standard doors

36013   Doors other than to standard sizes can be purpose-
made but they will be substantially more expensive
and will not conform with standard planning
modules. They ought not as a rule to be considered.

3602   Sliding doors v side-hung doors: General
considerations

36020   Except where the requirements of specific disabled
users indicate firmly the desirability of sliding
doors, side-hung doors are preferred.
General considerations relating to door mechanics,
acoustic and thermal insulation, costs and fire
protection favour side-hung doors. Considerations
relating to accident hazards, economic use of floor
space and ease of circulation favour sliding doors.

[1] Bib 93831

Door mechanics

36021 Closing and locking devices for side-hung doors are simpler and more reliable in use than those for sliding doors.

When opening a sliding door, users tend to pull it across the line of travel; this is done sometimes because they suppose the door is hinged, more often because the action of opening, particularly in the case of wheelchair users and other disabled people, is rough and unsympathetic. The consequence is to strain the sliding gear and in time for the door to become misaligned. This problem can largely, though not entirely, be alleviated by expensive door gear; the typical unsophisticated domestic installation is invariably vulnerable to uncaring treatment by disabled people. For this reason the general installation of sliding doors in residential homes and other buildings special for disabled people is not recommended.

Acoustic insulation

36022 Where a high level of acoustic insulation is required side-hung doors are recommended. Sliding doors to wc compartments can be embarrassing owing to ineffective acoustic insulation.

Thermal insulation

36023 Where the avoidance of draughts through gaps around doors is critical, side-hung doors are preferred since sliding doors are more difficult to insulate effectively.

Fire protection

36024 In situations where resistance to fire and spread of smoke are important considerations, side-hung doors are preferred.

Self-closing mechanisms for sliding doors are not always reliable in use and can be a hazard to disabled people.

Sterilization of space

36025 Where it is important that floor space is not sterilized sliding doors are indicated.

For comments on the sterilization of floor space by the swing of side-hung doors see 36143.

36026 Where it is important that wall space is not sterilized side-hung doors are indicated.

Doors sliding across wall surfaces may prevent the efficient utilization of walls, for example for storage purposes.

Position of adjacent walls

36027 The position of obstructions constraining approach, for example (particularly in respect of wheelchair users) a side wall close to the door handle where a side-hung door would open in, may indicate the preferability of sliding doors.

On the other hand the position of adjacent walls, particularly where circulation space is tight, may preclude the use of sliding doors, for example in areas serving cloakrooms, bathrooms or wcs.

Costs

36028 Sliding doors are more expensive than side-hung doors.

In a typical domestic situation where the choice is between (for example) a standard internal side-hung 0·900 doorset and a sliding door giving an equivalent clear opening width, the sliding door may cost twice as much or more. Cost notes: 90140.

3603 Sliding doors v side-hung doors: Disabled user criteria

36030 For ambulant disabled people sliding doors are commonly simpler to manipulate, but a side-hung door with a suitable lever handle need not be at all difficult to manage.

Where other factors suggest a side-hung door the manipulation of ironmongery is not as a rule a critical contra-indicating factor.

36031 For people with hand or arm impairments side-hung doors with suitable furniture need not be more difficult to manipulate than sliding doors.

36032 For wheelchair users, and particularly for independent wheelchair users, sliding doors are easier to manipulate and negotiate.

Accident hazards

36033 Accident hazards, for example to epileptics falling inside a small room, may indicate a sliding door if an out-opening door is not practicable.

36034 For blind people, side-hung doors left partially open are hazardous and sliding doors may be preferred.

3604 Sliding doors v side-hung doors: Wheelchair users

36040 For wheelchair users, sliding doors are often preferred but it is not advocated that they are used indiscriminately.

In many situations in buildings not planned with consideration for disabled people wheelchair users find that side-hung doors are placed in awkward or inaccessible positions. They therefore tend to suppose that sliding doors are always more satisfactory, which is not a valid generalization.

36041 In low cost housing, side-hung doors should be installed where no inconvenience will be caused by their use.

Space for convenient approach is important, see diagrams 24.9a-f.

Side-hung doors and wheelchair manoeuvre

36042 Where the wheelchair user approaches parallel to the face of a door opening in or out (for example as shown in diagram 24.10c) the amount of manoeuvring required will be no more than if a sliding door had been installed.

Where approach is face on, more complicated wheelchair manoeuvring is usually necessary.

36043 To minimize manoeuvring the clear wall space to the side of the door by the doorhandle should be not less than 0·300 wide, with a preferred dimension of 0·600.

36044 With a passageway 1·200 wide, a 0·900 doorset placed to one side allows the wheelchair user to approach relatively close, so minimizing reversing and manoeuvring (diagram 36.3a). Negotiating the door will be more difficult if the passageway is narrower, for example 1·000, or if the door is placed centrally (diagram 36.3b). It will also be more difficult and not less if the door is wider, for example if a 1·000 doorset is substituted (diagram 36.3c).

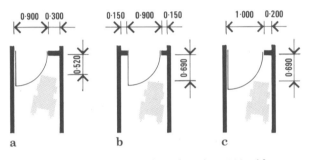

36.3 Wheelchair approach to door in 1·200 wide passageway (1:100)

36045 Diagram 36.4 shows how a person in a wheelchair may negotiate an in-opening door in a 1·200 wide passageway.

In diagram 36.4a he approaches close to the door, to reach the handle with his left hand. To allow clearance for the door to swing as he pulls it he has to reverse his chair (diagram 36.4b); if the door has a heavy spring closer it may be necessary to apply the brakes while this is done. He then passes through the door (diagram 36.4c), pulling the door to with his left hand. He may not be able to reach back far enough to shut the door behind him, though the fixing of an auxiliary horizontal rail (diagram 36.5) or D handle close to the door hinge (diagram 36.17) will help. Having passed through the door (diagram 36.4d) he may need to go down the passage, find a place to turn, and come back to close the door (diagram 36.4e). These operations may be complicated if, for example, he is carrying a loaded tray of spillable goods, or if someone has parked boxes or pieces of furniture in the convenient storage space to the side of the door.

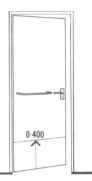

36.5 Pull rail to door

Bathrooms and wcs

36046 For bathrooms and wcs for wheelchair users, a sliding or bi-folding door may be more satisfactory than a side-hung door.

36047 The typical wheelchair user enters a small bathroom or wc compartment forwards and exits backwards. Turning of the wheelchair is done not inside the room but in the circulation area outside the door. An out-opening door may prevent this manoeuvre being undertaken economically and a sliding door is therefore preferred. An in-opening door is generally not suitable because of the hazard of falls and because when the wheelchair is in the room it may be impossible to close the door, or awkward manoeuvring will be necessary.

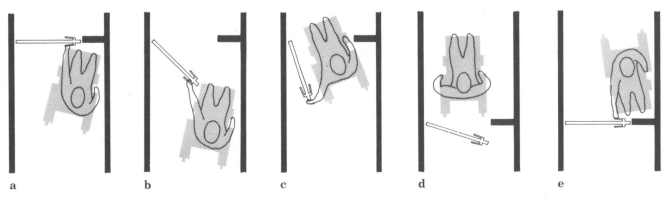

36.4 Wheelchair negotiation of in-opening door in 1·200 wide passageway (1:50)

3605 Sliding doors

36050 Single leaf straight sliding doors are preferred.

36051 Bi-parting doors operating sympathetically on a single track may be installed where there is not sufficient space for the door to slide to one side only. It is important that door rebates meet accurately or that an adequate draught excluder is fitted.

36052 Sliding doors may be controlled remotely by a cord and pulley; to be effective a counterweight should also be incorporated.

Bi-folding doors

36053 In situations where space is restricted bi-folding doors may be a solution.
An example may be the door to the bathroom or wc in a small flat, where an in-opening door would prevent wheelchair access, an out-opening door would conflict with circulation requirements and a sliding door would not be possible for lack of sliding space.

36054 Where bi-folding doors are installed, a wider doorset will be needed to give the clear opening width required than if a side-hung door is installed. Where for example an opening width of 0·770 as given by a 0·900 doorset is required, a bi-folding doorset having a length of 1·000 will be required (diagram 36.6).

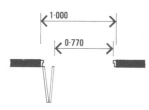

36.6   Bi-folding doors

36055 Bi-folding and other concertina doors have the disadvantage that sliding gear is easily damaged by careless use.
This problem is greater than for straight sliding doors. Bi-folding doors should be avoided in residential homes and other buildings used by a variety of disabled people. For discussion see 36021.

3606 Automatic opening doors

36060 Automatic opening doors are recommended.
Automatic opening doors can be electrically, hydraulically or pneumatically operated.
Operation is triggered by a sensing device which can be photo-cell or mat contact. Alternatively, operation may be by foot or hand pressure, pendant switch or push button. Costs are noted in 90141.

Door widths

36061 For wheelchair users, automatic opening doors should give a clear opening not less than 0·750 wide, preferred minimum 0·800.

36062 The majority of installations incorporate a time delay device whereby doors close automatically after a prescribed time lapse.
Such doors can be hazardous to wheelchair users and slow-moving ambulant disabled people.

36063 In the event of power failure it must be possible to move the door freely by hand.

Operating devices

36064 The most suitable operating device is the contact mat.
Doors are held open for as long as the area to either side is occupied. Mats must be sensitive to pressure exerted unevenly, for example by crutch users.

36065 Where automatic doors are operated by photo-electric cells a Z layout of light beams ensures that doors remain open if traffic moves slowly (diagram 36.7).

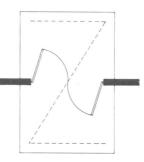

36.7   Automatic doors with photo-electric cells

Glazing

36066 Where doors are fully glazed an applied hazard cue must be incorporated, see 36215.

3607 Revolving doors

36070 Revolving doors are commonly installed in public buildings because they afford effective thermal insulation.

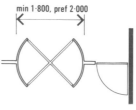

36.8   Revolving doors

36071 An auxiliary side-hung door must be incorporated by any set of revolving doors (diagram 36.8). Revolving doors are not usable (unless collapsed) by chairbound people. They can also be extremely hazardous to ambulant disabled people, old people and blind people.

36072 Revolving doors with narrow door leafs are hazardous. For a 4-leaf revolving door the diameter inside the circle should be not less than 1·800, preferred dimension 2·000.

3608 Door protection

36080 In private housing for wheelchair users the protection of door surfaces may be advantageous. Whether door protection ought as a matter of course to be incorporated in housing for disabled people is a matter of debate. Some wheelchair users who manage independently know from experience the exact geography of circulation spaces in their homes, and always avoid hitting surfaces. Other independent wheelchair users tend to be careless in their own homes, particularly when they are in a hurry to get things done; they may regularly hit door and architrave surfaces and protection is necessary. When they visit other people's housing the same people may be much more careful about how they manoeuvre their chairs, avoiding any possible damage. Because of this it is improbable, as might be supposed, that the liability of door surfaces to damage is a function of the width of door openings, indicating wider openings. No special study has been made, but it could be that as much damage occurs where door widths and passage widths are wide as where they are narrow.

36081 In residential homes for disabled people, in special schools for handicapped children, in social centres for the elderly or handicapped and in comparable buildings door protection is recommended.

Side-hung doors
36082 To protect side-hung doors against wheelchair footrests, a kicking plate should be fixed on the trailing face of the door to a height of 0·400 above floor level (diagram 36.5). A kicking plate is superfluous on the leading face of the door; the plate should be fixed only on the side the wheelchair user will kick against when he pushes open the door.

36083 To protect against all damage, including by wheelchair handles, protection will be needed to a height approx. 1·000 above floor level, see 3731.

36084 Double swing doors where installed should have kicking plates on both surfaces. Where double swing doors are glazed, toughened or wired glass is recommended.

Materials
36085 For door protection, heavy duty vinyl sheeting secured by contact adhesive is durable and resistant to impact. It can be dressed round door rebates. It is advantageous if the area protected extends above the door handle, allowing marks around the handle to be removed.

36086 Plastic laminate protection is satisfactory, but metal kicking plates are not recommended. Metal plates are easily scratched and can damage metal parts of a wheelchair.

Door frames
36087 Architraves and door linings should be of hardwood or protected by a metal angle. Wood domes at the foot of door frames are not recommended, see 3738.

36088 The hanging stile of an open door through which a wheelchair is turned (as shown in diagram 24.10e) is particularly vulnerable to damage, and should be suitable protected.

36089 Costs of door protection are noted in 90142.

361 Opening width of doors

3610 Opening width of doors: Side-hung doors

36100 Standard side-hung doors give a clear opening width 0·125 less than the width of the doorset (diagram 36.2). Allowing for tolerances in manufacture, the difference between doorset widths and opening widths ranges from 0·121 to 0·127.

36101 For a standard internal doorset the thickness of the doorleaf is 0·040 and the width of the doorstop 0·013. The actual clear width is also affected by the clearance between leaf and jamb; diagram 36.2 shows relevant dimensions for a standard internal doorset having a length of 0·900.

External doors
36102 Standard external side-hung doors give a clear opening width of 0·149 less than the length of the doorset. The clear opening width of (for example) an external 0·900 door is 0·751. The lesser opening width given by an external door by comparison with an internal door is because the door jamb is thicker and the doorstop is wider. External doorsets may also be specified with a thickness of 0·044 rather than 0·040. Allowing for tolerances in manufacture, the difference between doorset length and opening width ranges from 0·145 to 0·155.

3611 Opening width of doors: Sliding doors

Handles both sides

36110 Where, as is recommended in 36321, projecting handles are fixed to both sides of a sliding door, the width between door linings should not be less than 0·125 greater than the required clear opening width (diagram 36.9)
This allows a dimension of 0·052 from the face of the jamb to the centre line of the handle; assuming a handle cross-section of 0·024 the actual clearance will be 0·040, with the door in either the open or closed position. For people with impaired hands, manipulation of the door handles in such a position may be awkward and a wider clearance, say 0·060, is preferred.

36111 To give a clear opening width equivalent to that of a standard side-hung door the sliding doorleaf should be 0·100 longer than for the corresponding side-hung door.
Diagram 36.9 shows a 0·926 doorleaf giving a clear opening width of 0·775.

36112 To cater for people with hand impairments where the preferred clearance of 0·060 is provided at the door handle, the clear opening width will be reduced accordingly, in the case of the example shown in diagram 36.9 to 0·735.

Handle one side

36113 Where space is limited, for example to adapted existing openings, it is permissible if a projecting handle is fixed to one side only.

36114 Diagram 36.10 shows a 0·826 doorleaf giving an opening of 0·800.
This particular plan arrangement is shown because it is suitable for use with a standard 0·800 structural opening. The doorleaf overlaps the jamb by 0·013 on each side; this is not satisfactory either for acoustic or thermal insulation purposes, but where other criteria take precedence may be considered permissible.

36115 A projecting D handle should be fixed to the outer face of the door at the leading end, with a second handle fixed to the trailing end (diagram 36.9). For notes on door ironmongery see 3632.

Bi-parting doors

36116 For bi-parting sliding doors where projecting handles are fixed to both sides of each door, the width between door jambs should not be less than 0·180 greater than the required opening width (diagram 36.11). This assumes a clearance of 0·060 between handles when doors are in the closed position.

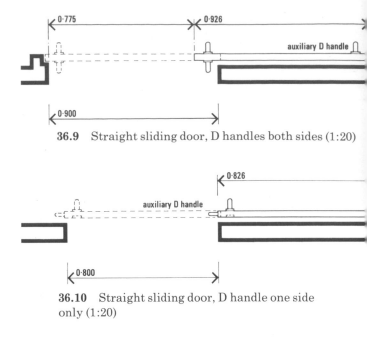

36.9 Straight sliding door, D handles both sides (1:20)

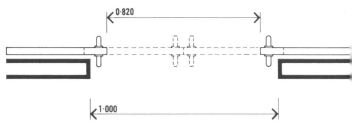

36.10 Straight sliding door, D handle one side only (1:20)

36.11 Bi-parting sliding doors (1:20)

3612 Opening width of doors: Beds

36120 Doors should give a clear opening width of not less than 1·120 to allow for the movement of beds where there is no turning.
To allow for turning a wider opening is required; a door opening into a passage 1·500 wide should have an opening not less than 1·420 (diagram 36.12).

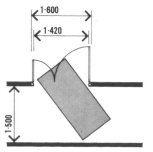

36.12 Door opening for beds (1:100)

36121 In the planning of residential homes or other buildings for disabled people it is unlikely that there will be any cause for having doors which are sufficiently wide to pass beds through.
The preferred routine is that disabled people who need to be moved are transferred from their bed to a wheelchair. Requests from fire officers for very wide doors should be resisted, see 1520.

3613 Opening width of doors: Ambulant disabled people

36130 Very narrow doors are awkward for stick or crutch users and for people using walking aids to negotiate.

36131 For ambulant disabled people, doors should give a clear opening width of not less than 0·670. This recommendation is based on the use of a 0·800 doorset: the alternative of a 0·700 doorset would give an opening width of 0·570 which would be inconveniently narrow for ambulant disabled people.

36132 Where the space available for approach to a door is restricted, a 0·800 doorset may be preferred to a 0·900 doorset.
The analysis of door widths convenient for wheelchair users (36045) is equally applicable to ambulant disabled people, particularly those using walking aids.

3614 Opening width of doors: Wheelchair users

36140 The minimum clear opening width of doors to allow for wheelchair users is 0·750. The preferred minimum is 0·770.
These requirements are determined, for reasons discussed below, by the characteristics of 0·900 doorsets.

Standard metric doorsets
36141 In respect of building design and optimum door widths for wheelchair users, the traditional precepts have been that doors must be wider than normal, that wide doors are preferable because they allow wheelchair users to pass through at an angle, and that the width of doors should be variable to take account of the width of passageways or the position of obstructions opposite the door. The introduction of standard metric doorsets means that these precepts have to be reexamined, since the dimensions of doorsets available become a primary determinant.

36142 Of the three doorset options of 1·000, 0·900 and 0·800, the 0·800 doorset gives a clear opening width of 0·675. While this is manageable for a standard chair up to approx 0·620 wide if the movement is straight in or out, it gives no latitude for manoeuvre and can be discarded.

36143 Thus possible doorset widths are 1·000 and 0·900. Many lay people, many wheelchair users, and some architects, working on a wider-the-better rule of thumb, will opt for 1·000 doorsets. The fact is however that, except where circulating space is very tight, 0·900 doorsets are satisfactory for wheelchair users; for discussion see 1702. Apart from the likelihood that 0·900 doorsets will be more economic than 1·000 doorsets, there are two practical reasons why they may be more suitable:

1. A 1·000 doorset does not fit the standard planning module of 0·300, whereas the 0·900 doorset does. This means that as a rule it is more economic to plan other components, such as partitions and windows, where 0·900 doorsets are used and not 1·000 doorsets.

2. A 1·000 doorset is extravagant on space, sterilizing approx 26 per cent more floor space than a 0·900 doorset. This factor can be critical where doors are in-opening to small rooms such as bathrooms or cloakrooms, or to rooms where the economic use of space is important, such as domestic kitchens or hostel bed-sitting rooms.

Suitability of 0·900 doorsets
36144 The 0·900 doorset is the preferred standard door size for normal housing purposes. It is advocated that the design of standard wheelchairs should take account of typical building constraints, particularly in housing. The implication here is that standard wheelchairs ought to be designed so that they are capable of passing through a 0·775 opening (ie a 0·900 doorset) from a 0·900 wide passageway. If wheelchair manufacturers observe this condition there will be little reason for using 1·000 doorsets in any circumstances. Thus the recommendations relating to side-hung doors throughout this book are based on the use of 0·900 doorsets.

36145 The proposition that wheelchairs should be designed to pass through 0·900 doorsets from 0·900 passageways does not mean that this standard ought to apply generally in buildings planned for wheelchair users. To operate comfortably most wheelchair users need more generous circulation spaces. The doorset size should remain constant, the variable being the passage width or the position of obstructions opposite or alongside doors.
For notes on circulation spaces and wheelchair turns through doors see 245.

Minimum clear opening
36146 The general use of side-hung doors giving a clear opening width of 0·770 (the actual dimension is approx 0·775, but to allow for tolerances 0·770 is the design limit) means that for other doors, such as sliding doors and automatic opening doors, there are advantages for the architect in working consistently to the preferred minimum clear opening width of 0·770 for wheelchair use.

36147 The absolute minimum clear opening width of 0·750 is determined by the admissibility of using 0·900 doorsets for external entrance doors. For discussion see 36102.

36148 For purposes of comparison with a 0·900 doorset giving a doorleaf of 0·826 and an opening width of 0·775, the Imperial size door recommended for wheelchair purposes in the second edition of this book was 2ft 9in, which is 0·838, giving an opening width of 2ft 7in, which is 0·787.

362 Self-closing doors

3620 Self-closing devices: General considerations

36200 Automatic door closers should be specified with care.
Floor springs, overhead door springs and spring hinges can make doors awkward to negotiate for wheelchair users and ambulant disabled people.

36201 Rising butt hinges are not recommended (36333) but are permissible to lightweight doors where a simple closing device is required.

Residential homes
36202 In residential homes for elderly or disabled people the need to install heavy self-closing fireproof doors, which in everyday use are an obstacle and a hazard, should be avoided.

36203 Doors held in the open position by magnetic catches linked to fire detectors may be advised. When the fire detector is activated the link breaks and doors close automatically. This provision can be valuable in homes for severely handicapped people. For discussion relating to fire protection see 6036. Cost notes: 90143.

36204 Lightweight spring closers are permissible in homes and institutions for blind people where doors left open can be dangerous.

3621 Swing doors: General considerations

36210 Heavy swing doors, either single or double leaf, should be avoided.
They can be hazardous to wheelchair users, blind people, and people using sticks or crutches.

Glazing
36211 Swing doors where installed should be glazed to minimize accident hazards.

36212 To allow for wheelchair users, the bottom of the glazing ought not to be higher than 1·010 above floor level (diagram 36.13a).
For standard external or internal doorleaves to BS4787[2] incorporating a glazed opening as shown in diagram 36.20, the dimension from the bottom of the door frame to the bottom of the glazing is 0·990. This gives a dimension from floor level of 1·010 when the threshold and clearance are allowed for.

36213 Alternatively a vertical strip of glazing 0·220 wide may be incorporated (diagram 36.13b).
This is a standard glazing opening for internal flush doorleaves to BS4787.

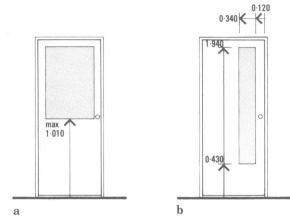

a   **b**

36.13 Glazed doors (1:50)

36214 In buildings for handicapped children glazing to doors should be continuous to the level of the kick plate.
A vertical strip of glazing may with advantage be installed to the side of the door.

36215 Where doors are fully glazed a hazard cue, such as an applied strip at approx 1·000 above floor level, should be incorporated to minimize hazards.

3622 Double-action swing doors

36220 Lightweight double-action swing doors may be suitable in buildings for disabled people.
Because these doors can be pushed open in either direction they can be helpful for people who can more easily push a side-hung door open than they can pull it open, for example some wheelchair users and some crutch users.

36221 Double-action doors may be fitted with a combined helical spring closer and check hinge, permitting the door to open through 180°.
These hinges are suitable for use in housing or institutions where people are using electric wheelchairs. Because of the spring action they are less suitable for people using self-propelled chairs.

[2] Bib 93831

House adaptations

36222 In existing dwellings a side-hung door may be awkwardly sited for wheelchair users (diagram 36.14a). It may be that the door can be replaced by a double action swing door which can be pushed open in either direction (diagram 36.14b).

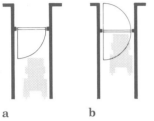

a   b

36.14 Adaptation with double action swing door

Flexible doors

36223 In certain special buildings for disabled people, double leaf flexible doors may be used. A semi-transparent pvc is suggested.
These doors have an industrial character. They ought not to be used where the aim is to maintain a domestic appearance.

3623 Door springs: General considerations

36230 The weight of spring closers to doors must be reduced as far as possible.
Where a hydraulic spring closer is specified the requirements of disabled people may be difficult to reconcile with other criteria. If too light a spring is specified, doors may not remain firmly closed in draughty conditions, which, apart from any discomfort caused, may mean that doors intended to be fire resistant may be ineffectual.

Resistances

36231 A resistance not exceeding 12Nm is recommended for external doors and 8Nm for internal doors.
In practice this may be impossible to achieve, for reasons discussed below.

36232 The pressure required varies according to the weight and width of the door and the adjustment of the door spring. As a rule a narrow door is more difficult to open than a wide door.
Closing devices currently manufactured do not as a rule allow for adjustments to be made. To vary the resistance it is necessary either to specify a heavier or lighter closer, or to fix the closer in other than the normal position on the door. The pressure is reduced the nearer that the door closer is moved towards the hinge; the actual weight of the door itself is not a factor of great significance.

36233 A medium light hydraulic spring closer, such as a Briton A, gives a 1·7kg pull on the training edge, equalling 13·77Nm for a 0·826 door. This is the minimum that can practically be used to hold a door against normal wind pressure.

External doors

36234 Where a door is in an exposed position and a heavy spring would otherwise be necessary, the door should be recessed or otherwise sheltered from prevailing winds.

36235 A heavy spring closer may be necessary for external doors, for example a Briton B which has a pull of 2·4kg on the trailing edge, giving a pressure of 19·45Nm on a 0·826 door and 21·80Nm on a 0·926 door.

36236 External doors in exposed positions may have single action springs and may open out.

3624 Delayed action devices

36240 Spring door closers should incorporate a delayed action closing device.
Delayed action closers are helpful for wheelchair users, ambulant disabled people, mothers pushing prams and people carrying baggage or pushing trolleys.

36241 For wheelchair users and ambulant disabled people, a time delay of between four and six seconds is suggested, with the door held at an angle of between 70° and 90°.
Longer time delays can be built in to the device, but may cause inconvenience to general users.

36242 Dual control valves are recommended, one governing door closing speed and the other giving adjustable acceleration over the last 10° of closing. This catching action can be useful to wide doors and where draughts are abnormal.

363 Door ironmongery

3630 Door handles: General considerations

36300 In buildings for disabled people, door handles should be at approx 1·000 above floor level; the standard fixing height of 1·040 is satisfactory (diagram 36.15).
1·040 is the height of door handles to internal doorsets to BS4787[3], given that the door handle is fixed centrally on a doorleaf 2·040 high, with a threshold of 0·015 and clearance of 0·005. For external doors to BS4787, the door handle will be at 1·025 above internal floor level, assuming a low threshold. Although some wheelchair users may find it more convenient if the door handle is at a level lower than 1·040, the advantages are unlikely to be significant.

---

[3] Bib 93831

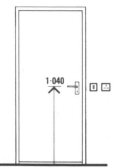

36.15 Door handle height (1:50)

Lever handles

36301 Where doors are latched, lever handles are preferred to knob handles.

Knob door handles do not provide an adequate grip for people with hand impairments. A lever handle can usually be operated with one or more fingers only, whereas a knob handle cannot easily be operated without the use of the thumb. A study published in 1966 of door handles tested by disabled people confirmed that lever handles are most suitable[4].

36302 A moulded lever handle which fits the hand comfortably and can be securely gripped should be specified.

A handle which is flattened in the horizontal rather than the vertical plane, and is curved convexly upward away from the pivot, ie moulded to fit into the palm of the hand, is suggested; diagram 36.16 illustrates a suitable example.

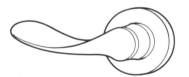

36.16 Lever door handle

36303 For people with deformed or stiff hands the clearance between the handle and the door face ought not to be less than 0·035.

Because clothes etc may catch on projecting handles, a wider clearance than 0·050 is not recommended.

Knob handles

36304 To avoid injury caused by knuckles grazing on door frames, knob handles ought not to be used on the outside of in-opening doors with narrow sash locks.

36305 A knob on one side of the door in combination with a lever handle on the other is not recommended; the stronger springing needed for the lever handle makes knob operation difficult.

[4] Bib 93832

3631 Door ironmongery: Side-hung doors

Auxiliary handle

36310 For wheelchair users a pull handle may be fixed to the trailing face of a side-hung door to enable the door to be pulled to as the person passes through. The pull handle should be aligned with the door handle, at a point approx 0·200 from the hinge side (diagram 36.17).

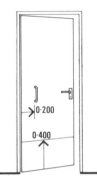

36.17 Auxiliary pull handle and kicking plate

Horizontal rail

36311 An auxiliary horizontal rail as shown in diagram 36.5 is more easily manipulated by wheelchair users and other disabled people than a short vertical handle.

The horizontal rail should be aligned with the door handle or bolt, or be at approx 1·000 above floor level if a catch only is provided.

36312 In institutions etc where there are several ambulant disabled people, horizontal push and pull bars in association with suitable roller catches may be preferred to lever handles to side-hung doors.

36313 Horizontal rails may also be helpful for wheelchair users whose reach is limited, by enabling them to open and close doors with the aid of a hook on a long portable handle.

Auxiliary pull handles, cost notes: 90144.

Amputees

36314 To permit doors to be conveniently manipulated by double amputees wearing twin split hooks, the diameter of rails or cross sectional depth of door handles ought not to exceed 0·030.

36.18 Elbow action handle

Self-closing doors

36315 Where side-hung doors are self-closing, a pull handle to both sides of the door should be provided in place of a push plate on one side and a pull on the other.

Elbow action handles

36316 For people with severe hand or arm limitations, hospital-type elbow action pull handles of the type shown in diagram 36.18 can be useful.
Because of the problem of clothes catching, these handles are not recommended for general purposes.

Door construction

36317 Internal doors having an eggcrate core, of the kind sometimes specified for low cost housing, are not suitable for the fixing of auxiliary handles or rails. For doors to wheelchair housing (8340) and special buildings for disabled people, doors having a solid frame, blockboard core or comparable construction should be specified. Cost notes: 90145.

3632   Door ironmongery: Sliding doors

36320 Standard sliding door flush furniture can be awkward for disabled and elderly people to manipulate.

D handles

36321 D handles should preferably be fixed to both sides of any sliding door.
Where a D handle is fixed to the outer side only, the door will be more difficult to open or close for those with hand impairments or reach limitations. Against this it should be noted that where D handles are fixed to both sides the width of the clear opening will be reduced by approx 0·095 (diagram 36.9); in some situations this may be too great a penalty.

36322 In the case of adaptations where the width of the door opening is limited, a sliding door with D handle to the outer side only may be necessary.

36323 A D handle should be fixed to the leading edge of a sliding door where there is a projecting handle on the outer side only (diagram 36.10).
A flush sliding door handle, preferably permitting a secure grip as shown in diagram 36.19, should be fitted to the inner face of the door.

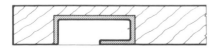

36.19   Flush sliding door handle

36324 On straight sliding doors an auxiliary D handle on the outer face can be a useful aid to wheelchair users (diagram 36.9).

Door gear

36325 Doors with top-hung self-lubricating track and bottom guide are recommended.

36326 Doors must be easily operable, for example with nylon wheels or roller bearings on aluminium alloy or similar track.

36327 The weight of the door must be within the capabilities of the sliding door gear. Heavy gear makes light work. Too light a gear makes operation impossible.

3633   Door ironmongery: Hinges

36330 Lift-off hinges are recommended to internal doors. Where door maintenance may be undertaken by a handicapped person, it will be easier if lift-off hinges are fitted rather than conventional paired hinges. A second factor is that where standard internal doorsets are specified they may be ordered with a 0·015 batten tacked to the bottom of the frame in place of the standard threshold (3420). If carpets are subsequently laid by the house-owner the battens will need to be removed, and this can be done more easily with lift-off hinges. A third factor, more likely to occur in normal housing than in wheelchair housing, is that restricted circulation spaces and narrow doors may prevent wheelchair access to rooms such as the bathroom and wc compartment. In such circumstances the temporary removal of the door, effectively increasing the width of the clear opening by approx 0·030 (diagram 36.2) may solve the problem.

Cranked hinges

36331 Wheelchairs are liable to conflict with the edge of the door stile adjoining the hinge; to minimize damage or where width is restricted, cranked hinges may be specified (diagram 36.20).

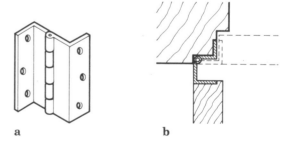

a   b

36.20   Cranked hinges

36332 In adaptation work, cranked hinges in place of existing butt hinges may obviate the necessity to dismantle the door and rebuild with a wider opening.

Rising butt hinges

36333 In housing for disabled people, rising butt hinges ought not to be used.
The common practice, both among wheelchair users and ambulant disabled people, is that doors are left open to facilitate circulation and the carrying of goods.

Blind people

36334 For blind people side-hung doors left partially open are a hazard and rising butt hinges may be specified.

Public buildings

36335 In wc compartments to public buildings rising butt hinges are recommended, see 63305.

3634 Door ironmongery: Locks, bolts, catches, holders

Locks and bolts

36340 Locks which require the simultaneous use of both hands should be avoided.

36341 Locks or bolts which can be opened from the outside in case of emergency should be provided to bathrooms and wcs.
Where doors to bathrooms or wcs do open in and may be blocked by a person falling inside (36004) lift-off hinges as well as an openable bolt should be specified. It can be helpful if, rather than having a single piece rebated frame, battens are loosely fixed as doorstops, allowing the door to be opened outwards.

36342 Diagram 36.21 illustrates an indicating bolt releasable by turning a small coin. Diagram 36.22 illustrates a bolt which can be released by pushing a pencil through the box section enclosing the indicator. Cost notes: 90146.

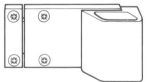 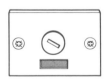

a   b

36.21 Coin operated bolt

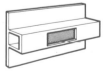

36.22 Releasable indicator bolt

36343 A throwover action bolt incorporating a bow handle on both sides, with provision for emergency opening, is recommended. Cost notes: 90146.

36344 Where floor fixing is required, for example for double doors, bolt handles should be sufficiently high above floor level to be comfortably reached; a height minimum 0·450 is suggested.

36345 A spring chain or monkey tail bolt can be more easily manipulated than a simple sliding bolt.

Magnetic door catches

36346 Magnetic door catches are suitable for cupboard doors but are not recommended for standard side-hung doors. 'Tutch' latches are also suitable for cupboard doors.

Door holders

36347 Push-pull automatic door holders are satisfactory if they are not too heavy. Manual and foot release holders are not recommended.

3635 Weatherstripping

36350 To minimize draughts and conserve heat the weatherstripping of doors is advised.

36351 It is important that weatherstripping does not cause any extra load when the door is opened or closed.

36352 A folded vertical bronze or similar strip tacked to the side of the door rebate is not recommended (diagram 36.23a).
The strip is effective by means of friction against the door stile. Extra effort will be needed to open the door and for some disabled users the sudden release of the door can be dangerously unbalancing.

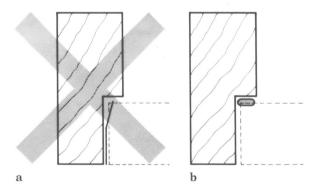

a   b

36.23 Weatherstripping to doors

36353 A vertical strip of flexible pvc or similar material fixed to the doorstop face of the rebate is preferred (diagram 36.23b).

37 Internal walls

370 Internal walls and partitions: Loadbearing requirements

3700 Apart from normal loadbearing duties such as carrying wash basins, sinks, cupboards and bookshelves, internal walls in buildings catering for disabled people may need to be suitable for the fixing of personal support rails.
These rails will be used by handicapped people to transfer for example from a standing to a seated position or vice versa, or to or from a wheelchair. In some situations where the person using them has paralyzed lower limbs they may need to carry the full weight of the body.

3701 Handrails, for example to passageways in residential homes for disabled people, are not as a rule required to support heavy loads, and fixings may be relatively less secure.

3702 A cause of complaint among disabled people is that support rails do not withstand the load they are required to carry. Failure may be attributable to the inadequacy of fixing screws, but is more often attributable to the inadequacy of the loadbearing capacity of the walls or partitions which rails are fixed to.

3703 Support rails should be fixed so as to be capable of carrying an applied load of 150kg; this allows for a person weighing 100kg with an allowance of 50 per cent for thrust.

Positioning of support rails
3704 Suitable positioning of support rails will depend on individual needs, which are variable and cannot reliably be predicted in advance.

3705 It is preferable that support rails are not fixed until individual requirements are established. It is therefore important that partitions should be capable of carrying supports at any point on the surface, or, if this is not possible, of giving a choice of fixing positions.

371 Internal walls and partitions: Materials

3710 Internal walls and partitions are generally either of prefabricated dry or wet fixed construction.

Wet fixed construction
3711 Partitions of wet fixed construction, for example bricks or concrete blocks, are recommended because they permit fixing at any point on the surface.
Bricks or blocks should have a thickness of not less than 0·075.

Prefabricated construction
3712 Prefabricated partitions without extra reinforcement are generally not suitable, since stability or thickness is likely to be inadequate.

3713 Domestic sandwich partitions, for example with a core of plaster board, flax board, polystyrene or glass fibre and a facing of asbestos wall board, hardboard, wood veneer or pvc fabric, are not satisfactory and should be avoided where possible.

3714 Chipboard partitions, particularly where there is plastic laminate facing, have more stability than cellular sandwich partitions. The disadvantage is that the thickness, not usually more than 0·025, does not allow for secure screw fixings.

Battens
3715 Where sandwich or chipboard partitions are installed, support rails should be fixed to timber battens not less than 0·050 thick. The battens should have a number of fixing points to spread the load, and ought preferably to be anchored to structural walls or columns.

Timber stud partitions
3716 Timber stud partitions are preferred to prefabricated partitions.
Studs should be minimum 0·050 thick, preferred minimum 0·075. It will not be possible to ensure that studding disposed across the panel caters for all requirements, and the use of timber battens fixed to the surface may be assumed.

Metal partitions
3717 Metal partitions, for example of double case 10–20 gauge steel with internal filler, are not suitable unless a batten can be fixed on the surface and bolted through, or secured to structural posts.

372 Acoustic insulation

3720 Partitions should give good acoustic insulation; this is particularly important in domestic housing and community homes for physically handicapped children who may be mentally handicapped and prone to noisy behaviour.

3721 The transmission of sound is primarily a function of superficial density, generally meaning that the heavier the partition the more effective acoustic insulation will be.

373 Protection of wall finishes: Institutions etc

3730 In special buildings for disabled people, and particularly where there are handicapped children, wall surfaces should be protected against damage from wheelchairs.
Children in wheelchairs, for example in a special school, are frequently careless about the way they handle their wheelchairs.

3731 Most marking of walls and doors is caused by projecting wheelchair footrests, and in particular by the protective rubber buffers at the outside corners of footrests. Other damage and marking is caused by shoes projecting beyond footrests, by hubcaps, handrims and wheelchair push handles. Damage can therefore be caused at any level up to about 1·000, though it most frequently occurs at levels between 0·100 and 0·450 above floor level.

3732 Owing to the virtual impossibility of protecting surfaces against all contingencies the fitting of renewable protective panels to vulnerable areas is recommended; self-adhesive laminated plastic sheeting is suggested.
Different wall finishes may be provided above and below dado level so that the lower area can be renewed independently.

Buffer rails

3733 The use of buffer rails to prevent damage to wall surfaces is not recommended.
In any special building for disabled people the height of wheelchair footrests will be very variable. A short-legged child using a large-wheel self-propelled chair may have footrests at up to 0·450 above floor level, and so also may an adult person with rheumatoid arthritis in an electric or attendant-propelled wheelchair. A buffer rail covering all contingencies, for example with lower edge at 0·100 and upper edge at 0·550 above floor level, will be visually obtrusive and will inevitably give an impression of institutionalism. Buffer rails will also complicate floor and wall cleaning. A further factor is that rails to both sides of a passageway will reduce the usable circulation width by up to 0·300; the width between wall surfaces may be increased to compensate but the consequence will be an uneconomic use of space.

3734 Where, despite these objections, it is decided to install them, buffer rails at 0·150 to 0·400 above floor level are suggested, projecting 0·100 from the wall surface (diagram 37.1).

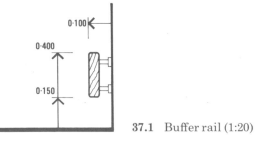

37.1 Buffer rail (1:20)

Bricks on edge

3735 Bricks on edge may be used as an alternative to a projecting buffer rail.
In some institutional settings bricks on edge at skirting level can be attractive and give good protection. Usable circulation space will not be compromised.

3736 Bricks on edge should be not less than 0·300 high. In most institutional settings this will not prevent all damage, and marking will occur on wall surfaces above.

Corners

3737 Exposed wall angles should be protected. Where corners are liable to damage by wheelchairs the insertion of a metal plaster bead to a height 0·600 above floor level is suggested (diagram 37.2).

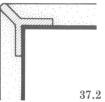

37.2 Metal bead to plaster corners

3738 Wood domes at the foot of corners are not recommended.
The purpose of these domes (diagram 37.3) is to guide wheelchair wheels away from the corner, so avoiding damage. The disadvantages are that the clear space for wheelchair manoeuvre is reduced, the domes are unattractive and, most seriously, they are a hazard to ambulant handicapped people.

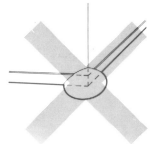

37.3 Wood domes to corners

Maintenance

3739 Wall finishes should be easy to clean and maintain. They should be chosen with a view to ease of making good where liable to damage by wheelchairs. Materials should be resistant to stains and marks.

374 Protection of wall finishes: Housing

3740 Consideration should be given to the protection of wall surfaces in housing which may be used by people in wheelchairs.

3741 There are differing views on the need for protection in private housing. On the one hand it may be contended that people are careful about not damaging their own property, on the other that they tend to be careless as a consequence of familiarity with the position of obstacles. These issues are discussed in relation to door protection (36080).

3742 On the basis that it is wise to insure against possible damage by wheelchairs, it is suggested that wall surfaces in private housing should be protected, for example by metal angles (diagram 37.2) and the use of hard plaster.

375 Internal finishes: Colour

3750 In respect of buildings for physically handicapped people, considerations relating to the use of colour are no different from those in buildings for use by any normal group of people. Apart possibly from the colour of floor surfaces (383) there are no disability-associated factors which need to be taken into account.

Therapeutic effects

3751 In the case of buildings for people who are mentally as well as physically handicapped, the way that colour is used may have a therapeutic effect. There is not however any reliable evidence about the use of colour in buildings for mentally handicapped people which indicates exactly how best colour ought to be used[1].

3752 Unless used intelligently, colours can be a source of irritation instead of pleasure. There is a particular danger where strong colours are used arbitrarily.

Emphasizing hazards

3753 Strong or contrasting colours may be used to emphasize obstructions or hazards, for example ramps, radiators and exposed beams.

3754 Colour changes may usefully be made at corners, where there is a break in plane, at the junction of stair tread and riser or where a ramped surface meets a level surface.

Glare

3755 Glare should be avoided. To reduce brightness contrast, white or a pale colour may be used on window walls. Similarly window frames and glazing bars may be painted white.

Buildings for partially sighted people

3756 In the case of buildings for people whose sight is impaired the considerations noted above should be given special attention.

[1] In this connection see for example Bayes and Francklin's discussion 'The therapeutic environment', Bib 93350, p24

380 Floor finishes: General considerations

3800 Because requirements for disabled people regarding the characteristics of floor finishes are frequently conflicting, generalizations about the preferability of one type of surface versus another are hazardous.

3801 There can be incompatible criteria between, for example, wheelchair users and ambulant disabled people and between blind and elderly people. Properties needed in the same floor may be difficult to obtain in combination, for example non-slip and easy-to-clean characteristics.

3802 According to what is known of user characteristics for any specific building, architects should decide which factors are most important, and specify floor finishes accordingly. Reference should be made to the comparative analysis of floor surfaces, table 38.1.

381 Floor finishes: Slip-resistance

3810 In any building planned for use by disabled people, a primary requirement is that floors are slip-resistant.
Although for chairbound people a slip-resistant surface is not required, it is more important that the danger of ambulant disabled people slipping and falling is minimized.

Slipperiness
3811 Slipperiness is due to (1) the nature of the floor surface, (2) the nature of footwear used, and (3) cleaning and maintenance treatments.

3812 Slippery surfaces can be hazardous to stick and crutch users, particularly where they may be wet. Rubber ferrules on wet surfaces or wet ferrules on slippery surfaces can slip easily.

Tiles
3813 In the case of certain tiled floors, for example those based on ceramics or concrete, the joints may afford a measure of friction to counter slipping.

3814 Most tiled floors, for example thermoplastic, vinyl asbestos, pvc, linoleum and rubber, are not less slippery because they are tiled than in situ flooring. Thin tiled floors are liable to curl if they become damp, and the lipped edges can be very hazardous.

382 Floor finishes: Resilience

3820 For most disabled people a comfortable floor in terms of resilience is desirable.
Floor finishes with a felt or sponge backing are satisfactory. Carpets are generally suitable (386). Cork flooring may be a suitable compromise where floor finishes are laid.

3821 For wheelchair users a non-resilient surface facilitates wheelchair propulsion.
This does not imply that resilient surfaces ought not to be prescribed where provision is made for wheelchair users; needlepunch textile flooring can for example be very suitable.

3822 For blind people, noisy and resonant floor surfaces are preferred, see 1423.

383 Floor finishes: Resistance to marks and indentations

3830 Dirt and marks are less conspicuous on a jointed or patterned surface than on a plain surface, and for the same reason an intermediate colour may be preferred to one which is very dark or very light.

3831 In residential homes, floors which are relatively dark may be preferred. Light coloured floors can be badly marked by wheelchair tyres.

3832 Warm colours are preferred where ceiling heating is installed, see 4235.

3833 For wheelchair users, floor surfaces should be resistant to residual indentations.

384 Floor finishes: Cleaning and maintenance

3840 In housing for disabled people, floors which require elaborate maintenance treatment should be avoided.

3841 The requirement that floors should be easy to clean is not easily compatible with the non-slip requirement. For ambulant disabled people the first consideration is that the surface should be non-slip. For this reason a rough surface may be preferred, despite the likelihood that it may be more difficult to keep clean. A very rough surface absorbs and holds dirt and grease, and ought to be avoided.

3842 The non-slip properties of a floor may be affected by faulty maintenance. Particular attention should be given to floors at building entrances, which may be dangerous when wet.

Incontinence
3843 In special buildings for handicapped people, particularly where users may be mentally as well as physically handicapped, floor finishes must be easy to clean when affected by incontinence stains.

385 'Warmth' of floor finishes

3850 Where floors are unheated, 'cold' materials should be avoided.

3851 Where the floor surface temperature is below approx 18°C, materials with high contact coefficients, for example marble or thermoplastic tiles, feel cold to the sole of the foot in comparison with materials with low contact coefficients, for example carpeting or cork.

386 Carpeting

3860 In housing for disabled people, carpets are recommended to rooms other than kitchens etc.

3861 Carpets have excellent non-slip characteristics, which is of primary importance to ambulant handicapped people. If falls occur, less injury is likely to be caused where a carpet is fitted than with any other floor surface. Carpets are also suitable for wheelchair users, provided that deep pile material is avoided.

3862 Carpets should be well-fitted and secured to the floor.
To minimize the risk of falls caused by tripping, wall-to-wall carpeting is preferred to loose carpets in rooms used by disabled people.

3863 Carpets inset into the floor, for example in the centre of a room, are rarely satisfactory. They soon become damaged at the edges, and are a hindrance to wheelchair users and other disabled people.

3864 Carpets are preferred where ceiling heating is installed, see 4235.

Residential homes
3865 In residential homes for disabled people, carpets are preferred to all areas where practicable, or comparable surfaces such as cord coverings and needlepunch textile flooring.

Incontinence
3866 In buildings where users are likely to be incontinent, carpets ought not to be ruled out. Mentally handicapped children tend to spend much of their time on the floor, and a comfortable surface is preferred.

3867 To facilitate the cleaning of incontinence stains, carpets where installed should be of non-absorptive nylon, acrylic or polyester fibres.
Needlepunch polypropylene or nylon textile flooring bound with acrylic resin is also suitable.

387 Kitchen floors

3870 For kitchen floors, a surface which can be kept clean by occasional washing with hot water and detergent is preferred.

3871 Kitchen floors should be resistant to spills of grease and fat. Rubber is not suitable. Pvc is satisfactory.

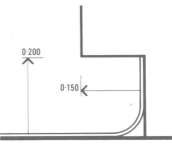

38.1 Skirtings to kitchen floor units (1:10)

3872 Coved skirtings are recommended to facilitate cleaning, especially to toe recesses to floor units (diagram 38.1).

388 Bathroom floors

3880 Bathroom floors should not be 'cold' or slippery when wet. Ribbed or studded rubber tiles or sheets can be suitable. Alternatively, ribbed pvc sheet may be used.

3881 Where the floor is heated, a 'cold' material, for example clay tiles, may be used. Glazed tiles should be avoided.

3882 For bathrooms in private housing, consideration may be given to the carpeting of bathroom floors.

3883 Where a shower is installed in a bathroom, other than in a tray having an enclosing kerb, a flush floor gully needs to be incorporated, which will facilitate the emptying of cleaning buckets.

Table 38.1 Comparative analysis of floor surfaces

	resistance to slipping			resilience	ease of cleaning	resistance to water
	dry	wet	polished (dry)			
carpet	G–VG	–	–	VG	F–G	VP–G
clay tile including quarry tile	G–VG	P–G	–	VP	G–VG	VG
composition block	G	P	G	P	G	G
cork carpet	VG	VG	G	VG	F	F
cork tile	VG	G	F–G	VG	F	F
granolithic concrete	G–VG	P–G	–	VP	G	VG
linoleum sheet and tile	G	P	F	G	G	F
needlepunch or fibre-bonded textile	VG	VG	–	VG	F	F–G
pvc sheet and tile, unbacked	G–VG	P	F	G	VG	G–VG
pvc sheet and tile, felt backed	G–VG	P	F	VG	G	F–G
pvc sheet and tile, foam backed	G–VG	P	F	VG	G	G
pvc (vinyl) asbestos tile	G	P	F–P	F	G	G–VG
rubber sheet and tile	VG	VP–P	F–G	G–VG	G	G–VG
terrazzo, in situ	P–G	VP	VP	VP	VG	VG
terrazzo tile	P–G	VP	VP	VP	VG	VG
thermoplastic tile	G	P	F–P	F	G	G–VG
timber, hardwood	G	P–G	P–G	P–G	G	P–G
timber, softwood	G–VG	F–G	F–G	G	P–G	P–G

VG very good   G good   F fair   P poor   VP very poor

In a number of cases a precise rating is not given; this is because the properties of a particular material may vary according to thickness, composition, environmental conditions, circumstances and method of laying and whether or not a backing is provided.

Technical officers of the Building Research Station have advised on the information given in this table.

resistance to wear	resistance to residual indentation	resistance to marking	warmth	suitable for underfloor heating	British Standard	Code of Practice
VP–G	VP–F	VP–G	VG	yes	–	–
G–VG	VG	G–VG	VP	yes	BS1286	CP202
VG	VG	VG	G	yes	–	–
G	F	F	VG	yes	BS810	CP203
G	VP–P	F	VG	yes	–	CP203
VG	VG	G	VP	only when laid monolithic	–	CP204
G	F–G	G	G	yes	BS810	CP203
F–VG	G	G	VG	yes	–	–
G–VG	G	F	F–G	yes	BS3261	CP203
G	F	F	G	yes	BS5085	CP203
G	G	F	G	no	–	–
G	F	G	F	yes	BS3260	CP203
G–VG	VG	G	G	no	BS1711	CP203
VG	VG	G	VP	no	–	CP204
VG	VG	G	VP	yes	BS4131	CP202
F–G	P	F	F	yes	BS2592	CP203
F–VG	F–VG	G	G	yes	–	CP201
G	F–G	P–F	VG	no	–	CP201

Services installations

4

40 Refuse disposal

400 Communal refuse systems

4000 In multi-storey housing schemes accommodating elderly or disabled people refuse disposal systems must be easily accessible and convenient to use.

Hoppers

4001 Access to hoppers serving refuse chutes must be unobstructed.
To allow for wheelchair users the clear space in front of hoppers should be not less than 1·500 deep (diagram 40.1b).

4002 To cater both for ambulant disabled people and wheelchair users the preferred height of hopper hinges is 0·600 above floor level (diagram 40.1a).

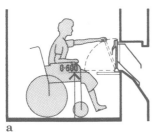

a

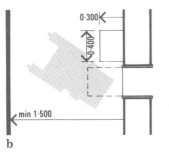

b

40.1 Access to refuse chutes (1:50)

4003 A shelf on which rubbish may be placed before disposal can be a useful aid to disabled people with hand or arm impairments; it should be adjacent to the hopper at the level of the hinge.

4004 Any supplementary refuse store for dry goods too bulky for disposal by chute should be accessible without the need to negotiate steps.

Garchey system

4005 The Garchey system, by which all kitchen waste can be disposed of at the kitchen sink, is advantageous.
It facilitates the disposal of food waste, making it a valuable aid for wheelchair housewives.

401 Dustbins

4010 In the planning of private houses the location of dustbins should be reachable under cover with no intervening steps.

4011 In the case of dwelling units for wheelchair users or other disabled people, the unobstructed area in front of dustbins should be minimum 1·200 deep, preferred dimension 1·500.

402 Kitchen waste

4020 The use of a portable kitchen waste receptacle may be avoided by planning the kitchen so that the dustbin is in a recess in the outside wall of the house (diagram 40.2). A chute or aperture gives access to the dustbin from inside the kitchen. A drawback is that the dustbin is used without its lid; in Britain this may not be approved by the local public health inspector.

4021 The aperture may be in a corner work surface where space might otherwise be wasted. The lid should have a tight smell-proof seal with a rebated edge. The diameter of the cover should be approx 0·250 (diagram 40.3).

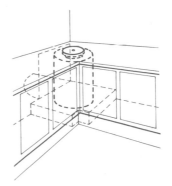

40.2 Dustbin recess

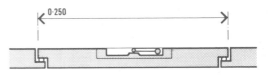

40.3 Lid to dustbin recess (1:5)

Sink waste

4022 Automatic sink refuse disposal units are recommended.
Where allowance is made at the sink for wheelchair access, the disposal unit and waste outlet should be set back to avoid obstruction. For recommended dimensions see 5153.

4023 The switch controlling the disposal unit should be accessible to a person seated or standing at the sink.

403 Central vacuum cleaning

4030   For domestic cleaning, a central vacuum cleaning
        unit may be considered but is not recommended
        for general application in housing for disabled
        people.
        Vacuum power is given through fixed piping to hose
        connections located throughout the home. In multi-
        storey dwellings or maisonettes this eliminates the
        need for carrying a portable cleaner up and down
        stairs. A lightweight plastic hose is used for which
        attachments are available. Dust and dirt are piped
        directly to a disposal container situated outside the
        living area.

4031   For many disabled people the equipment is too
        clumsy and complex to use easily, and there is also
        the problem of access to hose connection points.
        Where the system is installed, points must be
        conveniently located, serving all rooms including
        circulation spaces, bathroom and garage.
        Connection points should be at approx 0·750 above
        floor level.

41 Water services

410 Isolating valves (stopcocks)

4100 Stopcocks must be easy to manipulate and located in accessible positions. Access to stopcocks should be considered when pipe-runs are planned.

4101 The placing of stopcocks at floor level or at the back of kitchen cupboards must be avoided.

411 Thermostatic valves, water heaters

4110 The temperature of water drawn from a hot water cylinder should be thermostatically controlled. For elderly people and those with sensory disabilities it is important that the risk of injury caused by scalding water is minimized.

4111 Thermostatic valves may be provided to individual fittings but it is preferred that the temperature is controlled at the point of supply.

4112 Dependent on the length of draw-offs the temperature at the supply point should be between 43°C and 50°C, giving a temperature at the point of delivery of approx 40°C.
Thermostatic valves, cost notes: 90200.

Immersion heaters.
4113 The immersion heater on/off switch should be easily accessible.

4114 Immersion heater switches must be conveniently located.

Boiling water heater
4115 A boiling water heater adjacent to the sink can replace the use of kettles.
For some disabled people the lifting of kettles can be difficult and hazardous.

412 Shower valves

4120 Shower fittings must have thermostatic mixing valves.
This is particularly important for people with sensory disabilities or who are not able to move quickly.

4121 Manual mixing valves are not recommended. Where cold and hot water supplies are unequal in pressure, as happens when the cold supply is drawn from the mains, the water temperature of the shower may fluctuate rapidly.

4122 An alternative to a mixing valve is an electric shower heater fed from the cold supply and thermostatically controlled. See 54861.

413 Use of taps by disabled people

4130 For people with weak or arthritic hands conventional screw-down tap fittings may be difficult to use.

4131 The Leicestershire survey provides data about the use of taps by wheelchair users[1]. Among 378 people responding to questions, 45 per cent said they could use screw-down taps with either hand easily, 11 per cent said with either hand with difficulty, 21 per cent said with one hand easily, 6 per cent said with one hand with difficulty and 12 per cent said they could not manage taps at all. Others said they had not tried.

414 Specification of taps

Toggle action taps
4140 A toggle action self-closing tap may be suitable for people with arthritic hands or poor coordination. Taps with non-concussive valves should be specified.

4141 Large ball heads which require only a slight forward movement to operate the valve are suggested (diagram 41.1). Toggle action valves are also available with extended levers and insulated handles.
Lever and toggle action valves, cost notes: 90201.

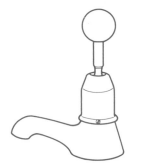

41.1 Toggle action ball head tap

Spring-loaded taps
4142 Spring-loaded self-closing taps, which need to be pushed down for operation, should be avoided.

Screw-down fittings
4143 Screw-down fittings where installed should have a head which allows a secure grip.
Owing to the variability of manual handicap among disabled people there is no particular kind of head which will always be satisfactory. The type of fitting shown in diagram 41.2a will usually be preferred to that shown in diagram 41.2b.

---

[1] Bib 93232, p96

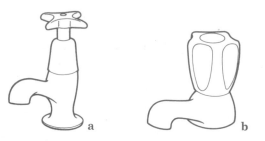

41.2   Screw-down taps

4144   Where screw-down taps are installed a fitting
having a plastic thread requires less effort to open
and close than a conventional metal thread.
A fitting with a broad dome head, for example as
shown in diagram 41.3, may be comfortably
operated by a handicapped person using the palm of
the hand. Cost notes: 90201.

41.3   Dome head tap

415   Lever action taps

4150   For people with weak hands a lever action fitting is
preferred to a screw-down valve. A valve where the
return of the lever is retarded to avoid concussion
should be specified.
For domestic purposes, water authorities in Britain
may not allow lever action valves to deliver cold
water directly from the mains; this ruling is
commonly relaxed in respect of housing and
institutions for disabled people.

4151   Taps where a single lever action controls both
temperature and flow of water are recommended.
The example shown in diagram 41.4 pivots both
horizontally and vertically. Cost notes: 90201.

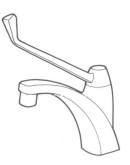

41.4   Single lever action tap

4152   An alternative is a single lever action tap which
delivers a constant spray of hot and cold water, the
temperature being controlled by the position of the
lever (diagram 41.5). Cost notes: 90201.

41.5   Constant spray lever action tap

4153   Quarter-turn lever action taps suitable for domestic
use are available; these can be served from the
mains supply (diagram 41.6).
The seal-off is applied pressure, and the spindle
does not revolve. This fitting can be used to replace
conventional screw-down taps in domestic kitchens
and bathrooms. Cost notes: 90201.

41.6   Quarter-turn lever action tap

4154   Where lever fittings with long arms are installed,
the arms when in the closed position ought not to
project over the basin.
Projecting arms may obstruct access to goods
standing on the basin shelf.

416   Location of taps

4160   For basin and sink taps there should be a clear
dimension of not less than 0·035 between the tap
handle and any adjacent vertical surface (diagram
41·7).

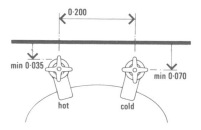

41.7   Location of taps to wash basins (1:10)

4161 Vertical bib and pillar tap spindles should be centred not less than 0·070 from any adjoining wall surface.

4162 The hot water tap should be placed to the left of the cold water tap.
This aids location; if invariably applied it will be advantageous to blind and partially sighted people.

417 Remote control valves

4170 For people with restricted reach, remote control valves can be a useful aid.
Some wheelchair users are not able to reach taps placed at the back of sinks or wash basins.

4171 Tap valves alongside basin fascias are recommended.
An alternative to the conventional arrangement of a fixture incorporating both valve and nozzle is the rerouting of supply pipes close to the fascia of the basin with valves, preferably with lever action controls, placed in an easily reached position (diagram 41.8).

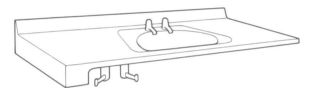

41.8   Tap controls below basin fascia

Foot controlled valves

4172 Foot controlled valves may be helpful for some upper limb amputees and others with impaired arm function, but will be unusable by wheelchair users. They are not recommended where provision is made for disabled people in general.

4173 In practice, capable double upper limb amputees learn to adapt to their environment so that conventional equipment can be used; devices such as knee and foot action taps have a limited application. Where it is proposed that they may be used a check should be made with the local water authority.

418 Electric valves

4180 Hot and cold water supplies to sinks and basins may be controlled by electrically operated valves.

4181 The electrical supply should be transformed down by a double wound transformer to 24v.
The transformer may also be used for the electrical supply to mechanically operated hoists in bathrooms. Additional safety may be obtained by providing a centre tap to earth.

Controls

4182 A solenoid valve on each water service with strainer on input side and drain valve may be actuated by either push button control or ordinary di-pole rocker switch stop.

4183 For disabled people, rocker switch operation is more convenient than push buttons.
Buttons on which continued finger pressure is needed to maintain water flow are awkward to use; for some arthritics and others with weak hands they can be unmanageable.

4184 Any electric valve should have a manual valve upstream to facilitate maintenance and control the water flow.

4185 Electric valves should be fully insulated.

4186 Cost notes on electric valves are in 90202.

419 Waste outlets

4190 Where provision is made at a basin or sink for wheelchair users it is important that the waste outlet trap does not obstruct knee access.
The outlet should be positioned towards the rear of the fixture.

4191 For fixtures where the outlet cannot be set back it may be possible to avoid an obstructing trap by incorporating a simple bend below the outlet and placing the trap against the rear wall, as shown in diagram 41.9.

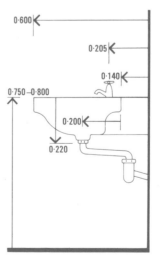

41.9   Waste outlet to wash basin: Provision for wheelchair access (1:20)

420 Heating: General considerations

4200 The design of any heating installation should take account of varying individual thermal requirements.

4201 It is important that diabled people are able to exercise some control over their environment. In institutions this may not be practicable, but where possible background heating should be controllable locally, or supplementary local heaters should be provided.

4202 For domestic purposes, background heating should be available throughout the home, with local heaters for topping up to suit individual requirements.
Disabled people, particularly those in wheelchairs, tend to leave doors open to facilitate circulation. Local heating to each room can provoke temperature gradients accompanied by draughts, and is not recommended as the sole means of heating. Background heating to principal rooms with inadequate provision to minor rooms and circulation spaces is also unsatisfactory.

Draughts
4203 It is important to minimize temperature variations and to reduce draughts.
Doors and windows should be weather-stripped, see 3635. Double glazing is desirable, see 3504.

Dust circulation
4204 Natural convection air currents are augmented by convectors, radiators, skirting heaters and heated air blown through grills.
Such systems may be unsuitable for bronchitics and others with respiratory complaints.

Old people
4205 For old people, who are more often at home during the day than younger people, the heating system should be able to maintain comfortable temperatures throughout the day.

421 Thermal requirements

4210 For disabled as for other people the optimum external temperature of the environment varies according to the part of the body concerned and the amount of activity being undertaken; the figures which follow are based on sedentary people.

4211 For the head the optimum air temperature is 16°C, for the hand it is 19°C and for the foot it is 21°C[1].

Preferred temperature levels
4212 For disabled people a heating installation should be capable of maintaining a temperature level of 22°C

in living rooms and dining rooms, and 17°C in kitchens, bedrooms and circulation spaces. These standards are the minima suggested for public authority wheelchair housing (83330). Where financial constraints are not stringent higher design standards may be advised.

4213 The temperature levels quoted should be obtained at and below 1·000 above floor level. In living areas a temperature of 21°C at a level 0·020 above floor level is desirable.

Bathrooms and wcs
4214 For paraplegics and some other disabled people, warmth in bathrooms and wcs is essential, not only for health reasons but also because so much time is spent there.

Air gradients
4215 Vertical gradients of air temperature can be uncomfortable, and should be eliminated as far as possible.

4216 Heating by means of radiators, radiant panel heaters, paraffin heaters, forced and gravity convectors or open fires often produces substantially higher air temperatures at head level than at foot level.

4217 To avoid chilling the feet, with consequent restricted blood circulation, it is important that the feet are not in a pool of cold air.
The provision of a 'warm' floor surface, for example cork or carpeting, may keep the soles of the feet warm, but unless there is an adequate air temperature immediately above floor level the ankles will still be cold and the resultant contrast will be uncomfortable.

Air temperature base
4218 The design of any heating installation should be based on a realistic minimum external air temperature; geographical and climatic conditions need to be taken into account and the conventional British design figure of –1°C may be inadequate.

422 Underfloor heating

4220 Underfloor heating has many characteristics which make it suitable for use in buildings for handicapped people, but its crucial disadvantage of inflexible response to control means that it cannot be recommended as a sole means of heating.

4221 Advantages of underfloor heating are that it does not produce vertical air gradients, and heat is transferred by conduction to the foot.
For handicapped people it can be most important to keep feet warm.

[1] Bib 93852, part 2, p53

4222 Where, as is the case among many disabled people, immediate response to adjustment of control is of first importance, an alternative system is preferred. The use of off-peak electricity makes control more difficult, meaning that supplementary heating must always be provided.

4223 To avoid discomfort the surface temperature of the floor should not be higher than 24°C.
In buildings for use by handicapped children who are frequently at or near floor level the floor temperature should not exceed 21°C.

4224 If these temperature limitations are observed additional means of heating will probably be necessary.

Institutions
4225 It has been suggested that, by making it more comfortable for handicapped people to go to and from the wc, underfloor heating can alleviate the problem of incontinence among disabled people in institutions[2].
This is less relevant where, as advocated in 70047, a wash room with wc is provided for each resident.

Carpeting
4226 Heat transfer by underfloor heating is affected by carpeting. To compensate for the loss of radiant heat the surface temperature of the structural floor should be higher than otherwise recommended.

Incontinence
4227 In buildings for mentally handicapped children, a warm floor surface is desirable for children who will often be lying or pushing themselves about on the floor. Many such children will however also be incontinent, and with heated floors smells may be unpleasant owing to vapour problems.
Additional heating should be incorporated such as a warm air system designed to give good air movement, preferably modulated with the fresh air supply and affording draught-free conditions.

423 Skirting heating, ceiling heating

4230 Skirting or ceiling heating installations can provide satisfactory environmental conditions.

Skirting heaters
4231 Skirting heating should be carefully designed, particularly in housing for wheelchair users. The casing may be susceptible to damage by wheelchair footrests.

4232 Where skirting heating is installed in wheelchair housing a possible problem is that the scale of provision may be affected by the installation of sliding doors.

[2] For example in Bib 93854

Ceiling heating
4233 Embedded ceiling panel heaters give sustained mean temperatures throughout the room and eliminate convection currents.
Careful control is required to avoid high running costs. Air thermostats in each room or space are essential.

4234 A satisfactory ceiling installation can be as low as 2·400 above floor level.

4235 Ceiling heating is recommended in buildings for handicapped children who may spend much of their time on the floor, and where underfloor heating may be unsuitable.

4236 Radiant heat from the ceiling is absorbed by the floor and other surfaces so that all surfaces become warm. The warmth of horizontal surfaces is dependent on colour and texture. Warm soft surfaces absorb heat, whereas cold and hard surfaces do not. Colours such as brown, red and orange are preferred to light blue or green.
In buildings where children may be incontinent, underfloor heating can cause unpleasant vapour odours from foul patches; with ceiling heating the effects will be less unpleasant.

Housing
4237 Where a ceiling heating system is installed in a housing scheme, careful attention must be given to the planning and design of windows in living spaces.
The principle on which ceiling heating is satisfactory, ie the absorption of radiant heat by the floor surface and, reradiation upwards, can be defeated by the masking effect of downdraughts from windows, the result being a pool of trapped cold air at low level. The problem may be avoided if the window area is not large and there is effective thermal insulation, for example double glazing.

424 Radiators, storage heaters

4240 Heating by means of radiators is generally satisfactory, but there is the disadvantage of cold air currents at floor level.

Panel radiators
4241 Panel radiators where the surface temperature is low and the front panel can be safely touched are recommended.
With modern microbore systems the surface temperature may be considerably lower than the flow temperature.

Location of radiators
4242 Where panel radiators are installed the requirement for low-level window sills in housing for disabled people (3510) may mean that radiators need to be placed on wall surfaces other than below windows.

4243 In housing for disabled people radiators should be set at levels to give most efficient thermal conditions.
Although radiators do not have to be placed below windows to give suitable heating conditions it is important that they are placed as low as possible on walls. Where windows are double glazed and down draughts are eliminated, no advantage is obtained by placing radiators below windows.

4244 In most situations the minimal risk of damage, inconvenience or the hazard of burns means that it is not necessary for panel radiators to be raised above the level where they might come in contact with wheelchair footrests or the feet of chairbound people.

Radiators and circulation spaces

4245 Where the placing of a panel radiator on a wall in a circulation area might critically affect wheelchair manoeuvre the underside of the panel should be at approx 0·250 to clear feet and footrests.
This factor may be important in mobility housing, see 8232. A typical panel radiator projects 0·065 from wall to front face.

Storage heaters

4246 Off-peak electric storage heaters are not recommended.
The principal disadvantage is inflexibility of control.

425 Blown warm air

4250 Blown warm air heaters may provide satisfactory conditions, provided that the circulation of dust is minimized by the use of properly maintained fine filters or low-speed fans.

4251 Care should be taken to avoid draughts, particularly at low level.
Warm air outlets should be located where they offset the effects of cold radiation from windows.

426 Local heaters

4260 Where central heating is installed there should also be supplementary local heaters, see 4202.

4261 Where a central heating installation cannot quickly give desirable temperature levels, supplementary heating is required for cold days when the main installation is not in use.

4262 Where convector heaters are installed, care should be taken to minimize the staining of adjacent decorated surfaces by convection currents.

Radiant heaters

4263 A radiant source of heat gives immediate warmth to the skin, inducing a feeling of comfort.
A disadvantage for some handicapped people affected by catarrh or sinus complaints is that radiant heat can cause discomfort.

427 Solid fuel heating

4270 In housing for disabled people, solid fuel heaters ought not to be installed.
Many disabled people find it difficult to feed and service solid fuel appliances. It is also difficult to design a solid fuel store from which fuel can easily be withdrawn by a disabled person.

4271 Open fireplaces are hazardous and must be provided with fixing points for fire guards.

4272 Where an open fireplace is installed a large capacity ashpit with easily accessible removable ashpan should be incorporated.

428 Heater controls

4280 Heater controls must be easy to reach and manipulate. Controls ought not to be lower than 0·500, preferred minimum 0·700, above floor level.

4281 The calibration of thermostat controls on a 1 2 3 4 index may be preferred to an index by degrees of temperature.
This will mean that the user sets the control by perception of comfort rather than a preconceived notion of the required temperature.

4282 Programme units for heating controls may need to be fixed at a prescribed height on a wall to ensure correct operation of the thermostat. Where these units incorporate switches, the prescribed height may be beyond the reach of a chairbound person. In family housing where another member of the household is available to operate switches this is not a critical matter. In housing where a chairbound person may be on their own the switches should be resited at low level.

4283 Gas fires are available with special handles to aid disabled people. Those with controls on top of the appliance are preferred.

Prepayment meters

4284 Prepayment gas and electric meters must be easily accessible, see 4364.
Gas boards in Britain can supply lever action controls for prepayment meters to aid people with hand disabilities. Boards can also arrange for the relocation of inaccessible meters.

43 Electrical services, lighting

430 Location of light switches

4300 All light switches must be conveniently located.

4301 Switches by doors should be horizontally aligned
with door handles (diagram 36.15).
In Britain door handles have traditionally been
located at approx 1·000 above floor level, whereas
light switches have been at approx 1·400. It has
perhaps been considered more important that the
light switch should be easily seen, whereas for the
door handle rough rules of comfortable reach have
applied. In European countries light switches are
commonly aligned horizontally with door handles,
so that the locating of the switch relies on its direct
relationship with the door handle.

Fixing height

4302 The recommended fixing height of light switches is
1·040 above floor level.
This recommendation applies equally to ambulant
handicapped people, elderly people, wheelchair
users and able-bodied people. The level of 1·040 is
fixed by the position on all standard doors of the
lock/latch, see 36300.

Ceiling switch cords

4303 Knob pulls for ceiling switch cords should be at
1·000 above floor level.
Where for any special reason a higher position is
preferred, the pull should be at maximum 1·200 for
wheelchair users and 1·500 for ambulant disabled
people.

4304 Ceiling switch cords beside walls should pass
through a screw eye.
Disabled people may have difficulty catching hold
of a swinging knob pull, particularly in the dark.

431 Specification of light switches

4310 For people with finger or hand impairments, and for
disabled people generally, rocker action switches
are recommended.

4311 To permit easy manipulation, switches should be as
wide as possible; a width of not less than 0·010
across the dolly is suggested.

43.1 Rocker switchplate **43.2** Neon locator switch

4312 For people with severe hand impairments or lack of
coordination, a switch where the whole plate
operates as a rocker is recommended.
Diagram 43.1 shows an example. Cost notes: 90210.

Illuminated switches

4313 An illuminated switch or surround identifying the
switch position can be a help where switches may
need to be located in darkness.
Diagram 43.2 shows a neon locator switch which
gives a permanent pale red glow. Cost notes: 90211.

Protection against marking

4314 In residential homes, special schools and similar
buildings, wall surfaces around switch plates
should be protected against marking by people who
cannot control hand movements. A transparent
acrylic plate approx 0·150 × 0·150 is suggested.

Multi-gang switchplates

4315 Not more than two switches should be grouped
together.
Multi-gang switchplates can be confusing,
particularly to elderly people and people with
mental impairment.

Surface switches

4316 In some situations, for example in adapted housing
where there are projecting architraves, surface
switches may be preferred to flush switchplates.
People who cannot easily control hand movements
may find that surface switches are easier to grip
and operate than a rocker switch. Toggle switches
if incorporated should project clear of the
switchplate for firm manipulation.

Ceiling switch cords

4317 For ceiling switch cords, a knob pull which is a ball
of rubber or plastic is preferred. A diameter
between 0·025 and 0·040 is suggested.

Low voltage switching

4318 A low voltage switching system with lighting
circuits controlled by switches operating on low
voltage at low current reduces the risk of injury
from electrical accidents.

432 Supplementary switches

4320 Two-way switches and intermediate switches
should be generously provided in buildings for
disabled people.

Master switching

4321 In residential homes the provision of master
switches controlling selected fittings may be
considered.
Master switching may cause confusion and
inconvenience. It is not often suitable in private
dwellings.

Footpress switches

4322 Footpress switches may be linked with manual
switches.
They may be suitable for ambulant disabled people
who find it difficult to carry goods and operate
switches at the same time.

4323 Care should be taken that footpress switches on the floor are not a hazard.

433 Immersion heater switches

4330 In maisonettes or two storey houses where allowance is made for disabled people and there is an upstairs immersion heater, twin switch units, each with an indicator light, should be provided so that the heater can be controlled at either floor level.

4331 Where a two-way switch is not provided a signal light at the lower level will indicate whether the upstairs immersion heater switch is on or off.

434 Socket outlets: General considerations

4340 In any housing for disabled people there should be an ample provision of socket outlets.

4341 The minimum provision recommended for ordinary housing is detailed in 8046. The provision recommended as desirable in the Parker Morris report *Homes for today and tomorrow*[1] is as follows:

working area of kitchen 4
dining area 2
living area 5
first (or only) double bedroom 3
other double bedrooms 2
single bedrooms 2
hall or landing 1
store/workshop/garage 1

4342 All socket outlets must be switched and shuttered. For safety reasons it is commonly advised that socket outlets should not be switched. In the case of disabled people the inconvenience and possibly greater hazard of using unswitched sockets indicates that on balance switched fixtures are preferred.

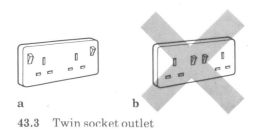

a   b

43.3   Twin socket outlet

Twin socket outlets
4343 To minimize the need for adaptors, twin socket outlets are recommended in locations where more than one appliance may be connected.

[1] Bib 93720, p27

4344 Manipulation of switches sited between plugs can be awkward; fixtures with switches located at either end are preferred (diagram 43.3).

Surface type socket outlets
4345 It is easier to locate a socket and insert a plug in a surface type outlet giving adequate hand purchase than in a recessed outlet fitting flush with the wall. Surface type fittings may be preferred where the socket is in a low or not easily accessible position.

Switch controls
4346 Toggle switches may be preferred to rocker switches.
With rocker switches it is less easy to discern whether the switch is in the on or off position.

4347 Switching by remote control can be a useful aid, see 4440.

Hooks
4348 Small hooks may be provided adjacent to socket outlets on which plugs when not in use may conveniently be hung.

435 Location of socket outlets

4350 Socket outlets must be carefully positioned in places where they are most needed.

4351 Where there are two sockets in a room they should preferably be placed on opposite walls.

4352 Socket outlets in low positions are difficult to reach, and may be hazardous to elderly people and others prone to dizziness.

Fixing heights
4353 Wherever possible, socket outlets should be at the same level as light switches and door handles, ie at approx 1·040 above floor level; see 4302.

4354 Because of the hazards of trailing flex, lower fixing heights may be preferred in some positions, but no socket outlet should be lower than 0·500 above floor level.

Kitchens
4355 Socket outlets over kitchen worktops may be difficult for handicapped people to reach; a location on the fascia of the worktop may be considered. This is most relevant for wheelchair users, particularly where, as is recommended in 5123, the depth of the worktop is 0·600. Where the depth is 0·500, outlets over worktops may be more easily reached, but for wheelchair users with poor hand control there will be hazards.

4356 Socket outlets to be reached by wheelchair users over worktops should be relatively low, but not so low that they are obscured by goods placed towards the back of the worktop.
A height approx 0·200 above worktop level is suggested (diagram 43.4).

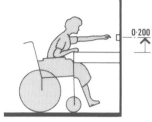

43.4 Socket outlets over worktops (1:50)

4357 In kitchens to be used by elderly or ambulant handicapped people, and where allowance is not made for wheelchair users, the preferred height for socket outlets over worktops is approx 1·200 above floor level.

436 Distribution boards

4360 Fuses and isolating switches should be placed in accessible positions.

4361 For ambulant disabled people, fuses etc ought not to be higher than 1·500 above floor level.

4362 For wheelchair users, fuses etc ought not to be higher than 1·200 above floor level.

Circuit brakers
4363 Circuits protected by a time delay tripping mechanism are suggested; when a fault has been corrected current is restored by simply replacing the switch controlling the affected circuit. There is no need to withdraw and replace blown fuses. Cost notes: 90212.

Prepayment meters
4364 Prepayment meters where installed should be easily accessible.
Coin slots should not be higher than 1·400 above floor level, and not lower than 0·800.

437 Lighting equipment

4370 Lampholders on wall brackets in accessible positions may be preferred to pendants.
Many disabled people may be unable to reach pendant fittings to replace faulty bulbs. In family housing this factor is less important than in single or two person housing.

4371 In grouped flatlet schemes the supervising authority may be responsible for the provision of light fittings and the replacement of bulbs. Where lighting is the tenant's responsibility, unsuitable equipment may be used and bulbs of inadequate wattage fitted, with a consequent risk of accident.

438 Lighting requirements

4380 Many handicapped people, particularly those who are elderly, require better artificial lighting conditions than non-disabled people.

4381 Disabled people with restricted mobility may not easily be able to take their work to the light, and enhanced general illumination levels may be warranted.

Deaf people
4382 For deaf people a high level of illumination is needed for lip reading.

Illumination levels
4383 The following levels of general illumination, based on the recommendations of the Illuminating Engineering Society[2], are suggested where provision is made for disabled people:

entrance halls, passageways 110 lux
staircases 160
sitting rooms 160
kitchens 215
bathrooms 110
bedrooms 110

4384 Supplementary lighting should be provided at local areas where background lighting does not give adequate illumination levels. The following local illumination levels are suggested:

sitting room, for sewing and darning 750 lux
kitchen, at preparation centre and over sink and cooker 325
bathroom, over mirror 325
bedroom, at bedhead 160

[2] Bib 93870

440 Public telephones

4400 Standard public telephone kiosks are not commonly accessible to chairbound disabled people.
Where kiosks are not accessible, wheelchair users must rely on someone else to operate the appliance for them, or make arrangements to use a private telephone which they can operate independently.

4401 It is not advised that all public telephones should be usable equally by ambulant and chairbound people. For a standing person the optimum level for a telephone receiver in a kiosk is approximately 1·200 above floor level. Receivers at a lower level, as needed by chairbound people, will be inconvenient for many ambulant people.

Allowance for wheelchair users
4402 Where a series of public telephones is installed, one appliance may be fixed at a lower level to serve seated people, with access for wheelchair users. Acoustic canopies or shields, where provided, should not obstruct access for wheelchair users.

4403 For wheelchair users, the telephone receiver should be not higher than 1·000 above floor level, and coin slots not higher than 0·900 (diagram 44.1a).
In practice some compromising of these fixing levels may be necessary according to the nature of the telephone appliance.

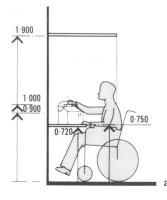

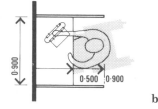

44.1   Public telephones for wheelchair users (1:50)

4404 There should be a shelf having a front rim at approximately 0·750 above floor level, with knee access not less than 0·720 high to cover wheelchair armrests.
Where an extended shelf is incorporated it may be helpful for part of the shelf to be splayed to facilitate reference to directories etc.

4405 The telephone appliance should be placed to one side of the compartment and forward of the rear wall so that it can be comfortably reached. Appliances hung in the conventional position on the rear wall are not easily accessible to wheelchair users. The most suitable positioning will depend on the characteristics of the telephone installation and the space available. Diagram 44.1 indicates suggested fixing parameters.

Hearing disabilities
4406 For people with hearing disabilities, selected receivers may be equipped with amplifiers.

441 Private telephones

4410 Local social services authorities, in order to meet the needs of handicapped people, may, under section 2 of the Chronically Sick and Disabled Persons Act 1970, make arrangements for 'the provision for that person of, or assistance to that person in obtaining, a telephone and any special equipment necessary to enable him to use a telephone'.
Although this is a statutory responsibility under the Act there is no direction to local authorities about the circumstances in which a telephone must be provided. Guidelines for telephone issue suggested by DHSS are stringent and some local authorities have adopted more generous criteria, based on individual circumstances and the judgement of social workers rather than on strict rules.

4411 Access to a telephone can be a critical safeguard for many severely handicapped people. For discussion see 895.

4412 In homes for disabled people who have limited mobility or who are liable to falls, the provision of more than one telephone receiver is advantageous. People who when they fall down are not able to get themselves up may place the telephone in a position where they can crawl to it and reach the handset to summon assistance.

442 Private telephones: Special appliances

4420 Special appliances are available from the Post Office for handicapped people who are unable or find it difficult to use standard equipment. For some items additional rental is chargeable. Information concerning special apparatus for handicapped people can be obtained from local telephone managers[1].

---

[1] A descriptive leaflet *Help for the handicapped* (DLE 550) is available from the Post Office

Hard of hearing people

4421 An amplifying handset is available for people who are hard of hearing, used in place of the standard handset. Sound is boosted by a transistorized amplifier inside the handset, and the volume can be regulated.

4422 An extra earpiece enables a person who is hard of hearing to listen to incoming speech with both ears, so reducing interference from other noises. This device enables another person with normal hearing to listen to the incoming speech and repeat the message so that it can be understood, for example by lip-reading.

4423 For people with hearing disabilities, extension bells located throughout the home can be a useful aid. The Post Office has a range of bells of varying loudness, including a 'cow-gong' bell which has a distinctive note more easily heard by some handicapped people.

4424 Several different arrangements of lamp-signalling can be provided in addition to the telephone bell. An example is a small neon lamp under a clear plastic cover in the back of the handset. The lamp glows in step with the ringing.

People with speech disabilities

4425 A faint-speech amplifier is available for people with partial loss of voice, to amplify outgoing speech to a normal level. The device can be switched on and off as required, so that the telephone can be used at normal voice level.

People with hand disabilities

4426 For people unable to operate the normal dial, arrangements can be made for the telephone to be connected direct to the local exchange when the handset is lifted. A loudspeaking telephone is available for people unable to use a handset.

Blind people

4427 Blind people do not as a rule have any difficulty using standard telephones, and require no special appliances.

4428 People who are partially sighted may be unable to read dialling digits and a card on which large numbers are printed may helpfully be placed round the dial.

443 Alarm call systems

4430 The role of alarm call systems for handicapped people in housing, whether scattered in the community or grouped under the supervision of a warden, is discussed in sections 893–899.
With regard to handicapped people living in scattered housing, the conclusion is that no alarm call device can be satisfactory; the comparative advantages of the telephone, in terms of security,

reliability and social benefits, are substantial. The notes which follow relate to alarm call systems and devices in residential homes and grouped housing schemes. Costs are noted in 90220.

Residential homes

4431 In residential homes for handicapped people, alarm call controls should be installed in each bed-sitting room, bathroom, wc and communal sitting area.

4432 An indicator board, with audible and visual signals, should be installed in a place easily accessible to the supervisory staff.

Grouped housing

4433 In grouped housing schemes supervised by a warden, alarm call controls should be installed in each resident's bedroom and bathroom. For discussion see 898.

Controls

4434 In bathrooms, controls must be pull cord, or push button on a suspended and insulated fitting. See 4303, 4317.
Suspended fittings in bathrooms should be coloured, or otherwise distinguishable from electric light pull switches.

444 Alarm call devices

Air-operated device

4440 A remote control switching system alarm call device is available which is air operated.
The aid comprises a control box containing a low pressure air switch, a 13amp socket and indicator light with cable connected to a 13amp plug, plastic tubing length 5·000, a control bellows with self-adhesive backing (for example for sticking to chair covers or bed linen), and a mouthpiece which can be used instead of the bellows. No specialist installation is needed, and the device can be used to operate more than one appliance simultaneously by fitting an adaptor socket.

4441 Light pressure on the bellows or a puff from the mouth operates the air switch inside the control box. This switches the power on and off with each alternate operation.

4442 The control bellows may safely be floated in a bath.

4443 The device can be used from a bed or chair to switch electrical appliances on or off, for example heaters and television sets. It can also be used to open doors. Costs are noted in 90221.

Radio transmitter

4444 A transistorized miniature radio transmitter may be worn around the neck or in a pocket, enabling a handicapped person to operate lights, buzzers and alarm calls.

445 Door call systems

4450 For people with restricted mobility, intercommunication between main rooms and the dwelling entrance door can be a valuable aid.

4451 At the front door a bell push and combined microphone/loudspeaker may be connected to an intercom telephone inside the dwelling, allowing two-way conversation. Visitors may be admitted by means of a remote control door lock. Door call systems, cost notes: 90222.

4452 A variety of devices are available for opening the front door in response to calls.

Deaf people

4453 For people who are hard of hearing, domestic entrance doors should have a loud door knocker or there should be an amplified doorbell. For deaf people a visual indicator, such as a flashing light, should be incorporated.

446 Electronic control systems

4460 Electronic control systems can enable even very severely disabled people to exercise independent control of their home environment.
The two units described below are those supplied by statutory agencies to disabled people in Britain; they are not unique and comparable units are available in Britain and elsewhere.

Possum mark 1

4461 The Possum mark 1 environmental control system for severely physically disabled people is operated by a microswitch or suction on a pneumatic tube; it can be used to control a range of equipment, such as an intercom, door opener, light switches, television programmes, telephone (including self-dialled calls), radio, typewriter, tape recorder, book page-turner and heating controls.

4462 The unit comprises an input control (normally either a flexible tube with pipestem mouthpiece or a microswitch which can be mounted on a wheelchair), a main control unit size $0.330 \times 0.250 \times 0.300$ having sockets into which the controlled devices are plugged, and a small remote indicator unit.
The indicator is labelled according to the devices which can be plugged in, and is usually housed in a cabinet in the room most frequently used. The unit has a capacity to switch on or off 11 electrical devices.

4463 The unit is operated by continuous depression of the microswitch or sustained suction on the pneumatic tube; this causes the panels on the indicator to be illuminated sequentially.
When the desired function is reached, releasing the pressure on the microswitch (or suction on the

tube) causes the device selected to be switched on or off. For people who do not have the capacity to manage even a pneumatic tube independently, the input control may be adapted to respond to whistling at a predetermined sound frequency.

4464 The unit can be supplied under the National Health Service through health authorities to severely handicapped people. The criteria for supply are rigorous.

Possum mark 2

4465 The Possum mark 2 unit is a less sophisticated aid developed for people who are not so severely handicapped. It has six switches for operation of an alarm system, intercom, door lock or other selected electrical devices. It comprises a switch panel, a distribution unit and a door lock intercom unit.

4466 The switch panel, size $0.394 \times 0.138 \times 0.113$, has six switches, which may be lever, rocker or pressure type. There is a microphone and loudspeaker on the panel face.

4467 The switch panel is connected by a lead to the distribution unit, which is put in a convenient place in the room most frequently used. This unit, size $0.378 \times 0.260 \times 0.140$, has four sockets into which electrical devices can be plugged.

4468 To operate the intercom or door lock the disabled person presses the appropriate switch on his panel. He can then communicate with his visitor and open the door to him. Using the same procedure, two-way conversation may be arranged with other rooms in the house. The switch panel also incorporates an alarm signal. If required, a subsidiary bell or buzzer may be fitted in a neighbouring house to operate separately or in conjunction with the general alarm.

4469 The Possum mark 2 unit may be supplied to handicapped people by social services authorities under section 2 of the Chronically Sick and Disabled Persons Act 1970. The criteria for supply are the disability of the individual and his home circumstances; no definitive guidelines are applied. Possum control units, cost notes: 90223.

447 Hard of hearing people: Induction loops

4470 In private housing, and in auditoria buildings, churches, lecture halls and similar buildings, induction loops may be incorporated for people using certain hearing aids.

4471 If a partially deaf person wishes to listen to the radio or watch television without increasing the volume to a level which is uncomfortable for others, an induction loop can be used. This loop is a wire run round the room or the house, and connected to electrical apparatus such as a radio. The loop sets up a magnetic field so that a person using a hearing aid with a special pick-up coil can hear the radio anywhere in the room or house. This avoids having to raise the sound level in the set, and at the same time ensures that the partially deaf person hears only the sounds from the radio and is not troubled by background noise.

Installations

4472 In public buildings the loop can be embedded in the floor screed, and wired to connect with loudspeakers.

4473 In private housing the loop may be installed at the time of building or subsequently, the cost of the installation being the same. The loop may consist of a household bell wire run round the room at any convenient height. For a radio, the two ends of the loop can be connected to the extension loudspeaker sockets of the set, if available. Where there are no extension sockets, as in television sets, an isolating transformer must be fitted between the set and the loop.

Associated light system

4474 For deaf people a flashing light system may be incorporated with the doorbell.
Relay contacts are required, with a control box in the main lighting circuit so that when the doorbell is pushed the lights go on or off. No extra wiring is needed; if provision is made for the installation of the contact box while the building is under construction the only cost is that of the control box when it needs to be installed. If provision is made subsequently there will be expenditure on the relay contacts. Cost notes: 90224.

45 Lifts etc

450 Lifts: General

4500 Provision of lifts: General considerations

45000 In multi-storey buildings catering for disabled people a lift provides the only satisfactory means of vertical circulation.

Lifts as a means of escape
45001 The admissibility of lifts as a means of escape from buildings in case of fire is discussed in section 60; see particularly 607.

45002 Where lifts are allowed as a means of escape special consideration needs to be given to the protection of lift enclosures.

Cost factors
45003 The installation of a lift in any building scheme may be determined by cost considerations. In Britain at the present time (1975) the cost of installing a standard passenger lift in any building will be not less than £10000, which in the case of small schemes will be a sizable proportion of the overall cost. The cost viability of a scheme planned for disabled people may therefore be compromised by the incorporation of a lift.

Public buildings
45004 Many of the recommendations which follow relate to the design of lifts in public buildings. General requirements for lifts in public buildings catering for chairbound people are detailed in 6423; for comments on the planning of lifts in public buildings see 617.

Residential homes
45005 In residential homes, social centres, holiday homes and similar buildings for disabled or elderly people, the problems that arise in public buildings as a result of conflicting criteria between disabled and non-disabled people are of less account. Lifts should be designed to satisfy the optimum criteria of disabled people.

45006 In residential homes for blind people the need for lifts to be used should be avoided where possible. Blind people, particularly those who are elderly, may be confused or frightened by lifts.

Provision of two or more lifts
45007 In buildings designed to accommodate disabled people, and where circulation is dependent on the use of lifts, at least two lifts should be installed, to allow for the mechanical failure of a lift or occasions when a lift is being serviced.

4501 Lift lobbies

45010 For chairbound people, either independent or accompanied, it is important that there is sufficient clear space in front of the lift door to propel the wheelchair directly into the lift.
Generous space is advisable not only for wheelchairs but also for mothers with prams and furniture removers.

Standard wheelchairs
45011 Where lifts cater for standard wheelchairs the unobstructed space in front of the door should be not less than 1·500 × 1·500 (diagram 45.2).

45012 At ground level in buildings where traffic is heavy, the unobstructed space should be not less than 1·800 deep (diagram 45.3).

Large wheelchairs
45013 In residential homes etc where lifts cater for people with large wheelchairs, the unobstructed space should be not less than 2·100 deep (diagram 45.4).

4502 Lifts: Levelling

45020 Lifts must be automatically self-levelling and should stop precisely at floor level. A tolerance of 0·005 is permissible.
Single speed and two-speed motors have a levelling accuracy of ±0·025, which is not a problem for able-bodied people but can be a hazard to those who are unsteady on their feet and an obstacle to wheelchairs.

Variable voltage motors
45021 Where provision is made for wheelchair users, variable voltage motors, which are capable of accurate levelling within the suggested tolerance, should be installed.

45022 Variable voltage motors ensure more comfortable acceleration and deceleration than single or two-speed motors, and are preferred where provision is made for disabled people.
Lifts which accelerate and decelerate suddenly can impose physical strains on people, and are a hazard to people who are unsure on their feet.

4503 Lift cars: Handrails and walls

45030 Handrails may be fixed to the side and rear walls of lift cars.
Rails should be fixed at a level which will aid standing handicapped people rather than wheelchair users, ie at approx 1·000 above floor level.

45031 In public buildings the projection of handrails from the face of walls should be minimized; 0·040 is suggested.
A flat section is indicated, dimensions approx 0·010 × 0·075.

45032 In special buildings for disabled people a more solid handhold is preferred and a greater projection is permissible. A circular section, diameter approx 0·030, is suggested.

Walls

45033 Car walls should be resistant to damage by wheelchairs.
Any protection incorporated to counter vandalism by small children and others will be sufficient. A laminated plastic surface is recommended.

4504 Oil hydraulic lifts

45040 In housing schemes for old people, homes for handicapped people, social centres for handicapped people and comparable buildings, an oil hydraulic lift may be preferred to an electric lift.

45041 The important factor is cost. Where for cost reasons the alternative is no lift at all, an oil hydraulic lift, costing substantially less than an electric lift, may be a possibility.
The cost is less largely on account of simpler building provisions. The machine room can be remote from the shaft and the pit depth below the lowest level served need not be greater than 0·500.

45042 Advantages for handicapped people of oil hydraulic lifts are that levelling is accurate and car movement is smooth.

45043 Disadvantages for general purposes of hydraulic lifts are that they are slower than electric lifts and the travel range is limited.
The normal speed of an oil hydraulic lift is approx 0·150 per second but 0·500 per second is possible. Typical speeds for electric lifts in offices and similar buildings range from 1·200 to 3·000 per second or faster. Oil hydraulic lifts usually have a travel range up to approx 9·000, with a maximum of about 20·000.

451 Lift sizes

4510 Lift dimensions: General considerations

45100 Dimensions of standard lifts are detailed in table 45.1, with notes on the suitability for disabled people of lifts of different sizes.
The lifts detailed in table 45.1 are the standard sizes specified in BS2655[1]. These standards are current United Kingdom and European practice.

Non-standard lifts

45101 Although there is no reason why, for particular purposes, lifts having dimensions which are non-standard should not be specified, it should be recognized that the cost of a special-size lift will be more than the cost of a standard lift having comparable dimensions.

Wheelchair criteria

45102 Where lifts are suitable for wheelchair users a distinction is made between standard-wheelchair criteria and large-wheelchair criteria (see 240).

45103 For most housing and public building purposes the observance of standard-wheelchair criteria will mean that wheelchair users are catered for. Only in special buildings catering for severely handicapped people, such as residential homes and hospital units, is the observance of large-wheelchair criteria necessary.

Internal dimensions

45104 Table 45.1 follows BS2655 practice in listing internal dimensions of lifts between opposite car faces. This means the dimension between front and rear faces of the car, rather than the actual clear dimension, which is from the inside face of the car door to the face of the rear wall.
The actual clear dimension includes the width of the car wall reveal, which is not as a rule less than 0·110. This additional 0·110 can make a critical difference to the usability of a lift by a wheelchair user.

Residential homes

45105 In residential homes and institutions for disabled people, the installation of a stretcher/passenger lift to accommodate a wheelchair carrying a person in a semi-reclining position is recommended.
Where an 8 person stretcher/passenger lift to BS2655 is used it should always be specified with the cupboard extension having the car roof at normal height, with car sides extended to provide support. (BS2655 allows, for the purpose of accommodating a stretcher, a cupboard extension at a reduced height.) The 12 person lift does not have a cupboard extension.

4511 Lift dimensions: Standard wheelchairs

45110 To cater for standard wheelchairs the nominal depth of the lift must not be less than 1·100 and the internal width must not be less than 0·900.
A width of 0·900 gives little space for standing occupants; the preferred minimum width is 1·100.

---

[1] Bib 93890

Minimum lift sizes

45111 The smallest standard lift which satisfies these criteria is the 6 person light traffic passenger lift (diagram 45.1).
This lift gives a clear internal dimension of only 1·210, and its admissibility for wheelchair users is therefore questionable.

45112 The length of a standard wheelchair (table 23.2) is not as a rule more than 1·080. Given a clear internal dimension of 1·210, this allows 0·130 for feet projection beyond footrests, which is more than adequate for most wheelchair users.
In the case of large people with large feet and large standard chairs the problem of excess length can normally be overcome by shifting the feet sideways, and failing that it is normally possible to swing the footrests or to detach them. For the wheelchair user who is accompanied, the use of a 1·100 deep lift means that an attendant standing behind the chair will have very little room for manoeuvre.

45113 On balance a 1·100 deep lift is considered permissible, but only in situations where for reasons of space or finance it is not possible to install a deeper lift.

Public buildings

45114 In public buildings which are to be accessible to wheelchair users the internal depth of the lift must not be less than 1·400 (diagram 45·2).
To allow space for an attendant and other users a 1·100 deep lift is not suitable for public buildings. In cases where two lifts are installed of which one gives adequate space for wheelchair use, the second may be 1·100 deep. For requirements for lifts for wheelchair users in public buildings see 642.

Entering and leaving

45115 For the user with a standard rear-propelled wheelchair the normal procedure is to enter the lift forwards, and to reverse the chair when leaving. When reversing commences, the front castor wheels swing round from the forward-movement position to the reverse-movement position. This requires clearance to either side of the castors of approximately 0·090, and the manoeuvre cannot in any event be controlled as economically as where the wheelchair is being driven forward. Thus although a lift having an internal width of 0·800 is theoretically manageable, a width of 0·900 is the minimum to allow comfortable maneouvring. A width of 1·100 is preferred.

45116 The experienced independent wheelchair user may prefer to enter the lift backwards, in order to be facing forwards (to watch the controls) and to be in a position to wheel himself out quickly when the doors open at the required level. For this procedure space requirements are not different from those of the user who enters forward.

Wheelchair manoeuvre inside lifts

45117 While it is advantageous for the wheelchair user to be able to turn inside the lift to minimize delay on leaving, turning space is not essential.
The notes in table 45·1 on the suitability of lifts assume that the chair user enters forwards and reverses to leave.

45118 For users with standard wheelchairs the clear space inside the lift to permit turning through 180° should be not less than 1·500 × 1·500.
The smallest standard lift which meets this condition is the 12 person general purpose passenger lift.

45119 For certain small wheelchairs, for example car chairs (2330) and small electric chairs such as the Epic (2341) and the Sleyride (2342) a space 1·300 × 1·300 is sufficient for turning.
The smallest standard lifts to meet this condition are the 10 person light traffic and general purpose passenger lifts.

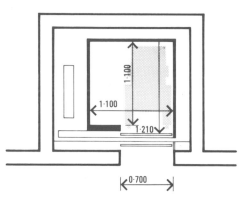

45.1 6 person light traffic passenger lift (1:50)

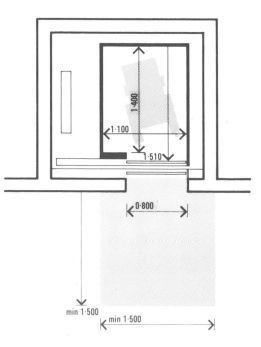

45.2 8 person light traffic passenger lift (1:50)

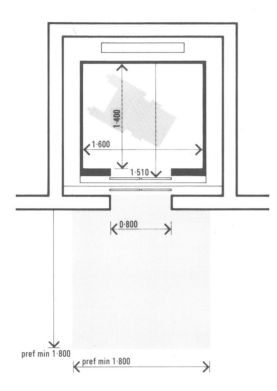

45.3 12 person general purpose passenger lift (1:50)

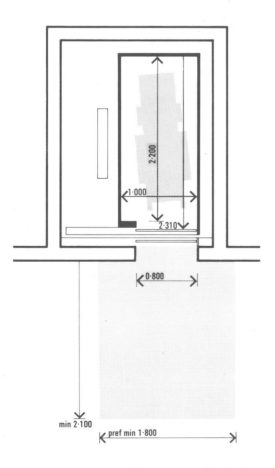

45.4 12 person stretcher/passenger lift (1:50)

4512 Lift dimensions: Large wheelchairs

45120 For severely handicapped people using large wheelchairs, a lift should have an internal depth of not less than 1·800, and a width of not less than 1·000.
The great majority of disabled people using large wheelchairs are accommodated without difficulty in a lift having an internal depth of 1·600. There are however a few people, for example people severely disabled by rheumatoid arthritis and others using wheelchairs with legrests fully extended, for whom a dimension of 1·800 is necessary. A nominal dimension of 1·800 gives an overall depth of 1·910.

45121 The only lifts listed in table 45.1 which satisfy these criteria are the 8 and 12 person stretcher/passenger lifts (diagram 45.4) and the 20 person hospital bed/passenger lift.
It is not essential that large-wheelchair criteria are observed in typical public buildings. They need to be observed in residential homes, centres for the handicapped and other institutions for disabled people, where a stretcher/passenger or bed/passenger lift might be requested in any circumstances.

45122 Doors should give a clear opening width of not less than 0·800, see 45201.

45123 In the case of people using large wheelchairs, the wheelchair is either driven in and reversed out or vice versa.

45124 To permit large wheelchairs to be turned inside the lift the clear space should be not less than 1·800 × 1·800.
The smallest lift to meet this condition is the 20 person general passenger lift.

4513 Lift dimensions: ISO standards

45130 The International Standards Organization has issued (1975) a draft standard for lift installations for residential buildings[2]. It proposes the restriction of standard lift cars to three, with a single width enabling product ranges to be simplified and facilitating the design of wells.

45131 The internal width of each lift car is 1·100, with a depth of 0·950 for a car with a rated load of 400kg, 1·400 for 630kg and 2·100 for 1000kg.

45132 The car having a depth of 0·950 is suitable for ambulant disabled people, but not for wheelchairs. For the suitability of the car having a depth of 1·400 see table 45.1. The car having a depth of 2·100 is suitable for all wheelchairs, but does not allow for a chair to be turned inside the car. All three cars have a door giving a clear opening width of 0·800.

[2] Bib 93894

452 Lift doors

4520 Lift doors: General considerations

Standard wheelchairs

45200 For standard wheelchairs the preferred minimum clear opening width for lift doors is 0·800.
The standard 4 and 6 person light traffic passenger lifts give an opening of only 0·700 (diagram 45.1) which, although tight, can be negotiated with a wheelchair. Given a standard chair 0·635 wide there will be a clearance of only 0·030 on each side of the chair, and manoeuvre will be awkward, particularly for independent wheelchair users leaving the lift. The complications described in 45115 mean that the wheelchair tends not to take a straight course in reverse, being likely to jam against the side wall. When this happens the wheelchair may get stuck across the opening, with hazard to the user when the door closes. Thus the preferred clear width of the landing door is 0·800, as provided with an 8 or 10 person light traffic passenger lift.

Large wheelchairs

45201 For large wheelchairs the minimum clear opening width for lift doors is 0·800.

45202 An opening of 1·000 is preferred to allow space for an attendant to pass alongside the wheelchair, and to permit the chair to enter at an angle where the depth is restricted.
In standard 16 and 20 person general passenger lifts, which are wider than they are deep, the 1·100 door opening allows for large wheelchairs to be accommodated.

Manually operated doors

45203 In residential homes for disabled or elderly people the landing door may be manually operated. Manually operated doors should be side-hung and not sliding; sliding doors, particularly those with heavy spring closers, can be difficult for disabled people to manipulate.

4521 Door closing

Speed of closing

45210 Where allowances are made for disabled people the speed that doors close should be specified.
A door closing suddenly may unbalance a disabled person, and speed of closing is therefore the important factor rather than time taken for doors to close.

45211 In residential homes and other special buildings for elderly or handicapped people the closing speed of lift doors should not be faster than 0·300 per second.
A 0·800 single sliding door will take just under three seconds to close at this speed.

45212 In other buildings where provision is made for disabled people the closing speed of lift doors ought not to be faster than 0·500 per second.
A 0·800 single sliding door will take 1½ seconds to close at this speed.

Photo-electric cells

45213 Photo-electric cells built in to lift doors are recommended to control door closing.
To cater for slow moving disabled people the timing device can be set for a suitable time delay, for example two seconds.

45214 Where landing and car doors open and close automatically the car door should be fitted with a sensitive edge, whereby doors are stopped and reopen when they are held.

Time delays

45215 Where allowance is made for disabled people and a photo-electric cell is not installed, timing devices should permit automatic closing doors to remain open for six seconds to cater for ambulant disabled and elderly people.
Where no special allowances are made, lift installations usually provide for doors to remain open for four or five seconds, which is convenient for able-bodied users. Non-disabled people normally take 0·8–1·75 seconds to enter or leave a lift[3].

45216 In buildings not used regularly by disabled people, lifts may be programmed to suit able-bodied people. Disabled people who can move slowly may need to ask someone else to hold lift doors open for them.

45217 Any adjustments made to reduce the door closing speed or extend the time that doors remain open may prejudice the convenience of a lift installation for able-bodied people.
If the speed of travel of the lift is accelerated to compensate in part for a longer time delay the cost of the installation will be significantly increased.

453 Lifts: Controls and indicators

4530 Specification of controls

45300 Lift controls must be easy to manipulate.

45301 Touch-light controls are recommended; where installed they should be at minimum 0·030 centres. For most handicapped people touch-light controls are easier to activate than buttons. They have the advantage of visual registration. In that they are sensitive to heat and not to contact, it could be objected that a double upper-limb amputee might find them inoperable. On the other hand the independent double amputee is typically a resourceful person; in the event of there being no one at hand to act on his behalf he could probably use his nose.

---

[3] Bib 93891, p749

Table 45.1 Standard lifts to BS2655: Dimensions and notes on suitability for wheelchair users

| | persons | load | internal dimensions of lift car | | | entrance | | notes |
			width	nominal depth	actual depth (approx)	clear width of opening	type of door	
Light traffic passenger and perambulator passenger lifts	4	300kg	1·100	0·800	0·910	0·700	single sliding	Not large enough for wheelchairs
	6	450kg	1·100	1·100	1·210	0·700	single sliding	Diagram 45.1. Can accommodate standard wheelchairs but not comfortably, see 45112.
	8	600kg	1·100	1·400	1·510	0·800	single sliding	Diagram 45.2. Smallest standard lift suitable for standard wheelchairs.
	10	750kg	1·300	1·400	1·510	0·800	single sliding	Suitable for standard wheelchairs. Allows for some small wheelchairs to be turned through 180°.
General purpose passenger lifts	8	600kg	1·100	1·400	1·510	0·800	2 panel centre opening	Suitable for standard wheelchairs.
	10	750kg	1·300	1·400	1·510	0·800	2 panel centre opening	Suitable for standard wheelchairs. Allows for some small wheelchairs to be turned through 180°.
	12	900kg	1·600	1·400	1·510	0·800	2 panel centre opening	Diagram 45.3. Suitable for standard wheelchairs and some large wheel-chairs. Allows for standard wheel-chairs to be turned through 180°.
	16	1200kg	2·000	1·400	1·510	1·100	2 panel centre opening	Suitable for all wheelchairs. Allows for standard wheelchairs to be turned through 180°.
	20	1500kg	2·000	1·700	1·810	1·100	2 panel centre opening	Suitable for all wheelchairs. Allows for standard and most large wheel-chairs to be turned through 180°.
Stretcher/passenger lifts	12	900kg	1·000	2·200	2·310	0·800	single sliding	Diagram 45.4. Suitable for all wheelchairs.
Bed/passenger lifts	20	1500kg	1·400	2·400	2·510	1·200	2 panel side opening	Suitable for all wheelchairs.

45302 Call buttons should project rather than be recessed or flush.
The faces of buttons should be concave or flat, with a diameter of not less than 0·015.

Alarm calls

45303 In addition to an alarm signal, a battery operated emergency telephone may be provided.
To avoid abuse the telephone should be connected to the house switchboard or direct to the telephone exchange.

Blind people

45304 In buildings which may be used by blind or partially sighted people who are alone, the incorporation of embossed digits on lift buttons, or on the panel immediately beside the lift buttons, is suggested.
In buildings which they use regularly, blind people, although they may accustom themselves quickly to the disposition of lift buttons on control panels, will be aided by the provision of embossed digits. There are some blind people who use independently buildings with which they are unfamiliar, and it is advantageous if they are not obliged to request assistance to use lifts. This recommendation therefore applies to multi-storey housing, office buildings, employment buildings and public buildings generally.

45305 Not all blind and partially sighted people read braille, and embossed digits ought not to be written in braille.

4531 Location of lift controls

45310 A horizontal arrangement of lift controls is not advocated for general purposes, for reasons discussed in 1115. For ergonomic reasons most ambulant people, and in particular blind and partially sighted people, can more easily manage a conventional vertical arrangement of controls.

Public buildings

45311 In public buildings the preferred maximum height of lift control buttons or switches is 1·600 (diagram 45.5a).
This allows for reaching by ambulant handicapped people with impaired arms. The reasons for recommending a maximum height which is beyond the reach of some chairbound people are discussed in 1115.

45312 For general purposes a mean height of controls of 1·400 is suggested.
In connection with the specification for lifts in public buildings which may be attendant-controlled, passenger electric lift attendant is one of two designated occupations under the Disabled Persons (Employment) Act 1944 which are reserved for registered disabled people (the other is car park attendant). Although lift attendants will be

ambulant handicapped people they may often need to use a chair or stool inside the lift, and it is therefore important that controls are not at high level.

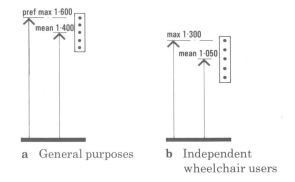

a   General purposes   b   Independent wheelchair users

45.5   Height of lift controls (1:50)

Chairbound people

45313 Lift controls to be operated independently by chairbound disabled people must not be higher than 1·300 above floor level (diagram 45.5b).
Although, as discussed in 2047, the majority of paraplegic chairbound people can reach controls at 1·600, these people are not representative of all chairbound people, and in situations catering particularly for wheelchair users, for example residential homes, an upper limit of 1·300 is suggested.

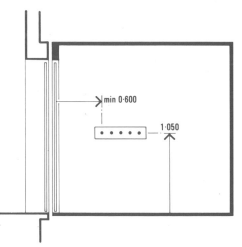

45.6   Residential homes: Lift controls for chairbound people (1:50)

45314 The mean height of controls on a panel catering for chairbound people should be approximately 1·050 above floor level (diagram 45.6).

Disposition of control panels

45315 Where only one control panel is installed in a lift car it is not critical that all controls are within reach of chairbound people.

45316 Where there are two control panels it may be convenient to arrange one of the panels at a lower level so that controls are within reach of chairbound people.

Residential homes
45317 In residential homes for severely disabled people a horizontal arrangement of lift controls is preferred. A height of 1·250 above floor level is suggested. Where it is expected that the majority of users will be chairbound a height of 1·050 is recommended.

45318 For wheelchair users, controls are more convenient if they are placed on a side wall rather than on the door wall.

45319 To allow wheelchair users to reach lift controls comfortably, controls on side wall panels ought not to be closer than 0·600 to the face of the car door (diagram 45.6).

4532 Lifts: Information indicators

45320 Where lifts are installed in buildings to be used by disabled people, careful consideration must be given to information regarding lift movements, location etc.

Indicators at landings
45321 There should be a 'lift coming' or 'call accepted' indicator at each landing.

45322 Where there is a bank of lifts, directional arrows should indicate when a car is approaching. People who can only move slowly should have time to reach the lift they require.

45323 For the benefit of blind people an audible signal may be given as a lift approaches; the sound should be varied according to whether the lift is travelling up or down.

45324 On the landing wall opposite the lift car there should be a clear indication of the floor level, visible when the lift door opens.

Indicators inside lift cars
45325 An indicator inside the lift car should signal clearly the direction of travel, and the floor level at which the lift is. The indicator should be visible from any position inside the lift car.

45326 In department stores, hotels, offices and comparable buildings, notices indicating the whereabouts of different departments, facilities, offices etc must be clearly displayed in lift cars for the benefit of deaf people.

454 **Vertical circulation: Special installations**

4540 Paternosters

45400 Paternosters are not recommended. A paternoster installation consists of an endless chain of lift cars moving continuously. No doors are provided.

45401 Where a paternoster is proposed it must be established that no disabled person will need to use it. If there is any doubt an alternative lift installation accessible to disabled users should be provided. Paternosters are occasionally installed in industrial buildings where it is assumed that all users are able-bodied.

4541 Passenger conveyors

45410 For wheelchair users and many ambulant handicapped people a passenger conveyor is more easily managed than an escalator. Passenger conveyors are known as travelators, movators, or moving sidewalks.

45411 Passenger bands should be not less than 0·800 wide, preferred minimum 1·000.

45412 The gradient of passenger conveyors should not exceed 12° (1:4·7).

45313 Passenger conveyors are hazardous for ambulant handicapped people who need to place one foot in a stable position before moving the other. For such people the only suitable means of vertical circulation is a lift.

4542 Escalators

45420 Where escalators are installed a lift should be available as an alternative. Escalators are hazardous to many elderly and ambulant disabled people. They are unusable by chairbound people, with the exception of the small number of independent wheelchair users who can ride up forwards and down backwards; the technique is to let the wheels drop into place as steps form, at the same time holding the side rails securely.

45421 Escalators may be hazardous for blind people. For blind people able to cope independently, escalators pose no problems. For those using guide dogs they can be difficult, in that dogs must be carried when travelling on escalators.

4543   Lifts in private houses

45430   A variety of electrically powered lifts are
manufactured which are suitable for installation in
existing private homes where practicable. They can
be installed to serve two or three floors. These lifts
are commonly not sufficiently large to accommodate comfortably a chairbound person in a
standard chair; care should be taken when
ordering.

45431   The lift shown in diagram 45.7 will accommodate
two adults or an adult in a small wheelchair. No lift
shaft, pit or motor room is required. Control is by
push button. Comparable lifts may be installed in
enclosed shafts. Cost notes: 90230.

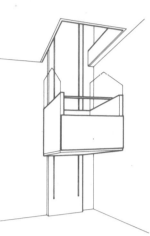

45.8   Home lift with bottom hinged gate

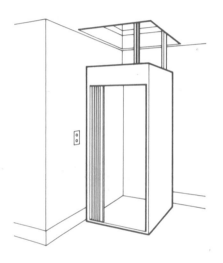

45.7   Home lift with lattice gate

45432   The lift shown in diagram 45.8 can carry a
wheelchair, the floor space required being 0·815 ×
1·475. The model having a fixed seat requires a
space 0·715 × 1·070. The builder's work is a ceiling
aperture and safety gate at first floor level. The
bottom hinged lift gate folds forward to give access.
The electric power unit is fixed to the wall at the
head of the mechanism. Operation is by push
button, with pull cord emergency control.
Cost notes: 90230

Counterweight lift

45433   For house adaptations where economy is of first
concern, a manually operated lift having
counterweights concealed in the supporting
columns may be a possible solution (diagram 45.9).
The floor aperture is the only structural work
necessary. Safety devices are incorporated but the
lift can only be used when there is the correct load
on the platform (including a wheelchair if desired).
The operating handle may be controlled either by a
person on the platform, or by an attendant on the
ground floor. There are two platform sizes:
0·685 × 0·510 for a standing passenger and
0·685 × 1·015 for a passenger with wheelchair.
Cost notes: 90231

45.9   Manually operated counterweight lift

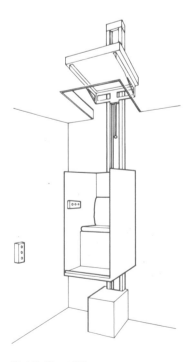

45.10   Seat lift

45.11 Stairlift for wheelchair use

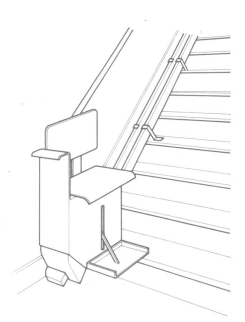

45.12 Stairlift for seated use

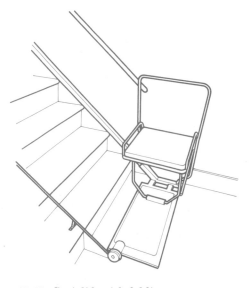

45.13 Stairlift with folding seat

Seat lift

45434 The seat lift shown in diagram 45.10 is designed for use in two storey houses where a stairlift is impracticable. The upholstered seat is in a compact lift box 1·220 high × 0·485 wide × 0·760 deep, which rises and descends on aluminium track guides fixed to the wall. The small control unit placed on the lower floor is shaped so that the seat fits over it. A self-sealing trap cover, size 0·595 × 0·895 (aperture 0·610 × 0·915), is installed at first floor level; it rises as the lift box rises, and drops into place as the box returns to the lower floor. An emergency lowering crank is usable in the event of a power failure. The only builder's work necessary is making the trap cover and cutting the aperture. Cost notes: 90232.

4544 Stairlifts

45440 For house adaptations for people not able to climb stairs it may be possible, according to the design of the existing staircase, to install a stairlift. These are not normally suitable for carrying a wheelchair, though the example shown in diagram 45.11 is an exception.

45441 Stairlifts of the type shown in diagrams 45.11–45.13 rely on maintaining a consistent angle for the supporting rails, ie they can as a rule only be installed where the staircase is a single continuous flight.

45442 The stairlift shown in diagram 45.11 is designed to carry one passenger standing or in a wheelchair, the size of the platform being varied as required. Where it is used to carry a wheelchair the staircase must be at least 0·180 wider than the wheelchair to be carried. The platform can be folded back when not in use. The driving gear is in the box at the corner of the platform.

45443 The example shown in diagram 45.12 is a chair carried on two driving rollers running on a guide rail at the side of the staircase. The footrest can be folded when the chair is not in use. Control is by two-way directional switches at each terminal point and on the chair arm.

45444 The example shown in diagram 45.13 is a stairlift for seated use; the seat can be folded away when not in use. It is operated by a constant pressure switch located under the armrest, with call buttons at the foot and head of the staircase. An aluminium support rail is fitted to either side of the stairs to guide and support the platform. The drive mechanism is normally positioned under the stairs.

45445 Costs of the stairlifts illustrated are noted in 90233.

4545   Short rise hydraulic lifts

45450 To cater for changes of level where the provision of
a ramp is not practicable, it may be possible to
install a short rise hydraulic lift, either manually or
electrically operated. The installation may be
suitable in an existing house where the ground
floor is at a higher level than the external
pavement, or than the garden.

45.14 Short rise hydraulic lift

45451 Diagram 45.14 shows a typical example. The lift
may be electrically operated, movement being
controlled by a push button. Alternatively, it may
be manually operated, in which case control is by
the operation of a hand pump, with lowering
controlled by an adjustable valve. To bring the
platform flush with ground level the lift is fitted in a
shallow pit. Cost notes: 90234.

General spaces

5

50 Entrances

500 Approach to buildings

5000 Requirements for approaches to public buildings are detailed in 631 for ambulant disabled people and 641 for chairbound people.

Housing

5001 Where practicable, entrances to ordinary housing should be ramped to the standards prescribed for mobility housing in 821. For related discussion see 1705.

In the case of mobility housing it may be difficult to achieve the recommendations for platforms at the head of ramps (501), while at the same time ensuring protection against water penetration; it is permissible that the entrance ramp rises to the line of the door threshold.

5002 Cost notes on ramped approach to housing are in 90300.

Single steps

5003 Where it is impossible to avoid steps at the entrance to a building it is preferable, for reasons discussed in 3114, that there is a single step rather than two consecutive steps.

Canopies

5004 Where the entrance door is not recessed a canopy should be provided at the entrance to a building. For wheelchair users the canopy should project not less than 1·000.

5005 In housing for wheelchair users, access from the garage to the entrance should be under cover, see 5700, 83202.

Access covers

5006 Where an access cover to services is located along the approach route to an entrance door, the position and detailing of the cover should cause minimum interference to wheelchair wheels, sticks and crutches.

501 Ramped entrances for wheelchair users

5010 At entrances to buildings where allowance is made for wheelchair users there should be a platform at the head of any approach ramp.

For drainage purposes the platform may be graded at an incline not steeper than 1:20. See also 64113.

5011 Where the ramp gives a frontal approach the platform should be not less than 1·200 deep (diagram 50.1a).

5012 Where the ramp gives a lateral approach platforms should be planned according to diagram 50.1b or 50.1c.

5013 Where the entrance door opens out the platform should be planned according to diagram 50.1d.

502 Loading bays

5020 At social centres for handicapped people, and at schools for handicapped children, the provision of a loading bay for disabled people using buses having tail lifts is recommended.

For discussion on loading bays for social centres see 70412.

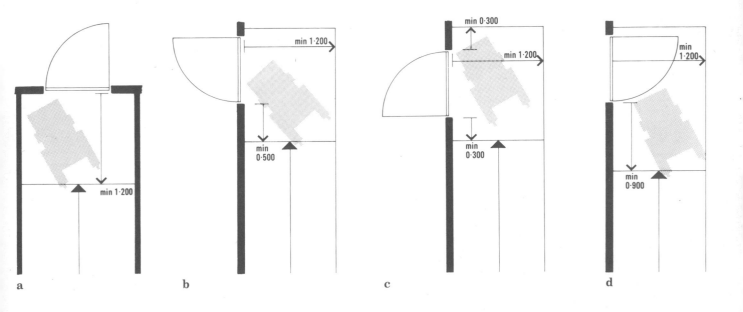

a   b   c   d

50.1 Building entrances for wheelchair users: Platforms at head of approach ramps (1:50)

Height of bays

5021 The preferred height of loading bays above road
level is 0·620 (diagram 50.2).

The floor height of buses fitted with tail lifts ranges
from approx 0·560 for minibuses to 1·350 for
conventional single deck buses. Conventional
buses are now rarely used for transporting
handicapped people, and may be ignored. Among
small buses floor heights range from approx 0·560 to
0·680. The mean of 0·620 is therefore suggested; it
will be advantageous if loading bay heights are

standardized at this level, with manufacturers
bearing it in mind when adapting existing
equipment or designing new equipment.

Hazard prevention

5022 Unless it is known that buses of a standard type
only will use the facility, it is not recommended
that a concrete kerb is incorporated against which
rear wheels strike.

5023 The exposed side of the loading bay may be
protected by gates.

5024 Loading bays must be sheltered from the rain,
allowing undercover access to the building.

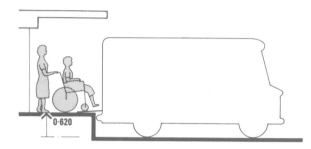

50.2 Loading bays for handicapped people's buses
(1:100)

503 Entrance doors, lobbies

5030 To prevent draughts and reduce heat losses
weatherstripping should be fitted to external doors,
see 3635.

5031 To allow for wheelchair users raised thresholds
must be avoided, see 340.

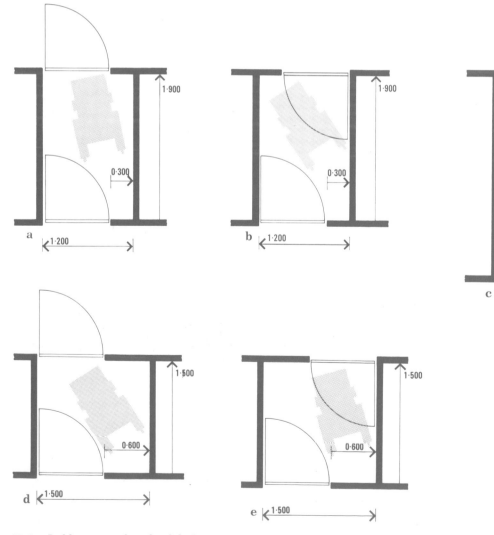

50.3 Lobby spaces for wheelchair users (1:50)

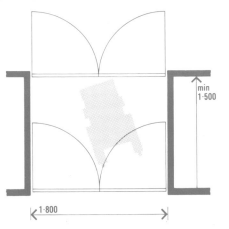

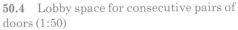

50.4 Lobby space for consecutive pairs of doors (1:50)

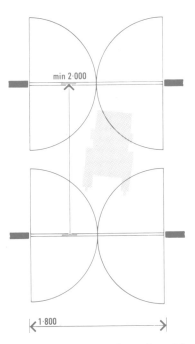

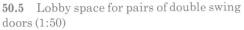

50.5 Lobby space for pairs of double swing doors (1:50)

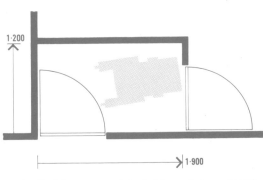

50.6 Lobby space with right angle turn (1:50)

Air curtains

5032 In public buildings an air curtain at the entrance door is recommended.
An electrically heated air curtain unit is fitted at ceiling level close to the entrance doors. A flow of warmed air is directed downwards to counter air turbulence when doors are opened and closed. In public buildings where there is considerable traffic, for example department stores, the provision of an air curtain may mean that entrance doors can be left open, so assisting accessibility for disabled people. In exposed situations or in cold climates the need for two sets of doors will be avoided.

Lobbies

5033 Where entrance lobbies are incorporated in housing or public buildings catering for wheelchair users adequate space must be provided between doors.

5034 Spaces between consecutive single side-hung doors, for example entrance lobbies to domestic housing or cloakroom lobbies in public buildings, should be planned as shown in diagrams 50.3a-e.

5035 Where both doors open into the lobby, for example as shown in diagrams 50.3b and e, the wheelchair user may have to reverse and reposition before the second door is opened.
A space as shown in diagram 50.3c is preferred if wheelchair manoeuvring is to be minimized.

Lobbies with pairs of doors

5036 In public buildings where there are consecutive pairs of doors the lobby space should be not less than as shown in diagram 50.4.
Where there are pairs of double swing doors the lobby space should be not less than as shown in diagram 50.5.

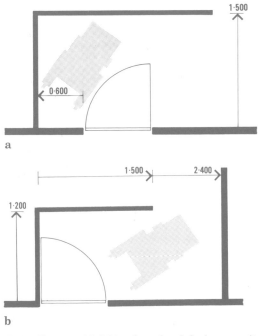

50.7 Screened lobbies for wheelchair users (1:50)

5037 Where a right angle turn is made the lobby space should be not less than as shown in diagram 50.6.

5038 In public buildings where there is a substantial amount of traffic lobby spaces should be increased.

Screened lobbies

5039 Diagrams 50.7a and b show suggested layouts for cloakrooms where there are screen walls to limit sightlines.

504 Doormats, letter boxes

5040 External and internal doormats should be recessed to lie flush with the adjacent floor surface.
Mats must be close-fitted to ensure that sticks, wheelchair wheels and stiletto heels do not become wedged at the edges.

5041 Loose doormats laid on floors are a hazard to wheelchair users and other disabled people.

5042 A coir (coconut fibre) close rubber link or fibre link mat is preferred to a chain or metal link mat.

Letter boxes

5043 A large aperture letter box, for example 0·280 × 0·075, is recommended.
The lower edge should not be lower than 0·750 above floor level.

5044 An internal letter basket prevents having to pick up letters from the floor.
The underside of the basket should be between 0·600 and 0·700 above floor level (diagram 50.8).

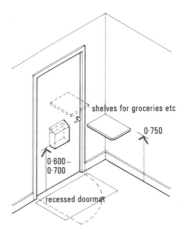

shelves for groceries etc

0·750

0·600 – 0·700

recessed doormat

50.8 Entrance facilities for housing

Blind people

5045 In housing for blind people a conventional letter box will not be adequate for the delivery of braille books. A delivery cupboard as described in 5050–5051 is preferred.

505 Entrances: Storage facilities

Cupboard for deliveries

5050 Milk bottles and other deliveries left regularly at the door should not be placed at ground level where they may be beyond the reach of a disabled person. A suitable solution is the provision of a cupboard, which can serve also for the reception of parcels and groceries, beside the door.

5051 The cupboard should have an external door and an easily accessible internal door. If required, a cupboard for the reception of letters and newspapers may be incorporated below the cupboard for deliveries.
Suggested floor heights are, for the letter cupboard 0·600 above floor level, and for the delivery cupboard 0·800 above floor level.

Shelf

5052 An external shelf may be provided adjacent to the door.
This may be used by disabled persons for placing groceries etc while the door is being opened.

5053 The preferred height for the external shelf is approx 0·750 above floor level. A shelf inside the door at similar height is also useful (diagram 50.8).
The space below the shelf should be unobstructed to permit wheelchair manoeuvre.

Coat racks

5054 Coat racks should be fixed at varying levels. For ambulant handicapped people a height above floor level of approx 1·300 is preferred, and for wheelchair users approx 1·100.

5055 Where provision is made for wheelchair users there should be a clear space approx 1·200 × 1·200 in front of coat racks.

506 Passages, corridors

Housing

5060 Where housing provision is made for ambulant disabled people, for example in mobility housing, passages should be not less than 0·900 wide.
In ordinary housing the general rule is that passages are 0·900 wide.

5061 In housing for wheelchair users passages should be not less than 1·200 wide.
For guidance on utilization spaces in relation to wheelchair manoeuvre through doors see diagrams 24.9a–f.

5062 To facilitate wheelchair manoeuvre, doors to either side of a passage should be directly opposite as shown in diagram 50.9a, rather than staggered as shown in diagrams 50.9b and c.

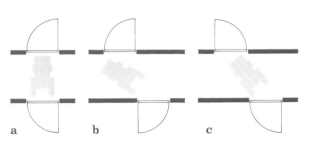

50.9 Wheelchair manoeuvre between doors to either side of passage

5063 Wheelchair manoeuvre between doors to either side of a passage is simplified if doors are hung so that the distance between door handles is minimized. The layout shown in diagram 50.9c is preferred to that in diagram 50.9b.

Public buildings, buildings for handicapped people

5064 In public buildings and in special buildings for handicapped people, such as residential homes and social centres, passages should be not less than 1·200 wide.

5065 A passage 1·200 wide is not sufficiently wide to allow two wheelchairs to pass; for this purpose passages need to be not less than 1·700 wide (diagram 24.3).
In practice major circulation routes in public buildings are commonly 1·800 or wider.

5066 Where passages are relatively narrow, for example 1·400 or less, the provision of passing bays is recommended.

Supplementary data

5067 For further information regarding the planning of passages and circulation spaces see:

Circulation spaces for ambulant disabled people: 25.
Wheelchair circulation spaces: 241–245.
Doors and wheelchair manoeuvre: 36042.
Lift lobbies: 4501.
Circulation areas in public buildings: 6321 (ambulant disabled people); 6422 (chairbound people).
Passages and door widths in mobility housing: 1702, 8230.
Passages and door widths in wheelchair housing: 8321.
Passages and door widths in housing for severely disabled people: 8433.

This section contains practical guidance and associated commentary on the planning of kitchens where provision is made for disabled people. Broader tactical issues relating to the planning of kitchens in housing for wheelchair users are discussed in 834.

510 Kitchen planning

5100 Kitchen use by disabled housewives

51000 The notes which follow (51001–6) summarize some of the findings of Phyllis Howie's comparative study of disabled and non-disabled housewives *A pilot study of disabled housewives in their kitchens* [1]. Although the methodology of the inquiry was unscientific the study affords the only evidence about the use of kitchens by disabled housewives in Britain, and is therefore reported here.

51001 Howie's study found that during a typical working day the aggregate number of visits to the various working areas of the kitchen was significantly less for disabled than for able-bodied housewives; for disabled housewives the modal figure for visits was 85, against 140 for able-bodied housewives. For each of the working areas of the kitchen the typical disabled housewife made fewer visits than the able-bodied housewife, the relative number of visits to each area being similar for both groups.

Relative use of work areas

51002 For the 60 housewives in the study the relative frequency of visits to different working areas of the kitchen was as follows, in terms of percentages:

sink   20
storage   20
hob   18
preparation centre   18
table   15
refrigerator   6
oven   3

Movements between work areas

51003 Diagram 51.1 shows the relative frequency, indicated by the width of linking arrows, of movements between principal fixed working areas of the kitchen. This diagram excludes movement to and from storage provision, which is distributed around the kitchen and is shown diagrammatically in diagram 51.2. In the diagrams cooker implies both hob and oven.

51004 Diagram 51.1 shows that among disabled housewives the highest incidence of linked movements is between sink and cooker. Of movements between sink and cooker, a large proportion were for filling a kettle and putting it on the hob.

[1] Bib 93920. Evidence reported in the following paragraphs is drawn from p19 (51001), p21 (51002), p22 (51003 and 51006), p23 (51004) and p24 (51005).

51005 The relative frequency of movements between the sink and dining table was significantly higher for disabled housewives than for able-bodied housewives. This was accounted for by the disabled housewives being able to carry articles only singly or in small quantities between sink and dining table.

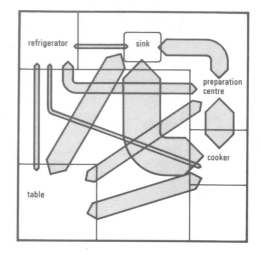

51.1   Disabled housewives: Relative frequency of movements between fixed working areas of kitchen (source: Howie)

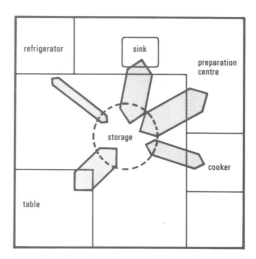

51.2   Disabled housewives: Relative frequency of movements between kitchen storage provision and fixed working areas (source: Howie)

Storage

51006 The intensity of movement between storage facilities and the preparation centre, sink and dining table was similar (diagram 51.2).

5101 Kitchen layouts: General considerations

51010 For disabled housewives, the working area of the kitchen must be free of interference from other traffic in the home. A cul-de-sac plan is preferred.

51011 Although the merits of corridor plans are subsequently discussed, it is preferable that the work sequence is unbroken, comprising work surface/sink/work surface/cooker/work surface, arranged in an L or a U.

Doors
51012 The number of doors serving the kitchen should be kept to a minimum.

51013 Where space in the kitchen is limited an out-opening door is preferred.
Where the swing of an out-opening door makes wheelchair access awkward a sliding door may be advisable.

Kitchen window
51014 The kitchen window may be over the sink.
The disabled housewife may spend more time at the sink than elsewhere in the kitchen, and may need to watch what is going on outside, to see people coming to the door and to oversee children playing.

51015 Where space in the kitchen is limited it may be preferred to use the area behind the sink for storage, for example for a pan or dish rack.
An alternative position for the window may be beside the dining table.

51016 With the sink in a corner position the window may be placed as shown in diagram 51.6.
This layout may permit a wheelchair user to reach window controls; where the window is behind the sink a remote control opening device may be necessary.

Extract fan
51017 An extract fan is suggested, particularly where the working area of the kitchen is in the same space as dining or living areas. It will give additional ventilation, and may reduce the need to open and close windows.

Dining provision
51018 Allowance should be made for at least two people to eat in the kitchen. In small kitchens the dining provision may be a pull-out board below one of the working surfaces.
For disabled people whose mobility is limited it is important that dining space is available in the kitchen. Where no allowance is made it is probable that an inconvenient or inadequate eating position will be improvised [2].

Kitchen trolley
51019 Space should be available in the kitchen for keeping a kitchen trolley.
A trolley facilitates the movement of food and equipment, and can serve as an additional work surface or parking place for items used in the preparation of meals. It may also be used as a walking aid by ambulant handicapped people. A

[2] For relevant evidence see Bib 93731, p31.

suggested provision is a compact portable storage unit running on castors (diagrams 51.26, 51.27) kept when not in use in the knee recess of the preparation area (diagrams 51.4–51.8).

5102   Kitchen layouts: Ambulant disabled people

51020 Except where a kitchen is planned for an ambulant disabled housewife whose specific needs can be established in advance, it is not recommended that kitchens in housing for disabled people are planned for ambulant disabled people and not made accessible for chairbound people.

51021 For mobility housing the kitchen may be planned as for normal housing, see 8233. It should be accessible to a chairbound person, but not planned for use by a chairbound housewife. It should be possible for fittings etc to be adapted to suit the individual requirements of an ambulant disabled housewife.

Corridor layout
51022 A corridor layout as shown in diagram 51.3 may be suitable.
An advantage is that fixed floor units can be used for support to either side. This can be achieved equally with a U layout, which may be preferred.

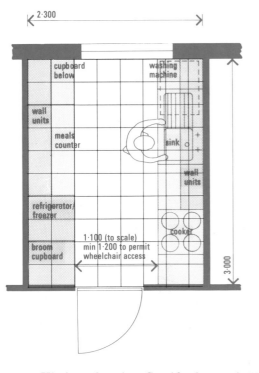

51.3   Kitchen planning: Corridor layout (1:50)

51023 The distance between parallel floor units should be not less than 1·100, and preferably not more than 1·200.
A clear width of 1·200 ought not to be exceeded if movements by an ambulant disabled person are to be minimized.

Modification of wheelchair kitchens

51024 A plan arrangement allowing space for wheelchair
manoeuvre can usually be adapted so that it is
convenient for an ambulant housewife.
A table can be placed where it will afford support
to insecure ambulant people, provide an additional
work surface at an alternative level and reduce
the space between work areas, so benefiting
housewives with impaired reach or mobility.

5103   Kitchen layouts: Chairbound housewives

51030 General principles for the planning of kitchens in
housing designed for use by chairbound housewives
are discussed in 834.

Small dwelling units

51031 In small units, ie for one or two person households,
a compact kitchen is preferred, allowing for the
chair to be driven in and reversed out, but not for
turning. Diagram 51.4 is an example.
For notes on kitchens in special units for severely
disabled people see 847.

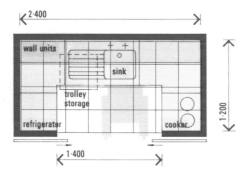

51.4   Compact kitchen for small dwelling units
(1:50)

Family units

51032 In units for households of three or more persons a
kitchen with an L layout of fixtures is preferred,
for example as in diagrams 51.5 and 51.6.
The advantages of an L layout are that it allows
for goods to be moved across surfaces without
lifting, and permits the placing of a dining table
conveniently related to sink and cooker.

Fokus kitchens

51033 Diagrams 51.10a and b illustrate the kitchen layout
recommended by the Fokus Society in Sweden for
special housing units for chairbound people.

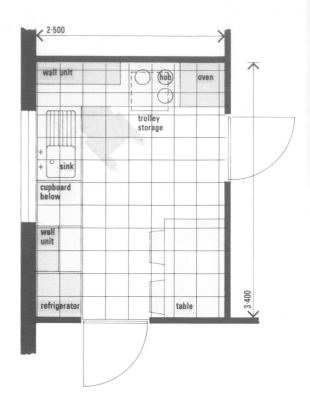

51.5   Kitchen planning: L layout (1:50)

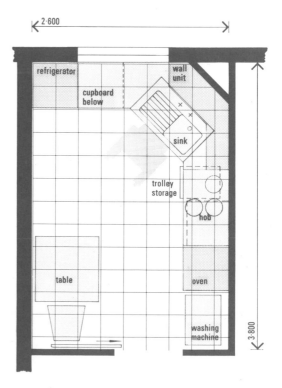

51.6   Kitchen planning: L layout with sink placed
diagonally (1:50)

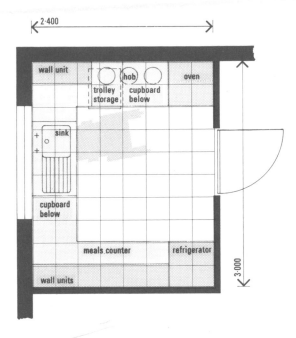

←— 2·400 —→

↕ 3·000

51.7   Kitchen planning: U layout (1:50)

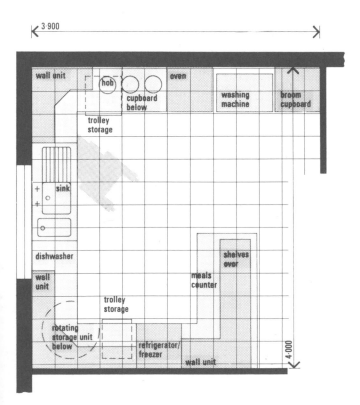

←— 3·900 —→

↕ 4·000

51.8   Kitchen planning: Comprehensive layout (1:50)

5104   Kitchen layout and wheelchair manoeuvre

51040   To allow for comfortable wheelchair turning inside a kitchen there should be an unobstructed space not less than 1·400 × 1·400 where toe recesses are provided below low-level fixtures, and 1·500 × 1·500 where they are not.
For notes on toe recesses see 5125.

51041   To avoid excessive wheelchair manoeuvring, circulation spaces ought not to be exaggerated; a maximum clear dimension of 1·800 is suggested. Diagram 51.7 illustrates an example.

Placing of sink

51042   Placing the sink in a corner position, as shown in diagram 51.6, can be advantageous.
The amount of work surface and storage accommodation accessible from a single position is maximized.

51043   Kitchen planning may be on the basis that wheelchair turning is achieved by a 3 point turn, utilizing the knee access space below the sink and preparation centre.
Diagrams 51.5 and 51.6 are examples.

51044   A corridor layout may be usable by a chairbound housewife where there is generous knee access space to the sink on one side.
The layout shown in diagram 51.3 allows for a 3 point turn where the clear width is 1·200, and not 1·100 as shown. Because of problems of lifting and carrying, an L or U layout is preferred. A further disadvantage with a corridor layout is that the distance to the dining table may be extended.

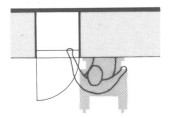

51.9   Access for chairbound housewives to oven etc

Access to storage

51045   To allow a chairbound person to reach inside a refrigerator, oven or built-in cupboard, the space alongside should have unrestricted knee access below the work surface, as shown in diagram 51.9.
While this is theoretically practicable for all the oven and refrigerator positions shown in diagrams 51.4–51.8, an effect will be to reduce the volume of storage accommodation below worktops; on balance this may be too big a penalty.

a

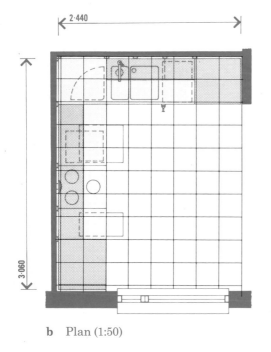

b   Plan (1:50)

51.10 Fokus Society (Sweden) kitchen for special
housing

511 Kitchens: Work levels

5110 Kitchen work levels: General considerations

51100 Suggested levels for standing work surfaces are given in table 51.1.
These figures need to be interpreted with caution, owing to the conflicting evidence discussed below on optimum work surface heights.

51101 In special housing for disabled people it must be possible to fix kitchen fittings at the level most convenient for the disabled housewife.
Given that no single level can be satisfactory for all users, this can be achieved by (1) adjustable-height fittings, (2) delaying the fixing of units until individual requirements are ascertained, or (3) installing units at a height which may be suitable, and refixing them if required. These alternatives are discussed further in 5112–5114.

Conflicting criteria
51102 Although for any disabled housewife there is an optimum level at which work surfaces may be fixed, any solution will involve compromise.
This is because there are conflicting criteria for activities carried out on work surfaces, for example between cutting up vegetables and stirring a bowl. It is also not possible to reconcile optimum levels for sink rim/drainer and sink invert; unless the sink bowl is inconveniently shallow it will happen that either the drainer is uncomfortably high for chairbound housewives or the invert is uncomfortably low for ambulant housewives.

51103 In kitchens for disabled housewives work surfaces should be at a consistent level.
Although surfaces at alternative heights may be indicated to cater for different activities, any advantage will be outweighed by the problem of having to move goods by lifting rather than by sliding. There is also the hazard of spillages where surfaces at different levels are adjacent.

51104 To provide alternative working levels, pull-out boards below work surfaces are recommended, see 5122.

Table 51.1 Kitchens: Work surface heights

	ambulant disabled housewives	elderly housewives	chairbound housewives
preferred height, surfaces at consistent level	0·900	0·850	0·800
range of levels for comfortable working	0·850–1·075	0·825–1·000	0·600–0·800

5111 Work levels for general purposes

51110 For general purpose housing the standard height of kitchen floor units is 0·900, as recommended in BS1195 [3] and in the draft international standard [4]. For housing for old people a height of 0·850 is recommended by the Department of the Environment [5].

51111 These standard levels have evolved from traditional usage adapted to the constraints of metric dimensional practice; while some studies suggest that they are appropriate from an ergonomic point of view, others suggest they are not. Where evidence conflicts it is on the basis that standard levels are too low for comfortable working.

51112 Saville from his research among able-bodied people indicates that, for fixed levels, heights of 0·975 for sink rim and draining boards and 0·900 for other work surfaces are most suitable, giving comfortable use for about 75 per cent of women [6]. Ward's evidence supports this, suggesting that the height of work surfaces should be related to elbow height, and that they are conveniently about 0·076 below elbow level [7]. Thompson, reporting a large-scale anthropometric study among able-bodied women, records that elbow heights range from 0·885 (0·910 with 0·025 allowed for shoes) at the 1st percentile to 1·125 (1·150) at the 99th percentile; from this he concludes that no one level can cater for all users [8]. On the basis that the comfortable work surface level for any individual is between elbow level and a height 0·076 below elbow level he suggests that work surfaces at a level of 1·000 will accommodate 58 per cent of the adult female population, work surfaces at 0·960 with an alternative at 1·040 will accommodate 88 per cent, and work surfaces at 0·925 with alternatives at 1·000 and 1·075 will accommodate 98 per cent.

5112 Variable work levels: Built-in adjustability

51120 Where housing is planned for disabled people and kitchen units need to be variable in height to suit a chairbound housewife, an ambulant disabled housewife or an able-bodied housewife, the preferred solution is built-in adjustability. Of the three options possible this is the most sophisticated and also the most expensive.

51121 The principle is that fittings are carried on a structural support system of horizontal brackets locked to wall-fixed uprights; a variety of proprietary systems is available.

[3] Bib 93902
[4] Bib 93903
[5] Bib 93630
[6] Bib 93905
[7] Bib 93765
[8] Bib 93971, referring to Bib 93764.

Advantages and disadvantages

51122 The advantage of built-in adjustability is flexibility, allowing for floor units, sink units, wall units and split level hob units to be readily repositioned with no structural alteration work required.

51123 The only disadvantage is the expense. The special components required are more expensive than standard floor or wall units, and the telescopic plumbing required for sink waste and water supply pipes is also expensive.

51124 A reservation is that, from such little evidence as is available it is doubtful whether in practice the advantages of the system will be properly exploited [9]. The impression is that preliminary fixing is often determined by a rough estimate of the most suitable levels. Subsequently checks may not be made to confirm that levels are appropriate, for example when a disabled housewife is no longer able to manage kitchen work and activities are taken over by an able-bodied helper.

Fixing parameters

51125 To allow for all potential disabled or able-bodied housewives the system should allow for work surfaces to be fixed at any point between 0·600 and 1·075 above floor level.
Where a system is installed which allows for horizontal brackets to be locked in only at fixed incremental points, fixing intervals should preferably be not less than 0·025, maximum 0·050.

51126 To avoid an awkward and dirt-collecting trap at the back of work surfaces, vertical support channels should be inset rather than projecting from the wall surface.
This will involve blocking pieces and the fixing of a false-front wall surface where supports are supplied.

51127 Diagrams 51.11a and b illustrate the fixing procedure for the Fokus kitchen units shown in diagram 51.10.

5113 Variable work levels: Delayed fixing

51130 The second option is to delay the fixing of units until the specific requirements of the disabled housewife are established.

Assembly of components

51131 Where this is to be done a system where kitchen units are built up from an assembly of components is suggested.

51132 The inclusion or omission of drawer units, alternative plinth heights and alternative heights for the cupboard unit allow for variability of working surfaces.
Diagram 51.12 illustrates how work surfaces ranging from 0·650 to 1·050 can be obtained by using plinth units 0·100 or 0·150 high, cupboard units 0·450, 0·550 or 0·650 and a drawer 0·100.

51133 An alternative is to employ a system of kitchen units where worktop level can be varied by having supporting legs to cupboard units which are available in different heights.

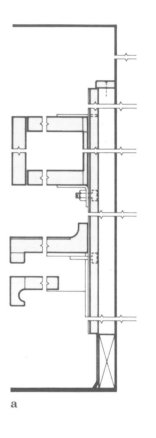

a

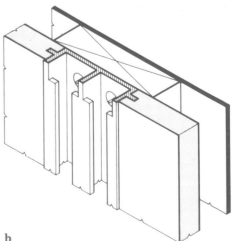

b

51.11 Fokus system adjustable kitchen units: Fixing details

---

[9] In the DoE survey of purpose-built housing (Bib 93122) 28 people had adjustable kitchen fittings of some kind. Fewer than half of these had actually had their units adjusted to suit the person who used them most.

51.12 Kitchen units: Variable work levels obtained from assembly of components (1:50)

51134 The disadvantage of the delayed fixing option is that it may not be practicable to wait until individual requirements are known.
Where fixing is delayed additional expense will be involved because the work of the tradesmen is difficult to coordinate and it can be costly to arrange for carpenters, plumbers and decorators to return to carry out minor works.

5114 Variable work levels: Fixing and refixing

51140 The third option is to fix standard units at the levels suggested in table 51.1, ie 0·900, 0·850 or 0·800, and subsequently to alter the fixing height if it becomes necessary.

51141 Where this procedure is adopted it is recommended that units comprising an assembly of components are used.
The disadvantages are as for delayed fixing described above.

Comparative costs
51142 No reliable evidence is available regarding comparative costs of these three options. The first option is likely to be the most expensive. Where it is expected that the tenant's requirements can be determined in advance the second option is recommended; where this is not likely the third option, taking into account the possibility of refixing and associated structural alterations, is likely to be more economical. The number of units in a scheme and the ready availability of tradesmen are factors which need to be considered.

5115 Work levels: Ambulant disabled and elderly handicapped people

51150 Where housing is planned for ambulant disabled or elderly handicapped people and kitchen units are to be at a fixed height, the levels recommended are those listed in table 51.1, ie 0·900 and 0·850 respectively.

Elbow height and work level
51151 The advice here that architects should endorse the standards of conventional practice rather than those suggested by the ergonomic studies mentioned above (51112) is arguable. No relevant

study of ambulant disabled people has been made and in its absence it might seem reasonable to apply Thompson's recommendations for able-bodied housewives. On the other hand it is questionable whether Thompson's underlying assumption is valid, ie that the lowest acceptable working level is 0·076 below elbow height and the highest acceptable level is at elbow height. Without firm evidence here, the impression is that for the majority of household tasks a work level at elbow height is too high for comfort, and for some tasks it is too high at 0·076 below elbow height. For certain activities, for example cutting up and preparing vegetables, a work surface at 0·076 below elbow height may be appropriate; for others, for example rolling pastry, using a whisk, stirring bowls or using an electric mixer, a lower working level is likely to be more satisfactory.
In the second edition of this book figures were given of optimum working heights for different kitchen activities [10]. These were based on largely untested evidence, for example that given by Walley [11]; because of the lack of authoritative evidence they are not repeated here.

51152 Data from the Swedish Consumer Institute indicate that for a housewife of average height (1·630) the most comfortable level for the sink rim is 0·920, and for other work surfaces 0·860 [12].

Sink rim and invert
51153 In practice the optimum level of work surfaces will be affected by the requirement (51103) that sink rim and work surfaces are at the same level.
Ideally the sink invert should be at about the same level as other work surfaces, but with a typical bowl 0·150 deep this is not attainable. A further complication is that if the sink invert were to be at a comfortable working level the sink rim and drainer would be above the elbow height of short people. It is inevitable, as happens in practice, that for standing housewives the typical sink is too low for comfort.

[10] Bib 93002, table 51.1.
[11] Bib 93907
[12] Bib 93910

Surfaces at consistent level

51154 From these conflicts of criteria and evidence the recommendation is made that for a standing housewife the preferred height for surfaces at a consistent level is at about 0·130 below elbow height.

Thompson's data indicate that the mean elbow height of adult women wearing shoes is 1·040, meaning that a woman of average height would be best suited by work surfaces at 0·910 [13]; this is not significantly different from the officially recommended level of 0·900. In respect of elderly people aged 66 or over Thompson's figure for the mean elbow height is 1·010, indicating that an elderly woman of average height would be best suited by work surfaces at 0·880. This is marginally above the officially recommended level of 0·850. Given that short people are more likely to be inconvenienced by having surfaces which are too high than tall people by having them too low, the evidence sustains the case for recommending work surfaces at the officially approved levels.

51155 On the premise that the important variable of elbow height is not significantly different as between disabled and non-disabled ambulant people, there is no cause for advocating that fixed levels in housing for ambulant disabled people, for example mobility housing (8233), are other than 0·900 for general purpose housing and 0·850 for old people's housing.

Use of stools

51156 Some ambulant disabled housewives may perch on a stool for support when working in the kitchen. While this may indicate that lower work surfaces would generally be suitable, no evidence is available on the usage of stools by ambulant disabled housewives and, for the purposes of determining fixed work surface heights, it is suggested that this factor is discounted.

5116 Work levels: Wheelchair users

51160 For chairbound housewives there is no single level for work surfaces which can be recommended as generally suitable.

Optimum work levels

51161 For wheelchair users, optimum work levels are determined not by elbow level but by the clear height required below the working surface for knee access. The requirement that the sink rim and work surfaces are at a consistent level means in practice that the optimum level is the lowest which permits knee access below the sink bowl.

51162 For housewives using standard wheelchairs the mean height of the thigh at the point where chair arms obstruct (diagram 20.9) is approx 0·605. Assuming a sink bowl 0·150 deep overall (see 5151) the sink rim will be not lower than 0·755. Because this is significantly higher than mean elbow level

(0·690) work surfaces will inevitably be higher than they ought to be for comfort.

Knee recess

51163 A knee recess giving a clear height of 0·605 will not admit housewives whose thighs are above average level; to cater for large women the minimum clear height should be 0·655, giving a sink rim and work surfaces at 0·805.

51164 The only satisfactory course is to adjust the height of the sink and work surfaces when individual requirements are known. Where units have to be fixed provisionally in advance, the compromise of 0·800 is suggested (diagram 51.15).

51165 The impossibility of achieving comfortable work surface levels emphasizes the need for pull-out boards below fixed surfaces to afford an alternative working level.

Work levels for chairbound and ambulant people

51166 It is not possible for fixed work surfaces to be at a level which will simultaneously be convenient for chairbound and ambulant disabled housewives; any compromise will be inconvenient for one group or the other.

51167 In practice, kitchens in housing for disabled people are more likely to be used regularly by ambulant than by chairbound housewives. This might suggest that if units are to be provisionally fixed they should be at a level convenient for ambulant rather than chairbound users.

In the DoE study of purpose-designed housing it was found that none of the basic kitchen tasks, for example meal preparation and washing up, was carried out by more than 40 per cent of disabled people interviewed [14]. Of those disabled people who did do household meal preparation and washing up, less than half were chairbound.

51168 On the basis that the chairbound housewife will be significantly more inconvenienced by having work surfaces at 0·900 than the ambulant housewife will be by surfaces at 0·800, the advice is that where units in wheelchair housing units have to be fixed in advance the compromise height of 0·800 is adopted.

[13] Bib 93971
[14] Bib 93122

512 Kitchen fitments

5120 Provision for seated kitchen work

51200 In all kitchens to be used by disabled housewives provision should be made for work to be done from a sitting position.
In kitchens for ambulant disabled people allowance should be made for the use of an adjustable-height kitchen chair, of the type shown in diagram 51.13.

51.13 Adjustable-height kitchen chair

51201 Provision for seated work should be made at the preparation centre.
It is desirable that this is by means of a knee recess. Where there is no recess pull-out boards should be incorporated, see 5122.

51202 For ambulant housewives any knee recess should be unobstructed to a level not lower than 0·150 below the work surface (diagram 51.14).

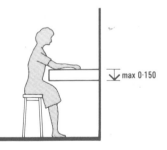

51.14 Knee recess for ambulant housewife (1:50)

51203 The clear height should be not less than 0·650. Where there is a recess the clear width should be not less than 0·600.

5121 Knee recesses for wheelchair users

51210 For wheelchair users provision for seated work must be made at the sink (5153) and at the preparation centre. Provision at the hob is not so essential; where it is made care must be taken to minimize the hazard of spillages.

Height

51211 To allow for knee access the minimum unobstructed height of any knee recess should be 0·650 (diagram 51.15a).

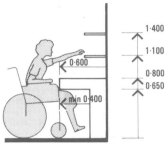

a

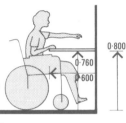

b

51.15 Knee recess for chairbound housewives (1:50)

51212 To allow for closer approach to the work surface, allowance should be made for clearance over wheelchair armrests. The clear height should be not less than 0·760 (diagram 51.15b).

Depth and width

51213 To allow for close approach the recess should have a depth of 0·600 (diagram 51.15b).
Where allowance is made only for knee access the depth should be not less than 0·400 (diagram 51.15a).

51214 Utilization of space in a corner of the kitchen for a knee recess is suggested, as shown in plan diagrams 51.5–51.8.

Portable storage

51215 A knee recess may be used to accommodate a portable storage trolley (diagrams 51.26–51.27) as shown in plan diagrams 51.4–51.8.
When knee access is required the unit can be easily moved out and positioned alongside the seated housewife.

5122 Pull-out boards

51220 In kitchens for chairbound housewives pull-out lap boards should be incorporated at the preparation centre so that work can be done at a lower level than the fixed worktop.

Board dimensions

51221 Where there is a knee recess allowance may be
made for sliding pull-out boards to be used at
varying levels to suit individual requirements
(diagram 51.16).
The height of boards should be adjustable from a
point 0·600 above floor level to a point 0·050 below
the fixed work surface.

51222 The width of pull-out boards should be not less than
0·500. They should be designed to project at least
0·300 in front of any adjacent vertical surface such
as a cupboard door (diagram 51.17a).

51223 A stop should be incorporated to prevent boards
being pulled out accidentally.
It should be possible for boards to be lifted out for
cleaning.

51224 To allow for cutting operations boards should be of
teak or have an otherwise suitable surface.

Auxiliary board with apertures

51225 It is advantageous if there are two pull-out boards
at the preparation centre, one to have apertures in
which mixing bowls may be placed for beating and
stirring.

51226 Suggested aperture diameters are 0·140 and 0·200
(diagram 51.17a).
Where there is one aperture only, 0·170 is
suggested.

51227 To afford more effective purchase for bowls set in
the apertures, a slightly elliptical aperture section
is suggested (diagram 51.17b).
The greater dimension of the ellipse should be
parallel with the worktop fascia.

51228 A flexible edging, for example of pvc, may be fixed
inside the aperture, to counter slippage of bowls.

5123 Depth of kitchen units: General considerations

51230 In kitchens for disabled housewives a depth of 0·600
is recommended for work surfaces.
A depth of 0·600 is standard for domestic kitchen
units, and is therefore more economical than any
alternative.

Ambulant disabled people

51231 For ambulant disabled housewives floor units 0·600
deep, with 0·300 deep wall units above, are
generally satisfactory, allowing a generous area of
usable working surface (diagram 51.18).
Access to cupboards over is not significantly less
difficult than where the work surface is shallower.

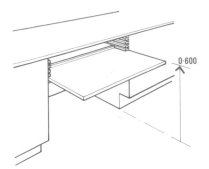

51.16 Adjustable-height pull-out boards

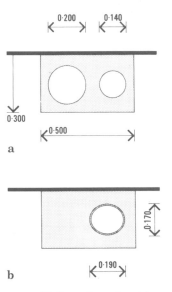

51.17 Pull-out boards with apertures (1:20)

Old people

51232 In housing for old people where kitchens are small,
units having a depth of 0·500 may be preferred to
save space, but they have no significant practical
advantages.

Narrow fitments

51233 Narrow fitments, for example of 0·300 or 0·400, may
be used for meal counters, peninsular units and
cupboards extending from floor to ceiling.

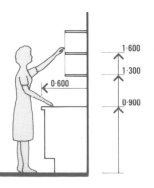

51.18 Kitchen units: Ambulant disabled housewives
(1:50)

5124 Depth of kitchen units: Wheelchair users

51240 For chairbound housewives kitchen units 0·600 deep are generally preferred (diagram 51.15a).

51241 For some wheelchair users shallower floor units, for example 0·500, may make it easier to reach wall units above, but there will be no advantage for the majority.
The amount of high level storage that can in any circumstances be suitably located is very limited, and as Howie points out (51313) there are hazards when chairbound people reach to high shelves.

51242 Units 0·600 deep give generous space at worktop level for preparation work, and for setting down utensils and ingredients.
The typical wheelchair housewife uses only the front 0·350 or so of the work surface for preparation. work, leaving the rear 0·250 for setting down goods. In practice she may use the work surface for the general storage of regularly used items; the effect may be untidy but will be more economic than relying on high or low level storage.

51243 Where the worktop clears wheelchair armrests a depth of 0·600 will ensure that close approach for working is possible (diagram 51.15b).

5125 Toe recesses

51250 In kitchens for chairbound housewives floor units should have relatively high and deep toe recesses.

51251 To allow for wheelchair footrests and give more space for wheelchair manoeuvre the preferred dimensions of any toe recess are 0·200 high and 0·150 deep (diagram 51.19).
Where a compromise is necessary it is better that the depth is reduced rather than the height.

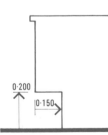

51.19 Toe recesses: Chairbound housewives (1:20)

51252 Where storage accommodation in floor units is limited and a high toe recess would significantly reduce the amount available it may be permissible to have no recess.
This would be the case only where a kitchen is planned for a chairbound person to work parallel with rather than facing units.

51253 In kitchens for ambulant disabled housewives a toe recess may be useful but is not essential.

51254 Cleaning and food cupboards at floor level should have unobstructed access.

5126 Support rails

51260 For some ambulant disabled housewives rails along the length of counter tops afford a useful means of support (diagram 51.20).

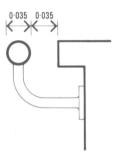

51.20 Support rails to kitchen units (1:5)

51261 Rails must not project above the work surface.

51262 These rails are not recommended for general purposes.
They may hinder the sliding of trays etc direct from work surface to portable trolleys, and for wheelchair users may reduce the area of accessible work surface. Utensils in drawers immediately below the work surface will be less easy to take out and put away.

513 Kitchen storage

5130 Kitchen storage: General considerations

51300 For public authority housing units for 3 or more persons the officially recommended minimum provision for kitchen storage is 2·3m³, and for 1 or 2 person units 1·7m³ (8045).

51301 On the basis of a survey of kitchen storage in family dwellings Thompson suggests that the volume should be approx 2·5m³ [15].

51302 For storage area Thompson suggests approx 15·0m² for articles used at least once each week, and a further 3·0m² for items used less frequently [16].

51303 For notes on kitchen storage for wheelchair housing see 8345.

[15] Bib 93971, p164.
[16] Bib 93971, p165.

5131 Kitchen shelf heights

51310 For housewives who are disabled, storage accommodation for articles used regularly must be within comfortable reach.

Restricted zone of reach

51311 In the case of chairbound housewives, and commonly of ambulant disabled housewives also, the restricted zone which can comfortably be reached, in conjunction with competing criteria for other kitchen activities, may make it difficult or impossible to achieve adequate accessible storage. This problem is acute for chairbound housewives. Fixed cupboards above standard depth work surfaces are not generally accessible, and requirements for knee access at the sink and preparation centre mean that storage provision at low level has to be limited.

51312 The shelf heights indicated in diagram 51.21 are derived from the anthropometric data in section 20, and from evidence in relevant reports [17]. Bearing in mind practical applications, they have been rounded to the nearest 0·100.
In respect of chairbound people the important proviso has to be made that the figures in diagram 51.21 are based on the performance of wheelchair users with relatively unimpaired upper limbs. People with severe arm impairments are excluded. One survey has reported that 60 per cent of wheelchair users have weak arms (2273).

Reach constraints of disabled housewives

51313 Howie, in her study of disabled housewives, says:

'Housewives who are stiff, weak or incoordinate need to have the shelves lower than might at first be thought, if they are to lift articles off safely. Housewives with weakness of grip tend to drop things and have to make sure of sustaining a hold of the article before lifting it down. Housewives with disabilities cannot summon up the extra mobility, stretch and resilience of the able-bodied housewife, and to reach, balance and manipulate at the same time needs strength and control of muscles in all parts of the body. The shelves they are able to use, rather than merely to reach, are therefore lower than might have been expected.' [18]

51314 For chairbound people there is often little or no usable space in standard wall cupboards over worktops (diagram 51.15a), and only a small amount in standard cupboards below worktops.

Inaccessible storage

51315 For chairbound housewives with severe arm impairments, there is no possibility of achieving adequate easily accessible storage accommodation. It will be unavoidable that, even where the data in diagram 51.15a are carefully applied, a proportion of storage provision is beyond reach.

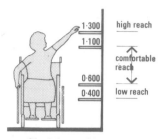

a Chairbound housewives

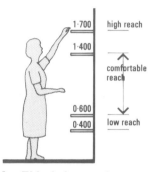

b Elderly housewives

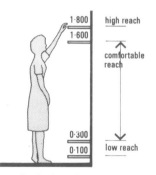

c Ambulant housewives

51.21 Kitchen shelf heights (1:50)

51316 In kitchens for disabled people it is permissible for shelves to be installed at high level.
It can be assumed that another person, for example a member of the family or home help, can be called on when necessary to reach goods on high level shelves. In single person dwellings high level shelves may be used for infrequently used articles, or for those needed only when visitors call.

51317 To minimize accidents, kitchen shelves ought not to be higher than 1·800 above floor level.

[17] In particular Paulsson (Bib 93931), Howie (Bib 93920), Thompson (Bib 93764) and Floyd (Bib 93500).
[18] Bib 93920, p53.

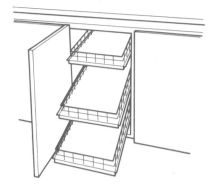

51.22 Kitchen storage: Sliding drawers with low sides

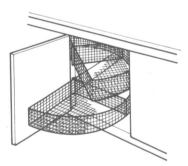

51.23 Kitchen storage: Basket drawers

51.24 Kitchen storage: Cupboards with rotating shelves

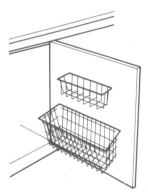

51.25 Kitchen storage: Baskets to inside of cupboard doors

5132 Fixed storage: Cupboards and shelves

51320 Shallow cupboards and shelves may be preferred. Reaching to the back of a deep shelf at high level is difficult and hazardous.

51321 Open shelves approx 0·150 deep can be useful. The storage of goods in single rows allows for accessibility, immediate visibility of what is available, and the avoidance of the need to rearrange goods to reach those behind. More shelves may be required than where wider shelves are fitted but it may not be necessary to use more wall space; deep cupboard units involve a large proportion of dead space to allow articles at the back to be lifted over those in front.

Blind people

51322 For blind people it is advantageous if open shelves have lipped front edges.

Wheelchair users

51323 For chairbound housewives, standard cupboards permitting frontal access only are not satisfactory. As shown in diagram 51.21a, cupboards and shelves should have space alongside for lateral approach, allowing goods to be more easily reached.

5133 Fixed storage: Drawers etc

51330 At low level, pull-out drawer units are preferred to open cupboards.

51331 Sliding drawers with low sides, as shown in diagram 51.22, facilitate the transfer of goods in and out.
Where deep drawers in cupboards have solid fronts it is helpful if the side panel on the exposed side, ie where a wheelchair may be positioned, is omitted or reduced in height.

51332 Wire basket drawers, as shown in diagram 51.23, have the advantage that goods at the back of low level drawers can be more easily located.

Corner units

51333 Corner cupboards may accommodate semicircular rotating shelves, as shown in diagram 51.24.

51334 Open shelves rotating independently on a corner post, of the kind designed for Fokus kitchens in Sweden (diagram 51.10), are recommended.

Door storage

51335 Storage on the inside of cupboard doors can be conveniently accessible, for example as in diagram 51.25.

51336 Costs of selected storage units are noted in 90311.

5134 Portable storage units

51340 Portable floor units running on castors are a valuable aid for disabled housewives.

51341 Diagram 51.26 shows a portable storage trolley designed for use in Fokus kitchens (diagram 51.10). Trolleys of this kind can be pushed around by a chairbound housewife without difficulty, and can be positioned alongside the wheelchair during meal preparation.

51342 Diagram 51.27 shows a trolley designed to carry cleaning utensils and equipment.

51343 In wheelchair kitchens storage trolleys can be kept in spaces below the sink and preparation centre giving knee access for wheelchair users.

5135 Kitchen storage accommodation: Doors and ironmongery

51350 For cupboards at low level, sliding doors may be preferred to side-hung doors.
The disadvantage of side-hung doors is that they can obstruct wheelchair manoeuvre, and may be a hazard to ambulant handicapped people.

High level storage
51351 At high level, side-hung doors are generally preferred to sliding doors.
A disadvantage of sliding doors is that they restrict the cupboard space which is simultaneously visible and accessible.

51352 For blind people, side-hung doors at high level may be a hazard, but not to the extent that they should be ruled out.

51353 For high level storage, pairs of adjacent vertically sliding cupboard doors which operate sympathetically may be used (diagram 51.28). Lightweight or counterbalanced roller shutter doors are also satisfactory.

Handles and knobs
51354 Door handles or knobs to high level cupboards should be fixed at the bottom of doors (diagram 51.29).

51355 Knobs or handles to low level cupboards should be fixed at the top of doors. No knob or handle should be lower than 0·450 above floor level (diagram 51.29).

51356 Magnetic door catches are recommended.

51357 Drawer pulls must be easy to manipulate. Full-width pulls are suitable where drawers slide easily. Recessed handles should be avoided.

51.26 Portable storage trolley

51.27 Storage trolley for cleaning utensils

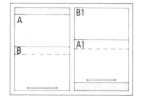

51.28 Kitchen cupboard with sympathetically sliding doors

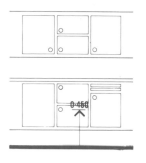

51.29 Kitchen cupboards: Position of handles

5136 Refrigerators, food storage

51360 For small households a refrigerator built in at a convenient level is preferred to a floor unit fitting below the worktop.

51361 For large households a large floor unit incorporating a freezer compartment is preferred, to give adequate cold storage.
In large households, where non-disabled members can help, it is not critical that all parts of the refrigerator are accessible to a chairbound housewife.

51362 Suggested limits for shelf dimensions are indicated in diagram 51.30.
In the case of tall refrigerator/freezer units some compromising of the preferred levels may be necessary.

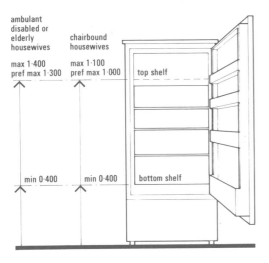

51.30 Built-in refrigerators

Chairbound housewives

51363 For chairbound housewives there should be a clear space alongside the refrigerator, allowing for side reach as shown in diagram 51.9.
Allowance for frontal approach only is less satisfactory.

51364 The door must be side-hung on the side away from the normal direction of approach.

51365 A pull-out board below the refrigerator may be helpful for transferring goods.

51366 Where planning is for lateral approach the refrigerator door should open through 180°, as shown for ovens in diagram 51.31.

Freezer

51367 Where space permits, allowance should be made for a freezer.
A freezer can be of value to handicapped housewives, enabling food to be stored when shopping is difficult, for example during illness or cold weather.

Cool cupboard

51368 If a cool cupboard is provided for storing perishable food the floor surface should be flush with the adjacent floor surface in the kitchen.
Allowance may be made for a portable vegetable rack on castors to be stored inside the food cupboard.

514 Kitchen cookers

5140 Kitchen cookers: General considerations

51400 In kitchens for disabled housewives, split-level cookers, where oven and hob are separated, are preferred to all-in-one floor units.
For many disabled people an oven at low level is awkward to use and to clean, and it is difficult to reach to the base of the oven to transfer goods to a higher level. It is also more difficult to slide oven shelves in and out where they are at low level.

Wheelchair housing

51401 In wheelchair housing, where it is not known whether the housewife will be disabled or not, it is suggested that space should be allowed where a floor unit can be placed or a split-level unit built in; see 8344.

51402 In housing units for one or two people a limited budget may necessitate the provision of a table top cooker with a small capacity oven.

51403 Hot plates should be level with adjacent work surfaces. The grill should be operable independently of the hot plates.

5141 Gas and electricity

51410 On balance electric cookers are preferred to gas cookers for disabled users, principally on account of accident hazards associated with naked flames and (where town gas is still used) poisonous gas. There is also a greater hazard of fat catching fire with gas cookers.
Surveys have shown that approx 30 per cent of old people cannot reliably recognize the odour of town gas where it is present in dangerous quantities [19]. There is also a proneness to accidents owing for example to arthritic hands incompletely closing valves.

51411 Loaded saucepans when being moved on flush electric plates are less likely to be tipped over than on typical gas rings, though with most modern gas hobs the hazard is minimal.

[19] Bib 93775

Blind people

51412 For blind people, partially sighted people and those with sensory disabilities, the heat remaining in electric rings when the current is switched off can be a potential hazard.

For blind people gas has advantages, in that it can be heard and located when the supply is switched on.

Gas cookers

51413 Gas cookers should always incorporate a safety device which automatically closes the valve when the flame is blown out or the gas supply is cut off.

51414 A gas hob is more flexible in use than an electric hob.

Heated pans can be left standing on a gas hob when the power is turned off, without the risk of liquids boiling over.

5142 Ovens

51420 A built-in oven unit is preferred, with the middle shelf at about the level of the adjacent work surface.

For chairbound housewives the bottom shelf may be better placed at about the level of adjacent work surfaces, for reasons discussed in 51425.

Oven doors

51421 For disabled housewives, whether ambulant or chairbound, it is not generally critical whether the oven door drops down or is hinged at the side.

An advantage of a drop-down door is that it gives a platform on which goods can be temporarily placed. On the other hand, a side-hung door may permit closer approach for housewives in wheelchairs.

Pull-out board

51422 Where the oven has a side-hung door a pull-out board can usefully be fitted below the oven to transfer goods.

A pull-out board may also usefully be fitted below the work surface to one side of the oven, as shown in diagram 51.31.

51.31 Wheelchair access to oven

51423 Where pull-out boards are not provided there should be a clear space to one side of the oven to allow for side reach, see diagram 51.9.

Door hinges

51424 Side-hung doors should be hinged on the side further from the source of light, and on the side which does not obstruct approach when the door is open.

51425 Side-hung oven doors should open through at least 140°. For wheelchair users doors should open through 180°, to avoid obstruction to wheelchair manoeuvre (diagram 51.31).

With a split-level cooker the need for the oven door to open through 180° is not critical, provided that the lower edge of the oven door is above the level of the wheelchair armrest. The recommended height above floor level for the lower edge of the oven door is therefore not less than 0·740.

Door handles

51426 Oven door handles should be easy to manipulate. Lever handles are preferred.

51427 Push-pull opening handles are awkward for some handicapped people to manipulate, and should be avoided. With some cookers it may be necessary to adjust the oven door catch, so that the pull needed to open it does not exceed about 4kg.

51428 The door handle to a floor unit oven should not be less than 0·500 above floor level.

Oven shelves

51429 Oven shelves should be pull-out and non-tip. A stop should be incorporated to ensure that shelves cannot accidentally be pulled right out.

5143 Hobs

51430 To allow for the sliding of pans, hot plates must be flush with the adjacent hob surface and with adjoining work surfaces.

Where surfaces are not flush there is a danger that pans may catch on supports or ring edges and tip over. This is usually a bigger hazard with gas cookers than with electric cookers.

Planning of hot plates

51431 The risk of burns caused by reaching across heated hot plates is minimized where rings are arranged in a straight line.

51432 Hot plates should preferably be at the rear of the work surface. The dimension from the front edge should be not less than 0·250 (diagram 51.32). This allows space in front for preparation and for transferring goods to either side. It is also easier if plates are at the back rather than the front to pull pans off when liquids are boiling, and there is a lesser hazard of accidental arm burning. Hot plates at the back are also safer in homes where there are small children.

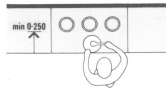

min 0·250

51.32 Hot plates at rear of work surface (1:50)

51433 A factor sometimes cited in favour of hot plates towards the front of the work surface is that chairbound people may not be able to see whether saucepans set at the back are beginning to boil over. For the majority of chairbound housewives this will not be a problem; diagrams 51.15a and b show that the eye level of a chairbound person of average height is well above saucepan level.

Staggered planning of hot plates
51434 Where a hot plate is required towards the front to suit individual preferences, a staggered arrangement is suggested, for example as shown in diagram 51.5.

51435 There should be a clear surface minimum 0·300 wide to one side of the hob, and preferably both sides. This allows for the projection of pan handles and for placing loaded pans beside the hob before or after cooking. It is particularly necessary where hot plates are at the front of the work surface.

Electric hot plates
51436 It is more important that simmer plates are alongside work surfaces than high speed plates. The simmer plate is used for food preparation which may take some time, and it is advantageous if pans can be easily moved on and off it.

Standard floor unit cookers
51437 Standard floor unit cookers are commonly provided with four plates, two at the front and two at the rear. Where for financial reasons a split-level cooker is not feasible, a standard unit of this kind is admissible, provided the work surface to either side is at the same level as the hot plates.

5144 Grill and plate warming

51440 Waist level grills are preferred to eye level grills. Eye level grills are hazardous for wheelchair users and people with limited reach or poor hand control.

51441 With split-level cooking units, the grill may be combined with the hob or the oven.
In units where the grill is incorporated with the oven it is improbable that all facilities and controls will be easily accessible to chairbound people.

51442 Plate warming on racks above the hob is not desirable.
The preferred provision is for plate warming inside the oven.

5145 Cooker controls

51450 Controls to the hob should be at the front of the unit at hob level, rather than above or behind it.

Electric controls
51451 Electric socket outlets should be fixed to one side of the cooker, rather than behind the hob.

51452 Electric cooker controls should have adjacent warning lights to indicate appliances turned on.

Gas controls
51453 Controls to gas cookers should have automatic ignition.
It should not be necessary to reach down to the base of the oven to ignite the oven flame.

51454 Controls should be easily identifiable when they are turned on.
Taps to gas cookers with a wide flange and contrasting colour to the underside are preferred. Flanges grooved on the underside are advantageous to blind people and those with sight impairment. It can be helpful for blind people if controls have an audible click.

Blind people
51455 For blind people, braille thermostats are available for many gas and electric cookers.

515 Kitchen sinks

5150 Sinks: General considerations

51500 For wheelchair users it is essential that there is a knee recess at the kitchen sink. For ambulant people it is not essential.
While it is advantageous for all disabled housewives if work at the sink can be done from a seated position, practical and economic constraints may mean that in ordinary housing, including mobility housing (8233), the kitchen sink is a conventional floor unit. There should be provision elsewhere, for example at the preparation centre or meals counter, for seated work to be undertaken.

Insulation
51501 For some wheelchair users the insulation of the underside of the sink bowl may be indicated. For paraplegics and others affected by loss of sensation, there may be a hazard where the underside of the sink becomes hot and there is direct contact with the thighs. This hazard is however minimal: first, because burning will occur only when the temperature of the underside surface reaches approx 50°C, which is unlikely to happen with normal washing-up water temperatures, and second, because clothing normally prevents direct contact. Where provision is made a sheet of self-adhesive polystyrene or insulating board is suggested (diagram 51.33).

51502 There is no danger of burns from exposed water pipes below the sink and insulation is not necessary.
It is important that hot water supply pipes are not positioned where there may be bodily contact.

Sink rim

51503 A moulded or slightly projecting edge to the drainer and sink bowl is permissible.
The projection should not be higher than 0·010 (diagram 51.33).

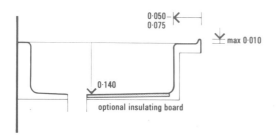

51.33 Sink bowl section for wheelchair users (1:10)

51504 Bowls set in a level surface may be preferred for chairbound housewives.
The width of the level surface in front of the sink bowl should be minimum 0·050, maximum 0·075 (diagram 51.33).

51505 A deep fascia on the line of the front edge of the sink rim hinders close approach to the sink by chairbound housewives.
The fascia must be shallow, with the lower edge not lower than 0·750 above floor level to allow for wheelchair armrests. Alternatively, and preferably, the fascia should be recessed (diagram 51.33).

Overflow

51506 A sink overflow aperture must always be provided.
The possibility of overfilling the sink may be greater among disabled housewives than others, owing to problems of controlling taps, particularly where bowls are shallow.

51507 Standpipe weir overflows ought not to be used as sink outlet plugs.

5151 Sinks: Bowl depths

Wheelchair housewives

51510 For wheelchair housewives, requirements for knee access, in association with the need to keep the sink rim low for comfortable working, indicate a shallow sink, for example 0·120.
In practice wheelchair housewives may find that shallow sinks are not satisfactory, owing to insufficient capacity for the variety of washing activities. Housewives who have been accustomed previously to deep sinks may find it difficult to adapt to the discipline of using a shallow sink.

51511 For wheelchair users a sink approx 0·140 deep internally is suggested.
This will cater better for general washing-up and food preparation activities than a bowl depth of 0·130 or 0·120.

51512 An internal depth of 0·140 implies an overall depth of approx 0·150 from sink rim to underside bowl; this is the basis for dimensional recommendations for work levels for wheelchair users (5116).

Ambulant housewives

51513 For ambulant disabled housewives a sink depth of between 0·140 and 0·165 is suggested.

Double bowls

51514 For a double bowl sink unit different depths are suggested, for example a deep bowl of 0·150–0·180 for washing and a shallow bowl of 0·110–0·130 for rinsing.

51515 Costs of shallow sink bowls are noted in 90312.

5152 Sinks: Fixing heights

51520 In public authority housing the height of the sink should be adjustable to suit individual requirements.
Flexible plumbing may be incorporated. For discussion on variable work levels see 5112–5114.

51521 To cater for chairbound housewives the suggested height for a fixed sink is 0·800 (diagram 51.34). For discussion see 5116.

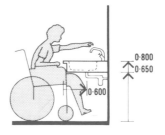

51.34 Kitchen sink for chairbound housewives (1:50)

51522 For ambulant disabled housewives the suggested height for a fixed sink is 0·900, and for elderly people 0·850. For discussion see 5115.

51523 No compromise fixing height can be recommended which will generally be suitable for chairbound housewives and at the same time for ambulant housewives.

5153 Sinks: Knee recess for wheelchair users

51530 The knee recess below the sink should be not less than 0·900 wide, and preferably not less than 1·200 (diagram 51.35).
It is advantageous if the recess to the sink is extended below the preparation centre, as shown in diagrams 51.5–51.8.

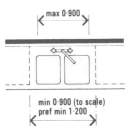

51.35 Kitchen sink: Double bowl (1:50)

51531 For wheelchair users the clear height should be not less than 0·650 (diagram 51.34).
A height of 0·650 permits knee access, but close approach to the sink is prevented by the front edge of wheelchair armrests. It is not suggested that the clear height should be sufficient to clear wheelchair armrests.

51532 The depth at toe level should be not less than 0·400, preferred minimum 0·500 (diagram 51.15a).
A recessed fascia to the sink permits closer approach.

Waste outlet

51533 The waste outlet should be at the back of the sink bowl, preferably in one corner.
For notes on waste outlets see 419.

51534 The minimum dimension from sink fascia to waste pipe should be not less than 0·250 (diagram 51.34).
This recommendation should also apply where a waste disposal unit is fitted.

5154 Sinks: Double blowl units

51540 For disabled housewives double bowl sink units are recommended.
There is no special disability-associated reason for this recommendation; it is simply that for all housewives double bowl units are preferred to single bowls. For suggested bowl depths see 51514.

51541 For ambulant disabled housewives the width across both bowls ought not to be more than 0·900 (diagram 51.35).

51542 For chairbound housewives the width across bowls should be limited to allow for reaching to either side of the bowls without having to move the wheelchair. The minimum width should be 0·700.

5155 Sinks: Taps and mixer fittings

51550 To permit saucepans and kettles to be placed for filling on the adjacent drainer or work surface, a swivel arm mixer fitting may be placed to one side of a single bowl sink (diagram 51.36a).

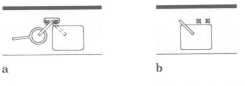

a   b

51.36 Kitchen sink: Mixer fitting for single bowl

51551 While available evidence (51004) confirms the importance of facilitating kettle filling, the layout in diagram 51.36a may have disadvantages. Problems can occur when the water flow has to be turned off, in that manual access to the top control on the bowl side of the swivel arm may be obstructed by cascading water.

Location of tap controls

51552 The preferred arrangement is that tap controls are located away from the swivel arm, as shown in diagram 51.36b.

51553 For housewives with reach limitations, tap controls may be located below the counter rim to one side of the sink bowl, as shown in diagram 51.37.
See also notes on remote control valves: 417.

51.37 Kitchen sink: Tap controls on fascia

51554 For a mixer fitting to be used for filling pans and kettles, the radius of the swivel arm ought not to be less than 0·150.

Double bowl units

51555 With a double bowl unit the two bowls may be planned at right angles to each other, allowing the mixer fitting to be used for filling pans as shown in diagram 51.38.

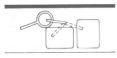

51.38 Kitchen sink: Mixer fitting for double bowl

Spray attachment

51556 To facilitate the cleaning of sink and drainer and
the rinsing of dishes a pull-out spray attached to a
flexible hose is recommended.
This attachment may also be useful for filling
cleaning buckets. Cost notes: 90313.

5156   Sink accessories

51560 For paraplegic housewives who are able to stand in
calipers a safety belt fixed to the sink fascia is an
aid for standing exercise (diagram 51.39).
This aid should be installed only for specific users
who may benefit from it; it ought not to be provided
for general purposes.

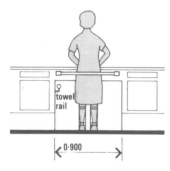

51.39 Kitchen sinks: Provision for standing
paraplegics (1:50)

51561 A towel rail may be fixed to one of the side walls of
the knee recess below the sink bowl (diagram 51.39).

5157   Dishwashers

51570 For disabled housewives with families automatic
dishwashers are a valuable labour-saving aid.

51571 A front-loaded machine may be easier to use than a
top-loaded machine.
Where the machine is loaded from the top it may be
necessary to remove the upper rack before the
bottom rack can be loaded.

51572 Machines with loading trays which slide in and out,
allowing for front, side or top loading, are
recommended.

51573 Dishwashing machines should be connected
directly to the water supply and to the drain outlet.

51574 For chairbound housewives it is advantageous if
the dishwasher is placed alongside the knee recess
to the sink, allowing for comfortable side reach.

52 Living rooms, dining rooms

520 Living rooms

5200 Living rooms in housing for disabled people need not be larger than in housing for general purposes.

5201 For wheelchair users attention should be given to the probable placing of furniture to ensure that adequate space is provided for manoeuvre and circulation.

5202 Sufficient space should be available to turn a wheelchair through 180° in a single movement, see 2435.

5203 Windows should be planned to allow for seated people to see out, see diagram 35.1.
Where possible, alternative aspects should be available. Bay windows are appreciated.

5204 Careful attention should be given to the location of radiators, see 4242.

521 Chairs

5210 The seating requirements of disabled people are very variable.

5211 In residential homes for elderly or disabled people there should be a variety of chairs to meet diverse requirements.

5212 For disabled people who have difficulty regaining a standing position the chair seat needs to be high; levels ranging from 0·400 to 0·550 above floor level are suggested. For some people a portable or retractable footrest may be needed. Some disabled people are more comfortable when seated in an erect position, in which case the depth of the chair seat should be comparatively shallow; a dimension approx 0·400 may be suitable. Armrests should be approx 0·180 above the chair seat, extending forward to allow for pushing up to a standing position. The chair should provide adequate lumbar support, and preferably head support also. Crossbars beneath the front edge of the seat should be avoided.

522 Dining areas: Private houses

5220 In housing where the housewife may be disabled, the dining area should be within the kitchen or immediately accessible.
Where the main dining area is not within the kitchen allowance should be made for at least two people to eat in the kitchen.

Hatch

5221 The provision of a hatch to facilitate the passing of food etc between kitchen and dining area is not generally recommended.

It is preferable that there is direct access between kitchen and dining area, making a hatch superfluous.

5222 In adapted dwellings where access between kitchen and dining area is not direct the installation of a hatch may be useful.
The floor of the hatch should be at the same level as the adjacent kitchen worktop.

Space requirements

5223 For wheelchair users a space minimum 0·900 wide is required at the dining table (diagram 52.1).
The position at the head of the table is commonly convenient.

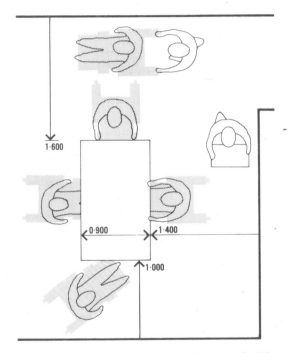

52.1 Dining areas: Space requirements (1:50)

5224 For lateral approach to the dining table by the wheelchair user a space minimum 1·000 should be allowed (diagram 52.1).
Where table legs may obstruct lateral access the space should be minimum 1·100 wide.

5225 To allow for someone to walk behind a wheelchair a clear dimension of 1·300 is required.
To allow for someone carrying a loaded tray the dimension should be 1·400 (diagram 52.1).

523 Dining areas: Residential homes

5230 In residential homes for disabled people an area approx 2·0m² should be provided for each resident, see 70060.

5231 The planning of dining areas in residential homes should assume the use of small tables for four or six people, rather than the use of long bench tables.

Some severely disabled people, for example rheumatoid arthritics, may not be able to use conventional tables and may require individual tables adjustable in height.

5232 Provided that overall space is sufficient, the architect should not attempt to determine exactly how tables will be arranged.
It can be expected that ad hoc arrangements will be made to suit the varying needs of people in the home.

5233 To allow wheelchair users to pass behind wheelchairs at a dining table there should be a clear dimension of 1·600 (diagram 52.1).

524 **Dining tables**

5240 In residential homes for disabled people dining tables may need to be at varying levels.
Some severely handicapped people, for example rheumatoid arthritics, may be unable to use conventional tables, being able to feed themselves only from a tray attached to the wheelchair or from a table fitting over the chair.

5241 For ambulant people the surface of the dining table should be approx 0·700 above floor level.

5242 Assuming a chair seat 0·430 above floor level the construction of the table should give an unobstructed height minimum 0·640 to allow for thigh access.

Wheelchair users

5243 For wheelchair users tables should allow thigh access, giving an unobstructed height minimum 0·670.
Any table which allows for clearance over wheelchair armrests will be too high to use comfortably; for this reason thigh access only is advised. Low level crossbars to dining tables must be avoided.

Table dimensions

5244 To allow wheelchair users to sit facing each other dining tables should be minimum 0·900 wide (diagram 52.2a), and preferably 1·050 wide (diagram 52.2b).
Because the reaching ability of wheelchair users is limited tables wider than 1·050 are not advised.

5245 Square tables for four people in residential homes for disabled people should be not less than 0·900 wide (diagram 52.2a).
Where it is expected that nearly all residents will be in wheelchairs tables 1·050 square are preferred.

5246 For tables for six people dimensions 1·650 × 1·050 are suggested (diagrams 52.2b, 52.2c).

5247 Where it is not anticipated that the preponderance of users will be in wheelchairs, smaller tables are preferred, for example 1·500 × 0·900 for six people.

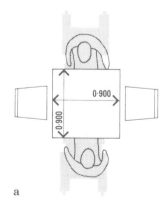

a

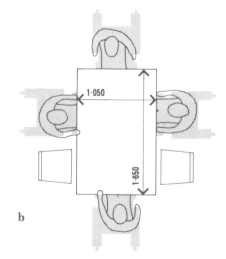
b

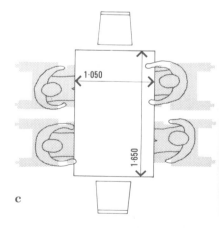
c

52.2 Dining tables (1:50)

53 Bedrooms

530 Bedrooms: General considerations

5300 Bedrooms must be adequately heated.
This is particularly important for housing for old people; the risk of hypothermia (9150) is highest among old people living on their own.

Windows

5301 Bedrooms should be planned so that there is a choice of bed positions, at least one of which allows for a view through the window to be obtained.

5302 To avoid uncomfortable glare it should be possible for beds to be placed parallel with and not opposite to a window.
In small rooms this recommendation may not be practicable.

5303 Window sills should be at a level so that a person in bed can see out.
The mean eye height of a person lying in bed is approx 0·660, and of a person seated in bed 0·890.

Bedridden disabled people

5304 For bedridden disabled people, provision may be made for moving the bed outside where there is a garden or suitable balcony. To give adequate clear width double doors are recommended.
For dimensional guidance see 3612.

5305 For a bedridden handicapped person it is advantageous to have a communicating door or openable partition between bedroom and living area, allowing for involvement in family conversation and activities in the living area.

Telephone point

5306 Where bedrooms are planned for severely handicapped people a telephone point should be provided beside bed positions.

Bed sizes

5307 In determining room dimensions for diagrams 53.1–53.8 the single beds shown are 0·900 wide × 2·000 long and double beds are 1·500 wide × 2·000 long.
These are the bed dimensions which bedrooms planned to the mandatory requirements of MHLG Circular 27/70 [1] must accommodate. In practice, traditional usages in Britain are single beds 0·762 × 1·981 (2ft 6in × 6ft 6in) and double beds 1·372 × 1·981 (4ft 6in × 6ft 6in). Thus bedrooms similarly planned to those shown in the diagrams may in actuality give more generous circulation spaces than indicated by the dimensions.

5308 Bedroom plans shown in diagrams 53.1–53.8 show furniture to the minimum amenity standards of MHLG Circular 27/70, detailed in 8048.

531 Bedmaking

5310 To allow for bedmaking from a wheelchair substantial extra space is required in bedrooms; for this and reasons discussed below the examples shown of bedroom planning for wheelchair users do not allow for access to three sides of beds.

5311 As a general rule it will be wiser, where cost constraints limit the amount of space which can be provided, for spare space resources to be allocated to living areas and perhaps to the bathroom rather than to bedrooms to permit wheelchair bedmaking.

5312 Because of the effort it involves, handicapped people, particularly those in wheelchairs, may seek to economize on bedmaking.
A possible consequence is that, both in private homes where there is a disabled person and in residential homes, lightweight quilts will increasingly be used which are much simpler to manage than conventional tuck-in sheets and blankets.

Family housing

5313 In family units, even where the housewife is in a wheelchair, it will not normally be necessary to allow for bedmaking from a wheelchair.
Where beds are not easily accessible it can be assumed that another member of the family will do the bedmaking.

5314 In single or two person units, bedroom planning should allow, where beds are placed against walls, for beds to be slid out easily to facilitate bedmaking.

Double beds

5315 To permit bedmaking from a wheelchair the width of the clear space to either side of a double bed should not be less than 1·100.
A space 1·100 wide will permit the wheelchair user to work parallel to the bed or diagonally to it, but will not allow for wheelchair turning.

532 Bedroom planning: General considerations

5320 In wheelchair housing bedrooms should be usable, ie allowing for wheelchair turning and for access to dressing tables, wardrobes etc; for practical guidance see 8351.
In mobility housing bedrooms should be accessible but need not necessarily allow for wheelchair turning.

---

[1] Bib 93712

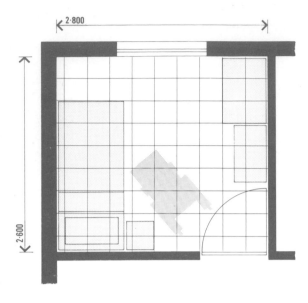

53.1 Bedroom planning: Single bed, wheelchair use (1:50)

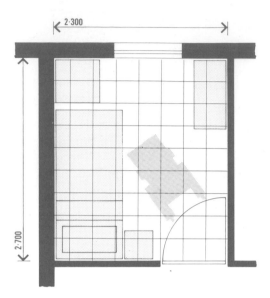

53.3 Bedroom planning: Single bed, wheelchair access (1:50)

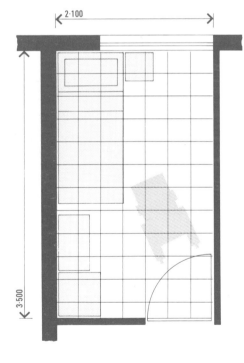

53.2 Bedroom planning: Single bed, wheelchair use (1:50)

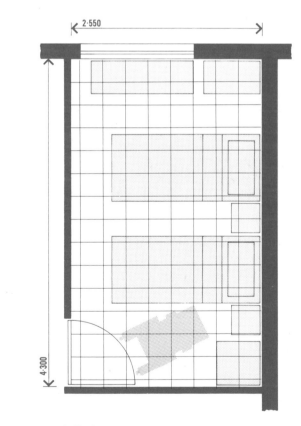

53.4 Bedroom planning: Two single beds, wheelchair access (1:50)

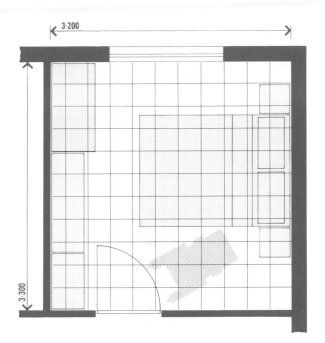

53.5 Bedroom planning: Double bed, wheelchair access (1:50)

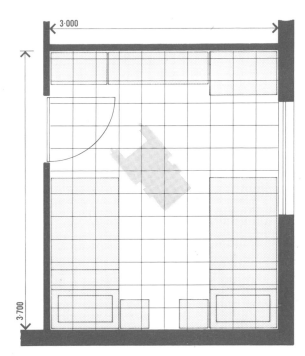

53.7 Bedroom planning: Two single beds, wheelchair use (1:50)

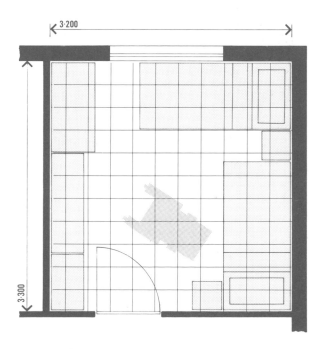

53.6 Bedroom planning: Two single beds, wheelchair use (1:50)

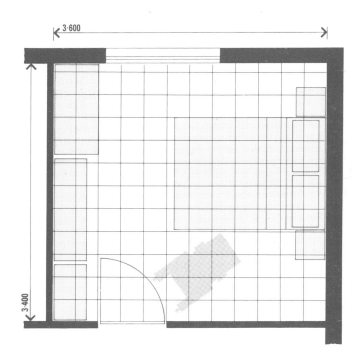

53.8 Bedroom planning: Double bed, wheelchair use (1:50)

5321 For domestic housing for disabled people six bedroom planning conditions can be identified:

1. Single bed, wheelchair access.
2. Single bed, wheelchair use.
3. Two single beds, wheelchair access.
4. Two single beds, wheelchair use.
5. Double bed, wheelchair access.
6. Double bed, wheelchair use.

5322 Dimensional considerations for bedroom planning are discussed in 533 and 534. There are three points to note:

1. Where provision is made for wheelchair access only, bedroom sizes need not be in excess of those for ordinary housing.
2. A room with two single beds which is accessible will be convenient for wheelchair use with one bed.
3. A double room which is accessible will allow for wheelchair use with two single beds.

Wheelchair turning

5323 To allow for comfortable wheelchair turning there should be a clear space in the bedroom not less than 1·450 wide (diagram 53.1).

5324 Where the size of the bedroom is limited by planning constraints a clear width of 1·400 may be considered admissible (diagram 53.3).
For reasons noted in 5307, it may be assumed that the bed will in practice be narrower than 0·900, and that the structure of the bed gives access for wheelchair footrests, see 5382.

5325 Alternatively, planning may allow for a 3 point turn.
The three arms of the turn should be not less than 1·100 wide (diagram 53.7). Where one arm is the door opening the other two arms should be 1·200 wide (diagram 53.8).

Examples of bedroom planning

5326 Diagrams 53.1–53.8 illustrate examples of bedroom planning. These are not intended to be definitive or exhaustive; in many instances equal convenience in similarly sized rooms may be achieved by alternative positions for the window or door, or by rearranging beds and furniture.

533 Bedroom planning: Single rooms

5330 For single bedrooms to be accessible the only essential requirement is that the doorset is 0·900. It is preferable that planning allows for wheelchair approach parallel to the bed, for example as shown in diagrams 53.2 and 53.3, rather than requiring a sharp turn. The door should be hinged in the corner of the room.

5331 For a single bedroom for wheelchair use a plan which is approximately square is preferred.
The example shown in diagram 53.1 has an area of 7·28m². A square plan of this kind facilitates access and maximizes manoeuvring space.

5332 In practice the constraints of house planning may require narrow rooms with the window on the end wall.
Diagram 53.2 shows how a room 2·100 wide, giving an area of 7·35m², can be made usable by allowing for wheelchair turning inside the door.

5333 The plan shown in diagram 53.3, giving an area of 6·21m², is admissible for wheelchair use but should preferably be used for access only. Apart from the limited turning space the disposition of furniture may make it awkward to pull the bed out, and the bedside table prevents a convenient approach to the door.

534 Bedroom planning: Double rooms

5340 Diagram 53.4 is an example of a room with two beds allowing for access but not usability.
Any room with two beds planned for access will also be accessible if there is a double bed. The placing of a single bed on the long wall will also mean that such rooms allow for wheelchair use by one person.

5341 Diagram 53.5 is a room with a double bed allowing for access. The plan shown does not allow for wheelchair use because convenient approach to wardrobe etc is not practicable.

5342 Diagram 53.6 is an example of a room with two single beds which is usable.
The plan here is identical to diagram 53.5, having an area of 10·56m². While two single beds occupy 20 per cent more floor space than a double bed they can be arranged more economically, giving a clear space in the middle of the room for wheelchair manoeuvre.

5343 Diagram 53.7 is an example of a usable room with parallel single beds.
While this plan is satisfactory for two single beds it is not adequate for use with a double bed, and is not therefore suitable as the principal bedroom in a family house. The area is 12·21m².

5344 Diagram 53.8 is an example of a usable room with double bed.
This example demonstrates the penalties of allowing for access and circulation round a double bed; the area at 12·24m² is 15·9 per cent greater than the accessible double room shown in diagram 53.5. If allowance is made for bedmaking the clear width on the window side of the bed would need to be increased from 0·700 to 1·100, increasing the overall area to 14·04m².

535   Transfer from wheelchair to bed

5350   Where bedrooms allow for access only the clear dimension at the side of the bed should preferably be not less than 1·100 (diagrams 53.4, 53.5). The assumption here, in line with the principles of mobility housing (1707), is that the handicapped person will be able to stand to transfer from his wheelchair, if need be with someone to help. In circumstances where space in bedrooms is limited it is possible for transfer to be achieved with the wheelchair parallel with the bed (diagram 53.9a), but where space is constrained the helper may not be able to position himself satisfactorily.

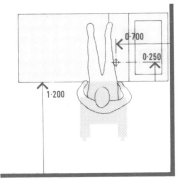

a

b

53.9   Wheelchair transfer to bed (1:50)

5351   Where bedrooms are planned for wheelchair use the clear dimension to the side of the bed should be not less than 1·200 (diagrams 53.7, 53.8). A person who is chairbound needs more room for transfer than a person able to stand.

Paraplegics

5352   Bedrooms planned for paraplegics should allow for the wheelchair to approach at right angles to the bed (diagram 53.9b). A clear dimension of 1·200 is adequate but more generous manoeuvring space will be advantageous.

5353   An accepted routine for high level paraplegics is that the user approaches the side of the bed, locks the brakes, lifts one leg on to the bed, and then the other, releases the brake, moves the chair forward so that the front of the seat meets the side of the bed, and then, pushing on the wheelchair armrests, shifts gradually across on to the bed. If there is a gap between bed and chair seat a sliding board may be used. The return is accomplished by sliding backwards into the wheelchair.

536   Bedrooms: Equipment, aids

5360   To cater for severely disabled people a beam may be fixed to the underside of the ceiling to carry a hoist on which the disabled person can transfer from wheelchair to bed and vice versa. This provision is only rarely required, and a beam ought not to be fixed until its need is established. For notes on hoists and ceiling structures see 261, 262.

5361   For some paraplegics, transfer to or from the bed may be effected by using a stirrup grip suspended from a ceiling eye bolt. This provision ought not to be made unless a specific need is established. Where an eye bolt as described in 260 is fixed it should be positioned approx 0·250 from the side of the bed and approx 0·700 from the head end (diagram 53.9b).

537   Bedroom storage

5370   Storage accommodation for disabled people should be available by the bed. Allowance may need to be made for the storage of prostheses etc in addition to the storage of clothes.

5371   Wall hooks for the hanging of sticks etc may be fixed to the wall adjacent to the bed. A drop-down shelf may be provided for the temporary placing of clothes.

5372   A drawer unit for storage of clothes etc may be built in below the bed frame (diagram 53.10). This can be helpful for disabled people who dress or undress seated or lying on the bed.

53.10   Bed with storage drawer

538   Beds

5380   For wheelchair users the mattress should be at
about the same level as the wheelchair seat, ie
approx 0·480.
This level is also convenient for many ambulant
handicapped people, being sufficiently high for
them to push up relatively easily to a standing
position.

Wheelchair transfer

5381   The transfer technique described in 5353 requires
unobstructed space below the bed frame.
Some beds may be unsuitable, for example divans
with side panels or built-in drawers.

5382   For paraplegics and others able to transfer
sideways, the structure of the bed is not important,
though it is desirable that there is a clear space at
floor level not less than 0·200 high to give access for
wheelchair footrests.

Residential homes

5383   In residential homes for disabled people beds which
are adjustable in height may be preferred.
For nursing supervision a convenient mattress
height is approx 0·650 above floor level. In
residential homes nursing considerations ought not
however to take precedence over other criteria;
rather than use beds which are clinical in
appearance it is preferred that ordinary beds of
varying heights are available for different needs.

Headboard

5384   A headboard with upper edge at approx 0·250 above
mattress level may be used by an ambulant
handicapped person to push himself up to a
standing position.

Castors

5385   To facilitate moving and making the bed, bed legs
should have free-running castors. At least one
castor should have a simply operated brake
attachment.

54 Wcs, bathrooms etc

540 Cloakroom and bathroom provisions: General considerations

5400 Public buildings

54000 Principal requirements for cloakroom provision in public buildings are detailed in section 633 for ambulant disabled people and 643 for chairbound people. Desirable provisions are detailed in 628, and notes on the planning of wc compartments are in 618.

5401 General housing: Bathrooms and wcs

54010 Recommendations for bathroom and wc provision in wheelchair housing are in 836.

54011 In wheelchair housing the wc usable by the disabled person should be conveniently accessible from usable bedrooms.
The Building Regulations require that any room containing a wc must, if it has direct access from a bedroom, have an alternative access bypassing the bedroom except where another wc is available in the dwelling [1].

54012 In dwelling units having a single bedroom only it may be advantageous to plan the bathroom off the bedroom without alternative access; a relaxation of the regulations should be obtained from the local district council, see 6005.

5402 Private dwellings for specific disabled people

Wcs
54020 In a house planned for a particular disabled person one wc should be designed to suit his or her specific requirements. Other wcs in the home need not be specially planned or equipped.

54021 Where there is one bathroom only in the home the wc suitable for use by the disabled person should be in a separate room.
This is particularly desirable in the case of traumatic paraplegics. For discussion see 83631.

Wash basins
54022 One wash basin should be designed so that it is suited to the particular needs of the disabled person.
While it can be helpful if other wash basins in the home are usable by the disabled person, the convenience of other members of the household ought not to be compromised. Where the disabled person is chairbound it is suggested that other basins should be suitable for use by ambulant people, see 54413.

---

[1] Bib 93800, regulation P3(3).

Baths and showers
54023 The bath, and shower if provided, should be suited to the particular needs of the disabled person. Baths and showers may have refinements not needed by the other members of the household, but these will not cause inconvenience.

Other facilities
54024 Other facilities, for example bidets, mirrors and medicine cupboards should be specified so that they are convenient both for the disabled person and other members of the family.

541 Planning of wc compartments

5410 Wc compartments: Ambulant disabled people

54100 In certain circumstances, for example in ordinary housing, small size wc compartments not specifically designed for use by disabled people may with advantage be planned so that they are as convenient as possible for disabled people to manage, including wheelchair users. See 8215 and diagram 82.1.

Wcs with out-opening doors
54101 For ambulant disabled people, wc compartments should be minimum 0·800 wide × 1·500 deep where the door slides or opens out (diagram 54.1).
This assumes the use of a close-coupled low level cistern. Where the cistern is outside the compartment the depth should be not less than 1·300.

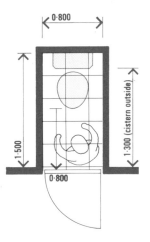

54.1 Wc compartment for ambulant disabled people, door opening out (1:50)

54102 The dimension from the face of the wc bowl to the face of the door should be not less than 0·800.

Wcs with in-opening doors
54103 Where the door opens in, the wc compartment should be minimum 0·800 wide × 1·700 deep (diagram 54.2).
Where the cistern is outside the depth should be not less than 1·500.

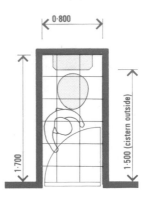

54.2 Wc compartment for ambulant disabled people, door opening in (1:50)

Epileptics

54104 Where a wc compartment may be used regularly by an epileptic person a larger space is warranted. It can be dangerous if a seizure occurs in a restricted and enclosed space.

Wcs for incontinent children

54105 In certain situations, for example ordinary primary schools catering for handicapped children (7243), a small sluice sink and drainer may be installed in the compartment in place of a basin (diagram 54.3). A drying rack should be installed over the basin. An attendant may leave the child seated on the wc, returning after an interval to clean the child and help him off. According to the hanging of the door and its position a curtain screen inside the door may be desirable.

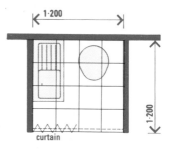

54.3 Wc cubicle for incontinent children (1:50)

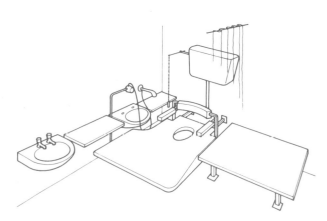

54.4 Sanitary unit for spina bifida children

Sanitary unit for spina bifida children

54106 To cater for the special requirements of families with a growing spina bifida child who is incontinent and paraplegic the Department of Design Research at the London Royal College of Art has designed an experimental sanitary unit with support surfaces for dressing, showering, wc use and washing. A prototype arrangement is shown in diagram 54.4.

5411 **Wheelchair users: Transfer to wc**

54110 In the planning of wc compartments for disabled people, important considerations are whether users are likely to be chairbound, and what techniques they use to transfer from wheelchair to wc.

Leicestershire survey

54111 In the survey made of people with wheelchairs in Leicestershire in 1968, specific questions were asked about the use of the wc [2]. In answer to the question 'How often do you use your wheelchair for going to and from the toilet in your home?' 26 per cent of 402 people who responded said always, 4 per cent said often, 8 per cent said sometimes and 63 per cent said never.

54112 In answer to the question 'Do you usually transfer from your wheelchair on to the toilet?' 40 per cent of 322 people who responded said yes, 56 per cent said no, and 4 per cent said sometimes. For the 139 people who answered yes or sometimes the question was then asked 'If you transfer on to the toilet do you need help to get from your wheelchair on to the toilet seat?' 60 per cent said 'Yes, I transfer by myself' and 4 per cent said 'Sometimes, I transfer by myself'. 30 per cent said 'Yes, I need someone to help me' and 4 per cent said 'Sometimes, I need someone to help me'.
The same group of people was asked 'If you usually transfer from your wheelchair on to the toilet seat do you find your wheelchair gets in your way or causes you to have difficulty getting on or off the toilet?' In answer to this question 64 per cent said no and 22 per cent said yes. The main reasons given for difficulty were lack of space to manoeuvre, non-removable footrests getting in the way during transfer, brake levers protruding and brakes not holding.

Other studies

54113 In a study made by the Loughborough Institute for Consumer Ergonomics in 1973 among 34 wheelchair users, there were 15 who used a frontal approach to the wc, 7 an oblique approach and 12 a lateral approach [3]. Of the 34, there were 8 who said they were able with difficulty to use an alternative technique for transfer.

[2] Bib 93232
[3] Bib 93960, p28.

54114 A study made at the Nuffield Orthopedic Centre at Oxford in 1966 [4] suggested that the majority of wheelchair users would prefer to have space available for a lateral transfer, and also sufficient space inside the wc compartment for an attendant to help.

5412 Wc compartments: Transfer from wheelchair

54120 A wc compartment for general use by disabled people should allow for either a frontal, an oblique or a lateral transfer from the wheelchair, with room for an attendant to assist.
In addition to notes below, utilization space for the wc is discussed with reference to bathroom planning (5454) and illustrated in diagram 54.55.

Frontal transfer

54121 Frontal transfer, with the wheelchair facing the wc, is usually employed by wheelchair users who are able to stand, with if need be an attendant positioned to one side to help him up and down. The normal practice is to fold the wheelchair footrests so that they do not get in the way.
The clear dimension from the rear wall should be minimum 1·900 and preferably 2·000 (diagram 54.5a). Where the cistern is external the dimension should be minimum 1·750, preferred 1·850.

Oblique transfer

54122 Oblique transfer, often employed by wheelchair users who can take some weight on their feet but cannot stand, is usually done by shifting to the front of the chair seat and then across to the wc seat. An attendant may help, positioned to prevent the feet sliding or the wheelchair shifting.
The preferred clear dimension from the centre line of the wc to the side wall is 1·100, minimum 0·950 (diagram 54.5b). The preferred clear dimension from the rear wall is 1·800, minimum 1·500, or 1·650 and 1·350 where the cistern is external.

Lateral transfer

54123 Lateral transfer is used by people with strong arms who are not able to stand, and can lift themselves across from wheelchair to wc seat.
This technique normally requires a wheelchair with removable armrests. Some chairbound people carry with them a sliding board to form a bridge between wheelchair seat and wc seat.

54124 The clear dimension from the centre line of the wc to the side wall should be minimum 0·950 (diagram 54.5c). The dimension from the rear wall to the front edge of the wc seat should be minimum 0·720.
For further notes on lateral transfer see 54152.

[4] Bib 93572

min 1·900
pref 2·000 (to scale)

a   Frontal transfer

d   Transfer through back of chair

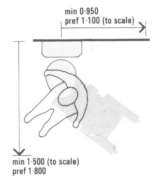

min 0·950
pref 1·100 (to scale)

min 1·500 (to scale)
pref 1·800

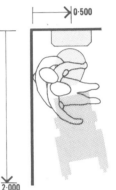

0·500

2·000

b   Oblique transfer

e   Attendant-assisted transfer

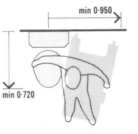

min 0·950

min 0·720

c   Lateral transfer

54.5   Transfer from wheelchair to wc seat (1:50)

Hemiplegic users

54125 Hemiplegic wheelchair users and others with alateral impairments can more easily transfer if a secure grip is available on their 'good' side; the plan arrangement shown in diagram 54.7 is suited to a person with a right hemiplegia who transfers laterally.
The typical hemiplegic wheelchair user is able to put some weight on at least one foot, and is usually able to transfer obliquely with the aid of an attendant. It can be helpful for him to have a secure fixed rail on the wall behind the wc.

Transfer through back of chair

54126 Some chairbound people transfer on to the wc seat by pushing from the wheelchair seat through the back of the chair (diagram 54.5d).
This is done by means of a zip in the canvas of the backrest. It is a technique used occasionally by high level paraplegics or low level tetraplegics. Low level paraplegics can transfer laterally or obliquely by pushing up and across, and high level tetraplegics must be lifted by an attendant or use a hoist.

Space for attendant behind wc

54127 To allow space for an attendant assisting from behind the wc seat, the preferred dimension from the centre line of the wc to the side wall is 0·500 (diagram 54.5e).

54128 There are conflicting requirements here. On the one hand, there needs to be comfortable space for an attendant to lift a disabled person on to the wc seat from behind, indicating a clear dimension of about 0·700. On the other, it is important that the side wall is close to the wc, to afford efficient use of horizontal and vertical support rails fixed to the wall. Where the first condition is the more critical, a possible solution is the provision of a hinged horizontal support of the kind shown in diagram 54.30, with no allowance for a vertical rail. But on balance the preference is for rails fixed to the wall, with the clear space limited to not more than 0·500. With the side wall at 0·500 a horizontal or slightly inclined rail can conveniently be used for pushing up to a standing position; beyond 0·500 the disabled person has to lean too far sideways to obtain effective thrust.

54129 The clear dimension from the centre line of the wc to the side wall must not be less than 0·400.
With a 0·400 dimension, as shown in most of the wc diagrams in this book, space is tight but manageable. In wc compartments 1·400 wide, the dimension may be between 0·400 and 0·450 (diagrams 54.8, 54.9). In wc compartments 1·500 wide (diagram 54.7), and in bathrooms where space is available, a dimension of 0·500 is recommended.

5413 **Wc compartments for wheelchair users: General planning considerations**

54130 For general purposes where provision is made for chairbound people, for example in public buildings (643), it is not essential that wc compartments are planned with sufficient space for the wheelchair to be turned through 180°.
While for people with small chairs there will normally be room to turn, it may be assumed that people with large chairs will either drive in and reverse out, or vice versa. Where there is not space inside the wc compartment for turning, it is essential that the adjoining area outside allows for wheelchair manoeuvre.

Hand rinse basins

54131 In wc compartments for wheelchair users in public lavatories or special buildings for disabled people, and in housing where a wc compartment is separate from the bathroom, a hand rinse basin should be installed. For notes on location etc see 5446.

Amenities

54132 Because chairbound disabled people, particularly traumatic paraplegics, spend a great deal of time sitting on the wc, the provision of amenities which help to pass the time may be considered. A bookcase is suggested.
For functional reasons a paraplegic person may not be able to hold a book while using the wc. A sophisticated bespoke provision might be a bookrest on a hinged arm fixed to the wall to one side of the wc seat.

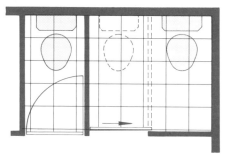

54.6 Adaptation of existing wc compartments (1:50)

Adaptation of existing wc compartments

54133 In existing public cloakrooms it may be possible to provide for chairbound people by combining two wc compartments, for example as shown in diagram 54.6.
Structural or planning constraints may mean that a sliding door needs to be substituted for an existing side-hung door.

54134 For notes on the planning of wcs in wheelchair housing see 8365, and in public buildings see 618.

5414 **Wc compartments for wheelchair users: Standard plan arrangements**

54140 The standard wc compartment size 2·000 × 1·500 recommended for public buildings (diagrams 54.7, 64.2) allows for transfer either (1) laterally across one side of the wheelchair, (2) frontally, or (3) obliquely.
This plan arrangement permits an assistant to stand in front or to one side of the disabled person being helped to or from his wheelchair. It also allows sufficient space for a man in a wheelchair to manoeuvre and position himself so that the fixture is used as a urinal.

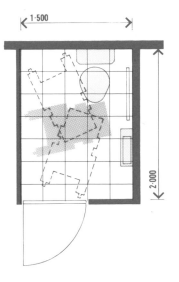

54.7 Standard wc compartment for wheelchair users (1:50)

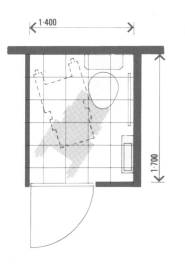

54.8 Small wc compartment for wheelchair users, internal cistern (1:50)

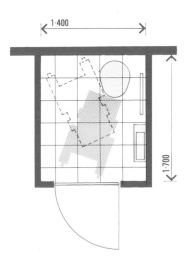

54.9 Small wc compartment for wheelchair users, external cistern (1:50)

54141 The small wc compartment size 1·700 × 1·400 (diagrams 54.8, 64.3) gives less space for manoeuvre and allows only for lateral or oblique transfer. The restricted space of this compartment does not comfortably cater for an attendant assisting with transfer.

Cistern outside

54142 A wc compartment size 1·700 × 1·400 caters better for frontal wheelchair transfer where the cistern is outside, as shown in diagram 54.9.
This plan has the slight disadvantage that there is less space for direct lateral transfer. The compensating gain in general manoeuvring space means that on balance it is preferred to the plan shown in diagram 54.8. It also caters better for an attendant assisting with transfer.

Door planning

54143 The preferred door positions are as shown in diagrams 54.7 and 54.8.
Where planning conditions make it necessary, the door may be located on the side wall (opposite the basin towards the corner); the disadvantage is that awkward manoeuvring is needed to place the chair for frontal transfer. Where the plan is as in diagram 54.8 (which does not permit frontal transfer) a side door is admissible, in effect giving a handed version of diagram 54.10.

54144 The preferred door hanging is as shown in diagrams 54.7 and 54.8.
If required the door may be hinged away from the corner (as in diagram 54.10). The disadvantage is that the wheelchair user has to reach across to the corner to open the door from inside. It is helpful if the door reveal is approx 0·200 wide, as shown in diagram 54.9.

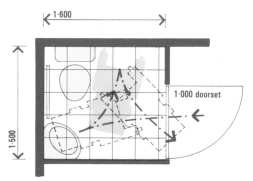

54.10 Small wc compartment for wheelchair users: Alternative plan (1:50)

Wc parallel with door

54145 As an alternative to the recommended layout shown in diagram 54.8, a compartment with the wc planned parallel with the face of the door is admissible (diagram 54.10). To allow for a 3 point turn the width of the compartment must be not less than 1·500 and depth not less than 1·600.
This arrangement does not give adequate space for an attendant, nor does it allow for frontal transfer;

it should be used only where the preferred layout is not practicable or where there are alternative facilities. The door should slide or open out. Where it opens out a 1·000 doorset is recommended to facilitate wheelchair manoeuvre; where it slides the clear opening should be not less than 0·850 wide.

54146 With the plan arrangement shown in diagram 54.10 it is advantageous if the cistern is outside the compartment.

5415 Planning of wc compartments for wheelchair users: Flexibility

54150 In respect of wheelchair housing units there is no single planning arrangement for the wc, whether placed in a bathroom or in a separate compartment, which can be guaranteed to suit all users.
This suggests that at design stage allowance should be made for fixing the wc in alternative positions to suit differing requirements. But for practical and economic reasons complete flexibility may not be feasible. For reasons discussed below, the recommendation is therefore that the wc position should be fixed, within a plan layout which will meet most requirements.

54151 There are three situations where a wc designed to suit disabled people generally may be unsatisfactory for a particular person. These are:
1. Where lateral transfer is required to the right and the wc is placed to the left, or vice versa.
2. Where additional clear space is required behind the wc to permit comfortable lateral transfer.
3. Where the position of the wc is inconvenient for a person with stiff hips.

Lateral transfer one side only
54152 Regarding situation 1, the planning of the bathroom or separate wc compartment in a wheelchair housing unit does not as a rule allow for the simple inversion of the plan to afford lateral access to the wc from the side other than that on which the design is based. The position of the door is invariably fixed by other planning constraints, precluding the general rearrangement of fixtures. Even where the resiting of fixtures is in theory practicable, plumbing and other servicing considerations are likely to mean that the cost is prohibitive.

54153 The lateral transfer condition is of most concern to hemiplegic people (54125), but the possibility that the user will have to transfer from the 'wrong' side will not as a rule be critical.
Most hemiplegic people who can cope independently are able to stand to transfer; if, for example, a person with a left hemiplegia has to use a wc compartment planned with fixed rail to the left, as in diagram 54.7, he can probably manage if there is a hinged horizontal support rail (of the kind shown in diagram 54.30) on the exposed side of the

wc. For the hemiplegic person who needs personal assistance to transfer to or from the wc it is not usually essential that a fixed support rail is available on his good side.

54154 No reliable estimates are available of the proportion of wheelchair users who have to be able to transfer laterally to one side rather than the other; the probability is that it is a fraction of 1 per cent of the total wheelchair population.

Fokus wc
54155 One practical way of achieving flexibility for either a left or right side transfer to the wc is shown in diagram 54.11.
Designed for Fokus housing schemes in Sweden, the principle is that the shower and basin units are interchangeable. For a person who needs to transfer to the left, the shower is placed as shown in the diagram, leaving the floor space on that side clear.

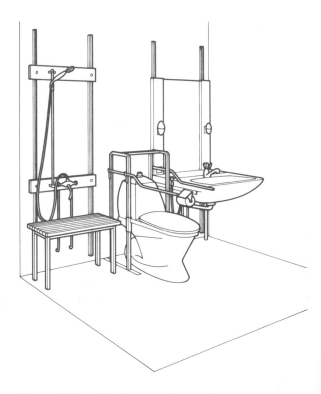

54.11 Fokus (Sweden) sanitary unit

Clear space behind wc
54156 Regarding situation 2, the critical factor is that the wheelchair can be positioned sufficiently far back for the rear propelling wheel not to be in the way of direct transfer from wheelchair seat to wc seat; for illustration see diagram 54.5c. There may be a requirement for more space behind and to one side of the wc than is provided by a standard fixture, particularly in the case of a corbel closet or wc with external cistern.

No reliable data are available indicating how many wheelchair users need to have extra space behind the wc for lateral transfer; they may be of the order of 1 or 2 per cent of the wheelchair population.

54157 There are two reasons why as a general rule it may not be advisable for the wc to project to give added space behind:
1. Some disabled people may need to have rails fixed to the back wall to pull or push up; for such people the wc needs to be close to the wall.
2. In a typical wc compartment or domestic bathroom the extended projection of the wc fixture will reduce the amount of space available for wheelchair manoeuvre.

54158 Where for a specific disabled person added space is required, it may be obtained by fixing a corbel closet to a box platform, as shown in diagram 54.18, or (where the cistern is external) positioning the wc as shown in diagram 54.19.

People with stiff hips
54159 Regarding situation 3, it can happen that for specific disabled people a comfortable posture is dependent on the position of the wc in relation to the wall behind.
A typical low-level suited may be unmanageable for a person with stiff hips, who needs a semi-reclining seat (as in diagram 54.26) and the cistern set back. The preferred solution may be to project the wc away from the wall. To allow for repositioning the wc a P trap is preferred to an S trap.

5416 Wc compartments not planned for assisted transfer

54160 Wc compartments not allowing space for an attendant to help are not recommended where general provison is made for wheelchair users. There are however some independent chairbound people who are able to use a wc compartment planned for ambulant disabled people; in the planning of selected cloakroom facilities in public buildings this possibility may be taken into account.

Frontal transfer
54161 A wc compartment planned for ambulant disabled people, as shown in diagrams 54.12 and 63.2, may be manageable by wheelchair users who are able to transfer frontally (diagram 54.5a) or who transfer through the back of the chair (diagram 54.5d). There is not sufficient space in the compartment for the door to be closed behind the wheelchair. Some wheelchair users may be able to leave the chair outside; for others who do not have an attendant to help, the only course will be to use the wc with the door left open.

54162 To allow space for a wheelchair in a narrow compartment the dimension from the edge of the bowl to the face of the door should be not less than 1·050 (diagram 54.13).
The minimum internal depth of the compartment should be 1·800, or 1·650 where the cistern is external.

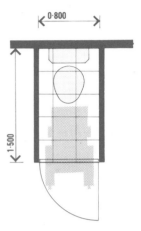

54.12 Wheelchair use of wc compartment for ambulant disabled people (1:50)

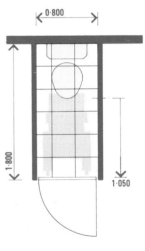

54.13 Wheelchair access to narrow wc compartment (1:50)

54163 Some chairbound people can use conventional wcs in narrow compartments by transferring from a direct frontal position and sitting astride the wc facing the rear wall.
The configuration of wc pans is not designed for this atypical posture, and it would be impossible to design a wc for both front and rear facing users without compromising its function.

Support rails
54164 It is helpful in narrow wc compartments if support rails on side walls are extended towards the door. This allows people with wheelchairs who are able to stand with the aid of fixed supports to leave the wheelchair outside the door. It is also generally advantageous for ambulant disabled people.

Oblique transfer

54165 A slightly wider compartment (minimum 1·000) with the door opening out or sliding provides sufficient space for a wheelchair user able to transfer frontally or obliquely.

In-opening doors

54166 Wc compartments with in-opening doors are not recommended, but slightly increased dimensions may allow for wheelchair use.

54167 A compartment minimum 1·800 deep (1·650 with external cistern) and 1·300 wide (diagram 54.14) allows for a person with a standard wheelchair able to transfer obliquely to drive in and close the door behind.
Where external approach is direct a 0·800 doorset is suggested to maximize the amount of manoeuvring space internally.

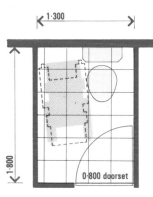

54.14 Wc compartment with in-opening door allowing wheelchair access (1:50)

54168 A wc compartment minimum 1·800 deep × 1·300 wide allows space for an independent wheelchair user with a small chair to transfer laterally (diagram 54.14).

54169 None of the solutions illustrated in diagrams 54.12, 54.13 or 54.14 should be used if an alternative allowing for assisted transfer is practicable.

5417 Flexibility of wc design

54170 As noted above (54150), allowance should be made where practicable for positioning the wc to suit individual requirements.

54171 Allowance ought also to be made for variation of seat height, within the range 0·350–0·500 above floor level.

54172 The required flexibility may be achieved by one of three methods:
1. Flexibility of component design.
2. Postponing the installation of fixtures until individual requirements are ascertained.
3. Installing fixtures in positions which are likely to suit most users, removing and refixing them if they are subsequently found to be not satisfactory.

54173 The issues involved are similar to those for kitchen units (5110–5114). Method 1 will invariably be precluded on economic grounds, though diagram 54.11 shows how it can be done. Method 2 is preferred but for adminstrative reasons will not as a rule be practicable. Method 3 may be the only possibility. In most situations removal and refixing will not be necessary; probably at least 90 per cent of wheelchair users can manage satisfactorily in a wc compartment where the wc is set close to the wall, with the seat at approx. 0·475, and with space for frontal, oblique or lateral transfer.

5418 Wc compartments: Freestanding wcs

54180 In residential homes, social centres and other special buildings for disabled people at least one wc compartment should be planned with the wc in a freestanding position.
This permits attendants to work from in front of, to either side of, or behind the fixture while assisting with transfer, cleansing or the adjustment of clothing. It also gives sufficient space for a portable hoist to be used.

Planning considerations

54181 The compartment should be minimum 2·100 wide × 2·100 deep (diagram 54.15).

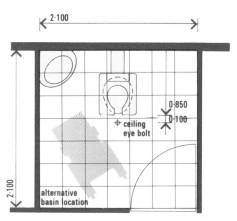

54.15 Wc compartment with freestanding wc (1:50)

54182 The position of the door is not critical; the generous internal space means that the door may conveniently open in.

54183 To allow an attendant to help from behind the wc it is helpful if the wc projects into the room as shown in diagram 54.15.
In this case there will be no cistern for support, and a backrest of the type shown in diagram 54.19 should be incorporated.

54184 In these compartments there should be no obstructions which may impede attendants helping a handicapped person on or off the wc.
It is not necessary that any support rails are fixed. A ceiling eyebolt may be provided for the suspension of a stirrup grip, see 2603, 54282.

Wash basin

54185 A wash basin or small sluice should be provided, but it is not necessary that it can be reached by a person seated on the wc. It should be placed in a corner where it is not in the way of a person being transferred on to the wc.

54186 The basin should be located in a corner of the room. Where it is placed as shown in diagram 54.15 it may impede lateral transfer from wheelchair to wc but there is the advantage that it is convenient for an attendant needing to wash while helping.

Residential homes

54187 In residential homes etc freestanding wcs should be planned to cater for people of both sexes.

542 Wc appliances

5420 Wc specifications: General considerations

54200 In housing and public buildings generally, a wc with low level cistern and relatively high seat will be suitable for most disabled people.

54201 In public buildings a corbel wc may be preferred, where planning permits and the structure is suitable.
In typical low cost low-rise housing schemes structural considerations usually make it easier to install a close-coupled wc suite than a corbel wc.

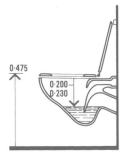

54.16 Corbel wc for wheelchair users (1:25)

Criteria for cleansing

54202 Desirably the vertical distance between water level and bowl rim should not be less than 0·200, preferred minimum 0·230 (diagram 54.16).
Many disabled people need to cleanse themselves without rising from the wc seat. A further consideration is that paraplegics and others who are incontinent may use manual techniques to empty the bowels (see 9152). It is therefore important that the water level is not close to the rim of the bowl. A dimension greater than 0·260 is not recommended because of the possibility of splashing.

54203 The configuration of conventional wc fixtures is not suited to the needs of disabled people in respect of cleansing.
There is insufficient space either at the front or at the back of the fixture for free access. What is needed, particularly in the case of people who have to be cleansed by an assistant, is a clear space between the top of the bowl and the underside of the seat. The practice of using seat extensions may help solve this problem, but raises others. A cut-away seat is helpful, but ideally the wc bowl should have a much larger opening at the rear. Kira [5] suggests an experimental wc which satisfies these criteria and which with modifications would be generally suitable for disabled people.

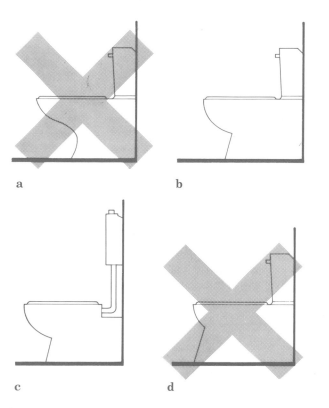

a   b

c   d

54.17 Configuration of wc bowl and cistern

[5] Bib 93951, p72.

Shape of wc bowls

54204 A wc bowl which recedes sharply, for example as shown in diagram 54.17a, is not recommended. A configuration of the type shown in diagram 54.17b is preferred.

In public cloakrooms, more particularly those used by men, there is a hazard that infections can be transmitted if genital organs are in contact with the fixture. The majority of currently available wc fixtures are unsatisfactory in this respect. A bowl configuration of the type shown in diagrams 54.17b and 54.17c is also preferred to facilitate manual cleansing.

Back support

54205 Where the wc is positioned away from the rear wall, to give additional space for lateral transfer from a wheelchair (see 54156), a back support should be incorporated, as shown in diagram 54.18 and detailed in diagram 54.19.

54206 A back support with its upper face not higher than 0·300 above the wc bowl is suggested, so that it can be used by a disabled person for pushing up to a standing position.

54207 It is essential that the back support is securely fixed.

The fixing apertures provided on a standard wc fixture for attaching the seat may be unsuitable for fixing the back support, owing to the liability of the fixture to fracture when weight is applied. The technical problems of arranging alternative fixing in the preferred position mean that, unless there is special cause for a projecting fixture, a standard wc suite with low level cistern will normally be the most appropriate solution.

54208 For alternative ad hoc facility see diagram 54.35.

5421 Corbel wcs

54210 For wheelchair users a corbel wc, of the type shown in diagram 54.18, may be preferred.

It permits close frontal approach and gives room below the bowl for the swing of wheelchair footrests; this makes it easier for men in wheelchairs to use the wc for urination.

Fixing

54211 Corbel wcs can be fixed to suit individual users. In housing for disabled people where a corbel wc is incorporated its fixing should if practicable be delayed until the preferred height is determined.

54212 A corbel closet can be fixed easily only where the wall behind the wc is of solid construction having a thickness of not less than 0·200.

Where the back wall does not give adequate fixing, U-shape cast iron or steel supports must be used. To ensure rigidity the base of any supports must be set into the concrete floor slab, with the screed and

floor finish over. Care is needed with installation where there are underfloor services or heating.

Box platform

54213 To allow for comfortable lateral transfer (diagram 54.5c) a corbel wc may be attached to a box platform (diagram 54.18).

The depth of the platform should be approx. 0·200. The width should be not more than 0·400 so as not to reduce usable space behind the wc for an attendant assisting a disabled person.

54.18 Corbel wc with box platform and back support

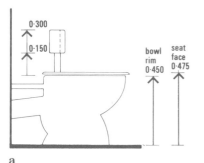

a

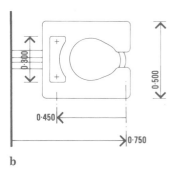

b

54.19 Back support to wc (1:25)

High level cisterns

54214 The traditional wc with high level cistern and chain-operated flush has similar advantages to the corbel wc.

It allows for flexibility of fixing position, for the placing of a horizontal support rail behind the fixture and, with the wc placed away from the wall, space behind for an attendant to assist. It is not now commonly manufactured and unless its use is strongly indicated a corbel or low level wc is preferred.

5422   Low level wc suites

54220   The contemporary low level close-coupled wc suite placed against a wall is generally suitable for disabled people.

54221   The fixture should have a cistern which, with the seat cover leaning against it, gives back support. A slim panel cistern of the type shown in diagram 54.17c may be suitable.

54222   To help wheelchair manoeuvre, a wc fixture which recedes towards its base as shown in diagram 54.17c is preferred to the type shown in diagram 54.17d.

5423   Clos o mat wc

54230   A proprietary combined wc and bidet appliance known as the Clos o mat can be helpful for severely handicapped people who are unable to cleanse themselves manually, or to do so only with difficulty.
The cleansing of the anus and the adjoining area is done without the use of hands, by means of an electrically controlled warm water douche and warm air flow. Manual control is incorporated, meaning that the appliance can be flushed in the conventional manner and used as an ordinary wc.

54231   Three versions of the Clos o mat are manufactured, the two main ones being the Clos o mat 61 (diagram 54.20) and the more recent Clos o mat Samoa (diagram 54.21). For handicapped people the easier switch control and greater fixing flexibility of the Samoa mean that it is generally preferred. Costs are noted in 90320.

54.20 Clos o mat 61   **54.21** Clos o mat Samoa

Clos o mat 61

54232   The warm water douche of the Clos o mat 61 is activated by the user depressing the foot button on the base of the pedestal. For the handicapped person who cannot use his heel to operate this switch, a toggle switch or lever switch on the wall, or a ceiling pull switch, may be wired in parallel.

The power supply is only connected when the user is seated on the wc.
Because a single switching device has to be used for the three operations of washing, flushing and drying, the washing phase cannot be controlled by a simple on-off switch. The switch has to be kept depressed, usually about 25 seconds but if required up to 40 seconds. For arthritics and others with severe weaknesses or lack of coordination, careful attention must be given to the positioning and operation of the switch. Following the washing and flushing phases, the switch needs no further activation, since drying continues for a predetermined period of up to three minutes, or until the user rises from the seat, so disconnecting power.

Clos o mat Samoa

54233   The warm water douche of the Clos o mat Samoa is activated by the user depressing one of two operating levers on the appliance with his hand, elbow or upper arm. The lever is kept depressed until the washing phase is complete.

Water and hot air

54234   The cold water supply to the appliance may be high or low pressure. No external warm water supply is needed. Because of the complex cleansing cycle it is necessary that flushing always occurs first time; for this reason the Clos o mat has a flushing valve rather than the more usual syphon. The appliance is approved by water authorities for installation in hospitals, residential homes and where required for physically handicapped people, but in some areas the relaxation of by-laws may be required.
The warm water and hot air systems are controlled by a thermostat, and an overriding safety device is incorporated. The thermostat is normally preset at between 35 and 37°C.

Soil pipe connections

54235   The Clos o mat 61 is connected to the soil pipe only by a standard S trap. The centre line of the floor socket is between 0·250 and 0·300 from the rear wall, compared with approximately 0·200 for an ordinary wc fixture.
For the Clos o mat Samoa, soil pipe connectors are available in seven variations of standard S and P traps (diagram 54.22b). The normal installation is an S trap centred at 0·150 from the rear wall or a P trap centred at 0·220 above floor level.

54236   When planning wc layouts or installing ordinary wcs which may be replaced by Clos o mats to meet specific individual needs, constraints of soil pipe connections must be considered.
Plumbing should be planned on the basis of simple connections through the floor or rear wall. With the Samoa the position of the water heater means that a side connection with the soil pipe cannot be made to the right; it can if necessary be made to the left, though it is not recommended. With the Clos o mat 61 there is less flexibility.

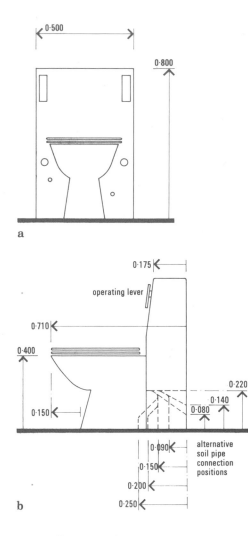

54.22 Clos o mat Samoa (1:20)

Suitability for users

54237 A Clos o mat can be of value to people affected by haemorrhoids, cystitis or other urinary infections, and people with muscular dystrophy, double amputees, severe arthritics and others who would otherwise need to be cleaned and wiped by another person.

The advantage of the appliance in a residential home or hospital is that the care staff workload may be reduced, by avoiding the need for two people to assist (one to do the lifting, the other to do the wiping). A disadvantage is that the fixed position of the douche arm means that the Clos o mat cannot be used with normal sani-chairs, though special wheeled sanitary chairs have been designed for the purpose.

54238 A Clos o mat installed in a dwelling for a specific disabled person may be more satisfactory in use than one installed in an institution for general purposes.

Because of the sophisticated mechanism of the appliance, alterations and adaptations, for example to the switching, can most effectively be made to suit a specific person; it is less easy to incorporate adaptations suiting different types of user

simultaneously. Similarly, raising the level of the seat, which has to be done by fixing the appliance on a base, may be necessary for a specific disabled person but unsuitable for others. A possible disadvantage in institutions is that the length of time taken for the full cleansing cycle, up to five minutes, may cause inconvenience to other users who are waiting.

54239 The effective use of a Clos o mat will depend a great deal on the motivations of individual users, and, where relevant, the readiness of care staff to cooperate.

The appliance can be a valuable aid to severely disabled people who want to be as independent as possible, and for whom independence in personal cleansing is psychologically important. In institutions where residents or patients may be less concerned about independence, and where some may insist on being aided by care staff, it may be less successful.

5424 Specification of wc seat

54240 For disabled people a wood seat may be preferred to a plastic seat.

The advantages of a wood seat are that it is warmer than a plastic seat and does not have sharp edges; these considerations are relevant to people with sensory impairments. A potential disadvantage of a plastic seat is that, being brittle, it is liable to be broken or cracked by a disabled person who lands on it very heavily.

Bench seat

54241 To aid pushing up to a standing position and facilitate transfer from a wheelchair, a bench seat 0·450–0·500 wide is suggested (diagram 54.23). The seat must be stoutly hinged: a piano hinge may be unsuitable for reasons of cleaning difficulties. Costs are noted in 90321.

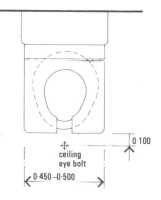

54.23 Bench seat to wc

54242 The front of the seat should have a cut-out to facilitate cleansing by hand and the manipulation of appliances.

Piloseat

54243 A proprietary foam-filled plastic-covered wc seat known as the Piloseat may be preferred by paraplegics and others prone to skin injury. Cost notes: 90321.

Blocking for seat raising

54244 The recommendations regarding dimensions between seat and water level (54202) and between bowl and underside seat (54203) indicate that it may be preferable to achieve a higher seat by raising the seat on blocks above the wc bowl rather than by raising the level of the wc bowl.

54245 Where a seat height of approximately 0·475 is required, a standard pedestal unit may be used, without the need for building up the base or raising the seat on blocks.

54246 Alternatively, a standard unit with a bowl rim at approximately 0·400 may be used, with blocks to raise the seat to 0·475 as shown in diagram 54.24. This has the advantage that the fixture may more easily be used by chairbound men as a urinal. For wheelchair housing it is a practicable alternative to a fixture with a bowl rim at 0·450.

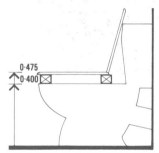

54.24 Raised wc seat (1:25)

54.25 Polypropylene raised toilet seat (underside up)

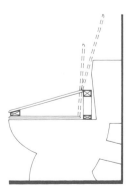

54.26 Wc seat for people with stiff hips (1:25)

Seat extensions

54247 For disabled people who cannot conveniently use a wc at its fixed height, a detachable ring seat may be fitted to raise the seat level.

54248 A polypropylene raised toilet seat may be fitted to standard wc bowls (diagram 54.25). It can be lifted off when not in use. Cost notes: 90322. Detachable seat extensions are not a satisfactory solution to the problem. They are commonly insecure, or else look insecure and are therefore psychologically unsuitable.

Inclined seat

54249 For people with stiff hips an inclined seat may be fixed on blocking pieces, as shown in diagram 54.26. The inclined seat should be fitted as a supplement to the normal horizontal seat, and not as a substitute for it.

5425   Height of wc seat: General provision

Wheelchair users

54250 In wc compartments in public buildings and elsewhere where provision is made for disabled people in general, including wheelchair users, the seat should be between 0·460 and 0·500 above floor level, with a preferred height of 0·475, ie with a bowl rim at approx 0·450.
To facilitate shifting from wheelchair to wc and vice versa the seat levels should correspond, or the wc seat should be slightly lower than the wheelchair seat. The seat height of wheelchairs in common use ranges from 0·470 to 0·490 (table 23.2).

Ambulant disabled people

54251 Where provision is made for ambulant disabled people and not for wheelchair users, the wc seat should be between 0·420 and 0·450, with a preferred height of 0·445 (diagram 63.2), ie with a bowl rim at approx 0·420.

Posture

54252 The wc seat heights recommended for disabled people are higher than those of standard wc fixtures, and are higher than is physiologically desirable for normal able-bodied people.

54253 To encourage the defecation process Kira suggests that a semi-squat posture at approx 0·250 above floor level is preferred[6]. He points out that contemporary wcs do not permit the adoption of this posture and suggests that they have contributed to the prevalence of constipation in civilised societies.
Discussing the requirements of elderly people Kira says: 'The solution has been to provide seat extenders of various sorts to raise the height, or to provide higher water closets. This has obviously

[6] Bib 93951, p61.

helped the problem of raising and lowering the body, but it has just as obviously aggravated the functional and physiological problems of defecation. Admittedly the problems of the aged will not be resolved by expecting them to use a squat plate, but it is not unreasonable to suppose that the use of a substantially lower water closet over a period of years will provide us with some of the exercise we need and keep the problems from assuming such major proportions in our later years. In short, the more apathetic we are about making the necessary effort, the more difficult it will become'.[7]

Disabled users: Evidence on seat heights

54254 In an unpublished survey made for the Department of the Environment, 25 people, representing 10 per cent of disabled users in the sample, said that their wc seat was too low[8]. In all of these cases the seat was at 0·460 or below. It may be that had wc seats been generally higher some would have said that seats were too high. But so far as it goes this evidence supports the recommendation that for disabled people generally a seat height of 0·475 is appropriate.

54255 The recommendation for a relatively high wc seat as necessary for wheelchair users, and to make it easier for ambulant disabled people to regain a standing position, is specifically disability determined. There is here a conflict of criteria, in that for able-bodied people a lower seat is preferred.

54256 The use of a portable footstool may permit an efficient posture to be adopted by a person using a high wc seat.

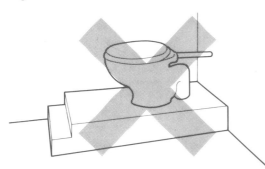

54.27 Built-up platform for wc

Built-up platform

54257 The use of a built-up platform as shown in diagram 54.27 is not recommended.
A platform can obstruct wheelchair approach and is likely to be a trip hazard to ambulant disabled people.

54258 Where a standard wc fixture needs to be raised the preferred solution is a purpose-designed moulded plinth. Cost notes: 90323.

Controlling dimensions

54259 The recommendations above assume the use of a standard wc where the seat is approx 0·025 above the level of the bowl rim. Where seat-raising devices are incorporated appropriate adjustments should be made to the recommended level of the bowl rim.

5426 Wc heights: Special purposes

Use of wc as urinal

54260 It is not esential when considering wc specifications to take account of the possible use of the wc as a urinal by male wheelchair users.

54261 For a typical male adult seated in a wheelchair the level of urine emission is approx 0·440–0·460; a contemporary wc bowl at approx 0·380 is therefore conveniently usable as a urinal and a bowl at 0·420 is usually manageable. A bowl at 0·450 is not satisfactory.
Because of the awkwardness of wc bowls and the difficulty of close approach in a wheelchair, the customary practice is to use a portable urine bottle which is discharged into the wc.

Sanitary chairs

54262 In hospitals and institutions for disabled people allowance should be made for the use of sanitary chairs.
A sanitary chair is a variant of a standard wheelchair, incorporating a ring seat designed to pass over the wc. The vertical clearance is usually approx 0·470 above floor level. Diagram 54.28 illustrates a typical example.

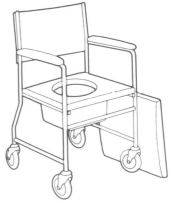

54.28 Sanitary chair

[7] Bib 93951, p62.
[8] Bib 93122.

5427 Wcs: Support rails

54270 General design notes on support rails are in 333. For recommendations for rails to wcs in public buildings see diagrams 63.2, 64.2 and 64.3. For notes on the fixing of support rails to partition walls see 370. Costs of support rails are noted in 90324.

54271 In housing for disabled people the fixing of support rails should be delayed until requirements are known, or a slightly inclined rail should be fixed, as shown in diagram 54.29a.

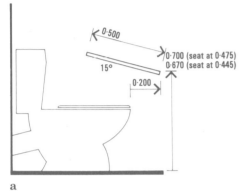

a

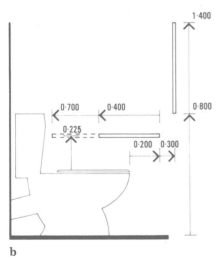

b

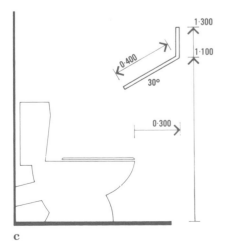

c

54.29 Support rails to side wall by wc (1:25)

54272 It is desirable that there are fixed supports to both sides of the wc so that both upper limbs can be used for raising the body.
The wc seat is often used by disabled people for pushing up, but it is helpful if fixed support is at a higher level. A back support as shown in diagram 54.19 can aid pushing across to or from a wheelchair, and rising to a standing position.

Horizontal rails

54273 A horizontal rail may be fixed to the side wall by the wc, at a height approx 0·225 above seat level, as shown in diagram 54.29b.
The minimum length of this rail should be 0·400; it is preferred that it is extended towards the rear wall to aid people who pull themselves across from the wheelchair, as shown in diagram 54.5c. Where there is no low level cistern or back support a similar horizontal rail may be fixed to the rear wall.

Hinged support rails

54274 For general use by disabled people, one side of the wc needs to be clear to permit wheelchair transfer. It is advantageous to have a hinged horizontal support rail on this side.
A rail folding up vertically against the wall when not required is suggested, as shown in diagram 54.30. Alternatively a rail swinging back against the wall may be used, as shown in diagram 54.31. Cost notes: 90325.

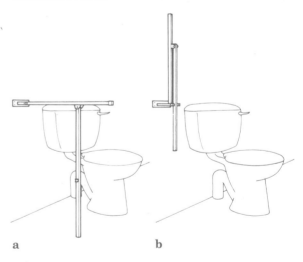

a   b

54.30 Hinged support rail folding vertically against wall

54.31 Hinged support rail swinging back against wall

Inclined side rails

54275 Where a pushing rail is fixed to the side wall it may be slightly inclined to support the lower arm, as shown in diagram 54.29a.

The preferred position for this side rail is slightly higher than for a horizontal rail, since the weight of the person pushing is carried by the arm and not the hand. The advantage of an inclination at approx 15° as shown is that it more easily allows weight to be transferred to the feet when rising. It also has the advantage that weight can be applied at different positions suited to the height of the person pushing up.

54276 The length of an inclined rail ought not to be less than 0·500, with the lower end not less than 0·200 in front of the line of the wc.

In narrow wc compartments rails should be fixed to both side walls.

Vertical rails

54277 For pulling up to a standing position a vertical rail as shown in diagram 54.29b is suggested.

The minimum length of the rail should be 0·400, extending from 1·000 to 1·400 above floor level.

54278 An alternative is a cranked rail of the type shown in diagram 54.29c, with the inclined section used for carrying the weight of the arm while the hand pulls on the vertical section.

54279 Vertical support rails are not as important as horizontal rails; in wc compartments for general use by disabled people the essential requirement is the fixing of horizontal or inclined rails for pushing against.

5428 **Wcs: Other lifting aids**

Portable aids

54280 A portable aid, for example as shown in diagram 54.32, may serve as a substitute for fixed horizontal rails.

Aids of this kind may be helpful for people who are temporarily disabled but are not recommended for permanent use. Because the legs may obstruct wheelchair approach they are not generally suitable for use by chairbound people.

Side support aid

54281 A wc aid designed to give side support and eliminate the danger of falling forward off the seat is shown in diagram 54.33.

The device is fixed to the standard wc seat mounting apertures. The front support arms fold out sideways for the user to get on and off the wc. The side supports give assistance for raising and lowering. Cost notes: 90326.

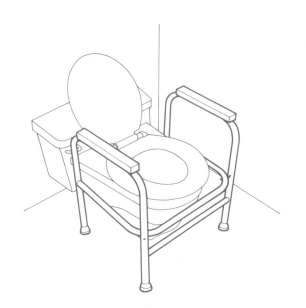

54.32 Portable lifting aid for wc

54.33 Side support aid for wc

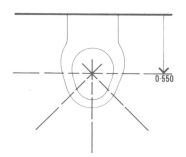

54.34 Positioning of ceiling track for hoist serving wc

Eye bolt

54282 For reasons discussed in 260, ceiling eye bolts to carry suspended grips are not commonly used by disabled people, and it is not recommended that they are generally provided in wheelchair housing.

54283 Where for a specific disabled person an eye bolt is required it should be fixed to the ceiling in a position above a point approx 0·100 in front of the wc seat (diagram 54.23). See also diagram 26.1.

Ceiling track for hoist

54284 Where a ceiling track is installed for carrying a patient hoist it should pass directly over the wc seat (diagram 54.34). For notes on ceiling tracks see 261.

5429 Wcs: Fixtures and equipment

Flushing devices

54290 Flushing devices to wcs must be easily accessible and convenient to manipulate.
For most disabled people the specification of the flushing device is not a critical matter: it is not significantly more or less difficult to press a lever than to depress a knob, pull a knob, or pull a chain.

54291 Foot pedal operating devices are not usable by chairbound people and are unsuitable for others who are disabled. They ought not to be specified.

54292 The flushing device should be accessible to a person either standing by the wc or seated on it.
For wheelchair users the preferred maximum height is 1·200 above floor level.

Flushing devices to low level cisterns

54293 For wheelchair users and people whose reach is limited, the lever handle on the face of a low level cistern should be on the side which affords lateral wheelchair approach; for example with layouts as shown in diagrams 54.7 and 54.8 the lever should be on the left side of the cistern.
The invariable practice is that the flushing handle to low level cisterns is on the right. This standardization is an aid to blind people.

54294 In wheelchair wc compartments where the handle needs to be on the left a cistern should be specified which is designed so that the tank and flushing mechanism can be transposed.
Where the cistern is external and the wc compartment is planned as in diagram 54.9 the flushing handle should be on the left side.

High level cisterns

54295 Where a high level cistern is installed the chain should have a large pull ball, at approx 0·800 above the level of the wc seat. A sleeve to contain the lower end of the chain may be advantageous.

Back support

54296 For a disabled person who needs comfortable back support when seated on the wc an ad hoc removable device fitting over the top of the cistern is suggested, as shown in diagram 54.35.
In this case the seat cover will need to be removed.

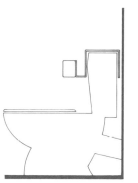

54.35 Back support fitting over wc cistern

Toilet tissue

54297 The toilet tissue holder must be easily reachable by a person seated on the wc.
A convenient location is below the side rail as shown in diagram 64.2a.

54298 A roll holder is suggested.
Soft tissue (normally manufactured in rolls) is generally preferred by disabled people. A roll holder is available with a locking mechanism which allows one sheet only to be torn off at a time; this may be easier for single-handed people than a conventional roll. Cost notes: 90327.

Heated wc seat

54299 For disabled people sensitive to cold surfaces a heated wc seat may be specified. Cost notes: 90328.

543 Cloakroom fixtures and fittings

5430 Urinals

54300 The conventional wc fixture is basically unsuited to standing male urination because of the soiling of the fixture and adjacent areas which invariably occurs.
This is particularly relevant in the case of blind people, ambulant disabled people with faulty coordination and elderly men generally.

Wheelchair users

54301 As discussed in 54261, a common practice among chairbound people is to use a portable urine bottle; where this is done the general preference is to use it inside a wc compartment.

Bowl urinals

54302 In public lavatories and in cloakrooms in public buildings, wall-fixed bowl urinals should give a choice of levels, for example 0·380 and 0·500 above floor level.

A bowl at 0·500 (diagram 54.36) is suitable for adults of average height, and is preferred to the customary fixing height of 0·600. Apart from its possible suitability for wheelchair users a bowl at 0·380 is satisfactory for small boys.

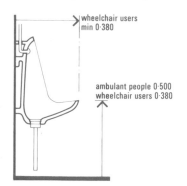

54.36 Bowl urinal (1:25)

54303 A bowl urinal may be suitable for chairbound people where the rim is low and the fixture projects sufficiently far from the wall to allow for access below by wheelchair footrests.

The preferred height of the rim above floor is 0·380. The projection should be not less than 0·380 (diagram 54.36). For cost notes on bowl urinal for wheelchair users see 90370.

Stall urinals

54304 Where stall urinals are provided a high step or threshold must be avoided. Steps where necessary ought not to be higher than 0·180, and not less than 0·400 wide (diagram 54.37).

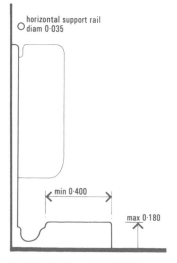

54.37 Stall urinal (1:25)

Support rails

54305 For ambulant disabled people a horizontal support rail may be fixed above the urinal fixture (diagram 54.37).

54306 For wheelchair users, short vertical rails may be fixed beside wall urinals.

These are useful to permit the chairbound person to pull himself up close to the urinal; they are recommended in institutions, social centres and similar buildings for disabled people.

5431 Drinking fountains

54310 In public buildings where drinking fountains are installed they should be usable by disabled people.

54311 Where no provision is made for chairbound people the lip of the drinking fountain should be approx 1·100 above floor level.

54312 For chairbound people, the lip should be not higher than 0·900 above floor level (diagram 54.38). The suggested level to cater for both chairbound and ambulant people is 0·900.

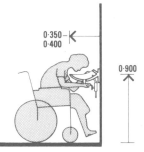

54.38 Drinking fountain for chairbound people (1:50)

54313 For chairbound people, drinking fountains should be wall-mounted, and lateral approach must be unobstructed. To aid access, a relatively deep (front to back) fixture is advised.

The normal practice will be that the chairbound person approaches the fixture laterally rather than frontally as shown in diagram 54.38; design requirements are similar.

Cup dispensers

54314 For wheelchair users, paper cup dispensers ought not to be higher than 1·200 above floor level.

5432 Incinerators

54320 Incinerators in women's cloakrooms should be accessible to disabled people and should be easy to operate; the need to use both hands simultaneously should be avoided.

54321 For wheelchair users, incinerator controls ought not to be higher than 1·200 above floor level.

5433 Mirrors

54330 For ambulant people the head of a wall-fixed mirror ought not to be lower than 1·800 above floor level. The base ought not to be higher than 1·300.
In diagram 54.39 the standing figure represents a tall man at about the 95th percentile (see diagram 20.2), with eye level at 1·740.

54331 For wheelchair users the base of the mirror should be not higher than 0·900 above floor level, and preferably at approx 0·750. The head of the mirror should be at a convenient height for ambulant people.
The wheelchair figure in diagram 54.39 represents a small woman at about the 5th percentile (see diagram 20.10), with eye level at 1·060.

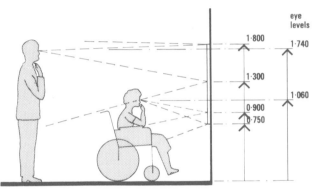

54.39 Mirrors (1:50)

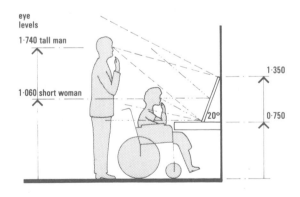

54.40 Inclined mirror to dressing table (1:50)

54332 Where a mirror is fixed over a dressing table it may with advantage be splayed, as shown in diagram 54.40.
An alternative is a pivoted mirror as shown in diagram 54.42.

5434 Towel dispensers

54340 Towel dispensers should be comfortably reachable by disabled people.

54341 For ambulant disabled people the preferred fixing height is approximately 1·400 above floor level.

54342 For wheelchair users the preferred fixing height is approximately 0·800. Where a dispenser is to be used by both chairbound and ambulant people, a height of 1·100 is suggested.

54343 In public cloakrooms where more than one dispenser is installed alternative fixing heights are suggested, for example 1·000 and 1·400.

54344 For wc compartments in public buildings a suggested location is shown in diagram 64.2a.

544 Wash basins

5440 Wash basins: General considerations

54400 Basins which are wider (from front to back) than is conventional are suggested; the length (from side to side) is not so crucial.
Wider basins are generally convenient for all users, to accommodate hand, face and hair washing.

Water source
54401 A mixer fitting having a single lever controlling both water delivery and temperature is recommended, see 4151.

54402 The water source should preferably be positioned not less than 0·100 clear of any rear obstruction, and approximately 0·100 above the basin rim to allow room for hand rinsing (diagram 54.41a). Conventional basins commonly give a clearance of only approximately 0·030 between the water source and rear wall of the basin, and the water source is at about the same level as the rim.

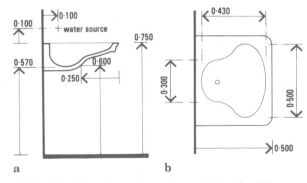

54.41 Wash basin configuration advised by Kira, modified to suit chairbound users (1:25)

54403 Where the water source is at high level the depth of the basin should be increased to contain splash. For this reason, and to provide adequate space for hand washing, an invert of up to 0·200 is indicated at the back of the basin. The front half, which needs only to catch drips from arms, can be relatively shallow. The water supply should preferably be aerated to minimize splash.

The basin dimensions shown in diagram 54.41 are as suggested by Kira in his report on bathrooms [9].

Shelf space

54404 For disabled people it is important that there is shelf space integral with the basin.

Shelves ought not to be fixed over the basin.

54405 Basins set in a desk top are recommended, as shown in diagram 54.42. The fascia should be recessed to permit close approach.

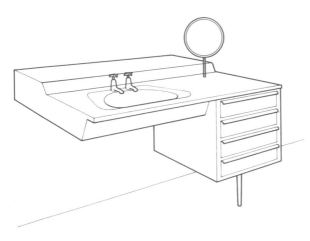

54.42 Wash basin in desk top

54406 Moulded or contoured basins which do not incorporate any convenient integral shelf space should be avoided.

For this reason a basin such as that shown in diagram 54.45 is not recommended.

54407 The soap tray ought not to be obscured by a tap fitting.

Fixing

54408 Basins must be securely fixed.

Many disabled people use the basin as a means of support; brackets supporting the basin ought preferably to be built into the wall and not attached by plugs.

5441   Wash basins: Ambulant disabled people

54410 For ambulant disabled people the suggested height for the basin rim is 0·900 above floor level (diagram 54.43).

Kira reports that for ambulant people optimum basin rim heights are 0·910–0·960 for hand washing,

0·860–0·910 for face washing and 0·910 for hair washing; the preferred level for the three activities is therefore approximately 0·910 [10].

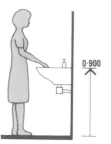

54.43 Wash basin for ambulant disabled people (1:50)

54411 A height of 0·910 may be preferred where considerations of dimensional coordination do not indicate 0·900.

Public buildings

54412 In public buildings basins may with advantage be fixed at varying levels, for example 0·700, 0·800 and 0·900.

Basins at lower levels are more convenient for children and wheelchair users.

Housing for disabled people

54413 In dwelling units for disabled people where there is more than one basin, the basin not for use from a wheelchair should have a rim at approximately 0·900.

Where there is one basin only it should be convenient for wheelchair use, see 5443.

5442   Wash basins for wheelchair users: Planning

54420 In wheelchair housing the wash basin for wheelchair use should be placed in a bathroom so that it can be approached directly, avoiding the need for an awkward turn immediately inside the door.

The basin positions shown in diagrams 54.57–54.64 are satisfactory.

54421 In the Loughborough study of bathroom space requirements 25 subjects used the basin from a frontal position, 8 from an oblique position, and 2 from a lateral position [11]. The two who used the basin from a lateral position had chairs with elevated legrests.

As with the bath (54521), this evidence indicates that in housing for wheelchair users basins should be planned to allow alternative means of approach.

[9] Bib 93951, p14.
[10] Bib 93951, p14.
[11] Bib 93960, p28.

54422 The basin should be planned to allow an oblique approach where a lateral approach is not practicable because of space limitations.

54423 For convenient wheelchair access to the basin the clear utilization space in front of the basin should be minimum 1·150 × 1·050, as shown in diagram 54.54.

5443 Wash basins for wheelchair users: Dimensional data

54430 Owing to the variability of wheelchair users there is no single height for a wash basin which will be generally convenient. In housing for disabled people it is preferred that the fixing of the basin is delayed until the optimum height for the disabled user is established. If this is not possible the basin should be fixed and altered subsequently if necessary.

Basin height

54431 For chairbound people convenient heights for the basin rim range from approximately 0·670 to 0·820. Where the basin has to be fixed in advance a rim height of 0·750 is suggested (diagram 54·44).

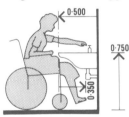

54.44 Wash basin for chairbound people (1:50)

54432 On the basis that the most convenient fixing level for a chairbound person is where the underside of the basin is just high enough to clear the thighs, it might be supposed that the optimum level for a fixed basin is the point at which its underside clears the thighs of a large person in a wheelchair. In practice this gives a basin rim which is excessively high for most chairbound people. A typical basin has an invert of about 0·180–0·200, giving a dimension from rim to underside of 0·200–0·220. For a large person with thighs at approximately 0·660 (diagram 20.7) this indicates a rim at say 0·870. But at 0·870 the rim will be intolerably high for a small person with thighs at approximately 0·520, and for most people will involve lifting the arms to an uncomfortably awkward position. In the Loughborough study of bathroom requirements 13 of the 35 wheelchair subjects considered the basin too high at the test height of 0·825 [12].

54433 Where a basin has to be fixed to cater for chairbound people, or for someone whose requirements cannot be established in advance, it is preferred that it is fixed at a relatively low level where for some users knee access may be impossible, rather than at a relatively high level where for most users it will be impossible to lift the arms comfortably over the rim.

Section

54434 To some extent the problem can be mitigated by specifying a basin with shallow shelving section, as shown in diagram 54.44. A section giving a shallow front and deep rear, of the type shown in diagram 54.41, is most satisfactory.

Unobstructed depth

54435 The unobstructed depth at toe level should not be less than 0·450, with a preferred dimension of 0·500 (diagram 54.44).
Standard basins having a depth of 0·400 or less do not permit close approach.

54436 Where a basin is set into a desk top, for example as shown in diagram 54.42, a depth of 0·600 is suggested.
This will cater for chairbound people with extended legrests. It will also give usable space behind the bowl for toiletries. The effect may be untidy, but as with kitchen work surfaces (51242) alternative storage space may not be conveniently accessible.

54437 The dimension from basin fascia to the waste trap should be not less than 0·300, preferred minimum 0·350 (diagram 54.44). To minimize interference with knees a P trap is preferred to an S trap. See 419 and diagram 41.9.

5444 Special basins

54440 A special basin with a recessed front edge to permit close approach by wheelchair users has been designed for spastic people (diagram 54.45).

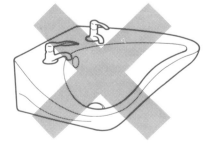

54.45 Basin for spastic people

54441 This basin is not generally recommended for wheelchair users; it has no integral shelf space and does not permit close approach. Cost notes: 90330.

[12] Bib 93960, p29.

5445 Wash basins: Residential homes

54450 In cloakrooms for general use in residential homes for elderly or handicapped people, basins should be fixed at different levels to cater for varying needs. A rim height of 0·900 is preferred for ambulant people, and 0·750 for chairbound people; where two basins only are installed these heights are suggested.

Bed-sitting rooms

54451 In individual bed-sitting rooms the wash basin ought not to be fixed until the room has been allocated and user requirements are known. There will be considerable variability among residents. The characteristics of wheelchair users may not correspond closely to those of the wheelchair population as a whole; there are likely to be proportionately many more people with unusual physical characteristics, meaning that it will be impossible to cater satisfactorily for all residents by installing basins at the same height throughout.

54452 Basins which are adjustable in height are suggested, but if it is not expected there will be many changes of use in the rooms it may be more economical to install a fixed basin, designed in such a way that it can be taken out and refixed at a different level when the room passes to another disabled person.

54453 Where in a residential home for disabled people it is necessary to install basins at a specific height, the likely preponderance of wheelchair users indicates that a level suitable for a typical wheelchair user will be more satisfactory than installing basins at a compromise height to suit both ambulant people and wheelchair users. A level of 0·750 is suggested, see 54431.

5446 Hand rinse basins

54460 In wc compartments for wheelchair users in public lavatories (6435) and in housing where a wc compartment is separate from the bathroom, a hand rinse basin should be fixed where it can conveniently be reached by a person seated on the wc.
If the basin is not within reach the disabled person must transfer back into his chair before washing his hands, and may not avoid fouling wheelchair armrests or handrims.

54461 A shallow basin having a single mixer fitting with lever control is recommended.

54462 The basin should be placed where it can be reached by a standing person as well as from the wc seat.

Position of support rail

54463 Where there is a side support rail the basin should be fixed forward of it, as shown in diagram 64.2a. It is important that the basin does not interfere with the use of the side support rail. For this reason the layout suggested in CP96 for wc compartments for chairbound people [13], in which the side rail is placed some 0·300 clear of the side wall in order for the basin to be positioned in between, is not recommended.

54464 The basin should be fixed as close to the wc as the side rail allows.
The position of the mixer fitting is important; it ought not to be further forward of the wc bowl than 0·550.

Rim heights

54465 Where a hand rinse basin is to be usable either from a standing position or by a person seated on the wc, the suggested rim height is 0·750 above floor level.

54466 In wheelchair wc compartments where hand rinse basins are installed specifically for wheelchair users the rim may be at a lower level; 0·600 is suggested.
Whether or not the basin is beside the wc fixture a person in a wheelchair will use it from a lateral position, and a low rim is therefore convenient.

Basin below side rail

54467 In a wc compartment in a private dwelling planned particularly for use by a chairbound person the basin may be fixed below the side rail, as shown in diagram 54·46.
This allows only for use by a person seated on the wc, and the basin rim may be as low as 0·350 above floor level.

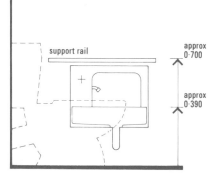

54.46 Hand rinse basin to side wall by wc (1:25)

Width of hand rinse basins

54468 In diagrams 54.7, 54.8 and 54.9 a narrow (front to back) hand basin is shown, the purpose being to ensure that the basin projection does not obstruct wheelchair approach to the wc.
Where the wc compartment is not planned for direct frontal or assisted transfer, for example as in diagram 54.10, a wider basin may be preferred.

[13] Bib 93000, p27.

5447   Wash basins: Hair washing

54470   Wash basins specified so as to be convenient for
hand and face washing are unlikely to be suitable
for hair washing, whether for ambulant disabled
people or wheelchair users.
While a desk top basin is preferred for ordinary
domestic use, a basin of the type shown in diagram
54.45 may be more suitable for handicapped people
who wash their hair in a front-rest position,
provided it projects to give adequate knee space.

54471   In social centres for handicapped people, basins for
hair washing should be adjustable in height, or
installed at alternative fixed heights; see 70461.

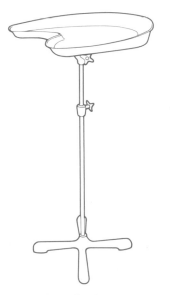

54.47   Portable bowl for hair washing

54472   Because of the difficulty of arranging fixed basins so
that they are convenient for hair washing, a
portable bowl on an adjustable-height stand is
suggested (diagram 54.47).

545   Planning of bathrooms

5450   Bathroom planning: General considerations

54500   Diagrams 54.48 and 54.57–54.64 illustrate bathroom
layouts for different purposes; they are commented
on in the following discussion.

54501   For wheelchair housing (8360) the recommendation
is that bathroom planning should allow for the use
of a shower as well as a bath, though it is not
essential that a shower is installed initially.
The provision of a floor gully is recommended;
diagrams 54.57, 54.59, 54.60 and 54.62 are examples
of suitable planning. See also notes on bathroom
floors (388) and showers in bathrooms (54814).

54502   A warm bathroom is essential for disabled people,
and in particular for paraplegics.
For recommended temperature levels see 4212.

Ceiling track for hoist

54503   In wheelchair housing the planning of bathrooms
should take account of the possible requirement for
a ceiling track with hoist for personal transfer to
and from the wc or in and out of the bath.
Recommended track lines for the wc are shown in
diagram 54.34, and for the bath in diagram 54.49.
Notes on electric hoists are in 261, and on ceiling
structures in 262. For additional notes on
suspended supports to baths see 5473.

54504   The simple requirement is for a straight track
between the wc and the bath where the wheelchair
can be positioned between appliances, allowing the
individual to be moved one way or the other.
Dependent on a suitable ceiling structure, this
provision is not difficult with any of the plan
layouts shown in diagrams 54.57–54.62.

54505   The more difficult requirement is for a track
running from the bedroom through to the
bathroom. The route may be through the bathroom
door or by opening up the partition between
bedroom and bathroom, as noted in 83515.
Bearing in mind the constraints on track routing
noted in 261, the preference is that the track goes
first to the wc and then to the bath, on the basis that
the wc is the appliance more often used.

Bathroom planning: Ambulant disabled people

54506   In low-cost family housing it is not as a rule feasible
to plan bathrooms to the standards for wheelchair
housing detailed in 5451–5456. But in line with the
principles of mobility housing, discussed in section
82, it is desirable that allowance is made for access
for ambulant disabled people, including people
using wheelchairs who are not chairbound.

54507   Bathrooms in typical low-cost contemporary
housing are often uncomfortably small and could
with advantage be larger. A bathroom survey made
in 1968 reported that a bathroom floor area of $3.7m^2$
or over is likely to be satisfactory for housewives;
below this figure satisfaction will tend to
decrease[14].

54508   For ambulant disabled people, for example those
using walking aids, the suggested minimum
bathroom size is 1.700×2.100, giving an area of
$3.57m^2$ (diagram 54.48).
With a 0.900 doorset this allows for wheelchair
access, though there is not sufficient space to close
the door with the wheelchair inside. The National
Building Agency metric house shell plans[15]
indicate minimum dimensions of 1.700×2.000 for
bathrooms having this layout.

[14] Bib 93950, p4.
[15] Bib 93733, 93734.

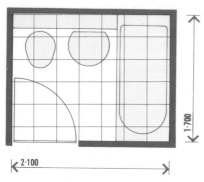

54.48 Minimum size bathroom for ambulant disabled people (1:50)

54509 Where practicable it is desirable that there is a platform at the head end of the bath, giving dimensions 2·100 × 2·100, ie 4·41m². With an out-opening door this layout is shown in diagram 54.64.

5451 Wheelchair bathrooms: Utilization spaces: General

54510 Diagrams 54.51, 54.54 and 54.55 show utilization spaces for baths, wash basins and wcs in bathrooms in wheelchair housing.
With minor exceptions discussed below, the bathroom layouts shown in diagrams 54.57–54.64 conform with these space requirements.

54511 Where practicable the plan should give an unobstructed space for each fixture according to the dimensions indicated, ie 1·800 × 1·200 for the bath, 1·150 × 1·050 for the wash basin and (including the wc fixture) 1·900 × 1·400 for the wc.

Overlapping spaces
54512 In prescribed areas, shown by a dotted line on diagrams 54.51 and 54.55, it is admissible that adjacent fixtures overlap utilization spaces, provided there is no overlapping at floor level where the swing of the wheelchair footrests would be obstructed.
Desirably also there ought not to be any obstruction between 0·600 and 0·850 above floor level, to allow for rear propelling wheels and push handles.

54513 The variations in the dimensions for frontal approach, ie 1·200 for the bath, 1·050 for the wash basin and 1·150 for the wc, take account of the additional space for wheelchair footrest access at the basin and wc by comparison with the bath.

54514 The spaces shown in diagrams 54.51, 54.54 and 54.55 will be handed where approach is from the other direction to that shown.

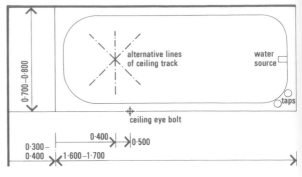

54.49 Bath plan (1:25)

Bath dimension variables
54515 In the majority of bath plans illustrated in this section the bath and associated platform are shown occupying a space 2·100 × 0·800.
This is the preferred metric planning envelope to ensure adequate overall space for wheelchair use; in certain circumstances the bath/platform space may be reduced to 2·000 × 0·700.

54516 The preferred bath length is 1·700, minimum 1·600. The preferred width is approx 0·760, minimum 0·700. The preferred platform depth is 0·400, minimum 0·300 (diagram 54.49).
For notes on length of baths see 5461, on width see 5462, and on platform dimensions see 5458.

54517 In bathrooms for old people or others where the bath/platform space is reduced to 2·000 long or 0·700 wide the overall dimensions of the bathroom may be reduced as indicated in diagrams 54.57–54.64.
In the case of diagrams 54.57 and 54.62 the reduction of the bath length will reduce wheelchair manoeuvring space, and the door should slide or open out.

54518 Variants of bath/platform spaces are shown in diagram 54.50.

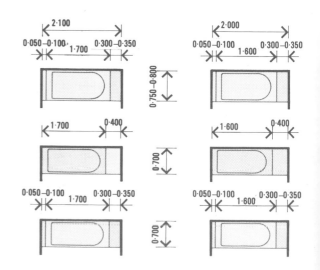

54.50 Variants of bath/platform spaces (1:100)

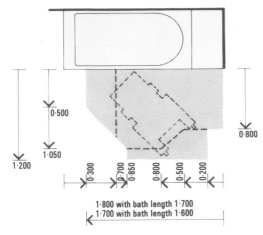

54.51 Bath: Wheelchair utilization space (1:50)

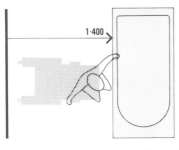

54.52 Direct frontal transfer to bath (1:50)

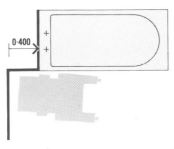

54.53 Access to bath taps by chairbound person (1:50)

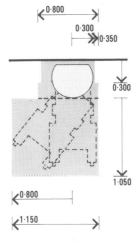

54.54 Wash basin: Wheelchair utilization space (1:50)

5452   Wheelchair bathrooms: Utilization spaces: Baths

54520 The utilization space for the bath shown in diagram 54.51 allows for lateral transfer using the platform at the head end, oblique standing transfer, or transfer by means of a mechanical hoist.
For notes on access to the bath see 5457, 5458.

54521 Among 34 wheelchair users in the Loughborough study who expressed a preference for means of transfer into the bath, 20 transferred from an oblique position, 8 from a frontal position and 6 from a lateral position[16]. Only 8 said they could use an alternative transfer.

Direct frontal transfer

54522 The space shown in diagram 54.51 does not allow for direct frontal transfer to the bath. Where planning permits, the clear dimension in front of the bath should be not less than 1·400, as in diagram 54.52; examples which conform are 54.57 and 54.59–54.62.
While provision for frontal transfer is preferred, it may be assumed that users will not be critically handicapped by having to use an oblique transfer, as may be the case with the examples shown in diagrams 54.58, 54.63 and 54.64.

Access to taps

54523 The spaces shown in diagrams 54.57–54.64 do not allow for a chairbound person outside the bath to comfortably reach taps in the conventional position at the foot end of the bath.
In wheelchair housing it will not as a rule happen that a disabled person who is severely handicapped, and therefore unable to reach to the taps, takes a bath without an attendant to assist. While it may therefore be admissible that taps are located as for use by an able-bodied person, it is preferred that taps are located in a more accessible position; see 5474.

54524 To afford closer approach the bath panel should be recessed, as shown in diagram 54.68.

54525 Where provision is made for a chairbound person to reach taps at the foot end of the bath, the clear space beyond the end of the bath should be 0·400, as shown in diagram 54.53.

Platform size

54526 Diagrams 54.57–54.64 show a platform 0·400 deep at the head end of the bath, as advised in 5458.
Where platforms of alternative depths are incorporated, overall dimensions of the bathroom may be adjusted accordingly.

[16] Bib 93960, p34.

5453 Wheelchair bathrooms: Utilization spaces: Wash basins

54530 The utilization space shown in diagram 54.54 allows for frontal or oblique approach to the wash basin.

54531 To facilitate washing, many wheelchair users prefer an oblique approach to the basin. Where there is an option, the basin may be positioned off-centre within a space, as shown in diagram 54.63.

Knee recess
54532 The knee recess to the basin should be not less than 0·800 wide at the front, and 0·700 at the rear. The basin should be positioned so that its centre line is not closer than 0·300 to any side obstruction at low level.
The example shown in diagram 54.62 does not strictly conform, in that the wc overlaps the basin utilization space. The plan as shown has compensating advantages, and may be considered admissible.

Depth of basin
54533 Diagrams 54.57–54.64 indicate a basin 0·500 deep from front rim to rear wall. Where deeper basins are used appropriate planning adjustments should be made.

54534 Desk top basins having dimensions 0·600 wide × 0·500 deep (front to back) may be incorporated in bathroom layouts as shown in diagrams 54.57–54.61, 54.63 and 54.64. Where wider or deeper basins are used appropriate adjustments should be made.

5454 Wheelchair bathrooms: Utilization spaces: Wcs

54540 The utilization space shown in diagram 54.55 allows for lateral or oblique transfer to the wc, as shown in diagrams 54.5b and c.

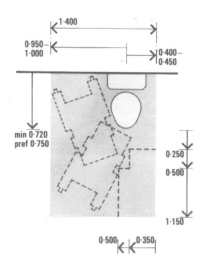

54.55 Wc: Wheelchair utilization space (1:50)

54541 It is desirable that planning also allows for direct frontal transfer to the wc, as shown in diagram 54.5a and provided for in diagrams 54.58, 54.61, 54.62 and 54.64.
Space constraints, in particular the placing of the wash basin, may prevent this; see 54552.

54542 Where practicable, planning should allow for approach at right angles to the axis of the wc, as shown in diagram 54.60.

54543 The bathroom layouts shown conform with diagram 54.55 with the exception of diagram 54.64 which does not allow for lateral transfer. This layout ought only to be used in family housing where a second wc in a separate compartment allows for lateral transfer.

Space for lateral transfer
54544 To permit lateral transfer to the wc the preferred clear dimension from rear wall to front of wc bowl is 0·750, with a minimum of 0·720.
All diagrams show a dimension of 0·750, with the exception of diagram 54.60; in this case a dimension of 0·720, in conjunction with a bath panel recess of not less than 0·030 and bath 0·760 wide, gives the required utilization dimension of 1·150. The example shown in diagram 54.62 does not conform, but it allows for reversing the rear wheels of the chair below the basin.

5455 Wheelchair bathrooms: Relationship of wash basin to wc

54550 Where a bathroom is planned for chairbound people and incorporates a wc, it is desirable that the wash basin is reachable by a person seated on the wc. For comment see 54460.

54551 The basin water source should not be further than 0·550 on plan from the front edge of the wc. Wheelchair users and others with no upper limb impairments can usually reach the basin where the water source is at approx 0·800 from the front edge of the wc bowl. For those with impaired upper limbs, or with a trunk impairment which restricts reach, the dimension needs to be 0·550 or less.

Obstruction of approach to wc
54552 In practice it is likely to happen that the placing of a conventional basin so that it can be reached from the wc will preclude direct frontal approach to the wc as advised in 54541.
Diagram 54.56 shows that where the centre line of the basin is at 0·800 from the front edge of the wc, an oblique approach is manageable. If the basin is brought forward to 0·550, as shown by the dotted line, it becomes much more difficult. In neither case is frontal approach practicable. As shown in diagram 54.56 the dimension between side wall and wc centre line is 0·500; if it is reduced to 0·400 approach is more difficult.

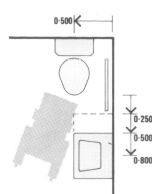

54.56 Relationship of wash basin to wc (1:50)

Side wall staggered

54553 To obtain a more direct frontal approach to the wc, the side wall may be staggered, for example as shown in diagram 54.60.

With this plan arrangement it is not recommended that the basin centre line is closer than 0·550; the side wall beside the wc needs to extend not less than 0·250 for the fixing of horizontal and vertical support rails. Diagram 54.60 shows that where the front to back dimension of the basin is 0·500 and the wall setback is 0·150, wheelchair approach still has to be oblique rather than frontal.

54554 To permit frontal approach to the wc, the line of the side wall carrying the wc needs to be set back not less than 0·300, as shown in diagram 54.58.

While this layout is preferred, a consequence is that the basin water source is less accessible than with the layout as shown in diagram 54.60.

Continuous side wall

54555 Where the side wall plane runs through (as in diagram 54.57), it is not recommended that the clear dimension from the front edge of the wc to the opposing side face of the basin is reduced to the minimum of 0·500 required by diagram 54.55 unless necessitated by space limitations.

Where this dimension is 0·500 and the centre line of the basin is at 0·800 (as in diagram 54.57), it cannot be assumed that most wheelchair users will be able to reach the water source.

54556 Placing the basin further away, as for example in diagram 54.59 where the centre line is at 1·000, allows for more direct frontal approach to the wc, and also gives more comfortable space for a 3 point turn inside the bathroom.

With the layout shown in diagram 54.59 the basin may alternatively be placed diagonally across the corner, or on the wall opposite the wc.

Other layouts

54557 With the basin as shown in diagram 54.62 the water source will be reachable from the wc by people with unimpaired upper limbs.

54558 With the basin as shown in diagram 54.64 the water source will be reachable from the wc by most users.

Supplementary basin

54559 A possible solution to the problems discussed above is to install a hand rinse basin alongside the wc for the benefit of chairbound people (diagram 54.46), in addition to a conventional wash basin for general purposes.

Such a facility will be advantageous for all users, whether disabled or not.

5456 Wheelchair bathrooms: Manoeuvring space

54560 In wheelchair housing where bathrooms accommodate a bath, wc and wash basin it will invariably happen, on account of space requirements for transfer to wc and approach to bath, that there is adequate space for a wheelchair to be turned through 180°.

Wheelchair turning inside bathrooms

54561 To allow for wheelchair turning the clear space in the bathroom should be not less than 1·400 wide. The examples shown in diagrams 54.57, 54.59, 54.60 and 54.62 allow for comfortable turning. Examples shown in diagrams 54.58, 54.61 and 54.64 allow for turning provided there is clearance for wheelchair footrests below wc and basin, and a recessed panel to the bath.

54562 Layouts as in diagrams 54.59 and 54.61 allow more comfortably for a 3 point turn than for a complete turn through 180°.

For related discussion see 243.

Bathrooms not planned for lateral transfer to wc

54563 In bathrooms where the wc is not planned for lateral transfer, space for turning may be tight. The minimum size bathroom shown in the NBA plans for a layout similar to diagram 54.64 is 2·000 wide[17]; assuming a 0·760 wide bath this does not give adequate turning space. The modified example shown in diagram 54.64 is 2·100 wide, which with a recess to the bath panel is admissible.

Doors

54564 Where manoeuvring inside the bathroom is limited the door must slide or open out.

54565 Where internal space is generous, for example as in diagrams 54.57 and 54.62 the door may open in, provided it can be opened from outside in the event of emergency (36341), and the bath length is not reduced (54517).

In the example shown in diagram 54.59 floor space is adequate but the clear dimension by the door handle is not sufficient to allow the door to open in (see diagram 36.2).

---

[17] Bib 93733, 93734.

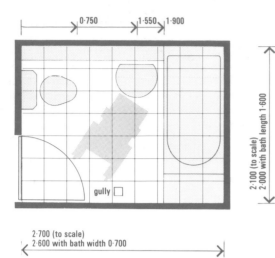

0·750 1·550 1·900

2·100 (to scale)
2·000 with bath length 1·600

gully

2·700 (to scale)
2·600 with bath width 0·700

54.57

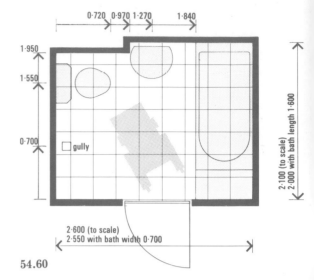

0·720 0·970 1·270 1·840

1·950

1·555

0·700

gully

2·100 (to scale)
2·000 with bath length 1·600

2·600 (to scale)
2·550 with bath width 0·700

54.60

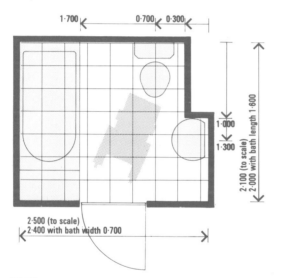

1·700 0·700 0·300

1·000

1·300

2·100 (to scale)
2·000 with bath length 1·600

2·500 (to scale)
2·400 with bath width 0·700

54.58

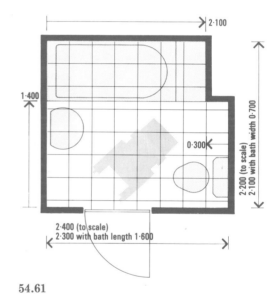

2·100

1·400

0·300

2·200 (to scale)
2·100 with bath width 0·700

2·400 (to scale)
2·300 with bath length 1·600

54.61

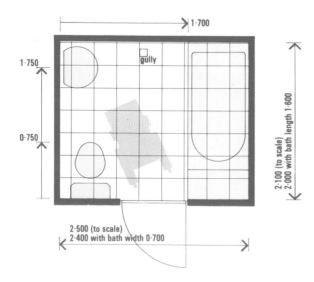

1·700

1·750

0·750

gully

2·100 (to scale)
2·000 with bath length 1·600

2·500 (to scale)
2·400 with bath width 0·700

54.59

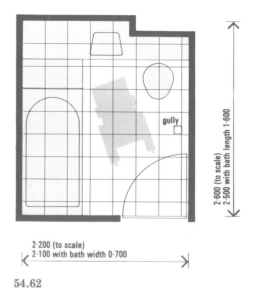

gully

2·600 (to scale)
2·500 with bath length 1·600

2·200 (to scale)
2·100 with bath width 0·700

54.62

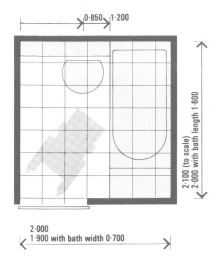

0·850 1·200

2·100 (to scale)
2·000 with bath length 1·600

2·000
1·900 with bath width 0·700

54.63

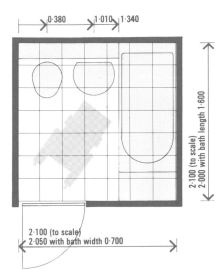

0·380 1·010 1·340

2·100 (to scale)
2·000 with bath length 1·600

2·100 (to scale)
2·050 with bath width 0·700

54.64

54.54–54.64 Bathroom layouts illustrating planning considerations for chairbound users (1:50)

54566 Where there is not adequate space for turning inside the bathroom it must be possible to turn immediately outside the door.
This will mean that the door should slide, as shown in diagram 54.63.

Alternative access
54567 In wheelchair housing, particularly for severely disabled people, it may be helpful to plan the bathroom so that direct access from a bedroom is obtained, allowing for the fixing of a track to carry a hoist from bed to bath and wc.
This will mean the provision of two doors to the bathroom, or a partition wall which can if required be removed. The floor gully if incorporated may need to be relocated. For related comment see 54503.

5457   **Access to bath: General considerations**

54570 Entering and leaving a bath is particularly hazardous for disabled people, and baths and fittings must be specified which minimize hazards. Auxiliary support devices must be provided, see 5470–5473.
Although there are disabled people who are unable, despite the aid of special equipment, to use the bath on their own, the majority, including some wheelchair users, can manage a bath independently where suitable provision is made.

Methods of access
54571 There are three basic methods of getting into a bath:
1. Stepping over the rim from a standing position.
2. Bending forward to support the body while holding on to the rim and swinging the legs over behind.
3. Sitting on the rim or near ledge and lifting the legs over in front.

54572 Disabled people with lower limb impairments may be unable, because of insecure balance, to use methods 1 or 2 without hazard. Lower limb amputees necessarily use method 3.

54573 Method 3 is the only safe way for people with lower limb impairments to get in and out of a bath, and it is therefore the criterion for bath planning for disabled people.

Height of bath rim
54574 Where there are no auxiliary support rails a bath having a relatively high rim is preferred for ambulant disabled people, for example up to 0·650 above floor level.
For ambulant disabled people a traditional high-sided bath is safer for access than the modern low bath, since the rim can be used for steadying as described in method 2.

54575 Where a bath with a low rim is installed it is essential to have auxiliary support rails.
A bath having a very low rim, for example 0·400 as recommended for old people in DoE Design Bulletin 1[18], is unsafe because the rim is too low to use for support.

54576 Where a vertical pole is provided (54712) an upright position can be maintained when entering the bath, and a low rim is preferred, suggested maximum height 0·400.
This is only acceptable for people without severe lower limb impairments.

54577 To avoid imbalance as a result of confusion regarding levels, the rim height must never be less than the inside depth of the bath.

[18] Bib 93610.

Bath cleaning

54578 A bath with a low rim is difficult to clean. Many disabled people find it impossible to clean the bottom of a bath comfortably. A low rim is therefore convenient only in institutions where an attendant is available, or in private dwellings where a domestic help or other member of the family undertakes the cleaning of the bath.

Small children

54579 A bath with a low rim is awkward for mothers (or fathers) bathing small children; for this purpose a traditional high rim bath is preferred.

5458 Access to bath: Platform provision

54580 To assist seated transfer into the bath by disabled people, a detachable seat fitting over the bath may be used (diagram 54.81) but the preferred provision is an integrated platform at the head of the bath.

54581 The platform should be at the same level as the bath rim and should be of equal width.
From a seated position on the platform the user transfers either to a seat placed at a level midway between top and bottom of a bath, or directly to the bottom of the bath.

Depth of platform

54582 The platform should be not less than 0·300 deep. A depth of 0·400 is generally preferred, as shown in diagrams 54.57–54.64.
There are two design considerations: first, that the depth allows the rear wall to give satisfactory back support while the user is seated on the platform; and second, that, with a wheelchair positioned against the back wall, lateral transfer (with armrest removed) can be achieved without the rear propelling wheel being inconveniently obstructive. Regarding the first, a depth of 0·300 is most comfortable, taking account of the rear ledge approx 0·050 deep at the head end of the bath; 0·400 is serviceable. Regarding the second, 0·300 is too short; 0·400 is reasonable, though the wheel will be partially obstructive, as shown in diagram 54.65a. On this basis 0·400 is generally advised. But where space is restricted, for example because blocking out at the tap end is needed to accommodate plumbing (as shown in diagrams 54.61a, b, e and f) the depth may be reduced to 0·350 or 0·300.

54583 Where the platform depth is increased to 0·600, as shown in diagram 54.65b, more convenient lateral transfer is possible, but back support against the wall is precluded.

Rear wall set back

54584 The setting back of the rear wall, as shown in diagram 54.61, allows the chair seat to align with the platform.
The layout shown in diagram 54.62, which allows the wheelchair to be reversed with the rear wheels passing under the front of the basin, has the same advantages. A minor disadvantage in both cases is that a vertical pulling up rail (see 54710) cannot be fixed in the preferred position.

Platform extension

54585 For some wheelchair users and ambulant disabled people it can be advantageous if the platform is extended at the side, as shown in diagram 54.65c. This can permit a more convenient placing of the wheelchair for lateral transfer to the platform. In bathrooms where space is limited the provision ought not to be made where the extension of the platform obstructs wheelchair manoeuvre through an adjacent door.

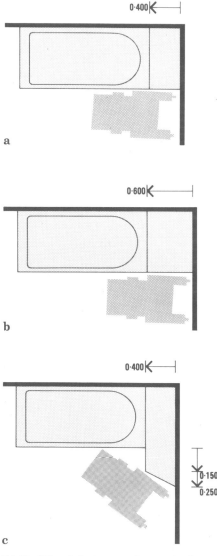

54.65 Wheelchair transfer to platform at head end of bath (1:50)

54586 For specific disabled people, for example rheumatoid arthritics and tetraplegics, a deeper platform up to 1·500 deep may be used as a drying bench.
This provision may be appropriate in institutions; in private dwellings it is not normally warranted.

Materials

54587 A warm surface for the platform is advised, for example cork.
Where the platform is tiled the use of a cushion may be assumed.

Secondary functions

54588 The platform has the important secondary function of enabling the disabled person to adopt a seated posture while washing feet and legs; this is a difficult activity to perform in a conventional bath. The dead space below the platform may be used for storage.

Hemiplegics

54589 Where a bathroom is planned for a specific disabled person with alateral weakness, such as a hemiplegic, a platform should be on the good side when transferring.

5459   Bathroom planning: Residential homes

54590 In institutions for disabled people a minimum of three baths should be provided to cater for residents with varying disabilities:
Bath 1 should be freestanding to allow for attended bathing (diagram 54.66a). For design notes see 5463.
Bath 2 should be placed against a wall, with a platform at the head end to allow for lateral approach from the left (diagram 54.66b).
Bath 3 should be as bath 2 but allowing for lateral approach from the right (diagram 54.66c).

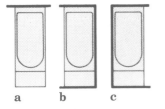

a   b   c

54.66 Baths in residential homes

54591 Bathroom planning in institutions should be on the basis that any bath may be used by either males or females.

Platform both ends

54592 In place of alternative baths for lateral approach from either side a bath may be provided with a platform at both ends and the water source at the centre, as shown in diagram 54.67.
This kind of bath should have two 'head' ends to allow for comfortable use. The outlet should be to one side below the water source.

Drying bench

54593 A bench approx 1·700 long × 0·700 wide may be provided for handicapped people to be dried by attendants after bathing.
This provision may take the form of a portable trolley.

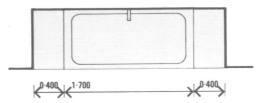

|←0·400→|←1·700→| |←0·400→|

54.67 Bath with platform at both ends (1:50)

Shower provision

54594 For ambulant handicapped people a shower compartment with a folding seat should be provided, see 5483, 5484.

54595 Part of the bathroom should be planned for a shower to be taken using a portable chair, see 5481.

54596 For general notes on bathrooms in residential homes see 70074.

546   Baths

5460   Bath height

54600 In housing for disabled people, and for wheelchair users in general, the preferred height of the bath rim is 0·450 above floor level (diagram 54.68). For a wheelchair user to shift laterally it helps if the platform is at a slightly lower level than the chair seat, for which the norm is approx 0·490.

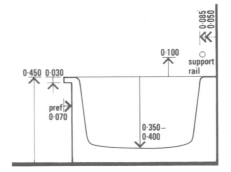

54.68 Bath section (1:20)

54601 For ambulant disabled people a bath rim at 0·500 or 0·550 may be preferred.

54602 For some severely disabled ambulant people, for example rheumatoid arthritics, a higher rim may be helpful, up to 0·650 above floor level.
This allows the user to lean against the rim and gradually shift to a seated position.

Assisted bathing

54603 Where a bath is installed for a specific disabled person who has to be helped with washing, a relatively high bath, up to 0·650, may be preferred. Where the rim is high it is essential there is a platform at the head end.

54604 For further notes on both bath rim height see 54574–7.

5461 Bath length

54610 In family housing for disabled people a bath length of 1·700 is suggested.
Although for specific disabled people a shorter bath may be more manageable this will not always be the case. An important factor in family housing is that other members of the household will probably prefer to have a 1·700 bath rather than one which is shorter. Where baths to standard Imperial dimensions are available a length of 5ft 6in (1·676) is satisfactory.

54611 For some disabled people a bath length of 1·600 is preferred.
In a long bath there is a tendency for the body to slide down to where the feet find support. If the bath is long a disabled person may find it difficult to maintain a secure seated position for washing.

Old people
54612 For old people in general a bath length of 1·600 is preferred; the recommendation of MHLG Circular 82/69 [19] that baths should not be longer than 1·550 (see 8058) may be disregarded.

54613 Baths shorter than 1·500 ought not to be installed for any users.

Relaxation
54614 For many disabled people a warm bath is valuable for relaxing the muscles and relieving discomfort. It is therefore often important that the bath should be sufficiently long for immersion of the body.

5462 Bath section and width

54620 An internal bath depth of approximately 0·400 is suggested (diagram 54.68).
For some disabled people a shallower bath, for example 0·350, may make it easier to push out of the bath up to the platform.

Bath bottom
54621 The bath must have a flat bottom to minimize the risk of accidents caused by slipping.
For notes on non-slip strips see 54765.

54622 A bath section as shown in diagram 54.69a is preferred to that in diagram 54.69b, to allow the feet to be wedged against the side when pushing up.

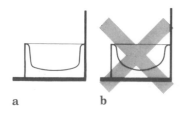

a   b

54.69 Bath sections

Toe recess
54623 A toe recess should be provided at the side of the bath to permit close approach by wheelchair footrests.
The bath panel may be splayed or set back, as shown in diagram 54.68. The preferred minimum depth of the recess is 0·070.

Rim
54624 To allow the hand to grip the rim comfortably the side panel should be recessed, with a fillet fitted into the rim as shown in diagram 54.68.

Bathing small children
54625 If the criteria for a bath suitable for disabled people are observed, ie high rim, shallow invert, platform at head end and toe recess, baths will be more convenient for the bathing of small children than is the case with conventional fixtures.

Bath width
54626 The preferred bath width is approximately 0·760, with a minimum of 0·700.
In the NBA metric house shell plans [20] all baths are contained in a 0·700 wide envelope, and for comparability the same practice could have followed in diagrams 54.56–54.64 and elsewhere. But for many disabled people (as for many able-bodied people) a bath 0·700 wide or less can be uncomfortably narrow. The preferred minimum is 0·750.

54627 The standard bath manufactured in Britain is about 0·760 wide, ie 2ft 6in; a space 0·800 wide is required to accommodate it with metric planning, and this is shown in most diagrams.
In some cases, for example diagrams 54.56, 54.60 and 54.64, a bath 0·760 wide is shown because it permits utilization space criteria to be observed within given overall dimensions.

54628 In housing for old people a bath 0·700 wide is admissible if bathroom space is restricted.

5463 Freestanding baths

54630 In institutions for disabled people at least one freestanding bath should be provided for users who need two attendants to help them in and out of the bath, or who are unable to wash themselves when in the bath.

54631 The freestanding bath must not be regarded as a generally acceptable substitute for the wall-fixed bath.
For disabled people able to bath independently or with limited assistance the wall-fixed bath with suitable support rails has advantages and is preferred.

[19] Bib 93630.
[20] Bib 93733, 93734.

Invert and rim

54632 To make it easier for attendants who help disabled people in and out of the bath and assist with washing, the bath invert should be at approximately 0·450 above floor level. The bath rim should be at approximately 0·800 above floor level (diagram 54.70).

A bath invert lower than 0·450 may cause strain and injury to bath attendants when lifting disabled people. This is most relevant in institutions where women assist with bathing.

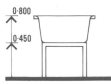

54.70 Freestanding bath for assisted washing

54633 The preferred provision is a bath which can be raised and lowered by a hydraulic jack or similar arrangement.

The equipment should be capable of raising the bath rim to 0·900 above floor level.

Split level planning

54634 Steps to a lower level enable the bath rim to be at a convenient height for attendants (diagram 54.71).

Platform

54635 There should be a platform at the head end of the bath. For transfer from a wheelchair the platform should be at approximately 0·450 above floor level (diagram 54.71a).

In this case the bath rim at the lower level may be higher than where the floor is flat, for example 0·850.

54636 A disadvantage of the layout shown in diagram 54.71 is that it is not convenient for use with a portable hoist.

A possible solution is for the platform at the head end to be unfixed, so that it can be moved out of the way when a hoist is used. The upper floor level should continue under the head end of the bath, to permit the use of the kind of hoist shown in diagram 26.6.

Bath length

54637 The preferred bath length is 1·600.

To allow for relaxation a bath length of 1·700 is suggested for general purposes (54610). A freestanding bath has to cater primarily for the job of washing by attendants and not for relaxation, and a shorter bath may therefore be appropriate.

Utilization space

54638 To allow for wheelchair approach and access by attendants the clear dimension between platform and rear wall should be not less than 1·200. The clear dimension to either side of the bath should be not less than 0·800 (diagram 54.71b).

Where space is provided as shown in diagram 54.71b the door may open in.

54639 A wash basin should be placed in the corner of the room, as shown in diagram 54.71b.

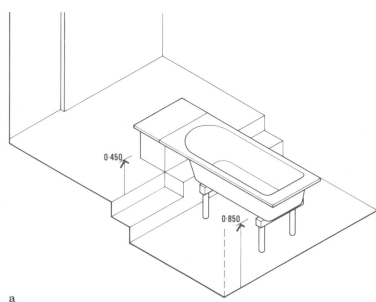

a

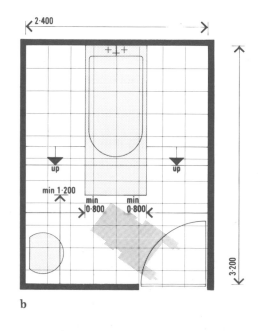

b

54.71 Freestanding bath: Split level planning (1:50)

5464 Proprietary sit baths

Medicbath

54640 A proprietary walk-in seat bath known as the Medicbath may be preferred by some elderly and ambulant handicapped people to a conventional bath or shower (diagram 54.72).
Costs are noted in 90340.

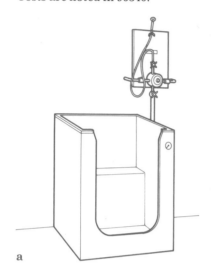

a

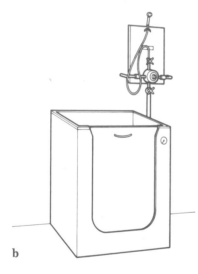

b

54.72 Medicbath

54641 The unit, 0·914 long × 0·686 wide × 0·864 high, is made of glass fibre reinforced plastic. Support legs are adjustable and the unit is secured by angle plates to the floor.
The user steps in, closes and seals the door, sits down, fills the bath and uses it. After washing, the bath is emptied by the floor drain outlets, the door is opened by depressing the seal valve and the user steps out.

Door

54642 The unit has a door with a sill at 0·100 above floor level. It can be supplied with a hinged door or with a removable sliding panel. The door is pneumatically sealed using either a hand pump or an electric compressor motor beneath the seat. Where an electric motor is fitted it should be operated by a ceiling mounted pull switch, fixed over one side of the bath.

Water supply

54643 Although the bath can be filled from wall taps served directly by the hot and cold water supplies, it is advantageous if it is equipped with a wall-mounted thermostatic control valve assembly, together with a shower spray attachment and flexible hose.
The bath is filled through an inlet just below the seat.

Disabled user applications

54644 The bath is designed for convenient use by elderly and ambulant handicapped people. It is not suitable for paraplegics and wheelchair users who cannot stand.

54645 The unit is not recommended as a substitute for a conventional bath in special housing units designed for disabled people; other users in the household may prefer an ordinary bath, and so also may the handicapped person if a purpose-designed bath can be installed.
It is more suitable for house adaptation work, for example where there is no bath or the existing bath is inaccessible. It may be possible for a unit to be installed temporarily by an agency providing equipment for handicapped people, and reused by another handicapped person when it is no longer needed.

54646 The unit is more suitable for installation in hospital units, old people's homes and homes for handicapped people, where it may be one of a range of bathing facilities available.
Its effective use will depend on the readiness of residents or patients to use it and on the willingness of care staff to help; to bath a patient in the unit requires more time to be spent by the care staff than using an ordinary bath or giving a bed bath.

Heating

54647 A possible disadvantage of the unit for some handicapped people is that they become uncomfortably cold during the period that the bath is emptying. To counter this, the room should be kept warm, with perhaps a supplementary radiant heater.

Arjo roll-in bath and shower

54648 The Arjo roll-in sit bath made in Sweden is used in conjunction with the Arjo lift ride-chair (diagram 26.5). It has a sliding seat for direct transfer and a self-sealing door.

54649 The Arjo roll-in shower cabinet (diagram 54.73) is similarly designed.
Costs are noted in 90341.

54.73 Arjo roll-in shower cabinet

5465 Special baths

Sitz baths

54650 A sitz bath is a short high-sided bath used in a sitting position. It is not recommended for general use by disabled people.
The semi-squat washing position required by the low seat is awkward for most disabled people, and less comfortable than the high seat of the Medicbath. The high side makes access difficult or impossible unless a platform is incorporated, in which event space would be adequate for a more satisfactory conventional bath.

54651 A relatively low proprietary sitz bath is shown in diagram 54.74. Dimensions are 1·220 long × 0·710 wide × 0·475 high, not including the platform at the head end.
A bath of this kind may be a necessary compromise in an adapted bathroom where space is limited. Costs are noted in 90342.

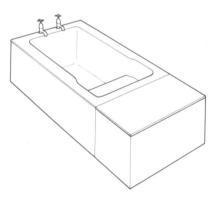

54.74 Sitz bath with platform at head end

Old people's baths

54652 For old people a shallow flat-bottomed bath with low rim may be suggested, but is satisfactory only if installed in conjunction with adequate support rails. Cost notes: 90343.

Handicapped children

54653 In units for handicapped children, for example special schools, the provision of a bath/shower unit is suggested; see 5489.

5466 Baths: Materials

54660 By comparison with cast iron baths, acrylic baths have the advantage for disabled people that they have a relatively non-slip surface. A disadvantage is that where exceptionally hot water is used the plastic can warp.

54661 Plastic baths, either acrylic or grp, are liable to fracture where portable bath seats are used. Plastic baths are not suitable for adaptation work where there is no platform at the head end.

54662 Where provision is made for transfer by a platform at the head end a plastic bath may be satisfactory.

5467 Sauna baths

54670 For disabled people a sauna bath can be valuable therapeutically as well as for cleansing.
Sauna baths are normally installed by specialist contractors, who can advise on their suitability and design for disabled users.

Wheelchair users

54671 The room temperature of the sauna may rise to 75–100°C; at this level the metallic parts of a wheelchair will become dangerously hot after a short time and it is not therefore practicable for wheelchair users to remain in their chairs in the sauna. Either the chair is left outside and they are carried in, or an attendant wheels the chair in, transfers the disabled person to the bench and immediately removes the chair.

Floor

54672 The sauna floor should be at the same level as adjoining floors outside and there should be no raised threshold at the door.

54673 The clear space between floor battens should be not more than 0·005.
This is to avoid the jamming of wheelchair tyres, trolley tyres, and stick or crutch ferrules.

Bench

54674 For disabled users bench seating should be at approximately 0·500 above floor level. A bench 0·450 deep and not less than 2·000 long is suggested.

54675 Handrails should be fixed to walls at the end of benches to aid handicapped people. They should be of timber, with timber brackets.

Room area

54676 The floor area of the sauna will depend on the number of users to be accommodated. It is not necessary that there is sufficient floor area for a wheelchair to be turned inside the sauna.
Where a wheelchair may be brought into the sauna the door should give a clear opening width of not less than 0·770.

547 Bathroom fixtures and fittings

5470 Bath support rails: General considerations

54700 Support rails to baths may be fixed to aid two
activities:
1. Getting in or out of the bath in a standing
position.
2. Raising or lowering the body to or from a seated
position in the bath.

54701 For activity 1 there should be a vertical rail,
accessible from inside or outside the bath.
Examples are described in 54710 and 54715.

54702 Activity 2 usually requires that both hands are used
for support, one on the outer bath rim or platform at
the head end of the bath, the other on a horizontal
or slightly inclined rail fixed to the side wall over
the bath.
With this kind of support it is usually possible for
the user to take part of his weight on his lower arm,
which is supported by the rail, or to loosen his grip
sufficiently to allow his hands to slide along the
rail, enabling him to ease himself gently into the
bath.

54703 An inclined rail on the side wall rising steeply away
from the head end of the bath and designed for the
user to pull himself up by a hand-over-hand
technique is not recommended.
This is dependent on maintaining a secure footing,
with the feet acting as a pivot around which the
body rotates. The normal bath surface does not
provide the necessary degree of stability for this.

54704 For notes on support rails see 333.

5471 Baths: Vertical supports

Bath with platform
54710 Where there is a bath platform a vertical rail
should be fixed to the side wall approximately 0·300
away from the edge of the platform (diagram 54.75).
The rail should extend from 0·900 to 1·500 above
floor level. Where the bathroom layout is as in
diagram 54.59 or 54.60 this rail may be fixed to the
back of the bathroom door.

54711 Where there is a bath platform it is not essential
that an additional vertical rail is fixed to the side
wall over the bath.
To aid disabled people who prefer to stand to
transfer rather than use the platform, a vertical rail
may be fixed as shown in diagram 54.76.

Bath without platform: Vertical pole
54712 Where there is no platform to the bath a vertical
pole diameter approximately 0·035 may be fixed on
the access side of the bath (diagram 54.77).
The pole is used as a pivot, allowing the body to
turn through 90° when entering or leaving the bath.

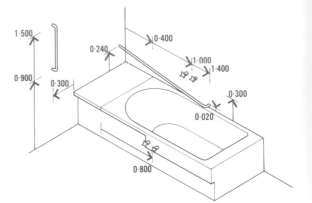

54.75 Bath with platform: Support rails and tap
location (1:50)

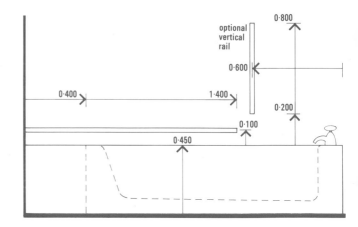

54.76 Bath with platform: Wall-fixed rails (1:25)

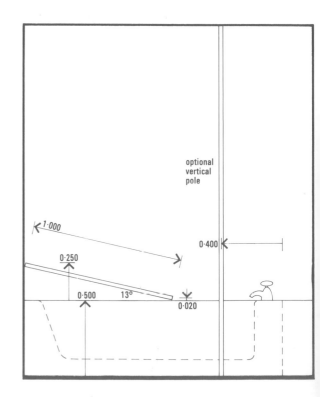

54.77 Bath without platform: Inclined rail and
vertical pole (1:25)

54713 The pole should be positioned approximately 0·400 from the foot end of the bath.
This allows the pole to be reached from a seated position in the bath, and also to be used when reaching over to operate controls at the foot end.

54714 The useful length of the pole ranges from approximately 0·700 to 1·300 above floor level, the most convenient height being approximately 1·000.

54715 A vertical pole should be installed only where a specific need is established.
It is not recommended for general use by disabled people; for people with stiff hips it can make access to the bath difficult or impossible. It may also obstruct access to taps.

Bath without platform: Other vertical supports
54716 Where a pole is installed no other vertical rails need to be fixed. Where it is not, a vertical rail should be fixed to the side wall as shown in diagram 54.76.

5472 Baths: Horizontal supports

54720 For secure hand support the panel on the access side of the bath ought not to be flush with the bath roll. A fillet should be fixed inside the bath roll (diagram 54.68).

54721 A support rail fixed to the wall over the bath should preferably be slightly inclined, rising towards the head end of the bath, or else horizontal.
A slightly inclined rail is recommended in the Research Institute for Consumer Affairs report *Bath Aids* [21].

Inclined rails
54722 Where no platform is provided the preferred length of an inclined rail is 1·000, angled at approximately 13° (diagram 54.77).
This arrangement is appropriate where support rails are fixed beside an existing bath in a corner position.

54723 Where there is a platform the preferred length of an inclined rail is 1·400, angled at approx 10° (diagram 54.75). This assumes a platform length of 0·400; where the length is 0·500 the rail length should be extended to 1·500, and so on.

54724 In each case the centre of the lower end of the rail should be approx 0·020 above the bath rim and the upper end approx 0·240.

Horizontal rails
54725 The preferred height for horizontal rails where installed is 0·100 above the bath rim (diagrams 54.76, 54.78, 54.68).

[21] Bib 93961.

54726 Where there is no platform the suggested length of the rail is 0·600, extending from 0·300 to 0·0900 measured from the head of the bath (diagram 54.78).

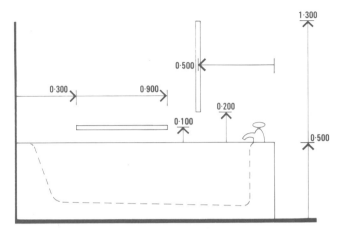

54.78 Bath without platform: Wall-fixed rails (1:25)

54727 Where a platform is provided the suggested length is 1·400 (diagram 54.76).
This rail should extend across the length of the platform to the rear wall. Where the platform length is 0·500 the length of the rail should be 1·500, and so on.

Cross rails
54728 A cross rail fitting over the bath at, or slightly above, rim height is not recommended.
Aids of the kind shown in diagram 54.79 are among the most common fitted to existing baths for disabled people. They provide neither suitable support on which to press down with flexed arms while pushing up out of the bath, nor for pulling with outstretched arms when raising the body. They have two further disadvantages. First, bath taps are used for anchorage, for which they are not designed. Second, unless the rail is hinged, the rail gets in the way of legs when getting in or out of the bath, a particular disadvantage for people with stiff hips. The only advantage they have is to enable a handicapped person lying on his back in the bath to raise his trunk to a vertical position preparatory to getting out of the bath.

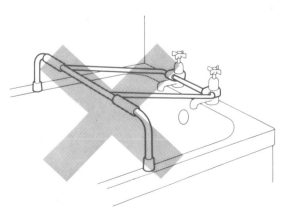

54.79 Cross rail fitting over bath

5473 Baths: Suspended supports

Eye bolt

54730 For some paraplegics with strong upper limbs it can be advantageous to fix an eye bolt to the ceiling for the suspension of a chain and stirrup grip. For reasons discussed in 2602, this is not a provision which is generally suitable for disabled people.

54731 An eye bolt where fixed to the ceiling should be positioned over the bath rim at approx 0·500 from the head end (diagram 54.49).

Ceiling track for hoist

54732 For severely disabled people not able to transfer independently a hoist carried on a track fixed to the ceiling may be required. For notes on ceiling tracks in relation to bathroom planning see 54503.

54733 The track should be positioned over the centre of the bath at approx 0·400 from the head end (diagram 54.49) so that a disabled person can be raised or lowered directly into the bath.

Existing bathrooms

54734 In an existing bathroom it may not be possible to obtain an adequate ceiling fixing for the hoist or eyebolt. A possible solution is to span a length of galvanized barrel across the bathroom, see 2607.

5474 Location of bath controls

54740 The customary position for bath controls is at the foot end of the bath. Although, as discussed below, alternative positions may be preferred the location of controls is not always of critical significance; where a standard bath is installed, repositioning is not advocated unless a specific requirement is established.

Family housing

54741 In family housing it may be expected that a severely disabled person will rely on assistance for the preparation and use of the bath, indicating that it is more important that controls are easily accessible to an assistant standing outside the bath than that they are within comfortable reach of a disabled person seated in the bath. On the other hand this cannot be taken for granted, and since there are obvious hazards if a person seated in the bath attempts to use controls which cannot be easily reached or manipulated, the more important criterion is that they can be reached from within the bath.

54742 Bath controls and water source fittings should be in a position where they can be reached for testing water temperature from inside and outside the bath.

54743 Where taps are at the foot end of the bath, it is preferred that they are positioned in the corner on the access side, as shown in diagram 54.49.

54744 For comment on access by wheelchair users to taps at foot end of bath see 54525 and diagram 54.53.

People with reach limitations

54745 For people with severe reach limitations controls may be placed below the bath rim on the access side at approx 0·800 from the head end (diagram 54.75). This location is recommended where economics permit. For technical reasons it may be more practicable to place the controls nearer the foot end. Controls must not project so as to cause a hazard.

54746 Alternatively, controls may be placed on the wall surface over the bath. A suggested position is approx 0·300 above the rim of the bath at approx 0·600 from the head end (diagram 54.75). This location is not suitable for people with arm impairments reaching across the bath, but where a platform is provided people without reach limitations can comfortably manage such controls from outside the bath, from the platform and from inside the bath.

Water source

54747 The water source should be at the foot end of the bath. A nozzle projecting from the side wall may be a hazard to a person entering or leaving the bath.

Institutions

54748 Baths in institutions should be specified in the expectation that disabled people who can bath independently will do so. It is therefore important that controls are, so far as is practicable, usable by a person seated in the bath.

54749 Controls which can only be key-operated ought not to be specified. The intention of these devices is that potentially hazardous controls will be operated only by an attendant, preventing any risk to the handicapped bather. While on safety grounds this may seem reasonable it denies to handicapped people the opportunity to act responsibly for themselves.

5475 Specification of bath controls

54750 In general screw-down tap fittings are satisfactory for baths. For some disabled users lever action fittings may be preferred but it is not essential that they are fixed initially. For baths the specification of tap fittings is not usually so critical as for basins or sinks, which are more often used independently. In the case of the bath there may be someone else to assist; if there is not the disabled person is not likely to be so handicapped as to need special tap fittings.

54.80 Portable seat fitting inside bath

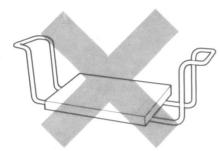

54.81 Suspended bath seat

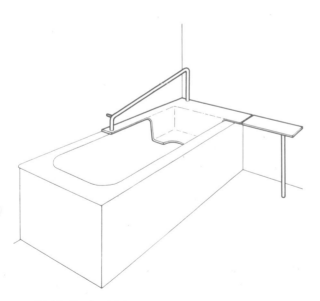

54.82 Bath aid fitting over standard bath

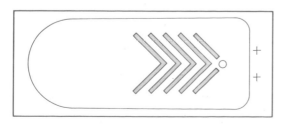

54.83 Adhesive strips to bath bottom (1:25)

Supplementary valves

54751 Where alterations need to be made to existing bath fittings it may be possible to install supplementary valves to draw-off pipes in positions more convenient to the disabled user.
These valves would not replace existing valves, which would normally remain in the open position. For illustration see diagram 41.8.

54752 Bath taps may be electrically remote controlled. Where valves are electrically controlled, switch operation in bathrooms is not generally permitted by electricity authorities in Britain, although waivers may occasionally be obtained in the case of alterations to homes of disabled people. For notes on electric valves see 418.

5476 Baths: Equipment, aids

54760 A soap holder should be built into the side wall of the bath, not further than 0·700 from the head end.

Portable bath seats

54761 For handicapped people not able to transfer directly to or from the bath bottom a portable seat may be used.
Because handicapped people tend to let themselves down heavily the seat must be secure and strong. A seat which stands on the bottom, for example as shown in diagram 54.80, or is supported by the side of the bath is preferred to a seat suspended from the bath rim as shown in diagram 54.81.

Detachable bath bench

54762 Where there is insufficient room to build in a platform at the head of the bath, for example to existing baths, a detachable bath bench is a useful aid. A bath bench overlapping the side of the bath by approx 0·500 is suggested.

54763 The bath aid developed by the Loughborough Institute for Consumer Ergonomics (diagram 54.82) can be fitted over most standard baths.
Similar aids may be made up by a carpenter to suit a particular person.

Self-closing waste plug

54764 The bath plug may be balanced by a counterweight attached to a length of chain, opened and closed by a light pull.
This can be useful to people with reach limitations, as are pop-up wastes controlled at high level.

Non-slip strips

54765 Self-adhesive plastic strips may be placed on the bottom of the bath to give a non-slip surface. These strips should be placed in the zone where a firm foot grip is needed for pushing up (diagram 54.83). They ought not to be fixed at the head end where they may be abrasive on the skin of the buttocks. Cost notes: 90344.

548 Showers

5480 Shower versus bath

54800 It is sometimes supposed by non-disabled people that people who are disabled find it easier to use a shower for washing rather than a conventional bath. As a generalization this is not valid and there is no evidence in Britain to support it.

Disadvantages of shower

54801 It is often as difficult to transfer from a wheelchair on to a shower seat or bench as it is to transfer into a bath, and having transferred it is invariably less convenient.

For paraplegics and others affected by loss of sensation a slatted board seat is hazardous; with the upholstered covering which is needed to prevent skin damage it is soggy and unpleasant to sit on. For a person with poor balance a shower seat is precarious and it may be necessary to hold firmly to a support rail while washing, making it impossible to do body scrubbing simultaneously, let alone direct the shower spray. For people who are unstable, including by definition most wheelchair users, the bath with its solid sides affords security, making it easier for the disabled person to manage the business of washing himself.

Evidence on use of showers

54802 In the survey undertaken by the Department of the Environment of disabled people in purpose-designed accommodation the evidence was that baths were more popular than showers; of the 19 per cent of people with showers fewer than half actually used them[22]. The English cultural tradition of preferring to wash in a bath rather than under a shower is solidly entrenched, and it is no doubt as prevalent among disabled people as it is among those who are not.

54803 In the Norwich sample of 233 people living in private housing there was no one who used a shower for washing[23]. People were asked whether, given convenient provision, they would prefer a bath or shower; in many cases the question was hypothetical since it was a matter for conjecture whether any kind of facility would be manageable. Of those from the subsample of 155 identified as needing wheelchair housing, 77 expressed a preference for a bath, against 6 preferring a shower.

54804 A study of the prototype sheltered housing scheme for old people at Stevenage, where showers were installed as an alternative to baths, reported that elderly people were commonly reluctant to attempt to use the shower[24].

[22] Bib 93122.
[23] Bib 93230. The Canterbury survey (Bib 93221, p6) confirms the disinclination of handicapped people to use showers.
[24] Bib 93631, para 299.

Cost considerations

54805 Because of the need for a thermostatic valve and the requirements of water authorities regarding the equalization of hot and cold water pressures, a shower installation for a disabled person in Britain will invariably be considerably more expensive than a bath.

5481 Shower compartments: Wheelchair access

54810 Where a shower compartment is planned for use by a handicapped person seated in a portable chair, for example similar to that shown in diagram 54.28, it is desirable that there is no plinth, kerb or similar obstacle to wheelchair access.

To prevent water flooding out of the compartment the preferred practice is that there is an enclosing dampproof membrane not less than about 0·060 high. For wheelchair use this poses a technical problem which is not easily resolvable. Where the shower is in a bathroom it is important to prevent water seeping below the side panel of the bath, and an integrated dampproof upstand is therefore required. This may cause problems regarding access to services behind the bath panel.

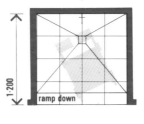

1·200

ramp down

1·200

54.84 Shower compartment for wheelchair access (1:50)

0·150

0·040

54.85 Ramp to shower compartment (1:5)

Controlling water spread

54811 For wheelchair use the suggested provision is that the floor of the shower area is set about 0·040 below the adjoining floor, with a shallow ramp as shown in diagram 54.85. Inside the shower area the floor should be laid to fall to a gully.

Where a shower space is incorporated in a bathroom or wc compartment a ramp at the entrance will impede wheelchair manoeuvre for other purposes, and on balance a floor laid to a gentle fall is preferred, despite the risk of flooding.

54812 A continuous grating over a channel at the edge of the shower area is not recommended.
Apart from collecting dirt, gratings can easily be dislodged, causing a hazard to ambulant disabled people. They may also interfere with the movement of wheelchair wheels.

Shower area
54813 The minimum dimensions of a shower area or compartment planned for chair access should be 1·200 × 1·200 (diagram 54.84). Where space permits, an area 1·500 × 1·500 is preferred.
For cost notes on proprietary shower tray for wheelchair users see 90350.

Showers in bathrooms
54814 Where there is a floor gully in the bathroom so that a shower can be used, for example as shown in diagrams 54.57, 54.59, 54.60 and 54.62, the floor should be laid to a fall of not more than 1:20.
To prevent water flooding out through the door the preferred gully position is on the far wall, as shown in diagram 54.59.

Shower/wc compartments
54815 Because of the problems of providing a shower in the bathroom it may be preferred in family housing to install the shower in the wc compartment separate from the bathroom.

54816 The minimum area of the compartment should be 1·700 × 1·600, with a preferred area of 1·900 × 1·700 (diagram 54.86).
The door should preferably be as shown in diagram 54.86, but it may be on the wall opposite the basin if required. The floor should be laid to a consistent gentle fall.

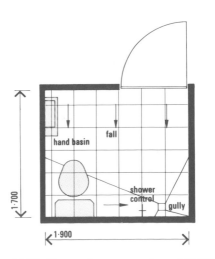

54.86 Shower/wc compartment (1:50)

54817 Some disabled people can conveniently take a shower seated on the wc.
In this case a portable shower spray on a flexible hose will be used, with control on the spray rose.

Dressing space
54818 In private housing where the shower space is planned for use with a portable shower chair, the normal practice will be that the disabled person dresses and undresses in the bedroom. It is not therefore essential to incorporate dressing space adjacent to the shower area.

54819 For an example of a changing cubicle containing shower and wc see diagram 73.1.

5482 Shower compartments not planned for wheelchair access

54820 A shower compartment not designed for direct wheelchair access may have a low kerb to contain water spillage.
A kerb approx 0·060 high is suggested (diagram 54.90); a kerb higher than this is likely to obstruct the swing of wheelchair footrests.

54821 The floor inside the compartment should be at the same level as the floor outside.
This is to minimize hazards to ambulant people with poor balance.

Floor finishes
54822 The floor surface inside the shower compartment should be impervious and slip-resistant.
This is more feasible than for the bath, where the tactile qualities of the surface need to be considered relative to sensitive parts of the body.

5483 Shower compartments: Planning

54830 For normal ambulant people a typical shower compartment is 0·900 × 0·900 (diagram 54.87). The preferred minimum size is 1·050 deep (in the direction of the shower stream) × 0·900 wide.
It is not possible to bend over comfortably in a compartment only 0·900 deep, or to move out of the shower stream while washing. Kira advises dimensions of 3ft 6in (1·070) × 3ft 0in (0·915)[25].

Planning for seated use of shower
54831 The examples shown in diagrams 54.88, 54.89 and 54.90 are for ambulant disabled people, or for users with wheelchairs who transfer across to the shower seat. The normal practice is that the wheelchair is pushed out into the dressing area while a shower is being taken.

54832 A shower compartment for disabled users should have a bench seat, with the dimension across the compartment minimum 1·050 (diagrams 54.88, 54.89). The width of 1·050 allows ambulant people to bend over when using the compartment, and to support the feet on the bench while washing.

[25] Bib 93951, p45.

54833 Wheelchair transfer is facilitated where the bench is on the approach side, as in diagram 54.88, rather than on the wall side, as in diagram 54.89.

54834 A curtain which can be easily handled should be provided to the unenclosed side of the compartment.

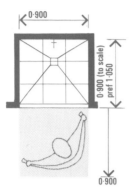

54.87 Shower compartment and dressing space for ambulant people (1:50)

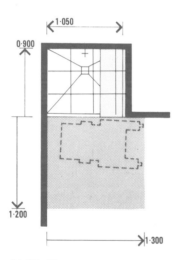

54.88 Shower compartment with bench seat on approach side, showing wheelchair utilization space (1:50)

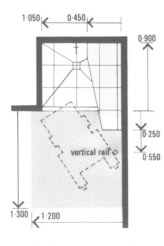

54.89 Shower compartment with bench seat on non-approach side (1:50)

Depth of compartment

54835 For disabled users in general the preferred depth of a shower compartment is 1·100 (diagram 54.90), to give ambulant disabled people room to move out of the shower stream while washing.
A depth of 0·900 (diagrams 54.88, 54.89) is more manageable by people not easily able to push across the seat, and may be preferred where planning is specifically for non-ambulant people.

Dressing space

54836 For wheelchair users the dressing space outside the compartment should be minimum 1·300 × 1·200 (diagrams 54.88, 54.89).
Although dressing may be done elsewhere (54818) a space approximately 1·300 × 1·200 will be needed for wheelchair approach.

5484   Shower seat

54840 The suggested height of the shower seat is 0·400 above the level of the floor outside the compartment.
Although this will normally be lower than the wheelchair seat, and will therefore make transfer more awkward, a seat higher than 0·400 will make it difficult for short people to place their feet on the ground and bend over to wash. A further factor is that the floor inside the compartment may be lower than outside, making the actual seat height more than 0·400.

54841 Where provision is made for a specific disabled person the fixing of the shower seat may be deferred until the optimum height is determined.

Planning of shower seat

54842 The seat should be placed on a side wall rather than on the rear wall, allowing for transfer by wheelchair users.

54843 Where, as in diagram 54.89, the seat is not on the approach side, it may with advantage be extended approximately 0·250 outside the compartment.

54844 The suggested depth (front to back) of the seat is 0·350 (diagram 54.90c).
To cater for varying requirements the seat may be splayed on plan, as shown in diagram 54.89.

Seat draining

54845 The seat should be self-draining.
Slatted board seats are uncomfortable for many handicapped people and the use of an air cushion may be assumed.

Seat hinge

54846 In small compartments the seat should be hinged so that it can be folded against the wall when not in use (diagram 54.90a).

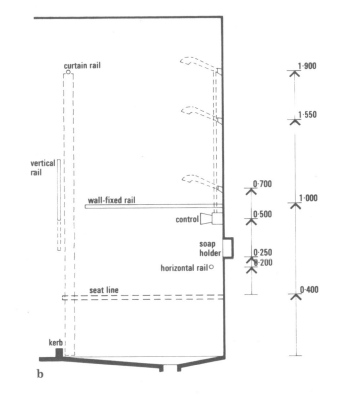

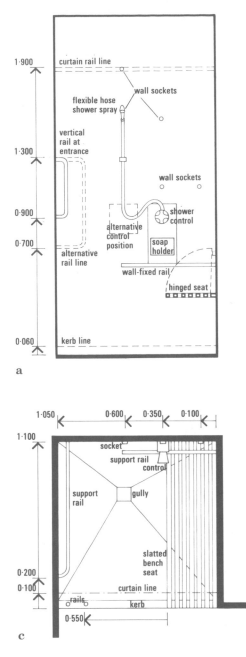

54.90 Shower compartment with bench seat (1:25)

5485 Shower compartments: Support rails

Vertical rails

54850 A vertical rail should be fixed at the entrance to the compartment on the wall opposite the shower seat, extending from 0·900 to 1·300 above floor level (diagram 54.90a).

54851 To allow the rail to be used by a person pulling up from the shower seat the dimension on plan between seat and rail should not be more than 0·550, as shown in diagram 54.90c.

54852 Where the wall behind the seat continues, as shown in diagram 54.89, a vertical rail may be fixed at approximately 0·300 from the edge of the seat.

54853 Additional vertical rails should be fixed when individual requirements are determined.

Horizontal rails

54854 A horizontal rail may be fixed to the rear wall over the shower seat, at approximately 0·200 above seat level (diagram 54.90b).
This is for ambulant people to push up to a standing position, and for non-ambulant people to pull across the seat when transferring from the wheelchair.

54855 For ambulant disabled people a horizontal rail should be fixed to the side wall opposite the seat, at approximately 1·000 above floor level (diagram 54.90b).

Apart from being an aid for balancing while washing, this rail can be valuable if the user has to move out of the shower stream in the event of a sudden temperature change.

54856 A similar horizontal rail may be fixed above the back of the seat, but will need to be at a height where it does not inconvenience seated users.

5486 Shower fittings: General considerations

54860 The temperature of the shower stream must be thermostatically controlled. It is important, even with the most sophisticated thermostat devices, that controls are easily accessible and operable.

Instantaneous shower units
54861 Where for reasons of expense a thermostatically controlled valve is not installed, a possible alternative is an electrically heated shower unit served direct from the cold water main.

54862 For the unit shown in diagram 54.91 the incoming water supply is plumbed directly into the inlet pipe located inside the casing. Control valves are regulated by concentric hand controls, enabling the water temperature to be adjusted as required. A hand spray is supplied with 1·220 length of flexible hose. Cost notes: 90351.

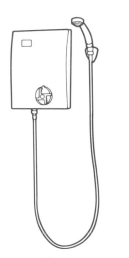

54.91 Instantaneous shower unit

54863 For instantaneous shower units a 30amp electrical circuit is normally required, with operation by ceiling pull switch.

54864 *Shower spray*
A portable shower spray attached to a flexible hose is recommended.

54865 Wall sockets or a rise and fall fitting should be provided so that the shower spray can be fixed in different positions. The spray should be detachable to allow for hand control.

54866 The shower spray should be controllable by means of a diverter mechanism on the handset.
It is important for disabled people to be able to protect themselves against misdirection of spray.

Storage shelf
54867 A shelf, preferably recessed, should be provided for soap, brushes etc at approximately 0·650 above floor level and within reach of a person on the seat (diagram 54.90b).

5487 Shower compartment controls

54870 The control to the main shower stream should be positioned where it can be comfortably reached by a standing or seated person. A height approximately 0·900 above floor level is suggested.
The control shown in diagram 54.90b is on the same wall as the spray. This is normal practice, but ideally the control should be elsewhere to avoid reaching across the shower stream to handle it.

Wall sockets
54871 Where wall sockets are installed suggested fixing heights to serve seated disabled people are 0·700 above the shower seat and 1·550 above floor level (diagram 54.90b).

54872 The fixing of these sockets is inexpensive; where they are installed they should be provided generously.

Ambulant people
54873 Where the shower spray is fixed the preferred level is approximately 1·900 above floor level (diagram 54.90b).
Where the spray fitting can be adjusted vertically the range should be from approximately 1·500 to 1·900 above floor level.

5488 Shower fittings with baths

54880 A shower incorporated with the bath is suitable for disabled people only where there is a floor gully for water falling outside the bath.
The only way that a shower can be used satisfactorily inside a bath is by having the shower stream directed centrally along the length of the bath, with the user standing at the foot end. Even here, unless a shower curtain is installed to contain spray within the bath, some water spillage is inevitable, and the problems of waterproofing the floor described in 54810 will occur. With the shower spray in any other position there will always be water spillage outside the bath. Since for most disabled people standing in the bath will, if manageable, be extremely hazardous, it is necessary that the bathroom floor is waterproof,

with a gully to collect overflowing water (diagram 54.92); the recommendations which follow assume this is done.

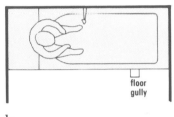

a

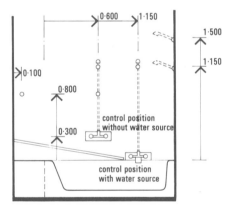

b

54.92 Shower to side wall over bath with platform (1:50)

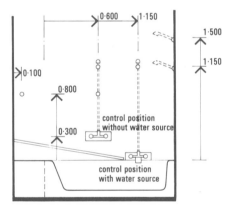

54.93 Location of shower spray sockets over bath (1:50)

54881 Some disabled people who prefer a shower will be catered for satisfactorily only by having a shower compartment allowing chair access or a compartment with a bench seat.

Seat for bath shower

54882 For disabled people not able to stand in the bath the only convenient showering position is seated on a platform at the head end, or on a portable bath seat placed across the bath.
In this event the shower spray in the conventional fixed position at the foot end will be unsuitable, necessitating fixing points on the side wall over the bath. A shower stream directed at right angles over a bath of standard width will spray over and outside the bath, and will be unsuitable for washing under.

54883 An adjustable rose on the side wall is suggested so that the shower stream can be angled obliquely, as shown in diagram 54.92.

Controls

54884 A hand spray attached to a flexible hose with control on the spray arm is recommended.
This facility is also useful for cleaning the bath.

54885 A mixing valve at 0·300 above the bath rim at 0·600 from the head end of the bath is preferred where there is a platform at the head end and where the water source is separate (diagram 54.93).
This allows the user to operate controls when standing or seated in the bath, or seated on the platform.

54886 A mixing valve above the bath rim at 1·150 from the head end is suggested where the water source for the bath is combined with the mixing valve (diagram 54.93).
There is no convenient place where the combined unit can be placed without conflicting with the side support rail. This means that the controls will be beyond the reach of a person seated on the platform, and there is no advantage over the conventional control position at the foot end of the bath. For disabled users the only satisfactory solution is therefore that the water source is separate from the mixing valve.

Sockets for shower spray

54887 For a person seated on the platform the suggested position for a wall socket is at 0·800 above the bath rim at 0·600 from the head of the bath (diagram 54.93). For back washing an additional socket may be fixed on the side wall at 0·100 from the corner.

54888 To give alternative fixing positions for the spray the provision of more than two sockets is recommended.

54889 For a person standing in the bath suggested wall socket positions are at 1·150 and 1·500 above the bath rim.

5489   Shower provision: Handicapped children

54890 In units for handicapped children, for example special schools, a shower tray may be used in place of a bath. The suggested fixing height is 0·600 above floor level, with a shower tray approximately 0·170 deep.
A portable shower spray attached to a flexible hose should be installed, with drying bench at the same level as the tray rim (diagram 54.94).

54891 The proprietary bath/shower unit shown in diagram 54.95 may be suitable for this purpose. Cost notes: 90352.

549 Domestic bathrooms: Fixtures and fittings

5490 Bidets

54900 A bidet is a valuable facility for disabled people affected by haemorrhoids or who have difficulty cleansing the perineal region.
The use of a combined bidet/wc fixture may be considered, see 5423.

54901 The conventional bidet is impossible for many disabled people to use.
It can be awkward to sit on, and it is also difficult to transfer to or from a wheelchair.

Wheelchair users

54902 Because of differing means of wheelchair transfer and the various aids which may be used, it is not possible to make general recommendations on the planning of the bidet for wheelchair users.
The facility is not incorporated in public authority housing in Britain; where it is installed it will be to suit a particular user, and it can be established in advance whether transfer will be lateral or frontal, and how much clear space is needed in front of the fixture.

54903 The suggested height from floor to bidet rim is 0·400 (diagram 54.96a).
Standard bidets have a height in the range 0·320–0·400. For wheelchair users the preferred height might be assumed to be as for wcs, ie 0·475. This will however involve raising the base, which for technical reasons may be complicated, and will make the fixture physiologically unsuitable for other users. It will also probably happen that any wheelchair user able to transfer to use a bidet at a height of 0·475 will be able to manage also with a height of 0·400.

Planning of bidet in freestanding position

54904 For some users the bidet needs to be in a freestanding position, as shown in diagram 54.96b. The normal arrangement is that the rear edge of the bidet abuts the wall, with the user sitting astride the fixture facing the wall. For wheelchair users the problem is that convenient lateral transfer from the chair seat is impossible, and clear space behind the fixture is required.

54905 The clear dimension between the rear face of the fixture and the adjacent wall surface should be 0·400 (diagram 54.96b).
This is desirable also for ambulant people with lower limb impairments to give adequate space when sitting down or regaining a standing position. A technical complication will be that services need to run below the floor instead of being drawn through the adjoining wall or running along it.

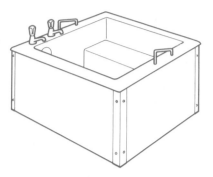

54.94 Shower tray for bathing handicapped children (1:50)

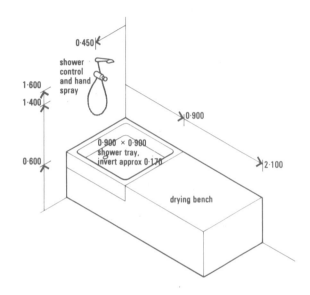

54.95 Bath/shower unit for handicapped children

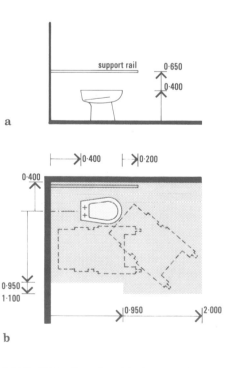

54.96 Bidet for wheelchair users (1:50)

54906 To serve all contingencies a large utilization space is necessary, as shown in diagram 54.96b.
One side only of the bidet should be clear for wheelchair manoeuvre.

Support rails
54907 A horizontal support rail should be fixed to the unexposed side of the fixture, as shown in diagram 54.96b.
For secure fixing of this rail the bidet may be placed parallel with a side wall; the dimension from centre line of the fixture to the side wall ought not to be less than 0·400 to allow for satisfactory use.

54908 A vertical rail may be fixed to the wall in front of the fixture for pulling up to a standing position. The position on plan of this rail will depend on individual requirements.

54.97 Maternity bidet
Maternity unit
54909 For some disabled people a maternity bidet may be more convenient to use than a standard fixture. The proprietary unit shown in diagram 54·97 is designed to give more support and seating area than a conventional bidet. The user sits with his back to the wall. Plumbing is concealed in the pedestal. Cost notes: 90360.

5491 Towel rails

54910 Heated towel rails should be suitably placed to minimize the danger of burns to people with sensory impairments.

54911 Towel rails should not be positioned where disabled people might be encouraged to use them for support.

54912 Towel rails ought not to project so as to cause a hazard.

5492 Medicine cupboards

54920 Medicine cupboards should where practicable be within comfortable reach of disabled users, and should be lockable in homes where there may be young children.

54921 For ambulant disabled people the preferred maximum height for medicine cupboard shelves is 1·550 above floor level, and for chairbound people 1·250.

54922 Narrow shelves for the storage of articles in single rows are recommended.

55 Laundries

550 Communal laundry rooms

5500 In grouped housing schemes for elderly handicapped people, and in residential homes where residents are encouraged to do some or all of their own clothes washing, the laundry room should be located where it can be conveniently reached from residents' flats or bed-sitting rooms.

5501 Generous circulation space should be provided, with room for two or three people in wheelchairs.

5502 In grouped housing schemes it is preferable for social reasons to have one large laundry room rather than two small ones.

5503 According to circumstances, the following provisions may be incorporated:
1. Laundry sink with double draining board.
2. Shelves 0·600 deep for laundry baskets and stacked clothing.
3. Ironing board with two electric sockets at approximately 1·040 above floor level.
4. Light industrial type laundry equipment, comprising hydro-extractor, tumbler dryer and washing machine.
5. Drying racks.
6. Extractor fan.
7. Bench seats.

551 Clothes washing: Private housing

5510 In private housing for disabled people it is desirable that a separate laundry/utility room is provided.

5511 In housing for disabled people there are three reasons why it may be preferred that clothes washing is not carried out in the kitchen:
1. The kitchen sink will be comparatively shallow, and not therefore suitable for soaking dirty clothes.
2. The kitchen working area will need to be economically planned, meaning that washing equipment is better kept out of the kitchen.
3. It is important that kitchen floor surface does not become wet or slippery.

Public authority housing

5512 In public authority housing in Britain designed to minimum space standards a separate laundry/utility room is not normally incorporated. Space is provided in the kitchen for a clothes washing machine.

552 Laundry sinks

5520 There is no single fixing height for a laundry sink which can be expected to cater well for all disabled people. Where possible fixing should be deferred until individual requirements are known.

5521 In wheelchair housing where it is necessary to fix the sink in advance, the suggested heights above floor level are 0·580 to the sink invert and 0·780 to the sink rim (diagram 55.1).

5522 It may not be practicable to provide knee access below laundry sinks; planning may allow for lateral approach rather than frontal approach.

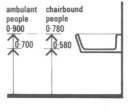

55.1 Laundry sinks

5523 For ambulant users suggested fixing heights are 0·700 to the sink invert and 0·900 to the rim (diagram 55.1).

553 Washing machines and dryers

5530 A combined washing and drying machine is recommended, to minimize the need to handle wet and heavy clothes.

5531 For ambulant people it is easier to feed wet clothes into a top loaded machine. For wheelchair users a front loaded machine may be preferred. As a rule it will not be critical for disabled users whether machines are top or front loaded.

5532 It is desirable that fixed plumbing connections are made for washing machines, rather than relying on the emptying of machines by means of flexible hosing discharging into a sink.

554 Heated cabinets, clothes dryers

5540 Racks or shelves in heated cabinets to be comfortably reached ought to be not higher than 1·600 for ambulant handicapped people, and 1·250 for chairbound people.

5541 The switches to electrically heated cabinets must be conveniently located.

Open air clothes drying

5542 An adjustable-height rotary clothes dryer may be used for drying clothes outside. The centre post turns in a socket in the ground, and clothes can be pegged out from one position without walking or stretching. Cost notes: 90380.

5543 Clothes lines to be within comfortable reach should be adjustable down to 1·400 above ground level.

555   Ironing

5550   A securely fixed drop down ironing board is
recommended.
Portable boards are often unsteady and difficult to
erect.

5551   The height of the board should be adjustable.
Suitable working heights range from 0·600 to 0·820.

5552   Where the height of the board is fixed suggested
work heights are 0·800 for ambulant people, and
0·650 for wheelchair users (diagram 55.2).

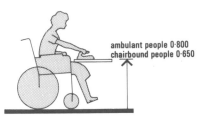

ambulant people 0·800
chairbound people 0·650

55.2   Ironing boards

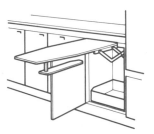

55.3   Hinged and folding ironing board

5553   A hinged and folding ironing board may be built
into a kitchen unit (diagram 55.3).

56 Storage

560 Storage: General considerations

5600 Recommendations for general storage provision in wheelchair housing are made in 837, for kitchen storage in wheelchair housing in 8345, and for kitchen storage generally in 513.

5601 In housing for disabled people overall storage provision should be to standards equal to that for general purpose housing.
Standards for general storage space in public authority housing are incorporated in table 81.3.

561 Wheelchair access to storage

5610 In housing for disabled people storage accommodation used regularly ought not to be in corner positions which are awkward to reach. For chairbound people, fixed cupboards and drawers placed closer than 0·300 to a corner are not easily accessible (diagram 56.1).

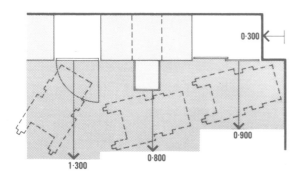

56.1 Wheelchair access to storage space (1:50)

5611 Adequate space for circulation and manoeuvre should be provided in front of storage accommodation.

5612 To give adequate room for a chairbound person to approach frontally and manoeuvre, the minimum dimension between a cupboard face and any opposing obstruction should be 1·300 (diagram 56.1).

5613 Where pull-out drawers are installed the dimension between the face of the extended drawer and any opposing obstruction should be not less than 0·800 (diagram 56.1).

5614 Where cupboards have sliding doors or open shelves, the width from the cupboard face to any opposing obstruction should be not less than 0·900 (diagram 56.1).

562 Wheelchair storage

5620 Storage space where allocated for a wheelchair should be not less than 1·200 × 0·700 wide. For notes on wheelchair storage in wheelchair housing see 8370.

5621 When folded a standard DHSS model 8L wheelchair occupies a space 0·935 high × 1·080 long × 0·270 wide. A model 9L car chair occupies a space 0·970 high × 1·030 long × 0·270 wide. A model 13 attendant-propelled chair occupies a space 1·090 high × 0·700 long × 0·410 wide.

563 Clothes storage

5630 In housing for disabled people clothes storage provision should be not less than that provided for general purpose housing.
In public authority housing (8049) the recommended space is 0·600 hanging space per person, with cupboards not less than 0·550 deep internally.

5631 The space below clothes rails ought to be unobstructed to floor level.
Because of the limited reaching and stooping ability of disabled people drawers or shelves should not be provided at low level below hanging clothes.

Clothes rails
5632 For the majority of clothing articles (jackets, blouses, skirts, shirts etc) a rail at 1·050 above floor level is satisfactory.

5633 For longer articles (overcoats, long trousers, dresses etc) a rail at 1·400 is suitable, or 1·500 to allow for ankle-length dresses.

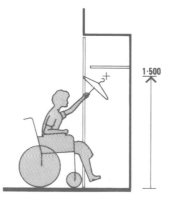

56.2 Clothes rails (1:50)

5634 For wheelchair users rails at approximately 1·500 above floor level may be manageable with the aid of long handle coat hangers (diagram 56.2).

564   Drawers

5640   Drawers should be designed to pull out easily,
without the need to use both hands simultaneously.

5641   For elderly and ambulant disabled people, drawers
to be comfortably reached should not be higher
than 1·300 above floor level.

5642   For chairbound people, drawers to be comfortably
reached should not be higher than 1·000 above floor
level.

565   Cleaning cupboard

5650   In housing for disabled people the floor to any
cleaning cupboard should be unobstructed and
flush with the adjacent floor surface.
This obviates the need to lift the vacuum cleaner
and other heavy equipment in and out.

5651   Shelves and drawers should be easily accessible.
Sliding racks are suggested.

566   Linen cupboard

5660   In housing for disabled people, the linen cupboard
may allow for storage of articles in single rows, in
which case shelves may be not more than 0·400
deep.

5661   Where space is restricted a deeper cupboard may be
necessary, for example a standard 0·600 unit.

5662   To facilitate the movement of stored clothing,
slatted boards inside the linen cupboard should run
at right angles to the cupboard door.

57 Garages

570 Garages: General considerations

5700 Where there is a door giving direct access from the garage to the interior of the dwelling, it must be a self-closing fire door and the floor level of the garage must be not less than 0·100 below the floor level of the dwelling to the other side of the door, to comply with regulation E18 of the Building Regulations.

In the case of special wheelchair housing units a relaxation of these regulations may be sought, see 6005. Although the variation in floor level may be dealt with by a ramp rather than a step, the gradient of the ramp may need to be at least 1:12, ie steeper than a chairbound person may be able to manage independently. The only satisfactory solution is for the floors to be at virtually the same level.

DHSS and social services authorities

5701 Until 1972 it was the practice of the Department of Health that invalid tricycles issued by them should be kept under cover, either in a garage available to the client or in a small shed provided by the Department. With the general issue of glass fibre vehicles this practice is discontinued. The only exception is in respect of electrically powered invalid tricycles; where the client does not have suitable storage accommodation the DHSS will supply a shed so that battery charging can be carried out under cover, and will also pay for a concrete base to be laid.

5702 In respect of cars issued by the DHSS (2700) the Department does not provide or pay for garages or hardstandings.

5703 For disabled people with cars or invalid tricycles where kerbside or other parking is difficult, social services departments may, under section 2 of the Chronically Sick and Disabled Persons Act 1970 (8023), provide hardstanding or carry out other structural alterations to permit vehicles to be parked conveniently.

571 Car garages: Dimensional data

5710 Suitable garage dimensions for a disabled person are affected by the size of the car he uses. The recommendations which follow are based on the dimensions of a 'standard design car' and a 'small design car', as described in MHLG Design Bulletin 12[1] and detailed in table 57.1. Dimensions of selected cars in common use are detailed in table 27.2.

In diagrams 57.1–57.6 the car outline is that of a Morris Marina, which at 4·220 × 1·645 is marginally larger than a small design car. In diagrams 57.2 and 57.4–57.6 the outline is superimposed on a tinted area representing the dimensions of a standard design car. For purposes of comparison, the dimensions of a standard design car are approximately those of a Jaguar XJ6 at 4·845 × 1·770 or a Citroen DS at 4·750 × 1·780. In effect therefore, what is called a small design car is a medium size family saloon, and a standard design car is a limousine. While, for financial reasons, it may in practice happen that households with a disabled member tend to have small cars rather than large ones, the design data which follow are based on a standard design car. No contingency space is provided for in the utilization areas recommended.

5711 Suitable garage planning for a disabled person is affected first, by whether he is a car driver; second, by whether he is chairbound, and third, by whether, if he is chairbound, he goes out independently.

5712 Utilization spaces incorporated in the diagrams are as follows:
1. Assisted transfer for wheelchair user to driver's seat or front passenger seat: 1·200.
2. Independent transfer by wheelchair user to driver's seat or front passenger seat: 1·000.
3. Wheelchair manoeuvring space to side of car: 0·900.
4. Wheelchair manoeuvring space at either end of car: 0·900.
5. Circulation space for ambulant disabled person: 0·900.
6. Circulation space to side of car for able-bodied person: 0·400.

5713 Criteria for these spaces are discussed further in the notes which follow.

Table 57.1 Standard and small design cars: Dimensional data

	standard design car	small design car
length	4·750	4·100
width	1·800	1·600
height	1·700	1·500
door opening clearance		
full	0·900	0·900
normal	0·500	0·500
minimum	0·400	0·400
turning circle diameter		
between kerbs	13·000	11·000
between walls	14·000	no evidence

Source: Bib 93980, p4.

[1] Bib 93980.

572 Transfer procedures

5720 The procedure normally used by wheelchair passengers and by independent chairbound drivers is to enter the car through the door for the front passenger.

Independent chairbound drivers

5721 Chairbound car drivers who can manage independently usually transfer from the wheelchair seat on to the passenger seat and then slide across to the driving seat. The backrest of the passenger seat is then tipped forward and the wheelchair, which has been folded up by the driver when seated on the passenger seat, is pulled in behind it on to the floor in front of the rear seat.

This procedure is more easily accomplished where the car has two doors rather than four; such cars have wide doors, and to allow them to open fully a clearance of 1·100 is desirable.

5722 Some wheelchair users who are car drivers transfer direct into the driving seat, following which the chair is left in the garage or placed in the boot of the car by the helper.

Ambulant disabled people

5723 Where space is allowed for wheelchair manoeuvre and transfer, ambulant disabled people using walking aids will be catered for.

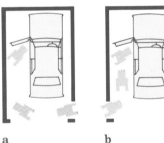

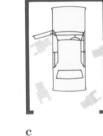

a   b   c

d   e   f

g

57.1   Garage planning: Access for chairbound people (1:200)

573 Garage planning criteria

5730 In wheelchair housing, for reasons discussed in 83202–3, it is essential for drivers using wheelchairs that access from the garage to the dwelling entrance is under cover. For the same reasons it is desirable that chairbound passengers can be transferred into the car without going outside.

Driver and passenger considerations

5731 To accommodate all kinds of disabled drivers or passengers there has to be space in the garage for wheelchair approach to either the offside or the nearside of the car, and space behind or in front of the car for a wheelchair to be manoeuvred from a house door which is on the opposite side of the garage to that where transfer is made to the car.

5732 If provision is made in the garage for a chairbound person who is not the driver to transfer into the car, there needs to be space on the passenger side for assisted transfer, and on the driver's side for the driver to get in and out.

5733 Where the driver is a wheelchair user who transfers independently on the driver's side, or who is helped by an attendant, it is not essential, any more than it is for garages for normal purposes, that space is provided on the passenger side for access.

Access door to dwelling at front of garage

5734 Diagrams 57.1a and b show garage plans where the door giving access to the dwelling is at the front of the garage.

In diagram 57.1a the car is shown positioned with wheelchair access on the passenger side with the dwelling door on the opposite side. Space behind the car is available for wheelchair manoeuvre.

5735 In diagram 57.1b the car is shown with access on the passenger side on the same side as the dwelling door.

In this instance it is not essential that there is space for wheelchair manoeuvre behind the car, and the normal practice will be for the car to be parked just inside the garage door rather than against the rear wall. But since it cannot be assumed that in practice wheelchair access will not be needed on the driver's side the garage plan allows for wheelchair manoeuvre behind the car.

Access door to dwelling at rear of garage

5736 Diagrams 57.1d and e show garage plans where the access door to the dwelling is at the rear of the garage. This arrangement is less satisfactory than that shown in diagrams 57.1a and b. The reason is that when the wheelchair enters the garage it will invariably be propelled in a forward direction, and, unless the length of the garage is extended, there may not be room to turn through 180° so that the chair is facing in the right direction for transfer into the car.

In theory this problem can be resolved by assuming that the car is reversed into the garage instead of being driven in forwards. This is not a realistic proposal; not all disabled (or able-bodied) drivers have the expertise to reverse a car into a garage with precision.

5737 Diagrams 57.1d and 57.1e show alternative positions for a door at the rear of the garage. The preferred location is on the end wall, on the driver's side of the car as shown in diagram 57.1d.
In practice it may happen that wheelchair access to the passenger side is required, in which case the wheelchair will need to be turned in front of the car just inside the door, as shown in diagram 57.1e. To facilitate turning, a 1·000 doorset is preferred to a 0·900 doorset.

Dwelling access door at centre of garage

5738 There are complications where the door to the dwelling is located centrally on one of the side walls. Wheelchair transfer may be required either on the passenger's side or the driver's side, ie not necessarily on the side of the dwelling access door. In this case wheelchair manoeuvring space will be needed on both sides of the car and behind it, as shown in diagram 57.1c.
The consequence will be that the width of the garage is exaggerated. Because of this it is not recommended that the access door is placed centrally. Where it is done it is suggested, in view of the limited space that may be available beside the car for wheelchair manoeuvre, that the doorset width is 1·000 to facilitate wheelchair turning.

Preferred garage dimensions

5739 Although it cannot be guaranteed to cater for all contingencies, a garage having internal dimensions 5·700 × 3·400 (as shown in diagrams 57.1a, b, d and e) is suggested where comfortable garage provision is required for disabled users.
The preferred layout is as shown in diagram 57.2.

574   Garage planning: Economic considerations

5740 The criteria discussed in 573 have significant space implications. Whereas a typical garage for normal purposes having dimensions 2·400 × 4·800 has an area of 11·52m², a garage 3·400 × 5·700 has an area of 19·38m², ie an increase of 68 per cent.
In the case of low cost housing it may well be that cash resources would be more effectively deployed than by providing a large garage, and alternatives need to be considered.

5741 The recommended solution (discussed in 579 and elsewhere) is a carport rather than an enclosed garage, but where a garage is required some saving of space may be admissible.

5742 Space can be saved if the garage is planned so that access is only through the garage door, as shown in diagram 57.1f.
In this case manoeuvring space is not required behind or in front of the car. The example shown allows for wheelchair access on either the passenger or driver's side.

5743 To allow for undercover access from the dwelling there will need to be a canopy in front of the garage, extending across the width of the door opening. The incorporation of a canopy will mean that there is probably only a small cost saving by comparison with the example shown in diagram 57.2.

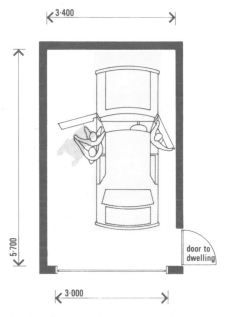

57.2   Garage plan allowing for access to car by chairbound driver or passenger (1:100)

Access one side only

5744 A more economic alternative is to allow for access to one side of the car only, as shown in diagram 57.1g.
Access to both sides of the car, as allowed for in diagram 57.1f, is advantageous only where an able-bodied driver gets into the car after a wheelchair passenger has transferred in.

5745 While the planning provision shown in diagram 57.2 is preferred, the only practicable solution may be to assume passenger transfer outside the garage. The car will be reversed out of the garage, following which the disabled person will be helped in. Similarly, if the disabled person is the driver and transfers with help on the driver's side, his attendant will get into the car after it has been reversed out.

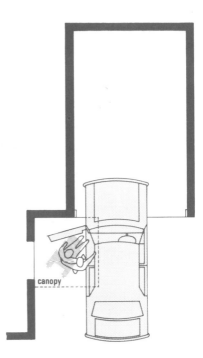

57.3 Garage plan with canopy to dwelling entrance (1:100)

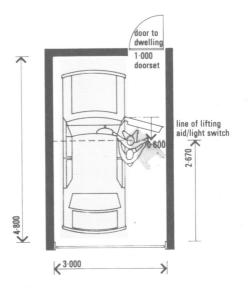

57.4 Garage plan to minimum dimensions allowing for access to car by chairbound person (1:100)

Canopy outside garage

5746 Where planning permits, the provision of a canopy outside the garage door on the passenger side is recommended, as shown in diagram 57.3.
In this case the driver reverses the car part way out of the garage, and then helps the disabled passenger into the car.

575 Garages: Low cost housing

5750 For general purpose public authority housing in Britain enclosed garages are not now normally provided, in line with instructions to local authorities given in Department of the Environment Circular 24/75[2].
Garaging provision for public authority wheelchair housing is discussed in 838.

5751 For low cost wheelchair housing units a garage having internal dimensions 3·000 × 4·800 is suggested, as shown in diagrams 57.1g and 57.4.
This plan arrangement assumes that:
1. Access is possible to one side of the car only, which may be either the driver's or the passenger's side.
2. The normal approach will be through the garage door.

5752 On this plan the clear dimension for transfer is reduced to 1·000.
This will normally be sufficient for independent chairbound drivers, but for drivers needing assistance it may not be adequate. On the other hand, planning assumes a car 1·800 wide, whereas most family cars are approximately 1·600–1·650 wide (table 27.2). It also assumes a clearance on the non-access side of 0·200; in practice most drivers can manoeuvre cars to tighter tolerances, for example 0·100.

5753 Although wheelchair access through the garage door is assumed, it will be helpful if there is an ancillary door at the rear of the garage giving access to the dwelling, as shown in diagram 57.4. Space provision for a standard design car will mean that where the disabled person drives a small car there will be room for a 3 point wheelchair turn inside the rear door. To facilitate turning a 1·000 doorset is suggested.

Double garages

5754 To serve a pair of wheelchair housing units, space can be saved by having a double garage without a party wall, as shown in diagram 57.5.
While the plan arrangement shown in diagram 57.5 does not cater for all possible contingencies, it is most unlikely in practice that adjoining disabled tenants will require more space than is shown. It is more likely that they will in fact be able to cope with less; if this is so the party wall may be installed after completion.

5755 Where a double garage is provided for a single household having a disabled member it may be planned to the dimensions shown in diagram 57.5.

[2]Bib 93717

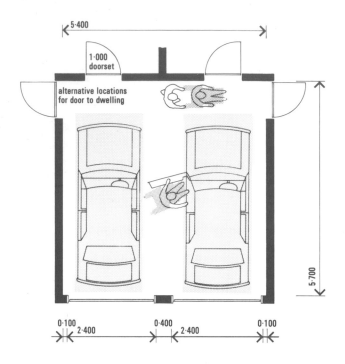

57.5 Double garage serving pair of wheelchair housing units (1:100)

Piers

5756 In low cost housing garages may be of single leaf brick construction. Supporting piers will be outside the prescribed space envelope, but it is desirable to place them so that they do not interfere with the opening of car doors or the positioning of wheelchairs.

576 Garage doors

5760 Where garage doors are manually operated, up and over doors are preferred to sliding or side-hung doors.
For many disabled people, manually operated sliding, folding or side-hung garage doors are difficult to manage.

Up and over doors

5761 Where an up and over door is specified it ought not to project outwards while being opened.
For chairbound people and others with limited mobility it ought not to be necessary to reverse or step back when the door is opened.

5762 Where the door projects in the open position it should be designed to throw settled water clear of the operator when being closed.

5763 A lightweight glass fibre garage door may be preferred to a heavy metal door.

5764 For up and over doors, handles close to ground level should be avoided. A door handle at about 0·750 above ground level is suggested.

Door widths

5765 Where pedestrian access is through the garage door the door should be within a wide structural opening. A width of 3·000 is recommended, as shown in diagrams 57·2 and 57·4.
For wheelchair users it should be possible to manoeuvre round the side of the door when the rear bumper is close to the garage door.

5766 Where the garage is planned so that the car can be driven in to permit wheelchair transfer on either side the opening should be not less than 3·000.

5767 In circumstances where these constraints do not apply the structural opening should be not less than 2·400, as shown in diagram 57·5.

577 Automatic garage door openers

5770 Although automatic garage door openers are a valuable aid, it needs to be recognized that there is rarely a need for them to garages to wheelchair housing units. For comment see 83803.

5771 Garage doors may be controlled by the car driver approaching the garage by one or other of the following means:
1. From a keyed switch on a post accessible to the car driver.
2. By a magnetically operated switch buried in the drive.
3. By an ultrasonic beam.
4. By a trip pad in the drive.
5. By the shining of headlights on a sensitive control incorporated in the door.
6. By breaking a photo electric cell.
7. By radio control.

5772 The issuing of a licence for a radio-controlled garage door opener may be refused by the Post Office in Britain if interference may be caused by other equipment operating on the same frequency, for example in local hospitals.

Control switches

5773 Where switches or push buttons are employed for automatic door operation they should be conveniently accessible to a disabled person in the driving seat of the car. A suggested location is on a post beside the driveway at approximately 1·100 above ground level.
Any controls inside the garage should also be easily accessible.

5774 Where posts with keyed switches are installed on family housing estates materials should be specified which minimize vandalism.
One hazard is that children may make switches unworkable by stuffing chewing gum into the key aperture.

5775 Costs of garage door openers are noted in 90390.

578 Garages: Fixtures, equipment

5780 Where individual requirements can be established in advance, a pull switch for the garage light may be positioned within reach of the driver seated inside the car. A two-way switch permitting control from inside the house is recommended.

5781 An external light illuminating the garage door having a two-way switch controlled from inside the garage and inside the house is advantageous.

5782 For disabled drivers with electric vehicles a socket outlet should be installed in the garage for battery charging.

Lifting aids

5783 For some chairbound disabled people a lifting aid fitted inside the garage may be helpful, such as a stirrup grip and chain suspended from a ceiling eye bolt or from a galvanized barrel fixed across the garage.
This aid will not be required to the same extent as, for example, comparable lifting aids for baths and wcs. The reason is that the handicapped person will also need to be able to transfer in and out of the car in places where no overhead aid is available; an alternative portable aid is likely to be preferred, such as an attendant-operated ratchet hoist fitted across the roof of the car.

5784 Where a fixed aid is installed it should cater for chairbound people who transfer into the car either on the driver's side or passenger's side. A galvanized barrel fixed across the garage may be a suitable solution, see 2607.

Positioning of aids and switches

5785 Barrels, ceiling eye bolts and light pull switches, where required, should be positioned approximately 0·600 behind the hinge to the front door of the car.
For a standard design car the dimension to this point from the rear bumper is approximately 2·670 (diagram 57.4).

579 Carports

5790 In public authority housing for disabled people carports are generally preferred to enclosed garages. For discussion see 8381.

5791 For chairbound people using carports the likelihood is that transfer into the car will be on the passenger side, and planning should be on this basis.
Evidence suggests that of disabled people potentially in need of wheelchair housing about 90 per cent are not car drivers, see 83802.

Carport dimensions

5792 The preferred undercover area of the carport is 5·700 × 3·400, minimum 5·400 × 3·000 (diagram 57.6).

5793 Where a long side is exposed, as in diagram 57.6, the width of the cover may be 3·000. Where there are walls to both sides the width should be not less than 3·400.

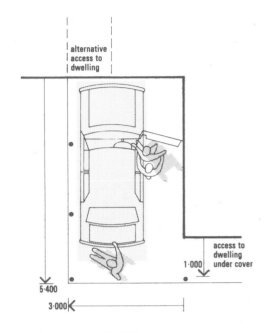

57.6   Carport (1:100)

Space for wheelchair transfer

5794 According to circumstances, the normal routine will be for the wheelchair user to transfer on the exposed side of the carport, but there should be sufficient space for transfer under cover on the unexposed side, as shown in diagram 57.6.

5795 With a standard design car and planning as shown in diagram 57.6 the clear dimension will be approximately 1·000, which is not adequate for assisted wheelchair transfer. It may be assumed that the car is reversed into the carport.

5796 Problems of access to both sides of the car, as discussed with refference to diagram 57.1c, ought not to occur with carports.
Where it is the passenger who is disabled the advantage of the carport is that it allows space for the car to be manoeuvred into a convenient position for assisted transfer.

5797 A carport length 5·400 allows undercover wheelchair access to the car boot of a small design car, as shown in diagram 57.6.
To cater for users of standard design cars the length should be 5.700.

Posts

5798 The clearance at posts etc should be not less than 1·000 (diagram 57.6).

5799 Access from the carport to the dwelling entrance must be under cover. For comment see 83810.

580 Car parking spaces

5800 In car parks used by the general public or in special car parks such as those to employment buildings, provision should be made for disabled drivers and cars carrying disabled passengers.

5801 Special spaces located at the end of a row of parking bays, leaving one side clear for disabled people to get in or out of the vehicle, need not be wider than standard bays for general purposes.

5802 In Britain the standard parking bay is approximately 2·400 wide.

Special parking spaces

5803 To allow for assisted wheelchair users the preferred width of special spaces allocated for disabled drivers is 3·600, minimum 3·200 (diagram 58.1).

5804 To allow for ambulant disabled people the preferred width of parking spaces is 3·000, minimum 2·800 (diagram 58·1).
While manoeuvring space may be tight, a width of 3·000 will in practice cater for independent wheelchair users.

5805 Where adjacent spaces are reserved for disabled drivers, an access area 1·200 wide may be marked on the ground to indicate that cars should be parked to either side (diagram 58.2).
This will allow for access on one side to the driver's door of a car, and on the other to the passenger's door.

Signposting

5806 Car parking spaces for use by disabled people should be suitably signposted, see 653.

5807 To deter non-disabled drivers from using the spaces, the international symbol may be painted on the ground, with the legend 'Disabled drivers' (diagram 58.2).

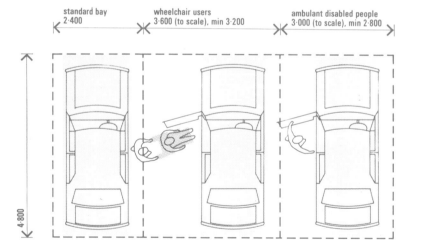

58.1 Car parking spaces (1:100)

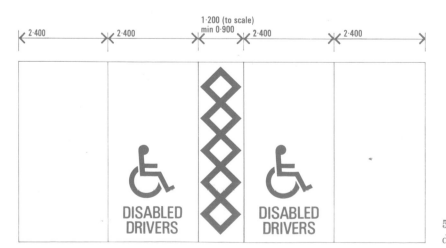

58.2 Parking spaces marked for disabled drivers (1:100)

581 Gardens

5810 Gardens should be accessible and easy to maintain.

Raised flower beds

5811 Raised flower beds are suggested. A height approximately 0·600 above ground level is generally convenient.
A bed width of approximately 1·200 is suggested where there is access from both sides. Where access is from one side only the width should be maximum 0·800.

5812 Raised flower beds may be formed in situ of blocks, bricks or concrete slabs. Alternatively prefabricated beds are available.

Garden paths

5813 To allow for wheelchair users garden paths should be not less than 1·000 wide, preferred width 1·200.

5814 For the majority of disabled people it is desirable that garden paths should have a roughened or corrugated finish, to give a non-slip surface. For chairbound people a relatively smooth finish is preferred.
For a chairbound person who propels his own chair, a roughened finish may impede mobility. On inclined paths the surface should not be so smooth that traction is difficult to obtain.

Sitting-out area

5815 A paved sitting-out area in a sunny and sheltered position having direct access from the house will be appreciated by disabled people.

Maintenance

5816 A waterpipe laid through the garden is suggested. Watering can then be done by pushing a short lightweight length of hose into sockets at strategic points.

5817 Grass banks are difficult for handicapped people to maintain and the alternative of terraced flower beds, which can be tended without stooping, is suggested.

Greenhouses

5818 A greenhouse to be used by a gardener in a wheelchair should be minimum 2·400 long × 1·950 wide. The clearance down the centre should be minimum 0·750 wide and the shelf for plants on each side should be 0·600 wide. The door should give a clear opening width of not less than 0·750. The path outside the door should be not less than 1·350 wide to allow for wheelchair manoeuvre.

Lawn mowing

5819 A suitably protected socket outlet should be provided in an accessible position for lawn mowing. Disabled people who cannot control a manually operated or petrol driven machine may be able to use an electric lawn mower.

582 Balconies

5820 In multi-storey flats which may be used by handicapped people, it is desirable that balconies with suitable access for wheelchairs are provided.

5821 Where allowance has been made for a wheelchair to be turned through 180° the balcony should be not less than 1·500 wide.

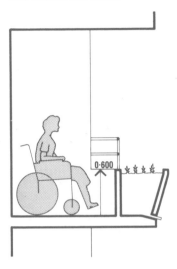

58.3 Balconies (1:50)

5822 To allow for view from the balcony by a person seated in a wheelchair the solid front panel of the balcony ought not to be higher than 0·600 above floor level (diagram 58.3).

5823 A flower box may be built in with the balcony. To allow for tending from a wheelchair the suggested height is 0·600 above floor level (diagram 58.3).

583 Fuel stores

5830 It is not possible to design a solid fuel store from which fuel can be easily withdrawn by a disabled person.
Solid fuel heaters ought only to be installed where a helper or able-bodied member of the family will be available to draw fuel.

5831 Approach from the dwelling to the fuel store must be under cover.

Public buildings:
General

6

600 Statutory building controls: General

6000 Parts 6 and 7 of this book detail the provisions which ought to be made in public buildings if they are to be usable by disabled people.
In this context 'public buildings' means not only buildings which give general services, but also those which disabled people may use for employment, business, transport, health or social services, refreshment, recreation, entertainment, worship, education or cultural activities. For practical reasons, recommendations for accommodation provided in hostels or institutions are also included, with reference to detailed information in previous sections. Virtually all types of building are therefore covered, with the exception of private housing which is examined in part 8.

6001 For the architect designing new buildings or adapting existing ones, the practicability of making suitable arrangements for disabled people may be hazarded by the statutory requirements of building legislation and associated regulations, and in particular those relating to means of escape in case of fire. It is therefore important to understand at the start what positive controls there are which can help achieve building usability for disabled people and, similarly, what controls may have a negative effect.

6002 There are on the English statute book a great many pieces of legislation affecting the construction of buildings and the ways they are used. Many of these statutes are complicated and obscure, and to attempt to detail all those which conceivably have a bearing on the use of buildings by disabled people would be a demanding exercise. Reference is therefore made only to those pieces of legislation which have a particular relevance; to avoid confusion reference is made only to legislation operative in England and Wales.

Statutory authorities
6003 The distinction between building authorities, fire authorities and planning authorities needs to be understood.

1. Building authorities
are responsible for the administration of building regulations under the Public Health Acts and the Health and Safety at Work etc Act; these are both pieces of legislation on which the Department of the Environment advises. Building authorities are generally second-tier local authorities, ie district councils, metropolitan district councils and London borough councils. For the inner London area the building authority is the Greater London Council.

2. Fire authorities
are responsible for the administration of the Fire Precautions Act, on which the Home Office advises. They are generally first-tier authorities, ie county

councils and metropolitan regional councils. For all London boroughs the fire authority is the Greater London Council.

3. Planning authorities
are responsible for the administration of planning legislation, on which the Department of the Environment advises. They are generally second-tier local authorities.

6004 The administration of the Chronically Sick and Disabled Persons Act is the concern of all local authorities. At central government level the Act is the concern of various departments. On section 4, dealing with access to public buildings, local authorities are advised by the Department of the Environment.

Relaxation of Building Regulations
6005 There are occasions when suitable provision for disabled people in public buildings may not always be compatible with the requirements of the national Building Regulations. When this is the case it may be possible to obtain a relaxation of the regulation concerned, provided there is no additional hazard for other building users.

6006 Where there appear to be problems the matter should be discussed at an early stage with the local authority building inspector. In cases of doubt informal advice can be obtained from the Department of the Environment.

6007 Applications for relaxation, in cases where the observance of regulations is considered unreasonable, must be made to the district council on an official form obtainable from the council. In most cases the local authority can itself decide whether or not the relaxation is allowed, but in certain cases, mainly those concerning structural stability and fire precautions in larger buildings, the application has to be referred to the Secretary of State for the Environment. If the applicant is a local authority the application in all cases must be made to the Secretary of State for the Environment.

6008 If the local authority refuses an application which it has power to determine the applicant can appeal to the Secretary of State for the Environment.

601 Access provision: The Chronically Sick Act

6010 The only piece of English legislation dealing specifically with access to public buildings for disabled people is section 4 of the Chronically Sick and Disabled Persons Act 1970. It reads:

'Any person undertaking the provision of any building or premises to which the public are to be admitted, whether on payment or otherwise, shall, in the means of access both to and within the building or premises, and in the parking facilities and sanitary conveniences to be available (if any), make provision, in so far as it is in the circumstances both practicable and reasonable, for the needs of members of the public visiting the building or premises who are disabled.'

6011 The interdepartmental government circular 'The Chronically Sick and Disabled Persons Act', commenting on the implementation of section 4, reads:

'"Provision" is not defined in the Act. In its ordinary meaning it covers not only new construction but also the conversion of existing buildings. Public halls, public libraries, theatres, cinemas and shops are obvious examples of buildings to which the public are to be admitted. The Section places an obligation on anyone undertaking the provision of buildings to which it relates to make provision for the needs of disabled persons in so far as it is in the circumstances both practicable and reasonable to do so. The provision is to be made in relation to both internal and external means of access and to any parking facilities and sanitary conveniences that are to be made available to the public visiting the building. So far as local authorities are concerned, the Section in effect makes it mandatory to do what they were asked in MHLG Circular 71/65 to do on a voluntary basis, and have in many instances been doing already.' [1]

Comment on section 4

6012 As discussed in the commentary (1406) section 4, because of the qualifying clause 'in so far as it is in the circumstances both practicable and reasonable', is legally weak. In the event of any dispute contested in the courts it is most improbable, as demonstrated by the Liverpool cinema precedent (1407), that it would withstand legal scrutiny. Its merit, which ought not to be underestimated, is its political serviceability. Its legislative intention – that buildings are made accessible to disabled people – is explicit, a point which can be used to advantage by individuals and organizations working on behalf of people with disabilities.

CP96

6013 In the United Kingdom the British Standard Code of Practice *Access for the Disabled to Buildings; Part 1: General recommendations* [2], commonly referred to as CP96, is the primary reference for standards of accessibility to buildings. It is cited in the official circular giving advice on the implementation of the Chronically Sick and Disabled Persons Act [3]. It does not itself carry any legal authority, though it could be that, in the event of a dispute over the interpretation of legislation regarding accessibility, its recommendations might be used as a yardstick. Its application and the shortcomings of the 1967 version are discussed in 612.

602   Access provision: Other legislation and regulations

The Public Health Acts

6020 Section 59 of the Public Health Act 1936, as amended by the Public Health Act 1961, covers access to buildings from the point of view of general safety and security. It applies to (1) theatres, halls and similar buildings, (2) restaurants, shops, stores or warehouses to which members of the public are admitted and where more than 20 people are employed, (3) clubs which are subject to the Licensing Acts, (4) schools not exempted from building regulations, and (5) certain churches, chapels and other places of worship. Subsection 59(1) reads:

'Where plans of a building or of an extension of a building are, in accordance with building regulations, deposited with a local authority . . . the authority shall reject the plans unless they show that the building, or, as the case may be, the building as extended, will be provided with such means of ingress and egress and passages or gangways as the authority deem satisfactory, regard being had by them to the purposes for which the building is intended to be, or is, used and the number of persons likely to resort thereto at any one time.'

The Health and Safety at Work etc Act

6021 Section 61 of the Health and Safety at Work etc Act 1974 empowers the Secretary of State for the Environment to make building regulations 'with respect to the design and construction of buildings and the provision of services, fittings and equipment in or in connection with buildings'. The purposes for which regulations may be made include (subsection (2) (a)) 'securing the health, safety, welfare and convenience of persons in or about buildings'.

6022 While the Department of the Environment does not at present (1975) have any immediate plans for introducing regulations relating specifically to access provision for disabled people, there is potential under section 61 for it to do so.

Town and Country Planning Acts

6023 In the second edition of this book the admissibility of using planning legislation to ensure accessibility was discussed, with reference to section 17 (1) of the Town and Country Planning Act 1962. Section 29 of the Town and Country Planning Act 1971 has now replaced section 17 of the 1962 Act, but it is in

[1] Bib 93200, para 22. The Ministry of Housing and Local Government circular referred to is *Access to public buildings for the disabled* (Bib 93001) which gives brief practical recommendations on access provision.
[2] Bib 93000
[3] Bib 93200, paras 28, 33

essence identical. Subsection 1 reads (in abbreviated form):

'Where an application is made to a local planning authority for planning permission, that authority . . .
(a) may grant planning permission, either unconditionally or subject to such conditions as they think fit, or
(b) may refuse planning permission'.

6024 The question is whether a reasonable interpretation of this section is that accessibility for disabled people to buildings is a planning consideration for which it is fit to impose conditions. It was previously suggested that it might be, and that a planning authority, faced with an application for permission to erect a building which disabled people would want to use, could properly take into account access arrangements in making a decision [4]. The matter has not been tested in the courts but the consensus of advice is that it is not a fit planning condition. The Encyclopaedia of the Law of Town and Country Planning (with reference to section 17 of the 1962 Act) says:

'the local planning authority cannot do *just as they wish* in exercising their discretion to add conditions to a planning permission, and subsection 1 does not mean this when it says the planning authority may add to a planning permission such conditions "as they think fit". This means that the conditions must be thought to be "fit" (ie meet, fit, proper, requisite, etc) *from a planning point of view*'. [5]

6025 In the second edition of this book the passing by local authorities of council resolutions requiring that planning permission only be granted to schemes making suitable provision for disabled people was discussed [6]. If it is the case that accessibility is not a fit condition for refusing planning permission it follows that any such resolutions are legally invalid, in that what they require is not within the power of the local authority to determine. There is however no reason why local planning authorities should not exhort private developers to make their proposed buildings accessible, and the interdepartmental circular on the Chronically Sick Act (quoted in 6011) specifically asks them to do so.

The Council of Europe resolution
6026 In 1972 representatives of governments of eight European nations – Austria, Belgium, France, West Germany, Italy, Luxembourg, the Netherlands and the United Kingdom – were signatories to resolution AP(72)5 of the Coucil of Europe resolution 'Planning and equipment of buildings with a view to making them more accessible to the physically handicapped'. Following the preamble the resolution reads:

(The representatives) 'considering it desirable to make buildings more accessible to physically handicapped persons, who constitute an appreciable proportion of the population in each country,
I. Draw attention to measures which can be taken to construct or adapt new buildings in such a way as to facilitate access to and use of such buildings;
II. Recommend that governments of the seven States parties to the Partial Agreement and that of Austria should take all necessary measures, in particular those referred to in the appendix to this resolution, to ensure that public buildings, including privately-owned buildings to which the public has access, should be constructed and fitted out in such a way as to make them more accessible to the physically handicapped;
III. Invite the said governments to inform faculties of architecture and town planning and schools of building of the measures referred to in the appendix to this resolution'.

6027 The appendix referred to [7] contains a number of recommendations which display faulty drafting or an unrealistic understanding of the practicalities involved, for example doors are to have a minimum width of 0·900 but it is not made clear how door width is defined; lift control buttons are to be at a maximum height of 1·200 above floor level and telephone booths are to have minimum dimensions of 1·200 × 1·200.

6028 There is no evidence that architects in the United Kingdom have taken account of the terms of the resolution. It has no legal authority, although, in that it was signed by a representative of the British government, it has more authoritative endorsement than CP96.

603 **Structural fire precautions**

6030 There are two sets of building requirements relating to fire protection. The first relates to structural fire precautions, ie constructional provision which minimizes the risk of fire occurring or limits its spread when it does occur. The second, which is complementary, relates to means of escape in case of fire, ie suitable provision throughout the building for people to get out quickly and easily when a fire occurs. Both are important in connection with the use of buildings by disabled people, the second in particular.

Designated uses
6031 Structural fire precautions for areas outside inner London are prescribed in the national Building Regulations, issued by the Secretary of State for the

[4] Bib 93002, para 6081
[5] Bib 93803, p2987
[6] Bib 93002, para 6080
[7] Bib 93060

Environment in exercise of his powers under section 4 of the Public Health Act 1961 and other statutes [8].

Part E of the Building Regulations deals specifically with fire precautions; it designates different kinds of buildings according to their use, the purpose being to classify buildings in respect of fire hazards and to define fire resistance requirements of the structure and the resistance of finishes to spread of flame. In relation to fire hazards, the area of the building at risk is an important factor and there are thus regulations for countering the spread of fire by compartmentation, ie by dividing buildings into cells with fire-resistant walls and floors.

6032 The eight designated purpose groups are:
I   small residential
II   institutional
III other residential
IV   office
V   shop
VI   factory
VII other place of assembly
VIII storage and general

6033 Purpose group II covers all institutional buildings having sleeping provision and which cater for the treatment, care or maintenance of elderly or disabled people. It includes hospitals, residential homes, residential schools and holiday accommodation specifically designed to cater for disabled people.
In respect of accommodation for disabled people it can be important whether a building is designated group I, II or III. All buildings registered under part III of the National Assistance Act 1948 (1504) are automatically group II. The converse, that all buildings erected under housing powers are either group I or group III, does not necessarily apply. But as a general rule self-contained dwellings, including grouped flatlet schemes supervised by a warden, are designated either group I or group III.

Fire-resisting doors
6034 The mobility of disabled people within and around buildings may be constrained by heavy fire doors in compartment walls. As a general rule the longer the period of fire resistance which doors are required to satisfy, the heavier they will be.
In the majority of single storey buildings ½-hour fire doors only are required by the regulations, and in the case of most other buildings 1-hour doors are required. For high buildings, requirements are dependent on the use, height and size of the building. Except in one and two storey private houses, where there is no compartmentation requirement, doors in compartment walls must be automatically self-closing.

6035 There will be occasions when multi-storey buildings, including two or three storey institutional buildings, need to be usable by disabled people. In this connection there are

possibilities under the regulations for fire doors to be held in an open position. Regarding fire-resisting doors, regulation E11(3)(b) reads:

'No means of holding any such door open shall be provided other than a fusible link or, if the door is so constructed and installed that it can readily be opened manually, an electro-magnetic or electro-mechanical device susceptible to smoke.'

6036 Fusible links are usually fitted in conjunction with doors hung on a descending track and the door is normally held in the open position, closing only when the link is affected by heat. When prescribing requirements in relation to means of escape, fire officers insist that door-closing devices must be activated by smoke detectors rather than heat detectors, meaning that electro-magnetic or electro-mechanical devices must be installed.

6037 Regulation E11(2) of the Building Regulations reads:

'"Electro-magnetic or electro-mechanical device susceptible to smoke" refers only to any such device which will allow the door held open by it to close automatically upon the occurrence of each or any one of the following –
(i) detection of smoke by automatic apparatus suitable in nature, quality and location:
(ii) manual operation of a switch fitted in a suitable position:
(iii) failure of electricity supply to the device, apparatus or switch:
(iv) if a fire alarm system is installed in the building, operation of that system.'

Doors to protected shafts
6038 Where self-closing doors normally held in the open position by fusible link devices give access to a protected shaft (ie a lift shaft or stairway shaft) a normal side-hung door or doors must be provided in the same openings. These auxiliary doors can however be fitted with certain electro-magnetic devices which allow them to be held open under normal circumstances and actuate closing when a fire occurs.

Regulations in London
6039 In the inner London boroughs (the old London County Council area) the Building Regulations do not apply. Instead the Greater London Council administers regulations under the powers of the London Buildings Acts. The requirements of the GLC Constructional By-Laws must be observed [9]; it is the job of district surveyors appointed by the GLC to see that these by-laws are observed.

---

[8] Building regulations currently in force (1975) are the Building Regulations 1972 (Bib 93800). Part E of the 1972 regulations has been replaced by Schedule 1 Regulation 16 of the Building (First Amendment) Regulations 1973 (Bib 93801).
[9] Bib 93804

604 Means of escape provision

6040 Fire protection requirements relating to means of escape from buildings are complex. In effect there are two types of requirements: first, building requirements in respect of means of escape, and second, requirements regarding the use of buildings with reference to means of escape.

Although these two sets of requirements have different purposes they become enmeshed in practice. In particular, with important implications for the use of buildings by disabled people, requirements regarding the use of buildings are commonly determined, among other things, by the physical provisions made for means of escape.

Effects on building use by disabled people

6041 Building requirements for means of escape are designed to ensure that, for building users in general, adequate means of escape are built into the structure. In respect of regulations covering the use of buildings, the difficulty, so far as disabled people are concerned, is that building requirements for means of escape devised to cater for general occupancy can mean that in certain circumstances the arrangements are not suitable for disabled people, and in particular for wheelchair users. Because of this there is always the possibility that regulations for the use of buildings may be imposed which specifically exclude disabled people or severely curtail the extent to which they are allowed to use buildings.

Means of escape requirements outside London

6042 Outside inner London, building requirements for means of escape in respect of certain buildings (detailed in 6020) are enforced under sections 59 and 60 of the Public Health Act 1936. In the case of certain new flats, maisonettes, shops and offices, requirements are enforced under the Building Regulations, as detailed in 6044. In the case of buildings where neither the Public Health Act nor the Building Regulations apply, the normal practice is to seek the advice of the local building authority and fire officer.

Requirements in inner London

6043 In the case of buildings in inner London the GLC issues Codes of Practice which advise on building requirements for means of escape in case of fire [10]; these are not mandatory but afford a basis for discussion with architects. The approval of means of escape is in the hands of the GLC, who have powers to impose such conditions as they consider appropriate.

Building regulations requirements

6044 Under section 11(1) of the Fire Precautions Act 1971 the power of the Secretary of State for the Environment to make building regulations under section 4 of the Public Health Act 1961 was extended to include power to impose requirements as to the provision of means of escape in case of fire. In the exercise of that power the Building (First

Amendment) Regulations 1973 came into operation on 31 August 1973; part EE of this amendment covers means of escape, limited specifically to certain flats and maisonettes, and to shops and offices, but excluding small shops and certain high office buildings.

6045 Regulation EE3 reads:

'In any building or part of a building to which this regulation applies there shall be provided –
(a) means of escape consisting of exits and escape routes of such number, size, layout, design and construction as may reasonably be required in the circumstances of the case to enable the occupants to reach a place of safety in the event of fire; and
(b) such other works (other than means of fighting fire) as may be necessary for securing that such means of escape can be safely and effectively used at all material times.'

6046 The intention is that further amendments to the Building Regulations will be issued in respect of other building types, using the simplified procedure given by section 61 of the Health and Safety at Work etc Act 1974 (6021).

CP3

6047 The requirements of the regulations under part EE are deemed to be satisfied if the building complies with the relevant recommendations of the British Standards Institution's Code of Practice CP3 *Precautions against fire* [11].

6048 The three parts of CP3 issued to date adopt a common approach to the design of means of escape. The aim is to enable people to escape by their own unaided efforts should a fire occur, using protected routes built into the structure and without relying on outside assistance. It is not assumed that it is always essential to evacuate the entire building; buildings can be designed so that people are able to move to adjoining protected fire compartments, but if they do so they must be free to move to safe areas via stairs. CP3 does not permit the use of lifts as a means of escape.

605 Regulations for the use of buildings relating to means of escape

6050 The Fire Precautions Act 1971, which applies equally to inner London as to areas outside London, is concerned with buildings as they are occupied and used, in relation to their planning and the protection that they provide.

The Act gives to the fire authority – in effect to the fire inspectors appointed by them – substantial powers to control the use both of existing buildings and new buildings when they are completed.

[10] Bib 93806
[11] Bib 93812–93814

Although the fire inspector is not obliged to make any firm decision until the building is ready for occupancy it is advisable that at an early stage in the design process the architect discusses his proposals with him.

Controls under the Fire Precautions Act

6051 Under section 1 of the Act, fire authorities must issue fire certificates for buildings for particular uses. Buildings which can be so designated by the Secretary of State (for the Home Office) comprise virtually all buildings for public use, or where people using them may be at risk in the event of fire. Crown buildings are not exempted under the Act. Places of work can be designated under an amendment to the Act (see 6057); other classes of use for which designation orders can be made are:
a. use as sleeping accommodation
b. use an an institution providing treatment or care
c. use for entertainment, recreation or instruction, or for purposes of any club, society or association
d. use for teaching, training or research
e. use for any purpose involving access to the premises by the public whether on payment or otherwise

6052 Under section 6(1) of the Act, a fire certificate issued for a building has to specify the particular use or uses to which the premises may be put, and the means of escape in case of fire with which they are provided. Under section 6(2) the certificate may impose requirements for limiting the number of people who may be in the building at any one time, and may prescribe other precautions which have to be observed in relation to fire hazards to people using the building. Under section 10 the fire authority can, if it thinks there is a serious risk to people using the building, apply immediately to the magistrates' court for an order to be issued prohibiting or restricting the use of the building.

6053 It is apparent that under section 6 fire authorities are legally entitled to prescribe what kind of disabled people may use a building, and under what circumstances. Under section 10 they have powers to prohibit disabled people from particular buildings.

Designated usage

6054 To date (1975) the only usage designated under the Act is hotels and boarding houses, by means of the Fire Precautions (Hotels and Boarding Houses) Order 1972 [12].
In connection with the administration of the Act and more specifically of this order the Home Office issued in 1972 a guide *Hotels and boarding houses* [13]. The Home Office emphasizes that this guide has no legal force. No reference is made to the use of hotels by disabled people but paragraph 1.3.8 of part II says 'Lifts are not acceptable for means of escape'.

Offices, Shops and Railway Premises Act

6055 The Offices, Shops and Railway Premises Act 1963 is more embracing than its title suggests. Apart from offices and shops it covers for example public restaurants. Local authorities are required under section 29 of the Act to issue fire certificates, among the conditions for which is 'that the premises are provided with such means of escape in case of fire for the persons employed to work therein, or proposed to be so employed as may reasonably be required in the circumstances of the case'. Although there is no specific reference here to disabled people, this section may be interpreted as meaning that if it is proposed to employ disabled people the authority must first be satisfied that the means of escape are adequate.

Use of lifts for escape

6056 Although under building regulations lifts are not permitted as a means of escape (6048), it may be possible in certain circumstances in the case of existing buildings for arrangements to be made with the fire inspector for disabled people to be employed in the building and to rely on the lift for escape purposes.
Stringent conditions may be imposed, for example relating to the protection of lift lobbies, the number of disabled people in wheelchairs who may be employed and the areas of the building where they may have their regular work stations.

Health and Safety at Work etc Act

6057 Section 78 of the Health and Safety at Work etc Act 1974 amends the Fire Precautions Act 1971, to enable it, among other matters, to extend to places of work.
The intention is that the means of escape and general fire provision of the Factories Act 1961 and the Offices, Shops and Railway Premises Act 1963 should be repealed, and that control over these matters in those premises to which the two Acts apply should be exercised instead under the Fire Precautions Act 1971, except in respect of a limited number of high hazard premises. The repeal of the relevant provisions of the 1961 and 1963 Acts will coincide with a new designation order, under section 1 of the 1971 Act, applying to factories, offices and shops.

Licensing Acts

6058 The use of buildings which have to be licensed for public use can be controlled by the conditions of licences.
Cinemas and theatres are licensed by local authorities under the Cinematograph Acts of 1909 and 1952, and the Theatres Acts of 1843 and 1968; for discussion regarding conditions of use of these buildings by disabled people see 7402. Public houses and licensed restaurants are controlled by the Licensing Acts of 1961 and 1964; although in the case of these buildings it is unlikely that licensing conditions might be imposed regarding disabled people there is the possibility that they could be.

[12] Bib 93811
[13] Bib 93810

School buildings

6059 Halls in school buildings to which the public may be admitted are subject to the Home Counties Music and Dancing Act 1926, under which conditions of use may be imposed.

In respect of other school buildings the current (1976) position is that fire inspectors have no statutory authority to impose conditions regarding use; the matter is one for the education authority to determine. But under the Fire Precautions Act (1976) position is that fire inspectors have no one of the uses that may be designated; when this is done fire officers will have power to inspect school premises, and fire authorities will have power to impose conditions regarding use.

606 Disabled people and fire regulations: Comment

6060 In line with the intentions of section 4 of the Chronically Sick and Disabled Persons Act, and for reasons discussed in the commentary, it ought to be a firm principle when public buildings are planned, first, that they will be accessible to disabled people, and second, that people who are disabled are not prevented from using them on account of conditions imposed for fire protection reasons.

Strategies

6061 The introduction of any official code of practice or set of rules governing the use of buildings by disabled people or means of escape from buildings by disabled people ought on principle to be discouraged.

The use to which buildings are put, whether they are used regularly or intermittently by disabled people, the kind of disabled people using them, the availability of people who could help disabled people in the event of an emergency; these and other circumstances vary so much among different buildings and in respect of the same buildings that it would be unwise to establish any general negative or inhibiting rules. If there have to be rules they ought to be positive ones, prescribing what needs to be done to enable people with disabilities to use buildings. It will inevitably happen that negative rules exacerbate problems for disabled people generally, reducing the latitude for reasonable ad hoc solutions.

Tactics

6062 The following tactical guidelines emerge:

1. There should be no extension of CP96 *Access for the disabled to buildings* to cover egress from buildings.

2. Where amendments to building regulations are made in respect of precautions against fire for specific building types no special conditions should be incorporated relating to disabled people.

3. The issuing of guidelines from management associations or similar organizations setting down rules for the use by disabled people of particular building types, such as cinemas, theatres, hotels, shops and employment buildings, should be discouraged.

607 The use of lifts as a means of escape: Comment

6070 The fact that lifts are not considered permissible as a means of escape in case of fire poses a threat to the use of multi-storey buildings by disabled people. No official guidelines on this matter have been issued but it is believed that the general advice from the Home Office to fire authorities is that where people in wheelchairs may use buildings regularly, for example for employment, they should be restricted to the ground or first floors. It needs however to be recognized that although CP3 is firm on this issue (part 1 says 'Lifts cannot be considered for escape purposes' and part 2 says 'Lifts should be disregarded for escape purposes') there is no mandatory requirement, either under Building Regulations or the Fire Precautions Act, which positively forbids the use of lifts as a means of escape.

Reasons for not using lifts

6071 There are seven reasons which may be cited why lifts ought not to be permitted as a means of escape:

1. The fact that certain lift controls are heat sensitive, meaning that lifts may automatically converge on the point where a fire outbreak occurs.
2. The possibility that when an outbreak of fire occurs in a building someone may suppose it is helpful to turn the electricity off at the mains, so leaving people stranded in a lift car half-way up a shaft.
3. The need for lifts to be commandeered by the fire brigade when a fire occurs.
4. The possibility of smoke spreading via the lift shaft.
5. The possibility of mechanical or electrical failure of the lift.
6. The delay which may be experienced waiting for a lift to answer a call.
7. The limited capacity of lifts.

6072 Of these reasons, point 1 can be insured against by technical means. Point 2 can be resolved by putting the lifts on a separate electrical circuit from the rest of the installation.

Immobilization of lifts

6073 Regarding point 3, the normal practice would be that only one lift is commandeered by the fire brigade for fire-fighting purposes. A switch in a glass-fronted box is provided at ground level, operating a control whereby firemen can use the lift without interference at landing call points. This means that other lifts may still be usable. There is in any event nothing to prevent lifts from being used as a means of escape before the fire brigade arrives to immobilize them.

Hazards of smoke and mechanical failure

6074 Regarding point 4, although there is a negligible risk of fire inside a lift shaft, there is a risk of smoke spread in a lift shaft if the fire has penetrated the lobby or corridor. The natural ventilation at the head of a lift shaft encourages the flue action. It is therefore essential that lift lobbies can be kept clear of smoke, as discussed in 6077.

6075 Regarding point 5, the possibility is remote that a fire will commence in a protected lift shaft, causing electrical or mechanical failure of the lift. Although modern lifts are not always 100 per cent reliable, their unreliability is not such as to warrant not using them in the event of an emergency.

Capacity of lifts for escape purposes

6076 The two most cogent points – 6, possible delay while a lift is obtained, and 7, limited lift capacity – are associated. When an emergency occurs the response of able-bodied people will be to escape as quickly as possible by means of the stairs, without thinking to wait for a lift. It will only be handicapped people not able to use stairs at all who will rely on the lift.

The limited capacity of lifts is a relevant factor here; if lifts are to be permitted as a means of escape it may be appropriate that the number of non-ambulant disabled people regularly using the building at any one time should be limited to the number who can be accommodated in say two lift loads.

6077 If lifts are to be permitted as a means of escape by disabled people it is essential, given the possibility that there may be a delay waiting for the lift to arrive, that protected lift lobbies are kept free of spreading smoke.

The practice recommended in CP3 is that lobbies should be ventilated by means of permanent openings or openable windows giving direct access to the open air; the intention is to avoid a concentration of smoke accumulating in the lobby. Smoke in lobbies may not however disperse quickly, particularly for example in tall buildings where narrow internal air shafts can create draughts which prevent air escaping at all. To afford security, more sophisticated technical solutions are needed.

Pressurization

6078 A possible solution is pressurization. This means maintaining by mechanical means a positive air pressure in the lift lobby so that smoke is deterred from getting in. By means of ventilating fans the equipment ensures that the air pressure in the lobby is always higher than in adjoining areas; air pushed into the lobby space will find its way out

through closed doors, walls, cracks and crevices. By this means smoke will be kept out.

The preparation of a British Standard Code of Practice on positive pressure is currently (1976) under consideration.

6079 Where a protected lift is installed in a building and it is arranged that it can be used as a means of escape, a notice may be fixed to the lift, bearing the international symbol (654) and a legend such as 'In the event of fire this lift is to be used as a means of escape only by disabled people'.

608 Alternatives to lifts for means of escape

6080 In multi-storey buildings designed specifically for the use of disabled people, for example residential homes and social centres, it will probably not be feasible to rely on lifts as a means of escape, and alternatives have to be found. One possibility is the system of horizontal compartmentation applied to hospital buildings, whereby people can be moved from an area where fire occurs to a protected area at the same level which affords temporary safety, sufficiently secure for the period that the fire brigade needs to deal with the incident.

6081 Alternatively, it may be possible for people to be moved horizontally by means of a connecting link to an adjoining but separate building. In certain circumstances the fire authority may allow an open terrace at high level to be used as a temporary place of safety, permitting disabled people to congregate while the incident is dealt with; this arrangement is not normally permitted.

Ramps

6082 In low rise two or three storey buildings it may be practicable to incorporate external ramps as a means of escape. They will however be expensive and an extravagant use of space.

6083 In its code of practice *Means of escape in case of fire* [14] the Greater London Council requires that ramps which afford a means of escape should have a gradient of not more than 1:10 (3213).

Such a gradient is uncomfortably steep for disabled people; it is not easy to control a loaded wheelchair on an extended decline of 1:10. While a maximum gradient of say 1:16 might be preferred, there would be substantial penalty in terms of construction costs; in the circumstances a 1:10 ramp is permissible despite possible hazards.

Chutes

6084 In existing buildings, for example those used as residential homes for handicapped people, ad hoc arrangements may be necessary, of a kind which might be ruled out in the case of new buildings. Slides or chutes may be installed, but they may not

[14] Bib 93806

be easily manageable in the event of an emergency evacuation. It is unlikely that anyone severely crippled or deformed by, for example, tetraplegia, muscular dystrophy or rheumatoid arthritis will be able to slide comfortably down a chute. In this connection, there are possibilities for using instantly inflatable rafts for the purpose of sliding handicapped people down chutes.

Single storey buildings

6085   In single storey ground level buildings used by disabled people it will not as a rule be difficult to arrange suitable means of escape. Ground level buildings used by gatherings of non-disabled people, for example sports buildings, schools and meeting halls, are planned on the basis that although there may be a relatively high risk of fire occurring in the space there will be a generous number of escape routes, allowing the building to be evacuated very quickly. By avoiding steps at exit points in such buildings it ought also to be possible to ensure that disabled people can move out quickly, and there should be no cause for restrictions on the use of the building.

609   **Fire precautions: Summary of tactics for building use by disabled people**

6090   Regarding the administration of fire regulations in relation to the use of buildings by disabled people, three situations are identified:
1. Buildings specifically designed for use by disabled people.
2. General purpose buildings incorporating special provision for users who are disabled.
3. General purpose buildings used by disabled people on the same basis as non-disabled people.

Special buildings

6091   In respect of special building types, for example residential homes, social centres, sheltered workshops, and schools for handicapped children, it is necessary that each case is considered on its merits.
Appropriate provision for means of escape will be dependent on a variety of factors, for example the number of disabled people regularly using the building, the severity of their handicap and their likely awareness of fire hazards. For these buildings it would be inappropriate to set down general standards for matters such as travel distances to exit doors.

Buildings with special provision

6092   In respect of general purpose buildings where special provision is made for disabled people, for example theatres and cinemas having areas allocated for chairbound people and hotels with rooms equipped for disabled guests, the requirement will be for a direct escape route, by means of a protected lift if the special provision is not at ground level.

6093   Where a lift is used as a means of escape it will be a reasonable condition to limit the number of non-ambulant people permitted to use the special provision at any one time, having regard to the capacity of the lift or lifts and the number of journeys that can be made within the time allowed for evacuation of the building.
Disabled people who prefer to use normal facilities rather than the special provision should be treated in the same fashion as all other users of the building, without discrimination.

General purpose buildings with no special provision

6094   In respect of general purpose buildings where no special provision is required, the general rule should be that no special conditions are imposed regarding use by disabled people, and that they are treated on the same basis as all other users.

6095   In respect of new multi-storey buildings it will be advantageous if a protected lift can be installed which is possible as a means of escape. In the case of existing buildings it should be assumed that disabled people can if necessary use stairways as a means of escape, either unaided or with the assistance of others.

6096   In employment buildings, procedures for means of escape by staff who are disabled should be determined by the management in cooperation with the fire inspector, having regard to the nature of disability among the people concerned.

6097   In auditoria buildings and other places of assembly, the management should be asked to exercise generous discretion regarding the admission of disabled people. It should be the job of the management to see that disabled people using the building are aware of possible hazards, and the procedures to be followed in an emergency.

Modification of conditions

6098   Where it appears that the conditions proposed by the fire officer are not in the circumstances reasonable, it may be possible by discussion and negotiation to obtain their modification.
Where for example there is a general ruling that chairbound people are not to be admitted, it may be helpful to discuss with the fire officer the actual nature of the hazard, the evidence offered that a hazard clearly exists, and the relative degree of the supposed hazard by comparison with admitted hazards to other groups of users against whom no controls are enforced.

6099   Where there is doubt, it may be wise to establish that under the legislation the fire officer concerned is authorized in writing by his fire authority to impose conditions. If he is not, reference may be made to the relevant committee of the local authority. If he is, and the conditions seem unreasonable, an appeal may be made to the magistrates' court and, if not upheld, subsequently to the crown court.

610 Purpose and scope of recommendations

6100 The practical recommendations prescribed for new buildings in sections 62–64 can in most situations be applied equally to alterations or additions to existing buildings. Some compromising may be necessary where physical constraints mean that the ideal is unobtainable; such compromises should be based on a commonsense interpretation of the recommendations, and will be more satisfactory than making no provision at all.

Convenience for all

6101 While the recommendations are based on the requirements of disabled people, it is emphasized that compliance will make buildings more convenient for non-disabled people, and in particular for elderly people, to use. Their implementation will be of benefit to mothers with prams, and ought also to contribute materially to the avoidance of accident hazards in buildings.

Defining disabled people

6102 For the purposes of this discussion and associated practical recommendations the operational definition of disabled people is 'those people who on account of physical impairment are handicapped in their use of traditionally designed buildings by the lack of suitable facilities'. These are in the main people with locomotor disabilities, in particular impairment of lower limbs.

6103 Many people with lower limb impairment have other disabilities also. Practical recommendations are therefore formulated so that the implementation of the recommendations for either of the two principal categories of ambulant disabled and chairbound disabled will mean that people with upper limb or hand impairments, or who are blind or partially sighted, are also assisted.

6104 The guiding rule is that provision for chairbound people is as comprehensive as possible. It is not always sufficient to rely exclusively on this rule, and separate attention to the needs of ambulant disabled people is warranted. There are two main reasons for this. First, opposing criteria may, for reasons discussed in the commentary (1111–1115), occur between ambulant disabled and chairbound disabled people. Second, there are practical reasons why it is not possible to make every part of a building accessible to chairbound people (for example in auditoria buildings, discussed in 7400); areas of buildings not accessible to wheelchairs will none the less be used by ambulant handicapped people, and it is important that any such areas are as conveniently manageable as possible.

Definitions: Ambulant and chairbound

6105 In the context of public building design it is meaningful, for reasons discussed in the commentary (1117), to regard ambulant disabled people as tail-enders of the normal population, meaning people who, on measures of physical performance, are at the tail end of the normal distribution statistical curve. Chairbound disabled people can be regarded as outsiders, meaning that on measures of physical performance they are outside the normal distribution, constituting a separate subpopulation.

6106 Among the total population, the continuum of physical impairment across a broad spectrum means that it is impossible to draw any clear dividing line between modals (meaning able-bodied people in the centre of the normal distribution) and tail-enders, or between tail-enders and outsiders. In the context of public building design the divisions are finally determined by the constraints of design specifications; these are analyzed in 613 and 614.

Ambulant disabled parameters

6107 The parameters of the ambulant disabled population are identified at the lower (least handicapped) end by the traditionally inconvenient characteristics of typical buildings, and at the upper (most handicapped) end by the design specifications. Thus a person at the lower end is, for example, someone who cannot comfortably stoop to reach low level socket outlets. A person at the upper end is someone who can cope with steps only if they are easily graded and have handrails to either side, and who can use a wc only where support rails are installed.

Chairbound disabled parameters

6108 Anyone whose lower limb impairment is such that he is not catered for by provisions made for ambulant disabled people must, for mobility purposes, be regarded as chairbound disabled, whether or not he actually uses a wheelchair. This defines the lower end of the chairbound population. The upper end is exemplified by a person who cannot propel his own wheelchair and can only use a wc if someone is with him to help with transfer, and if the compartment is large enough to accommodate his wheelchair.

611 Wheelchair criteria

6110 In the recommendations for public buildings in the second edition of this book a distinction was made between small-wheelchair criteria and large-wheelchair criteria. Small wheelchairs were standard folding self-propelling chairs and comparably sized electric attendant-propelled chairs. Large wheelchairs were upholstered chairs, and in particular the model 13 used mainly by old people.
Although the model 13 is still issued by DHSS its use is steadily declining among old people, for reasons discussed in 23311, to the point where it can be disregarded when determining space standards for general wheelchair purposes in public buildings.

6111 The general recommendations for chairbound people in section 64 and elsewhere in this book are governed by the characteristics of what were previously called small wheelchairs and are now called standard wheelchairs.

6112 People who have large electric wheelchairs or modified versions of standard chairs, for example with extended legrests, may not be conveniently provided for by the observance of standard wheelchair criteria. This means it is desirable where possible to have wider passageways and larger lift cars; the use of wider doors is not always recommended, for reasons discussed in 36143.

6113 In the case of some buildings, such as hospitals, residential homes for old people or handicapped people and social centres for old or handicapped people, space provision needs to take account of wheelchairs which are larger than standard; special requirements are itemized under the relevant headings in part 7.

612   CP96

6120 The general recommendations for public buildings in section 62, together with the requirements for ambulant disabled people in section 63 and chairbound disabled in section 64, are comparable with the recommendations of the British Standard Code of Practice *Access for the Disabled to Buildings; Part 1: General recommendations* [1], commonly referred to as CP96.

Shortcomings

6121 In its original 1967 version, which is the way it is still (1976) being applied, CP96 has shortcomings. It prescribes general recommendations only, and until guidance is given on how, in varying circumstances and in respect of varying types of building, the recommendations are to be applied, it is impossible for practising architects to use it with precision.

6122 The intention in 1967 was that Part 1 should be followed by further parts, detailing how the recommendations should be observed in (for example) offices, shops, theatres or transport buildings. In the event, no further parts have yet been drafted. Nor has the British Standard *Indication signs for the use of buildings by disabled people*, which was noted in CP96 as being in course of preparation, yet been issued. The updating of CP96 to conform with metric practice is at present (1976) under discussion; publication of the revised code is expected during 1977 or 1978.

Change to metric

6123 CP96 was drafted with Imperial measures in mind, on the basis of Imperial components and standard equipment. Throughout the construction industry the introduction of metric measures has meant the redesign of standard components. The dimensions of these standard components affect the establishment of performance standards, meaning that operational standards based on Imperial practice are not automatically valid under metric practice. Two important examples are the width of doors and the size of lift cars.

Door widths

6124 For doors catering for wheelchair users CP96 requires a clear opening width of 2ft 7in (metric equivalent 0·785) which was based on the use of a standard 2ft 9in door. With metric practice the 0·900 doorset is the basic unit on which recommendations for circulation spaces are made, for reasons discussed in 361. The internal 0·900 doorset gives a clear opening width of 0·775 and the external doorset 0·751. Although for external doors there will generally be advantages, both for wheelchair users and others, if wider doors are used, a clear width of 0·751 is adequate for chairbound people, given that external doors to public buildings invariably have an unobstructed approach on both sides, allowing a wheelchair to pass through without turning. For consistency a clearance of 0·750 is prescribed for internal doors also, the effect – that doorsets less than 0·900 wide must not be used – being the same.

6125 For ambulant disabled people the clear opening width of doors is not as a rule a critical matter. To afford reasonable limits an opening width of 0·750 is required for entrance doors (ie a 0·900 doorset), and 0·670 for internal doors, meaning that where space is restricted, for example to wc compartments, 0·800 doorsets may be used.

Lift dimensions

6126 The lift dimensions prescribed in CP96 (paragraph 4.4.5) were based directly on the use of standard lifts complying with the 1965 version of BS2655. While not being arbitrary, the lift dimensions of CP96 were not immediately determined by the space requirements of wheelchair users. The change to metric has resulted in revisions to standard lift dimensions, making the recommendations of CP96 obsolete. The change has been beneficial, in that the standard sizes prescribed in the 1971 version of BS2655 [2] are generally more economic for wheelchair users than those of the 1965 version. Relevant criteria are discussed in section 45.

Other departures from CP96

6127 As a result of the change to metric there is a small discrepancy between the width of passageways recommended in CP96 and those recommended here. CP96 required that corridors and passageways should be not less than 4ft 0in wide, metric equivalent 1·220. Owing to the use of the

---

[1] Bib 93000
[2] Bib 93890

basic metric planning module of 0·300 a standard passage width is 1·200, and since for wheelchair manoeuvre the difference between 1·200 and 1·220 is not significant, a width of 1·200 is acceptable. Similarly, ramp widths of 1·200 are acceptable.

6128 There are discrepancies between the dimensions for wc compartments recommended in CP96 and those now recommended; these are discussed in 618.

6129 Other variations between recommendations here and in CP96 are the same as found in the second edition, relating to the height of switches and controls (see comment to 6230), the height of lift control buttons (6270) and the avoidance of open risers to staircases (6132).

613 'Must' specifications for ambulant disabled people

6130 The aim of the specifications detailed in sections 63 and 64 is to ensure that in buildings to which they are applied disabled people are satisfactorily catered for. The observance, where appropriate, of specifications containing the word 'must' will satisfy a basic usability criterion. The reasons why this criterion is preferred to one of independence are discussed in the commentary (1401); the primary objective is to guarantee that situations where failure to cope might occur are avoided.

Avoidance of failure-to-cope situations
6131 In respect of ambulant disabled people, must specifications are included in section 63 to avoid the 'failure-to-cope' situations which may occur when:

1. The only way into the building is by way of a revolving door (63131) or a door having a clear opening of less than 0·750 (63130).
2. The only approach to the building is by way of a ramp having a gradient steeper than 1:12 (63114).
3. An escalator or passenger conveyor is installed, with no alternative lift or staircase available (63200).
4. Internal doors give an opening of less than 0·670 (63211).
5. Steps or staircases which have to be used have a gradient exceeding 35° (6312, 6323).
6. Handrails are not provided to both sides of any steps or staircases (63123, 63236).
7. The door to a wc compartment opens in (63311).
8. Support rails are not provided beside wcs (63312).

6132 There is one must specification the non-observance of which would be unlikely to mean failure to cope, but which is included because it represents good practice and is in line with the recommendations of CP96. This is that passageways are not less then 1·200 wide (63210).

6133 All these specifications, with the possible exception of that relating to wc doors, represent good practice whose observance would be of benefit to all building users.

People excluded
6134 Observance of all must requirements in section 63 does not guarantee that all ambulant people are catered for. Among them will be ambulant disabled people who cannot cope with stairs, and can manage only if a lift is available. For such people the size of lifts is unlikely to be critical and it is not essential that wheelchair standards are observed. If vertical circulation criteria for chairbound people are observed all ambulant disabled people are automatically catered for; it is therefore appropriate to categorize ambulant people who cannot climb stairs with chairbound people. For further discussion on stairs see 616.

6135 CP96(1967) requires that open risers to staircases are avoided. This is not a potential failure to cope situation, and the specification here (63231) is a should rather than a must.

614 'Must' specifications for chairbound people

6140 As discussed in the commentary (1111) there are three factors which handicap chairbound people in their use of buildings: (1) the personal physical disability; (2) the obligation to operate always at low level, and (3) the characteristics of the wheelchair. The handicapping effects of the first two can be mitigated by having an able-bodied assistant to perform activities such as pushing the chair, opening doors and reaching for light switches. The effects of the third cannot so easily be countered.

Avoidance of failure-to-cope situations
6141 The significance of wheelchair handicapping effects is shown by the must specifications in section 64. They are designed to counter failure-to-cope situations that may occur when:

1. The only approach to the building is stepped (64100).
2. The width of the approach ramp is less than 1·200 (64111).
3. A steep approach ramp does not have a level platform at its head (64115).
4. An exposed ramp or platform does not have a safety kerb (64117).
5. Raised thresholds are higher than 0·015 (64122).
6. Doors give a clear opening of less than 0·750 (64210).
7. Corridors are less than 1·200 wide (64220).
8. A lift is not available for vertical circulation (64230).
9. Lifts have internal dimensions less than 1·400 × 1·100 (63231).

10. The clear space in front of lift doors is less than 1·500 × 1·500 (64232).

11. Cloakroom lobby spaces are too confined (64301).

12. There is insufficient space inside wc compartments to accommodate wheelchairs (6432).

13. The wc seat is not at a convenient level (64330).

14. Support rails are not provided beside wcs (64340).

15. A wash basin is not provided in the wc compartment (64350).

6142 Of these must requirements, the wash basin facility is simply good practice, which in the case of chairbound people is essential. All other requirements, with the exception of that for wc support rails, are determined by the characteristics of wheelchairs rather than by the characteristics of their users. The critical ones – those regarding door widths, passage widths, lift sizes and wc compartment sizes – are exclusively wheelchair-determined.

Ramping of kerbs

6143 A supplementary must requirement relates to the ramping of kerbs (6210). This is important in respect of the overall environment rather than of individual buildings. The absence of one kerb ramp is unlikely to mean failure to cope, but the cumulative effect of unramped kerbs over a wide area may do so.

Scope of requirements

6144 The observance of all must requirements will guarantee that, apart from exceptional circumstances, buildings are usable by chairbound people. Failure may occur among people who use very large or atypical wheelchairs, but to guard against all contingencies is not possible.
In terms of tactical measures to minimize occurrence of failure, it would be wiser for wheelchair manufacturers to adapt to the constraints of building standards rather than to encourage enhanced standards; this topic is discussed in relation to housing, see 1701.

615 Usability and independence criteria

6150 Observance of must specifications will not ensure that people in wheelchairs can always cope independently, but only that failure to cope will be avoided if someone else is available to help, for example with opening doors and pushing a wheelchair up a ramp.
The reasons for this are discussed in 1401–2. An important exception is the planning of wc facilities, where it is considered essential that people who are potentially capable of managing independently should be able to do so.

Ramp gradients

6151 In respect of ramps (64110), gradients are permitted which will not be manageable by chairbound people who use buildings independently; the reasons for this are discussed in 321. In some building types, for example large office buildings, public lavatories and special buildings for use by handicapped people, more stringent criteria for ramp gradients should be observed; these are noted in part 7.

6152 Observance of all must specifications, guaranteeing usability, should be regarded as the minimum provision acceptable. The additional observance of all should recommendations will satisfy an ease-of-help criterion and is recommended, see 1402.

Blind and deaf people

6153 For blind people, there are no special provisions which must be incorporated in public buildings to guarantee usability, for reasons discussed in 1307. To assist blind people who use buildings on their own, it is suggested (6271) that control buttons in lifts should have embossed digits.

6154 For deaf people there are no essential special provisions to guarantee usability of public buildings, but it is useful if there are adequate notices around buildings indicating the whereabouts of facilities (6291).
Such notices will help deaf and hard of hearing people to find their way about without having to enquire, and they will also benefit people who are not handicapped.

616 Stairs and ramps

6160 For ambulant disabled people, a suitably graded flight of steps is permitted at building entrances, and stairs are allowed for internal circulation. This is the only significant difference between circulation requirements for ambulant disabled and chairbound people, and in the circumstances it might be advocated that wheelchair criteria, meaning ramps and lifts, should be applied. There are three reasons why this is not done:

1. In some public buildings, planning considerations and topography may indicate that the principal entrance has to be stepped. If only wheelchair criteria were to be observed it could be that only a side entrance to the building would be usable by disabled people, with no allowance at the principal entrance. In practice, many ambulant disabled people would use the principal entrance, and to cater for them it is important that steps are suitably graded with handrails to either side.

2. In auditoria buildings, access to certain areas may unavoidably be by means of steps. To accommodate ambulant disabled people it is not therefore sufficient to rely on wheelchair criteria, which would make only limited areas accessible.

3. Even where a lift is available inside a building, it is desirable that stairs are convenient for ambulant disabled people to use. Dependent on the location of lifts, reliance on lifts may involve extended walking distances and for those who can walk only slowly it may be more convenient to use stairs. It may also happen that the mechanical failure of lifts makes necessary the use of stairs.

6161   The requirements for ramps at entrances to buildings are, in all important respects, identical for chairbound and ambulant disabled people. This is because any approach to a building which caters for chairbound people will also be used by ambulant disabled people, for whom it should be suitable. An exception is that in the rare circumstance of a ramp being provided only for ambulant disabled people, a platform at the head is not required. This is because where the ramp gradient exceeds 1:12 an alternative stepped approach is automatically provided, and where the gradient does not exceed 1:12 the surface is not so steep as to cause discomfort to ambulant disabled people and warrant the provision of a platform. In the case of ramps for chairbound people a platform has to be provided where the gradient exceeds 1:12.

617   Lifts

6170   The only mandatory requirement for lifts in public buildings catering for chairbound people relates to internal dimensions (64231); there is also a general recommendation (6270) that no lift control is higher than 1·600. These recommendations vary from those in CP96. The matter of lift dimensions has already been discussed (6126); regarding the height of controls the recommendations of CP96(1967) that they are between 0·910 and 1·370 above floor level are considered inappropriate, for reasons discussed in 1115.

6171   In practice, as discussed in section 60, the usability of multi-storey buildings by disabled people may be governed not by lifts being available but whether they are admissible as a means of escape. Where in a public building a lift is installed which can be used by disabled people it ought in any event to be manageable by people in wheelchairs.

6172   A situation ought never to occur where for economic reasons only one lift is installed, of a size which caters only for ambulant people and not for wheelchair users.

6173   It is not advocated that in public buildings special lifts are installed exclusively for the use of disabled people. Nor, as a rule, will it be desirable to incorporate provisions suited to disabled people, for example extended time delays (45212) and slower closing of doors (45216), which are at variance with requirements for able-bodied people.

618   Wc compartments

6180   Requirements for wc compartments for ambulant disabled people are detailed in 633, and for chairbound people in 643.

6181   The ambulant disabled compartment is a modified standard wc compartment; apart from a minor variation of the positioning of support rails it is not different from that recommended in the second edition of this book and in CP96(1967).

Minimum dimensions for chairbound people

6182   For chairbound people the minimum wc compartment size is 1·700 × 1·400, with preferred dimensions of 2·000 × 1·500.
The minimum size should be regarded as a tolerable compromise rather than a satisfactory provision. To cater comfortably for all people who use wheelchairs the preferred size compartment should be incorporated; for certain building types, itemized where appropriate in part 7, this is considered essential.

Comparison with CP96

6183   The preferred size wc compartment is some 25 per cent larger than the wc compartment required by CP96(1967) and recommended as a minimum in the second edition of this book.
The CP96 dimensions were based on the evidence of studies made at Oxford [3]. There has been no evaluation of wc compartments designed to them, and only a small amount of feedback on their use. There have been complaints that the 1·750 × 1·370 dimensions are not generous enough to turn a wheelchair through 180° inside the compartment [4], but that was not the intention. A more pertinent complaint has been that the 1·750 depth does not allow sufficient space in front of the wc fixture for a person who drives his chair in to face the seat, pushes to a standing position, swivels and sits down. To cater for such people, and to provide more room for general manoeuvre, a deeper compartment is needed, and one which is marginally wider. For these reasons the internal dimensions recommended are 2·000 × 1·500, which have the additional advantage that they will make it easier for a helper assisting a handicapped person to or from a wheelchair.

6184   The minimum size wc compartment at 1·700 × 1·400 gives an area of 2·38m²; this is only marginally less than the area of 2·40m² given by a wc compartment designed to CP96(1967).

[3] Bib 93231, 93232
[4] Personal communications

619 **Implementation of requirements**

6190 Recommendations in part 7 are referenced to headings or paragraphs in section 63 in respect of provision for ambulant disabled people, and to section 64 in respect of provision for chairbound disabled people.

6191 Because it is important that where provision is made for chairbound disabled people, ambulant disabled people are also accommodated, there are some requirements (for example 6311 and parts of 6411) which are identical for both groups. To facilitate application of these requirements they are repeated in both sections. There are also general recommendations, listed in section 62, which should be observed in all buildings where provision is made for disabled people.

6192 The implementation of recommendations in part 7 where the word must occurs will satisfy the usability criterion; the additional implementation of should recommendations will satisfy the ease-of-help criterion. Must recommendations are usually followed by a colon and an instruction such as 'observe 631', meaning that the must recommendations in section 631 have to be complied with.

6193 The requirements of sections 63 and 64 and recommendations in part 7 have purposely been made definitive, more so than is warranted by available evidence of what is appropriate; this is done to give architects clear and unambiguous performance standards which are realistic, practicable, and can be expected to meet the needs they are designed to satisfy. In circumstances where their rigid implementation may be inappropriate they should be interpreted in a commonsense fashion.

62 Public buildings: General recommendations

The recommendations made in this section should be observed in all buildings where provision is made for disabled people. With the exception of the requirement for ramped kerbs (6210) these provisions, while desirable, are not essential to enable disabled people to use buildings. Provisions which are essential are detailed in section 63 (ambulant disabled people) and 64 (chairbound people).

620 Parking bays

6200 Parking bays reserved for the use of disabled people should be close to a building entrance.

6201 Reserved parking spaces should be not less than 2·800 wide, and should be suitably identified. See 5804, 654.

621 Ramped kerbs

6210 At suitable locations road and pavement surfaces must be blended to a common level, or the height of the kerb reduced to not more than 0·030 above the adjacent channel level. The gradient of any ramped surface should not exceed 1:10.
Methods of ramping kerbs are shown in diagram 30·3. See Ramping of kerbs, 302. For discussion see 1224.

622 Entrances, doors

6220 Entrances to buildings should be easy to negotiate. Entrance lobbies should be generously planned; in all situations provision as required for chairbound people (64221) is suggested. Air curtains are recommended, see 5032.

6221 Automatic opening doors are recommended. See 3606.

6222 Raised thresholds should be avoided. For chairbound people this is mandatory, see 64122. See also 340.

6223 The lower edge of vision panels to swing doors should not be higher than 1·010 above floor level. Frameless glass doors should have hazard markings.
See 36212. CP96 recommends that the bottom of any vision panel is not less than 1·220 above floor level.

6224 For spring closers to doors a resistance not exceeding 12Nm is preferred for external doors, and 8Nm for internal doors.
For practical reasons this may not be easy to observe, see 3623.

6225 Door handles should be at approx 1·000 above floor level. Lever handles are preferred to knob handles. See 36300.

623 Switches and controls

6230 Switches and controls for light, heat, ventilation and fire alarms should be not higher than 1·600 above floor level and should be easy to manipulate. CP96 recommends that switches and controls should not be higher than 1·070; this is of doubtful merit and will be difficult to implement. For discussion see 1115.

6231 Socket outlets should be not lower than 0·500 above floor level.
See 435.

624 Handrails

6240 Handrails should have a cross section not wider than 0·050.
See 331.

625 Floor surfaces

6250 Floor surfaces should be slip-resistant. See 381.

626 Telephones

6260 Telephones for public use should be at approx 1·200 above floor level. For chairbound people, selected telephones should be not higher than 0·900 above floor level.
See 440.

627 Lifts

6270 Lift control buttons or switches should be not higher than 1·600 above floor level.
CP96 recommends levels between 0·910 and 1·370. For discussion see 1115.

6271 Digits on lift buttons or on the panel beside lift buttons should be embossed.
See 45304.

6272 The closing of lift doors should be controlled by photo-electric cells.
See 45213.

628 Cloakroom provision

6280 Where access to a cloakroom is through a lobby
with two doors in sequence, both doors should open
in the same direction.
See also 64310, 64321.

6281 Coat racks should be reachable by disabled people.
See 5054.

6282 High steps to stall urinals should be avoided.
See 54307.

629 Identification of facilities

6290 Facilities which are suitable for disabled people, for
example special wc compartments, should be
identified by special signs.
See 651, 652.

6291 Notices should be displayed in the entrance halls of
buildings and other strategic positions to indicate
the whereabouts of different departments, facilities
etc.
See 6154.

63 Public buildings: Ambulant disabled people

630 Requirements for ambulant disabled people

6300 Summary
63000 Where provision for ambulant disabled people is to be made in a building all appropriate specifications under 631, 632 and 633, together with requirement 6210 (ramped kerbs) must be observed. Attention should be given to other recommendations in section 62.
For discussion on the distinction between should and must specifications see 1401–2, 613.

631 Ambulant disabled people: Approach

6310 Summary of approach requirements
63100 The approach to at least one entrance to the building from the adjacent street and/or car park must be level, ramped in compliance with 6311, or stepped in compliance with 6312. The entrance door must comply with 6313.
A level approach is one where the gradient does not exceed 1:20.

6311 Ramped approach
63110 Where the approach is ramped the following recommendations must be observed.

Dimensions
63111 The gradient of the ramp should not exceed 1:12.
A ramp is defined as an inclined surface having a gradient exceeding 1:20.

63112 The width of the ramp must be not less than 1·200.

Handrails
63113 A handrail at approx 1·000 above ramp level should be provided to any exposed side of a ramp or platform.
For discussion on handrails to ramps see 323.

Alternative stepped approach
63114 Where the gradient of the ramp exceeds 1:12 an alternative stepped approach must be provided, in compliance with 6312.
An alternative stepped approach is needed where the gradient is steep because some ambulant disabled people have difficulty negotiating ramps (1112, 1224). An example of a suitable arrangement is shown in diagram 64.1. It is desirable that the stepped approach is adjacent to the ramped approach.

6312 Stepped approach
63120 Where the approach is stepped the following recommendations must be observed.

Goings and risers
63121 Step goings must be not less than 0·280. Risers must be not more than 0·165. Goings and risers in any flight must be of uniform depth and height.
See 316. For discussion on stepped approaches to buildings see 6160.

Total rise
63122 The vertical rise of any flight of consecutive steps should not exceed 1·200. Long flights of steps should have platforms at intervals.

Handrails
63123 A handrail must be provided to each side of the steps.
A single rail down the centre of a flight is permissible.

63124 Handrails should be extended not less than 0·300 beyond the nosing of the top step.
See 3131, 3322. For detailed guidance on handrails see section 33.

6313 Entrance door
63130 At least one entrance door must give a clear opening width of not less than 0·750.
See 6124–5.

63131 Where revolving doors or turnstiles are installed, an auxiliary side-hung door or gate giving a clear opening width of not less than 0·750 must be provided.

632 Ambulant disabled people: Internal planning

6320 Accessible areas
63200 Areas to be accessible to ambulant disabled people must be served by circulation areas complying with 6321. They must be at the same level as the entrance door (6313) or must be reached by a lift (6322) or a staircase complying with 6323.
For comment on vertical circulation see 6160.

6321 Circulation areas
63210 Passageways must be not less than 1·200 wide.
See 506, 6127. For notes on circulation spaces for ambulant disabled people see section 25.

63211 Doors must give a clear opening width of not less than 0·670.
See 6125.

63212 Ramps to circulation areas should have a gradient not exceeding 1:12.

6322 Lifts
63220 Where a lift is provided its floor at entrance level should be at the same level as the entrance door complying with 6313.
See also 627. For comment see 617. For detailed guidance on lifts see section 45.

63221 The lift door should give a clear opening of not less than 0·700.
See 4520.

6323 Staircases
Treads and risers

63230 Stair goings must be not less than 0·250. Risers must be not more than 0·170 high. Goings and risers in any flight must be of uniform depth and height. For comment on vertical circulation see 6160. For design notes see 314.

63231 Open risers should be avoided. CP96(1967) says 'Open risers shall not be permitted'. For comment see 6135.

Total rise

63232 The vertical rise of any flight of consecutive steps should not exceed 1·800. A maximum of 1·800 is suggested rather than 1·200 as for external steps (63122) because internal stairs are protected from the weather.

Handrails

63233 A handrail must be provided to each side of any steps or stairs. See 3301.

63234 Handrails should be extended not less than 0·300 beyond the nosing of the top step of any flight. See 3131, 3322.

633 Ambulant disabled people: Cloakroom provision

6330 Wc compartments

63300 Wc compartments for ambulant disabled people should be in accessible areas complying with 63200.

Internal dimensions

63301 The preferred wc compartment width is 0·800. A comparatively narrow compartment is preferred to allow ambulant disabled people to use support rails to either side to push themselves up to a standing position.

63302 The depth should be not less than 1·500 where the door slides or opens out. Where the cistern is outside the compartment the depth may be 1·300. See 54101.

Door

63303 The door to the wc compartment must open out or slide, and give a clear opening width of not less than 0·670. See 36004, 36341, 6125.

63304 Where the wc compartment is approached laterally the door should be hinged on the side away from the direction of approach. A wc compartment for ambulant disabled people in a public cloakroom may conveniently be located at one end of a row of cubicles, as shown in diagram 63.1.

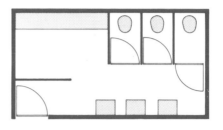

63.1 Layout of cloakroom showing possible location of wc compartment for ambulant disabled people

63305 The door should be hinged on rising butts and provided with a ball or roller catch and suitable indicator bolt. It should be openable from outside in the event of an emergency. For notes on ironmongery see 3634. CP96(1967) recommends that a horizontal pull rail is provided to the internal face of the door; this is not an essential provision for ambulant disabled people.

Wc fixture

63306 The upper face of the wc seat should be approx 0·445 above floor level. This means that the height to the rim of the pedestal will be approx 0·420. For design notes see 5425.

63307 The wc should be placed so that the seated user can support himself against the rear wall or low level cistern.

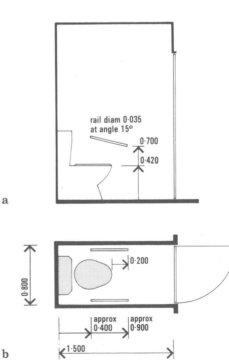

63.2 Wc compartment for ambulant disabled people (1:50)

Support rails

63308 A support rail having a diameter not less than 0·030 or more than 0·045 must be fixed to each side wall, as shown in diagram 63.2.

CP96(1967) recommends the provision of both horizontal and vertical rails to each side wall; a single inclined rail as shown in diagram 63.2 is preferred for reasons discussed in 54275.

6331 Other cloakroom provisions

Wash basins

63310 The preferred height of wash basin rims is 0·900 above floor level.

See 54410.

63311 To cater for people with varying disabilities, basins may be fixed at alternative heights, for example 0·700 and 0·800.

640   Requirements for chairbound people

6400   Summary

64000 Where provision is to be made for chairbound people in a building, appropriate requirements under 641, 642 and 643 must be complied with, together with requirement 6210 (ramped kerbs). Attention should be given to other recommendations in section 62.
Ambulant disabled people will automatically be catered for where provision is made for chairbound people. For discussion on the distinction between should and must specifications see 1401–2, 6141, 6150.

641   Chairbound people: Approach

6410   Summary of approach requirements

64100 The approach to at least one entrance to the building from the adjacent street and/or car park must be level, or ramped in compliance with 6411.

6411   Ramped approach
Dimensions

64110 The gradient of the ramp should not exceed 1:20. It must not exceed 1:12, other than in exceptional circumstances and only where an alternative stepped approach is provided in compliance with 64116.
For comment see 6151, 6161, 321, 322, 1112, 1224.

64111 The width of the ramp must be not less than 1·200, preferred minimum 1·500.
See 3220.

Handrails

64112 A handrail at approx 1·000 above ramp level should be provided to any exposed side of a ramp.
For discussion on handrails to ramps see 323.

Platform at head of ramp

64113 Where the gradient of the ramp exceeds 1:12 a platform having a width and depth of not less than 1·200 must be provided at the head of the ramp. To allow for drainage of surface water the platform will not be absolutely level, and a platform is not therefore required where the ramp gradient does not exceed 1:12. For platform plans see diagrams 50.1a–d.

Foot of ramp

64114 At the foot of any ramp whose gradient exceeds 1:12 the surface should be level for a distance of not less than 1·800.
See 3227.

Kerbs

64115 A kerb not less than 0·050 high must be provided to any exposed side of a ramp or platform. This is required to prevent wheelchair castor wheels dropping over the edge, see 324.

Alternative stepped approach

64116 Where the gradient of the ramp exceeds 1:12 an alternative stepped approach must be provided; the requirements of 6312 must be complied with. An example of a suitable alternative stepped approach is shown in diagram 64.1; for discussion see 616.

6412   Entrance door

64120 At least one entrance door served by an approach complying with 64100 must give a clear opening width of not less than 0·750.
See 6124.

64121 Where revolving doors or turnstiles are installed an auxiliary side-hung door or gate must be provided giving a clear opening width of not less the 0·750.

64122 Thresholds must not be raised more than 0·015 above the level of the floor to either side of the door.
See 340.

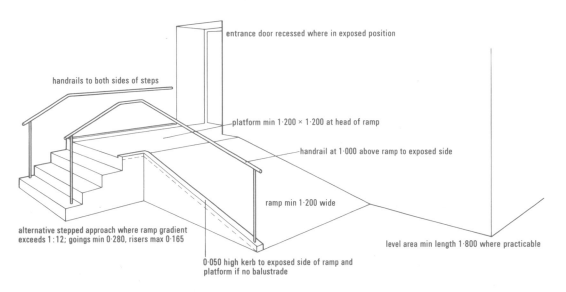

entrance door recessed where in exposed position

handrails to both sides of steps

platform min 1·200 × 1·200 at head of ramp

handrail at 1·000 above ramp to exposed side

ramp min 1·200 wide

alternative stepped approach where ramp gradient exceeds 1:12; goings min 0·280, risers max 0·165

level area min length 1·800 where practicable

0·050 high kerb to exposed side of ramp and platform if no balustrade

64.1   Building approach for chairbound and ambulant disabled people where ramp gradient exceeds 1:12

642 Chairbound people: Internal planning

6420 Accessible areas

64200 Areas to be accessible to chairbound people must be at the same level as the entrance door (6412) or as the floor of a lift (6423).

64201 Where variations in level are needed ramps should be incorporated. Gradients must be not more than 1:12.

6421 Doors

64210 Doors must give a clear opening width of not less than 0·750.
See 3614, 6124.

64211 On the leading side of any door the clear wall space to the side of the door by the door handle should be not less than 0·300 wide.
See 36043. For utilization spaces for wheelchair manoeuvre through doors see diagrams 24.10a–f.

6422 Circulation areas

64220 Passageways serving accessible areas must not be less than 1·200 wide, preferred minimum 1·500.
For comment see 6127.

64221 Where lobbies are incorporated between doors there must be space for wheelchair manoeuvre. Dimensions prescribed in diagrams 50.3–50.6 should be observed.

6423 Lifts

64230 Vertical circulation between floors must be by means of a lift. At entrance level the floor of the lift must be at the same level as the entrance door complying with 6412.
For detailed guidance on lifts see section 45.

64231 The internal depth of the lift must be not less than 1·400 and the width not less than 1·100.
CP96(1967) recommendations are obsolete and should be disregarded. For notes on lift dimensions see table 45.1. For comment see 617.

64232 The clear space in front of the lift doors must be not less than 1·500 × 1·500.
See 45012.

643 Chairbound people: Cloakroom provision

6430 Cloakroom planning

64300 Where a cloakroom is planned with wc provision for chairbound people it must be at the same level as an entrance door complying with 6412 or as a lift complying with 6423.

64301 Where access is through an enclosed lobby or partitions are installed to restrict sight lines, planning must allow for wheelchair manoeuvre. Dimensions prescribed in diagrams 50.3, 50.6 and 50.7 should be observed.

64302 Wc compartments for chairbound people must be designed in compliance with 6431–6436.

64303 A wc compartment for chairbound people in a public cloakroom may conveniently be located at the end of a row of cubicles.
For comparable example for ambulant disabled people see diagram 63.1

6431 Wheelchair wc compartments: Doors

64310 The door to any wheelchair wc compartment must give a clear opening width of not less than 0·750. This permits the use of 0·900 doorsets, see 6124. 1·000 doorsets may be used if preferred.

64311 The door must open out or slide, and should be positioned as shown in diagram 64.3 or 64.4. CP96(1967) allows an alternative position for the door on the side wall; it does not give comfortable space for wheelchair manoeuvre and is not recommended.

64312 Where the wc compartment is approached laterally the door should be hinged on the side away from the direction of approach.
For related example see diagram 63.1. For notes on door planning see 54143–4.

Door ironmongery

64313 The door should be openable from outside in the event of an emergency.
See 36004.

64314 The door should be hinged on rising butts and have a throwover indicator bolt or easily manipulated closing device.
See 3633, 3634.

64315 An internal horizontal pulling rail should be fixed to the door if it opens out.
See diagram 36.5, 36045.

6432 Wheelchair wc compartments: Planning

64320 For a wheelchair wc compartment the preferred dimensions are a depth not less than 2·000 and a width not less than 1·500.
See diagram 64.2b. The plan arrangements shown may be handed (laterally inverted). For comment see 618.

64321 The minimum dimensions must be a depth of 1·700 and a width of 1·400.
Diagram 64.3a shows a suitable layout where the cistern is within the compartment, and diagram 64.3b one where it is outside.

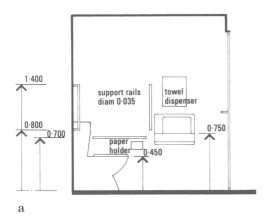

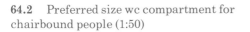

a

b

64.2 Preferred size wc compartment for chairbound people (1:50)

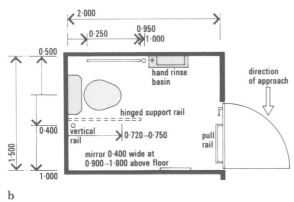

a

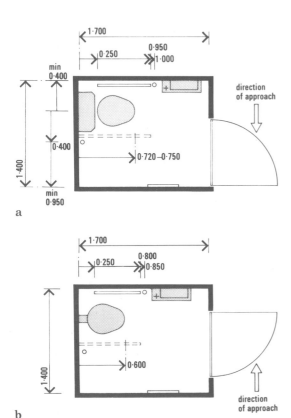

b

64.3 Minimum size wc compartment for chairbound people: Alternative layouts (1:50)

Space beside wc

64322 In a wc compartment having a width of 1·500 or more the dimension from the centre line of the wc to the nearer side wall must be not less than 0·500. This is to allow for an attendant; for discussion see 54127–8.

64323 In a wc compartment having a width of less than 1·500 the dimension from the centre line of the wc to the nearer side wall must be not less than 0·400. See 54129.

64324 The dimension from the centre line of the wc to the further side wall must be not less than 0·950. This gives space for wheelchair manoeuvre and lateral transfer, see 54123.

64325 In a wc compartment having a depth of 1·900 or more, the dimension from the rear wall to the front edge of the wc seat must be not less than 0·720. This is to facilitate lateral transfer; for discussion see 54123–4, 54156. In a wc compartment having a depth of less than 1·900, space for manoeuvring in front of the wc ought not to be reduced.

6433 Wc fixture

64330 The upper face of the wc seat must be at approx 0·475 above floor level. The height to the rim of the wc bowl will be approx 0·450, see 54259.

64331 The wc seat should not be brittle. A wood seat may be preferred, see 54240.

6434 Wc compartments: Support rails

64340 Horizontal and vertical support rails must be installed in wheelchair wc compartments. See diagram 64.2. For fixing dimensions of rails shown in diagram 64.2 see diagram 54.29b.

64341 The diameter of rails should be not less than 0·030 or more than 0·045.

Horizontal rails

64342 A horizontal rail should be fixed parallel with the wc, extending from the rear wall to a point not less than 0·200 in front of the wc. The provision of this rail is important to assist transfer to and from the wc. When its use may be complicated by the fixing of a hand rinse basin, the basin may be fixed elsewhere in the wc compartment, but it is preferred that it is within reach of a person seated on the wc.

64343 A hinged support rail should be installed to the exposed side of the wc. See 54274, diagram 54.30.

64344 Horizontal rails should be fixed at a level approx 0·220 above the wc seat. CP96(1967) recommends that these rails are at 0·280 above the wc seat; experience has shown that this can be inconveniently high for some users.

64345 Where there is no low level cistern a backrest should be incorporated behind the wc.
See 54205. The backrest should be designed to serve also as a support for pushing up to a standing position or transferring to or from the wheelchair.

Vertical rails

64346 A vertical rail should be fixed approx 0·300 in front of the wc and approx 0·280–0·330 from the centre line of the wc.
See diagram 54.29b. For notes on clearance between rails and wall surfaces see 3335.

64347 A second vertical rail should be fixed on the rear wall at a point approx 0·400 from the centre line of the wc.
See diagram 64.2.

64348 Vertical rails should extend from approx 0·800 to 1·200 above floor level.
CP96(1967) says that rails may be extended to floor and ceiling; this is not considered necessary or desirable.

6435 Wc compartments: Hand rinse basin

64350 A hand rinse basin must be provided inside the wc compartment, located where it can be reached by a person seated on the wc.
See 5446. CP96(1967) says that a basin need not be provided 'where space is severely restricted'; this qualification ought not to be considered acceptable.

64351 The basin rim should be at approx 0·750 above floor level.

64352 A single mixer valve with lever handle is suggested, located on the side nearer the wc.

6436 Wc compartments: Accessories

64360 The toilet paper holder should be located where it can be reached by a person seated on the wc.
A suggested location is shown in diagram 64.2a.

64361 The wc flushing handle should be easy to manipulate.
See 54290.

Mirror

64362 A mirror should be fixed, the bottom edge to be at approx 0·900 above floor level, the top edge at approx 1·800.
Diagrams 64.2b and 64.3 show suitable locations.

6437 Chairbound people: Other cloakroom provisions
Wash basins

64370 In public cloakrooms having a row of wash basins, one basin should be fixed at a level convenient for wheelchair users, ie at approx 0·750 above floor level.
This is in addition to the hand rinse basin in the wc compartment.

Drinking fountains etc

64371 Selected drinking fountains, incinerators, mirrors and towel dispensers should be fixed at a level convenient to chairbound people.
See 54312, 54321, 54331, 54342. Where a paper towel dispenser is fitted a disposal container should be provided, preferably hung on the wall to avoid limiting manoeuvring space at floor level.

65 Signposting

650 Signposting: General considerations

6500 Where arrangements to aid disabled people are incorporated in any building it is important that both people who visit the building and those who work in it know that they are there. The display of signplates advertising the facilities available for disabled people is advocated; as discussed in the commentary it is desirable both for practical and psychological reasons that these notices focus specifically on disabled people[1].

The international symbol of accessibility (diagram 65.1) should always be used on signplates; although there are reservations about the graphic merit of the symbol it is essential on tactical grounds that it is widely promoted and employed as extensively as possible.

The international symbol

6501 Since the international symbol was officially adopted at a meeting of the International Society for the Rehabilitation of the Disabled in 1969 no authoritative guidance has been published on its practical applications. This has handicapped effective promotion of the symbol, which has too often been used in an arbitrary or meaningless fashion. The use of the symbol in isolation as a door or window sticker is particularly unhelpful; it is invariably the case that to transmit its message an accompanying explanatory legend is essential, without which it is simply an object of curiosity. Also to be deplored is the practice of 'awarding' the symbol as an accolade to conscientious building managers or architects.

6502 Depicting as it does a stylized figure in a wheelchair, the symbol suffers by relating not to all handicapped people but to wheelchair users only. It is therefore inappropriate for use in respect of services for ambulant disabled people or people with non-overt disabilities only. In practice, it commonly occurs that facilities for ambulant disabled people are allied with facilities for wheelchair users, in which case they can be advertised by the symbol, provided that a suitable legend is incorporated.

Purposes and functions of signplates

6503 There are seven purposes for which signplates may be used:
1. Identifying accessible entrances to buildings.
2. Identifying manageable routes through buildings.
3. Identifying usable vertical circulation facilities.
4. Identifying usable cloakroom facilities.
5. Identifying reserved car parking places.
6. Advertising the availability of special services in buildings.
7. Advertising the arrangements made for disabled people to use buildings.

6504 Each signplate should have on it the symbol and an informatory legend, and, where appropriate, a directional arrow. Signplates have three functions:
1. Directional – incorporating an arrow directing to a specific facility.
2. Locational – an identifying sign at the place where the facility is provided.
3. Informative – advising about the availability of a facility or service for disabled people.

Criteria for application

6505 As a general rule, building facilities identified by signplates should conform to minimum requirements for chairbound people as detailed in section 64.

For example, entrances should be unobstructed by steps, circulation routes should have a minimum width of 1·200, doors should give a minimum clear opening of 0·750, lifts should have minimum internal dimensions of 1·400 × 1·100 and wc compartments should have minimum internal dimensions of 1·700 × 1·400.

6506 In practice, particularly in respect of existing buildings, some compromising of preferred standards may not significantly affect the usability of a facility and commonsense criteria for displaying signplates should be employed.

6507 Where there is doubt it is wiser to display a symbol than not to do so.

Copyright

6508 There are no copyright restraints on the use of the symbol.

British Standard

6509 When CP96 *Access for the disabled to buildings* was published by the British Standards Institution in 1967 it had a footnote saying that a British Standard *Indication signs for the use of buildings by disabled people* was 'in course of preparation' [2]. The BSI is still (1976) planning an official British Standard; when it is issued it will offer authoritative advice, superseding the recommendations which follow. Because there has been no proper guidance issued these recommendations are tentative. They are based largely on the careful work done by Peter Rea in his *Symbol application manual* [3] relating to the disused Norwich symbol.

651 Approved uses of the symbol: General

6510 The notes below (6511–5) list approved uses for the symbol on signplates, in situations general to public buildings.

---

[1] For discussion see 1404
[2] Bib 93000, p2
[3] Bib 93082

Entrances

6511 The identification of accessible entrances to buildings, for example an unobstructed side entrance where the principal entrance is stepped.

Horizontal circulation

6512 The identification of convenient routes through buildings or between buildings, for example where there is a ramped route as an alternative to a stepped route.

Vertical circulation

6513 The identification of usable vertical circulation facilities, for example (1) the possibility for disabled people of using on request a goods or staff lift in places where the normal facility is a staircase or escalator; (2) where there is a lift available as well as a staircase or escalator, but where its location may not be immediately apparent, and (3) where a lift in one place is too small to carry a wheelchair comfortably and there is an alternative larger lift elsewhere.

Cloakroom facilities

6514 The identification of usable cloakroom facilities, for example (1) cloakrooms which can be reached without using steps; (2) cloakrooms where there are wc compartments having support rails to aid handicapped people, and (3) cloakrooms where there are wc compartments large enough to accommodate wheelchair users.

Public telephones

6515 The identification of public telephone kiosks large enough to accommodate wheelchairs, or public telephones installed at low level and therefore convenient for wheelchair users and people with limited reach.

652 Approved uses of the symbol: Particular

6520 The following notes (6521–8) list approved uses for the symbol on signplates, in situations specific to particular building types.

Theatres etc

6521 The advertising of special arrangements made for wheelchair users in concert halls, theatres, cinemas etc, for example whether disabled people may sit and remain in their wheelchairs, how many are permitted to use the building at any one time, and arrangements for reserving places for wheelchairs in advance.

Where provision is made for wheelchair users the information given on signplates may be extended to advise about services suitable for other handicapped people, for example seats convenient for ambulant disabled people or facilities for people who are hard of hearing.

Exhibition buildings

6522 For drawing attention in exhibition buildings to restrictions imposed by the local fire authority on the use of the building by disabled people, for example the number of wheelchairs admitted at any one time, and the need for chairbound people to be accompanied.

Transport buildings

6523 The advertising in railway stations, air terminals and airport buildings of the availability of wheelchairs on loan to avoid the need to walk extended distances, portable ramps to enable chairbound people to board trains, and other special services for disabled travellers.

Sports stadia

6524 The advertising in sports stadia of special provision for disabled spectators, for example special seating facilities or arrangements for disabled people to sit in their wheelchairs or motor vehicles at the side of the sports arena.

Swimming pools

6525 The advertising at swimming pools of services for swimmers who are handicapped, for example club facilities for disabled swimmers, the times of regular club sessions and the address of the club secretary.

Hotels

6526 The advertising in hotels of the availability of bedrooms suitable for wheelchair users.

Restaurants

6527 The advertising, perhaps by placing the symbol on or alongside the menu card, of accessible restaurants and cafes, in buildings where it is not evident that facilities are available.

Wheelchairs for loan

6528 The advertising in department stores, art galleries, museums, zoos, botanical gardens etc of the availability of wheelchairs for loan to customers or visitors who are handicapped.

653 Road traffic signs, car parking facilities

6530 The symbol as approved by the Department of the Environment for use on road traffic signs is shown in diagram 65.1. Copies of the official drawing WBM228 detailing the exact design of the symbol may be obtained from the Traffic Engineering Division of the Department of the Environment [4]. The symbol design is different from that of the drawing attached to DoE Circular Roads 59/71 [5], which was the weak version of the original design (diagram 14.11); for comment see 1404.

---

[4] For address see 94
[5] Bib 93081

65.1 International symbol of accessibility, as approved by the Department of the Environment

65.2 International symbol of accessibility

6531 The notes on DoE drawing WBM228 say:
1. The grid lines do not form any part of any sign to which the symbol is applied, but overall size of tile relates to the black panel on which the symbol normally appears.
2. When used on a sign with a blue background the black panel shall be omitted and the symbol be set directly on the blue background.

6532 The centre point of the wheel is four stroke widths from the left side of the tile, and three from its base. One stroke width is equal to $\frac{1}{4}$ x height, ie the height of a lower case letter x of the legend on the signplate.

Road traffic signs
6533 Regulatory signs for display on public highways are prescribed in *The traffic signs regulations and general directions 1975* [6]. Approved uses for regulatory signs incorporating the symbol are:
1. Parking place reserved for disabled badge holders.
2. Signs indicating exemption for disabled badge holders to premises and land adjacent to prohibited roads.
3. Directions to public lavatories including facilities for disabled people.

Signs on private land
6534 The traffic signs regulations do not apply to signs on private land. Suggested uses for the symbol are:
1. On signs relating to reserved parking places for disabled drivers or passengers.
2. For painting on floor surfaces to emphasize the exclusiveness of reserved parking places.

654 Specification of the symbol

6540 The setting out of the symbol should be based on a square tile as shown in diagram 65.1 and 65.2.

6541 The symbol may be photographically copied from diagram 65.2, whether reproduced in white or light colours on a black or dark coloured background, or in black or dark colours on a white or light coloured background.

6542 The standard variant of the symbol is as shown in diagrams 65.1 and 65.2, with the pin head facing right. On signplates where the symbol is used in conjunction with a directional arrow pointing left the design should be inverted.

6543 There are no standard colour specifications for signplates incorporating the symbol, other than for road traffic signs.

655 Sizes of signplates

6550 A basic range of six sizes of signplates is suggested, three horizontal pattern and three vertical pattern. For each pattern there are small, medium and large sizes, with dimensions as detailed in the captions to diagrams 65.3a and b. Diagrams 65.4a–d illustrate applications.

6551 Where signplates have a directional or locational function a horizontal signplate will usually be more appropriate. Where they have an informative function a vertical signplate will be more appropriate, except where the legend is brief.

[6] Bib 93793

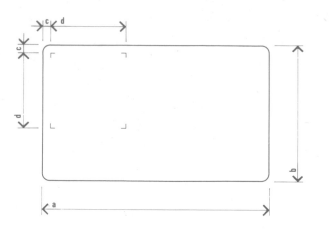

a Horizontal signplates

	a	b	c	d
small	0·225	0·135	0·0075	0·075
medium	0·300	0·180	0·010	0·100
large	0·450	0·270	0·015	0·150

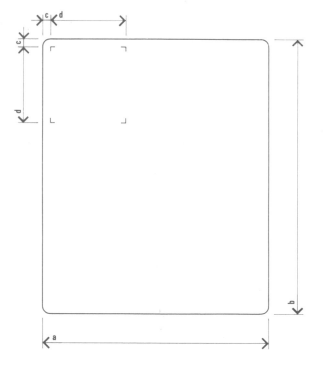

b Vertical signplates

	a	b	c	d
small	0·225	0·270	0·0075	0·075
medium	0·300	0·360	0·010	0·100
large	0·450	0·540	0·015	0·150

65.3 Signplate layouts

a

b

c

d

65.4 Signplate applications.
Normal design is white on dark background

Criteria for preferred sizes

6552 The preferred size of any signplate is determined by the nature of the facility identified, the function of the sign, the length of the legend and the distance from which it has to be read. The following guidelines are suggested:
1. For all directional signs, and for any other signs which may need to be read from a distance of more than 3·000, a large size signplate is recommended.
2. For external locational and informative signs which do not need to be read from a distance of more than 3·000 a medium size signplate is recommended.
3. For internal locational and informative signs which do not need to be read from a distance of more than 3·000 a small size signplate is recommended.

6553 These standard sizes, recommended for signplates when used in public buildings, are small when compared, for example, with road traffic signs. It is not essential that the legend on signplates is always readable from a distance. The intention is that the symbol on signs and notices is recognizable from a distance, and that people who need to know about the facility will approach closer to read the notice.

6554 In appropriate circumstances larger signs and notices may be installed.

656 Production of signplates

6560 Where a series of signplates is produced they should be of stove-enamelled aluminium plate or laminated plastic. For preparing single signplates a signwriting technique may be employed.

6561 For detailed guidance on the manufacture of signplates, signwriting techniques, methods of fixing and preparation of artwork and layouts for signs, reference should be made to Peter Rea's *Symbol application manual* [7].

657 Lettering, typeface, typestyle

6570 The recommended typeface for all signplates is Helvetica.

6571 It is suggested that headings to signplates, for example the name of the establishment or business providing the facility, are set in the lighter weight of typeface known as Helvetica regular, and the main legend in the heavier weight of typeface known as Helvetica medium.

6572 Lower case letters should be used throughout. Initial capitals should only be used for proper nouns or subjects, and for the first word of each new sentence.

6573 Punctuation should be kept to a minimum.

658 Location and positioning of signplates

6580 Signplates should be strategically placed, for example those relating to accessible entrances at a strategic approach point and at the entrance itself.

6581 Directional signs should be placed at focal points on main traffic routes. Signs should be sited to indicate a through route, with a locational sign at the destination.

6582 Directional legends should give one instruction at a time. Where appropriate, there should be a sequence of related signs, one at each change of direction or point of decision.

6583 The preferred height above floor level or ground level is between 1·400 and 1·700 to the lower edge of signplates. This allows for legends to be read from a standing or a seated (wheelchair) position. Road traffic signs, which should accord with official practice, are excepted.

659 Content of legend on signplates

6590 For its purpose to be achieved, a primary consideration in the design of any signplate is the content of its legend. The following guidelines are advised:
1. Be concise.
2. Avoid superfluous words, for example 'for disabled people' where the presence of the symbol and the context in which the signplate is displayed gives an unambiguous message.
3. In situations where facilities reserved for disabled people may be abused by able-bodied people the words 'for disabled people' or 'for wheelchair users' should be used.
4. The term 'disabled people' is generally preferred to 'handicapped people'. Where the facility is for wheelchair users only the term 'wheelchair users' should be used in preference to 'disabled people'.
5. For directional signs visual communication is preferred to verbal communication, ie arrows should be employed where possible rather than written instructions.

[7] Bib 93082, p48–9

660 Public lavatories: General considerations

6600 The recommendations in this section relate specifically to public lavatories managed by local authorities. They are also relevant to public cloakroom facilities in buildings such as railway stations, air terminals and department stores.

6601 The use of public lavatories by disabled people is discussed in the commentary (1219); among disabled people the accessibility of public lavatories is of greater importance than for any other building type (table 12.9).

6602 Since the second edition of this book was published the Ministry of Housing circular *Design of public conveniences with facilities for the disabled* [1] has been issued, and many local authorities have built public lavatories with the recommended unisex compartments.
The impression is that these facilities are only rarely used by people in wheelchairs, despite advertising by means of signs with the prescribed symbol. Local authorities ought not to be deterred from making further provision on this account; it is only if they are distributed in quantity that people in wheelchairs still be substantially aided.

6603 Detailed specifications for wc compartments for ambulant disabled people are in 633, and for chairbound people in 643. For comment on the internal dimensions of wheelchair compartments see 618.

Vandalism and supervision

6604 According to the character of the neighbourhood, equipment in unattended wheelchair wc compartments may be vulnerable to repeated vandalism. There is no simple answer to this problem; the more equipment is prescribed to be vandalproof, the less it is likely to be convenient for handicapped people. The recommendation is that wherever practicable special facilities should be supervised by an attendant.

6605 A supplementary advantage of supervision is that help may be given in an emergency, for example if a disabled person falls.

Provision for both sexes

6606 It is recommended that wheelchair wc compartments are usable by people of both sexes. This is because a husband may have to help his disabled wife to transfer to and from the wc, or a wife has to help her disabled husband.

6607 Where an attendant-supervised public lavatory is proposed, and where for planning reasons none of the arrangements shown in diagrams 66.1a–c is practicable, it is preferred that the special wc compartment is placed on the female side.

[1] Bib 93570

This is because it is relatively more important for chairbound women than for men that suitable wc provision is made, for reasons discussed in the notes on incontinence (9152). On the occasions when it is necessary for a chairbound man to use a wheelchair wc compartment on the female side it may be possible for the attendant to supervise the facility, so avoiding embarrassment.

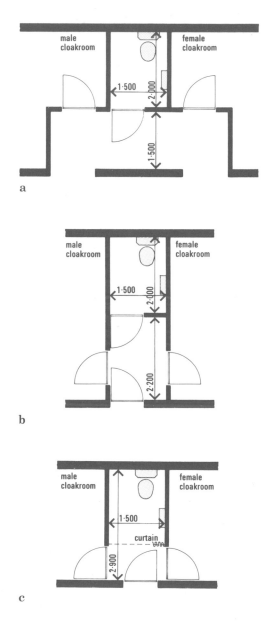

66.1 Public lavatory layouts with wheelchair wc compartment (1:100)

661   Public lavatories: Chairbound people

6610   The suggested aim is that in every locality having one or more public lavatories there should be at least one facility usable by chairbound people. This should be observed particularly in places visited by tourists, and most importantly at seaside resorts.

Siting

6611   Public lavatories catering for chairbound people should be on level sites.
The approach should be level or by a ramp having a gradient not exceeding 1:20.

6612   Car parking spaces should be available immediately alongside the facility.
This is important for chairbound people travelling alone by car. The facility should be identified by specific signs (6514) and should be signposted by traffic signs in the area (653).

Summary of requirements

6613   A public lavatory catering for chairbound people must incorporate at least one wc compartment to the preferred standards prescribed in 643, ie a depth of not less than 2·000 and a width of not less than 1·500. The wc compartment should be usable independently by those potentially able to do so; 'should' recommendations as well as 'must' recommendations of relevant specifications ought to be observed. See also 628.

6614   Wc compartments for chairbound people should preferably be usable by both sexes, see 6605 and discussion in 1219.

Access to wc compartments

6615   The door to the wc compartment must be shielded from external view.
Where the facility is for use by both men and women it should be shielded from direct view from inside male or female cloakroom areas.

6616   Diagram 66.1a shows a possible layout where approaches to male and female cloakrooms are adjacent, and the wheelchair wc compartment need not have independent access from male and female sides.

6617   Diagram 66.1b shows a possible layout where approaches to male and female cloakrooms are from opposite directions and the wheelchair wc compartment is accessible either from male or female sides, or direct from outside the building.

6618   Where space is limited it is permissible, though not recommended, that the wc compartment is separated from the adjacent lobby space by a curtain as shown in diagram 66.1c; the side doors may open in if preferred, provided that they are hinged on the side further from the wc.

Alarm call

6619   An alarm call, which may be push button or pull cord operated, should be located so that it is accessible to a person seated on the wc.
This is so that assistance can be summoned from the attendant in an emergency, but it will more commonly be used by a disabled person indicating to a companion waiting outside that he or she has finished using the wc and is ready to be transferred back to the wheelchair.

662   Public lavatories: Ambulant disabled people

6620   Where public lavatory provision is made for chairbound people it is desirable in addition that provision is made for ambulant disabled people, with one wc compartment for men and one for women.
This recommendation is made first, because of the preference which some disabled people have for a narrow wc compartment with support rails to either side and second, because there may be occasions, for example when handicapped people go on coach outings, when a single special facility is insufficient.

6621   New public lavatories not catering for chairbound people should be usable by ambulant disabled people, and wc compartments should be provided for male and female use.
These compartments should be accessible without having to negotiate steps. Where steps are provided the requirements of 6312 or 6323 must be observed.

Summary of requirements

6622   Where a wc compartment is provided in a public lavatory or cloakroom for use by ambulant disabled people, the requirements of 633 must be observed.
To facilitate independent use 'should' recommendations as well as 'must' recommendations of relevant specifications ought to be observed. See also 628.

Identification

6623   For wc compartments for ambulant disabled people the use of the international symbol showing a wheelchair will be inappropriate.

6624   The fixing of a notice saying simply 'Disabled people' or 'Wc for disabled people' will inevitably provoke complaints that the compartment is not big enough for wheelchairs. A preferred tactic might be to have a notice saying 'Wc for disabled people' incorporating directions to the nearest wc suitable for chairbound people. Ambiguous terms such as 'Semi-ambulant toilet' must be avoided.

663 **The street environment**

6630 In the planning of new towns, or new estates in existing towns, the street environment should be designed to avoid obstacles or hazards to disabled people.

6631 Kerbs at street intersections should be ramped. Both for mothers with prams and for pedestrians pushing loaded wheelchairs, it is important that there are no high kerbs. It should be possible, for example, for a husband pushing his wife out in a wheelchair to travel from his home to the local shopping centre and to principal public buildings in the area without having to negotiate any steps or high pavement kerbs. The importance of kerbs and ramps in connection with the use of buildings by disabled people is discussed in the commentary (1224). For methods of ramping kerbs see 3023.

Street furniture

6632 Street furniture should be located so as not to be hazardous to blind people or wheelchair users. Most blind people keep to the inside of pavements at approx 0·500 from adjacent walls. For comment on environmental provision for blind people see 1423.

6633 Posts for street lamps and traffic signs should be on the outside of pavements close to kerbs; they must not be placed in the centre of pavements.

Street surfaces

6634 Where street surfaces are planned to cater for wheelchair users and other disabled people the use of brick setts is permissible, subject to qualifications discussed in 3015.

6635 Brick setts if properly laid are not such a hazard to wheelchair users or ambulant disabled people that they should be discarded in favour of the smooth non-jointed surfaces generally indicated for wheelchair users; in wet or icy conditions the latter may be very hazardous for ambulant disabled people.

Benches

6636 Selected benches for rest purposes in pedestrianized areas, as in public parks, should be convenient for ambulant disabled people.
Seats should be relatively shallow, suggested maximum depth 0·500, and not lower than 0·420 above ground level. Fixed armrests should be at 0·200–0·250 above seat level.

Building types

7

70 Buildings for handicapped people

700 Residential homes for physically handicapped people

7000 General considerations

70000 The role of residential homes in the spectrum of accommodation services for physically handicapped people is examined in section 15 of the commentary. Planning and design tactics are discussed in 1515–1524.

70001 Advice from the Department of Health on the planning of residential homes is given in Circular LASSL(75)19 [1], to be read in conjunction with the building note on residential accommodation for elderly people [2]. For reasons discussed in the commentary, the provision suggested here is generally to a higher standard than that recommended officially. In that architects designing residential homes for social services authorities in Britain will be constrained by the cost allowances set down in the circular, it will not as a rule be practicable to achieve the preferred arrangements throughout, though to some extent additional expenditure on amenities for individual residents may be offset by savings on communal spaces.

70002 The recommendations made here assume a home for not more than about 30 residents, in line with the advice given in the DHSS circular.

70003 Matters of location are discussed in 1516 in relation to overall strategy.

7001 Siting

70010 For practical reasons a level site may be desirable but is not essential.

70011 A shelving site can have advantages, provided that immediate access to the building from roadway and parking areas is level. A shelving site affords variety of outlook, and also aids planning on more than one level. On a flat site it will not as a rule be sensible to plan a home for fewer than 30 people on more than one level, owing to problems of circulation and means of escape in case of fire.

7002 Approach

70020 The approach to the entrance serving parking areas used by residents must be level: a ramp of any gradient must be avoided if residents who have their own vehicles are to manage independently.

70021 All entrances to the home must be accessible to chairbound people: observe 641. At the principal entrance automatic opening doors are recommended, see 3606.

7003 Internal planning

70030 All areas of the home must be accessible to chairbound people: observe 642.

70031 To cater for residents using large or cumbersome wheelchairs the general use of 1·000 doorsets is advised.

70032 Main circulation routes should have a width of 1·800, see 5064, 2424.

Floor finishes

70033 Carpeting is suggested to residents' bed-sitting rooms, communal sitting rooms, circulation spaces and all other areas where practicable. Consideration may be given to carpeting in dining rooms. For discussion see 386.

Lifts

70034 Where lifts are incorporated at least one lift must have an internal depth of not less than 1·800 and width of not less than 1·000. The door should give a clear opening of not less than 0·800, preferred minimum 0·900. For further guidance see 45005, 4512 and detailed recommendations in section 45.

7004 Residents' bed-sitting rooms: Planning considerations

70040 Single rooms should be provided for 70 or 80 per cent of residents, and double rooms for the remainder. For discussion see 1517.

Planning of rooms

70041 Paired single rooms may be planned so that they can be converted into a double unit, but at least some of the 2 person units should be designed as such.

70042 Suggested minimum areas for residents' bed-sitting rooms are 14·0m² for single rooms and 20·5m² for double rooms.
The minimum standards recommended in the DHSS circular are 12·0m² for single rooms and 18·6m² for double rooms.

Placing of beds

70043 Rooms must be planned so that beds can be placed in alternative positions; fixed bedhead units should not be installed, see 1518.

70044 At least one bed position should allow a handicapped person lying in bed to see out of the window.

Furniture requirements

70045 Each bed-sitting room should be designed to accommodate a built-in cupboard (see 70054), a chest of drawers (which may be incorporated in the cupboard), a cupboard for crockery and cutlery, a bedside table and a desk or table which may be used for studying or hobbies, see 1518.
Double units should provide for a small dining table.

70046 Where practicable there should be provision in bed-sitting units for the preparation of light meals.

[1] Bib 93140
[2] Bib 93650

700 Residential homes for physically handicapped people *continued*

Washroom

70047 Where the budget permits, each unit should have a separate washroom, containing wc and wash basin. The fixing height of the basin, and if possible the positioning of the wc, should be flexible to suit individual requirements. For discussion see 1519.

Window boxes

70048 Window boxes are suggested for residents.

7005 Bed-sitting rooms: Beds, walls, storage
Beds

70050 Among residents there are likely to be requirements for various types and heights of bed. The provision of purpose-designed divan beds may be inappropriate; they can be awkward for anyone doing the bedmaking, and difficult for some wheelchair users to transfer on to, see 5381.

Walls

70051 Walls in bed-sitting rooms should be designed so that pictures can be hung or fixed to surfaces.

70052 There must be effective acoustic insulation between adjoining rooms, for example to allow a resident to sleep while his neighbour is playing records. The minimum level of sound insulation should be 45db.

Storage

70053 Storage provision in bed-sitting rooms should be designed so that it can be managed by a person with limited reaching ability.

70054 In single units, hanging space in clothes cupboards should be not less than 0·600, and in double units not less than 1·200.

70055 For notes on clothes storage see 563.

70056 At least one drawer should be lockable to enable residents to protect their private possessions.

7006 Communal areas

70060 The dining area should be usable for general social purposes by the residents; the suggested area per resident is 2·0m². For notes on dining table dimensions see 5244.
The DHSS circular recommends that an overall area of 5·1m² per resident is allowed for dining, sitting and hobbies.

70061 A hobbies room should be provided, minimum area 20·0m².

70062 Other sitting areas may be associated with circulation spaces.

70063 A public telephone should be available for the use of residents. An enclosed booth is preferred for privacy. For design notes see 440.

70064 A laundry room should be provided for residents, see 550.

70065 A communal refrigerator for the use of residents is suggested, see 1518.

70066 The main kitchen should be accessible to residents.

7007 Cloakroom provision

70070 Where wcs are not provided to individual living units they should be suitably located to serve bedrooms, in the ratio of not less than one wc to each four residents. The maximum travel distance from any resident's room to a wc should be 10·000.

70071 Additional wcs should be provided to serve communal areas, giving an overall ratio of not less than one wc to each three residents.

Wcs

70072 There should be a range of wc fixtures to cater for varying needs. At least one wc compartment for each sex should be planned for a left-hand lateral transfer, one for a right-hand lateral transfer and one with a freestanding fixture (5418). The provision of at least one bidet/wc of the kind described in 5423 is suggested.

70073 Selected wcs for each sex should be in narrow compartments with rails fixed to both side walls for ambulant disabled people.

Baths and showers

70074 Baths should be provided in the ratio of about one to each six residents. Alternative access-to-bath arrangements should be available, with at least one freestanding bath allowing for help from both sides, one wall-fixed bath for people who transfer more easily on the right, and another for people who transfer on the left. For design guidance see 5459. The DHSS circular recommends one bathroom to every 8 or 10 residents, and suggests 7·5m² for each bathroom.

70075 At least one shower unit, which can be used by people seated in portable shower chairs, should be provided, see 5481. A second shower compartment with a bench seat is advised, see 5482–5487.

Other fixtures and fittings

70076 Other sanitary fixtures and fittings, for example urinals, incinerators, mirrors and towel dispensers, should be designed to cater for people with varying disabilities. If duplicated in the same cloakroom, items such as wall urinals, incinerators and towel dispensers should be fixed at different levels.

7008 Staff accommodation

70080 It is recommended that no living-in accommodation is incorporated for permanent staff, see 1523. Provision may be made for short-stay staff. A staff duty room should be provided for general administrative purposes.

70081 There should be a staff dayroom with lockable cupboard for each staff member; cupboards should be provided on the basis that there will be at least one member of staff to each resident.

7009 Garaging, gardening

70090 Garaging should be provided for at least three vehicles. This accommodation should not be partitioned, allowing for economic usage of space among drivers of ordinary adapted cars, small invalid tricycles and those who need space to transfer into their vehicles from a wheelchair.

70091 Provision should be made for the overnight charging of electric vehicles and wheelchairs. Where garaging is provided for electric vehicles it may be required, for reasons of fire protection, that it is separated from garaging space for petrol vehicles.

70092 For comment on car accommodation see 1524. For design notes on garages see section 57.

Gardening

70093 A sitting-out area affording gardening opportunities for residents should be provided, with raised flower boxes; see 581.

701 Hospital units for physically handicapped people

7010 General considerations

70100 For reasons discussed in section 15 of the commentary it is not recommended that long-stay hospital units are provided for people who are physically handicapped. There is therefore no basis on which positive design guidance can be given.

702 Holiday hotels for physically handicapped people

7020 General considerations

70200 General principles for the planning and design of holiday hotels for physically handicapped people are discussed in the commentary, see 1527.

7021 Approach

70210 All approaches to the building must be accessible to chairbound people: observe 641.

7022 Internal planning

70220 All areas of the building used by guests must be accessible to chairbound people: observe 642. To cater for people using large chairs 1·000 doorsets are suggested.

70221 Where lifts are installed at least one lift must have an internal depth of not less than 1·800. For further guidance see 45005, 4512 and detailed recommendations in section 45.

7023 Accommodation for guests

70230 The preferred provision is individual rooms with a separate washroom containing wash basin and wc. The suggested ratio of double to single rooms is not less than 2:1, ie that 80 per cent of accommodation is in double rooms.

70231 Suggested areas are 16·5m² for double rooms and 11·5m² for single rooms.

7024 Communal areas

70240 It is improbable that at any one time more than 50 per cent of people using the restaurant will be in wheelchairs, and space standards need not be as generous as for residential homes. An area of 1·7m² for each diner is suggested.

70241 Sitting areas should generally be linked to circulation areas rather than being enclosed. Approx 2·0m² sitting space distributed throughout the building is suggested for each guest.

70242 Where a bar is provided, the counter may be at a lower level than normal to suit wheelchair users; a height of 0·850 is suggested.

70243 At least one public telephone booth must be accessible to chairbound people, see 440.

7025 Cloakroom provision

70250 Where individual wcs are not provided to each room there should be a minimum provision of one wc for each four guests in bedroom areas, with additional wc provision serving sitting and dining areas. Varying wc layouts should be provided. Where wcs are in individual washrooms flexibility should be obtained by alternative layouts.

70251 There should be a minimum of one bath for each six guests. Alternative bath layouts, including one freestanding bath, should be provided. At least one shower compartment should be provided.

70252 The preferred height for wash basins in guests' rooms or washrooms is 0·750, see 54453.

7026 Staff provision

70260 One general purpose room may serve as office and duty room for staff.

70261 Where provision is made for living-in staff, self-contained flatlets are suggested with bed-sitting room and washroom containing wc, basin and preferably bath.

7027 Other provision

70270 A wheelchair store should be provided, with facilities for charging electric wheelchairs.

70271 A laundry room may be required. For guidance see 550.

702 Holiday hotels for physically handicapped people *continued*

7028 Car parking
70280 For guests' cars, covered carports are suggested. Access from parking areas to the building must be under cover.

7029 External areas
70290 Sheltered external sitting areas accessible to wheelchair users should be provided. Ramp gradients should be not steeper than 1:20.

703 Medical rehabilitation units for physically handicapped people

7030 General considerations
70300 Planning requirements for medical rehabilitation centres for disabled people or rehabilitation units in general hospitals will depend on local circumstances, the role of the unit and the type of patients to be treated. Many of the recommendations for day centres (704) will be applicable and, if patients are resident, for homes for physically handicapped people (700).

7031 Training for daily living activities
70310 The daily living activities unit should be planned so that patients can be clinically assessed to determine what provision is appropriate in their homes, particularly for the bathroom and kitchen.

Bathroom equipment
70311 In respect of bathroom equipment there should be a variety of wcs installed in the unit, fixed at different heights and with alternative aids and support rails. The installation of one bidet/wc unit of the kind described in 5423 is suggested.

70312 Baths of differing lengths should be installed with a choice of shower equipment associated with baths or provided separately.

70313 Wash basins should be provided at different levels, or there should be one which is adjustable in height to determine optimum fixing level. It should also be possible to test different kinds of tap controls.

Kitchen equipment
70314 In respect of kitchen equipment there should be a sink adjustable in height to determine optimum fixing level. There should be a range of cooking and storage units for assessment purposes.

7032 Hydrotherapy pools
70320 Hydrotherapy pools should be planned with the help of specialists, taking into account the techniques of treatment and the kind of patients the unit will serve. Special attention must be given to access to the pool for disabled patients, for example by means of a hydraulic hoist, a ramp or a flight of shallow steps with rails to both sides.

70321 Changing areas should be generously planned, to cater for example for patients who need to lie on a bench when being helped. Floor finishes must not be slippery, particularly between changing areas and the pool. For supervision and instruction from outside the pool, a sunken walkway along one side may be helpful.

70322 Reference should be made to the recommendations for swimming pools (734) and the notes on hydrotherapy pools in schools for handicapped children (7269).

704 Day centres for physically handicapped people

7040 General considerations
70400 The recommendations which follow relate to day centres providing places for not less than about 60 physically handicapped people, or for a mix of physically handicapped and other client groups. Planning principles are discussed in the commentary, see 1420–1422.

70401 Clients will travel to the centre by private transport, hired car, special bus or public transport. A substantial proportion, including nearly all epileptics and mentally ill people, will come by public transport and the centre should be conveniently located for local buses.

7041 Approach
70410 All entrances to the building must be accessible to chairbound people: observe 641.

70411 Automatic opening doors (3606) should be installed at the principal entrance, and elsewhere if finance permits.

Loading bay for buses
70412 There should be a loading bay for special buses at the main entrance, the platform height to be approx 0.620 above ground level; see 502.
Depending on the kind of people using the centre and the transport arrangements made by the local authority, a sizable proportion of clients may be brought by small buses having hydraulic tail lifts. Lowering and raising the lift for each passenger is time-consuming, and there should be a loading bay for chairs to be wheeled directly to and from buses.

70413 There should be one main entrance only for vehicles, not separate approaches for the workshop and social centres.
Activity will be concentrated during the early morning arrival time and the afternoon departure time; the bay should be sufficiently long to cater for as many buses as the local authority may have in operation serving the centre.

70414 There should be a canopy over the loading bay, giving access under cover to the centre.

70415 Although a height of 0·620 for loading bays is suggested as generally convenient, the architect planning a new centre should check dimensions of special buses used locally.

7042 Internal planning

70420 All areas of the building must be accessible to chairbound people: observe 642.

70421 People using the centre are more likely than is the case with public buildings to have cumbersome chairs, and the provision of 1·000 doorsets is preferred. Passageways should be not less than 1·500 wide.

70422 Where lifts are installed at least one lift should have a depth of not less than 1·800. For detailed recommendations see section 45.

7043 Workshop area

70430 The workshop area should be relatively self-contained, allowing it to be closed off from other areas of the building.

70431 In the workshop approx 4·0m² should be provided for each worker; where the centre is for physically handicapped people only and the majority of users will be in wheelchairs the area per worker may be 4·5m².

70432 Other than that work will be manageable from a sedentary position, no reliable guidance can be given on activities in day centres. The normal practice is for contracts for outwork, such as component assembly and packaging work, to be arranged with local industry.

Work benches
70433 Work benches may be at alternative heights, or selected benches may be adjustable in height to cater for people with varying disabilities. For a small person in a wheelchair the preferred working level may be as low as 0·750, for a person with rheumatoid arthritis who stands or perches to work the bench may need to be at approx 1·100 above floor level.

Services
70434 All main services should be provided, including 3-phase electricity supply and compressed air.

Lighting
70435 Where the workshop is to be administered on industrial lines, it may be appropriate for there to be north-facing rooflights, with relatively few windows to side walls. Where activities will be in the nature of diversionary occupation windows giving a view outside are preferred.

Storage
70436 Generous storage accommodation should be provided, minimum 1·3m² per worker, preferred provision 1·6m². Space should be allowed for individual lockers for each worker.

7044 Assembly hall and social areas

70440 An assembly hall may cater for parties, whist drives, bingo, concerts, amateur dramatics and general meetings. It may also be used for table tennis and archery.

70441 An induction loop should be incorporated for people who are hard of hearing, see 447.

70442 Where there are other social spaces and activity areas in the centre it may not be essential that the assembly hall can be subdivided by means of partitions.

Stage
70443 The stage (if provided) should be accessible to wheelchairs. The maximum gradient of the ramp should be 1:6, preferred maximum 1:8. The width of the ramp should be not less than 1·200. Where a ramp will be extravagant on space the alternative of a simple electrically operated hydraulic platform hoist may be considered.

Dining area
70444 The dining area ought to be large enough to serve all people attending the centre at one sitting, particularly if precooked meals are brought in. While it will not be practicable to arrange self-service facilities for all, counter service is suggested; ambulant people without disabilities can help those who are handicapped, and people in wheelchairs can help others – it is easier to carry a tray balanced on a wheelchair than when using sticks or crutches.
For dimensional data on dining areas see 523–524.

Bar, library
70445 A bar may be provided, associated with social areas.

70446 Where a library is provided the preferred maximum height for bookshelves is 1·500.

Floors
70447 To reduce noise transmission and enhance the visual quality of spaces throughout the building, floors should be carpeted where possible. Carpeting should extend through circulation areas and social spaces, alternatives being used where a washable surface is needed to counter spillages or dirt.

7045 Activity areas

70450 Provision should be made for crafts and hobbies such as woodwork, metalwork, painting, pottery and photography.

70451 While it is recommended that separate spaces are allocated for each activity it may not be desirable that each has an enclosed room, apart from a darkroom for photography and a kiln for pottery. Movable partitions can be installed but it is probable that they will only rarely be moved, and there may be problems regarding acoustic insulation and servicing. Furniture or low level

704 Day centres for physically handicapped people
continued

partitions for screening may be preferred, so that linked areas can be supervised simultaneously. Some areas may need to be physically separated, for example woodwork and painting.

Sinks

70452 Where sinks are to be used mainly by staff or ambulant disabled people the rim height should be approx 0·900; where they are expected to be used frequently by people in wheelchairs the rim height should be approx 0·750.

Carpentry

70453 The carpentry area may have a practical role beyond catering for handicapped people doing woodwork. Among people in the locality who are handicapped, particularly those who are elderly, there is likely to be a steady demand for bath seat aids, of the kind shown in diagram 54.80. Social services departments are employing occupational therapists in increasing numbers; one of their jobs is to check whether bath aids may be useful, to measure what is needed and to arrange with a carpenter at the centre to make up suitable aids, aided by handicapped people working there. Other aids, such as cleaning trolleys and tap and door knob turners, may also be made at the centre.

Laundry and ironing

70454 A laundry and ironing room should be provided. Domestic type washing machines should be available for handicapped people who bring in their regular washing from home, and an industrial machine for the use of centre staff. For detailed guidance see 550.

Training kitchen

70455 The kitchen used for training for daily living purposes should be independent of any kitchen provision serving the main dining area. It should have adjustable height worktops for assessment purposes, giving levels between 0·650 and 1·000. One sink ought also to be adjustable in height.

70456 Kitchen equipment should generally be as found in ordinary homes, and not special for chair users.

70457 An area alongside the training kitchen should be set aside for the display of aids for daily living.

Billiards

70458 Where a billiards room is provided the clear space on all sides of the table should be not less than 1·500 wide to allow for players in wheelchairs.

7046 Hairdressing facilities

70460 For hairdressing, frontrest basins are usually more easily managed by handicapped people than backrest basins. Basins should be adjustable in height, or installed at alternative fixed heights.

70461 Where one basin only is provided the preferred rim height is 0·750 above floor level. With two basins levels of 0·680 and 0·780 are suggested; with three basins suggested levels are 0·650, 0·730 and 0·810.

70462 Where a backrest basin is installed it should be at a height to suit normal seated users, ie approx 0·750.

70463 Because of the difficulty of arranging fixed basins at height to suit all clients, the use of a portable hair washing bowl on adjustable height stand is suggested, see 54472.

7047 Bathing facilities

70470 There is likely to be a substantial demand at the centre for bathing and washing services for handicapped people with an inaccessible bath at home, being unable to bath themselves, or depending on domiciliary helpers.

Baths

70471 A variety of baths may be provided, catering both for bathing and assessment purposes. One freestanding bath only (5463) is suggested; other baths should be located against walls, though a bath of the walk-in type (5464) may be advised.

70472 Fixed baths should allow for alternative means of access; the incorporation of a built-in platform at the head end of all baths is recommended.

70473 Where a variety of baths is installed alternative lengths are suggested, for example 1·500, 1·600 and 1·700.

Showers

70474 At least one shower cubicle should be provided, allowing for use by disabled people, see 548. The preferred arrangement is that a portable shower chair is kept at the centre into which people can transfer from ordinary wheelchairs; the shower cubicle should be planned to allow for this.

7048 Cloakroom provision

70480 In the workshop area at least one wc compartment for male workers and one for female workers must be usable by chairbound people: observe 643.

70481 Elsewhere in the centre at least one wc compartment for men and one for women should allow for wheelchair use.

70482 A range of wc compartments may be provided, with alternative heights and positions of fixtures. There should be one peninsular wc, which may be in a compartment serving both sexes: see 5418.

70483 The provision of one bidet/wc of the kind described in 5423 is suggested, both for those who prefer using it and for assessing whether it might be a valuable aid for people not able to manage a conventional wc independently at home.

70484 In addition at least one wc compartment for each sex must be usable by ambulant disabled people: observe 633.

7049 Other provisions

70490 A shop may be provided in the centre, to serve as a general store for physically handicapped people not able to do their own shopping. Its floor area should be generous, allowing for management by a person in a wheelchair.

70491 Provision for gardening by handicapped people is recommended, see 581.

705 Sheltered workshops for physically handicapped people

7050 General considerations

70500 These recommendations relate to sheltered industrial workshops provided under the Disabled Persons (Employment) Act 1944, which are government sponsored (for example managed by Remploy Ltd), are managed commercially or by a local authority and which cater for physically handicapped employees.

70501 For sheltered workshops for blind people observance of the recommendations here will be advantageous; for guidance on specific facilities for blind people reference should be made to the appropriate sections of this book.

7051 Approach

70510 All entrances to the building must be accessible to chairbound people: observe 641.

70511 At least one entrance should have an area where parking for employees' vehicles is under cover, allowing for direct transfer to the building. A loading bay of the type suggested for local authority work centres is not needed.

7052 Internal planning

70520 All areas of the building must be accessible to chairbound people, including administrative offices: observe 642.

70521 The canteen should be conveniently planned for wheelchair use; gangways to self-service counters should be minimum 1·200 wide.

7053 Cloakroom provision

70530 At least one male and one female wc compartment for employees must be usable by chairbound people: observe 643. In addition at least one wc compartment for each sex should be usable by ambulant disabled people, see 633.

70531 Drinking fountains where installed should be usable by chairbound people, see 5431. Other cloakroom fixtures should be convenient for people with varying disabilities. Wash basins should be fixed at alternative levels.

7054 Other provisions

70540 Workshop equipment, for example clocking-in installations, should be convenient for use by chairbound people.

70541 Selected work benches may be adjustable in height for use by chairbound employees, see 70433.

706 Rehabilitation hostels and day centres for mentally ill people

7060 Hostels

70600 In line with the theme developed in the commentary (1309) it is preferred that people with mental illnesses rehabilitated from psychiatric hospitals are, when they return to the community, catered for in ordinary housing rather than in special hostels. Where new hostels are built or existing housing is adapted the people who will live there are no more likely to be physically handicapped than any normal group of adult people, and it is not therefore necessary that any special building provision is made. As in other hostels or housing, it is desirable that there is convenient access for wheelchair users.

7061 Day centres

70610 People affected by mental illness who attend rehabilitation work centres are not more likely than any other group of adult people to be physically handicapped. To cater for those who are, it is suggested that the recommendations for industrial training centres (783) are observed.

707 Hostels for mentally handicapped people

7070 General considerations

70700 As with rehabilitated mentally ill people, the preferred strategy for mentally handicapped people for whom an alternative is sought to subnormality institutions is that they are placed in ordinary housing rather than in special hostels; for discussion see 1308. Advice on the planning of hostels is given in a DHSS building note *Residential accommodation for mentally handicapped adults*[3].

70701 In hostels or housing for mentally handicapped people the incidence of physical disability may be relatively high. This is because conditions causing mental handicap often have physical effects also.

7071 Approach

70710 At least one entrance to the building must be accessible to chairbound people: observe 641.

[3] Bib 93360

707 Hostels for mentally handicapped people
continued

70711 Other entrances must be accessible to ambulant disabled people: observe 631.

7072 Internal planning
70720 All areas of the building should be accessible to ambulant disabled people, see 632.

70721 A proportion of bed-sitting rooms and all communal areas should be accessible to chairbound people, see 642.

7073 Wcs and baths
70730 Where wc provision is shared among residents at least one wc compartment should be accessible to wheelchair users, see 643.

70731 Baths should be equipped for use by handicapped people, for example with support rails and a platform permitting seated transfer. The aim will be to maintain a domestic character; this factor and the probability of limited staff resources indicate that a freestanding bath is not appropriate.

708 Day centres for mentally handicapped people

7080 General considerations
70800 Day centres for mentally handicapped people were until April 1971 administered by the health departments of local authorities and known as adult training centres; they are now administered by social services authorities and are usually known as senior training centres. Their primary role is to afford suitable employment to people who are too handicapped to manage successfully in a sheltered workshop (see 705) or in open employment. The current trend is increasingly for mentally handicapped people to be catered for in all-purpose day centres of the type described in 704, meaning that the emphasis is less exclusively on workshop facilities. In this context the guidance given in the DHSS building note *Adult training centres*[4] may be used as a basis for planning but need not be rigidly adhered to.

70801 A high proportion of users may be physically handicapped and suitable provision should be made.

Mentally handicapped children
70802 In line with the policy put forward in the commentary (1308) day centres for mentally handicapped children should preferably be educational facilities (see 728), rather than social services or health facilities.

7081 Approach
70810 At least one entrance to the building must be accessible to chairbound people: observe 641.

70811 Other entrances must be accessible to ambulant disabled people: observe 631.

70812 Provision should be made for the unloading under cover of people brought to the centre by special transport.

7082 Internal planning
70820 The workshop, dining area, social rooms and other rooms used by workers must be accessible to chairbound people: observe 642.

7083 Cloakroom provision
70830 At least one wc compartment for each sex or serving both sexes must be usable by chairbound people: observe 643.

70831 Suitable provision should be made for washing and cleaning the clothes of people who are incontinent.

709 Employment rehabilitation centres

7090 General considerations
70900 Employment rehabilitation centres, formerly known as industrial rehabilitation units, are administered by the Employment Service Agency of the Department of Employment. Their purpose, described in section 3 of the Disabled Persons (Employment) Act 1944, is to provide industrial rehabilitation courses for disabled people 'who, by reason of unfitness arising from their injury, disease or deformity, are in need of such facilities in order to render them fit for undertaking employment, or work on their own account, of a kind in which they were engaged before they became disabled or of some other kind suited to their age, experience and qualifications, or for making use of a vocational training course'.

7091 Approach
70910 At least one entrance to the building must be accessible to chairbound people: observe 641.

70911 Other entrances must be accessible to ambulant disabled people: observe 631.

7092 Internal planning
70920 All areas of the building must be accessible to chairbound people: observe 642.

7093 Cloakroom provision
70930 At least one wc compartment for each sex or serving both sexes must be usable by chairbound people: observe 643.

70931 Other wc compartments should be usable by ambulant disabled people, see 633.

[4] Bib 93343

71 Health and welfare buildings

710 District hospitals

7100 General considerations

71000 The general accessibility of hospitals to disabled people will usually be guaranteed by the need to make physical provision for moving patients around the hospital in beds, in wheelchairs or on trolleys, and for moving food and hospital equipment on trolleys. It is none the less important for architects to check that hospital buildings are accessible throughout, to cater for disabled patients, disabled visitors and disabled members of the hospital staff.

71001 Because of the nature of the work done there, the character of the physical environment and the immediate availability of medical services in the event of assistance being needed, hospitals are suitable places for disabled people to be employed. Among people with disabilities working in a hospital may be found administrators, telephonists, clerical workers, pharmacists, laboratory technicians, social workers and occupational therapists.

71002 The recommendations which follow relate to district hospitals catering for general needs. For special hospitals see 711.

7101 Approach

71010 All principal entrances to the hospital for staff and visitors must be accessible to chairbound people: observe 641.

71011 Car parking places for disabled staff and visitors should be strategically located around the hospital, preferably with access under cover to the building.

71012 Bus shelters for public transport should give adequate shelter, with a seat or bench usable by handicapped people.

7102 Services for staff and visitors

71020 Services in the hospital for staff, patients and visitors, such as shops, banks and canteens, must be accessible to chairbound people: observe 642.

71021 At least one public telephone, preferably located in the main concourse area, must be usable by chairbound people; see 440.

71022 Where public cloakrooms are provided, at least one wc compartment for each sex or serving both sexes must be usable by chairbound people: observe 643. Other wc compartments should be accessible to ambulant disabled people, see 633.

7103 Ward units

71030 The approach to ward units and all areas used by patients in side wards units must be accessible to chairbound people: observe 641 and 642.

71031 Wc compartments for ward patients should be usable by ambulant disabled people, see 633. Wc seats may be at varying levels to suit different needs.

71032 One wc should be at a height for use in conjunction with a sanichair, see 54262. At least one wc compartment should be usable by chairbound people, see 643.

7104 Out-patients' and therapy departments

71040 All areas of out-patients' and therapy departments must be accessible to chairbound people: observe 641 and 642.

71041 In cloakrooms for use by patients at least one wc compartment must be usable by chairbound people: observe 643. Other wc compartments should be usable by ambulant disabled people, see 633.

71042 For notes on hydrotherapy pools see 7032.

7105 Operating theatre suite, x-ray department

71050 All areas of operating theatres and x-ray departments used by patients must be accessible to chairbound people: observe 641 and 642.

7106 Administrative departments

71060 All areas of administrative departments must be accessible to chairbound people: observe 641 and 642.

71061 At least one wc compartment for administrative staff of each sex must be usable by chairbound people: observe 643.

7107 Pharmacy, pathology laboratories, central sterile supply department

71070 The approach to these and related departments must be accessible to chairbound people: observe 641.

71071 Areas where staff may be employed on sedentary work must be accessible to chairbound people: observe 642.

71072 At least one wc compartment serving staff of each sex must be usable by chairbound people: observe 643. Where departments are linked this requirement may be satisfied by the provision made for administrative departments.

7108 Staff accommodation

71080 Staff dining rooms must be accessible to chairbound people: observe 642.

71081 Where self-service catering is incorporated, gangways and check-out points should be planned to be usable by chairbound people.

71082 In nurses' living areas special provision for wheelchair staff is desirable but not essential. Provision should be made for chairbound visitors to enter any buildings and to use common rooms and

710 District hospitals *continued*

recreation rooms. It is also desirable that all areas of these buildings are accessible to ambulant disabled people, see 631, 632.

7109 Hospital kitchens, nurses' training schools, hospital stores, boiler room, mortuary, laundry

71090 It is desirable, but not essential, that provision is made in these areas for disabled people.

711 Special hospitals, nursing homes

7110 Special hospitals

71100 In special hospitals, for example psychiatric, maternity, children's and dental hospitals, requirements for disabled people are generally the same as for district hospitals. There is an equal likelihood that there will be disabled people, including wheelchair users, among the staff. Among patients there may be fewer people who are physically handicapped, although suitable provision is recommended to ward areas and treatment areas. The level of special provision should take account of the incidence of disability likely to be found among patients.

7111 Nursing homes, convalescent homes

71110 In nursing homes and convalescent homes, particularly those catering for long-stay patients, there may be a high proportion of patients who are disabled. Provision should be at least to the standards recommended for district hospitals, with all areas being accessible to wheelchair users. This, in conjunction with practical and economic problems relating to means of escape in case of fire, indicates that single storey planning is preferred.

712 Health centres

7120 General considerations

71200 The health centre has an important community role, being a place to which people can go for professional treatment and advice on a variety of health and welfare matters. It is therefore important that all areas are accessible to disabled people. There is also the possibility that among staff working in the building some will be disabled.

7121 Approach

71210 The principal entrance must be accessible to chairbound people: observe 641.

71211 Other entrances must be accessible to ambulant disabled people: observe 631.

71212 It should be possible for disabled people brought by car or special transport to be transferred in and out of the building under cover.

7122 Internal planning

71220 All areas of the building must be accessible to chairbound people: observe 642.

71221 Where the building is planned other than at ground level, special consideration may need to be given to means of escape in case of fire. For relevant discussion see 606–609.

71222 For recommendations for doctors' and dentists' surgeries see 713, 714.

7123 Cloakroom provision

71230 At least one wc compartment for each sex or serving both sexes must be usable by chairbound people: observe 643.

71231 Selected wc compartments elsewhere in the building should be accessible to ambulant disabled people, see 633.

7124 Other provisions

71240 A small room or recess should be provided where wheelchairs can be stored and made available to handicapped people attending the centre.

713 Doctors' surgeries

7130 General considerations

71300 Although chairbound people are frequently so severely handicapped that the doctor has to visit them at home, it is important in new surgery buildings that provision is made for wheelchair users. The general employment of wheelchair criteria will ensure that ambulant disabled people are also catered for, including those who cannot manage steps.

7131 Approach

71310 At least one entrance for patients must be accessible to chairbound people: observe 641.

71311 This entrance should be served directly from a parking area for patients. One or two parking bays may be identified for use by handicapped people, see 580, 6530.

71312 Other entrances must be accessible to ambulant disabled people: observe 631.

7132 Internal planning

71320 The waiting room and at least one consulting room, examination room and treatment room (if provided) must be accessible to chairbound people: observe 642. It is preferred that all consulting rooms are accessible.

7133 Cloakroom provision

71330 At least one wc compartment for the use of patients must be usable by ambulant disabled people: observe 633. It is desirable that this compartment is planned for use by chairbound people, see 643.

714   Dentists' surgeries

7140   General considerations
71400   In the case of dentists' surgeries, chairbound people tend to be restricted in their choice of dentist by the inaccessibility of existing premises, and it is important in new buildings that provision is made for wheelchair users.

7141   Approach
71410   At least one entrance for patients must be accessible to chairbound people: observe 641.

7142   Internal planning
71420   The waiting room and at least one dental surgery must be accessible to chairbound people: observe 642.

7143   Cloakroom provision
71430   A wc compartment for the use of patients should be usable by ambulant disabled people, see 633.

715   Old people's homes

7150   General considerations
71500   These recommendations relate to old people's homes registered under the National Assistance Act 1948 (see 1504) and administered by social services authorities or voluntary agencies.

71501   The planning of local authority homes is subject to cost controls administered by the Department of Health, meaning that the design standards of the building note *Residential accommodation for elderly people*[1] have to be observed and, apart from exceptional circumstances, cannot be significantly enhanced. As discussed in the commentary (1528) the social concepts on which these recommendations are based are outmoded and reasonable living provision for old people is difficult to achieve if they are acted upon. Ideally, provision ought to be similar to that recommended for residential homes for physically handicapped people (700).

71502   For the purposes of structural fire precautions under building regulations old people's homes are designated purpose group II (Institutional), meaning that stringent conditions in respect of the compartmentation of floors and walls must be observed. In conjunction with requirements of local fire inspectors in relation to means of escape in case of fire, the consequence is likely to be that any living accommodation for old people who are chairbound has to be at ground level.

7151   Approach
71510   The principal entrance to the building must be accessible to chairbound people: observe 641.

71511   Other entrances ought also to be accessible to chairbound people and must be accessible to ambulant disabled people: observe 631.

7152   Internal planning
71520   All communal rooms used by residents, for example dining rooms, recreation rooms and sitting rooms, must be accessible to chairbound people: observe 642.

71521   Staircases serving areas used by residents should be usable by ambulant disabled people, see 6323.

71522   Lifts where provided should be large enough for wheelchairs; internal dimensions should be minimum 1·100 wide × 1·600 deep.

7153   Residents' bed-sitting rooms
71530   All residents' bed-sitting rooms must be accessible to ambulant disabled people: observe 632. All bed-sitting rooms on upper floors must be at levels which are accessible by lift.

71531   To permit residents to visit each other all bed-sitting rooms should be accessible to chairbound people even if all rooms are not (because of fire protection requirements) planned for wheelchair users to live in.

71532   It ought not to be assumed that all residents will be able to cope with stairs, that they will not be severely handicapped and that there will not be some who are chairbound. Not less than 25 per cent. of all bed-sitting rooms should be planned for chairbound people to live in.

7154   Cloakroom provision
71540   At least one wc compartment for men and one for women located near communal rooms must be accessible to chairbound people: observe 643.

71541   The preferred provision for bed-sitting rooms is that, as recommended for homes for physically handicapped people, there is an attached washroom containing wc and wash basin. Where this is not done, there should be a range of wc compartments suitable for disabled people.

71542   Bathroom provision should be comparable to that recommended for homes for physically handicapped people (7006).

[1] Bib 93650

716 Old people's day centres

7160 General considerations

71600 Old people's day centres are discussed in the commentary (1420) in relation to centres for physically handicapped people; it is preferred that the two are not linked. While the facilities in an old people's centre will not be as extensive as those in a centre for the physically handicapped, it is important that they take account of the needs of people who are disabled or physically frail.

7161 Approach

71610 The principal entrance to the centre must be accessible to chairbound people: observe 641.

71611 Other entrances must be accessible to ambulant disabled people: observe 631.

7162 Internal planning

71620 All areas used by old people attending the centre must be accessible to chairbound people: observe 642.

71621 Where the hall has a stage it should be designed so that it can be used by people in wheelchairs, see 70443.

7163 Cloakroom provision

71630 One wc compartment for each sex or serving both sexes must be usable by chairbound people: observe 643.

71631 Other wc compartments should be suitable for ambulant disabled people, see 633.

71632 The provision of baths is recommended which can be used by people not able to bath at home or only with assistance, see 7047.

7164 Other provisions

71640 For guidance on other facilities, for example for crafts, hobbies and hairdressing, see 704.

717 Children's homes

7170 General considerations

71700 The Children and Young Persons Act 1969 provides for the reorganization of residential establishments for children in care in England and Wales. The intention is that a comprehensive system of community homes administered by social services authorities will replace the former pattern of children's homes, reception and assessment centres, nurseries, hostels, remand homes and approved schools. In these community homes there will be many children who are educationally retarded, socially handicapped or emotionally disturbed, and perhaps a higher proportion who are physically handicapped than among the normal child population[2].

71701 While it is desirable that in the planning of these homes consideration is given to the possibility that possibility that some children may be in wheelchairs or otherwise disabled, it is probably not warranted that suitable provision for children in wheelchairs is made throughout; the local social services authority may be able to give advice on this matter. Valuable design guidance on these homes has been published by the Department of Health[3].

[2] In this connection see Bib 93790, para 10.
[3] Bib 93740

72 Educational buildings

720 University buildings

7200 General considerations

72000 It is important that new university buildings are usable by students and staff who are disabled; section 8 of the Chronically Sick Act specifically requires that any person undertaking the provision of a new university building shall, in the means of access both to and within the building, and in the parking facilities and sanitary conveniences to be available (if any), make provision in so far as it is in the circumstances both practicable and reasonable, for the needs of persons using the building who are disabled. Policy issues relating to the planning of university buildings are discussed in the commentary (1417–1418).

7201 Approach

72010 At least one entrance to each building or block of buildings must be accessible to chairbound people: observe 641.

72011 All entrances to all buildings must be accessible to ambulant disabled people: observe 631.

72012 It must be possible to travel between all buildings on the university campus without having to negotiate steps. On campuses spread out over a wide area and where planning for ordinary users is on the basis of pedestrian circulation, consideration must be given to the mobility problems of disabled staff and students. Planning should allow for concessionary arrangements for disabled people to use personal vehicles.

72013 It is important that the accessible entrance to the library is the main entrance; the use of an alternative entrance may cause security problems, requiring that doors are locked with consequent inconvenience to disabled students.

7202 Internal planning

72020 All teaching, social and administrative areas, including libraries and laboratories, must be accessible to chairbound people: observe 642.

72021 In lecture theatres where seats are tiered, suitable arrangements should be made for chairbound people, see 7403.

72022 In buildings used by students for social purposes it is important that dining areas, bars and amenities such as public telephones are usable by students who are chairbound.

7203 Provision for blind and deaf students

72030 For blind students who rely on readers there should be a soundproofed carrel or other room in the library, see 7464. A carrel large enough for a wheelchair user will be convenient for a blind person and reader.

72031 For deaf students an induction loop should be installed to lecture rooms and selected teaching rooms, see 7405, 447.

7204 Cloakroom provision

72040 In each building or block of buildings at least one wc compartment for each sex or serving both sexes must be usable by chairbound people: observe 643.

72041 Other wc compartments may be usable by ambulant disabled people, see 633.

72042 These facilities should be conveniently planned in relation to buildings commonly used, for example social areas and libraries.

7205 Residential accommodation

72050 In new hostel buildings for students a proportion of rooms must be usable by chairbound people: observe 642. The minimum provision suggested for a university campus is that four rooms for students are specially designed for wheelchair use; the accommodation should be to rather higher space standards than that for general student use.

72051 Where student accommodation is planned in the form of flats shared by a group of students it is suggested that in each of four groups one bed-sitting room is planned for wheelchair use. The suggested minimum area for study bedrooms for disabled students is 12.0m^2[1].

72052 Wc compartments and bathrooms usable by chairbound people should be provided adjacent to special bed-sitting rooms.

7206 Other provisions

72060 In administration buildings, provision must be made for the employment of staff who are disabled.

72061 All recreational and sports facilities must be usable by disabled people, particularly where amenities are also available to people from outside the university. Recommendations in 733, 734, 735 and 736 should be observed as appropriate.

721 Polytechnics, technical colleges, colleges of further education

7210 General considerations

72100 In polytechnics, technical colleges and colleges of further education having courses in a broad range of disciplines, it is important that provision is made for students who are disabled, to standards comparable to those recommended for universities. For colleges of a specialist character recommendations are made in 722.

[1] The University Grants Committee (Bib 93378, p5) says that 8.9m^2 is not adequate for a single study bedroom, but does not suggest a reasonable minimum.

7211 Further education colleges for physically handicapped students

72110 As discussed in the commentary (1417) it is arguable that there is a need in Britain for further education colleges exclusively for physically handicapped students. Where a special college is planned, it can be expected that a proportion of students will be severely handicapped, perhaps using electric wheelchairs and with a strong ambition to cope independently. Design criteria may therefore be stringent; appropriate guidelines should be drawn from relevant sections of this book.

722 Education buildings: Special colleges

7220 General considerations

72200 The need for provision for disabled people in colleges having a special vocational role depends on the physical requirements (particularly in terms of mobility) of the vocation for which training or studying is undertaken. The recommendations which follow therefore discriminate between different types of college, but the distinctions are so subtle as to be arguably worth making. In the light of the general recommendation that provision is always made for staff who are disabled the preferred course is that buildings are accessible throughout.

7221 Provision in college buildings

72210 In the following buildings provision should be as for university buildings generally. This means that allowance must be made for chairbound students and chairbound staff, ie observance of 641, 642 and 643.
1. Colleges of accountancy, business management, insurance, etc.
2. Colleges of hospital administration.
3. Language colleges.
4. Law colleges
5. Secretarial colleges.
6. Theological colleges.

72211 In the following buildings provision must be made for staff who are chairbound, ie observance of 641, 642, and 643 in staff areas. Provision must be made for students who are disabled but not chairbound, ie observance of 631, 632 and 633 in student areas. In teaching areas provision ought also to be made for chairbound students; the inclusion of provision for chairbound staff will generally mean that this is obtained.
1. Colleges of architecture, planning, surveying, estate management etc.
2. Colleges of art, including departments of fine arts, graphics, interior design, furniture design, textiles, costume etc.
3. Colleges of engineering.
4. Schools of journalism.
5. Schools of librarianship.

6. Medical and veterinary schools, including schools of physiotherapy and occupational therapy.
7. Teacher training colleges.

72212 In the following buildings provision must be made for staff and students who are ambulant disabled, ie observance of 631, 632 and 633. Where possible provision ought also to be made for chairbound staff and students.
1. Schools of catering and hotel management.
2. Colleges of music.

72213 In the following buildings it is not essential that provision is made for students who are disabled. Provision ought however to be made for members of the administrative staff who are disabled. In administrative areas requirements for ambulant disabled people (631, 632 and 633) must be observed, and where possible requirements for chairbound people.
1. Colleges of drama.
2. Colleges of physical education.
3. Police and military training colleges.

723 Secondary schools

7230 General considerations

72300 As discussed in the commentary (1416) it is suggested that in each local education authority area provision should be made in selected secondary or comprehensive schools (normally catering for children aged 11 and over) for pupils who are disabled and who, if such provision were not available, might otherwise have to be placed in special schools. Observance of the recommendations below will also ensure the desirable objective of providing for teaching staff who are disabled.

72301 In other secondary schools it is not essential that special provision for disabled pupils is made in teaching areas, though it is desirable that architects bear the matter in mind when planning new schools. The aim should be to achieve a level of provision catering for ambulant disabled pupils and staff, ie observance of 631, 632 and 633.

72302 In all schools where there are joint-use facilities serving people from outside the school, for example for cultural, recreational, sporting and similar purposes, it is essential to cater for disabled people, including those who are chairbound.

72303 When planning new school buildings attention should be given to section 8 of the Chronically Sick and Disabled Persons Act, which requires that any person undertaking the provision of a school building must make provision, so far as it is practicable and reasonable, for disabled users.

7231 Approach

72310 At least one entrance to the main school building must be accessible to chairbound people: observe 641.

72311 Where there are detached buildings on the site all buildings must have at least one accessible entrance.

7232 Internal planning

72320 All teaching, social and administrative areas used by pupils and staff must be accessible to chairbound people: observe 642.

72321 Any sports hall, swimming pool, theatre, library and comparable areas must be accessible to chairbound people: observe 642. Where these amenities are available also to the general public, additional suitable access provision may need to be made. Reference should be made to recommendations for relevant building types.

7233 Cloakroom provision

72330 At least one wc compartment for each sex or usable by both sexes must be provided for pupils and staff who are chairbound: observe 643.

72331 Where facilities such as sports hall, swimming pool and theatre are available for public use, at least one wc compartment for chairbound people of each sex or usable by both sexes must be provided: observe 643.

724   Primary schools

7240   General considerations

72400 As for secondary schools, it is suggested that in each local authority area selected primary schools (for children aged 5 to 11 years) are planned to cater for children who are physically handicapped. The typical single-storey primary school on a level or near-level site needs little modification to make it manageable for disabled children, including those in wheelchairs, and the recommendations which follow are made on that basis. It is suggested that these standards apply to all new schools where site conditions are appropriate.

72401 The only special architectural provision likely to be needed in primary schools is a generously sized wc compartment. This is needed in particular for children with spina bifida (9183) where there may be a need for (1) a child in a wheelchair to get into a wc compartment, (2) space for a welfare assistant to change a child or provoke urination by pressure on the abdomen, and (3) space for a child in a wheelchair to manoeuvre to empty a urine bag (see 9152, 9151). Not all handicapped children are sensitive or embarrassed about the way they use the wc, but there are some who are and it is important that privacy can be obtained.

72402 The recommendation is that in primary schools designed to cater for children in wheelchairs, the cloakroom space should be planned so that it can be modified for the provision of a special wc compartment as described in 7243.
The placement of physically handicapped children in ordinary primary schools is discussed in the commentary, see 1413–1416.

7241   Approach

72410 The main entrance to the school must be accessible to chairbound children: observe 641.

72411 It is not necessary that any provision is made for loading and unloading handicapped children from special buses, as is recommended in the case of schools for physically handicapped children.

7242   Internal planning

72420 All teaching and social areas used by children inside the building must be accessible to chairbound children: observe 642.

7243   Cloakroom provision

72430 In primary schools where it is known that disabled children will be placed there should be a wc compartment allowing space for an attendant to assist a handicapped child.

72431 One compartment serving children of both sexes is suggested. Planning should generally be as required in 643, except that a small sluice sink and drainer may be installed in place of a basin, see 54105.

72432 The wc seat should be at approx 0·350 above floor level, with horizontal support rails at approx 0·550. The door to the compartment should open out or slide.

725   Day nurseries, nursery schools

7250   General considerations

72500 In England and Wales, day nurseries are provided by local health authorities for babies and small children of pre-school age who need day care, for example children of one-parent families or where home conditions are unsatisfactory. The role of nurseries is a caring one rather than an educational one. Nursery schools are provided by local education authorities for children aged between three and five; their role is educational, though there is not as a rule any formal teaching.

72501 Of very young children who are severely physically handicapped, the majority are also mentally handicapped, and the usual practice is for them to attend schools for severely subnormal children (728). There ought however to be suitable access provision in day nurseries and nursery schools for children using wheelchairs or walking aids. Special cloakroom provision is probably not warranted.

726 Schools for physically handicapped children

7260 General considerations
72600 The role of special schools for physically handicapped children is discussed in the commentary, see 1413–1415.

7261 Approach
72610 Principal entrances to the building must be accessible to chairbound children: observe 641.

72611 A loading bay should be provided for children brought to the school by special buses. The platform should be at approx 0·620 above ground level, see 502. Access to and from the school building must be under cover.

7262 Internal planning
72620 All areas of the school building must be accessible to chairbound children: observe 642.

7263 Wall and floor finishes
72630 Wall finishes should be washable. The use of exposed brickwork, which can cause injury to the hands of children with problems of coordination, should be avoided. Some protection may be needed to wall surfaces in particular locations but the general provision of buffer rails is not recommended, see 3733.

72631 Handrails should be fixed to walls only along main circulation routes; they ought not to be fixed indiscriminately.

72632 Floor finishes should be comfortable to play on, easily cleaned and pleasant to touch.
Compared with normal children, handicapped children may spend more of their time at or near floor level.

7264 Doors, windows, switches
72640 Door ironmongery should be simple for handicapped children to handle; special ironmongery will probably not be required.

72641 Doors should be protected from damage by wheelchairs on trailing faces only, see 36082.

72642 Some windows should have sills at or near floor level, allowing children lying or sitting on the floor to see outside.

72643 Light switches should be aligned with door handles, in positions where they can be reached by children in wheelchairs.

7265 Heating
72650 Special consideration must be given to heating; ceiling heating may be suitable, see 4233. Because of incontinence among children ventilation is also important.

7266 Fittings and equipment
72660 Equipment should be suitable for use by children in wheelchairs, for example allowing access to tables, woodwork benches and kitchen units in domestic science areas.
Although some concessions are needed, for example knee access to sinks, equipment in domestic science areas should generally be as found in ordinary housing in the locality.

72661 For young children, the provision of an internal sand and water play facility is suggested. External play equipment should generally be as for normal children in other schools.

7267 Cloakroom provision
72670 A range of wc provision should be incorporated, catering for children with varying disabilities.

72671 In boys' cloakrooms urinal bowls where provided should be at different levels; suggested heights are 0·350 and 0·500.

72672 For the cleaning of children who are incontinent a drainer tray associated with a sluice sink is suggested. There should be a drying table alongside. For a suggested facility see 54106.

72673 Drinking fountains where provided should be at a low level, at approx 0·800 above floor level.

7268 Remedial therapy
72680 The range and scale of therapy facilities will depend on the type of children in the school and their clinical needs. Accommodation may be required for:
1. An office, changing room and wc for physiotherapists.
2. A changing room for children, with bench seat, changing table and adjoining provision.
3. A remedial exercise room, with space for equipment including practice steps and practice ramp, walking frame, parallel bars, suspension rings and wall bars.
4. One or more individual treatment rooms.
5. Rest room.
6. Space for wheelchair parking.
7. Storage.

7269 Hydrotherapy
72690 There may or may not be a requirement for a hydrotherapy pool in the school. If there is, the provision related to it will depend on associated provision in the remedial exercise room.
Requirements may include:
1. Changing areas for boys and girls, with benches, changing cubicles and clothes storage provision.
2. Staff changing provision.
3. Shower area with precleansing foot-trough and by-pass for wheelchairs.
4. Hydrotherapy pool, approx 8·000 × 5·000 × 0·800 −1·200 deep. The water will be heated to approx 34°C. Access to the pool will be by shallow steps, a ramp, chute, or hydraulic or electric hoist. The

normal practice is for physiotherapists to enter the water for treatment and a sunken pool below ground level is normally preferred.

5. Drying area with mangle and drying cabinet.
6. Storage.
7. Wheelchair parking area.

727 Schools for mentally handicapped children

7270 General considerations
72700 Schools for mentally handicapped children are discussed in the commentary (1308). Those which used to be known as ESN (educationally subnormal) are now known as ESN (moderate) or as schools for slow learners. The incidence of physical handicap may be higher among children at these schools than in ordinary schools; recommendations made for schools for physically handicapped children will generally be relevant.

7271 Approach
72710 The principal entrance to the school must be accessible to chairbound children: observe 641.

7272 Internal planning
72720 All areas in the school used by children must be accessible to chairbound children: observe 642.

7273 Heating and ventilation
72730 Some children may be prone to accidents as a consequence of incontinence; special consideration should be given to heating and ventilation. Ceiling heating may be preferred, see 4233.

7274 Cloakroom provision
72740 At least one wc compartment for boys and one for girls should be usable by children who are chairbound, see 643, 54105.

72741 A sluice sink, drainer and drying table should be provided for children who are incontinent.

728 Schools for severely subnormal children

7280 General considerations
72800 Schools for severely subnormal children are now officially referred to as ESN (severe) schools. They are commonly known as SSN (severely subnormal) schools, and were what used before April 1971 to be Junior Training Centres. In some places they are called junior training schools; their role and administration is discussed in the commentary (1308).

72801 The incidence of physical handicap among children in these schools will be high. Recommendations for schools for physically handicapped children are generally applicable. Excellent design guidance on the planning of these schools has been published by the Department of Education[2].

7281 Approach
72810 All entrances to the building used by children must be accessible to chairbound children: observe 641.

72811 The provision of a loading bay for children arriving by special bus will not be required.

7282 Internal planning
72820 All areas used by children must be accessible to chairbound children; observe 642.

7283 Space for profoundly handicapped children
72830 An area of the school may be planned for use by children who are profoundly handicapped; these will nearly all be children who are non-ambulant and incontinent. Special consideration must be given to possibilities of stimulating awareness among them, bearing in mind the likelihood that they will spend all or most of their time on the floor.

72831 Use may be made of the ceiling as a surface for projection, and provision should be made, for example by cushioned raised platforms, for children lying down to see out of windows.

72832 Attention needs to be given to heating and ventilation in relation to the high level of incontinence, see 7265, 4233.

7284 Cloakroom provision
72840 Attached to the space for profoundly handicapped children there will be a special bathroom area, catering for children not able to do anything for themselves and needing to be changed, washed and attended to by adults.

72841 The area should include a changing table, with sluice and drainer, a large low sink for bathing small children and a sit-up type bath with adjustable shower attachment for older children, see 5489.

72842 Wc compartments should be either open or curtained, with low partitions. At least one wc cubicle should allow for wheelchair access, with wc seat at approx 0·350. Other wcs should have seats at different levels; suggested heights are 0·280 and 0·320.

72843 Elsewhere in the building there should be cloakroom provision for children who are able to manage more independently; one wc compartment affording privacy should be accessible to chairbound children.

7285 Other provisions
72850 Provision should be made for the storage of wheelchairs.

---

[2] Bib 93394

729 **Schools for maladjusted children**

7290 **General considerations**

72900 Maladjusted children are those who are so
emotionally disturbed that they need the resources
of a special school where they can be given
individual attention and help. Among them there is
not likely to be a higher incidence of physical
handicap than in ordinary schools. One of the
requirements for these schools is that there should
be a variety of spaces, volumes and planes giving
children a choice of areas to which they can
withdraw or where they can be sociable. To achieve
these requirements floors at different levels can
help, meaning that the kind of criteria used for
disabled children are inappropriate. Design
guidance for these schools has been issued by the
Department of Education[3].

[3] Bib 93741

73 Hotels, refreshment and recreation buildings

730 Hotels, motels

7300 General considerations

73000 For disabled people, and particularly those who are chairbound, the accessibility of new hotels is of major importance. The general accessibility of hotels to disabled people is desirable for arranging holidays, business and social visits, and for attending local business and social functions. As discussed in the commentary (1219), it is also important for disabled travellers that new hotel buildings are reliable places for finding accessible cloakroom facilities.

73001 In the planning of new hotel buildings, considerations of general convenience for guests will dictate that guestrooms are accessible without having to negotiate steps; it should be possible to transport baggage on a trolley from the car park or taxi setting-down point to any guestroom. Given this condition all guestrooms will be accessible to ambulant disabled people and it should be possible to arrange that they are accessible to wheelchair users also, the critical factor being the provision of 0.900 doorsets to bathrooms in bedroom suites. Such provision will cater for the large majority of wheelchair users, but for the few who are chairbound and severely handicapped more generous space will be required in the bathroom than is obtained as standard practice.

73002 The suggestion is that one or two specially equipped bedrooms for handicapped people should be incorporated in each new hotel.

7301 Fire protection

73010 The provision in a new hotel of one or two guestrooms specially equipped for handicapped people may raise problems regarding fire protection.

73011 For motels, where all or a large proportion of guestrooms are at ground level, there are likely to be no objections, since means of escape can be direct to the outside.

73012 For urban hotels on small sites where guestrooms are stacked at high level the fire authority may reject proposals for special rooms, on the grounds that means of escape for chairbound people are not adequate.
In such cases it may be tactically wise to rely simply on general provision to cater for disabled people, including wheelchair users; the fact that no rooms are specifically planned for disabled people should mean that means of escape provision is based on the assumption that building users are not disabled.

73013 For discussion on means of escape provision and regulations relating to means of escape see 604, 605.

73014 In respect of hotel buildings, fire certificates are required under the Fire Precautions Act 1971 (6054). In theory the issuing of a fire certificate under the Act might be conditional on no guests in wheelchairs being allowed to stay.

7302 Approach

73020 The principal public entrance must be accessible to chairbound people: observe 641.
This entrance should afford undercover loading and unloading from cars or taxis for people in wheelchairs.

73021 At least one entrance served from the hotel garage or car park must be accessible to chairbound people: observe 641.

73022 All other public entrances must be accessible to ambulant disabled people: observe 631.

7303 Internal planning

73030 Restaurants and bars must be accessible to chairbound people: observe 642. See also recommendations for restaurants, 731.

73031 Conference rooms, function rooms, ballrooms, shops and other public facilities must be accessible to chairbound people: observe 642.

7304 Guestrooms: General provision

73040 As discussed above, it is desirable that all guestrooms are accessible to ambulant disabled people and, given that bathrooms can have 0.900 doorsets, to most wheelchair users also. Where only some of the rooms in a new hotel building are accessible in this way a proportion of each type of guestroom, for example family rooms, double rooms, twin-bedded rooms and single rooms, should be suitably planned.

Bathrooms

73041 The normal practice in the planning of guestroom suites is that the bathroom door opens in; where the space internally is confined it may be impossible to close the door with a wheelchair inside. According to the layout of the room this may mean that the wc, bath or basin is not reachable by a chairbound person.

73042 A possible compromise, not recommended but permissible if there is no alternative, is that lift-off door hinges are specified so that the bathroom door can be temporarily removed; this will have the advantage that the clear opening width for wheelchair access is increased by approx 0.030 (diagram 36.2).

73043 Where for planning or economic reasons the bathroom has to have a 0.800 doorset it is also advisable that lift-off hinges are specified; the clear opening width obtained will be approx 0.715 which, while not being negotiable by people in large wheelchairs, will commonly be manageable by people with standard wheelchairs.

730   Hotels, motels *continued*

7305   Guestrooms: Special provision
73050   Guestrooms specially planned for handicapped people should have 0·900 bathroom doors opening off a circulation area not less than 1·200 wide.

Bathrooms
73051   There should be room inside the bathroom to enter in a wheelchair and close the door. The door to the bathroom should slide or open outwards.

73052   Inside the bathroom the layout should allow for lateral transfer to the wc.

73053   The wash basin should be of the desk type to allow for close wheelchair approach.

73054   A splayed or tilting mirror is suggested to suit seated and standing users, see 5433.

73055   The bath should have a platform at the head and for seated transfer, see 5458, with support rails to aid transfer in and out, see 5470–5472.

Other provisions
73056   In the planning of special guestrooms consideration should be given to the convenience of furniture for wheelchair users. For notes on beds see 538.

73057   For the disabled person travelling on his own and liable to falls, a refinement which may enhance security is the provision of call buttons at skirting level.

7306   Public cloakrooms
73060   In cloakrooms serving public areas of the hotel at least one wc compartment for each sex or serving both sexes must be usable by chairbound people: observe 643.

73061   At least one wc compartment in each public cloakroom should be usable by ambulant disabled people, see 633.

7307   Other facilities
73070   Administrative areas, offices, and reception areas should be planned so that they can be used by staff who are chairbound. No special provision is required for staff living areas.

73071   Where there is a swimming pool allowance should be made for chairbound users, see 734.

73072   Other facilities where incorporated should be accessible to chairbound people, for example shops, hairdressers' salons, gymnasia, sauna baths and games rooms.

731   **Restaurants, snack bars, cafés**

7310   General considerations
73100   New restaurant buildings ought always to be accessible to chairbound people. Restaurants are, however, commonly in converted premises where ideal access provision is impossible. In the case of large restaurants it is important that at least certain dining areas are accessible; the rough ruling suggested is that provision must be made where the number of diners accommodated exceeds 40.

73101   Where there are a number of eating facilities in the same building each area should allow for wheelchair access. The recommendations for cloakroom provision should be applied in respect of the building and not necessarily for each facility.

7311   Approach
73110   All public entrances must be accessible to ambulant disabled people: observe 631.

73111   Where any eating facility (restaurant, snack bar, café etc) is at ground level or caters for 40 or more diners at least one public entrance must be accessible to chairbound people: observe 641.

7312   Internal planning
73120   All public areas must be accessible to ambulant disabled people: observe 632.

73121   Where provision is made for more than 40 people, dining areas must be accessible to chairbound people: observe 642.

7313   Dining tables
73130   Where seating is fixed, selected tables in dining areas accessible to chairbound people must be usable without the need to transfer out of the wheelchair, for example by leaving one side of the table clear. Care should be taken that circulation spaces will not be obstructed by customers seated in wheelchairs.

73131   Although high tables may be preferred by wheelchair users to permit close approach they will often be inconvenient for other customers, and are not advised.

73132   In self-service restaurants counters should be at a level convenient for normal ambulant people, while at the same time allowing for approach by people in wheelchairs.

7314   Cloakroom provision
73140   In public cloakrooms at least one wc compartment for each sex should be usable by ambulant disabled people, see 633.

73141   Where provision is made for chairbound people at least one wc compartment for each sex or serving both sexes should be accessible, see 643.

732 Public houses, bars

7320 General considerations
73200 The recommendations here apply to pubs and also to public bars in for example restaurants, club buildings, theatres, concert halls, sports buildings, transport buildings and hotels.

7321 Approach
73210 At least one entrance must be accessible to chairbound people: observe 641.

73211 All other public entrances must be accessible to ambulant disabled people: observe 631.

7322 Internal planning
73220 All bars and other areas used by customers must be accessible to ambulant disabled people: observe 632.

73221 At least part of the public area must be accessible to chairbound people: observe 642.

7323 Cloakroom provision
73230 In public cloakrooms at least one wc compartment for each sex should be usable by ambulant disabled people, see 633.

73231 Where practicable at least one wc compartment should be usable by chairbound people, see 643.

733 Sports centres

7330 General considerations
73300 Among indoor sports activities in which disabled people can take part are archery, badminton, basketball, billiards, bowling, fencing, movement and dance, shooting, swimming, table tennis, volley ball and weight lifting. Among outdoor activities are angling, archery, bowls, canoeing, sailing, shooting and swimming.

Community use
73301 Increasingly, new sports buildings are being planned not exclusively for competitive sporting activities, but as recreational and social centres affording a variety of leisure opportunities for the local community. Because of this community role it is most important that provision is made throughout for disabled people, whether centres are developed independently or are part of bigger complexes such as schools or universities.

Provision by scale of centre
73302 The recommendations which follow detail the provision appropriate in comprehensive sports centres serving large populations. In small centres, economics and the scale of the building may dictate less ambitious provision for disabled users. For example, in low-cost buildings containing a single all-purpose dry sports hall and minimum ancillary

accommodation, including some changing rooms at first floor level, the incorporation of a lift may not be feasible.
In such cases it is essential that the sports hall is accessible, and that ad hoc arrangements can be made for entrance level rooms to be used for changing by chairbound and other disabled people. At least one shower room and one wc compartment must be at entrance level.

73303 For sports stadia where the emphasis is on spectator provision see 735.

73304 For supplementary design guidance reference may be made to Felix Walter's *Sports centres and swimming pools*[1].

7331 Approach
73310 The principal public entrance to the centre must be accessible to chairbound people: observe 641.

73311 All other entrances must be accessible to ambulant disabled people: observe 631.

73312 Parking provision for disabled drivers should be available close to an accessible entrance.

7332 Internal planning
73320 All areas where wheelchair users might wish to go must be accessible to chairbound people: observe 642. Areas of particular importance are social spaces, canteens and bars.

73321 Where turnstiles are used by the general public pass gates must be available for wheelchair users.

7333 Cloakroom provision
73330 At least one wc compartment for each sex or serving both sexes must be usable by chairbound people: observe 643.

73331 In all cloakrooms at least one wc compartment should be usable by ambulant disabled people, see 633.

7334 Other provisions
73340 Changing and shower areas must be usable by disabled people, including wheelchair users. The recommendations for swimming pools (7343) should be used as a guide. In centres where a swimming pool is incorporated and there are separate changing areas for swimming and other activities provision for disabled people should be made in both areas.

73341 In spectator areas where seats are tiered provision should be made for ambulant disabled people. The recommendations for auditoria buildings (7403) may be applied.

73342 Parts of spectator areas serving all activities must be accessible to chairbound people: observe 642.

---

[1] Bib 93580

734   Swimming pools

7340   General considerations
73400   These recommendations relate specifically to covered swimming pools administered by local authorities. They are also generally applicable to other swimming pools, for example at hotels, holiday camps, schools and club buildings.

73401   For general guidance on the planning of swimming pools reference may be made to the Sports Council's bulletin *Public indoor swimming pools*[2].

Use of main pool versus learner pool
73402   Among recreation buildings it is particularly important that swimming pools are accessible to disabled people. The primary aim should be to afford recreation rather than therapy, which is undertaken in special hydrotherapy facilities (see 7032). It is therefore important in new buildings that disabled people have access to large pools and are not restricted to using shallow learner pools.

73403   For some ambulant disabled people the learner pool may be unusable. Adult disabled people with impaired lower limbs need to keep the body from the neck down below water level in order to maintain buoyancy. This means a water depth of not less than approx 1·200, which is deeper than is provided in a learner pool.

73404   It is equally important that the learner pool is accessible to disabled people, to cater for handicapped children, and mentally handicapped and elderly people who prefer to use a shallow pool.

Swimming clubs
73405   Some blind, mentally handicapped and severely disabled people require continual assistance or supervision and cannot conveniently be catered for during public sessions at busy swimming pools. In response to their needs, swimming clubs for handicapped people have in recent years been established in many places. The customary arrangement is that the pool is reserved for the exclusive use of the club at specified times, usually for one hour during each week at a time when the pool is closed to the general public. Even if relatively independent, many disabled people prefer to use the pool at the reserved sessions when it is less crowded and special attention can be given to their needs.

73406   For supplementary guidance on the design of swimming pools reference may be made to Felix Walter's *Sports centres and swimming pools*[3].

7341   Approach
73410   The principal public entrance must be accessible to ambulant disabled people: observe 631.

---

[2] Bib 93742
[3] Bib 93580

73411   At least one entrance served from a car parking area must be accessible to chairbound people: observe 641.
If this entrance is not that used by the general public the normal routine for supervision and the issuing of tickets will not apply to disabled users.

73412   Handicapped people attending club sessions will usually be brought by private car, or by special vehicles used to transport disabled people. It is advantageous if loading and unloading can take place under cover.

7342   Internal planning
73420   All public areas must be accessible to ambulant disabled people: observe 632.

73421   The route from the wheelchair entrance to changing areas for chairbound people and to the pool area must be accessible to chairbound people: observe 642.

7343   Changing rooms
73430   The current trend in swimming pool design is away from individual cubicles, and towards open changing areas, using benches. Whether general provision is by cubicles or not, it is important that changing areas for each sex are accessible without the need to negotiate steps.

Use of normal provision
73431   Where provided, changing cubicles for general use in swimming pools are often small, for example approx 0·800 wide × 0·900 deep. Although many ambulant disabled people, particularly those needing personal assistance for drying and dressing, would be better accommodated in cubicles of larger than standard size, it may not be practicable to increase the size of cubicles for general use to satisfy the preferred requirements of disabled people.

73432   The majority of handicapped people attending club sessions will be able to use ordinary changing cubicles. Some, and preferably all, ordinary cubicles for each sex must be accessible without the need to negotiate steps.

73433   It may be assumed that where disabled people attending club sessions use cubicles to change, clothes will be left in the cubicle and not taken to a clothes store.

Special cubicles
73434   To cater both for chairbound people who are independent and those who need assistance with dressing and undressing, the provision of two special changing cubicles containing bench seat, shower, wc and wash basin is suggested.

73435   The wc should permit lateral transfer and support rails should be fixed to walls by seat and shower. A suggested layout is shown in diagram 73.1.

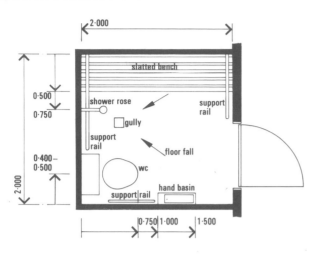

73.1 Changing cubicle for wheelchair users (1:50)

73436 Where special cubicles are provided they should be close to the pool.

Communal changing rooms

73437 Some changing accommodation other than in cubicles should be accessible to chairbound people. People who are severely handicapped may need to lie horizontally on a bench to be dressed and undressed. Communal changing rooms where provided, for example for the use of school parties, may be suitable for this purpose.

Disabled children

73438 Changing accommodation must be available which is usable by disabled children assisted by a parent of the opposite sex.
Such accommodation, sometimes referred to as family changing, may often be of benefit to normal users, for example mothers accompanying small boys or fathers accompanying small girls. Changing facilities should be provided supplementary to those exclusively for use by males or females.

73439 Separate changing room provision serving learner pools may be suitable for use by groups of disabled swimmers.

7344 Precleansing arrangements

73440 For wheelchair users the normal precleansing foot trough in association with showers is not a practicable proposition, and it may be hazardous or impossible for ambulant disabled people. For disabled swimmers a by-passing system will therefore be necessary, but it is not advised that planning assumes there will be no precleansing.

Precleansing facility for disabled swimmers

73441 The ICTA report *Sports and open-air facilities* recommends that a large shower compartment suitable for precleansing by disabled people should be included in the general shower area[4]. The

[4] Bib 93581, p24

suggested width is 1·800, with horizontal support rails on three sides at 0·800 above floor level. A footrest at 0·300 above floor level is recommended along the rear wall, with a shower control at 0·900 above floor level. Two shower roses are proposed, one at 1·750 for standing users and the other at 0·700 for users sitting on or near the floor.

Use of wheelchair changing cubicles

73442 Where on financial grounds it is not feasible to incorporate this kind of provision, the suggestion is that the shower in a wheelchair changing cubicle should be used for precleansing, with disabled swimmers changing in other places directed to it. This will not be an ideal solution, and in practice ad hoc cleansing arrangements may have to be made.

Normal precleansing provision

73443 To assist ambulant disabled swimmers to use normal precleansing provision, vertical support rails must be securely fixed to walls above steps or sills to foot troughs. For people who are unstable on their feet the preference is for a sill with floor level the same to either side, rather than a step up or down.

7345 Access to pool

73450 Where practicable, a continuous handrail should be provided to both sides of the route between changing area and pool; this is needed for ambulant disabled people who leave calipers or other walking aids in the changing area.

73451 For chairbound people a route from changing area to pool which by-passes the precleansing area must be available: observe 642.

Stepped access

73452 One access to the shallow end of the swimming pool should be by a flight of steps, for example as shown in diagram 73.2.
Care should be taken to ensure that the steps are not a hazard to general users; if they encroach on the circulation area securely fixed guard rails must be installed.

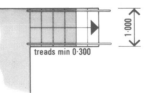

73.2 Stair access to pool (1:100)

73453 The incorporation of a stepped access to a swimming pool (in place of the traditional ladder access) ought not to be rejected on the grounds that it may be a hazard, for example to children running round the pool side.
Given careful design, hazards will be minimized, and the trend in swimming pool design from traditional rectangular competition pools to informal recreational pools will make suitable provision more compatible with other criteria.

734   Swimming pools *continued*

73454 Where suitably graded steps cannot be built in for
       entering and leaving the pool, the provision of a
       lightweight portable flight of steps may be
       considered. The top end of the steps should plug
       into sockets in the pool surround; when the steps
       are not in use these sockets are concealed by a
       hinged slat.

73455 Steps should be gently graded; risers of approx 0·140
       and goings of approx 0·300 are suggested. The width
       between handrails should be approx 0·600.
       Where portable steps of this kind are planned they
       will be used at the shallow end of the pool; adequate
       storage accommodation should be provided close by
       for when the steps are not in use.

Access chute

73456 As an alternative, or in addition to portable steps, a
       portable chute for access to the pool is suggested. A
       portable chute may be an aid for wheelchair users;
       the platform at the head of the slide should be at
       approx 0·450 above deck level to facilitate
       wheelchair transfer.
       As with portable steps, the chute should be
       designed so that it is held securely by floor sockets.

Ladder access

73457 Where there are conventional ladder steps for
       access, special consideration should be given to
       their design. Vertical rails to either side of the
       ladder should be kept inside the line of the pool
       wall, and extend down into the water (diagram
       73.3). Treads should be not less than 0·180 wide.
       Paired rails on pool decks are sometimes of varying
       height to discourage abuse, for example by
       somersaulting children; this is awkward for
       handicapped people, who are less likely to be
       unbalanced where rails are the same.

73.3   Ladder access to pool

Mechanical hoist

73458 A mechanical hoist for transferring severely
       disabled people into the pool is not normally
       required.
       Many disabled people dislike mechanical hoists,
       and many helpers find it easier to cope manually
       with disabled people who need to be assisted in or
       out of the pool.

73459 Where a hoist is provided elaborate equipment is
       not necessary. A portable hoist as shown in
       diagram 26.4b which fits into a floor socket,
       sealed when not in use, is suggested.

7346   **Pool specifications**
73460 The decision whether to have a main pool with
       conventional sunken water level and sidewall
       overflow channels or a pool with deck level water
       will normally be based on considerations other
       than the needs of disabled swimmers.
       For most disabled users the deck level water
       arrangement has the advantage: there is easier
       access in and out of the water, less upper limb effort
       is needed to climb out, and fewer steps are needed
       between pool floor and deck level. A possible
       disadvantage in respect of partially sighted
       swimmers is that the demarcation line between
       deck and pool is not so clearly marked where water
       is at deck level, and there is a consequent accident
       hazard.

Water temperatures

73461 For public sessions the water temperature in the
       main pool will normally be maintained at approx
       26°C.

73462 Architects when designing new swimming pools
       may receive requests from representatives of
       handicapped organizations that there must be the
       possibility of raising water temperatures very
       considerably for the benefit of handicapped
       swimmers.
       Apart from expenditure on a more powerful heating
       installation and the cost of boosting temperature
       levels, there will be practical difficulties. It is
       normal practice for the air temperature to be higher
       than the pool water temperature; allowance for this
       will mean that the whole fabric of the building will
       need to be insulated more effectively to prevent
       condensation occurring, with effects on the
       structure and its design.

73463 An investigation in Sweden reported that for
       handicapped swimmers a temperature of 27.2°C was
       generally suitable[5].

73464 For public sessions the water temperature of the
       learner pool is normally maintained at approx 28°C.
       To cater for handicapped children temperatures up
       to 32°C are preferred.
       In practice it may not always be possible for water
       temperatures to be boosted to the preferred levels
       for the occasions that the pool is used for
       handicapped people. These recommendations ought
       however to be borne in mind when the heating
       installation is specified.

[5] Bib 93581, p27

73465 For disabled swimmers who find that pool temperatures at or only marginally above normal levels are too uncomfortable, it has to be recognized that public pools are unsuitable and that the answer is the use of a therapeutic pool in a hospital or rehabilitation centre.
Water temperatures in therapeutic pools are normally maintained at approx 34°C.

Handrails
73466 Handrails where fixed in swimming pools must be resistant to corrosion from humidity or the effects of chlorine. Metalwork should be non-ferrous if exposed.

73467 Where used as a core, metal sections should be sealed and dipped in nylon or treated with impervious coating.

73468 Where timber sections are used, the surface should be sealed to avoid moisture absorption and expansion.

73469 Bracket supports should be strongly fixed.

7347 Cloakroom provision
73470 At least one wc compartment for each sex or serving both sexes must be usable by chairbound people: observe 643.
This wc compartment should be located where it is convenient for wheelchair users who are swimmers or spectators. It should be provided in addition to any wc provision for wheelchair users in special changing cubicles.

73471 Selected urinals should be usable without the need to negotiate steps, see 5430.

7348 Floor surfaces
73480 All floor surfaces should be slip-resistant. Surfaces which incorporate flutes or channels to allow water to drain are preferred to patterned surfaces which hold water. Surfaces should be textured to afford a grip to the flesh of the feet.

7349 Other provisions
73490 Storage space may be needed for the hoist, wheelchairs and other equipment used at handicapped club sessions.
Some ambulant disabled people use a wheelchair to reach the pool side when they have discarded prostheses or calipers. A wheelchair may be kept at the pool for them.

73491 The provision of sauna baths is recommended. For disabled people the sauna bath is beneficial for warming the body and relaxing muscle tension before entering the swimming pool, and for restoring circulation afterwards. For notes on sauna baths see 5467.

73492 No special provision for disabled people is required to staff areas.

735 Sports stadia

7350 General considerations
73500 The recommendations below relate to sports stadia, whether open or covered, accommodating more than say 1000 spectators. For smaller buildings the recommendations for sports centres (733) will generally apply.

7351 Approach
73510 At least one public entrance serving each part of the stadium must be accessible to chairbound people: observe 641.

73511 All other public entrances must be accessible to ambulant disabled people: observe 631.

7352 Internal planning
73520 All circulation areas serving spectator areas of the stadium must be accessible to ambulant disabled people: observe 632.
For further guidance see 7404.

Wheelchair places
73521 Provision must be made for chairbound spectators. One wheelchair place should be provided for each 1000 or portion of 1000 spectators accommodated up to 10000, and one space for each 2000 or portion of 2000 spectators accommodated in excess of 10000.

73522 A minimum of four such places should be provided. An area minimum 0·900 wide × 1·400 deep must be provided for each wheelchair space. Where provision is made for an able-bodied attendant to sit alongside in a removable seat the minimum width should be 1·400.

7353 Cloakroom provision
73530 In public cloakrooms at least one wc compartment for each sex should be usable by ambulant disabled people, see 633.

73531 At least one wc compartment for each sex or serving both sexes in cloakrooms to a part of the stadium accessible to wheelchair users must be usable by chairbound people: observe 643.

7354 Other provisions
73540 Office accommodation should be usable by staff who are disabled, see 760–762.

73541 Where restaurant and bar facilities are provided, at least one restaurant facility and one bar facility must be accessible to chairbound people: observe 642. See also 731, 732.

73542 All public bars, snack bars, restaurants, lounges etc must be accessible to ambulant disabled people: observe 632.

736   Sports clubhouses

7360   General considerations
73600   In clubhouses for specific sports, for example cricket, football, golf, rowing, sailing and tennis, provision must be made for disabled people who use the building as spectators or for social purposes. Depending on the character of the sport, it is not always essential that provision is made in participant areas such as changing rooms.

7361   Approach
73610   At least one entrance to the building must be accessible to chairbound people: observe 641.

7362   Internal planning
73620   Principal areas of social activity, for example clubrooms, bars and restaurants, must be accessible to chairbound people: observe 642.

73621   All areas of the building should be accessible to ambulant disabled people, see 632.

7363   Cloakroom provision
73630   At least one wc compartment for each sex or serving both sexes must be accessible to chairbound people: observe 643.

73631   In cloakrooms used by sports participants at least one wc compartment should be usable by ambulant disabled people, see 633.

7364   Other provisions
73640   Selected spectator viewing areas must be accessible to chairbound people: observe 642.

73641   All spectator viewing areas must be accessible to ambulant disabled people: observe 632.

737   Club buildings

7370   General considerations
73700   Club buildings, for example youth centres, youth clubs, social clubs, working men's clubs, vocational clubs and professional clubs, must be usable by disabled people.

73701   In general, provision for members who are disabled will ensure that the building is suitable for disabled people who work in the building, and no special provision in staff areas is necessary.

7371   Approach
73710   At least one entrance to the building must be accessible to chairbound people: observe 641.

73711   Other entrances to the building should be accessible to ambulant disabled people, see 631.

7372   Internal planning
73720   Principal areas used by club members, for example social areas, bars and meeting rooms, must be accessible to chairbound people: observe 642.

73721   All areas used by club members must be accessible to ambulant disabled people: observe 632.

7373   Cloakroom provision
73730   At least one wc compartment in the building must be usable by chairbound people: observe 643.

73731   Selected wc compartments should be usable by ambulant disabled people, see 633.

7374   Residential clubs
73740   In residential club buildings, bedroom accommodation for guests must be usable by disabled people. Provision should follow recommendations for hotels, see 730.

7375   Clubs for special groups
73750   For clubs for handicapped people see day centres for physically handicapped and mentally ill people, 704. For clubs for old people, see day centres for old people, 716.

738   Community centres, dance halls

7380   Community centres: General considerations
73800   Community centres, including for example village halls and church halls, must be usable by disabled people.
These buildings are commonly used by old people for social activities, and it is important that provision is made for those who are handicapped, particularly in cloakroom accommodation.

7381   Community centres: Approach
73810   At least one entrance to the building must be accessible to chairbound people: observe 641.

7382   Community centres: Internal planning
73820   Principal social areas must be accessible to chairbound people: observe 642.

7383   Community centres: Cloakroom provision
73830   At least one wc compartment in the building must be usable by chairbound people: observe 643.
This wc compartment should be to the preferred dimensions detailed in 64320.

7384   Dance halls
73840   Dance halls should be accessible to disabled people, not only for those, including wheelchair users, who participate, but also for those who attend for social purposes or as spectators.
As a rule dance halls will be part of buildings such as community centres, clubs or recreation centres, and access for disabled people will be ensured if appropriate recommendations for the building as a whole are observed.

739 Casinos, pier buildings, amusement arcades

7390 General considerations

73900 Amusement arcades and similar facilities are commonly very accessible buildings, for reasons associated with the requirement that it is easy for people to move in and out (see 1110). It ought not to be a difficult matter to incorporate suitable provision for disabled people.

7391 Approach

73910 At least one entrance to the building must be accessible to chairbound people: observe 641.

73911 Where in pier buildings turnstiles are installed there must be an alternative means of entrance for wheelchair users and other disabled people.

7392 Internal planning

73920 In pier buildings and amusement arcades all areas open to the general public must be accessible to chairbound people: observe 642.

73921 In casinos and similar buildings all areas for the use of club members or the general public must be accessible to chairbound people: observe 642. For requirements in respect of restaurants and bars see 731 and 732.

7393 Cloakroom provision

73930 At least one wc compartment for each sex or serving both sexes must be usable by chairbound people: observe 643.

74 Auditoria and cultural buildings

740 **Provision for disabled people in auditoria buildings**

7400 General considerations

74000 Buildings where seating is tiered pose problems. It is impossible to design them so that wheelchair users and others not able to manage steps can reach all seats, and special arrangements are required.

74001 Particular attention must be given to escape arrangements for chairbound and other disabled people. Wheelchairs may be a hazard in the event of hurried evacuation, and escape routes must not be obstructed. On the other hand, conditions ought not to be so strict as to prevent wheelchair users and other disabled people from using auditoria buildings at all, and requests by fire officers for unreasonable controls should be resisted.

7401 Provision for chairbound people

74010 In theatres etc special areas of the auditorium should be planned to accommodate wheelchairs, allowing chairbound people to remain in their chairs during performances. Space for wheelchairs needs to be more generous than for people using conventional seats, and an area minimum 1·400 × 0·900 is suggested.

74011 There should be space for able-bodied friends to sit alongside wheelchair users; the space for a wheelchair user and attendant should be minimum 1·400 wide. It may be possible for ordinary seats to be removable, and to be put in place when the area is not occupied by wheelchairs.

74012 People in wheelchairs usually sit higher above floor level than people on ordinary seats (see diagrams 20.7–20.10), and wheelchair spaces must be arranged to avoid obstructing the view of people seated behind.

74013 The minimum requirement for chairbound people detailed below (7403) is suggested for cinema, theatre, concert hall and congress hall buildings, and also in lecture theatres in, for example, university buildings, museums, public libraries and scientific institutes where seats are tiered. The suggested provision is varied for sports stadia, see 73521.

7402 Licensing conditions

74020 The number and location of places for chairbound people in theatres or cinemas may be governed by licensing provisions, see 6056.

74021 The conditions of licences are prepared on the advice of the fire inspector, who may require that places for chairbound people are sited alongside exit doors, so that in the event of fire wheelchairs do not impede the evacuation of the building. A general requirement is that wheelchair users must be accompanied by an adult able-bodied person who will occupy an adjacent seat in the auditorium; this requirement may apply whether or not the wheelchair users remains in his wheelchair.

7403 Chairbound people: Suggested minimum provision

74030 The suggested minimum provision for chairbound people in any auditorium is one wheelchair place for each 250 seats or portion of 250 seats for the first 1000 people accommodated, and one wheelchair place for each 500 seats or portion of 500 seats in excess of 1000.

74031 Not less than two such places must be provided, each minimum 0·900 wide × 1·400 deep. Where provision is made for an able-bodied attendant to sit alongside in a removable seat the minimum width should be 1·400.

7404 Ambulant disabled people

74040 Not all parts of an auditorium need be accessible to ambulant disabled people, ie access to all seats need not comply with the approach and circulation requirements of 631 and 632.
It may not, for example, be practicable to provide continuous handrails to each side of any steps. If circulation areas serving auditoria are accessible it will be possible for at least some sections of all parts of the auditorium to be reached without undue difficulty by ambulant disabled people.

74041 In an auditorium an ambulant disabled person who can manage steps only with difficulty is a hazard to other people in the event of an emergency. Special attention ought therefore to be given to means of escape by disabled people from parts of the auditorium which are most easily accessible.

74042 Seats at the end of rows are often particularly convenient for ambulant disabled people.

7405 People who are hard of hearing

74050 In theatres or concert halls provision may be made so that earphones can be plugged into sound amplifying equipment.

74051 Auditoria buildings should have built-in induction loops (see 447) so that hard of hearing people using their own hearing aids can benefit from improved reception. The facility should be suitably advertised, see 6521.

7406 Cloakroom provision

74060 In auditoria buildings comprehensive provision should be made in cloakroom accommodation for disabled people.

74061 It is most important that provision for chairbound people is made in concert halls and theatres. These buildings are often used for activities other than that served by the auditorium; they tend also to be used by people who travel further and spend more time away from home than those (for example) using cinemas.

74062 Where cloakroom provision is made for chairbound people it must be conveniently and quickly accessible from wheelchair places in the auditorium.

741 Cinema buildings

7410 General considerations

74100 In accordance with the requirements of section 4 of the Chronically Sick and Disabled Persons Act 1970, it is essential that in the planning of new cinema buildings suitable provision is made for disabled people.

This is equally important where existing large cinema buildings are remodelled to give two or three smaller auditoria; in this connection particular attention has to be given to means of escape.

74101 The use of cinemas by disabled people is discussed in the commentary in 1214 and 1409.

7411 Approach

74110 All public entrances to the building must be accessible to ambulant disabled people: observe 631.

74111 At least one entrance to the auditorium, preferably conveniently served from a car parking area, must be accessible to chairbound people: observe 641. According to circumstances it may be permissible that this entrance is an emergency exit rather than a normal public entrance.

7412 Internal planning

74120 All public areas must be accessible to ambulant disabled people: observe 632.

74121 Special places in the auditorium must be available for chairbound people, in accordance with the minimum provision suggested in 7403.

74122 Circulation areas between wheelchair places and the accessible entrance must be usable by chairbound people: observe 642. In buildings where public amenities such as a bar or restaurant are incorporated any such amenities should be accessible to chairbound people.

7413 Cloakroom provision

74130 At least one cloakroom must be accessible to ambulant disabled people: observe 633.

74131 At least one wc compartment for each sex or usable by both sexes should be accessible to chairbound people, see 643.

7414 Other provisions

74140 The availability of provision for disabled people should be suitably advertised, see 6521.

742 Theatre buildings, concert halls, opera houses

7420 General considerations

74200 The comments on the need for provision for disabled people in cinema buildings apply with even greater force to theatre buildings, concert halls and opera houses. Unlike cinemas, these buildings are invariably financed in part by a grant or loan from public funds, and it should be a condition of this aid that satisfactory arrangements are made for disabled patrons.

7421 Approach

74210 All public entrances must be accessible to ambulant disabled people: observe 631.

74211 At least one public entrance to the building must be accessible to chairbound people: observe 641. Parking bays close to an accessible entrance may be reserved for use by disabled people, see 580, 654.

7422 Internal planning

74220 All public circulation areas serving auditoria, bars, restaurants, cloakrooms and other facilities must be accessible to ambulant disabled people: observe 632.

74221 In the planning of auditoria, attention should be given to the needs of ambulant disabled people, see 7404.

Provision for wheelchair users

74222 Selected places in the auditorium should be planned for use by chairbound people, to a standard not less than that recommended in 7403.

74223 In small theatre buildings the minimum provision suggested should be exceeded, so that there are in any theatre at least four places for chairbound people; this will be advantageous for handicapped people attending in groups from clubs or residential homes.

74224 Circulation areas between the wheelchair places and the accessible entrance must be usable by chairbound people: observe 642.

74225 At least one bar must be accessible to chairbound people: observe 642.

74226 Where restaurants are provided at least one facility must be accessible to chairbound people: observe 642. See also 731.

7423 Cloakroom provision

74230 All cloakrooms should be accessible to ambulant disabled people, see 633.

74231 At least one wc compartment for each sex or serving both sexes must be usable by chairbound people: observe 643.

742 Theatre buildings, concert halls, opera houses
continued

7424 Other provisions

74240 Lecture rooms, committee rooms and similar facilities where provided must be accessible to chairbound people: observe 642.

74241 Where office accommodation is incorporated allowance should be made for the employment of disabled staff, see 760.

74242 The availability of provision for disabled people in the building should be suitably advertised, see 6521.

743 Congress and conference buildings

7430 General considerations

74300 In new congress and conference buildings it is important that all areas used by delegates or visitors are accessible to chairbound people. The scale of the building will as a rule ensure that this is practicable.

7431 Approach

74310 The principal entrance must be accessible to chairbound people: observe 641. Parking bays adjoining this entrance or an alternative entrance accessible to chairbound people may be reserved for handicapped people, see 580, 654.

74311 Other entrances must be accessible to ambulant disabled people: observe 631.

7432 Internal planning

74320 All halls, meeting rooms, exhibition areas, restaurants, bars and other areas used by delegates or visitors must be accessible to chairbound people: observe 642.

74321 In halls where seats are arranged in tiers special places must be available for chairbound people, in accordance with the provision suggested in 7403.

7433 Cloakroom provision

74330 At least one wc compartment for each sex or serving both sexes must be usable by chairbound people: observe 643. In large buildings it is desirable that more than one cloakroom has facilities for chairbound people.

74331 In public cloakrooms at least one wc compartment for each sex should be usable by ambulant disabled people, see 633.

7434 Other provisions

74340 Office accommodation must generally be accessible to staff who are chairbound, see 760.

74341 The availability of special provisions for disabled people in the building should be suitably advertised, see 651, 6521.

744 Exhibition buildings

7440 General considerations

74400 The recommendations which follow apply to exhibition buildings used for permanent or changing displays, including for example planetaria. They also apply to trade display buildings, such as centres concerned with building or household materials and equipment.

7441 Approach

74410 At least one entrance must be accessible to chairbound people: observe 641.
Parking provision should be available near this entrance.

74411 Other entrances must be accessible to ambulant disabled people: observe 631.

7442 Internal planning

74420 All circulation areas used by visitors, including conference rooms, lounges, restaurants and bars must be accessible to chairbound people: observe 642.

74421 Where display stands are mounted on temporary platforms the level of platforms should not be higher than 0·080 above fixed floor level.
For chairbound people a single step may be permissible in certain circumstances but not two steps or more; for discussion see 3114.

74422 Where practicable it is desirable that platforms to display stands are ramped.

7443 Cloakroom provision

74430 In public cloakrooms at least one wc compartment for each sex must be usable by ambulant disabled people: observe 633.

74431 At least one wc compartment for each sex or serving both sexes must be usable by chairbound people: observe 643.

7444 Other provisions

74440 Owing to the relatively high fire risk of temporary display stands in exhibition buildings, requirements for means of escape in case of fire are likely to be stringent, and may prejudice use of the building by disabled people.
Although careful consideration should be given to means of escape when the building is planned, it may not in practice be possible to guarantee that disabled people are always catered for, since licensing regulations for the building may vary according to the character of the exhibitions which are mounted and the numbers of people expected to attend.

74441 The arrangements made for disabled people to use the building should be suitably advertised, see 6522, 6528.

745 Museums, art galleries

7450 General considerations

74500 In any new museum or art gallery building it is essential that all display areas are accessible to disabled people, including wheelchair users; it is not sufficient that certain areas only are accessible. The consequence may be constraints on the architect planning a building where, for aesthetic reasons, there are advantages in having a variety of levels and volumes involving the incorporation of steps; with ingenuity it is probable that apparent irreconcilables can be resolved.

74501 To avoid unduly demanding conditions it is suggested that ramps may be used internally even though they will inhibit wheelchair independence. Wheelchair users visiting museums or art galleries will invariably be accompanied; if they are on their own museum attendants will be able to help them negotiate ramps.

7451 Approach

74510 At least one public entrance, preferably the main entrance, must be accessible to chairbound people: observe 641.

74511 All other public and staff entrances must be accessible to ambulant disabled people: observe 631.

7452 Internal planning

74520 All display areas must be accessible to chairbound people. In that ramps are considered permissible for internal circulation, some modifications of the strict specifications of 642 are warranted.

Steps and ramps

74521 Where there are changes in floor level, other than between storeys where vertical circulation must be by lift in accordance with 6423, there should be steps which are usable by ambulant disabled people in compliance with 632.

74522 Where such steps are incorporated there must also be a ramp for wheelchair users. The gradient of any internal ramp must not exceed 1:8; the preferred maximum gradient is 1:12 (see 321) and where the length of the ramp exceeds 6.000 a steeper gradient than 1:12 ought not to be considered permissible.

74523 Where there is a ramp in conjunction with steps, the steps will have handrails to aid ambulant disabled people and it is not necessary that handrails are provided to ramps.

74524 Ramps must be not less than 1·200 wide.

74525 Where the gradient of a ramp is less steep than 1:12 it is not essential that alternative steps are available. Where there are no steps and the ramp gradient is between 1:12 and 1:20 there should be a handrail to at least one side of the ramp; it is preferred in such cases that the ramp is not less than 1·800 wide.

Restaurants etc

74526 Any restaurants, shops or other amenities in the building must be accessible to chairbound people: observe 642 as modified.

Lecture rooms

74527 In lecture rooms where seats are tiered, special places should be provided for chairbound people in accordance with the provision suggested in 7403.

Staff areas

74528 Areas where staff may be employed on sedentary work, for example dealing with cataloguing or archives, must be accessible to chairbound people: observe 642.

7453 Cloakroom provision

74530 In public cloakrooms at least one wc compartment for each sex must be usable by ambulant disabled people: observe 633.

74531 At least one wc compartment for each sex or usable by both sexes should be usable by chairbound people, see 643. In large buildings, for example where the exhibition and display area exceeds 1000m², this recommendation should be treated as essential.

7454 Other provisions

74540 It can be expected that wheelchairs will be made available for loan to visitors; storage space not less than 3.0² should be provided. The availability of this and other provisions for disabled people should be suitably advertised, see 6528.

74541 Any suggestion that special means of escape provision should be incorporated in view of the possible use of the building by wheelchair users and other disabled people should be discouraged. For guidance on this matter see 609.

746 Library buildings

7460 General considerations

74600 The number of disabled people who use public libraries, or would do so if they had the opportunity, is small; for discussion see 1215. Despite this it is essential that library buildings are accessible to disabled people: first, because the requirements of the Chronically Sick Act (6010) ought to be implemented; and second, because it is important that disabled people are afforded every opportunity to make the most of their potential for living.

74601 The recommendations which follow apply in particular to public libraries administered by local authorities, but are relevant also to university and college libraries, company libraries, libraries for research or scientific institutes and all other general or specialist libraries.

7461 Approach
74610 At least one public entrance must be accessible to chairbound people: observe 641. Parking bays near this entrance may be reserved for handicapped people, see 580, 655.

74611 All other public and staff entrances must be accessible to ambulant disabled people: observe 631.

74612 For security reasons it is desirable that the accessible entrance is the main entrance. An alternative entrance may need to be kept locked, causing inconvenience to disabled visitors.

7462 Internal planning
74620 All principal public areas, for example lending library, research library, music library, reading rooms, lecture rooms and exhibition and display areas, must be accessible to chairbound people: observe 642.

74621 In lecture rooms where seats are tiered, wheelchair places must be provided, as suggested in 7403.

74622 Steps and staircases in public areas must be suitable for ambulant disabled people, see 6323.

7463 Bookshelves
74630 For reasons discussed in the commentary (1115) it is impossible to arrange bookshelves in public libraries so that they can be reached by all disabled people.

74631 To cater for disabled people and elderly people in general the planning of library spaces used by the public should be based on the condition that no bookshelf is higher than the eye level of an average-height woman, ie 1·500 above floor level. The lowest shelves ought not to be lower than 0·250 above floor level.

74632 In areas of the library used only by staff, or where it is routine for staff to obtain books for customers, bookshelves at higher levels are permissible.

7464 Provision for reading
74640 In new library buildings where reading carrels are provided, at least one carrel must be large enough to accommodate a person in a wheelchair. Such provision may also be suitable for blind students who rely on someone to read to them. For blind students with readers, and for any students whose disability means that they must use a typewriter, it is important that at least one carrel is soundproof, or that a soundproofed room is available.

7465 Staff provision
74650 In large library buildings there is a variety of opportunities for staff to be employed on sedentary work, for example cataloguing, indexing, reading and secretarial work. All rooms used for these and similar purposes must be accessible to chairbound people: observe 642. Any common rooms, refreshment rooms and recreation rooms must also be accessible.

74651 For branch public libraries and other small library buildings where less than ten or so people are employed, provision for disabled staff is not essential.

7466 Cloakroom provision
74660 In any library building where cloakrooms are provided for customers or where provision is made for chairbound staff at least one wc compartment for each sex or serving both sexes must be usable by chairbound people: observe 643.

74661 If cloakrooms are available for customers and the accessible wc compartment is in an area used only by staff a notice drawing attention to its availability may be displayed, see 6514.

747 Research and scientific institutes

7470 General considerations
74700 In buildings for research or scientific institutes the provision which it is appropriate to make for disabled people will depend on the character of work undertaken, for example whether it is suitable for sedentary operation, and the possibility that there may be visitors who are disabled.

748 Professional institute and learned society buildings

7480 Professional institute buildings: General considerations
74800 Professional institute buildings may afford a variety of services to members. In the planning of them an important factor to consider is that the professional person disabled by trauma or disease during working life may have to find employment which is not physically demanding, and a professional institute may offer suitable opportunities. Comprehensive provision ought therefore to be made.

7481 Approach
74810 At least one entrance to the building must be accessible to chairbound people: observe 641.

74811 Other entrances must be accessible to ambulant disabled people: observe 631.

7482 Internal planning

74820 All areas used by staff or members must be accessible to chairbound people: observe 642. For relevant guidance see recommendations for library buildings (746), museum buildings (745), restaurants (731) and office buildings (760).

7483 Cloakroom provision

74830 At least one wc compartment for each sex or usable by both sexes must be usable by chairbound people: observe 643.

74831 Other cloakroom provision should be usable by ambulant disabled people, see 633.

7484 Learned society buildings

74840 In buildings for learned societies provision should be made for disabled people; the recommendations for library buildings (746) should generally be observed.

749 Zoo buildings, botanical garden buildings

7490 General considerations

74900 All visitor areas in zoos and botanical gardens should be accessible to disabled people, including wheelchair users. Although on hilly sites this may be difficult to achieve, satisfactory arrangements will generally be possible with the aid of careful landscaping.

7491 External planning

74910 Pedestrian routes between buildings and around the site should be graded so that they are not steeper than 1:20. Where for topographical reasons this may be impossible the maximum gradient permissible is 1:12.

74911 Paths should be not less than 1·800 wide. Finishes should be suitable for wheelchairs; loose gravel must be avoided.
Where travel distances are extended seats should be provided for resting.

74912 Where there are steps on public routes they should be usable by ambulant disabled people: observe 6312. There must be an alternative route for chairbound people, with ramps having a maximum gradient of 1:12.

74913 Where the direct route between buildings or areas of interest involves the use of steps there should be signs indicating the alternative route available for chairbound people, see 6512.

74914 In public car parks selected parking bays in convenient locations should be reserved for handicapped people, see 580, 6535.

7492 Approach

74920 The principal entrance to any building must be accessible to chairbound people: observe 641.

74921 Other entrances must be accessible to ambulant disabled people: observe 631.

74922 In places where admission is controlled by turnstiles alternative gate access must be available through which wheelchairs can pass.

7493 Internal planning

74930 Inside individual buildings all areas open to visitors must be accessible to chairbound people. Where changes of route level are needed, other than between storeys, the incorporation of steps with ramps is permissible, as suggested for museum buildings, see 74521.

7494 Cloakroom provision

74940 At least one wc compartment for each sex or serving both sexes must be usable by chairbound people: observe 643.

74941 Other public lavatories should include at least one wc compartment for each sex usable by ambulant disabled people, see 633.

7495 Other provisions

74950 Wheelchairs should be available for loan to visitors and storage space adjoining the principal entrance should be provided for them.

74951 Buildings for administrative or research purposes should be usable by staff who are disabled. The recommendations for office buildings (760) and research and scientific institutes (747) should be observed.

75 Official administration buildings

750 Civic buildings

7500 General

75000 The recommendations below relate specifically to civic buildings such as the administrative headquarters of county councils and district councils. These buildings will incorporate administrative offices; in this connection requirements coincide with those for other public administrative offices, and appropriate provisions are detailed in 751.

75001 Civic buildings are used by members of the public for a variety of purposes. Section 4 of the Chronically Sick Act requires that in buildings used by the public suitable provision is made for disabled people, and local authorities have a moral obligation to ensure that their own buildings conform with the intentions of the Act. There is an opportunity in new civic buildings to demonstrate by example what in practice can be achieved.

7501 Approach

75010 The principal entrance must be accessible to chairbound people: observe 641.
Alongside this, or an alternative entrance accessible to chairbound people, there should be parking bays reserved for handicapped people, see 580, 6535.

75011 Other entrances used by members of the council or the general public must be accessible to ambulant disabled people: observe 631.

7502 Internal planning

75020 All areas used by the general public, for example enquiry offices, exhibition rooms and rooms for payment of rents, rates and licences, must be accessible to chairbound people: observe 642.

75021 Reception rooms, committee rooms, members' dining rooms and lounges, staff recreation rooms and restaurants must be accessible to chairbound people: observe 642.

75022 Council chambers must be accessible to chairbound people: observe 642. Public galleries to council chambers should also be accessible.

75023 In respect of other facilities which may be incorporated in the building reference should be made to appropriate sections: libraries (746), register offices (752), advisory offices (753), courtrooms (755).

7503 Cloakroom provision

75030 Cloakrooms should generally be accessible to chairbound people. At least one wc compartment for each sex or serving both sexes must be usable by chairbound people: observe 643.

75031 In all cloakrooms there should be at least one wc compartment for each sex usable by ambulant disabled people, see 633.

751 Public authority and national administrative offices

7510 General considerations

75100 The recommendations made here relate to the administrative offices of the following agencies.
1. Central government, for example national and regional offices of central government departments, and local offices dealing with services such as health, insurance and employment.
2. Local government, for example central and area offices of county councils and district councils.
3. Police, fire and ambulance authorities.
4. National boards controlling services such as water, fuel, transport and posts.

75101 Public authorities may be concerned with helping disabled people to obtain employment, and for political as well as social reasons it is therefore important that their own administrative buildings permit the employment of disabled people. The role of public authorities as both promoters and potential providers of employment opportunities for disabled people means that in the planning of their administrative buildings more stringent criteria are appropriate than in the private sphere where goals are primarily commercial. The provision proposed for public authority offices is therefore more extensive than that suggested for commercial offices, discussed separately in 760–762.

75102 In the case of existing buildings which are adapted it may be difficult to satisfy all the recommendations made below, and some compromises may have to be made. In new buildings it ought not to be necessary to compromise; in the case of 2 or 3 storey buildings it may be expensive to incorporate a lift which will permit the employment of disabled people not able to climb stairs, but such provision ought properly to be made.

75103 Special attention may need to be given to means of escape in case of fire. For discussion see 760.

7511 Approach

75110 At least one entrance must be accessible to chairbound people: observe 641.
This entrance should be adjacent to the car parking area used by employees.

75111 Other entrances must be accessible to ambulant disabled people: observe 631.

7512 Internal planning

75120 All areas used by the general public, for example reception areas, enquiry offices and interview rooms, must be accessible to chairbound people: observe 642.

75121 All offices and areas used by employees, for example recreation rooms and staff restaurants, must be accessible to chairbound people: observe 642.

7513 Cloakroom provision

75130 At least one wc compartment for each sex must be usable by chairbound people: observe 643.

75131 In all cloakrooms at least one wc compartment should be usable by ambulant disabled people, see 633.

752 Register offices

7520 General considerations

75200 In new register office buildings suitable provision should be made for disabled people attending marriage ceremonies, including wheelchair users.

7521 Access and use

75210 At least one entrance to the building must be accessible to chairbound people: observe 641. Rooms used by people attending marriage ceremonies must be similarly accessible: observe 642.

753 Official and advisory bureaux

7530 General considerations

75300 In order that disabled people have the same opportunities as others to exercise their privileges as citizens, it is important that the offices of agencies such as citizens' advice bureaux, housing advisory centres, legal aid centres and welfare rights offices are accessible. Employment exchange buildings (job centres) are covered under 751.

7531 Approach

75310 At least one entrance to the building must be accessible to chairbound people: observe 641.

7532 Internal planning

75320 Areas for public enquiry and interviewing must be accessible to chairbound people: observe 642.

75321 It is desirable that provision is made for staff who are disabled to be employed.

754 Police stations, fire stations

7540 Police stations: General considerations

75400 Because of the nature of activities performed in police stations, disabled people may not be so concerned about their accessibility as they are for other public buildings. It is recommended that ambulant disabled people visiting police stations are catered for, and that provision for chairbound people is made where it can be done without difficulty.

75401 In divisional police stations it is desirable that provision is made for clerical staff who may be disabled. The headquarters buildings of police authorities are covered under 751.

7541 Police stations: Approach

75410 The principal public entrance to the building must be accessible to ambulant disabled people: observe 631.

75411 Where provision is made for chairbound staff at least one entrance must be accessible to chairbound people: observe 641.

7542 Police stations: Internal planning

75420 Areas used by members of the general public, for example enquiry offices, interview rooms and waiting rooms, must be accessible to ambulant disabled people: observe 632.

75421 Where provision is made for chairbound staff appropriate areas must be accessible to chairbound people: observe 642.

7543 Police stations: Cloakroom provision

75430 Where provision is made for chairbound staff at least one wc compartment should be usable by chairbound people, see 643.

75431 In new police station buildings consideration may be given to the provision of a wc compartment serving chairbound visitors.
The general availability of accessible wc compartments in new police stations could be helpful for disabled travellers.

7544 Fire stations

75440 In local fire station buildings it is not necessary that any provision is made for disabled people. For recommendations for the headquarters buildings of fire authorities see 751.

755 Court buildings

7550 General considerations

75500 Court buildings in England comprise crown courts, which are used only for criminal cases referred to judge and jury, and magistrates' courts which are used for civil cases. The recommendations below (7551–7553) relate to magistrates' courts; comparable provision should be made in crown courts, and also in coroner's courts.

75501 Users of magistrates' courts comprise three groups: first, people who work in the building, including magistrates, solicitors, clerks, police, probation officers and administrative staff; second, the general public, attending as witnesses, visitors, or to pay fines or maintenance orders; third, defendants attending for trial.

755 Court buildings *continued*

75502 Among magistrates and court staff, disabled people may not be uncommon, and similarly among members of the public. The scale of magistrates' court buildings ensures that accommodation of disabled users will not impose unreasonable constraints.

7551 Approach

75510 All entrances to the building must be accessible to ambulant disabled people: observe 631.

75511 The principal public entrance must be accessible to chairbound people: observe 641.

75512 Where a car park is provided for building users at least one entrance from the car park must be accessible to chairbound people: observe 641.

7552 Internal planning

75520 All principal areas used by the general public, for example reception area, offices for payment of fines and maintenance orders, refreshment areas, adult and juvenile courtrooms, waiting rooms and interview rooms, must be accessible to chairbound people: observe 642.

75521 Areas used by people working in the building who may be disabled, for example magistrates' rooms, solicitors' rooms, conference rooms, probation officers' rooms, and administrative offices, must be accessible to chairbound people: observe 642.

75522 Special consideration should be given to the design of magistrates' benches, for example by the provision of an alternative ramped access where there is a stepped access.

75523 Areas used by defendants, for example custodial areas, should be accessible to ambulant disabled people, see 632.

7553 Cloakroom provision

75530 At least one wc compartment serving magistrates, solicitors and administrative staff must be usable by chairbound people: observe 643.
This compartment should be usable by both sexes or be duplicated for each sex.

75531 For public use, at least one wc compartment for each sex or serving both sexes must be usable by chairbound people: observe 643.
This facility may be omitted where the wheelchair wc compartment for administrative staff can be made available for public use.

75532 Selected wc compartments should be usable by ambulant disabled people, see 633.

7554 Inns of Court

75540 Provision for disabled people using inns of court should be comparable to that recommended for users of magistrates' courts.

756 Ceremonial representative buildings

7560 General considerations

75600 In ceremonial representative buildings, for example embassies, legations, consulates and high commission buildings, comprehensive provision should be made for disabled people.

7561 Approach

75610 At least one entrance must be accessible to chairbound people: observe 641.

75611 Other entrances must be accessible to ambulant disabled people: observe 631.

7562 Internal planning

75620 All areas used for official receptions and related purposes must be accessible to chairbound people: observe 642.

7563 Cloakroom provision

75630 At least one wc compartment for each sex or usable by both sexes must be accessible to chairbound people: observe 643.

75631 Selected wc compartments should be usable by ambulant disabled people, see 633.

757 Military buildings

7570 General considerations

75700 No special facilities for disabled people are needed in military buildings, for example barracks or military training schools, except that in office buildings where civilian staff are employed provision ought to be made for the employment of disabled people, see 760.

758 Prison buildings

7580 General considerations

75800 No evidence is available regarding the incidence of disability among the inmates of prisons. In the expectation that it may not be significantly different from other populations, and that disabled people are likely to be found among prison staff and visitors, consideration should be given when the brief is being prepared to the requirements of disabled users.

759 Public mortuaries

7590 General considerations

75900 In public mortuaries the public entrance, the waiting room and the viewing room should be accessible to chairbound people, see 641 and 642.

76 Commercial buildings

760 Office buildings: General

7600 Commercial offices: General considerations

76000 The specific recommendations detailed in 761 and 762 relate to commercial offices for private companies. In the case of offices for public authorities requirements are more stringent, and are detailed in 751.

76001 In all new office buildings it is important that disabled people can be employed. For the avoidance of stress and disturbance, and for the convenience of themselves and others using the building, disabled employees should be able to use office buildings independently; this means that, apart from observing the relevant 'must' requirements of the specifications in section 6, relevant 'should' recommendations ought also to be observed, for ambulant disabled or chairbound people as appropriate.

Disabled Persons' (Employment) Act

76002 The fact that under the Disabled Persons' (Employment) Act 1944 businesses employing 20 or more people are required to have among their employees 3 per cent who are disabled may be cited as a reason why office buildings should be conveniently accessible and usable.
On a practical level the logic here is not strong; only a small percentage of people who are registered as disabled are so physically handicapped as to require special arrangements in buildings and a large proportion of firms find it impossible, in part because of the decreasing number of people who are registered, to meet their 3 per cent quota[1]. The Act does however afford a basis for prompting or persuading building developers to incorporate provision for disabled people; in this respect the Chronically Sick Act, because it does not cover employment buildings, is weak.

76003 Under Section 15 of the Act the Department of Employment may provide financial assistance to an employer to enable him to install special equipment and meet other specific expenses connected with the employment of a disabled person.

Fire regulations

76004 It is important that possibilities for the employment of disabled people in new office buildings are not threatened by inhibiting requirements from the building or fire authority relating to means of escape by disabled employees in case of fire; for reasons discussed in the commentary (6093) it is considered appropriate that no special architectural provision is made in this connection.

7601 Buildings with lifts

76010 In large office buildings where lifts are installed to serve all floors it should be possible to cater for wheelchair users throughout. The recommendations detailed in 761 ought to be achievable in the case of all buildings where the area of office space exceeds 1000m², or where 50 or more staff are to be employed.

7602 Buildings without lifts

76020 In certain circumstances it may be impracticable to plan office buildings so that they are accessible to wheelchair users, for example small offices planned over a row of shops. Such buildings can however be made accessible to ambulant disabled people and the recommendations in 762 should be observed. In other cases, for example small buildings on infill sites, it may be possible to make the ground floor accessible to wheelchair users and other areas accessible to ambulant disabled people.

761 Large office buildings

7610 General considerations

76100 The recommendations below relate to office buildings having a lift or lifts serving all floors. They should also be observed for buildings where all office accommodation is at ground level.

7611 Approach

76110 At least one entrance serving the reception area must be accessible to chairbound people: observe 641.
To cater for people who use wheelchairs independently this entrance should have a level approach from the setting down point for visitors arriving by car and from a car park for employees.

76111 Other entrances must be accessible to ambulant disabled people: observe 631.

7612 Internal planning

76120 All areas used by office staff, including refreshment and recreation areas, must be accessible to chairbound people: observe 642.

7613 Cloakroom provision

76130 At least one wc compartment for each sex or serving both sexes must be usable by chairbound people: observe 642.

76131 The suggested provision is that there should be one wheelchair compartment for each sex for each 1000m² gross floor area of office space.

76132 The distance to be travelled from any office to a wheelchair wc compartment, excluding vertical circulation by lift, should be not more than 60·000.

---

[1] For discussion see 1306. At the time of writing (May 1976) a Bill is before Parliament which aims to amend the Chronically Sick Act to cover employment buildings.

761   Large office buildings *continued*

76133   Where wc compartments for wheelchair users are not available on all office floors they should be planned adjacent to lifts.

76134   Where an office building may be subdivided among various tenants wheelchair wc compartments should be provided on each floor.

76135   In addition to wheelchair wc compartments selected wc compartments in all cloakrooms should be usable by ambulant disabled people, see 633.

762   Small office buildings

7620   General considerations
76200   The recommendations below relate to small office buildings where a lift is not installed and where there is office accommodation other than at ground level.

7621   Approach
76210   All entrances must be accessible to ambulant disabled people: observe 631.

76211   Where there is ground floor office space at least one entrance should be accessible to chairbound people, see 641.

7622   Internal planning
76220   Where there is an accessible entrance complying with 641 ground floor areas must be accessible to chairbound people: observe 642.

76221   Other areas used by office staff must be accessible to ambulant disabled people: observe 632.

7623   Cloakroom provision
76230   At least one wc compartment for each sex should be usable by ambulant disabled people, see 633.

76231   Where ground floor office space is accessible to chairbound people one wc compartment for each sex or serving both sexes should be usable by chairbound people, see 643.

763   Shopping centres

7630   General considerations
76300   In the planning of new shopping centres it is most important that all shop buildings and associated facilities are accessible to disabled people, including wheelchair users, meaning that requirements relating to approach and internal planning for chairbound people (641, 642) are observed throughout.

76301   For discussion on the use of pedestrian precincts by disabled people see 1229.

7631   Car parking
76310   Parking areas serving shopping centres must allow for unobstructed access to all parts of the centre. Selected parking bays should be reserved for use by handicapped people, see 580, 6535.

76311   For guidance on car park buildings see 776.

7632   Pedestrian circulation areas
76320   Travel distances in shopping centres may be extended. For independent wheelchair users and people who have to push wheelchairs, main circulation routes ought not to be inclined at a gradient steeper than 1:20, and ought preferably to be level.
Topographical conditions may make this difficult but careful landscaping can assist.

76321   Where practicable there should be undercover access from parking areas to principal facilities.

76322   For guidance on floor surfaces and the street environment see 301, 663.

7633   Other provisions
76330   Where a public lavatory is incorporated it should include provision for chairbound people, as recommended in 660–662.

7634   Market buildings
76340   The recommendations above are generally applicable to covered or open market buildings.

764   Department stores, supermarkets

7640   General considerations
76400   Disabled people, including those who are chairbound, should be enabled to do their own shopping, without their choice being restricted by inaccessible buildings. The use of department stores and other shop buildings is discussed in the commentary, see 1207.

76401   In respect of department stores and supermarkets the scale of the building, along with the important commercial consideration of making it as simple as possible for people to move in and out of the building, will mean that there ought to be few problems of arranging suitable provision for wheelchair users; for discussion on shops as free movement buildings see 1110. In new stores where, in addition to ground floor provision, selling spaces are at basement or first floor level, it is a common practice for customer access to be by means of staircases only, or staircases in association with escalators. A goods lift may be usable (unofficially) by chairbound people, but this expedient ought not to be relied upon and the only satisfactory provision is for a customer lift to be installed.

7641 Approach

76410 The principal public entrance and any entrances directly approached from parking areas must be accessible to chairbound people: observe 641.

76411 Other entrances must be accessible to ambulant disabled people: observe 631.

7642 Internal planning

76420 All customer areas must be accessible to chairbound people: observe 642.

7643 Cloakroom provision

76430 Where cloakrooms are provided for the use of customers at least one wc compartment for each sex or serving both sexes must be usable by chairbound people: observe 643.

76431 At least one wc compartment in each public cloakroom should be usable by ambulant disabled people, see 633.

7644 Other provisions

76440 In buildings where more than 20 or so staff are employed on administrative office duties provision must be made for employees in wheelchairs: observe 641 and 642.

76441 Where there is cloakroom provision in the building for wheelchair customers it will not normally be necessary to provide a special wheelchair wc compartment for staff use.

76442 Both inside and outside the building facilities available for disabled people should be suitably signposted, see section 65. Consideration should also be given to the provision of notices which will help deaf people, see 6154.

765 Specialist shops

7650 General considerations

76500 In respect of specialist or small shops suitable access provision will be possible where customer areas are at ground level only and where the site is level or near-level. Problems are likely to occur where customer areas are on more than one level or where the site is awkward.

76501 Available evidence indicates that for disabled people not able to go out independently it is most important that accessibility is provided at shops giving a service which cannot be delegated; for disabled people who can go out independently access is important at all shops giving an essential service, meaning the majority of shop buildings.

76502 The use of different shop buildings by disabled people and the importance of access is discussed in the commentary; see 1207, 1220–1222.

7651 Higher priority specialist shops

76510 The requirements detailed below are for wheelchair accessibility and should be applied to all large shop buildings having a selling area of about 100m² or more. In respect of small shops they should be applied wherever practicable.

76511 Among specialist shops a distinction can be made between those providing a service which chairbound people are likely to require, and where access is most important, and those where the service is less likely to be required, and some compromise is admissible. The suggested priority list, where requirements for access (641) and internal circulation (642) should be observed, is as follows:

1 art dealers
2 antique shops
3 auctioneers' showrooms
4 bakers, confectioners
5 betting shops
6 booksellers, stationers
7 boutiques
8 building society offices
9 butchers
10 car showrooms
11 chemists
12 clothes and clothing accessory shops, for example milliners, shoe shops, tailors, wool shops
13 do-it-yourself shops
14 electricity showrooms, electrical accessory shops
15 fishmongers
16 florists
17 furniture and bedding shops
18 garages
19 garden equipment shops and horticultural suppliers
20 gas showrooms
21 general stores
22 grocers, greengrocers
23 handicraft shops
24 insurance agencies
25 jewellers, clock and watch repairers
26 laundries, dry cleaners
27 newsagents, tobacconists
28 medical and surgical equipment suppliers
29 music shops
30 office equipment shops
31 opticians
32 photographic studios
33 radio and television rental shops, suppliers and repairers
34 souvenir shops
35 toyshops
36 travel and tourist agencies
37 travel goods shops
38 wine shops, off-licence shops

7652 Lower priority specialist shops
76520 For other specialist shops it is desirable but not essential that access for chairbound people is provided. Where provision cannot be made, the requirements for ambulant disabled people in respect of access (631) and internal circulation (632) must be observed. Shops in this group are as follows:

1 accommodation agencies
2 advertising agencies
3 car accessory shops
4 car hire dealers
5 cycle accessory shops, suppliers and repairers
6 draughtsmens' shops, artists' materials suppliers, photographic equipment shops
7 driving schools offices
8 employment agencies
9 estate agents
10 funeral directors
11 furniture removers' offices
12 mother and babywear shops
13 petshops
14 publishers' offices
15 shoe repairers
16 sports equipment shops
17 theatrical suppliers

766 Hairdressing salons

7660 General considerations
76600 It is important that hairdressing salons and barbers' shops are usable independently by disabled people; for discussion see 1208.

7661 Approach
76610 The entrance must be accessible to chairbound people: observe 641.

7662 Internal planning
76620 At least part of any customer areas must be accessible to chairbound people: observe 642.

76621 For notes on the specification of basins where provision is made for disabled people see 7046.

767 Launderettes

7670 General considerations
76700 It is important both for social and practical reasons that launderette facilities are usable by disabled people; for discussion see 1222.

7671 Approach
76710 The entrance must be accessible to chairbound people: observe 641.

7672 Internal planning
76720 Customer areas must be accessible to chairbound people: observe 642.

76721 While it is desirable that washing and drying equipment is specified which can be used conveniently by people who are disabled, it may be assumed that help from staff or other customers will be available if needed.

768 Post offices

7680 General considerations
76800 The use of post offices by disabled people is discussed in the commentary, see 1210.

7681 Approach
76810 The principal public entrance must be accessible to chairbound people: observe 641.
As discussed in 1222, post offices are among buildings which independent wheelchair users may need to use on their own; it is desirable that the entrance has a level approach.

7682 Internal planning
76820 All customer areas must be accessible to chairbound people: observe 642.

7683 Other provisions
76830 In new post office buildings it is not essential that provision is made for staff who are disabled.

769 Bank buildings

7690 General considerations
76900 The use of banks by disabled people is discussed in the commentary, see 1210.

7691 Approach
76910 At least one entrance must be accessible to chairbound people: observe 641.
To cater for independent wheelchair users this entrance should have a level approach.

7692 Internal planning
76920 All customer areas, including offices used by the manager and other senior staff, must be accessible to chairbound people: observe 642.

7693 Provision for staff
76930 In large bank buildings employing 20 or more staff provision should be made for employees in wheelchairs. Areas where staff may be engaged on sedentary work must be accessible to chairbound people. Suitable cloakroom provision should be incorporated or allowed for.

77 Transport buildings

770 Public transport and disabled people

7700 Public transport: General considerations
77000 As discussed in 1412, public transport for disabled people is a means to an end rather than an end in itself, a factor to be taken into account both in the design of transport buildings and vehicles.

77001 In the case of chairbound disabled people it can be assumed that local journeys will generally be undertaken by private car or special buses and that longer journeys may be made by train or plane.

77002 For ambulant disabled people the position is different, in that for local journeys they may be expected to need to use public transport, for example buses or underground railways.

77003 Elderly people are commonly dependent on public transport, and so are other groups who can be categorized as handicapped, for example small children, epileptics and people who are mentally handicapped.

771 Railway station buildings

7710 General considerations
77100 Chairbound people who travel by train are invariably accompanied. Those who travel independently usually make advance arrangements with the railway authorities for assistance to be given as necessary.

77101 In stations where access to platforms for travellers involves the use of steps it is probable that alternative access, for example by special lift, will be available for goods traffic.
Notices should be displayed advising travellers that alternative access routes can be used if necessary, and also indicating other services for disabled people, see 6523.

77102 For discussion on the use of railways and station buildings by wheelchair users see 1217 and 1410.

7711 Approach
77110 The principal approach to the building must be accessible to chairbound people: observe 641.

77111 Other entrances must be accessible to ambulant disabled people: observe 631.

7712 Internal planning
77120 All public areas, for example booking halls, waiting rooms, refreshment rooms and enquiry offices, must be accessible to ambulant disabled people: observe 632.
These areas should be accessible to chairbound people wherever possible.

77121 In station concourses, services for the general public, for example newsagents, tobacconists, chemists, hairdressers and banks, should be accessible to chairbound people, see 642.

7713 Cloakroom provision
77130 In any public cloakroom at least one wc compartment for each sex should be usable by ambulant disabled people, see 633.

77131 In large station buildings at least one cloakroom, preferably supervised by an attendant, must have at least one wc compartment for each sex or serving both sexes which is usable by chairbound people: observe 643.
It is particularly desirable that suitable provision is made at terminus buildings, where disabled people may arrive following a journey of some hours during which they have not been able to reach a wc.

7714 Other provisions
77140 Where office accommodation is incorporated provision must be made for staff who are disabled, see 761 or 762 as appropriate.

77141 Where a car park building is incorporated the recommendations in 776 should be observed.

772 Underground railways and rapid transit systems

7720 General considerations
77200 For reasons discussed in 1411, it is not essential in the planning of stations for new underground railways and rapid transit systems that provision is made for chairbound people. It is important that special consideration is given to the needs of ambulant disabled people.

7721 Approach
77210 All entrances to station buildings must be accessible to ambulant disabled people: observe 631.

77211 Where turnstile ticket barriers are incorporated an alternative access gate must be provided.

7722 Internal planning
77220 All areas of the station should be accessible to ambulant disabled people, see 632.
For practical reasons it may be difficult to achieve the prescribed requirements for staircase gradients but it is essential that handrails are installed to both sides of any stairs.

77221 Where escalators are installed they should travel direct from platform level to street level.

772 Underground railways and rapid transit systems *continued*

77222 For handicapped people not able to use escalators with safety it is essential that an alternative staircase is available; see 45421.

77223 Lifts where provided ought desirably to travel from platform level to street level; where this is not possible the need to use stairs should be minimized.

7723 Cloakroom provision
77230 Where public lavatories are provided at least one wc compartment for each sex should be usable by ambulant disabled people, see 633.

773 Bus and coach station buildings

7730 General considerations
77300 As discussed in 1217, there are occasions when chairbound people may travel by coach on party outings, and it is desirable that provision is made in coach station buildings.

77301 For discussion on the design and use of buses see 1410.

7731 Approach and internal planning
77310 Principal public areas, for example concourses with associated amenities, must be accessible to chairbound people: observe 641 and 642.

7732 Cloakroom provision
77320 In any public lavatory at least one wc compartment for each sex should be usable by ambulant disabled people, see 633.

77321 At major coach stations at least one wc compartment for each sex or usable by both sexes should be usable by chairbound people, observe 643.

7733 Other provisions
77330 Guard rails should be installed where queues may form.

77331 Seats and benches for public use should have backrests.

7734 Bus stops
77340 Bus stops served by local bus services must give adequate shelter. A seat or bench suitable for handicapped people should be provided.

77341 Refuges should be designed so that buses may draw up close to the kerb, so minimizing problems of access to or from buses for people with lower limb disabilities.

774 Airports, air terminals

7740 General considerations
77400 Severely disabled people can as a rule travel long distances more conveniently by air than by car or train.
The principal advantage is that journeys can be completed quickly; this is of critical advantage to wheelchair users who, when using car or train, cannot always be sure of finding accessible public lavatories. Provided that airports are generally equipped with accessible public lavatories the likelihood is that wheelchair users will increasingly use air travel. Another advantage of quicker travel is simply that disabled people will be caused less discomfort than sitting for long periods in a car or train.

Passenger handling
77401 When considering the means of handling passengers, which will be directly related to the design concept, architects should take account of the needs of wheelchair users and other disabled people.
Except where there are telescopic bridges from waiting area to aircraft door, chairbound people will need to be carried up or down steps to transfer to or from an aircraft.

77402 In airport buildings the distance from the aircraft to taxi, bus or car is often considerable. Wheelchairs will invariably be provided by the airport authority for use by people who are handicapped, and their availability should be advertised; see 6523.

77403 Other provisions usable by disabled people ought also to be advertised, for example lifts which substitute for a staircase or escalator, and accessible cloakrooms.

7741 Approach
77410 The approach to the building from any taxi rank, coach or car setting-down point must be accessible to chairbound people: observe 641.

7742 Internal planning
77420 All steps and stairs serving public areas, including spectator areas, must be usable by ambulant disabled people: observe 632.

77421 All public areas used by passengers, for example concourses, check-in points, waiting rooms, baggage halls, customs areas, restaurants, banks and shops must be accessible to chairbound people: observe 642.

77422 Passenger conveyors serving public areas must have bands not less than 0·800 wide, see 4541.

77423 Where passenger transit through immigration combs involves passing through narrow gates, alternative routes must be available for chairbound people.

77424 Where airline passengers have to use staircases for transfer from the terminal building to the apron, alternative transfer arrangements must be available for chairbound people.

7743 Cloakroom provision

77430 In any public cloakroom at least one wc compartment for each sex should be usable by ambulant disabled people, see 633.

77431 At least one public cloakroom must have a wc compartment usable by chairbound people of both sexes, or one compartment for each sex: observe 643.

7744 Other provisions

77440 At any airport or air terminal building there will be a variety of opportunities for the employment of staff who are disabled; in areas where staff may be employed on sedentary work the requirements for public authority offices (751) should be observed.

77441 In public car park buildings where cars are parked by customers the requirements of 776 should be observed.

775 Sea terminal buildings

7750 General considerations

77500 In the planning of new sea terminal buildings it is important that consideration is given to disabled people, including wheelchair users, travelling by car ferry. In terminal buildings not associated with car ferries it is desirable, but not essential, that the recommendations below are observed.

7751 Internal planning

77510 Principal public areas, ie concourses with associated facilities such as shops and restaurants, must be accessible to chairbound people: observe 642. Where appropriate, immigration and customs halls ought also to be accessible.

7752 Cloakroom provision

77520 In public cloakrooms at least one wc compartment for each sex should be usable by ambulant disabled people, see 633.

77521 At least one wc compartment for each sex or serving both sexes must be usable by chairbound people: observe 643.

776 Car park buildings

7760 General considerations

77600 The recommendations here refer to multi-storey car parks where cars are parked by customers.

7761 Reserved parking bays

77610 Selected parking bays may be reserved for the use of disabled drivers or disabled passengers. These bays should be close to the entrance to the building and should preferably be at street level.

77611 The suggested scale of provision is one reserved bay for each 100 parking places, with a minimum of three.

77612 Reserved bays should be identified by special signs, see 6535.

7762 Approach

77620 The approach to the building must be accessible to chairbound people: observe 641.

7763 Internal planning

77630 All car parking areas must be at ground level or at the same level as a lift, or must be accessible from ground level or a lift by means of a ramp having a gradient not steeper than 1:12.

77631 All staircases must be usable by ambulant disabled people: observe 632.

7764 Cloakroom provision

77640 In public lavatories at car parks it is particularly desirable that provision is made for chairbound people, see 66.
Suitable provision should be made in all cases where public lavatories are to be supervised.

777 Road service stations

7770 General considerations

77700 For severely disabled people the convenience of travelling by car may be jeopardized by the lack of suitable wc facilities along the route. Where new road service stations are planned provision for disabled people should be made in cloakrooms; this is particularly important where service stations are on motorways and no alternative facilities are available locally.

77701 Where suitable provision is made for disabled people it is important that it is appropriately advertised, see 6514.

7771 Approach

77710 The principal entrance to the building must be accessible to chairbound people: observe 641. Where motorway facilities are duplicated on each side of the carriageway, public areas in each building must be accessible.

77711 Two or three parking bays adjoining the accessible public entrance must be reserved for disabled drivers or passengers, see 580.
These spaces must be suitably identified, see 653.

7772 Internal planning

77720 All principal public areas, for example restaurants, foyers and shops, must be accessible to chairbound people: observe 642.

7773 Cloakroom provision

77730 Where service stations are sited on principal roads in rural areas, for example on motorways or on trunk roads outside built-up areas, at least one cloakroom must be usable by chairbound people: observe 643.

This wc compartment must be usable by both sexes, so that a husband can help a disabled wife and vice versa. Where, for reasons of supervision, it has to be linked with a male or female cloakroom, it is preferred, for reasons discussed in 6607, that it is linked to the female cloakroom.

77731 At least one wc compartment for each sex should be usable by ambulant disabled people, see 633.

78 Industrial buildings

780 Factory buildings

7800 General considerations
78000 In new factory buildings the provision appropriate for employees who might be disabled is associated with the nature of the production work. There is no cause for special provision in factory buildings engaged on heavy manufacturing processes, whereas in those engaged in light manufacturing or component assembly the needs of disabled people must be considered.

78001 In single-storey structures at ground level, which comprise the majority of new industrial buildings, it ought to be possible to make satisfactory provision without difficulty.

Standard factories
78002 Standard factory buildings on new estates, planned for example by new town corporations or other public authorities, should always be designed so that disabled people can be employed there. Access and internal circulation arrangements should cater for chairbound people, and cloakroom provision must be at the same level as the production floor. Wc compartments should be designed so that they can be modified to suit disabled people if necessary.

7801 Access
78010 In new factory buildings where disabled people may be employed entrances should be usable by chairbound people, see 641.

7802 Internal planning
78020 Areas of factories where disabled people may be employed must be accessible to chairbound people: observe 642.

78021 Refreshment and recreation areas should be similarly accessible.

7803 Cloakroom provision
78030 Cloakrooms serving areas where disabled people may be employed should have at least one wc compartment usable by ambulant disabled people, see 633.

78031 Cloakroom provision should be planned so that it can be adapted to cater for chairbound people if required.

7804 Administrative areas
78040 In factory buildings where more than say 20 people are engaged on administrative work suitable provision must be made for the employment of disabled people. The recommendations for office buildings should be observed, see 761 or 762 as appropriate.

781 Warehouses, storage buildings

7810 General considerations
78100 In warehouses and storage buildings, requirements for the movement of goods will as a rule ensure that working areas are usable by disabled people. Special provision need not be incorporated, though cloakrooms should be designed so that wc compartments can be suitably modified if necessary.

782 Horticultural and farm buildings

7820 General considerations
78200 In general purpose horticultural and farm buildings it is not necessary that any special provision is incorporated for disabled people.

78201 In horticultural buildings with laboratories consideration should be given to employment facilities for disabled staff, see 786.

783 Industrial training centres

7830 General considerations
78300 Industrial training centres administered by the Department of Employment or other agencies may offer opportunities to disabled people to retrain for work suited to their capacities. Although only a minority of trainees may be disabled, it is desirable that comprehensive provision is made.

7831 Approach
78310 At least one entrance to the building must be accessible to chairbound people: observe 641.

7832 Internal planning
78320 All workshops, teaching areas, study rooms, laboratories, refreshment rooms, recreation rooms and other areas used by trainees must be accessible to chairbound people: observe 642.

7833 Cloakroom provision
78330 Selected wc compartments should be usable by ambulant disabled people, see 633.

78331 At least one wc compartment must be usable by chairbound people: observe 643.

784 Telecommunications buildings, telephone exchanges

7840 General considerations
78400 In new telecommunications buildings it is not necessary that areas used exclusively by engineering or maintenance staff, for example apparatus rooms, switch rooms and plant rooms, should be accessible to disabled people.

784 Telecommunications buildings, telephone exchanges *continued*

78401 Office areas may be used by disabled staff; the requirements of 761 or 762, as appropriate, should apply.

78402 Where areas such as canteens, games rooms and cloakrooms are used by both engineering and clerical staff, accessibility standards should be as for associated office areas.

Telephone switchboards
78403 The manning of telephone switchboards can often be done by handicapped people, including many who are blind and some who are chairbound. It is therefore important in new telephone exchanges that suitable provision is made.

7841 Telephone exchanges: Approach
78410 At least one entrance to the building must be accessible to chairbound people: observe 641.

7842 Telephone exchanges: Internal planning
78420 Areas used by switchboard staff must be accessible to chairbound people: observe 642.

7843 Telephone exchanges: Cloakroom provision
78430 At least one wc compartment for each sex or serving both sexes should be usable by chairbound people, or capable of being adapted.

785 Broadcasting studio buildings

7850 General considerations
78500 In television and radio broadcasting studio buildings provision must be made for disabled people who come in to take part in broadcasts, and, in buildings where there are more than about 20 administrative staff, for disabled employees.

7851 Approach
78510 At least one entrance to the building must be accessible to chairbound people: observe 641.

7852 Internal planning
78520 All studios and rooms used for hospitality purposes must be accessible to chairbound people: observe 642.

78521 In buildings where provision is made for staff who are disabled, all administrative areas, including refreshment and recreation rooms, must be accessible to chairbound people: observe 642.

7853 Cloakroom provision
78530 Where provision is made for staff who are disabled at least one wc compartment for each sex or serving both sexes must be usable by chairbound people: observe 643.

78531 Selected wc compartments may be usable by ambulant disabled people, see 633.

786 Laboratory buildings

7860 General considerations
78600 In laboratory buildings where technicians may be employed on sedentary work, provision should be made for staff who are disabled, including wheelchair users.

7861 Approach
78610 At least one entrance to the building must be accessible to chairbound people: observe 641.

7862 Internal planning
78620 Laboratories, staff common rooms, dining rooms, libraries and other areas used by staff must be accessible to chairbound people: observe 642.

7863 Cloakroom provision
78630 At least one wc compartment for each sex or serving both sexes must be usable by chairbound people: observe 643.

79 Religious buildings

790 Churches

7900 General considerations
79000 It is most important in new church buildings, including cathedrals, chapels, synagogues, mission halls and Quaker meeting houses, that provision is made for disabled people.

79001 The use of church buildings by disabled people is discussed in the commentary, see 1211.

7901 Approach
79010 At least one public entrance must be accessible to chairbound people: observe 641.

79011 Other entrances must be accessible to ambulant disabled people: observe 631.

7902 Internal planning
79020 All areas used by worshippers must be accessible to chairbound people: observe 642.

79021 Where for reasons of liturgical practice the convention is that steps are incorporated, for example to sanctuaries, it is desirable, for reasons discussed in 3114, that there is a single step only rather than two consecutive steps. Risers of such steps ought not to be higher than 0·120.

79021 Areas for congregations or meetings should have induction loops for the benefit of people using hearing aids, see 7405.

7903 Cloakroom provision
79030 Where cloakroom accommodation is incorporated at least one wc compartment should be usable by ambulant disabled people, and preferably also by chairbound people; see 633, 643.

7904 Church halls
79040 Where church halls are associated the recommendations for community centres should be followed, see 738.

791 Masonic temples

7910 General considerations
79100 In masonic temples there is a division between areas used for rituals, for example ceremonial spaces, temple, lodge rooms and associated lodge dining rooms, and areas open to members of the public on social occasions, for example dining room, ballroom and bars. In both areas provision ought to be made for disabled users.

7911 Approach
79110 All public entrances must be accessible to ambulant disabled people: observe 631.

79111 At least one entrance must be accessible to chairbound people: observe 641.

7912 Internal planning
79120 Principal areas must be accessible to chairbound people: observe 642.

7913 Cloakroom provision
79130 At least one wc compartment for each sex should be usable by ambulant disabled people, see 633.

79131 At least one wc compartment for each sex or serving both sexes must be usable by chairbound people: observe 643.

792 Crematoria

7920 General considerations
79200 In the planning of new crematoria buildings comprehensive provision must be made for disabled people.

7921 Approach
79210 At least one entrance to all buildings must be accessible to chairbound people: observe 641.

7922 Internal planning
79220 Crematoria chapels and all associated areas used by people attending ceremonies must be accessible to chairbound people: observe 642.

7923 External space
79230 Wreath courts and gardens of remembrance must be accessible to chairbound people: where steps are incorporated alternative ramped approaches must be available.

Housing

8

800 Housing options

8000 Strategic directions for housing for disabled people in the context of living accommodation generally are discussed in sections 16 and 17 of the commentary. Where circumstances permit it is preferred that adaptations are made to existing housing. Where there is a requirement for new housing or rehousing, the majority of handicapped people can be satisfactorily catered for in mobility housing. For the small proportion who are chairbound, purpose-designed wheelchair housing is required. For couples both of whom are handicapped, and for severely disabled people living on their own, suitable housing can be provided in association with comprehensive domiciliary support services.

8001 The ways by which statutory authorities in Britain can provide or adapt housing for disabled people are controlled by a variety of Acts of Parliament, affecting housing, social services and health authorities. The legislation detailed below relates only to England and Wales. For Scotland there is different legislation which is broadly comparable.

801 Legislation: Housing authorities

8010 The powers which local housing authorities work to when providing accommodation for disabled people are contained in sections 91 and 92 of the Housing Act 1957 and section 3 of the Chronically Sick and Disabled Persons Act 1970. Section 91 in part V of the Housing Act 1957 reads:

'It shall be the duty of every local authority to consider housing conditions in their district and the needs of the district with respect to the provision of further housing accommodation.'

8011 Regarding the mode of provision of accommodation under section 91, section 92 reads:

(i) The local authority may provide housing accommodation
(a) by the erection of houses on any land acquired or appropriated by them,
(b) by the conversion of any building into houses,
(c) by acquiring houses,
(d) by altering, enlarging, repairing or improving any houses or buildings which they have.
(ii) The local authority may alter, enlarge, repair or improve any house so erected, converted or acquired.'

The Chronically Sick Act
8012 Section 3 of the Chronically Sick and Disabled Persons Act 1970 reads:

'Every local authority for the purposes of Part V of the Housing Act 1957 in discharging their duty under Section 91 of that Act to consider housing conditions in their district and the needs of the district with respect to the provision of further housing accommodation shall have regard to the special needs of chronically sick or disabled persons; and any proposals prepared and submitted to the Minister by the authority under that section for the provision of new houses shall distinguish any houses which the authority propose to provide which make special provision for the needs of such persons.'

This section does not amend in any way the duties of housing authorities under the 1957 Act, it merely makes them explicit. The only new requirement is that housing units for disabled people are itemized when proposals are submitted to the Department of the Environment for approval for financial subsidy.

House renovation grants
8013 In respect of dwellings occupied by disabled people which are not adequate in terms of amenities, there may be an entitlement to an improvement grant under the Housing Acts of 1969 and 1974. The primary purpose of improvement grant legislation is to enhance the quality of housing by the improvement of old property or the conversion of existing properties. In respect of privately rented or owner-occupied dwellings, grants are obtained through the local housing authority. In respect of local authority dwellings, grants are obtained through the Department of the Environment. The normal rule is that grants are not given for dwellings built before 3 October 1961, but this is disregarded in the case of improvements to dwellings for disabled people.

8014 For the purposes of improving housing in terms of its general fitness for habitation there are four kinds of grants, detailed in part VII of the Housing Act 1974. These are summarized as follows:

1. *Improvement grants*. These are discretionary grants, the aim being to improve the property to a 10 point amenity standard. The dwelling must have a rateable value of £300 or less in Greater London, or £175 or less elsewhere in England and Wales.

2. *Intermediate grants*. These are made as a right, replacing what were known as standard grants under the 1969 Act, for the provision of missing standard amenities, ie (1) fixed bath or shower, (2) wash basin, (3) sink, (4) hot and cold water supply and (5) wc.

3. *Special grants*. These are discretionary for improving property where there is multiple occupancy.

4. *Repairs grants*. These are available in housing action areas and general improvement areas and attract a bigger subsidy from central government than improvement or intermediate grants in other areas.

Grant limits

8015 Grant limits are calculated on the basis of the 'eligible expense', ie the cost of the work accepted by the housing authority as eligible for grant. The applicant receives the appropriate percentage of the eligible expense, which is 50 per cent at the normal rate, 60 per cent in general improvement areas, and 75 per cent (or in cases of hardship up to 90 per cent) in housing action areas. The eligible cost limits are £3200 in the case of improvement grants, and £1500 for intermediate grants, made up of £700 for the provision of standard amenities and £800 for repairs.

In the case of 50 per cent grants, the amount contributed by the Government is 75 per cent, the remaining 25 per cent coming from the rates. In general improvement areas and housing action areas the proportions are 90 and 10 per cent.

Section 56

8016 Under the Housing Act 1969, grant entitlement was determined by the physical character of the dwelling; its occupancy was not a consideration. The position changed when an amendment was incorporated in the Housing Act 1974 to enable grants to be given in the case of disabled people living in dwellings not adequate for them on account of their disability.

The legislation affected was for England and Wales only; in Scotland section 56 does not apply and there is no equivalent power.

8017 Section 56 (2)(a) of the 1974 Act says that an improvement grant can be given for:

'In the case of a registered disabled person, works required for his welfare, accommodation or employment where the existing dwelling is inadequate or unsuitable for those purposes.'

On account of possible confusion regarding the interpretation of 'registered disabled person' this section was amended by the Housing Rents and Subsidies Act 1975, Schedule 5, paragraph 19(2). The effect is to include both people who are registered as handicapped under section 29 of the National Assistance Act 1948 (8020), or who in the opinion of the social services authority might have been registered.

8018 For the purposes of the 1974 Act an improvement grant cannot be made for work which can be undertaken entirely by means of an intermediate grant. Section 56 (2)(b) defines an intermediate grant as:

'In respect of works required for the improvement of a dwelling by the provision of standard amenities which it lacks or which in the case of a registered disabled person are inaccessible to that person by virtue of his disability.'

8019 The role of house renovation grants in the context of house adaptation work for disabled people is discussed in the commentary (1718); their administration is discussed in 864.

802 Legislation: Social services authorities

8020 Social services authorities have a general duty to adapt housing for disabled people where a need is established. The relevant powers are in section 29 of the National Assistance Act 1948 and section 2 of the Chronically Sick and Disabled Persons Act 1970. Section 29 (1) of the 1948 Act reads:

'A local authority shall have power to make arrangements for promoting the welfare of persons to whom this section applies, that is to say persons who are blind, deaf or dumb, and other persons who are substantially and permanently handicapped by illness, injury or congenital deformity or such other disabilities as may be prescribed by the Minister.'

Approved schemes

8021 The people defined in section 29 as 'substantially and permanently handicapped' are known as the 'general classes of the handicapped'. Under subsection 3 of section 29, social services authorities have power to introduce schemes to put into effect subsection 1, according to provisions prescribed in section 34 of the Act. All social services authorities in England and Wales now have approved schemes which contain the power to 'assist handicapped persons in arranging for the carrying out of any work of adaptation in their homes or the provision of any additional facilities, designed to secure the greater comfort or convenience of such persons, and if the council so determine defray any expenses incurred in the carrying out of any such work or in the provision of any such facilities'.

Means testing

8022 Section 29 (5) of the 1948 Act reads:

'A local authority may recover from persons availing themselves of any service provided under this section such charges (if any) as, having regard to the cost of the service, the authority may determine, whether generally or in the circumstances of any particular case.'

The Chronically Sick Act

8023 Section 2 (1) of the Chronically Sick and Disabled Persons Act 1970 reads:

'Where a local authority having functions under section 29 of the National Assistance Act 1948 are satisfied in the case of any person to whom that section applies who is ordinarily resident in their area that it is necessary in order to meet the needs of that person for that authority to make arrangements for all or any of the following matters, namely –

(e) the provision of assistance for that person in arranging for the carrying out of any works of adaptation in his home or the provision of any additional facilities designed to secure his greater safety, comfort or convenience.'

8024 The effect of section 2 of the 1970 Act is to make explicit the duties of social services authorities under the 1948 Act.

Old people

8025 Although section 2 of the 1970 Act does not explicitly refer to elderly people, it will in fact always happen that an elderly person who is handicapped and needs home adaptations is covered by the section. The powers that social services authorities have are therefore identical for elderly as for non-elderly handicapped people, and they cover also people who are mentally handicapped.

8026 For elderly people who are not handicapped, as well as those who are, social services authorities have broad powers under section 45 of the Health Services and Public Health Act 1968. Subsection (1) reads:

'A local authority may with the approval of the Minister of Health, and to such extent as he may direct shall, make arrangements for promoting the welfare of old people.'

Local Government Act 1972

8027 In connection with the reorganization in April 1974 of local government in England and Wales, amending legislation was introduced. Section 195 (3) of the Local Government Act 1972 reads:

'Schemes approved under section 34 of the National Assistance Act 1948 . . . shall cease to have effect; and the local authorities who . . . are the local authorities for the purposes of that Act may, with the approval of the Secretary of State, and to such an extent as he may direct shall, make arrangements for carrying out the functions to which those proposals and schemes formerly related.'

8028 Although section 195 of the 1972 Act substitutes the word 'may' for the word 'shall' in the 1948 Act, the effect is not to alter the duties which social services authorities have under the 1948 Act; the purpose was to make more flexible the administration of services between social services and housing authorities. In this connection section 194 of the 1972 Act gives to councils of counties (social services authorities) reserve powers to undertake housing in their areas, though without prejudicing the functions of district councils in relation to housing. Section 194 (2) of the 1972 Act reads:

'If requested to do so by the county of a district, or by the councils of two or more districts, within the county, the council of a county may, with the consent of the Secretary of State, undertake on behalf of the district council or councils the provision of housing accommodation in any manner in which the district council or councils might do so.'

8029 One of the underlying purposes of section 194 is to afford more flexibility in the provision of housing for people with special needs such as disabled people, bearing in mind that individual district councils may not within their own areas have sufficient demand to warrant the provision of special group schemes. The Secretary of State referred to in the section is the Secretary of State for Social Services, but when county councils undertake housing schemes they are submitted for approval to the Secretary of State for the Environment and are dealt with in the same fashion as submissions by housing authorities. The intention is that when social services authorities undertake housing schemes they are on completion transferred for management and administrative purposes to the district council in whose area they are located.

803 Legislation: Health authorities

8030 Under the broad powers of section 12 of the Health Services and Public Health Act 1968, health authorities can adapt housing on health grounds, for example for patients with kidney failure dependent on home dialysis. Section 12 (1)(a) says that health authorities may make arrangements for the provision, equipment and maintenance of residential accommodation for the care of persons with a view to preventing them from becoming ill, the care of persons suffering from illness and the after-care of persons who have been so suffering.

8031 Section 12 (5) of the 1968 Act reads:

'A local health authority may, with the approval of the Minister, recover from persons availing themselves of services provided in pursuance of arrangements made under this section such charges (if any) as the authority consider reasonable, having regard to the means of these persons.'

8032 The 1968 Act related to the functions of health departments in local authorities; with the reorganization of local government in April 1974 these functions have been transferred to area health authorities. Section 2 (2) of the National Health Service Reorganisation Act 1973 reads:

'It shall be the duty of the Secretary of State to provide throughout England and Wales, to such extent as he considers necessary to meet all reasonable requirements –

(e) such facilities for the prevention of illness, the care of persons suffering from illness and the after-care of persons who have suffered from illness as he considers are appropriate as part of the health service in place of arrangements of a kind which immediately before the passing of this Act it was the function of local authorities to make in pursuance of Section 12 of the Health Services and Public Health Act 1968.'

804 Public authority housing: Normal standards

8040 In connection with the recommendations which follow relating to standards for mobility and wheelchair housing it is important to understand first what is meant by normal standards. Normal standards for public authority housing are commonly referred to as Parker Morris standards, because they derive from the report of a subcommittee of the Central Housing Advisory Committee chaired by Sir Parker Morris and published in 1961 under the title *Homes for today and tomorrow* [1]. The standards have since been updated and issued in metric dimensions in Ministry of Housing and Local Government Circular 27/70 *Metrication of housebuilding: Progress* [2], published in 1970. Standards are based on minimum floor areas according to the intended size of the household and minimum room sizes are not specified. With regard to user requirements, designers are referred to the design bulletin *Space in the home* [3].

8041 The standards in MHLG Circular 27/70 relate to all schemes of public authority housing other than flatlets for old people and single person accommodation provided with communal facilities. The majority of standards prescribed in the circular are mandatory and must, under current administrative arrangements, be observed in order for schemes to receive subsidy.
As noted in 83010, administrative arrangements relating to space standards and associated cost controls are currently (May 1976) under review by the Department of the Environment.

Plan requirements
8042 In respect of plan arrangements the following standards are mandatory:
1. A dwelling shall have (i) an entrance hall or

[1] Bib 93720
[2] Bib 93712. In November 1970 the Ministry of Housing and Local Government was absorbed, with the Ministry of Transport and the Ministry of Public Building and Works, into the Department of the Environment. Certain Ministry of Housing circulars, including 27/70, continue to be operative.
[3] Bib 93723

lobby with space for hanging outdoor clothes and (ii) for 3 person and larger houses and 3 person and larger dwellings served by lift or ramp, a space for a pram (1·400 × 0·700).

2. Except in 1 or 2 person dwellings, access from bedroom to the bathroom and a wc shall be arranged without having to pass through another room.

3. The kitchen in a dwelling for two or more persons must provide a space where casual meals may be taken by a minimum of two persons.

4. In addition to kitchen storage, the sink and space for a cooker, a minimum of two further spaces shall be provided in convenient positions to accommodate a refrigerator and a washing machine. The latter may be in the kitchen or in a convenient position elsewhere. These spaces may be provided under worktop surfaces.

Space standards
8043 Standards of minimum net space and minimum general storage space are prescribed according to the number of people (bedspaces) the dwelling is designed for. Net space is the area on one or more floors enclosed by the walls of a dwelling measured to the inner boundaries of the zones for the main containing walls. It excludes the floor area of general storage space and dustbin store, fuel store, garage or balcony.
Minimum space standards for single storey houses and other dwelling units adaptable for use by disabled people are noted in table 81.3.

Wc and wash basin provision
8044 In respect of wc and wash basin provision one standard only is mandatory. This is that in two or three storey houses and two level maisonettes at or above the minimum floor area for five persons, and in flats and single storey houses at or above the minimum floor area for six persons, two wcs are required, one of which may be in the bathroom. The non-mandatory standards are:
1. In 1, 2, and 3 person dwellings, one wc is required, and may be in the bathroom.
2. In 4 person two or three storey houses and two level maisonettes, and in 4 and 5 person flats and single storey houses, one wc is required in a separate compartment.
3. Where a separate wc does not adjoin a bathroom, it must contain a wash basin.

Kitchen fitments
8045 Standards for kitchen fitments are not mandatory. For 3 person and larger dwellings the recommendation is that 2·3m³ of enclosed storage space should be provided in connection with (a) preparation of and serving of food and washing-up; (b) cleaning and laundry operations, and (c) food. For 1 and 2 person dwellings the provision should be 1·7m³. Part of this provision should comprise a ventilated cool cupboard and a broom cupboard.

Worktops should be provided on both sides of the sink and on both sides of the cooker position. Kitchen fitments should be arranged to provide a work sequence comprising worktop/cooker/worktop/sink/worktop, or the same in reverse order, unbroken by a door or other traffic way.

Socket outlets

8046 The non-mandatory recommendation is that electric socket outlets are provided as follows:

working area of kitchen 4
dining area 1
living area 3
bedroom 2
hall or landing 1
bed-sitting room in family dwellings 3
bed-sitting room in 1 person dwellings 5
integral or attached garage 1
walk-in general store (in house only) 1

This provision is not as generous as that recommended as desirable in the Parker Morris report (4341).

Space heating

8047 The minimum mandatory standard for space heating is an installation with appliances capable of maintaining kitchen and circulation spaces at 13°C, and living and dining areas at 18°C, when the outside temperature is −1°C.

Furniture

8048 Rooms have to be designed to accommodate the furniture detailed below. This provision is mandatory; architects when submitting plans must show the furniture drawn on.

1. Kitchen: small table unless one is built in.
2. Meal space: dining table and chairs.
3. Living space: two or three easy chairs, settee, tv set, small tables, reasonable quantity of other possessions such as radiogram and bookcase.
4. Single bedrooms: bed or divan (2·000 × 0·900), bedside table, chest of drawers, wardrobe or space for cupboard to be built in.
5. Main bedrooms: double bed (2·000 × 1·500) and where possible two single beds (2·000 × 0·900) as an alternative, bedside tables, chest of drawers, double wardrobe or space for cupboard to be built in, dressing table.
6. Other double bedrooms: two single beds (2·000 × 0·900), bedside tables, chest of drawers, double wardrobe or space for cupboard to be built in, small dressing table.

8049 Spaces for wardrobes or built-in cupboards should be on the basis of 0·600 hanging space per person. Cupboards should be not less than 0·550 deep internally.

805 Standards for old people's housing

8050 Standards for old people's housing are set down in MHLG Circular 82/69 *Housing standards and costs, accommodation specially designed for old people* [4].

Category 1 and category 2

8051 Circular 82/69 distinguishes between category 1 and category 2 schemes. Category 1 schemes, which comprise self-contained units to the same space standards as Parker Morris housing, are intended for relatively active old people. Category 2 schemes, commonly known as grouped flatlet schemes, are designed to cater for more frail old people; they are always warden-serviced, whereas category 1 need not be. The dwelling units in a category 2 scheme are all in a single block, with undercover access to any communal accommodation. Units in a category 1 scheme may be scattered among other housing. In category 2 schemes all units may be self-contained, but the usual practice is for single person units to have shared bathing facilities. Communal facilities are mandatory for category 2 schemes, optional for category 1, and common room space standards are more generous for category 2: 1·9m² per person compared with 0·95m². Dwelling amenity standards are generally the same; one difference is that a kitchen cooker is mandatory for category 2 and optional for category 1.

8052 The notes which follow relate to category 2 schemes.

Communal provision

8053 Communal facilities are to be provided as follows:
1. Self-contained warden's dwelling.
2. Emergency alarm system connecting each dwelling with the warden's flat.
3. Common room or rooms with minimum floor space 1·9m² per person, with associated tea kitchen, space for hats and coats, wc and hand basin, store.
4. Laundry room with sink, automatic washing machine, tumbler dryer, table for folding clothes.
5. Cleaning cupboard.
6. Telephone with seat for use by tenants.
7. Enclosed and heated circulation areas.
8. Delivery hatches to individual flats or, alternatively, grouped lockers.
9. Guest room (optional).
10. Warden's office (optional).

Space

8054 Space standards for dwelling units are set down in table 81.3. Of the general storage accommodation, 0·8m² in 1 person flatlets may be in internal communal stores, and 1·2m² in 2 person flatlets.

---

[4] Bib 93630

Kitchens

8055 Kitchen provision is generally as for family housing, with the following qualifications:
1. The refuse disposal point must be accessible under cover.
2. Food storage provision may include a refrigerator with minimum capacity 0·07m³.
3. Kitchen work surfaces to be max 0·850 above floor level, shelves to be max 1·520.
4. Suitable gas or electric cookers must be provided.

Heating

8056 The minimum standard for space heating is an installation capable of maintaining living area, bathroom, hall, bedroom, kitchen and communal rooms at 21°C and circulation areas at 15·6°C when the outside temperature is −1°C.

Wcs

8057 The wc compartment is to include a wash basin, the door is to open outwards and to be fitted with a lock openable from outside, and the wc is to be provided with at least one support rail at the side.

Bathrooms

8058 Bathrooms are to be provided on a shared basis of not less than one bathroom to four flatlets, except that for any group of not less than four bathrooms a shower compartment may be substituted for one of the bathrooms. Baths where provided must be flat bottomed and not longer than 1·550 with at least one support rail. Shower compartments where provided must have a non-slip floor, the shower must be thermostatically controllable to give a maximum output temperature of 49°C, spray outlets must be adjustable to varying heights and the shower compartment must contain a support rail and wall-mounted seat.

Access to dwellings

8059 Where access to dwellings involves a climb of more than one storey from the point of pedestrian or vehicular access a lift must be provided.

806 Fire protection

8060 Elsewhere in this book the effect of fire regulations on the use of public buildings by disabled people is discussed at length. It is suggested that where there is conflict between social criteria and fire protection considerations, architects should take account of all relevant factors, rather than automatically giving precedence to safety considerations.

8061 The same principle should be observed with domestic housing. In practical terms there is one significant difference. This is that in the case of housing no fire officer or other authority has legal power to require an architect to incorporate special provisions simply because some or all of the tenants may be disabled. For housing there is no certification procedures, as there is for example in the case of shops, offices, cinemas, theatres or hotels, by which the enforcing authority can impose conditions relating to use by disabled people.

8062 The only enforcable constraints are those structural or technical provisions which are general to housing and, according to circumstances, may be required under building regulations. In relation to use by disabled people this means structural fire precautions which involve automatically self-closing doors, or means of escape provisions which require self-closing doors and prohibit the use of lifts.
Structural fire precautions regulations are not inhibiting except where housing is three storeys or higher. Means of escape regulations, as detailed in part 1 of CP3 [5] are applicable only to flats or maisonettes in blocks over two storeys. There is no legal mandate by which self-closing doors can be required in houses or flats of one or two storeys.

Old people's housing

8063 When sheltered housing for old people is planned in accordance with the provisions of MHLG Circular 82/69, fire officers asked to advise may request the incorporation of smoke detectors in association with self-closing doors. In its cost yardstick calculations for old people's housing the Department of the Environment makes no allowance for special fire protection provision, and the architect who incorporates it will need to absorb the expenditure within tolerance, or compromise on standards elsewhere.

8064 If self-closing doors are used they will be an impediment to the day-to-day activities of disabled people, and tenants will invariably find a means of making them inoperative. A report published in 1973 on a sheltered housing scheme for old people is relevant:

'The kitchen and living room doors are intended to be self-closing fire doors which the tenant of each flat has found a way of propping open. Some doors are looped back with string, some are held open by a chair, some have their closers unscrewed and some are held back by the pile of the newly-fitted carpet which runs under them. I was told that the doors banged if they were not held back and that they were left open at night to allow air to circulate through the flat.' [6].

8065 At some future date, sheltered housing for old people may be designated a class of use under section 1 of the Fire Precautions Act (6051), in which event the issuing of fire certificates might be dependent on the incorporation of special

[5] Bib 93812. The regulations discussed here relate to areas outside London; for inner London the conditions under London by-laws are similar.
[6] Bib 93635, p505.

provisions. There is not at present (1976) any intention on the part of the Department of the Environment or the Home Office that this should be done. If it were to happen, single storey buildings would not be affected, since they are specifically excluded under section 3 of the Act.

Wheelchair housing

8066 In the case of housing specially designed for people using wheelchairs, careful consideration needs to be given to fire protection. The only realistic solution may be accommodation at ground level or where there is direct means of escape to the ground. Although in respect of single storey housing no regulations can be imposed for means of escape it is advisable that reasonable precautions are taken. The route out of the dwelling from any of the bedrooms ought not to pass through the high fire risk areas of the living room or kitchen; if it does an alternative escape from bedrooms should be available. The preferred provision is external doors which can be used for day-to-day purposes to give access to the garden or courtyard. Bottom-hinged collapsible doors which form a ramp when pushed outwards are not recommended; apart from the difficulty a handicapped person might have using them they are liable to be obstructed by furniture.

Use of lifts

8067 In the case of flats and maisonettes in blocks over two storeys the relevant recommendations of CP3 must be observed [7]. These say 'Lifts cannot be considered for escape purposes, primarily because of the delay that may be experienced before a lift answers a call, the limited capacity of the lift when it arrives and the possibility of failure of the electricity supply in the event of fire'.
In practice it may be possible by negotiation with the fire inspector of the local building authority to make suitable arrangements for lifts to be used as a means of escape, but there will be practical constraints and financial penalties. The probability is that the fire inspector will require at least two lifts, with deck access and alternative escape routes. Waiting areas will not as a rule be permitted. The number of dwelling units for disabled people will therefore be governed by the size of the lifts and the amount of time allowed for the evacuation of the building.

Self-closing doors

8068 Self-closing doors must not be used internally in wheelchair housing. Where in multi-storey housing with wheelchair units there is a requirement in circulation spaces for self-closing doors, they should normally be held in the open position by electro-magnetic or electro-mechanical devices as described in 6037.

[7] Bib 93812

81 Summary of suggested housing provision

810 General

8100 Detailed guidance on the planning of mobility housing is contained in section 82, independent wheelchair housing in section 83, housing for severely disabled people in section 84 and housing for disabled old people in section 85. For reference purposes and to aid comparison, summary information is given here on space and amenity standards, distribution of units by household size, and principal design recommendations.

811 Space standards

8110 Suggested space standards are listed in table 81.3.

Mobility housing
8111 For mobility housing, space standards are the same as for normal Parker Morris housing, as set down in MHLG Circular 27/70 [1] with modifications for old people as in MHLG Circular 82/69 [2].

Wheelchair housing
8112 For wheelchair housing, space standards are as recommended by the Department of the Environment in *Wheelchair housing* [3]. The suggested net space increase over the normal standard ranges from 4·6 per cent for 7 person two storey houses to 22·6 per cent for self-contained single person category 2 old people's units. In all cases net space only is enhanced for wheelchair units; the standard for general storage space remains as for normal housing.

8113 The areas are not maxima or minima, but standards which architects may expect to obtain with careful planning. With economic organization of space, reductions may be practicable; where they are significantly exceeded it may be that planning is not as efficient as it could be.

8114 The standards are based on:
1. An evaluation of spaces in typical Parker Morris housing, relying extensively on the National Building Agency Design Guides [4].
2. An analysis of wheelchair utilization areas in circulation spaces and living areas.

3. A desk appraisal of some 150 examples of wheelchair house planning; some of these are illustrated with comments in *Wheelchair housing* [5].

812 Distribution of wheelchair housing units

8120 Table 81.2 summarizes the suggested distribution of wheelchair housing units for a typical community having a total population of 100 000. Overall, the provision is one wheelchair unit per 1000 population, so that the figures listed can be interpreted in terms of percentages.

8121 Provision on the scale of 1 per 1000 is relatively generous, given that about one in about 350 of the total population is a wheelchair user, that less than one in two of the wheelchair population needs special wheelchair housing, and that a substantial proportion of chairbound people will continue to be catered for in owner-occupied, rented or adapted accommodation. The demand for special wheelchair housing may be reduced in localities where mobility housing is developed in quantity.

8122 The relative need for different types of wheelchair housing will vary according to local circumstances. In this connection the data in table 11.1 on the estimated incidence of handicapped people in different communities are relevant; in towns where there is a predominantly elderly population the percentage of units which should be for old people may rise to 40 per cent or higher, and the need for family accommodation and units for severely disabled people may be proportionately reduced.

8123 Estimates are not made of the amount of mobility housing which may be needed. As discussed in the commentary, the aim here should be to provide as much as possible, with no limit on absolute numbers.

[1] Bib 93712
[2] Bib 93630
[3] Bib 93120
[4] Bib 93733, 93734
[5] Bib 93120

Table 81.1 Suggested distribution of wheelchair housing units in typical population of 100 000

number of persons (ie bedspaces) per dwelling	1	2	3	4	5	6	7	total
single storey independent wheelchair housing units, including for severely disabled people	3	11	21	18	12	4		69
two storey wheelchair housing units						3	2	5
old people's warden-serviced wheelchair housing units	4	22						26
total	7	33	21	18	12	7	2	100

Table 81.2 Housing for disabled people: Summary of design recommendations

	mobility housing	independent wheelchair housing, single storey	housing for severely disabled people
Access			
ramp gradient from garage or road	max 1:12	max 1:20	max 1:20
lift access (where applicable)	lift car min 1·400 × 1·100 door width min 0·750	ground floor provision preferred	ground floor provision preferred
entrance door	0·900 doorset flush threshold	0·900 or 1·000 doorset flush threshold	0·900 or 1·000 doorset flush threshold
Internal circulation			
passage widths	min 0·900	min 1·200	min 1·200
internal side-hung doors, doorset width	0·900 to kitchen/living/ dining room and one bedroom	0·900 to all rooms	0·900 to all rooms, 1·000 where appropriate
sliding doors (where necessary), clear opening width	min 0·770	min 0·770	min 0·770
Kitchen			
kitchen provision	as for normal housing	planned with potential for wheelchair use, eg knee access to sink and preparation area	planned for wheelchair use, knee access if required
kitchen work levels	0·900 0·850 for old people's housing	provision for adjustability, 0·800 if fixed for wheelchair use	to suit individual requirements
Bathroom/wc			
bathroom/wc access	wheelchair access not essential	wheelchair access	wheelchair access
bath	1·600 or 1·700 long provision for fixing support rails	lateral/frontal wheelchair approach 1·600 or 1·700 long platform at head end provision for fixing support rails	lateral/frontal wheelchair approach 1·600 long platform at head end provision for fixing support rails
wash basin	rim at 0·900	rim at 0·750 if fixed preferred front to back dimension 0·600	to suit individual requirements
wc	as for normal housing provision for fixed support rails	seat height at 0·475 if fixed provision for fixed support rails	to suit individual requirements provision for fixing support rails
shower	no provision	provision for installing shower if required	provision for installing shower if required
Fittings and equipment	as for wheelchair housing where practicable	light switches and socket outlets aligned with door handles window and other controls at low level	as for wheelchair housing
Garaging	hardstanding	carport, covered access to dwelling	covered parking area serving cluster

Table 81.3 Wheelchair housing: Suggested space and amenity standards

number of persons (ie bedspaces) per dwelling		suggested space standards			suggested amenity standards
		mobility housing (Parker Morris standards) m²	wheelchair housing m²	net space increase %	kitchen

Single storey house/flats in multi-storey blocks

1	net space	30·0	35·5	18·3	
	storage, houses	3·0	3·0		
	storage, flats	2·5	2·5		
2	net space	44·5	49·5	11·2	
	storage, houses	4·0	4·0		
	storage, flats	3·0	3·0		
3	net space	57·0	63·0	10·5	
	storage, houses	4·0	4·0		
	storage, flats	3·0	3·0		
4	net space	67·0*	73·0	9·0	
	storage, houses	4·5	4·5		
	storage, flats	3·5	3·5		
5	net space, houses	75·5	86·0	13·9	
	net space, flats	79·0	86·0	8·9	
	storage, houses	4·5	4·5		
	storage, flats	3·5	3·5		
6	net space, houses	84·0	94·5	12·5	
	net space, flats	86·5	94·5	9·2	
	storage, houses	4·5	4·5		
	storage, flats	3·5	3·5		

Two storey houses

5	net space	82·0†	91·0	11·0	
	storage	4·5	4·5		
6	net space	92·5	101·5	9·7	
	storage	4·5	4·5		
7	net space	108·0	113·0	4·6	
	storage	6·5	6·5		

Old people's housing category 1

1	net space	30·0	35·5	18·3	
	storage, houses	3·0	3·0		
	storage, flats	2·6	2·6		
2	net space	44·5	49·5	11·2	
	storage, houses	4·0	4·0		
	storage, flats	3·0	3·0		

Old people's housing category 2

1	net space, without bath	27·0	32·5	20·4	
	storage	1·9	1·9		
1	net space, with bath	28·15	34·5	22·6	
	storage	1·9	1·9		
2	net space	39·0	46·5	19·2	
	storage	2·5	2·5		

Table 81.3 *(continued)*		Key to table 81.3

Key to table 81.3

* For 4 person flats other than those with balcony access the net space standard is 70·0m²

† For 5 person 2 storey intermediate terrace house the net space standard is 85·0m²

bathroom/wc	bedrooms

Kitchen

kitchen in recess off living area, usable from wheelchair

kitchen usable from wheelchair

kitchen accessible to wheelchair, not usable

Bathroom/wc

bathroom with wc allowing lateral or frontal transfer from wheelchair

bathroom with wc allowing frontal transfer from wheelchair only

wc with wash basin, wc allowing lateral transfer from wheelchair

wc compartment, not accessible to wheelchair

wc with wash basin, not accessible to wheelchair

Bedrooms

bed-sitting room, usable from wheelchair

main double bedroom, usable from wheelchair

double bedroom accessible to wheelchair, usable as single room

single bedroom usable from wheelchair

single bedroom accessible to wheelchair, not usable

double bedroom not accessible to wheelchair

single bedroom not accessible to wheelchair

421

813 Amenity standards and design recommendations

8130 Suggested planning provision for kitchens, bathrooms and bedrooms in wheelchair housing is shown diagrammatically in table 81.3.

8131 Principal design recommendations for mobility housing, independent wheelchair housing and housing for severely disabled people are summarized in table 81.2. In some instances these recommendations are subject to qualification, and reference should be made to detailed guidance elsewhere.

814 Surveys to assess housing needs

8140 Other than giving a general picture of the handicapped population by age and degree of disability the OPCS survey report *Handicapped and impaired in Great Britain* [6] does not provide data which can be directly applied, either on a national or local basis, to estimate the housing needs of disabled people. A possible alternative source of evidence is the collection of local surveys of the needs of handicapped people made by local authorities under section 1 of the Chronically Sick and Disabled Persons Act. The majority of these surveys have however used similar measuring techniques to the national survey, and are affected by the same shortcomings. Furthermore, they were made by social services departments who are not themselves responsible for housing, and only in a few cases was specific evidence on housing needs obtained.

8141 The responsibility for assessing housing needs lies with local housing authorities. The primary question for them is how much special wheelchair housing is required in their area, and how it should be distributed. To develop suitable housing in the ordinary housing sphere they need also to know something of the extent of the need for mobility housing, and how it should be distributed by household size.

Identification of people needing special housing
8142 The criterion of need for wheelchair housing is that a disabled person is in effect chairbound. The criterion of need for mobility housing is that a person on account of disability needs to have accommodation without steps.

8143 The basic information needed in any locality is how many people there are who are chairbound, and how many are not able to cope with steps. To identify these people a possible method is for the housing authority to carry out a survey of people in their area who are on the register of disabled people kept by the social services authority. While this would not by any means cover all disabled people in the locality it would be likely in practice to reach many of those in most need, simply because it is the need for special services which encourages people to register. A second and potentially more valuable way of reaching people in need of wheelchair housing is the records of people issued with wheelchairs by the local appliance centre of the Department of Health; the proviso must be made here that the Department normally insists that names and addresses on this list are confidential. A third possibility, and the only one which offers a chance of comprehensive coverage, is to undertake a house-to-house survey of all households in a particular locality.

Local surveys
8144 To carry out a preliminary house-to-house survey, voluntary interviewers might be enlisted, working under professional supervision. They could be given a short questionnaire, with instructions to make it clear to handicapped people visited that they were not being interviewed in order that they could be put on a waiting list for special housing, but simply as a local exercise to estimate needs for planning purposes. When making a call the kind of strategically critical question they would put would be 'Is there a handicapped person in the house, who on account of disability, needs to be living in a house which does not have steps?'. If the reply to this question were positive there would, prima facie, be a requirement for mobility housing, and the second question could be put relating to wheelchair housing needs 'Is this person in a wheelchair and does he need to be able to get his wheelchair into the bathroom and wc?'.

8145 In the case of handicapped people thus identified it ought in practice, using a straightforward single-sheet questionnaire form, to be able to assemble important data quickly and easily. The basic information needed might comprise:
1. Age and sex of handicapped person.
2. Composition of household.
3. Tenancy arrangement.
4. Cause of disability (to know whether the condition is likely to deteriorate or not).
5. Whether the handicapped person is a housewife, or uses the kitchen regularly.
6. Whether there is a car in the household, and if so whether the handicapped person drives it.

8146 Despite the unsophisticated methodology it is possible that inquiries of this kind could give valuable indicators for housing policies, regarding the amount of wheelchair housing needed, its distribution by household size, the division between single storey and two storey units and the need for garaging provision. At the same time useful practical evidence would be obtained regarding the need for mobility housing.

[6] Bib 93210, 93211

820 Mobility housing: General considerations

8200 Mobility housing is ordinary housing built to prevailing public authority housing cost limits and space standards, but designed so that it is convenient for disabled people to live in. The important features are that wheelchair access is possible to the entrance and principal rooms, and that the bathroom and wc are reachable without using steps. As discussed in the commentary (1707), mobility housing is potentially suitable for all ambulant disabled people to live in, including those who use wheelchairs but are not chairbound.

8201 All single storey dwelling units and flats accessible by lift can, given suitable site conditions, be planned to mobility standards. Two storey mobility housing is practicable where there is bathroom and bedroom provision on the ground floor, or where a stairlift can be used to reach the upper floor.

8202 Because for public authority housing minor modifications only are needed to achieve mobility standards, it is recommended that mobility housing should be provided in all situations where it is practicable. If it is available on a generous scale a substantial proportion will be occupied by households not having a handicapped member, so avoiding any impression that it is special housing.

8203 Evidence discussed in the commentary (1707) indicates that mobility housing has the potential to cater for some 96 per cent of people categorized as handicapped, although only some 15 per cent of handicapped people have impaired mobility and need suitable housing. The primary need is for small units; where a housing authority has a policy of distributing mobility housing units it is suggested that the aim should be to have 70 per cent in 1 or 2 person units, 20 per cent in 3 or 4 person units and 10 per cent in units for 5 persons or more.

8204 Official advice on the planning of mobility housing is given in the Department of the Environment report *Mobility housing* [1], supplemented by notes on two storey housing in *Wheelchair housing* [2].

8205 Design recommendations are summarized in table 81.2. Cost allowances for public authority mobility housing are noted in 871.

821 Siting

8210 No special conditions need be observed regarding the location of mobility housing in relation to shops, transport and other amenities.

8211 The eligibility of any proposed housing units for mobility standards will depend on topographical conditions. Although there is a requirement that there are no steps, the probability is that wheelchair users living in mobility housing will invariably be pushed out, and it is not critical that access is level. The approach ought not to be so steep as to be a hazard for ambulant disabled people or a strain for wheelchair pushers; the general rule should be that any ramp from the adjacent road or vehicle parking area to the front door should have a gradient not exceeding 1:12.

8212 The 1:12 approach condition will determine which dwelling units on a site are suitable for mobility treatment. Expensive site works to achieve mobility standards ought not to be undertaken. Wider paths are not warranted; if paths are adequate for mothers with prams they will also be satisfactory for people pushing wheelchairs.

8213 In the planning of estates incorporating mobility housing it is important that there are dropped kerbs at road intersections to aid people pushing wheelchairs.

822 Mobility housing: Access

8220 So far as is practicable, mobility housing should be planned to foster social interactions between handicapped and other people. In this respect balcony or deck access to flats may be more successful than internal access because of the greater number of regular social contacts which are likely to occur [3].

Entrance doors

8221 Thresholds to entrance doors should be not higher than 0·025, see 3401. Where there is no raised sill the provision of an internal mat recess is recommended.
A possible alternative is to have a standard external door sill approx 0·070 high, on the basis that the floor surface to either side can be ramped if necessary. On balance it is preferred that suitable provision is made initially. Two storey mobility housing may have a single step, see 8260.

Lifts

8222 Where approach is by lift the internal width of the lift car should be not less than 1·100, and the nominal depth should be not less than 1·400, see table 45·1. Lift doors should give a clear opening width of not less than 0·750.

Fire protection

8223 Where multi-storey blocks with lifts are potentially suitable for incorporating mobility housing units, any recommendation from the fire officer advising that mobility units ought not to be introduced on grounds of inadequate means of escape should be queried.

[1] Bib 93111
[2] Bib 93120, paras 8.01–8.06.
[3] For relevant evidence see Bib 93601, p1061.

In defence, it may be said that (1) the flats are standard housing provision and it is probable that only a proportion will be used by handicapped people, and (2) that handicapped people occupying them will by definition not be chairbound, and can in the event of an emergency be expected to manage the stairs as a means of escape. It may be appropriate to consider practical means by which it is permissible for the lift to be used as a means of escape (see 607), in which case it may be reasonable to impose conditions as to the number of people living in the block who may be reliant on the lift as a means of escape.

823   Internal planning

8230   Passageways and circulation spaces should be minimum 0·900 wide. Wider spaces are advantageous but they should not be incorporated if the effect is to increase the overall area of the dwelling unit. For discussion on this topic see 1702.

8231   Doorsets to principal rooms, ie living room, kitchen, dining room and at least one bedroom, should be 0·900 wide.

8232   Because the viability of mobility housing depends on the full use of 0·900 passageways in association with 0·900 doorsets, particular attention must be given to the placing of panel radiators; they can significantly reduce usable space (4245).

Kitchens
8233   While it is not recommended that kitchens are specially designed for use from a wheelchair, it ought to be possible for a person in a wheelchair to move into and around the kitchen. In family dwellings this ought to be practicable; the clear space in the kitchen should be minimum 1·400 × 1·400.

Bathrooms
8234   Where practicable, doorsets to bathrooms should be 0·900 wide; where this is done bathroom fittings should be arranged so that a person in a wheelchair can approach the basin, bath and wc.

Wc compartments
8235   Where there is a separate wc compartment it may not be practicable to provide sufficient space internally to accommodate a wheelchair. If the compartment has a 0·900 doorset it will be possible to manoeuvre a wheelchair part way in, so facilitating use of the wc, for example by a handicapped person able to stand and swivel to transfer. Preferably the door should be planned at right angles to the axis of the wc rather than parallel with it; even where the doorset is only 0·800 it will be possible for a person in a standard wheelchair to get close to the wc for transfer, provided that approach from the adjoining circulation space is direct (diagram 82.1).

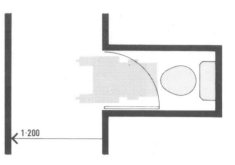

82.1   Wheelchair use of wc compartment with 0·800 doorset (1:50)

Bedrooms
8236   It is essential that at least one bedroom is accessible, but it is desirable that second and third bedrooms, where planned at entrance level, also have 0·900 doorsets. For notes on access to beds see 5330, 5340, 5341.

824   Mobility housing: Garaging

8240   In line with normal public authority housing (5750), the garaging provision for mobility housing will generally be a hardstanding.

8241   Where an enclosed garage or carport is provided, it is desirable but not essential that it is within the dwelling curtilage. It is not necessary that it is made wider to allow for wheelchair use.

825   Mobility housing: Other provisions

8250   The principle that mobility housing is ordinary housing means that it does not incorporate the variety of special provisions needed in wheelchair housing. The general rule should be to design for convenience without involving additional expenditure.

8251   Consideration should be given to the following provisions:
1. The hanging of doors to facilitate wheelchair manoeuvre in and out of principal rooms, ie doors to be hinged in corners (36002).
2. The positioning of socket outlets at waist level, aligned with light switches and door handles (4302).
3. Socket outlets to be generously distributed. Provision should be as recommended in MHLG Circular 27/70 (8046).
4. The placing of coin-in-slot meters where they can be easily reached by a handicapped person.
5. The specification of door and window ironmongery which is convenient to manipulate.
6. The layout of kitchen fitments to permit economic and efficient use.

7. The specification of kitchen equipment so that the height of work surfaces can be adapted to suit particular handicapped users.

8. A swivel tap at the kitchen sink which facilitates the filling of kettles (5155).

9. The specification of partition walls to the bathroom which allow for the fixing of support rails alongside the wc and bath.

10. The incorporation of a platform at the head end of the bath to allow for seated transfer (5458). If this is not practicable the use of a portable bath bench (54762) may be assumed; the preferred height for the bath rim is 0·450 (54600).

11. The specification of a wc having a relatively high seat, approx 0·445 above floor level (54251).

12. The specification of screw-down taps which can be replaced by lever taps if necessary.

13. The use of slip-resistant flooring materials. Carpeting is preferred to areas other than kitchen and bathroom.

14. The avoidance of threshold sills to internal doorsets (3430).

15. Convenient access to the dustbin location (401).

826   Two storey housing: Accessibility

8260   The traditional two storey dwelling with access by stairs to bathroom and bedrooms at first floor level should be accessible but will not be ideal for disabled people to live in.
In the case of a two storey family dwelling there is always the possibility that someone in the household will become disabled and have difficulty managing the stairs. It may not be realistic, particularly in the case of owner-occupied accommodation, to assume that the family can move to convenient single storey housing, and attention should be given to disability requirements.

Staircases

8261   Walls to staircases should be structurally satisfactory for the fixing of a second handrail, should it be required to facilitate access to the first floor.

8262   Standard staircases are generally advised. With a view to aiding disabled members of the household, it may be advocated that the staircase should have low risers and deep treads. The incorporation of a special staircase will be expensive (315) and the space used may compromise space standards elsewhere in the dwelling; on balance a standard staircase is preferred.

Wheelchair visitors

8263   Where practicable, two storey dwellings should be accessible to wheelchair visitors.
The difficulty of arranging the downstairs wc compartment so that it can be used by a chairbound person (1704) means that the case for requiring a flush threshold at the entrance is not strong. For

reasons discussed in 3114, a single step is considered admissible.

8264   The entrance should have a ramped or level approach and flush threshold, or single step not higher than 0·170.

8265   The wc compartment should have a 0·900 doorset, or 0·800 doorset with direct access as shown in diagram 82.1.

827   Two storey mobility housing

8270   There are two methods of planning two storey housing to mobility standards so that it is potentially convenient for disabled people to live in.
The first is to have a bathroom and at least one bedroom at entrance level, as shown for example in diagram 17.1. The second is to have a straight flight staircase on which a mechanical stairlift, of the kind shown in diagrams 45.11–45.13, can be installed if required. For discussion see 1706.

Ground floor provision

8271   The requirements for two storey mobility housing with ground floor provision are:

1. The entrance has a ramped or level approach and flush threshold.

2. The kitchen, living room and at least one bedroom are at entrance level and have 0·900 doorsets, with circulation spaces not less than 0·900 wide.

3. The bathroom and wc (in a separate compartment or in the bathroom) are at entrance level.

8272   Where practicable, the bathroom should have a 0·900 doorset, allowing wheelchair access.

Stairlift provision

8273   Typical proprietary stairlifts currently manufactured can be simply fixed to the side wall to a straight staircase, with no elaborate builder's work involved. They can be removed and refixed elsewhere when there is no longer a requirement for them. Most are designed to carry passengers without wheelchairs, but there are some which can take small wheelchairs.

8274   The requirements for two storey mobility housing with stairlift provision are:

1. The entrance has a ramped and level approach and flush threshold, or a single step not higher than 0·170.

2. The kitchen and any living rooms at entrance level have 0·900 doorsets, with circulation spaces not less than 0·900 wide.

3. There is a wc at entrance level.

4. There is a straight flight staircase, with top and bottom landings not less than 0·900 × 0·900 clear.

8275 To allow for the possibility of using a wheelchair at first floor level it is desirable that bedrooms and bathrooms have 0·900 doorsets, and that the top and bottom landings have a clear dimension of 1·200 in the direction of the stairs (diagram 82.2).

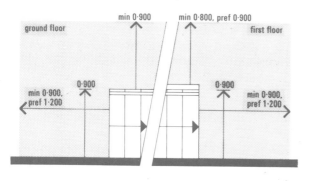

82.2 Planning of stairs for stairlift provision (1:50)

8276 The requirements in 8274 should be relatively easy to incorporate in typical low cost two storey housing, and it ought to be practicable to develop schemes of this kind in quantity. In practice, only a small minority of tenants may be expected to need the stairlift provision and it is therefore admissible that the entrance has a single step rather than a flush threshold. In the event that a wheelchair user occupies the dwelling and cannot manage the step, it ought to be practicable to ramp the step to facilitate access.

828 **Housing for blind and deaf people**

8280 The recommendations below are for group schemes for blind or deaf people. Where special units are provided for blind or deaf people it is recommended that they are planned basically to mobility standards. For the majority of blind and deaf people special housing is neither necessary nor desirable.

Blind people

8281 Where housing is planned to cater for blind people the following provisions are suggested:
1. An enclosed run for exercising guide dogs, with sanitary area which can be washed down.
2. Internal or external storage accommodation which can serve if required as a sleeping area for a dog.
3. A delivery cupboard suitable for braille books (5045).
4. Bathroom equipment which is easy to clean; this is particularly important in the case of the wc.
5. Suitable ironmongery; knob door furniture may be preferred to lever furniture to minimize the hazard of clothes catching.
6. Storage cupboards with sliding doors, or storage provision with open shelving.
7. Lighting arrangements to aid people who are partially sighted.

Deaf people

8282 Where housing is planned to cater for deaf people the following provisions are suggested:
1. An induction loop to aid hard of hearing people (447).
2. Lighting arrangements which will aid people who communicate by lip reading.

83 Wheelchair housing

830 Wheelchair housing: Planning principles

8300 Wheelchair housing: Tactical guidelines

83000 This section is concerned with housing for chairbound people who can manage independently or with family support. Housing for people not able to manage independently is discussed in section 84. Housing for old people using wheelchairs is discussed in 852. Space standards, household distribution and design requirements for wheelchair housing are summarized in tables 81.1–81.3.

83001 The preferred arrangement for wheelchair housing is that all parts of the dwelling are accessible, with design flexibility to cater for people with special needs such as chairbound housewives in kitchens. In practice, as discussed in the commentary (1708, 1711) a proportion of chairbound people who are members of family households do not need comprehensive provision, and can be conveniently accommodated if a bedroom and bathroom are accessible, with access to other rooms at ground level.

83002 The recommendations which follow are based on the tactical distinction between comprehensive single storey wheelchair housing, which is potentially suitable for all wheelchair users, including housewives, and two storey housing with wheelchair provision at ground level, which is not suitable for wheelchair housewives.

83003 The recommendations relate specifically to public authority housing in England and Wales, ie housing built by local authorities, by housing associations and by new town development corporations, subject to controls administered by the Department of the Environment. In the case of private housing these administrative controls do not apply, and, according to circumstances and client requirements, provisions of a more generous character may be appropriate.

83004 The recommendations made here are in accord with the advice given by the Department of the Environment in *Wheelchair housing* [1].

8301 Wheelchair housing: Space and cost determinants

83010 The guidance which follows has been prepared at a time (May 1976) when the planning of public authority housing continues to be governed by the twin constraints of mandatory minimum space standards and cost yardstick controls. The administration of the yardstick is under review by the Department of the Environment, and it may be that by the time of publication, or soon after, current procedures will have been superseded. The important factor in respect of wheelchair housing is whether cost allowances continue to be determined by the number of bedspaces provided in individual dwelling units; if they do not, some modifications of suggested planning arrangements may be warranted.

83011 Space standards are based on Parker Morris housing standards (table 81.3), with additional space allowing for wheelchair circulation; cost controls are based on the basic housing cost yardstick (related to density and the overall number of bedspaces) with an additional allowance for the extra space and special amenities. The cost allowances currently available are set down in DoE Circular 92/75 *Wheelchair and mobility housing: Standards and costs* [2]; their administration is discussed in section 87.

Underoccupation

83012 When planning wheelchair housing, the understandable inclination of the architect is to attempt to cater for all possible contingencies, for example by expanding the size of all bedrooms, incorporating sophisticated kitchen equipment and including alternative bathing and wc facilities. The consequence is that the special provision may exceed what can be obtained within cost limits. To avoid this, it is tactically wise when planning wheelchair housing to maximize what can be designated as basic housing provision. The practical technique for achieving this is to plan in the expectation that underoccupation will occur, for example that a 3 person unit will be occupied by a two person household, a 4 person unit by a three person household and a 5 person unit by a four person household.

83013 The propriety of planning deliberately for underoccupation is not challengeable. It is socially desirable for all households that there is at least one spare bed space, to cater for example for visitors or so that growing children can have separate bedrooms. In the case of disabled people there may be a need for an extra bedroom for a relative coming temporarily to care for the disabled person, or for the spouse of a person whose disability means that he needs a room to himself. The evidence of the DoE survey [3] indicates that in purpose-designed wheelchair housing underoccupation commonly occurs. Of the 102 dwelling units with two bedrooms 70 (69 per cent) were occupied by households of one or two people. Of the 71 dwelling units having three bedrooms 33 (46 per cent) were occupied by households having three or fewer members.

Bedroom planning

83014 The important tactical factor is bedroom planning. A single bedroom having sufficient space for wheelchair manoeuvre will often be almost as big

[1] Bib 93120
[2] Bib 93121
[3] Bib 93122

as a double bedroom for ordinary purposes, and it will be advantageous for yardstick purposes if it is, so obtaining the bonus of an additional bedspace.

83015 Two examples illustrate the point. A 3 person 2 bedroom unit will need to have both bedrooms enlarged if it is to be potentially satisfactory for either a husband/wife or a single person who is chairbound. The effect will be to bring the overall area close to the 4 person standard; it makes sense to slightly enlarge the second room and to designate the unit 4p2b. The second example is a 4p3b unit with the main bedroom and one single bedroom enlarged; it will be advantageous if the enlarged single room can accommodate two beds so that the unit can be designated 5p3b.

83016 Planning wheelchair housing on this basis means that a 4p2b unit will still be capable of accommodating a four person household or a 5p3b unit a five person household. Where it is a husband or wife who is chairbound the provision for the rest of the family will not be substandard by comparison with general purpose housing.

83017 The recommendations in 8302–8308 are made on this basis. Table 81.3 summarizes the recommendations diagrammatically.

8302 Single person households

83020 For single person households the suggested wheelchair housing provision is either a bed-sitting room unit or a unit with a separate bedroom. The suggested net space standard is 35·5m².

Bed-sitting room
83021 For a bed-sitting room unit the bathroom should allow for wheelchair manoeuvre. With careful planning the bed-sitting space will be sufficient for the bed area to be partitioned from the sitting area.

Separate bedroom
83022 In the case of a separate bedroom unit the requirement for increased space may make it uneconomic to plan within cost limits; it is preferable therefore that the bedroom is planned as a double room and the unit designated 2p1b. An advantage of a large bedroom is that when the disabled person is ill there is room for a friend or relative to stay temporarily.

8303 Two person households

83030 For a two person household the suggested provision is either a 2p1b or a 3p2b unit. The suggested space standard for a 2p1b unit is 49·5m², and for a 3p2b unit 63·0m² (table 81.1).

2p1b units
83031 The majority of two person households with a wheelchair member are spouses. It is therefore admissible that a substantial proportion of units planned for two person households are 2p1b. Of the 77 two person households in the Norwich study with a member assessed as needing or potentially needing wheelchair housing (table 17.2), there were 50 (65 per cent) comprising married couples.

83032 In the case of a 2p1b unit the bedroom should cater for a chairbound husband or wife, for example as shown in diagram 53.8.

3p2b units
83033 Some spouse households will have a requirement for a 3p2b unit, allowing for the disabled person to have a bedroom to himself, or for the second bedroom to be used for visitors or as a workroom.

83034 The suggested 3p2b unit will be suitable for a two person household not comprising husband and wife. The disabled person will use the large double room, the non-disabled person the small single room.

83035 The second bedroom in a 3p2b unit should allow for wheelchair access, and may be planned on the same basis as a small bedroom for ordinary housing. In the housing design guides published by the National Building Agency the smallest single bedroom conforming to Parker Morris standards has an area of 5·44m² [4].

83036 Where practicable, the second bedroom in a 3p2b unit may with advantage be planned for wheelchair usability, see 8463.

8304 Three person households

83040 For a three person household the suggested provision is a 4p2b unit. In this case the disabled person may be a spouse, or a single person such as a disabled child, adolescent or grandparent.

83041 The space standard is 73·0m². One of the two bedrooms should be a double room planned for wheelchair use. The second double room should be planned on the same basis as a bedroom for two single beds in ordinary housing; this will be large enough to accommodate a single chairbound person.

83042 For reasons discussed in 83015, 4p3b units are not as a rule economical to provide. Where for a particular reason a 4p3b unit is planned it may be possible to make one of the single bedrooms suitable for wheelchair use without substantially increasing overall space above the 4p2b standard.

[4] Bib 93733, 93734

8305 Four person households

83050 For a four person household the suggested provision is a 5p3b unit, having a space standard of 86·0m².
In this case the disabled person may be a spouse, or one of the other two members of the household. In the latter case it will probably happen that the disabled person needs a room to himself, for example where he or she is a grandparent in a three generation family.

83051 The bedroom provision should comprise one double room planned for wheelchair use, and a second double room and a single room planned for wheelchair access.
The disabled person if a spouse will use the large double room, if a single person the second double room.

8306 Five person households

83060 For a five person household the suggested provision is a 6p3b unit, having a space standard of 94·5m².
In this case the disabled person could be a spouse or any other member of the family.

83061 The main double bedroom need only be enlarged for wheelchair use.
This will cater for all contingencies; where the disabled person is not a spouse he or she will use one of the smaller double rooms.

83062 An alternative for five person households is a 6p4b unit.

83063 In 6p4b units the main double bedroom should be enlarged and also one single bedroom. The other double room and single room should be as for normal housing.

8307 Six person and larger households

83070 For a six person household a 6p4b unit will generally be satisfactory.
The bedroom planning arrangements suggested (83063) will cater for all contingencies.

83071 It is not advised that larger single storey units, for example 7p4b, are planned as part of the normal wheelchair housing stock.
It is unlikely in the case of a seven person household needing wheelchair accommodation that the chairbound person will be the housewife; it is more probable that he or she will be an ageing relative or one of the children. In such cases two storey accommodation will be suitable. Where a need for single storey seven person units occurs it should be met on an ad hoc basis.

8308 Two storey wheelchair housing

83080 Two storey wheelchair housing ought not to be planned on the basis that the chairbound person might be a housewife or mother.
Where a mother is chairbound it is essential that she has access to all family rooms, meaning that the only suitable solution is single storey housing. For the same reasons it is not recommended that two storey housing is intended for chairbound husbands.

Downstairs bedroom
83081 The accessible downstairs bedroom should always be a double room, allowing for wheelchair access; for an example see diagram 53.6. It is not essential that it is planned on the basis that there is wheelchair approach to all clothes cupboards, dressing tables etc.
If the bedroom is occupied by one person only it will be large enough for full wheelchair use. If it is occupied by two people it can be expected, on the basis that the disabled person will not be the housewife or mother, that wheelchair access to all cupboards etc is not essential.

83082 Two storey housing may be planned so that access to the first floor can be by stairlift or hoist, but this is not a desirable alternative.

Six and seven person units
83083 The preferred two storey wheelchair housing units are 6p3b and 7p4b.

83084 For a five person household the recommended provision is a 6p3b unit.
The dimensions of the two double bedrooms upstairs will be as for normal housing.

83085 For a six person household the recommended provision is a 7p4b unit.
The one single and two double bedrooms upstairs will be as for normal housing.

Five person units
83086 Although space standards for 5p3b two storey wheelchair housing are included in table 81.3, provision of this kind is not recommended in the overall distribution of wheelchair housing units detailed in table 81.1. The reasons are as follows:
1. Where the household comprises four people, single storey accommodation is preferred.
2. Where the household comprises five people, the preference is for a 6p3b unit.
3. Given that the downstairs bedroom will have two beds, it will not as a rule be economic to plan upstairs accommodation with one double and one single bedroom only.

831 Wheelchair housing: Siting, location

8310 Siting

83100 Wheelchair housing should be planned as an integral part of an ordinary housing scheme rather than as a separate colony of special units. The aim, at least in respect of wheelchair housing for younger people, should be to achieve assimilation so that the special units are not perceived as something peculiar or different.

Attitudes to disabled neighbours

83101 While colonies should be avoided, there may be advantages in grouping a small number of wheelchair housing units close to each other. In the DoE survey 238 of the 249 informants had disabled neighbours [5]. In response to the question whether they liked to have neighbours who were disabled 107 (45 per cent) said they did, 56 (24 per cent) said they would prefer not to, and 75 (31 per cent) did not have views either way. In general, those with minor disabilities were less likely to positively like having disabled neighbours and were more likely not to know them; the tentative interpretation here is that people who could sustain an appearance of normality were more sensitive about being categorized as disabled than those whose disabilities were relatively severe. Disabled people aged 50 or over tended to like having disabled neighbours more than those who were younger; this also is understandable.

83102 Among the reasons given by the 107 people who said they liked having disabled neighbours were 'mutual understanding' (37 per cent), 'can help each other' (22 per cent), 'doesn't feel odd one out' (13 per cent) and 'nice to know others with similar problems' (9 per cent). Twelve per cent said they liked disabled neighbours, but with reservations about the size of the scheme.

83103 Among the reasons given by the 56 people who said they disliked disabled neighbours were 'able people more help' (38 per cent), 'doesn't feel disabled' (14 per cent) and 'depressing' (14 per cent).

83104 From this evidence it can be suggested that the optimum arrangement is to put three or four wheelchair units in close proximity, with the proviso that if they are for old people the numbers can be increased.

Planning constraints

83105 The planning of integrated schemes is more easily achievable with two storey than with single storey wheelchair housing. By comparison with two storey housing, single storey units use more land and are less easily introduced in an ordinary housing scheme. Where practicable, units should be placed at the centre rather than the periphery of a development.

83106 To make efficient use of land, single storey housing should be compact. Narrow frontage patio units are generally more economic than detached or semi-detached bungalows.

83107 It is desirable, but not essential, that wheelchair housing is planned on flat sites. The important consideration is that any carport or garage within the curtilage is at the same level as the ground floor of the dwelling.

8311 Gardens

83110 Gardens where provided to wheelchair housing units should be small.
Among the 155 potential users of wheelchair housing in the Norwich study there were 125 who at the time of interview had a house with a garden; of these only 7 said they did any gardening themselves.

83111 For notes on garden facilities see 581.

8312 Location of wheelchair housing

83120 The location of shopping facilities need not be a critical determinant for the location of wheelchair housing units, but it is advantageous if local shops are within say a quarter of a mile.

83121 To aid people who push wheelchairs, pedestrian routes to local shops should be easily graded, with inclines not exceeding 1:12.

83122 For young families in particular it is desirable that wheelchair housing is sited close to places of employment.
It may be that a disabled wife relies on her husband for assistance in the middle of the day, for example helping her to use the wc, and it is important that he should be able to travel quickly from his home to his place of work. The same analysis applies in respect of a daughter in employment who is living with a disabled parent. The difficulties which family wage earners may face when seeking employment in a new locality is a further factor indicating easy accessibility to possible places of employment.

83123 Sheltered or quiet outlooks, for example on to internal courtyards, should be avoided.
Although disabled people, in common with others, may be distressed by constant noise outside, a peaceful alternative may also be trying. People who are housebound often like to have activities going on around them, to watch the traffic, to see children going to school or at play, and to look for the milkman and postman. Routine but varying happenings of this kind can make all the difference between day-to-day contentment and miserable boredom.

---

[5] Bib 93122

832 Wheelchair housing: Access and internal circulation

8320 Access

83200 Ramped approaches to wheelchair housing units should have a gradient not exceeding 1:20. For discussion see 3215.

83201 Any external door must have a flush or near-flush threshold; the height of the sill above floor level to either side should not exceed 0·015.

83202 Where a garage or carport is within the curtilage, access to the dwelling must be under cover.
Apart from considerations of convenience the lack of undercover access will mean that, when there is rain or snow, wet and dirty wheelchair tyres will stain floor surfaces.

83203 Where there is an integral garage the floor of the garage should be at the same level as the floor inside the house; some people who can manage wheelchairs independently are unable to cope with ramps. See 5700.

8321 Internal circulation

83210 For economic house planning, internal circulation areas should be reduced to a minimum, and not needlessly exaggerated to cater for wheelchair manoeuvre. Passageways should be not less than 1·200 wide, in conjunction with 0·900 doorsets.

83211 The issue of 0·900 versus 1·000 doorsets is discussed exhaustively elsewhere: in respect of mobility housing (1702), wheelchair circulation spaces (24) and doors generally (36). Clients or architects may prefer to incorporate 1·000 doorsets throughout for wheelchair housing, but this will not necessarily be advantageous.

83212 Passageways 1·200 wide allow for chairs to be negotiated through 90° from passageways into rooms or vice versa.
As a general rule it may be assumed that turns through 180° will take place inside rooms rather than in passageways. Where space is needed to turn at the entrance door, the width of the hall should be not less than 1·500.

83213 Unless floors are to be carpeted standard threshold sills to internal doors should be omitted, see 3420.

8322 Internal circulation: Two storey wheelchair housing

83220 In two storey wheelchair housing having an accessible bedroom and bathroom at entrance level, accommodation at first floor level need not be planned for wheelchair use and no special conditions need be observed in respect of door widths or circulation spaces.

83221 On the basis that a hydraulic hoist or stairlift may be installed to carry a wheelchair, the planning of modified two storey 5 or 6 person units with bathroom and/or bedrooms upstairs may be practicable.
For practical and economic reasons this tactic is not recommended for public authority housing. Where it is undertaken all doorsets at first floor level should be 0·900, with 1·200 passageways.

833 Wheelchair housing: Building elements, services and equipment

8330 Ironmongery

83300 Window and door ironmongery must be easy to manipulate.
Except in the case of the kitchen window in housing for wheelchair housewives, remote control window openers ought not to be installed until a need is established.

83301 Door handles should be at the standard height of 1·040 above floor level (36300).
In the DoE survey there were four people who said that their door handles were too high, all of them at 1·000 and above [6]. This evidence is not sufficient to warrant a lower fixing level for all wheelchair users; the additional expense involved would be out of proportion to the benefit.

83302 Kicking plates may be fixed to the trailing face of side-hung doors (36082).

83303 Door construction should be suitable for the fixing of auxiliary pull handles (36310, 36317).

8331 Taps

83310 Lever taps may be provided in place of screw-down taps to kitchen sink, wash basin and bath.
Most disabled people can cope without difficulty with conventional screw-down fittings. For the few who need lever taps it may therefore be more economic to install screw-down fittings initially, and to substitute lever taps when a need is established.

---

[6] Bib 93122

83311 For people whose reach is severely limited, tap controls may need to be on basin or sink fascias; see 4171.
This provision should be made only when a special need is established.

8332 Floor finishes

83320 Floor finishes throughout should be slip-resistant, see 3810.

83321 Carpeting is preferred wherever practicable, see 3861.

8333 Heating

83330 The heating installation should be capable of maintaining living and dining areas at 22°C, and kitchen, bedrooms and circulation spaces at 17°C, when the outside temperature is −1°C.
This is a higher standard than the mandatory requirement for general purpose housing (8047) and is comparable with the standard of 21°C throughout the dwelling required for flats for old people (8056).

83331 There is no empirical evidence affording a firm basis for preferred heating standards in housing for disabled people, but it is reasonable that they relate to standards regarded as suitable for old people. In large dwelling units the expense, both capital and running, of heating all areas to 21°C will be heavy, and a distinction is therefore made between living rooms and other areas.

83332 In all rooms the temperature should be controllable by the tenant.

83333 To reduce heat losses and cut the cost of fuel, special attention should be given to thermal insulation when selecting materials.

Two storey housing
83334 In accord with space heating requirements for general purpose housing prescribed in MHLG Circular 27/70 (8047), it is not essential in two storey wheelchair housing that accommodation at first floor level (which will not be accessible to the disabled occupant) is subject to the heating standards recommended in 83330.

8334 Electrical services

83340 Socket outlets should be generously provided. The minimum provision should be as recommended in MHLG Circular 27/70, see 8046. The desirable provision is as recommended in the Parker Morris report, see 4341.

83341 Light switches and socket outlets should be aligned with door handles.

8335 Provision for hoists

83350 The ceiling or walls in the bathroom should be structurally capable of carrying a track for an electric hoist (261) so that a person who is severely handicapped can be transferred from the wheelchair to the wc or bath and vice versa.

83351 In addition, it is desirable that a disabled person can be transferred from bedroom to bathroom by means of a hoist suspended from an overhead track, see 83515.
Where bedrooms and bathroom adjoin it may be practicable, where a track has to be installed, for the partition wall to be removed.

8336 Alarm systems

83360 It is preferred, for reasons discussed in 895, that telephones are used for alarm purposes.

83361 Where fixed alarm devices are installed their positioning may be deferred until individual requirements are ascertained.

834 Wheelchair housing: Kitchens

8340 Kitchen use

83400 A kitchen designed for a wheelchair housewife is not automatically equally suitable for other users. For ambulant housewives the worktops and sink levels will be too low, and the provision of adequate accessible storage at low level will be prejudiced by the requirement for wheelchair access at the sink and preparation area. The larger clear circulation space needed by the wheelchair housewife may be disadvantageous for ambulant kitchen users, for whom a smaller area can be more economical and efficient. For the housewife who is not disabled, or who has a disability but does not use a wheelchair, it is preferable that the kitchen is designed for normal use.

83401 Of the 155 people in the Norwich study identified as potentially in need of wheelchair housing, 67 used the kitchen regularly, and a further 6 might have done so had it been accessible or more easily manageable. There were 82 people who did not use the kitchen and would not have used it even had it been specially designed for them.
This evidence indicates that in the planning of kitchens in single storey wheelchair housing units it is wise to allow for flexibility, particularly in respect of work levels, so that the kitchen can be

organized for wheelchair use or not, as the requirement may be. For supporting evidence from the DoE inquiry see 51167.

8341 Kitchen planning

83410 Wheelchair kitchens should be planned economically, without an exaggeratedly large circulation area.

83411 For small households, ie for one or two persons, the kitchen may be planned as a recess off the living room, so that the wheelchair user drives in and reverses out. It is not essential that there is room to turn the wheelchair around.
Diagram 51.4 illustrates an example of a kitchen recess.

83412 In kitchens for larger households, ie for three or more persons, circulation space in the kitchen should allow for wheelchair turning. Where there are no obstructions at footrest level the clear width between parallel units may be reduced to 1·400; where there are obstructions the width should be not less than 1·500. For examples see diagrams 51.5–51.8.

Two storey wheelchair housing
83413 In two storey wheelchair housing units, the kitchen should be planned from the start for use by an ambulant housewife.
The kitchen should be accessible, allowing a wheelchair user to prepare snacks etc, and there should be space to turn a wheelchair inside the room.

8342 Dining provision in kitchens

83420 In single storey housing units, the dining table should be inside the kitchen, or immediately outside provided that it is directly accessible. A hatch between the kitchen and dining area is not an adequate substitute for direct access, see 5221.

83421 In two storey units, the dining area may be separate from the kitchen provided that, as recommended in the Parker Morris report, there is space in the kitchen for two or three people to sit down to eat [7].

8343 Kitchen work levels

83430 In single storey wheelchair housing units where kitchens are planned so that they can be adapted to meet the requirements of chairbound housewives,

the initial fixing for work levels may be at 0·900 to suit ambulant housewives.
Alternatively work levels may be fixed at the compromise height of 0·800; for discussion see 51166–8.

83431 In two storey housing units kitchen work levels should be at 0·900.

8344 Meal preparation

83440 The preferred cooking provision for a wheelchair housewife is a split-level unit with built-in hob and waist-level oven.
This provision would in practice be advantageous for all housewives. It is not the norm in public authority housing in Britain, an important factor being that the cooker is an item provided by the tenant, and in the planning of kitchens a space is left to insert a floor unit.

83441 The building contract may allow for building in hob and oven. An alternative is not to include the equipment in the contract but to allow when planning the kitchen for a split-level tabletop oven and hob to be obtained by the tenant.
The hob should be on a shelf so that it aligns with the surface of adjoining worktops. There can be a knee recess below the shelf; if it happens that the housewife is not disabled and prefers a conventional floor cooker unit the shelf can be removed and the floor unit put in place.

Sink
83442 There should be wheelchair access to the kitchen sink. A shallow sink is therefore preferred, but it may be a disadvantage for a non-disabled housewife who uses the sink for clothes soaking and other household activities. For design notes see 5151.

83443 Double bowl sink units are preferred.

83444 A swivel tap may be incorporated so that kettles need not be lifted off the worktop for filling, see 5155.

83445 As a general rule it is not necessary that the underside of the kitchen sink is insulated to insure against burns to paraplegics, see 51501.

83446 A waste disposal unit at the sink is desirable, but in most cases wheelchair housewives will be able to cope with refuse disposal by other means. If they cannot there will usually be someone else available to help when necessary.

Preparation area
83447 Knee access should be provided at the preparation area. Pull-out boards are recommended to give alternative working levels, see 5122.

[7] Bib 93720, para 33

8345 Kitchen storage

83450 Storage accommodation in a kitchen for a wheelchair housewife poses an insoluble problem. Wall units above worktops are unsatisfactory because they cannot be comfortably reached (51315), and adequate accommodation at low level is compromised by the need for knee access below work surfaces.

High level storage

83451 In wheelchair kitchens it will not as a rule be practicable to arrange all the regulation storage provision (8045) within reach of a chairbound person; it will therefore be necessary that some storage provision is not accessible.

83452 Wall units at high level should be incorporated, first because not all kitchen users will be chairbound, and second, because items used only infrequently may be stored at high level and handled by someone other than the wheelchair housewife.

Low level storage

83453 Knee access provision should be limited to the sink and preparation area, allowing for floor units to be fitted below other work surfaces.

83454 At low level the use of pull-out drawers is helpful, and revolving cupboards at high and low level are also recommended.
Wheelchair housewives may be unable to reach goods at the rear of wall or floor units.

Storage trolleys

83455 The use of portable pull-out trolleys is recommended (5134).
These trolleys will not as a rule be part of the building contract and it may be that they can be made up by handicapped people at a local work centre, in the same way that bath seats are made (70453).

835 Living rooms, bedrooms

8350 Living rooms, dining rooms

83500 The area of living rooms and dining rooms need not be exaggerated.
While it is important that the dining area is planned to allow convenient wheelchair access to the table, it is not necessary to increase overall space standards for the dwelling on account of wheelchair manoeuvring space in living rooms and dining areas.

83501 Windows in living rooms should allow for seated people to see out.
A structural sill height of 0·600 is suggested. Transomes must not be inside the zone 1·000–1·200 above floor level (351).

8351 Bedrooms

83510 Bedroom requirements for wheelchair housing are discussed in 8302–8. Examples of bedroom layouts are shown in diagrams 53·1–53·8.

Bedmaking

83511 It is not necessary to allow for bedmaking from a wheelchair by providing manoeuvring space on three sides of any bed.
For notes on bedmaking see 531.

Single beds

83512 Single beds may be placed with the long side against walls; as discussed in the commentary with reference to institutions (1518) this is preferred.

Bedroom storage

83513 Where bedrooms are planned for wheelchair use, clothes cupboards having unobstructed access and adjustable-height hanging rails are recommended, see 563.

Bedrooms and bathrooms

83514 The planning of bathrooms should allow for easy access from bedrooms to the wc.
In single bedroom units it may be convenient to plan the bathroom off the bedroom, see 54012.

83515 Where a bedroom for wheelchair use is planned alongside the bathroom, it may be practicable, if the need occurs, for part of the partition wall to be removed; it will then be possible to install a ceiling track to enable a disabled person to be carried in a suspended sling direct from bed to bath or wc.

836 Bathrooms and wcs

8360 Bathroom planning: Flexibility

83600 Where practicable, bathroom planning in wheelchair housing should afford flexibility to allow for the placing of fixtures to suit individual requirements. Initial planning should be for the provision of a bath, with the possibility of installing a shower if required.

83601 The bathroom should be planned to allow for turning a wheelchair, see 5456.

Shower provision

83602 Where a bath is installed it is helpful if a shower can if required be operated in conjunction with the bath, enabling a disabled person to take a shower seated on the platform at the head end of the bath; such a provision should be regarded as a supplementary rather than an alternative facility.

83603 Where for economic reasons a decision has to be made between a shower only and a bath only, the recommendation is in favour of the bath; for discussion on showers versus baths see 5480.

83604   Where there is a wc compartment separate from the bathroom which allows for wheelchair use it may be planned to accommodate a shower also, see 54815.

Partition walls

83605   Partition walls should allow for the fixing of support rails, see 370.

8361 Baths

83610   The preferred bath length is 1·600 or 1·700, see 5461.

83611   There should be a platform at the head end of the bath to aid transfer from the wheelchair (5458).

8362 Wash basins

83620   The wash basin should be planned for convenient wheelchair approach.
It ought not to be placed on the side wall directly inside the door so that an awkward right angle approach is necessary.

83621   Conventional wash basins with a narrow dimension from front to back are not usually satisfactory; a basin set in a desk top is preferred (5443).

83622   The fixing of the basin may be deferred until the requirements of the disabled tenant are ascertained.
Where the basin is fixed in advance the rim height should be 0·800 or 0·850 where the expectation is that disabled users will be ambulant; where they are likely to be in wheelchairs a height of 0·750 is suggested.

83623   The basin may be placed close to the wc so that a handicapped person can wash his hands when seated on the wc.
In practice this is not always feasible, first because some users are too severely handicapped to reach a basin which needs to be accessible for general use, and second because planning constraints may require alternative layouts.

8363 Wcs: General considerations

83630   Two factors affect wc provision in wheelchair housing: first the means of transfer from wheelchair to wc and vice versa (discussed in 5411), and second the amount of time which disabled people spend using the wc.

83631   For reasons discussed in the notes on incontinence (9152), wheelchair users in general and paraplegics in particular spend extended periods of time using the wc. The effect where there is only one wc in the home is to cause inconvenience to other members of the household. Where it is in the bathroom the consequence (dependent on cultural attitudes – there are usually more inhibitions in working class than in middle class households) is to sterilize the use of the bathroom for long periods. Ideally therefore there ought in wheelchair housing to be two wcs, with the one outside the bathroom planned for wheelchair use. The DoE survey confirmed that even in 4 person households inconvenience could be caused by having only one wc [8]. There is however a significant cost penalty in having two wcs in a single storey dwelling unit, particularly if the one in a separate compartment is planned for wheelchair use.

8364 Wcs: Provision by household size

83640   For 1, 2 or 3 person wheelchair dwelling units one wc only is suggested, in the bathroom.

83641   In 4 person dwelling units, where the household occupancy is expected to be three people, one wc only need be provided, in the bathroom.
MHLG Circular 27/70 recommends that for 4 person dwelling units there should be a wc compartment separate from the bathroom (8044) although this is not a mandatory standard. In wheelchair housing the expectation is that in 4 person units the household will be of three people only (83012–6), and the provision of a separate wc compartment is not therefore critical. In the case of 4 person households with a wheelchair member the preferred dwelling is a 5 person unit, which has two wcs.

83642   For 5 person single storey units there should be two wcs, the one in the bathroom to be planned for wheelchair use. The wc in a separate compartment need not be accessible to wheelchairs. Alternatively, where planning permits, the separate wc may be planned for wheelchair use. In this case the wc in the bathroom need not be planned for lateral transfer, for example as shown in diagram 54.64.

83643   For 6 or 7 person single storey units there should be two wcs. The wc compartment separate from the bathroom should be planned for wheelchair use; it should also be planned so that a shower can be installed if required, see 54815.

Two storey housing

83644   In two storey wheelchair housing units there should be a ground floor bathroom with wc planned for wheelchair use, and a room at first floor level containing wc and wash basin.

[8] Bib 93122

8365 Planning of wcs

83650 Where a wc for wheelchair use is in the bathroom it should permit lateral, oblique or frontal transfer, as shown in the examples in diagrams 54.57–54.62.

83651 Where a wc for wheelchair use is in a separate compartment the minimum dimensions should be 1·700 × 1·400 or 1·600 × 1·500 (diagrams 54.8–54.10). In either case it is not critical that there is sufficient space for frontal transfer, provided that the wc in the bathroom does allow this.

83652 In housing schemes where a number of wheelchair housing units are planned it may be helpful, to cater for hemiplegics, to plan half with wcs allowing for left side transfer, and the other half right side.
In practice, for reasons discussed in 54153, this provision is unlikely to be essential, and it ought not to take precedence over other criteria.

8366 Wcs: Fixtures and equipment

83660 The fixing of the wc for wheelchair use ought if possible to be deferred until the requirements of the disabled tenant are ascertained.

83661 Where the wc is fixed in advance the suggested seat height is 0·475.
For discussion on wc seat heights see 5425.

83662 The preferred provision to raise the wc seat height is a concrete plinth moulded to the configuration of the wc pedestal.
The use of portable seat raisers is not recommended for reasons of stability.

83663 A wc fixture where the dimension from water level to seat level is relatively generous is preferred; for discussion see 54202.

Support rails
83664 Allowance should be made for the fixing of support rails to the side wall adjoining the wc; rails ought not to be fixed until individual requirements are ascertained.

83665 On the exposed side of the wc the provision of a hinged horizontal rail is suggested, see 54274.

837 Wheelchair housing: Storage

8370 Wheelchair storage

83700 In the planning of wheelchair housing units a space should be allocated for wheelchair storage. The suggested area is 1·200 × 0·700, ie 0·84m². For dimensions of folded wheelchairs see 5621.

83701 MHLG Circular 27/70 requires that in housing units for 3 or more persons a space 1·400 × 0·700 is provided for a pram. In wheelchair housing planned for three, four or five people it is improbable that pram storage provision will be required, and the space allocated for a pram can duplicate for wheelchair storage.
With the current trend in Britain to collapsible push-chairs in place of the traditional baby carriage it may be that official standards could be amended; it also means that in 3, 4 or 5 person units where pram space is required, the recommended standard may cater for a wheelchair as well as a folded pram.

83702 For 6 or 7 person wheelchair units a space should be allocated for storage of both wheelchair and pram. To allow for a folding pram and non-folding wheelchair or vice versa, a space 1·800 × 0·700 is suggested.
For space standard calculation purposes this is net space rather than general storage space. In the net areas for 6 and 7 person units suggested in table 81.3 allowance has been made for it.

83703 For 1 and 2 person units, where Circular 27/70 does not require pram storage, additional space needs to be allowed for wheelchair storage. In the areas suggested in table 81.3 for 1 and 2 person units allowance has been made for this.

8371 General storage

83710 The areas detailed in table 81.3 for general storage space in wheelchair housing are the same as those required by Circular 27/70 for ordinary family housing and Circular 82/69 for old peope's housing.

83711 Where a carport is linked to the dwelling unit a proportion of the storage space may be associated with it.

Fuel storage
83712 The use of solid fuel in wheelchair housing is not recommended, and no provision need be made for fuel storage.

838 Wheelchair housing: Garaging

8380 The need for special garages

83800 In respect of garage provision, the most demanding condition is that of the chairbound disabled person who goes out independently, needs space in the garage to transfer from his wheelchair across the passenger seat to the driver's seat, pulls his chair in after him, and does not have anyone at hand to help him open and close the garage door. He needs a garage having more generous internal dimensions than those provided for normal use, with undercover access from the dwelling and an automatic garage door opening device.

83801 Elaborate provision of this kind may be suggested by a client or architect planning wheelchair housing, but it is arguable that it is appropriate. Even where it is incorporated there are still possible situations where it may be inadequate, for example families with two cars or with two car-driving disabled members.

Norwich data
83802 Of the 155 people in the Norwich survey identified as potentially in need of wheelchair housing, 19 (12 per cent) drove a vehicle themselves, and a further 31 (20 per cent) were in households having a car driven by someone else. It is only disabled car drivers, not invalid tricycle drivers, who might need extra-wide garages, and of the 19 there was only one – a double amputee able at the time of interview to walk – who drove a car. There was thus no one who at the time of interview needed a wider garage.
Given the possibility that the DHSS invalid tricycle will in time be phased out, it might be contended that the 18 tricycle drivers should be regarded as potential car drivers, with a need for additional garage space if chairbound. At the time of interview 4 of these 18 people were chairbound.

83803 The evidence does not support the case for automatic garage door openers. For disabled drivers who are members of 2 person or larger households the incorporation of an automatic door opener may be an attractive bonus but it is not as a rule a critical necessity. In Norwich there were only two drivers, both of invalid tricycles, who were living alone.

Use of resources
83804 In relation to other special provision in public authority wheelchair housing, a special garage is expensive. Given that the demand for special provision is minimal, it is questionable that garages ought to be provided at all. Available resources might instead be allocated to (for example) enhanced kitchen or bathroom arrangements, or additional space inside the home. In this context the desirability of having a garage for security reasons is irrelevant; vehicle security is not a matter which is influenced by disability determinants.

83805 In accordance with instructions in DoE Circular 24/75 enclosed garages are not provided for public authority housing in Britain [9].

8381 Carports

83810 For wheelchair housing units, attached carports are recommended.
In respect of wheelchair access and manoeuvring space, the carport has major advantages. The wheelchair user has convenient access to either passenger door or driver's door for getting in and out, along with access to rear doors and car boot for loading luggage; to achieve equal convenience inside an enclosed garage is virtually impossible. For the disabled driver it is important to avoid having to clear ice or snow from car windows; a carport linked to the dwelling should ensure this as capably as a garage.

83811 For single storey wheelchair housing, other than units in sheltered housing schemes for old people, integral carports should be provided in the ratio of 1:1.

83812 For two storey wheelchair housing a carport or other garaging facility may be provided outside the curtilage.
It is unlikely that a disabled person in two storey housing will be a car driver. The housing provision is most likely to be used for a mentally handicapped person, for an elderly person who is handicapped or for a child who is disabled. There is not therefore sufficient cause for requiring garaging within the curtilage. The recommendation is that hardstanding provision, a carport or an enclosed garage should be provided for the dwelling within comfortable reach (say 60·000), if possible by a level route.

83813 For notes on carport design see 579.

8382 Garages

83820 In housing schemes where carports are planned and it is decided for a particular tenant that a garage is necessary, it may be practicable to modify the planned carport so that it becomes an enclosed garage.

83821 On housing estates where enclosed garages are provided for general purpose housing, it will be reasonable that wheelchair units also have enclosed garages.

83822 For notes on garage design see 570–578.

83823 For notes on access from the garage to the dwelling see 83202–3.

---

[9] Bib 93717

840 General considerations

8400 Housing alternatives to institutions for people who are severely disabled are discussed in section 16 of the commentary. Design requirements are generally identical to those for wheelchair housing, the more significant factor being the management of social services. Decisions regarding social management can affect planning and design arrangements, for example in respect of siting, accommodation for supervisory staff and alarm call provision.

Need for special units

8401 The primary need is for special units for single severely disabled people and for couples who are both handicapped. There may also be some units where two or three people, who have perhaps known each other in institutions, may share together. Provision for two or three people to share will also cater for siblings, for example a brother and sister with muscular dystrophy.

8402 According to the way that support services are organized, special units may be either dispersed or clustered. If they are dispersed they may be scattered throughout a new estate when it is planned, and the same general criteria for siting and design provision apply as for independent wheelchair housing. Design guidance in this section relates primarily to clustered units.

8403 In the case of cluster schemes, planning decisions will depend on whether there is to be external support with staff coming in from outside, or internal support with helpers living in housing alongside. The aim should be to integrate special units among ordinary housing, avoiding any impression of a cripples' colony. It is therefore desirable that the number of special units in any scheme is as small as is practically viable; suggested distributions by numbers of clusters are detailed in table 84.1.

External support schemes

8404 Taking account of the efficient deployment of domiciliary staff and the possibility of mutually supportive relationships, it is suggested that for external support schemes the maximum number of units in a cluster should be six, with a preference for five or four.

Internal support schemes

8405 For internal support schemes, economic factors may mean that a cluster as small as six is not practicable. It is suggested that where there is one cluster only the minimum number of units should be eight; the alternative is for two or three related clusters, accommodating up to say 20 tenants in 14 units.

8406 In housing schemes incorporating one or more clusters of special units the aim should be to have not less than 50 ordinary housing units for each cluster of special units.

841 Distribution of special units

8410 It is suggested that cluster schemes of special units should be planned in the expectation that the ratio of households having one member to those having two will be of the order of 3:2.
There is no substantive evidence to support this recommendation. It is hoped that, with the development of a number of experimental projects, practical evidence will be steadily assembled. When it is available some modification of the recommendations which follow may be needed.

Bed-sitting room provision

8411 For single person households, an important practical issue is whether to plan bed-sitting room accommodation, or to opt instead for units having a separate bedroom. The practical and social advantages of the alternatives are discussed below (846), the conclusion being that bed-sitting room provision ought not to be discarded.

Table 84.1 Housing for severely disabled people: Suggested distribution of units and hypothesized tenancy arrangements

	units in scheme	clusters	units in each cluster and distribution by bedspaces provided	number of tenants (hypothesized) and distribution by household size
external support schemes	5	1	5: 2 bsr + 3 2plb	7: 3 single, 2 2 person
internal support schemes	8	1	8: 3 bsr + 5 2plb	11: 5 single, 3 2 person
	10	2	5: 2 bsr + 3 2plb 5: 1 bsr + 3 2plb + 1 3p2b	7: 3 single, 2 2 person 8: 2 single, 3 2 person
	14	3	5: 2 bsr + 3 2plb 4: 1 bsr + 3 2plb 5: 2 bsr + 2 2plb + 1 3p2b	7: 3 single, 2 2 person 6: 2 single, 2 2 person 7: 3 single, 2 2 person

8412 In relation to flexibility of tenancy allocation, the provision of separate bedroom units for two people can be advantageous; these units may cater for a married couple, for two people sharing a flat or for a disabled person on his own who prefers not to have a bed-sitting unit.

8413 For special housing units planned in one or more clusters, the number of bed-sitting units should be not more than 40 per cent of the total.
The calculations in table 84.1 regarding hypothesized tenancy arrangements are based on the expectation that among 2 person units about two-thirds will be occupied by two person households, the remainder by one person households. In two cases the incorporation of a 3 person 2 bedroom unit is suggested; it is assumed these will always be occupied by two people.

8414 If it is practicable, housing authorities should conduct investigations in advance, for example by checking local people in hospital units or residential homes, and by asking domiciliary social workers to examine their case records, so that a reasonable prediction can be made of the number of single, 2 person and 3 person units that may be required.

8415 Alternatives are possible and can usefully be examined. If the authority's policy is not to build bed-sitting units it may be that the size of separate bedrooms will be convenient for one disabled person, but not for couples who are both handicapped; in such cases it may be appropriate to have some variability of bedroom space standards; these are discussed in 846.

Space standards
8416 Suggested space standards for units for severely disabled people are as for independent wheelchair housing, see table 81.3.

Storage
8417 Suggested standards for general storage are as for category 2 old people's schemes, ie 1·9m² for 1p units and 2·5m² for 2p units. For 3p units the suggested standard is as for 3p flats, ie 3·0m².

842 **Special units: Siting and location**

8420 Guidelines for the location of clusters of dwelling units for severely disabled people are discussed in the commentary (1612). Reference should also be made to the recommendations for the location of independent wheelchair housing (8312).

Electric wheelchairs
8421 The planning of an estate containing clustered units should allow for disabled tenants to go out of their homes by electric wheelchair to reach local shops and other amenities.

8422 Currently (1976) independently operated electric wheelchairs issued by the Department of Health are for indoor use only; people to whom they are prescribed are asked not to use them outside the curtilage of their home, though in practice the rule is not always strictly observed. It is possible that in the future electric wheelchairs will be issued which, with suitable insurance arrangements, disabled people can use both inside and outside their homes.

Access to amenities
8423 Amenities within easy travelling distance (say 300·000) of clustered housing units should include a general store, a pub, a launderette and preferably a post office, a chemist and a betting shop. On routes between housing and these amenities, no ramp gradient should exceed 1:20 and there should be no vehicular roads to cross.

Other housing
8424 To aid social interactions between disabled tenants and others living nearby it is desirable that other housing is designed to be accessible to wheelchair users, ie to mobility standards.

843 **Access, internal circulation**

8430 A cluster of special units should be planned so that the tenant of one unit can visit the tenant of another by not going outside, or if going outside remaining under cover.

8431 Ramp gradients to all entrances must be minimal to allow for electric wheelchairs; the maximum gradient should be 1:20.

8432 There should be direct access from the living area of flats to the outside, either to individual patios or a communal garden.

Internal circulation
8433 The conditions recommended for independent wheelchair housing, namely 0·900 doorsets in conjunction with 1·200 passageways, will generally be satisfactory. There may however be some tenants with large electric wheelchairs, and for these it may be helpful in situations where right-angle turns have to be made for there to be 1·000 doorsets or sliding doors.

844 **Garaging provision**

8440 People who are so severely disabled as to need housing with special support are unlikely to be able to drive vehicles of their own.

8441 For units which are dispersed there should be no garaging provision, or space should be available where a carport or garage can be placed.

8442   For each cluster of four or five units there should be a covered parking area to cater for one large car or two small cars or invalid tricycles. There should be undercover access to all dwellings from the parking area.

845   **Communal rooms**

8450   As discussed in the commentary (1618), it is not necessary that a range of communal rooms is associated with special flats.

8451   In the case of internal support schemes only, the following communal rooms may be incorporated:
1. A hobbies room, area approx 14·0m².
2. A laundry room with clothes washing and drying facilities.
3. A general purpose room, to serve as office, meeting room and bed-sitting room for staff on duty, area approx 13·0m².

846   **Bedrooms**

8460   For severely disabled people living on their own, there are advantages in having the bed in a different space from the living and eating area; the sleeping area may be untidy and if visitors call it can helpfully be closed off. On the other hand, an open plan unit permits the more economic use of space, which for wheelchair users can be critical.

Comparison with old people's schemes

8461   In old people's housing schemes in Britain there is currently a trend away from bed-sitting rooms, and a general preference for flats with separate bedrooms. In this connection the situation of younger severely disabled people may not be analagous. Old people in flatlets have invariably been accustomed to separate bedrooms in their previous accommodation; they regard the sitting room as a sitting room, the bedroom as a bedroom, and have accumulated over the years furniture which they do not want to dispose of. Physically handicapped people on the other hand will come from institutions or family homes where they have been sheltered, and will have had very different experiences. They will have been accustomed either to dormitory living or having a small room of their own, and in either case a self-contained bed-sitting room unit will be a considerable improvement. It is also unlikely that they will have much personal furniture.

8462   Where it is decided that all units should have separate bedrooms it may be helpful if within a cluster there are some larger units which are potentially suitable for couples both of whom are handicapped, and some smaller units suitable for a wheelchair person living alone. In the case of the former, the bedroom should be an enlarged double room, and space standards will be enhanced elsewhere. In the case of the latter, the bedroom will be an enlarged single room, and space standards elsewhere need not be significantly higher than those of comparable normal units.

Two bedroom units

8463   Two bedroom units may be required to cater for two people sharing, or for a brother and sister who are both handicapped. To give flexibility, and to allow for the accommodation of three people if required, the recommendation is that both the double bedroom and the single bedroom should be planned for wheelchair usability (532).
By comparison with a 3p2b independent wheelchair housing unit (83033), the area occupied by bedrooms may be enlarged relative to living space.

8464   For three people sharing, a 3 person unit may be planned with three single rooms, each allowing for wheelchair use. In this case the rooms may be arranged as bed-sitting rooms, and there should be a small shared sitting and eating area.

847   **Kitchens**

8470   In special flats, careful attention should be given to the management of cooking and eating arrangements. There are likely to be people who cannot cope with a conventional kitchen in a confined space, and are not able to eat comfortably at conventional tables. They may also be people who, more than most in wheelchairs, need generous space for circulation.

8471   These conditions point to the provision of an integral kitchen/eating/sitting area, rather than having a separate enclosed kitchen. The working area of the kitchen may be confined to a fairly small recess which the wheelchair user drives into and reverses out of. Just outside the recess there should be a place for a dining table.

8472   Kitchens should be economically planned. Food preparation procedures will generally be unsophisticated, but facilities should be adequate to organize meals on occasion for say four people. A refrigerator must be incorporated; shopping trips are likely to be infrequent, and there is the possibility that meals-on-wheels (pre-cooked meals delivered to handicapped and elderly people at home) will increasingly come in frozen packages.

8473   The final fixing of kitchen fitments and work surfaces should be deferred until individual tenants' requirements are established. For discussion see 5112.

848 **Bathing and washing**

8480 The washroom to each flat should contain a wc, a wash basin and a bath or shower. For reasons discussed in 5480 the preferred provision is a bath, a shower being substituted only where there is a specific need.

8481 Final fixing of the wc and wash basin should be delayed until the tenant's requirements are established. For some users a bidet/wc of the kind described in 5423 may be needed.

849 **Equipment**

8490 It should be possible for handicapped people to be moved by hoist suspended from a ceiling track from the bed direct to the bath and wc.
The track should not be fixed until a need is established. According to the planning of the dwelling it may be an advantage to install a partition between the bedroom and bathroom, which can be removed if the need arises.

8491 For some tenants the opening of the entrance door may need to be remotely controlled from the wheelchair.
Special provision here will be by the health or social services authority and will not be a part of the building contract.

8492 An alarm call system to summon help in an emergency may be incorporated. For reasons discussed in 895, a telephone may be the simplest and most satisfactory solution. For notes on alarm systems in housing for severely disabled people see 899.

850 General considerations

8500 Although the incidence of disability is much higher among old people than among young people, and there is therefore a substantial need for suitable housing, the pattern of severe disability is dissimilar, with proportionately fewer people needing comprehensively planned wheelchair housing; for related discussion see 1712. The primary need among old people is for housing designed to mobility standards.

8501 All schemes of grouped flatlets for old people which are warden-serviced should be to mobility standards; in respect of ground floor accommodation this will not be difficult to achieve since MHLG Circular 82/69 requires that all accommodation is accessible by enclosed circulation areas [1].

Lift access

8502 The upper floors of flatlets schemes ought also to be mobility standards. A drawback is that in two storey housing a lift is not at present (March 1976) admissible for housing subsidy; it is only allowed for schemes of three storeys or higher.

8503 In the case of schemes by district councils a lift may be paid for by the county council under section 56 of the Local Government Act 1958 which says 'A county council may make any contribution the council think fit to expenditure of the council of a county district in the county'.
When a contribution of this kind is made by a county council to a district council the district council will benefit directly when its housing revenue account is in deficit or in balance; when it is technically in surplus the contribution will in effect go partly to the Government.

8504 It is also desirable that self-contained dwellings for old people (category 1 schemes) are to mobility standards, incorporating a lift in the case of two storey schemes.

851 Location of housing for disabled old people

8510 Some old people prefer to live in communities composed predominantly of other old people, and others prefer to live in communities where there are young families. Studies made of social needs have shown that there is no overwhelming preference for either arrangement, but that the preferences of individuals are correlated with the type of accommodation in which they happen to live, meaning that they prefer what they know rather than what they do not know [2].

Elderly neighbours

8511 No studies have been made among elderly disabled people to assess their preferences, but it may be that the majority would prefer to be in communities where their immediate neighbours are also elderly people rather than where there are young families. Elderly disabled people, even more than young disabled people, rely extensively on neighbours for physical, social and emotional support. They may depend on neighbours in the event of an emergency; if these happen to be young people not usually at home, their morale, self-sufficiency and security may be affected. A further point is that whereas non-disabled people may be able without difficulty to get out to local old people's clubs to satisfy their social needs, disabled old people are likely to be much more restricted in their mobility, and there is therefore among them perhaps a greater need to become socially involved with the group of people among whom they live.

8512 A suggested tactic for the siting of dwellings for elderly disabled people is that they should be part of a grouped scheme for old people, surrounded by housing occupied by families. In this way, elderly disabled people would have the benefit of the company of other old people but would also have a link with younger people, whom they could watch and talk to and who might help with the occasional household activities beyond the capacity of old people.

Social contact

8513 The need to devise solutions which facilitate social contact is emphasized here because studies have shown that among elderly people the satisfying of social needs is commonly of more importance than the satisfying of physical needs. The following comment comes from a study of the rehousing of old people:

'Old people's acceptance of the amount of contact which they had with other people tied in more closely (to their overall satisfaction) than their responses to such questions as the adequacy of heating or the size of rooms. The significance of this particular result is brought out by other, more general studies of old people which have shown that a variety of activities and contacts are related to their personal adjustment and morale. It seems therefore that provision for social contacts should be regarded as a central and not a marginal part of an architect's brief when planning a scheme.' [3].

Rehousing in same neighbourhood

8514 Where elderly disabled people have to be rehoused, their new homes should be located close to their old home. Because of their limited mobility, in conjunction with a lack of personal transport, elderly disabled people may find it difficult either to establish new social contacts or to maintain contacts with friends from the area in which they lived previously. If it is not possible to rehouse in the immediate vicinity of their previous home it is

[1] Bib 93630
[2] Bib 93616, p81; 93601, p62.
[3] Bib 93616, p82

desirable that elderly disabled people should be rehoused alongside former neighbours. The report quoted above says:

'It is clear that physical infirmity and not age is the important personal factor which affects activities outside the home and social contacts. The tendency of the housebound to be socially isolated has been amply documented in other studies. Although the proportion of old people with physical infirmities who are rehoused in independent accommodation is small, the present survey has revealed their particular vulnerability to this type of change. It is in general unwise to move them to outlying estates unless there are facilities or persons to assist them in re-establishing contacts. It seems that this infirm group is particularly suited to housing which forms part of the re-development of central areas.' [4]

852 Old people: Wheelchair housing

8520 Any wheelchair housing units for old people should be in schemes where there is a warden to give supervision.

Category 1 schemes

8521 In the case of category 1 schemes as described in MHLG Circular 82/69, where dwelling units are self-contained, with limited communal provision, space standards should be as for independent wheelchair housing, with an addition to allow for wheelchair circulation. Space standards are summarized in table 81.3.
At the current time (March 1976) space and amenity standards for old people's housing are under review by the Department of the Environment.

Category 2 schemes

8522 In category 2 schemes, where single-person dwelling units need not be self-contained and where there is undercover circulation throughout, with comprehensive communal facilities, space standards should be as for normal category 2 old people's units, with a slightly larger percentage increase for wheelchair circulation than for category 1 units.

8523 For old people's housing schemes, a larger proportion of units may be suitable for chairbound people than is recommended for general purpose housing; up to 25 per cent is suggested.

Kitchens

8524 Among old people who need wheelchair housing there is the possibility that some, for example those affected by hemiplegia or arthritis, may prefer to stand to work in the kitchen. The fixing of kitchen units should be delayed until tenants' requirements are ascertained.

[4] Bib 93616, p82

Garaging

8525 In an old people's housing scheme containing wheelchair units there is a possibility that some tenants will be issued with invalid tricycles by the Department of Health. It is however improbable that there will be so many that the normally recommended provision for old people's housing of one car space for each four units should be increased, and it is likely that such provision will be needlessly generous.

8526 The suggested provision is hardstandings, allowing for the incorporation of carports if required.

853 Communal facilities in grouped schemes

8530 In grouped schemes for old people where provision is made for wheelchair users it is not necessary in common room areas to increase the floor space required under MHLG Circular 82/69 (8053).

8531 The cloakroom adjoining the common room containing wc and hand basin should be accessible to wheelchair users.

8532 Communal rooms or areas used by tenants, for example pantry, kitchen, laundry room, guestroom and warden's office, should be accessible to wheelchair users.

8533 Where communal refrigerators are provided for the storage of tenants' milk, butter etc it must not be necessary for any tenant to walk up or down stairs to reach their refrigerator.

8534 The telephone for use by tenants should be planned for use by chairbound people.

8535 For notes on alarm call systems in grouped flatlet schemes for elderly disabled people see 898.

854 Welfare facilities in old people's schemes

8540 In the development of new sheltered housing schemes which include provision for disabled old people, the social services authority may consider it desirable to incorporate special welfare facilities in addition to, or to a higher standard than, the minimum required by MHLG Circular 82/69. In such cases, the grant may be either for capital expenditure or may be made annually if it is related to improved servicing. In other cases the housing authority or housing association may wish to improve the quality of provision generally, and although the additional cost may not be subsidizable and may not be attributable to specific welfare benefits the social services authority can if it wishes make a grant to reduce any deficit incurred.

860 House adaptations: General considerations

8600 As discussed in the commentary (1715) existing housing ought where practicable to be adapted, so that disabled people can stay in their own homes.

8601 Social services authorities have powers to adapt housing for disabled people, under section 29 of the National Assistance Act 1948 and section 2 of the Chronically Sick and Disabled Persons Act 1970. For details of the legislation see 802.

8602 Housing authorities have concurrent powers under housing legislation to adapt dwelling units which they own (8010). Under section 56 of the Housing Act 1974 they may make grants for improvements to private dwellings lived in by disabled people (8014).

Administration by social services authorities

8603 Where a request for adaptation work is made to the social services authority, the authority may agree to cover all expenses, or may ask for a contribution from the tenant or landlord.

8604 Among works of adaptation which may qualify for a grant from the social services authority are:

1. The provision of a ramped access in place of, or in addition to, an existing step access.
2. The widening or rehanging of doors, or the substitution of sliding doors for side-hung doors.
3. The provision of easily handled door or window ironmongery.
4. The fixing of an additional handrail to the staircase.
5. The fixing of support rails by the bath or wc.
6. The raising of the wc seat.
7. Extensions or alterations to ground level accommodation so that there is a bath and wc at ground level.
8. Alterations to kitchen fittings so that they can be conveniently used.
9. The substitution of lever handles for screw-down tap fittings.
10. The provision of a ceiling track carrying an electrically or manually operated hoist.
11. The installation of a stair lift.
12. The relocation of prepayment meters for gas or electricity.
13. The relocation of electric socket outlets and switches.
14. The provision of driveways and crossings for invalid tricycles.

8605 The majority of adaptation work is of an unsophisticated character, not necessitating the advice of an architect. It is carried out directly by the social services authority, or in the case of local authority housing by the direct works department of the housing authority working to instructions from the social services authority. In the case of more extensive adaptation work the social services authority will require a detailed estimate, or for competitive tenders to be submitted.

8606 Regarding the selection of equipment for adaptation work, architects and others are recommended to seek the advice of the Disabled Living Foundation (94).

861 Adaptations to existing local authority housing

8610 In respect of local authority housing, both social services and housing authorities have powers to adapt dwellings for disabled people.

Minor works

8611 The general practice is that works of a minor character, for example the fixing of a second rail to the staircase, the fixing of support rails by bath or wc or the raising of a wc seat, are undertaken by the social services authority. Initiatives will normally come from a domiciliary social worker who, with an occupational therapist, can determine what provision will be appropriate, and can arrange for the work to be carried out without delay. Most social services authorities have a ruling whereby adaptation works costing less than a certain sum (perhaps £100 or £200) can be put in hand with the approval of director or area director of social services and without reference to the committee, given of course that funds are available.

8612 Where a county council adapts a property owned by a district council it may make an agreement on the lines adopted by Cheshire, whereby the property is reinstated when the handicapped person moves out, provided that first, the adaptations mean that the dwelling is not suitable for use by a non-disabled tenant and second, that the district council is not able to let the dwelling to another handicapped person, or to a family having a handicapped member [1].

Structural adaptations: Subsidy arrangements

8613 The costs of specially approved items for new dwellings specifically designed for physically handicapped people are admissible for purposes of calculating reckonable expenditure for subsidy [2]. Housing authorities may also request subsidy for adaptations to existing accommodation to bring it up to a standard which would be acceptable under the recommended provisions for new dwellings for disabled people.

8614 Because no special subsidy is available to social services authorities when they carry out adaptations (the cost being met from the general rates fund) whereas the subsidy available to housing authorities under the Housing Rents and Subsidies Act 1975 is generous, it is advantageous for metropolitan district councils and London

---

[1] Bib 93108, p38
[2] Instructions are given in paragraph 15 (iv) of DoE Circular 59/74 (Bib 93715).

borough councils to transfer the cost of local authority house adaptations from their social services budget to the housing revenue account, and in county district areas for county councils and district councils to make a mutually satisfactory arrangement whereby major adaptations to local authority houses are paid for by the housing authority. Because of the administrative complexity of the procedure – requests for subsidy must be channelled through the DoE regional office and delays may occur – it will not as a rule be worth claiming subsidy for minor adaptations.

8615　At the time this advice is given (March 1976) it is unclear how the procedure for claiming subsidy will generally operate. It may be similar to that for special provision in new housing, whereby an estimate of the additional cost is submitted to DoE for approval. In the case of adaptations it is more difficult to establish suitable levels of expenditure on a theoretical basis. The expectation is that competitive tenders will have to be obtained from which the amount admissible for subsidy can be determined; in the event of overspending or underspending adjustments will need to be made.

8616　Works of adaptation which ought generally to be admissible for subsidy are broadly the same as items allowed as provisions in new dwellings for disabled people, detailed in tables 87.1 and 87.2.

862　**Adaptations to privately rented accommodation**

8620　The main responsibility for adapting privately rented accommodation lies at present (1976) with social services authorities.

8621　The arrangements made by Cheshire are that the county council meets the cost by a full grant, provided that, first, the owner is willing for the work to be carried out; second, there is a formal leasing arrangement which gives the tenant security of tenure; and third, the landlord undertakes not to increase the rent as a result of the adaptations [3].

8622　In practice there are often obstacles. The landlord may simply not want to have the work done. He may wish the tenant to move, and refuses to cooperate by pressing the social services and housing authorities to move the tenant to local authority accommodation. He may see the operation as a means of raising the rent without substantial expenditure on his part. If the tenancy is controlled, ie the rent of the sitting tenant cannot be legally raised, he may see it as a technique for decontrolling the tenancy by having the premises altered.

863　**Adaptations to owner-occupied accommodation**

8630　As with rented accommodation, social services authorities have power to adapt owner-occupied accommodation.

8631　The arrangements made by Cheshire County Council as described in *Made to measure* read as follows:

'Where an owner-occupied house is to be adapted to meet the needs of a handicapped person who is either the owner or a close relative of the owner, the county council will expect the owner to make a financial contribution towards the cost of the adaptation if he has adequate liquid assets to do so. If an applicant has the resources to pay the whole or part of the cost without hardship but is unwilling to make a contribution the application may be declined.

'In cases where the owner-occupier is unable to contribute in this way, the cost is met by grants and loans from the county council, as follows:
(i)　the first £300 of the cost is met by a grant in all cases.
(ii)　if the adaptations cost more than this, the amount by which the value of the property is enhanced is assessed, and this amount is offered as an interest-free loan to the owner, repayable to the county council on the sale or disposal of the property.
(iii)　any further sum required to meet the total cost is made as a grant.

'Thus where the value of the property is not increased as a result of the adaptation, the total can be met by a grant. Where a loan is involved, the county land agent assesses the enhanced value of the property and the clerk of the county council prepares the legal agreement with the owner covering the terms of the loan.

'If an owner-occupier is prepared to make his own arrangements to carry out the adaptation work, and can make a substantial contribution to the cost himself, the county council may consider making a grant, provided that the work is carried out to the satisfaction of the county architect and that it meets the need of the handicapped person.' [4]

8632　These arrangements could with advantage be followed by other social services authorities. If, in the long term, responsibility for adaptations to owner-occupied houses were transferred to housing authorities the administration would be similar.

[3] Bib 93108, p38
[4] Bib 93108, p38

864 Adaptations using house renovation grants

8640 Under section 56 of the Housing Act 1974, disabled people living in owner-occupied or rented accommodation may be entitled to improvement grants to help finance adaptations where their existing accommodation is not suitable for them, or where basic amenities are not accessible on account of their disability. The relevant powers are detailed in 8013–9.

8641 Examples of possible entitlements are for the building on of a downstairs bathroom where, in a typical detached or semi-detached house, the upstairs bathroom is inaccessible to a disabled person not able to walk upstairs, the building on of a bedroom for a child who is handicapped, or the building on of an office for a handicapped person who conducts his business from his home.

Conditions for grants
8642 The award of a grant will generally be subject to the normal conditions and terms. Apart from those noted in 8013–5, these include the following:

1. The dwelling must conform with requirements in respect of life and standards, though these can be waived by the housing authority if they are satisfied that the dwelling cannot be made to reach the standard at reasonable expense.

2. The applicant, who need not himself be disabled, must have the necessary title to the dwelling, ie own the freehold or a leasehold having at least five years to run.

3. In the case of owner-occupied property, the owner occupier will have to certify that the dwelling will be his only or main residence, and that it will be occupied for a period of five years by him or members of his household.

4. In the case of rented accommodation, the landlord will have to certify that for a period of five years the dwelling will be let or available for letting as a residence, and not for a holiday, to a person other than a member of his family.

5. If these conditions are breached, for example if the property is sold, the owner will be liable to refund the grant, plus compound interest, on demand by the housing authority. The authority may, at its discretion, demand a lesser sum or no sum at all.

8643 Apart from the rateable value bar noted in 8014, there would appear to be no circumstances where a house adaptation proposed by a social services authority for a handicapped client under section 2 of the Chronically Sick Act would not be eligible for an improvement grant under section 56 of the Housing Act 1974. In special circumstances the eligible cost limit could be raised by the housing authority, or the additional sum could be paid by the social services authority. Equally, the social services authority could under section 2 carry the share of the cost not covered by the grant, and normally paid by the applicant.

865 Adaptations to new local authority housing

8650 Adaptations to new local authority housing, meaning special provisions for individual disabled tenants, are admissible for subsidy under the Housing Rents and Subsidies Act 1975. As discussed in the commentary (1718) it is recommended that the cost of all provisions should be carried by the housing authority, rather than being paid in part by the social services authority.

866 Adaptations to housing by health authorities

8660 Health authorities in Britain are responsible for undertaking adaptations to housing for renal dialysis patients; for details see 88.

870 Public authority housing: Administration of costs

8700 The administration of cost allowances for housing for disabled people is detailed in DoE Circular 92/75 *Wheelchair and mobility housing: standards and costs* [1]. Additional allowances to supplement the basic yardstick may be claimed for dwelling units designed as wheelchair or mobility housing in conformity with the recommendations in DoE Housing Development Directorate Occasional Papers 2/75 *Wheelchair housing* and 2/74 *Mobility housing* [2,3].

8701 The administration of the housing cost yardstick is currently (March 1976) under review by the Department of the Environment. While the general administration of cost controls may be revised, it can be expected that any new system will continue to afford financial incentives to local authorities to develop wheelchair and mobility housing, and that the two stage procedure for wheelchair housing will be maintained.

871 Mobility housing

8710 An additional allowance, currently £50 per dwelling exclusive of regional variation, may be claimed for each dwelling designated as mobility housing. Planning must conform with recommendations in HDDOP 2/74 and paragraphs 8.01–8.06 of 2/75; these are as detailed in section 82, except that in two storey stairlift provision dwellings the entrance must have a ramped or level approach and flush threshold. An entrance step (8274) is not admissible.

8711 It may be expected that the additional allowance will be largely absorbed by the ramped entrance feature. Where it is not, spare resources may be used to improve the dwelling generally or on the incorporation of facilities listed in 8251.

Stairlift
8712 In that it is a removable and reusable piece of special equipment provided for a particular disabled person, a stairlift installed in a two storey mobility housing unit should be paid for by the social services authority rather than the housing authority. In exceptional cases where the housing authority can demonstrate that there is no realistic alternative if it is to meet its statutory obligations, a stairlift may be provided by the housing authority. In such cases a submission may be made to DoE for the capital cost to be subsidized, on the same basis as other approved adaptations to existing local authority dwellings for disabled people.

[1] Bib 93121
[2] Bib 93120
[3] Bib 93111

872 Wheelchair housing

8720 For wheelchair housing the intention is that the basic yardstick supplemented by the additional allowance will be sufficient to cover all essential provisions but not refinements. This is referred to in Circular 92/75 as stage 1. Subsequently, when the disabled person who is to occupy the dwelling is known and his specific requirements can be ascertained, ad hoc allowances may be claimed for special fittings or equipment needed; this is known as stage 2.

8721 Table 87.1 lists items which if they are required should be included at stage 1. Table 87.2 lists items which may be admissible at stage 2. There is no prescribed demarcation line between stage 1 and stage 2 items, and items in the stage 2 list may be incorporated at stage 1, given that finance is available.

8722 The stage 1 list includes:
1. Items which in ordinary housing are required to satisfy Parker Morris standards.
2. Items (including extra space) necessary to ensure that the accommodation is basically convenient for a tenant who uses a wheelchair.
Supplementary provision not qualifying under these two headings and not potentially entitled to a stage 2 allowance ought also to be incorporated at stage 1 if it is considered desirable. Such provision includes:
3. Items which are not mandatory for ordinary housing or regarded as essential for wheelchair housing.
4. Items which in ordinary housing would be paid for by the tenant, but which in wheelchair housing the architect decides to include in the building contract.

8723 Table 87.2 lists examples of special equipment which may be eligible for cost subsidy at stage 2; it is not intended to be exhaustive.

Social services authority items
8724 The following special provisions may be incorporated in new wheelchair housing but their cost should be met by the social services authority. They will not as a rule be included in the housing contract.
1. A hydraulically or electrically operated patient hoist.
2. A Possum mark 2 control unit for opening doors, turning on lights and controlling radio or television.

8725 In two storey wheelchair housing having an accessible bedroom and bathroom at entrance level, upstairs accommodation will not be planned for wheelchair use. In exceptional circumstances the incorporation of a stairlift may be required; it should be treated as an adaptation and paid for by the social services authority.

Health authority items

8726 Certain special provisions for disabled tanants in wheelchair housing are provided by the health authority. They include the installation of a Possum mark 1 control unit for opening doors, turning on lights, operating radio and tv, using the telephone etc, and the installation of an electrically operated turning bed.

Portable equipment

8727 Items of portable equipment which may be supplied through the social services or health authority and are not a part of the contract include portable ramps, portable shower chairs, bath seats, storage trolleys and cleaning trolleys.

Table 87.1 Wheelchair housing: Schedule of stage 1 items

Space
1. Dwelling area in excess of Parker Morris space standards, on the basis suggested in table 81.3.

Access
2. Ramped approach to any entrance door, with flush threshold.

Doors and windows
3. Doors of adequate width for wheelchair manoeuvre.
4. Sliding doors in place of side-hung doors where appropriate.
5. Suitable door ironmongery.
6. Door construction allowing for fixing auxiliary rails.
7. Vision panels to doors.
8. Cupboard at entrance door for delivery of letters, parcels etc.
9. Window furniture and ironmongery generally, including curtain track.
10. Windows giving view from wheelchair, including bay windows.

Walls and floors
11. Partition walls to bathroom and wc which allow for the fixing of support rails.
12. Ceiling and wall structures allowing for carrying a track for an electric hoist.
13. Structural walls etc affording effective thermal insulation.
14. Protection to salient angles of wall corners, or hard plaster.

Heating and electrical services
15. Heating installation capable of maintaining living and dining areas at 22°C, and other areas at 17°C.
16. Socket outlets generally, including for charging batteries to electric wheelchairs and invalid tricycles.
17. Rocker switch plates.
18. Emergency call system in warden-serviced schemes.

Floor and wall finishes
19. Slip-resistant floor finishes to kitchens and bathroom.
20. Carpeting to living rooms, bedrooms etc.
21. Tiling to bathroom walls.

Kitchens
22. Kitchen fixtures suitable for wheelchair use, or potentially adaptable.

Bathrooms and wcs
23. Suitable bath with platform at head end.
24. Suitable wash basin.
25. Suitable wc for wheelchair use.
26. Additional wc in single storey 5 person unit.
27. Plumbing services allowing for the subsequent installation of a shower.
28. Lever action taps in place of screw-down taps.

Bedrooms
29. Built-in cupboards allowing for wheelchair access.

External facilities
30. Rotary clothes dryers.
31. Wider garden paths.

Garaging
32. Integral carport allowing for wheelchair use.

Table 87.2 Wheelchair housing: Schedule of potentially admissible stage 2 items

1. Repositioning of fixed equipment to suit individual tenant requirements.
2. Electrically operated remotely controlled lock and latch to entrance door.
3. Remotely controlled window opening devices.
4. Kicking plates to internal side-hung doors.
5. Protective edgings to door frames, hanging stiles etc.
6. Support rails alongside bath and wc.
7. Ceiling track for electric hoist.
8. Supplementary electrical installations.
9. Special kitchen fixtures and equipment to suit individual tenant requirements.
10. Built-in refrigerator if required by disabled housewife.
11. Built-in split-level cooker if required by disabled housewife.
12. Waste disposal unit to kitchen sink.
13. Shower in place of bath, or supplementary to bath.
14. Remotely controlled taps to wash basin or kitchen sink.
15. Special wc appliances, for example a Clos o mat.
16. Alterations to wc fixtures to suit individual tenant requirements.
17. Enclosed garage for chairbound car driver.
18. Automatic opening doors to garage.

88 Home dialysis

880 Home dialysis treatment

8800 The job of the kidneys is to remove waste products and excess water from the body. These accumulate mainly as a result of the breakdown and use of food in the body; they are removed from the blood by the kidneys and are passed out of the body through the bladder as urine. When the kidneys fail to function as they should, waste products are retained in the body, a condition which is fatal if not treated. The preferred remedy is the transplantation of a healthy kidney from a donor, but for any patient in need of a transplant the likelihood of there being a matching kidney immediately available is small. The alternative is to employ an artificial kidney.

8801 An artificial kidney cleanses the blood by imitating the action of a natural kidney. Blood is pumped from an artery in the patient's arm and passes over a thin plastic membrane in a bath of dialysing solution of chemical concentrate and softened water. Water and waste products pass through the membrane (the dialyser) and the purified blood is then taken back into the veins.

Hospital versus home dialysis
8802 A typical dialysing regime is three eight hour sessions each week. In the early years of kidney machines, dialysis was carried out in special hospital units, a practice which still applies in many countries. There are three principal disadvantages of relying on permanent hospital dialysis: first, it is time-consuming for the patient to travel repeatedly from home to hospital and back again; second, the new hospital beds allocated to dialysis would soon be fully used and no new patients could be taken on; and third, there is the hazard of hepatitis (inflammation of the liver) from infected blood.

8803 The alternative, now the usual course of action in Britain, is to set up the dialysing machinery in the patient's own home. Hospital dialysis is a temporary measure only, the objective being to get the patient on to home dialysis as quickly as possible. From the time that the patient starts dialysing at hospital the programme of setting up the necessary equipment is put into operation; if all goes well he is able to transfer as soon as he has completed training at hospital, a course usually taking some three months.

8804 Advice on the administration of home dialysis is given in an official circular from the Department of Health and Social Security, HSC(IS)11 *Services for chronic renal failure* [1]. The material which follows draws extensively on the advice given in this circular, and on the report on home dialysis issued by the Scottish Local Authorities Special Housing Group [2]. Notes on the estimated need for home dialysis units are in 1719.

[1] Bib 93271
[2] Bib 93113

881 The management of home dialysis

8810 For home dialysis, an adapted room reserved exclusively for the purpose is required, or a cabin installed in the garden. Because of the infection hazard it is critically important that the room is used only for dialysing; before and after each session the room has to be thoroughly cleaned.

8811 A patient on dialysis can continue to do a full-time job, though he is not able to spend more than three or four consecutive days and nights away from home. He normally dialyses late in the day; when accustomed to the routine he can, after initial checks that the machinery is working properly, relax and go to sleep since the system has built-in alarms.

The dialysis room
8812 To the lay observer the sight of all the clinical equipment and associated paraphernalia in a home dialysing room is awesome. It appears that the apparatus of a hospital intensive care unit has been assembled there, and the fact that people without medical training are expected to cope with it seems daunting.

8813 In the middle of the room is the bed, on which the patient lies when he has connected himself to his control unit by means of injections and plastic tubing; as an alternative he may sit in an easy chair but a bed is more usual. The control unit is beside him, with knobs to control the flow and pressure of the blood, and dials, supplemented by alarm systems, to tell him whether all is going to plan, whether he is losing blood or not losing water. Associated with the machine is a blood pump to boost the flow of blood to the dialyser. There is a water supply to the dialyser, drawn off the mains with a non-return valve, and passing through a water softener.

8814 Beside the bed is a telephone, to call aid in the event of the machinery going wrong; if it does, the patient simply switches off and starts again later when the fault is corrected. There may also be an alarm call for summoning help from the family. In the rare circumstance that the patient is living on his own, he may have an intercom to the front door and a door opening device. If there is a risk of power cuts he will have an emergency electricity supply from an external generator.

8815 On one side of the room is a large sink and drainer for cleaning the dialysing membrane when the session is over. Because it is relatively inexpensive the normal facility is a reusable membrane, but some hospitals provide their patients with disposable membranes, in which case a standard domestic sink is sufficient. Around the room are rows of storage shelves for the variety of packages of sterilized materials and equipment used by the patient. Elsewhere are buckets and mops, a sphygmomanometer for the patient to take his own blood pressure, a weighing machine to check before and after session weight, and perhaps a television set (not provided by the hospital authority) to pass the time while dialysing is in progress.

882   Alternative provisions for dialysis

8820   Alternative means of providing a home dialysis unit are by:
1. Adapting an existing room.
2. Installing a prefabricated portable cabin alongside the house.
3. Building a purpose-designed extension.
4. Rehousing in more suitable accommodation, adapted as necessary.

Adapting existing room

8821   Of these, option 1 is preferred; the adaptation of an existing room, if one is available, is the most economical procedure. There is also the point that the dialysis room is part of the home rather than being an appendage, though there is the disadvantage that it is impossible to avoid the pervading odours generated in the room.

Portable cabin

8822   The advantage of a portable cabin is that when no longer needed it can be transported and reused for another patient. There is always the possibility that the person using it, or for whom it is intended, will receive a kidney transplant, and there is also the fact that the mortality rate among people on dialysis is significantly higher than among normal able-bodied people.

8823   The detachment of the cabin from the house is sometimes an advantage; for ordinary living purposes the patient has a normal home and can ignore the existence of the special unit. The principal disadvantage is the expense; apart from the cost of the cabin unit, services are likely to be more expensive than with a house adaptation, and on an awkward site foundation costs can be substantial. In the case of terraced housing the only way to get a cabin into the garden may be by means of a crane.

Purpose-designed extension

8824   Constructing a purpose-designed extension is not as a rule a viable proposition. If there is room for an extension there will also be room for a cabin which will invariably be preferred on account of the urgency with which the facility is needed. A doubtful alternative which has been promoted is the use of a standard demountable prefabricated extension [3]. In the long term an integrated room extension has the advantage that when the unit is no longer needed there is extra accommodation in the home.

[3] For example in Bib 93313

Rehousing

8825   If it happens that the patient's existing home does not have a room suitable for adaptation and there is no space for a cabin, the only solution is rehousing. In such cases local authorities are generally extremely cooperative, moving dialysis patients to the top of the housing list on health grounds. There is then a search for suitable accommodation which gives an extra room. Desirably the room should be on the ground floor, less desirably on the first floor; above this, services are expensive to incorporate. In rural areas, finding suitable housing may be relatively easy; in urban areas it can be a problem and in inner London boroughs extremely difficult.

Contingency planning

8826   A possible strategy for local housing authorities is to build contingency dialysis housing, planned with a downstairs room having the infrastructure of services which can be plugged in when needed. There might be administrative problems of insuring that such houses could be taken over at short notice for dialysis patients, but experiments could usefully be made. A possibility is that dialysis housing units could have a dual role as wheelchair housing, as discussed in the commentary (1711).

883   Requirements for adapted rooms

8830   Where there is no alternative, a room as small as 8.0m² can be adapted to take a home dialysis unit; the preferred minimum area is 11.0m². The room should be planned to accommodate the following furniture and equipment:
1. A single bed 2·000 × 0·900.
2. A bedside table.
3. A control unit approx 0·610 × 0·700 × 1·220 high.
4. A dialyser with container. This will be either (1) a mobile coil or disposable dialyser, either of which will be approx 0·400 × 0·500 × 1·200 high, or (2) a tilt trolley mounted board dialyser approx 1·000 × 0·500 × 1·200 high.
5. A water softener, approx 0·380 × 0·380 × 1·200 high.
6. A sink and drainer of glass fibre or stainless steel. The unit should be not less than 1·000 long if reusable membranes are to be used. Tap nozzles should be approx 0·450 above the rim of the sink.
7. Open shelving 0·300 and 0·350 deep, approx length 12·000. Where space is limited it is not necessary that all of this is in the dialyser room.

Services

8831   Services should be provided as follows:
1. Mains water supply, minimum water pressure 140kN/m², with non-return valve to serve water softener. Treated water should pass through plastic or stainless steel pipework diameter 0·013, terminating in a stopcock. The connection between the stopcock and the dialyser is by flexible plastic hose.

2. Mains water supply to sink, with water heater to hot supply if the domestic system is not adequate. Mains water supply is necessary to avoid contamination of water in a standing tank.

3. Trapped plastic waste connected to drainage for dialyser effluent.

4. Drainage outlet for water softener overflow.

5. 20A electricity supply to control unit. The trend in machine design is for operation from a 13A socket outlet.

6. Double 13A socket outlet. This is in addition to supplies for the control unit and water heater.

7. Two way light switch with drop cord switch by bed. A fluorescent light fitting is preferred.

8. Telephone point. The telephone, located on the bedside table, will be an extension to the house telephone.

9. Alarm call device. This may not be needed where the telephone can be used to summon assistance.

10. Intercom and remote control front door opening device. This will be required only when the patient may be alone when dialysing.

11. 3kW convector heater.

12. Extract fan. This may not be needed where ventilation is adequate.

13. Changeover switch for emergency generator, with suitable connections. This will be required only if there is a risk of electricity cuts.

Wall and floor finishes

8832 Wall finishes should be of washable vinyl. A tiled or plastic laminate splashback 0·500 high should be incorporated over the sink and drainer.

8833 The floor should be of jointless waterproof vinyl sheet with coved skirtings. The skirting, minimum 0·015 high, may be continued across the door opening to contain water when the floor is washed.

8834 The door may have a glazed inspection panel and cylinder night latch.

884 **Requirements for portable cabins**

8840 A typical portable cabin usable for home dialysis has dimensions approx 5·000 × 2·800 (diagram 88.1). It will be supplied fully finished to receive hospital equipment.

8841 Mains electricity, water and drainage should be supplied to the cabin.

885 **Home dialysis: Administration of services**

8850 In Britain, health authorities are responsible for the financing and administration of home dialysis services, through the agency of haemodialysis units associated with major hospitals. In cases where

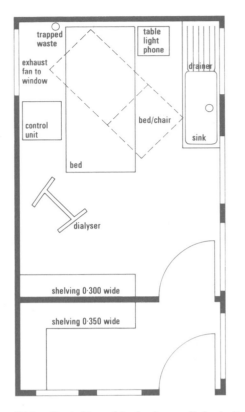

88.1 Portable cabin for home dialysis (1:50)

rehousing in, or adaptation of, local authority accommodation is involved, the health authority will coordinate adaptation work with the local housing authority. The social services authority will not as a rule be concerned.

8851 The area health authority responsible for the hospital unit will also be responsible for all capital and maintenance expenditure on the home unit. The only exception is that where the hospital unit and patient's home come under different area health authorities but the same regional health authority, it is for local decision which area authority takes financial responsibility.

8852 For dialysing the room temperature ought not to be less than 21°C, and to avoid damage to the kidney machine the room temperature ought never to fall below 4°C. It has been agreed by the Department of Health that the cost of maintaining a dialysis room, either in a house or portable cabin, at 21°C during dialysis and at 4°C at other times is carried by the area health authority [4]. Where electricity is used to heat the dialysis room, area health authorities are asked to arrange for the supply to be metered separately, provided the cost is reasonable. Where a house is centrally heated, the cost of supplementary electric heating can be met if it is needed to boost the room temperature for dialysis, but no contribution is made by the health authority to central heating costs.

[4] Bib 93271, appendix a, para 1.

890 The incidence of accidents in the home

8900 Deaths due to accidents in the home are recorded and analysed in the quarterly returns issued by the Registrar General. In the first quarter of 1974 there were 1793 deaths in England and Wales due to accidents in the home and residential institutions; of these 1085 (61 per cent) were falls. Of these falls, 750 (69 per cent) were by women. People aged 65 and over make up 14 per cent of the total population but account for 69 per cent of home accidents [1].

8901 The majority of non-fatal home accidents are not notified and comprehensive data on injuries are not therefore available. Surveys indicate that people who are very young, very old or disabled are particularly prone to accidents. Among accidents in the home, the most frequent are those which occur in the kitchen, followed by those in the living room and on staircases. Nearly all staircase accidents occur when the individual is descending.

8902 A survey made in 1963 found that the greatest incidence of injury from home accidents occurs among children aged under five, and that the greatest incidence of death occurs among old people [2]. It is estimated that for each fatal home accident there are 200 non-fatal injuries.

891 Design factors in the causation of home accidents

8910 Faulty planning and design can contribute to home accidents. An analysis of records of accidents made by the Building Research Station suggested that 8 per cent could be attributed to faulty design [3].

8911 In a survey of homes in Aberdeen where accidents had occurred the following potential causes of accidents were observed [4]:
1. Unguarded fires.
2. Non-safety taps on kitchen cooking appliances.
3. Highly polished floors.
4. Worn steps.
5. Poor staircase lighting.
6. Inadequate kitchen work surfaces.
7. Trailing flex.
8. Loose mats.
9. Multiple appliances on one plug.

8912 A study made for the British Medical Association discovered accident hazards in 914 out of 1602 homes studied, of which the following were most frequently noted [5]:
1. No handrails to stairs.
2. Sharp bends on stairs.
3. Too many steps inside the home.
4. No lighting to outside steps.
5. Dark passages.
6. Gas meters placed too high.
7. Kitchen shelves fixed too high.

The architect's role

8913 Architects can help to avoid unnecessary hazards by designing housing on the assumption that it will be used by disabled people. The observance of the accident prevention check list below is suggested; numbers in brackets refer to paragraph and section numbers in the main text.

892 Prevention of accidents in the home: Check list

8920 Staircases, steps
Avoid single steps (3111).
Avoid steps less than 0·100 high (3112).
Avoid open risers (3120).
Avoid winders (3121).
Provide handrails to each side of any staircase (3301).
Extend handrail horizontally beyond top and bottom steps (3322).
Illuminate staircases adequately (3124).

8921 Doors
Raised thresholds if provided to be at step nosings (3400).
Avoid internal threshold sills if no carpet (3420).
Avoid inswinging doors to bathrooms and wcs (36004).
Doors to bathrooms and wcs to be openable from outside (36341).

8922 Windows
Windows at upper levels to be safe for young children (3513).
Out-opening windows at ground level to be planned to avoid hazards (3503).
Window controls comfortably reachable (3531).
Allow for access to windows for cleaning (3506).

8923 Floor finishes
Floor surfaces to be slip-resistant (3810).

8924 Water services
Hot water to be thermostatically controlled to reduce scalding risks (4110).

8925 Heating
Adequate space heating to be provided to avoid use of portable heaters (420).

8926 Electrical services, lighting
Two way light switches to be generously provided (4320).
Socket outlets to be switched and shuttered (4342).
Socket outlets to be in accessible positions (4352).
Illumination levels to be adequate (4383).
Allow for easy access to prepayment meters (4364).

[1] Data here are drawn from Bib 93781, p29.
[2] Bib 93772
[3] Bib 93776
[4] Bib 93773, p63
[5] Bib 93772

8927 Kitchens
Working area of kitchen to be efficiently planned (51010).
Work surfaces to be planned to minimize need for lifting or carrying hot liquids etc (51103).
Work surface to be provided to either side of hob (51136).
Hot plates and cooker controls to be arranged to minimize hazards (51430, 51450).
Provide adequate accessible storage accommodation (51310).

8928 Bathrooms, wcs
Baths to have flat bottom (54621).
Support rails to be fixed adjacent to baths and wcs (5427, 5470).
Medicine cupboard to be lockable (54920).

893 The role of alarm call systems

8930 Alarm call systems installed in the homes of elderly or handicapped people need to be regarded as one component of the broad range of services which can be made available to support people whose resources – both physical and emotional – are limited. They ought not to be regarded simply as mechanical devices whose purpose is to ensure that in the event of an accident help can be summoned.

Security against isolation
8931 People who need alarm systems are in the main elderly or handicapped people living alone. In some cases an alarm installation may be valuable for a handicapped person who, while not living alone, is often left alone, but such cases are relatively rare; merely to share a household is to have the basis of security whose absence it is the role of alarm systems to counter.

8932 Invariably the pre-eminent need of elderly or handicapped people living alone is for supportive social relationships which combat isolation, loneliness, depression and insecurity. There is a need for regular calls from social workers, relatives, friends or voluntary visitors. Voluntary workers can be particularly valuable, giving companionship, helping with odd jobs about the home. In addition, many social services authorities in Britain now administer good-neighbour schemes on an organized basis, whereby elderly people are employed to visit and help other old people who are living alone.

8933 Regular and reliable visiting will mean that housebound people have an important measure of psychological and physical security. No alarm system can hope, or should be expected, to perform as a substitute for this service. Alarm systems may in practice be counter-productive, in that they may appear to afford a greater security than they do, so that friends and relatives become less bothered about making regular visits.

894 The reliability of alarm systems

8940 No mechanical alarm system can hope to guarantee 100 per cent security to handicapped people living alone. As discussed in the pages which follow, there are a variety of sophisticated systems available, aimed at insuring against almost any eventuality. The goal is not an achievable one, and it needs to be recognized that no one, whether handicapped or not, is immune to unpredictable hazards. Most normal people are not obsessively neurotic about the possibility of sudden distress; it does not occur to them that they ought for example always to wear a sensitive device against the body which raises an alarm when there is a sudden shift of heart-rate. Similarly, handicapped people are generally equally unneurotic, and it is unsurprising that they frequently reject the clever gadgetry designed to help them.

8941 Only in an institution where there are supervisory staff constantly at hand is anything approaching 100 per cent security obtainable. Old or handicapped people who opt instead to carry on living in ordinary houses are consciously electing to live at some hazard; they choose to do so because, as discussed in the commentary in relation to institutions and housing alternatives for severely disabled people, there are benefits, in terms of managing their own lives in their own places, which more than compensate for any lack of protection.

Evidence on incidents warranting alarm systems
8942 No reliable evidence is available about the nature and extent of incidents for which the use of an alarm call might be advantageous. It is not possible for example to estimate how many accidents or events causing injury to people living alone might have been averted or alleviated had the people concerned been equipped with aids for summoning assistance. This lack of pertinent evidence means that it is not difficult for manufacturers of alarm devices to claim for them an effectiveness out of proportion to their actual potential.

Old people at risk
8943 There are from time to time widely publicized cases of old people who have died unnoticed in the midst of a housing estate, and have been undiscovered for weeks after [6]. Such happenings might have been prevented by the issuing of alarm devices, but there is no simple prescription. It seems that many old people who live alone resolutely resist seeking aid when they need it, whatever the consequences.

---

[6] There was extensive press publicity in January 1973 when two such cases occurred during the same week.

8944 The moral issues here are not simple to resolve. If old people are fiercely independent and positively do not wanted to be helped, is there an entitlement on the part of others to intervene and prevent the occurrence of death, even if it only serves to prolong the life of someone who has no urge to carry on living? The answer has to be that intervention is warranted: people cannot be ignored, however cantankerous, bloody-minded, ill-tempered and ungrateful they may be. But if there is intervention it needs to be unobtrusive, on the basis that help is offered and it is up to the individual to decide whether or not it is accepted.

Deliberate non-use of alarm devices

8945 In the study of alarm systems made by the Institute for Consumer Ergonomics it was found that many old people equipped with alarm devices deliberately made no use of them, never intended to use them and put them out of action [7]. They allowed the batteries of their devices to run out and did not replace them, they left their portable aids lying in drawers, they tied pull-cord switches so that they were out of reach, or obscured them by furniture. The reasons they gave were that they did not want to disturb the person who supervised the alarm, they did not admit they were at risk, they did not like to have to ask people to come to their aid even when in need, and they did not like the way that the aid drew attention to their dependence. Of the people in the study who had experienced an emergency, less than one in four of those with alarm systems used them to summon assistance.

8946 Even if people equipped with alarm devices are willing to use them when necessary, it is essential if they are to serve their purpose that there is someone to respond when a call is made. In housing schemes where there is a resident warden this is not usually a problem. In the case of people at risk who are scattered in the community it is often very difficult to guarantee that help can be summoned. In the field study carried out by the Institute of Consumer Ergonomics, 130 cases of emergencies were recorded; in 54 of these the person concerned had been unable to draw attention to their predicament. Half waited for more than an hour for help to come, 14 for more than six hours, and for 17 help never came [8].

895 Alarm systems: Telephones

8950 The usefulness of the variety of special alarm devices available needs to be critically examined. Flashing lights, two way communication systems, buzzers and sirens, portable transmitters and the installations known as habit cycle alarms; all these have shortcomings. In the circumstances there is a powerful case for rejecting special alarm devices and opting instead for the installation of telephones.

8951 The issuing of telephones by social services authorities to handicapped people is specifically allowed for under section 2(i)(h) of the Chronically Sick and Disabled Persons Act 1970. Some social services authorities have a consistently good record for the provision of telephones, prescribing them on the recommendation of social workers; others are less generous.
A survey made by the Department of Health of aids to households showed that in the Greater London Council area in the year 1972–73 the number of telephones provided under the 1970 Act to handicapped people ranged from 12 per 100 000 total population in one London borough to 255 in another [9].

Advantages of telephones

8952 The major bonus of the telephone, by comparison with any other alarm system, is its potential for social support. For handicapped people living on their own it can be used to keep in touch with family and friends. In an emergency it can also be used to call aid with greater reliability than any alarm device. It has the further advantage that it is not perceived as a symbol of dependency, and has none of the unattractive connotations of other alarm devices.

Disadvantages

8953 Its principal disadvantage is that it is expensive. It may also be difficult for people who are deaf or hard of hearing to use, though a variety of special aids available from the Post Office (442) mean that it is a great deal more versatile than might be supposed. For deaf people a teleprinter print-out machine can be associated with a telephone, enabling them to 'talk' by telephone with other people having similar machines.

8954 The other disadvantage of the telephone as an alarm system is that it may not be to hand in places such as the bathroom or kitchen where a handicapped person may fall and need to call aid; this is however a disadvantage shared with most other devices. On balance it is evident that, particularly for handicapped people living on their own in the community, the telephone has substantial advantages over any other alarm system.

The Hull project

8955 Overwhelming evidence on the value of the telephone, both as an alarm system and as a social support, is provided by Peter Gregory's account of a project in Hull *Telephones for the elderly* [10]. One hundred housebound or near-housebound old people were issued with telephones and monitored for a year, and a control group of comparable old

[7] Bib 93881, 93882
[8] Bib 93882, p6
[9] Bib 93242
[10] Bib 93683; Bib 93684 is a brief report of the main findings.

people was checked. The results were remarkable. The telephone helped to keep old people in touch with their families, it was invaluable in emergencies, it could be used for calling the doctor and it made shopping much easier. It made no significant difference to the frequency of visiting by children or grandchildren. While it reduced visiting by other relatives, any such effects were more than offset by increased contact with friends and family. Fears that the telephone might be difficult to manage owing to lack of dexterity, coordination or worries about the strange instrument were found to be unwarranted. The evidence was not conclusive, but there were firm indications that by enabling people to look after themselves more effectively the telephone helped to keep them out of institutions. Most importantly, comparing telephone users with the control group, there was powerful evidence that the telephone was a life saver. Furthermore, of the five telephone users who died, all but one died with others about them. Of the ten in the central control group who died, four died on their own and were found on the floor some time after.

8956 In the face of this evidence of the unique worth of the telephone it seems superfluous to examine alternative alarm systems further. It also exposes clearly the fallacy of regarding alternatives simply as mechanical devices to summon aid in the event of an emergency. The notes which follow on the efficacy of alarm devices need to be read in this context.

896 Supervised alarm systems

8960 Alarm systems can be categorized by whether they rely for responses to calls on a fully supervised service, for example with a warden serving a call board, or on ad hoc means of summoning aid, for example from someone passing outside. Of the systems discussed below, two way intercoms and habit-cycle systems have to be supervised. Radio transmitters are not necessarily supervised, but in view of the likelihood that people using them will be at significant risk it is appropriate for the purposes of the discussion to assume that they are.

Two way intercom systems

8961 When installed in ordinary homes which are not part of a grouped scheme a two way intercommunication alarm system will be wired from a central control point to some 30 or more individual dwellings. The system is relatively expensive to install and there is the probability, particularly where it is provided in owner-occupied or rented accommodation, that it will not be needed by a subsequent tenant when the person to whom it is issued has died. Its advantage over the telephone is that communication can take place in all rooms of the home. It does not however have the social advantage or versatility of the telephone.

Habit-cycle alarms

8962 Habit-cycle alarm systems operate on the negative principle that the alarm is raised if the person at risk fails to act rather than doing something positive such as activating a buzzer. One example is a wired connection to the flushing handle of the wc, whereby the alarm is raised if the wc is not used during a cycle-period of say 12 hours. A second example is a pressure mat fitted on the floor or under a carpet, for example outside the kitchen door, which sends a signal when stepped on. The warden servicing the scheme has a control board of illuminated lights, normally set late at night. Each time the person flushes the wc or steps on a mat his light on the board is cancelled. An alternative habit-cycle system, operating on a positive rather than negative basis, is that each tenant has a switch to activate; if they do not do so during a 12 or 24 hour cycle the alarm is raised.

8963 On their own these habit-cycle devices do not give adequate security, particularly where they are installed in scattered dwellings. There may be good reasons why the device is not activated, for example that the handicapped person uses a commode by the bed, chooses not to get up in the morning or spends a day away from home visiting relatives. A second disadvantage is that an incident needing emergency help can occur, but remains undiscovered for many hours.

8964 In grouped housing schemes there is a danger that habit-cycle alarms may be regarded as an adequate substitute for personal surveillance. In scattered housing the elaborate system of monitoring means that a telephone will be simpler and more reliable.

Radio transmitters

8965 An alarm device with potential for people at high risk is a remote control battery operated transistorized transmitter, carried around in handbag or pocket. When activated it sends out a radio call to a receiver, converted automatically to an alarm call. The receiver is normally an aerial in the home, but it may be an inductive loop, in which case the transmitter must be inside the loop. To cover falls outside, the loop must embrace the garden as well as the dwelling.

8966 The disadvantages of a transmitter are that it is easily damaged, it can be broken if dropped and uses a battery which needs regular replacement. An inquiry made by the Department of Health among people using transmitters reported that drawbacks were that they could be inadvertently activated by high frequency radio signals, they were too bulky and were often left in a drawer by their users [11]. Further prototypes are being tested, but it is doubtful, even if a lightweight model is developed, whether the system can be suitable for general use.

[11] Reported in Hansard (House of Commons), 9 February 1973, column 948.

Other devices

8967 Pull cord alarm systems may be installed in non-grouped housing for handicapped people, but the extensive electrical servicing required usually makes them uneconomic. A disadvantage is the high risk of false alarms; visitors may suppose that the alarm is the bathroom light and the warden will be called out on an unnecessary errand.

897 Unsupervised or part-supervised alarm systems

8970 For handicapped people scattered in the community, the only feasible alarm system may be one which relies on a neighbour to respond to calls, or someone who happens to be passing. Examples are a radio transmitter or pull cord system where the alarm is sounded in the neighbour's house, a hand-held alarm buzzer or whistle which the neighbour next door can hear, or flashing lights or an illuminated sign saying 'Help' which passers-by may respond to.

8971 Systems of this kind are intrinsically unreliable. Handicapped people may not wish to ask neighbours to monitor the alarm; both sides may suspect that the alarm might be used frequently and could cause disturbance between them. If there is a neighbour willing to monitor the alarm she (or he) will either have to ask someone to sit in when she goes out or leave the handicapped person at risk.

8972 No system which relies on a passer-by hearing or seeing an alarm call can be regarded as satisfactory. Nor should there be reliance on a 'street warden' who is meant to keep a lookout for flashing light signals or similar calls. On their part, handicapped people are unlikely to want an illuminated sign outside their home advertising their vulnerability, saying (for example) 'Help, please call police'.

Access to dwelling

8973 A problem common to all alarm systems for people at risk scattered in the community is access to the dwelling by a person responding to a call. A possibility is for a neighbour to keep a key, but there are occasions when an alarm may occur, the neighbour is out and no key is available. This is a further factor in favour of issuing telephones; the handicapped person can arrange with a friend or relative living some distance away to keep a key.

898 Alarm systems: Grouped flatlet schemes

8980 In the case of warden-serviced public authority grouped flatlet schemes for old people it is mandatory that an alarm system is installed, see 8053. According to circumstances a two way intercom or pull cord buzzer and light system may be preferred.

Intercom systems

8981 A demerit of an intercom system is that it may be perceived by the handicapped person as an interference with privacy. In its favour is greater security; some intercom systems are sufficiently sensitive to pick up sounds throughout a dwelling. There is also the advantage that when a tenant calls for help the warden can make an immediate phone call if an outside service is required. An intercom system may also reduce the time which the warden needs to spend visiting tenants; this may be an advantage for the warden but not for the tenants.

8982 Where a two way intercom system is installed it should preferably allow the warden to listen in only with the tenant's knowledge. A system of this kind is noted with costs in 90220.

Buzzer and light call systems

8983 Where a buzzer and light call system is installed there should be a control board at the warden's office, with an audio and visual link to the home of any resident who serves as deputy when the warden is out. It is advantageous if the control board is outside the warden's flat so that the warden can lock his flat while he is away. Cancellation of calls should be possible only at the source of calls.

Location of alarm devices

8984 Care should be given to the location of alarm activating devices in each dwelling. It is important that an alarm can be reached by someone using the bath, and desirably the wc also. There should also be a device which can be reached by the handicapped person in bed, though it will not always be known in advance exactly where the bed will be. It is less important that an alarm call is provided in the living room.

8985 A contingency which ought to be guarded against is the handicapped person who falls and is not able to get back to a standing position but can crawl to reach an alarm call at low level. A push button on the skirting board is suggested; a suitable location is in the living room, perhaps close to the door. Care should be taken that the button is not fixed in a place where it is likely to be obscured by furniture.

8986 It may be possible to confine the alarm call for the bath and wc by fixing a protected alarm rail, of the kind used to ring bells in buses. For the bedroom a remote controlled air-operated device is suggested, as described in 4440; this device also has the advantage that it can be floated in the bath.

899   Alarm systems: Housing for severely disabled people

8990   Where a cluster of housing units is provided for severely disabled people, as described in section 84, telephones are preferred to an intercom system for calling assistance. The tenants, while being severely disabled, will generally be intelligent and capable people for whom a telephone is essential for social and other contacts. Problems may occur in respect of people with speech or hearing disabilities, or who cannot use conventional telephone equipment. The use of the equipment is the more important factor; if it can be controlled some means of transmitting messages can probably be devised. Possum equipment (446) and selected special telephone equipment for handicapped people may be prescribed.

8991   A two way intercom system might seem advantageous in the case of disabled people liable to fall and unable to summon aid by telephone. Frequent routine calls from helpers will mean however that there is a regular check, and in the circumstances a telephone should afford adequate insurance.

8992   Rather than installing a two way intercom system a possible supplementary insurance is an emergency alarm buzzer within the cluster, whereby a person at risk can summon a co-tenant who can in turn call for someone who is able to help physically. Such a system may be unsophisticated; a hand bell may serve as well as a fixed alarm.

8993   Where fixed alarm devices are installed in housing for chairbound people, their positioning should be deferred until individual requirements are ascertained.

Warden-serviced schemes

8994   In grouped housing schemes for handicapped people where staff are always on call within the building, a two way intercom system is recommended. It is helpful if the system incorporates alternative buzzers, one call to be used in the event of an emergency, which staff know they must answer immediately, and the other to be used for routine request calls.

Appendices

9

In the principal data sections of this book reference is made to selected fittings and equipment suited to disabled users. In some cases these are proprietary goods specifically designed for disabled people, in others they have a general application. The notes which follow give some indication of the cost of their provision.

In the main, prices quoted are for the supply of goods only, excluding delivery charges, value added tax and installation costs. They were checked with manufacturers and suppliers, and were those obtaining in March 1976. Prevailing market trends mean that they will in many cases be outdated by the time this book is published or soon after, and the prices noted should be regarded as giving a relative rather than an absolute indication of actual costs.

In some cases the product of a particular manufacturer is noted as an example; this does not imply that it is necessarily preferred to similar goods by other manufacturers. The cost implications of certain general recommendations are also noted, for example relating to suitable doors and ramped entrances. These have been prepared with the assistance of a chartered quantity surveyor; prices are at a level comparable with average competitive rates obtainable in the London area in early 1976.

Information regarding the current availability of proprietary goods specifically suited to the requirements of disabled people may be obtained from the Disabled Living Foundation, see 940. Reference may also be made to the catalogue *Sanitary, kitchen and ironmongery fixtures for the physically handicapped* issued by Nicholls and Clarke Ltd, Niclar House, 3/10 Shoreditch High Street, London E1 6PE.

900   Ancillary equipment

9000   Lifting aids

90000 Manual lifting aids
Chain and stirrup grip with ceiling plate, as diagram 26.2: £12·00
(Kimberley Bingham and Co Ltd, Birmingham; a similar aid is manufactured by Hoskins Ltd, Birmingham)

90001 Electric hoists
Electric hoist with traversing motor, as diagram 26.3, excluding track and fixing: £162·50
(Wessex Medical Equipment Co., Romsey; similar equipment is manufactured by J A Carter Ltd, Wiltshire; Railvalift, Hertfordshire; Delta Designs, Hertfordshire)

90002 Portable hoists
Patient lifter, as diagram 26.4a: £130·00
Upper section (without trolley base), with steel bathroom socket, as diagram 26.4b: £101·42
(Zimmer Orthopaedic Ltd, Bridgend: similar equipment is manufactured by F J Payne and Sons, Oxford; Easicarri Ltd, Cheltenham)

Hoist/mobile seat, as diagram 26.5: £350·00
(ARJO UK, Wokingham)

Lifting aid for bathing, toileting and sling lifting, as diagram 26.6: £364·00
(Mecanaids Ltd, Gloucester)

90003 Walking frames
Walking and stair climbing frame, as diagram 25.3: £16·52
(Rowen Community (South Wales) Ltd, Neath)

901   Building elements

9010   External elements

90100 Pavings
Patented rubber treaded flags, as described in 3014: Cost on quotation
(Shap Granite Co Ltd, Shap)

Non-slip epoxy or bauxite grit floor coating for internal or external surfaces: £2·50–£2·90 per m^2 laid
(Tretol Ltd, London)

90101 Ramp heating
Mineral insulated 750w heating cable, load density approx 160w/m^2 for ramp 1·200 wide $\times$ 4·000 long. Supply lay and test, London area (pro rata: £45·00
Air thermostat control in weatherproof box: £11·00
(G A Brooks Partners Ltd, London)

Control sensitive to ice
for public ramps: £70·00
for road heating: £170·00
(Findlay, Irvine Ltd, Edinburgh)

90102 Portable ramps
Ramp of expanded steel mesh, as described in 3263, 1·930 long $\times$ 0·915 wide, weight approx 63kg: £57·00
1·930 long $\times$ 0·760 wide, weight approx 59kg: £52·49
(Expamet Industrial Products Ltd, Hartlepool)

Folding portable ramp in two mild steel channel sections, length 1·520, for rise up to 0·230: £24·00
(Homecraft Supplies, London: similar ramps are also available from Kimberley Bingham and Co Ltd, Birmingham; Nottingham Handcrafts Ltd, Nottingham; Rootes (Maidstone) Ltd, Maidstone)

9011 Handrails

90110 Additional rails
Additional handrail to standard domestic straight flight staircase, with brackets and fixing: £18·00

Horizontal extension to handrail end, length 0·300, including brackets and fixing: £4·00

9012 Thresholds

90120 Flexible threshold
Flexible threshold for external door, as diagram 34.1, 0·090 wide,
length 0·830: £3·68
length 0·930: £3·98
(Duraflex Housecrafts Ltd, Cheltenham)

90121 Threshold seal
Threshold seal with resilient neoprene insert, as diagram 34.2, length 1·000: £7·14
(Sealmaster Ltd, Cambridge)

90122 Hinged water bar
Hinged water bar as diagram 34.4, satin chrome finish, for 0·900 doorset: £17·39
(James Gibbons Ltd, Wolverhampton)

90123 Draught excluders
Retractable seal draught excluder, as diagram 34.5, length 0·830,
for internal door: £2·80
for external door: £2·95
(Chamberlain Weatherstrips Ltd, Chessington)

Parabar positive action draught excluder, aluminium anodized, for 0·900 doorset: £1·90
(Expandite Ltd, Bracknell)

9013 Windows

90130 Louvre windows
Window with louvred fanlight section, as diagram 35.2, 0·900 wide × 1·200 high with 0·230 louvre and 0·800 drop rod control, including glazing: £24·25
(Pillar Naco (UK) Ltd, Slough)

90131 Winding gear
Remote control winding gear, as diagram 35.3, 0·800 drop from fanlight to control, supply and fix: £24·70
(Teleflex Morse Ltd, Basildon)

90132 Cord control gear
Cord control gear to standard fanlight, per set: £1·75
(Teleflex Morse Ltd, Basildon)

90133 Window stays
Telescopic friction stay, satin chrome finish: £4·72
(Newman-Tonks and Co Ltd, Birmingham)

90134 Cam stay control
Aluminium duplex cam stay control, as diagram 35.5, link bar 0·250,
throw 0·150: £2·32
throw 0·300: £2·43
(E D Hinchliffe and Sons Ltd, West Bromwich)

9014 Doors

90140 Side-hung and sliding doors
Door giving 0·750 clear opening width, including ironmongery, frame and fixing,
side-hung: £33·00
sliding: £46·00

90141 Automatic opening doors
Pair of bi-parting sliding doors, unit 2·130 wide × 2·300 high giving 0·900 opening, including frame, electric operator and carpet activator control, supply, deliver and install London area: £2300·00
(Stanley Automatic Doors Ltd, Slough)

Automatic door unit and control box (doors not supplied) for single sliding door giving opening up to 1·500, activator operated by mat, photocell or push button: £450·00
(Besam Ltd, Guildford)

90142 Door protection
Cotton-backed vinyl sheeting for contact adhesion to door surface: £2·00 per m²
(Nairn Coated Products Ltd, Lancaster)

Plastic laminate kicking plate 0·400 high, to one side only 0·826 doorleaf, excluding fixing: £2·00

90143 Fire protection
Magnetic door release unit, per door: £14·00
(Gent and Co Ltd, Leicester)

Fusible link, per door: £2·00
(Mather and Platt Ltd, Manchester)

90144 Pull rail
Auxiliary horizontal rail diameter 0·030, length 0·500, for fixing to trailing face of side-hung door: £2·20
(Nicholls and Clarke Ltd, London)

90145 Door cores
0·826 × 2·040 plywood faced door
0·040 thick, honeycomb core: £7·00
0·044 thick, solid timber core: £19·00

90146 Door ironmongery
Coin-operated indicating bolt, as diagram 36.21, extruded aluminium alloy: £2·20
(Josiah Parkes and Sons Ltd, Willenhall)

Throwover indicating bolt, satin chrome: £6·55
(Parker Winder and Achurch Ltd, Birmingham)

902 Services installations

9020 Water services

90200 Thermostatic valves
Mixing valve for single-point application, with
thermostatic control knob and flexible hose,
exposed fitting: £68·20
built-in fitting: £80·03
with lever handle on thermostat, extra: £8·00
(Walker Crosweller and Co Ltd, Cheltenham)

Shower mixing valve for handicapped and elderly,
with half-turn control lever: £73·77
(Barking Brassware Co Ltd, Barking)

90201 Taps
Ball head non-concussive toggle-action pillar valve,
as diagram 41.1, chromium plated, per pair: £21·95
(Barber Wilsons and Co Ltd, London)

0·013 plastic screw-down basin taps, broad dome
head, as diagram 41.3, per pair: £4·04
(IMI Opella Ltd, Birmingham)

Single lever action mixing tap, as diagram 41.4:
supply only £24·35
(Dent and Hellyer Ltd, Andover)

Constant spray lever tap, as diagram 41.5: £39·00
(Walker Crosweller and Co Ltd, Cheltenham)

Quarter-turn lever action tap, as diagram 41.6,
0·012 bibcock, per pair: £9·50
0·012 sink high neck pillar, per pair: £12·00
0·012 headwork conversion to fit existing taps, per
pair: £4·60
(IMI Opella Ltd, Birmingham)

90202 Magnetic valves
Electro-magnetic valve, as described in 418, for
0·013 pipe,
low pressure: £13·45
high pressure: £14·86
(Danfoss (London) Ltd, Greenford)

9021 Electrical services

90210 Rocker switches
Gira rocker action switchplate, as diagram 43.1,
size 0·100 × 0·100: £1·30
(BBI Lighting Ltd, Basingstoke)

90211 Luminous locator
Neon locator for fitting to plate switch, as diagram
43.3: £0·77
(MK Electric Ltd, London)

Single gang flush-mounted switchplate as described
in 4313, satin chrome: £1·71
(Walsall Conduits Ltd, West Bromwich)

90212 Circuit breakers
Consumers' control unit, 4 rewirable fuses: £5·70
Consumers' control unit, 4 circuit breakers: £13·60
(J A Crabtree and Co Ltd, Walsall)

9022 Communications services

90220 Speech/call systems
'Talkback' communication system for warden-
serviced housing units, catering for dwellings
within operational range of 2·7km, using portable
control unit for contact along primary network
cable. Typical installation incorporating radio
entertainment channel and fire detection link,
scheme covering 20 dwellings: £1220·00
scheme covering 50 dwellings: £2690·00
(Tunstall Byers and Co Ltd, Doncaster)

Visual call and intercom system for warden-
serviced housing. Typical installation for scheme of
not less than 20 dwellings, with speaking facility
(wall unit with telephone headset) in living or bed
area, pull call switch in bathroom, master station in
warden's office, cost per dwelling: £60·00–£70·00
(Zettler UK Division, Harrow)

90221 Air-operated switches
Unit as described in 4440, 13amp: £19·14
(Herga Electric Ltd, Bury St Edmunds)

90222 Door call systems
Entrance instrument for single door, including
power supply unit, entrance lock mechanism,
telephone wiring and flat telephone, supply and
install, London area: £85·00
(Sterdy Telephones Ltd, Hoddesdon)

90223 Possum systems
PSU3 system, replacing mark 1 system as described
in 4461, specification to suit individual
requirements: Cost on quotation
PSU2 system, replacing mark 2 system as described
in 4465, basic unit controlling door lock, intercom,
alarm and four outlets: £164·00
(Possum Controls Ltd, Aylesbury)

90224 Systems for deaf people
Control box for doorbell flashing light system for
deaf people, as described in 4474: £9·78
(Hector Tanner and Co, Bristol)

9023 Lifts

90230 Home lifts
Lift with lattice gate as diagram 45.7, internal car
dimensions 0·890 × 0·840, lifting capacity 159kg,
installation serving two floors, supply and deliver
London area, excluding builder's work: £2400·00
(Hammond and Champness Ltd, London)

90230   Home lifts *continued*
Lift in enclosed shaft, internal car dimensions
1·015 × 1·010, door opening 0·800, installation
serving up to three floors, supply and deliver
London area, excluding builders' work: £4000·00
(Hammond and Champness Ltd, London: similar
lifts are manufactured by W J Furse and Co Ltd,
Nottingham; Marryat and Scott Ltd, Hounslow;
Otis Elevator Co Ltd, London)

Home lift to carry wheelchair as diagram 45.8,
serving two floors, supply and deliver London area,
excluding builder's work: £1350·00
(AMP Engineers Ltd, Hitchin)

90231   Counterweight lift
Manually operated counterweight lift, as diagram
45.9, supply and install, Manchester area: £400·00
(Terry Personal Lifts, Knutsford)

90232   Seat lift
Seat lift as diagram 45.10, serving two floors,
supply, deliver and install London area, excluding
builder's work: £725·00
(Wessex Medical Equipment Co, Romsey)

90233   Stairlifts
Stairlift to carry a wheelchair as diagram 45.11,
supply, deliver and install, London area,
chain hauled: £1230·00
cable hauled: £1323·00
(Stairlift Engineering Ltd, Reading: comparable
stairlifts are manufactured by Gimson and Co Ltd,
Leicester; W J Furse and Co Ltd, Nottingham;
T Dooley and Co Ltd, Bridlington)

Stairlift comparable to that in diagram 45.12,
suitable for straight of 16 steps, deliver and install
London area, excluding builder's work: £600·00
(Wessex Medical Equipment Co, Romsey:
comparable stairlifts are manufactured by South's
Mechanical Handling, Burnley; W J Furse and Co
Ltd, Nottingham; Minivator Sales Ltd, Dunstable;
Project and Design Co Ltd, Redcar. The stairlift by
Hammond and Champness Ltd shown in diagram
45.12 is temporarily (April 1976) unavailable)

Stairlift with folding seat as diagram 45.13, supply,
deliver and install London area, excluding builder's
work: £835·00
(Gimson and Co Ltd, Leicester: comparable
stairlifts are manufactured by Bennie Metal
Products Ltd, London; T Dooley and Co Ltd,
Bridlington)

90234   Short rise hydraulic lift
Electrically operated lift with safety rails as
diagram 45.14, platform dimensions 0·610 × 1·270,
rise 0·200–0·940 to lift 750kg, supply and install
London area, excluding builder's work: £700·00
(Power Lifts Ltd, Watford: comparable lifts are
manufactured by Trepel (UK) Ltd, Sheerness;
Becker Equipment Ltd, Wembley; Brumpex-Eccles
Ltd, Camberley; Hymo-Lift Ltd, Northampton)

903   **Dwelling spaces**

9030   **Entrances**

90300   Entrance ramps
Ground floor entrance provision to typical
individual house,
incorporating step and standard threshold to
external door, rise approx 0·300: £86·00
with approach ramp 4·500 long × 1·200 wide, level
platform at head 1·200 × 1·200, no kerbs or rails,
modified external doorset with flexible threshold as
noted in 90120: £160·00

9031   **Kitchens**

90310   Kitchen units for wheelchair users
Owing to the range of variables and variations
among requirements relating to household size and
individual needs, requirements, it is not practicable
to make reliable cost comparisons between kitchens
for wheelchair users and normal users.
(Kitchen units designed to suit wheelchair users
are manufactured by Geo A Moore and Co Ltd,
Wetherby; Metric (built-in) Units Ltd, West
Drayton; Paramount Kitchen Furniture Ltd,
Carlisle. Units with low level work surfaces or
otherwise suitable for disabled users are also
manufactured by Multyflex Kitchens Ltd, Llanelly;
W and G Sissons Ltd, Sheffield)

90311   Kitchen storage facilities
Three sliding shelves on roller bearing runners, as
diagram 51.22: £26·75
Two vegetable storage baskets on roller bearing
runners, as diagram 51.23: £25·50
Carousel corner unit with rotating shelves, as
diagram 51.24: £87·25
Baskets to inside of cupboard door, as diagram
51.25: £5·25
(Multyflex Kitchens Ltd, Llanelly)

90312   Shallow sink bowls
Stainless steel sink bowl
without drainer, 0·483 × 0·381 × 0·114 deep: £12·00
with single drainer, size 0·914 × 0·533: £50·00
(W H Paul Ltd, Derby)

Stainless steel sink and drainer, overall size
1·067 × 0·533, round bowl 0·406 top diameter, 0·292
base diameter, depth 0·127: £29·13
(W and G Sissons Ltd, Sheffield)

Stainless steel sink top with rectangular bowl 0·125
deep,
1·000 × 0·600: £23·43
1·000 × 0·500: £20·00
(Nicholls and Clarke Ltd, London)

90313   Sink spray attachment
Sink spray attachment as described in 51556: £51·00
(Barking Brassware Co Ltd, Barking)

9032 Wcs

90320 Bidet/wc
Clos o mat 61, as described in 54232: £485·00
Clos o mat Samoa, as described in 54233: £516·00
(Clos o mat (Great Britain) Ltd, Sale)

90321 Wc seats
Hardwood wc seat 0·584 deep × 0·457 wide,
without cover: £8·50
with cover: £13·50
(Atkinson and Kirby Ltd, Ormskirk)

Foam-filled plastic-covered wc seat, as described in
54243: £6·50
(Kimberley-Bingham and Co Ltd, Birmingham)

90322 Wcs, seat raising devices
Standard pedestal pan, vitreous china: £6·00
Corbel pan, vitreous china: £18·00

Special heavy duty wc suite comprising washdown
closet in white fireclay 0·508 high, low level cistern
and fittings, plastic open front seat: £40·50
(Doulton Sanitaryware Ltd, Stoke-on-Trent)

Raised wc seat with shield, fixed to bowl by bracket
clamps, adjustable up to 0·175: £11·50
(Carters (J and A) Ltd, Westbury)

Polypropylene raised wc seat, as diagram 54.25:
£5·00
(Carters (J and A) Ltd, Westbury)

90323 Wc plinth
Purpose-designed 0·075 high white glazed fireclay
plinth to raise standard pedestal wc: £10·00
(Twyfords Ltd, Stoke-on-Trent)

90324 Wc support rails
0·025 diameter plastic coated rail 0·710 long: £1·40
(Homecraft Suppliers, London)

0·030 diameter chromium plated rail with knurled
finish and adjustable flanges.
0·455 long: £6·50
0·610 long: £7·07
0·815 long: £9·89
(Carters (J and A) Ltd, Westbury)

Support rails made to measure for wheelchair wc
compartments, according to recommendations of
MHLG Circular 33/68, to give two horizontal and
two vertical supports, chromium plated finish:
£44·00
(Kimberley Bingham and Co Ltd, Birmingham:
comparable made to measure support rails are
available from Dent and Hellyer Ltd, Andover;
Reginald Tampkin Ltd, Chelmsford; Ryders Ltd,
Bolton; Nicholls and Clarke Ltd, London)

90325 Hinged support rails
Wall-mounted lift-up wc support rail as diagram
54.30,
with self-locking drop-down leg: £11·00
with variable height leg: £13·00
(Renray Products (UK) Ltd, Belfast)

Wall-mounted hinged horizontal support, as
diagram 54.31: £17·00
(Renray Products (UK) Ltd, Belfast)

90326 Wc side support aid
Support aid as diagram 54.33: £35·00
(Mecanaids Ltd, Gloucester)

90327 Toilet roll holder
Toilock roll holder as described in 54298: £3·63
(Burn Bros London Ltd, Orpington)

90328 Heated wc seat
12-volt thermostat-controlled heated wc seat, with
automatic cut-off: £20·00
(Reginald Clayton Ltd, St Leonards)

9033 Wash basins

90330 Basin for spastics
The basin in diagram 54.45, formerly manufactured
by Adamsez Ltd, is not now (April 1976) available.

Comparable basin size 0·584 × 0·457 with concave
front and shallow bowl, vitreous china: £12·76
(Nicholls and Clarke Ltd, London)

90331 Desk top basins
Typical wall-hung vitreous china basin with taps,
including fixing: £33·00
Typical vitreous china basin for installation in desk
top, including taps and fixing, excluding top: £40·00
Vanitory top and legs for above, by builder: £35·00

1·067 × 0·533 plastic laminated top for basin, fascia
0·100 deep: £33·27
Inset basin for above: £16·10
(Nicholls and Clarke Ltd, London)

90332 Hand rinse basins
Hand rinse basin for building into wall, 0·430 long
× 0·270 high, projection 0·150, vitreous china: £7·16
(Doulton Sanitaryware Ltd, Stoke-on-Trent)

9034 Baths

90340 Medicbath
Bath as diagram 54.72, with waste connections,
chain and plug,
with hand-inflated seal on hinged door: £149·00
with electrically inflated seal on hinged door:
£174·00
(Medic-Bath Ltd, Manchester)

90341 Roll-in shower and bath
ARJO roll-in shower cabinet as diagram 54.73, with
water control unit: £360·00
Roll-in sit-bath, as diagram 54.73, with self-sealing
access door, water control unit: £455·00
(ARJO UK, Wokingham)

90342 Sitz bath
Acrylic sitz bath as diagram 54.74, with side and
end panels: £53·00
(Heatons Plastics Ltd, Rotherham)

90343 Old people's bath
Flat-bottomed bath for old people, size 1·500 × 0·700
× 0·380, reinforced acrylic: £49·10
(Chloride Shires Ltd, Leeds)

90344 Anti-slip bath strips
Pack of 7 stippled pvc self-adhesive strips, 0·305
long × 0·019 wide, for fixing to bath bottoms etc:
£0·48
(Expandite Ltd, Bracknell)

9035   Shower provision

90350 Shower trays
Acrylic shower tray as described in 54813, size
0·815 × 0·815 × 0·140 deep (0·040 fall), front and
centre back outlet, 0·038 strainer waste, 0·038
P trap: £47·80
(Armitage Shanks Ltd, Armitage)

Glass fibre shower base, size 1·200 × 1·200, with
shallow fall to corner waste outlet: £49·00
(Nicholls and Clarke Ltd, London)

90351 Instantaneous shower units
Shower unit as diagram 54.91: £38·55
(IMI Santon Ltd, Newport, Gwent)

90352 Bath/shower unit for handicapped children
Acrylic bath/shower unit as diagram 54.95, size
0·914 × 0·914 × 0·457 high: £56·50
(Heatons Plastics Ltd, Rotherham)

9036   Bidets

90360 Maternity bidet
The maternity bidet in diagram 54.97, formerly
manufactured by Adamsez Ltd, is not now (April
1976) available.

Vitreous china bidet 0·457 high, designed to assist
wheelchair users, with thermostatic mixer and
ascending spray: £108·08
(Nicholls and Clarke Ltd, London)

9037   Urinals

90370 Urinal for wheelchair users
Fireclay bowl urinal with extended front for
wheelchair users, 0·800 high × 0·360 wide, 0·500
projection, with integral cistern: £75·21
(Doulton Sanitaryware Ltd, Stoke-on-Trent)

9038   Laundry facilities

90380 Rotary clothes dryer
3-arm rotary clothes line, diameter 2·850, line space
36·600: £24·75
with winding mechanism for raising and lowering:
£37·95
(Hills Industries Ltd, Caerphilly)

9039   Garages

90390 Automatic opening garage doors
Electro-mechanical unit for fixing to garage roof,
with portable or car-mounted transmitter: £340·00
(Automatic Doors Ltd, Isleworth)

Electric motor for single garage door: £118·75
Remote control pack set with hand transmitter:
£61·75
(Hillaldam and Coburn Ltd, Surbiton)

Autoray remote control unit: £103·50
Push button operated control carried in car: £77·50
(P C Henderson Ltd, Romford)

Remote control unit for lightweight garage door:
£97·50
Key switch: £12·50
Radio control, receiver and aerial: £54·50
Ultra-sonic car transmitter: £26·95
Metal door, 2·130 wide × 1·980 high, supply and
deliver: £35·15
Glass fibre door, 2·130 wide × 1·980 high, supply
and deliver: £56·00
(Bolton Gate Co Ltd, Bolton)

Electronic remote control for garage doors,
including modulated light transmitter: £120·00
(Scott Automatic Ltd, Edgware)

Ray control unit: £67·55
Hand transmitter set and aerial: £87·25
(Westland Engineers Ltd, Yeovil)

9100 Ageing

It is more meaningful to regard ageing as a physical than as a chronological phenomenon. Although elderly people as a group are subject to a progressive decline in physical and mental health, many continue to lead physically active and busy lives. While they will invariably benefit from building provisions made for people who are disabled, it ought to be recognized that only a minority are in urgent need of them. It is a mistake to equate, as is sometimes done, old age with physical disability. Data in the OPCS survey indicate that more than three in four of those aged 65 and over, and more than three in five aged 75 and over, have no physical problems and are not describable as either handicapped or impaired[1]. In a survey made in 1957–61 among old people in England and Wales admitted to local authority residential homes as being in need of care and attention, Peter Townsend estimated that 52 per cent could have cared for themselves in a suitable environment[2].

The following conditions may occur as a consequence of the ageing process:

1. Height diminishes, involving a decrease in the range of reach.

2. Mobility and physical agility are impaired, and reactions are slower.

For old people, walking is more of an effort than for young people, even though the speed is slower. An old person tends to walk with head forward, spine flexed, and hips and knees slightly bent. Steps are small and feet tend to shuffle along the ground. When turning, steps become even smaller and leg movements are less effective.

Because of the tendency to drag the feet, obstructions at floor level, such as uneven paved surfaces, are hazardous. Stepping down from stools and benches is often difficult for old people; the need to use stools, for example to open windows, must be avoided.

3. Ligaments become stiffer and muscles weaker, affecting ability to grip or stoop.

4. There is a tendency to giddiness.

Stooping may cause a loss of balance, and giddiness can occur when the standing position is regained.

5. Bladder control is weakened.

In a study of old people made by Sheldon, 31·5 per cent reported frequency and urgency of urination, women being more affected than men[3].

Attention must be given in housing to the placing of wcs in relation to bedrooms. See also Incontinence, 9152.

6. Sensory faculties are impaired, with greater susceptibility to cold.

7. Vision, hearing and the sense of smell are impaired.

The number and proportion of people in Great Britain aged 65 and over is rising, though the trend will not continue indefinitely. At present (1976), people aged 65 and over represent 14·2 per cent of the total population. Population projections indicate that, on the basis of a central projection of fertility, the proportion will increase to 14·8 per cent in 1981, fall to 14·6 per cent in 1991, and then drop substantially to 13·6 per cent in 2001. On the basis of a high variant of fertility the projected percentages are 14·6, 14·3 and 13·3, and on a low variant 14·9, 15·1 and 14·6. The aggregate number of old people, at present 7·75m, is expected to rise to 8·07m in 1981 and 8·24m in 1991, and then to fall to 7·91m in 2001[4].

Among people who are very old the trend is for numbers to continue to increase. The population in Great Britain aged 85 and over, at present estimated at 510 000, is expected to rise to 537 000 in 1981, 673 000 in 1991 and 736 000 in 2001. The predicted figure for the year 2001 represents an increase of 44 per cent over the 1976 figure [5]. Inevitably, a substantial proportion of these very old people will be frail and handicapped, and these statistics are particularly relevant to the formulation of housing policies for elderly people who need care and support.

An old person who has a disability is often multiply handicapped, for example an amputee who is also affected by arthritis and heart disease. This means that, in respect of architectural design for handicapped old people, consideration needs to be given to general needs and not only to specific ones.

9101 Amputation

The removal of the whole or part of a limb.

Of the 4826 amputee patients who attended limb centres in England and Wales for the first time in 1973, 72 per cent were aged 60 or over. The ratio of leg to arm amputations was 18:1. Of all amputations, 85 per cent were attributable to disease, of which arteriosclerosis accounted for about 70 per cent and diabetes 20 per cent; 12 per cent were caused by accidents, and 3 per cent were due to congenital disabilities or other causes [6].

Among lower limb amputees the disability per se is commonly minimal, no more than a tolerable inconvenience. Much more distressing is the phantom pain, a fiercely real sensation of the non-existent foot that pain-killing drugs, short of destroying all sensibility, are incapable of defeating.

Prostheses
An artificial leg can match more closely the usefulness of the original than an artificial arm. In the case of upper

[1] Bib 93210, p5
[2] Bib 93640, p262
[3] Bib 93686
[4] Bib 93780, p15–18
[5] Bib 93780, p16
[6] Bib 93273, p126–7

limb amputees the removal of the hand leaves a functional arm which can hold or carry, whether or not a prosthetic appliance is fitted. Where a prosthesis is employed, a simple hook attachment is of greater practical value than a cosmetic hand.

Young versus elderly amputees
In terms of personal mobility and building requirements there are broad differences between young amputees and those who are older.

The young person is commonly able to adapt successfully to the wearing of a prosthesis, and double lower limb amputees may be able to walk.

Among old people where amputation has been necessary on account of peripheral vascular insufficiency, there is the probability that the remaining limb is tending to fail, and there is a greater likelihood of multiple handicap, particularly of the cardiovascular and respiratory system. As a consequence elderly people invariably rely for mobility on a wheelchair. Hamilton and Nichols report that among elderly amputees rehabilitated and trained to cope independently a follow-up inquiry found that many made little use of their prostheses, and some did not use them at all[7].

Lower limb amputees can more easily manage steps than ramps, see 1224, 3201. For design factors relating to upper limb amputees see Hand and arm disabilities, 9145.

9102   Ankylosis

The fusion of two bones at a joint, due to disease.

9103   Ankylosing spondylitis

See Spondylitis, 9185.

9104   Aphasia

Loss of the power of speech. A person severely affected by aphasia may be unable to speak or write, understand speech or writing, or communicate by signs. Aphasia is caused by brain damage, resulting for example from a stroke or head injury.

9105   Apoplexy

A lay term, synonymous with stroke. See Hemiplegia, 9147.

9106   Arteriosclerosis

Hardening of the arteries. When the condition is serious the flow of blood is reduced. Diseased leg arteries may be replaced by vein grafts or plastic tubes; in some cases amputation may be necessary.

9107   Arthritis

A general term for conditions where there is inflammation of the joints. The chief diseases are osteoarthritis and rheumatoid arthritis, which between them account for the prescription of more wheelchairs than any other disabling condition (table 22.2).

Osteoarthritis
Painful degenerative changes of the joints. In the majority of cases there is no disability and osteoarthritis does not usually involve the severe crippling caused by rheumatoid arthritis.

Osteoarthritis of the hip joint is painful, causing impairment of gait. The pain is most acute while walking and eases on resting. People affected generally avoid movement as much as possible, the lack of exercise contributing to muscle weakness, obesity and general deterioration. Surgical replacement of one or both hips can give good results.

For people with osteoarthritis of the hip, provision should be made for work to be done from a seated position.

Rheumatoid arthritis
Rheumatoid arthritis is the most crippling of the rheumatic diseases. It affects people of all ages but is most common among the middle aged, and is some four times as prevalent among women as it is among men. The peak incidence is between the ages of 35 and 40; 80 per cent of cases occur between the ages of 25 and 50[8].

The disease usually starts in the small joints of the hands or feet, later involving other peripheral joints including the shoulders and hips. Affected joints are painful, becoming swollen and stiff.

It cannot usually be predicted when the disease will flare up, and it may therefore be impossible to plan employment or other physical activities in the confidence that they will be achievable.

Cold and draughts can cause discomfort to rheumatoids. A comfortable thermal environment is essential, see 421. Double glazed windows are recommended. Rails, taps, handles, etc should be easy to grip. Provision must be made for work to be done from a seated position wherever possible.

9108   Arthrodesis

The fusion of joints by surgery.

9109   Arthrogryposis

A condition where joints are deformed at birth, hands and feet being most affected.

---

[7] Bib 93412, p98
[8] Bib 93291

9110 Asthma

A respiratory complaint characterized by paroxysms of difficult breathing and wheezing.

Housing on low level, damp or exposed sites may be unsuitable.

9111 Ataxia

Incoordination of the locomotor system. The ataxic gait is clumsy and falls are common. Ataxia may be due to cerebral palsy, multiple sclerosis or other causes.

The hereditary ataxias (for example Friedrich's ataxia, see 9140) are rare conditions which run in families. The part of the nervous system controlling muscular coordination steadily degenerates, causing paralysis and death.

9112 Athetosis

Involuntary movements. Athetosis is often a symptom of cerebral palsy. There is frequently a loss of direction during simple movements, and delicate movements are difficult.

9113 Atrophy

Wasting of the muscles. Atrophy may be caused simply by not using muscles, or by disease, for example polio.

9114 Autism

Self-absorption in one's own fantasies.

The autistic child has a world of his own, not relating or responding to other children, to his parents or to happenings about him. He appears insensitive to pain. He is hyperactive (hyperkinetic), alternating between periods of intense physical activity and periods of impenetrable calm. While he is not aggressive, he needs to be constantly supervised, to see that he does not damage objects about him or injure himself or other children.

It is impossible to devise any physical environment which can directly control the behaviour of the autistic child. In special schools it is wise to avoid surfaces which are potentially damaging, for example to use toughened or wired glass to low level glazing.

Autism among adults, a common symptom of schizophrenia, has similar characteristics.

9115 Blindness

The National Assistance Act 1948 defines a blind person as one 'so blind as to be unable to perform any work for which eyesight is essential'.

In England and Wales nearly all blind people are registered with local social services authorities and comprehensive statistics are available. The 98 141 blind people who were registered at March 1974 represented 2·1 per 1000 of the total population; of these, 72 per cent were aged 65 or over [9].

A survey made in 1965 of registered blind people found that among those aged 16–64, 26 per cent were totally blind (not able to tell where windows are in a room): for those aged 65–79 the figure was 19 per cent [10].

The handicapping effects of blindness in relation to deafness are discussed in 1307. The environmental problems of blind people are discussed in 1423. Housing for blind people is noted in 8281.

9116 Brittle bones (Fragilitas ossium)

A rare inherited disease which can cause severe deformity. Among children, fractures may frequently be caused by trivial falls. The liability to fractures diminishes with age; if there have been repeated fractures the lower limbs may not develop normally, and the person affected may become chairbound.

9117 Bronchitis

Chronic bronchitis involves inflammation of the bronchial tubes, causing coughing and shortness of breath. It occurs most frequently among elderly people, especially men.

Acute bronchitis often develops during the winter following exposure to cold, particularly where accompanied by damp. It is particularly dangerous to old people.

Cold bedrooms can exacerbate bronchitis. On the other hand, some bronchitics may be discomforted by air-conditioned environments, requiring instead cool constantly circulating air.

9118 Calipers (Braces)

Calipers may be short, to give support to weak feet and ankles, or long to give support to weak knees, thighs or calf muscles.

9119 Cardio-vascular diseases

Diseases associated with the heart and circulatory system are the most common type of chronic disability. Common causes include arteriosclerosis, coronary heart disease, high blood pressure, and rheumatic carditis.

The degree of heart disorder varies from conditions where ordinary physical activity causes no discomfort to those

[9] Bib 93244
[10] Bib 93330, p19

where it is impossible to perform any activity without discomfort. Heart diseases may be classified according to the amount of work which the physician permits, varying from no restriction of physical activity to complete rest.

For people with severe heart disorders the conservation of energy and avoidance of excessive physical activity are important. The energy expended in climbing stairs can be considerable, and the need to climb stairs should be avoided where possible.

Storage and equipment should be planned to minimize bending, reaching, lifting and carrying. Provision should be made for household activities to be undertaken from a seated position.

9120 Cerebral haemorrhage

The rupture of a blood vessel in the brain. Cerebral haemorrhage may cause aphasia where the lesion is in the speech centre of the brain, and hemiplegia where the lesion involves the motor pathways. Mental faculties may also be affected.

9121 Cerebral palsy

A variety of injuries causing damage to the brain at birth or faulty development of the growing brain tissues. Those affected are popularly known as spastics. According to the location of the injury, varying disabilities occur. The most common is spastic cerebral palsy. Other types include athetosis (the next most common) (9112) and flaccidity.

The effects of cerebral palsy are permanent, and regular treatment is necessary to prevent disabilities and deformities becoming more severe. Among children, apparent improvements occasionally occur, but this is usually because latent abilities have not been able to develop owing to the previous lack of effective treatment. Depending on the degree and location of brain damage, mental and sensory faculties may be affected.

The likelihood of a child with cerebral palsy having a motor disability only is small. Surveys of cerebral palsied children report that half have intelligence at educationally subnormal level or below; three quarters or more have some degree of speech defect; a quarter have poor vision, a quarter have hearing loss and an unknown number have epilepsy[11].

In Britain cerebral palsy is not a notifiable condition and reliable statistics are not available. The OPCS survey estimates that about 1 in 2500 of the adult population has a physical impairment due to cerebral palsy[12].

9122 Club foot

A congenital deformity of the foot and ankle. If treated early in childhood it can often be completely cured.

9123 Colostomy

An artificial opening in the abdomen. The large intestine (colon) is diverted to empty into a plastic bag held in place by adhesive and a belt worn across the abdomen. The operation is sometimes performed where there is bowel incontinence, for example among young people with spina bifida. See also Ileostomy, 9151.

9124 Congenital disabilities

Disability present at birth, or manifest soon after.

9125 Contracture

The permanent or temporary shortening of a muscle or ligament, limiting normal joint movement. Contractures may occur with arthritis and neurological conditions, especially where there is spasticity.

9126 CVA

CVA, meaning cerebro-vascular accident, is caused by cerebral haemorrhage, thrombosis or embolism. A consequence may be hemiplegia, see 9147.

9127 Cystic fibrosis

An uncommon disease of young children causing progressive lung damage.

9128 Cystitis

Inflammation of the urinary bladder.

9129 Deafness

Deaf people are not obliged to register and comprehensive statistics are not available. It has been estimated that there are some 30 000 or 40 000 people in Britain who were born totally deaf or became deaf at an early age, and a further $1\frac{1}{2}$ million people who are hard of hearing[13].

For hard of hearing people, amplifiers to telephones and doorbells can help. In auditoria buildings and private housing, induction loops may be incorporated for people using certain hearing aids, see 447. For deaf people facilities in public buildings should be signposted, see 6154. In special buildings for deaf people, audible alarms, for example in case of fire, may be accompanied by visual signals.

---

[11] Bib 93302; contribution on congenital amputees by N Gibbs, p36
[12] Bib 93210, p218
[13] Bib 93202, p60

9130 Dementia

Serious loss of mental capacity which may develop in old age. It may be associated with arteriosclerosis (9106) or hemiplegia (9147).

9131 Diabetes

A disorder in which the body is unable to control the use of sugar as a source of energy. In severe cases, nerve degeneration may impair walking ability; in extreme cases diabetic gangrene may develop and a leg amputation may be necessary. Diabetes can be a cause of progressive sight impairment.

9132 Disseminated sclerosis

See Multiple sclerosis, 9162

9133 Dwarfism

Seriously retarded or stunted growth. A dwarf's mental development may be normal or retarded, and his body well proportioned or deformed, depending on the cause. Among causes are poor nutrition, disease, hormone disturbances and inherited factors or abnormalities present at birth.

There is no generally agreed definition in terms of stature of dwarfism. An inquiry made in 1961 suggested that there are about 2000 people of restricted growth in Britain [14].

Design factors
Problems of dwarfs using buildings are usually associated with short stature and restricted reach, though they may also be psychological. Difficulties may occur for example with reaching shelves, cupboards, window openers, door handles, light switches etc at levels suitable for normal people, with using deep sinks, basins or worktops at normal heights, and with coping with high steps. These difficulties are substantially alleviated where provision is made for disabled people, and in particular for wheelchair users.

In public buildings no special provisions need be incorporated specifically for dwarfs. Problems of accessibility are generally catered for by the incorporation of requirements for chairbound people, or where attention is given to the needs of young children.

In private housing it is not necessary that any standard provisions are incorporated specifically to suit dwarfs. Adaptations may be necessary to suit specific people, for example low level switches and ironmongery, and altered work heights.

9134 Dystrophy

See Muscular dystrophy, 9163.

9135 Embolism

Sudden blockage of a blood vessel by a clot, which if in the brain may cause hemiplegia (9147).

9136 Encephalitis

Degeneration of brain cells. Residual effects may be slowness of movement, shuffling gait, slow speech and difficult articulation (post-encephalitic Parkinsonism). Mental faculties are not usually affected.

9137 Enuresis

Involuntary passing of urine, bedwetting.

9138 Epilepsy

A disease of the nervous system characterized by fits and/or sudden loss of consciousness. A warning of an attack may be recognizable, and between attacks the individual is normal. In the great majority of cases the condition is not handicapping.

The problems of people with severe epilepsy in relation to the external environment are discussed in the commentary (1427). For individuals who are affected, there are a variety of precautions that can be taken in the home to minimize injury from falls. Situations where it may be difficult to obtain assistance should be avoided, for example doors to bathrooms and wcs should be openable from outside (36331) and spaces ought not to be confined (54104). Floors should be carpeted, furniture should be carefully selected and upholstered where possible, and furniture and equipment in the kitchen and bathroom, where hazards are greatest, may be protected by foam or rubber coverings. Open fires or exposed electric fires should be avoided.

9139 Fibrositis

A lay term applied to painful muscles, especially in the back.

9140 Friedrich's ataxia

A rare disease of the nervous system, appearing in childhood or early adolescence. In the early stages walking is unsteady. As the disease progresses muscles become weak, there is lack of control of movement and vision is impaired. Mental faculties are not affected.

9141 Fragilitas ossium

See Brittle bones, 9116.

---

[14] Bib 93235, p6

9142   German measles

See Rubella, 9178.

9143   Haemophilia

A hereditary disease in which the blood only clots very slowly, so that a minor cut or bump can cause prolonged bleeding. It affects males but is transmitted by females. It has been estimated that it affects one person in 35 000 in Britain[15].

In severe cases of haemophilia internal bleeding erodes the joints of arms or legs; if not treated the resultant deformities may make the use of a wheelchair necessary.

In housing for haemophiliacs it is important to avoid steps or thresholds which may cause bumping to a person in a wheelchair. Because haemophiliacs are only rarely completely chairbound, and because, being men, they are not usually housewives, they will as a rule be satisfactorily accommodated in mobility housing rather than in special accommodation for wheelchair users.

9144   Haemorrhoids

Haemorrhoids, or piles, are varicose (dilated) veins about the lower end of the bowel which may protrude or bleed, and can be extremely painful. Frequent warm bathing can relieve pain; the provision of a bidet (5490) is advantageous.

9145   Hand and arm disabilities

People with hand and arm disabilities may be grouped as follows:

1. Entirely dependent on one hand and arm, for example high level amputees to whom a prosthesis cannot be fitted.

2. Limitation in both hands and arms, for example arthritics.

3. One good arm and a partial disability of the other, for example hemiplegics or arm amputees using prostheses.

Many people in group 3 are able to use the affected arm for holding purposes. The amputee usually has good strength in the remaining portion of his arm, and can carry normal loads with the aid of a prosthesis.

Design factors
Operations involving the simultaneous use of both hands should be avoided as far as possible. Careful attention should be given to the specification of door locks and latches, window opening devices, sliding door ironmongery and heater appliance controls. Door handles, water taps and other valves should be easy to manipulate. Footpress switches may be used in conjunction with manually operated switches (4322).

[15] Bib 93292, p236

9146   Heart diseases

See Cardio-vascular diseases, 9119.

9147   Hemiplegia

Paralysis of one side of the body, customarily referred to as a stroke. It may be caused by damage to the brain due to thrombosis, embolism or cerebral haemorrhage, or, less commonly, head injury or a brain tumour.

The brain has two hemispheres which make up the cerebrum. These hemispheres are mirror images of each other, each chiefly concerned with the movement and sensation of the opposite side of the body. The right side is controlled by the left hemisphere, and vice versa. Speech is controlled by only one hemisphere, the so-called dominant one, which also controls the dominant hand. Thus the left hemisphere is dominant in a right-handed person. A right-handed person who has a stroke affecting the left side of his brain may lose the use of the right arm and leg, and also the power of speech. A stroke affecting the right side of the brain may cause the loss of use of the left side but will not impair speech. On the other hand, perceptual problems are greater with a left than with a right hemiplegia.

The paralysed side is referred to as the hemiplegic or involved side. In some cases paralysis is only temporary and recovery is complete. Recovery is more likely to occur in the leg than in the arm.

The extent of paralysis varies considerably. Speech may be affected and also the muscles of one side of the face. The hemiplegic drags his paralyzed leg and tends to support the affected side on the good side. Because of body imbalance the ambulant hemiplegic often uses a stick. A caliper may be used to support the foot. The arm may be partially or totally paralyzed but can often be used for holding purposes.

Mental as well as physical changes may be associated with hemiplegia. These vary from complete change in personality to minor deviations in behaviour. Apart from damage incurred by the silent areas of the brain, resulting in personality changes, damage can take place in areas concerned with memory and facilitation. There may also be incontinence.

The person with a severe hemiplegia is obliged to use a wheelchair. A one-arm drive chair is available, but few hemiplegics are easily able to control it, for reasons discussed in 23182.

Design factors
The hemiplegic, whether chairbound or ambulant, needs firm support for lateral transfer, for example to bath or wc (54125); it is easier if support rails are on the good side. Handrails should be provided to both sides of steps or stairs (3301). For vertical circulation, steps are easier to use than a steep ramp (3201). Door and window ironmongery should be controllable with one hand. See also Hand and arm disabilities, 9145.

9148   Huntington's Chorea

A rare hereditary disease which is progressive and usually familial. Symptoms are involuntary movements, ataxia, slow slurred speech and mental deterioration.

9149   Hydrocephalus

The abnormal accumulation of fluid in the brain, often associated with spina bifida (9183). Surgical treatment is possible to arrest the condition but lost brain function cannot be restored.

Common characteristics are spasticity of the legs and, less frequently, of the arms, and there may also be ataxia, tremor, imbalance and clumsiness of fine finger movements. There is a close relationship between hydrocephalus and mental impairment, those with severe hydrocephalus commonly being mentally severely incapacitated.

9150   Hypothermia

A term used to describe the condition where the body is unable to generate sufficient heat to maintain body temperature or regulate skin temperature. It is most prevalent among elderly people living in inadequately heated houses.

Exposure to cold is a principal cause of hypothermia, so that incidence is highest during the winter months. The condition is most likely to occur among old people who have a tendency to fall, for example when getting out of bed.

Those who are socially isolated are most at risk; where falls occur in unheated bedrooms people may remain exposed for several hours [16]. In the exceptionally cold period of the first three months of 1963 hypothermia was cited as a direct or contributory cause of death in 438 cases in England and Wales, of whom 307 were aged 70 or over and 55 were aged under one year [17].

A study made among more than 1000 old people in Britain in the winter of 1972 found that body temperatures of people at risk were at their lowest early in the morning and so were house temperatures, indicating the importance of protection from exposure to cold during the night [18].

9151   Ileostomy

An ileostomy operation is similar to a colostomy (9123), but the opening is made higher up in the bowel. It involves bringing out a loop of the ileum through an opening in the abdominal wall to create an artificial anus, wastes being emptied into a removable plastic bag worn on a belt and attached to the body by adhesive.

9152   Incontinence

The inability to control movements of either bowels or bladder, or both.

It is not a simple matter to define incontinence, or to categorize people as either incontinent or not. The most common form is inability to control the bladder. The maintenance of bladder control in association with lack of bowel control is rare. The usual difficulty is inability to retain urine but some people have the problem of retention, meaning that they cannot pass urine when they wish to.

The discussion which follows concentrates on incontinence of the bladder. Among people who are incontinent, bowel control is often not a serious problem, as most handicapped people can with practice develop a regular timetable for defecation.

Disability associations
Disabling conditions which cause incontinence include traumatic paraplegia and spina bifida, in each of which the lesion of the spinal cord causes paralysis of the muscles controlling urination and defecation. Incontinence, or a need to urinate at frequent intervals, is also common among people affected by multiple sclerosis. It is prevalent among elderly handicapped people, where loss of functional capacity is associated with the normal ageing process. For data on disability conditions associated with incontinence see table 13.1.

Wheelchair users
Among wheelchair users the incidence of incontinence is high, affecting about one person in three. In the Leicestershire survey the questions were put 'Can you control your bladder?' and 'Can you control your bowels?'. Of those in the sample who answered both questions 34 per cent had some lack of control; 12 per cent were not able to control either bladder or bowels, 16 per cent could control bowels but not bladder and 6 per cent said they could control bladder but not bowels[19].

Women and men
Incontinence is invariably very much more handicapping, physically, socially and psychologically, among women than it is among men. The reasons are anatomical and physiological. For men, incontinence appliances are available which are manageable, efficient and sanitary, whereas for women no effective appliance for external control has yet been devised.

In the case of men, the apparatus is in three parts: first, an appliance, most usually a condom, which encloses part of the penis; second, a delivery tube, and third, a bag, normally worn inside the trouser leg or else lying in a cutaway portion of the cushion on the wheelchair seat.

[16] In this connection see Bib 93687, p11
[17] Bib 93784, p166
[18] Bib 93688
[19] Bib 93232, p141–2

For women, the only effective appliance is the indwelling catheter which is socially and psychologically uncongenial, and which when used over long periods becomes increasingly problematical to manage. There is also the constant hazard of urinary infection. Indwelling catheters are not normally prescribed for girls or young women; the more common solution is an ileal loop operation whereby an artificial opening is made in the abdomen and urine is passed into a bag attached to a belt, see 9151.

Intermittent incontinence
Many women and some men with intermittent incontinence wear padding and protective pants. To be effective the padding has to be bulky and the pants non-porous. Apart from the hazards of skin pressure sores, there are consequences which inhibit the use of public buildings and public places, for example problems of disposal and the possibility of antisocial odours.

Paraplegics
For many disabled people, and more particularly women, the planning and accomplishment of urination is troublesome. Among paraplegics, the usual method of provoking urination is by manual pressure on the lower abdomen.

Waiting on the wc to achieve urination can be extended. In terms of time spent using the wc, the problem is aggravated by medical exhortations to paraplegics to consume large quantities of liquid each day in order to keep the kidneys in good order.

Design factors
Where a family house is to be used by someone who is incontinent, and particularly by a paraplegic or someone with a colostomy or ileostomy, it is desirable that a second wc is provided to prevent others in the household becoming irritated, inconvenienced or frustrated. If there is one wc only it is preferable that it is separate from the bathroom.

The influence of incontinence and the lack of accessible cloakrooms on the use by disabled people of public buildings is examined in the commentary (1219).

9153 Incoordination

The inability to coordinate movements or control regular movements. Disabilities affecting coordination include cerebral palsy, Parkinson's disease and multiple sclerosis.

For people who lack coordination, careful attention should be given to the positioning and specification of controls, for example door handles, light switches and socket outlets. Projecting thresholds and other hazards at floor level should be avoided. Provision should be made for the sliding of articles, for example in the kitchen.

9154 Kidney disease

When chronic kidney failure occurs there are two possibilities for survival; a kidney transplant or the use of an artificial kidney machine. Where a machine is installed at home special provision is needed, discussed in section 88.

9155 Lesion

Damage due to injury or disease.

9156 Locomotor ataxia (Tabes dorsalis)

A disease of the central nervous system (a form of late syphilis) involving destruction of nerve fibres in the spinal cord, causing an inability to coordinate movement. The disease can cause incontinence and disturbance of vision.

9157 Low back pain

Low back pain may be caused by a lumbar disc lesion, commonly known as a slipped disc. Pain may be referred down the leg, when it is known as sciatica.

In private housing, fittings and equipment should be designed to avoid stooping or reaching to low level.

9158 Meningitis

Inflammation affecting the membranes of the brain or spinal cord.

9159 Mongolism

A congenital condition, known medically as Down's syndrome. Mongol children, who are usually born to older mothers, are mentally handicapped and often very affectionate. Physically, fingers are short and muscles are weak.

9160 Monoplegia

Paralysis of a single limb.

9161 Motor neurone disease

A rare disease of the central nervous system causing rapid and progressive physical deterioration. Onset is usually in middle age, with weakness and wasting of the upper limbs and weakness of the legs. There may be incontinence but there is no sensory loss and mental faculties are not affected. Different syndromes, which may occur singly or in combination, are amyotrophic lateral sclerosis, progressive muscular atrophy and chronic bulbar palsy, the last associated with difficulty of articulation and swallowing. The cause of the disease is not known.

9162   Multiple sclerosis

The most common organic disease of the central nervous system, formerly more often known as disseminated sclerosis. It can cause locomotor paralysis, incoordination, incontinence, vertigo, slurring of speech, loss of sensation, deafness, blindness, impotence and impairment of mental faculties[20].

Incidence
Multiple sclerosis is not inherited, though it is sometimes familial. It is a disease of civilization, whose prevalence is low in primitive communities with poor levels of sanitation and environmental hygiene. The suspicion is that, like polio, the infecting agent is a virus. But, unlike polio, the interval between infection and the onset of symptoms is prolonged.

There is an association with latitude: the further the move from the equator towards the poles, the higher are the rates of multiple sclerosis. The prevalence throughout the world is of the order of 30 per 100 000 total population. In the United Kingdom the prevalence is about 65 per 100 000, in Scotland 100, and in parts of the Orkney Islands 300. Women are more susceptible than men. The disease appears most often among people in their 20s and 30s, with a mean age of onset of 32 years. The earlier the onset the more slowly the disease progresses.

Symptoms and prognosis
The manifestations of multiple sclerosis stem from disturbance to the life mechanisms of nerve cells. The myelin sheath, which protects and insulates the nerve fibres of the central nervous system, is destroyed. Scarring (sclerosis) of the myelin sheath follows, and the resulting plaques of damage affect the functioning of the nerve tracts. Early symptoms include double vision, incontinence, a proneness to trip and fall without warning, and lack of coordination. Subsequently paralysis may become general and vision may be lost. Speech may also be affected. Exacerbations of the disease tend to happen at times of emotional stress, for example during pregnancy. In some cases deterioration is steady, but the more likely happening is that following the initial attack there will be a complete or almost complete remission.

The improvement may be sustained, but usually the disease is characterized by attacks and remissions. In some cases attacks are not severe, and there are people with multiple sclerosis who go through life without being severely disabled. In other cases, deterioration may be intermittently progressive over a period of 30 years or more. The prognosis is not predictable, and exacerbations of the disease cannot be anticipated. Donnelly reports that in any group of cases studied at one time, about half will be moderately disabled and the other half severely disabled. About one third of people affected have the progressive form of the disease, and about two thirds the cyclical form with remissions succeeding exacerbations.

Comparison with muscular dystrophy
Surridge reports a study of a group of people with multiple sclerosis compared with a control group of muscular dystrophy[21]. Whereas intellectual deterioration,

predominantly loss of memory for recent events and impairment of conceptual thinking, had occurred in two-thirds of the multiple sclerosis group it had occurred in none of the dystrophy group.

This is relevant to the provision of aids and appliances. To cope well with disability the individual concerned has often to think of alternative means of tackling problems, employing his remaining assets to best advantage. Whereas people with muscular dystrophy were resourceful and inventive in this direction, people with multiple sclerosis were not.

Surridge found that about one in four people with multiple sclerosis were depressed. By contrast a similar number were euphoric, a mood more commonly supposed to be associated with the disease. The external appearance of cheerful complacency was not however borne out by people's own account of their feelings; many who gave an outward impression of high morale and euphoria were subjectively severely depressed; this group tended to be intellectually impaired, severely disabled and incontinent. There was also a proneness, both among euphorics and depressives, for people to be unrealistic about their circumstances, denying that problems existed where self-evidently they did.

Donnelly also reports that euphoria is less common among people with multiple sclerosis than is often supposed, less than 20 per cent of people affected showing signs of it. He records that there is an 8 per cent suicide rate among people with the disease.

Pathological phenomena
People with multiple sclerosis may be irritable and apathetic, being disinclined to do things for themselves. Surridge's evidence is that depression, euphoria, intellectual deterioration, irritability and apathy are all pathological phenomena, the consequence of damage to the central nervous system, rather than responses to physical disablement. Deleterious personality changes occur frequently, causing great distress to relatives. Eventually the only solution may be transfer to a residential home or hospital, and when that happens it is not uncommon, with the partner left behind suddenly relieved of appalling stress, for the relationship to disintegrate finally.

Unpredictability
Apart from the unpredictable prognosis of the disease, its effects are often unpredictable from day to day. On a good day a person with multiple sclerosis may feel fit and capable, able to go out and do a full day's work; the next day may be a poor day, when no physical or mental effort can be made at all. This day-to-day uncertainty, in conjunction with incontinence, vulnerability to fatigue and all the psychological and emotional problems discussed above, make it difficult for people with multiple sclerosis to make plans ahead, for example for outings involving the use of buildings or public services. There is

---

[20] The notes here on the aetiology of multiple sclerosis draw extensively on Bib 93289, and on D J Donnelly's paper, Bib 93288
[21] Bib 93302, p85

a tendency among people with multiple sclerosis to blame their lack of achievement on inadequate environmental provision, for example of accessible public lavatories. In many cases, because of the nature of the disease, it is improbable that people would be motivated to use buildings if suitable provisions were made.

Both outside and inside the home the need among people with multiple sclerosis for supporting aids may vary from week to week. On some days a wheelchair may be needed inside the home, on most not; equally there are days when the individual can cope only if the kitchen, bathroom and rest of the home is wheelchair-oriented, whereas on most days no special provision will be wanted.

Need for aids
The answer regarding aids and architectural props is that it is probably best to provide for all contingencies, dwellings being planned for example so that they are equipped for full management from a wheelchair. At the same time it needs to be recognized that people with multiple sclerosis, because of the characteristics of the disease, sustain a pretence of personal independence and normality, rejecting aids or supports which imply recognition of their loss of ability. Architects concerned with the provision of facilities for people with multiple sclerosis need to exercise patience, and ought also to realize that their hopes for constructive response may not be fulfilled.

Exceptions
While the prognosis for people with multiple sclerosis is commonly poor, there are some, even those with severe disability, who remain alert, lucid and tolerant. For these people, physical aids from architects and others are welcomed wholeheartedly and used constructively.

9163   Muscular dystrophy

Muscular dystrophies are a group of hereditary diseases causing progressive muscle weakness. Some are seen in childhood, others in adolescence or early adulthood. There are three main types:

1. The Duchenne type or pseudohypertrophic muscular dystrophy. This affects boys only, usually between the ages of two and five. Walking ability is usually lost by the age of 12, and death usually occurs before adult life is reached. No specific treatment is available for this or other types of muscular dystrophy.

2. Limb girdle dystrophy. This occurs in men or women, starting during teens or early adult life. It involves muscles of the shoulder and hip girdles. People affected usually survive to middle age but are severely disabled.

3. Facioscapulohumeral dystrophy. This also occurs in men or women, starting in teens or early adulthood. The prognosis is better; the person affected may have a normal life span although becoming increasingly disabled.

No reliable data are available on the incidence of muscular dystrophy. The OPCS survey, which did not study children, estimated that it affects about 1 per 5000 of the adult population [22].

Design factors
A child or adult with muscular dystrophy usually needs a wheelchair as muscle power deteriorates, and eventually an electric wheelchair may be necessary. As a rule, help will be needed to transfer from wheelchair to car seat, bed or wc seat. A hoist may be necessary for transfer.

9164   Myasthenia gravis

A disease causing muscle weakness. It commonly affects eye muscles and those needed for swallowing.

9165   Neuritis

See Polyneuritis, 9173.

9166   Osteoarthritis

See Arthritis, 9107.

9167   Osteomyelitis

Acute infection in a bone, mainly occurring among children.

9168   Paget's disease

A bone disease of unknown cause, in which one or more bones are thickened, become painful and occasionally fracture spontaneously.

9169   Paraplegia

Total or partial paralysis of both lower limbs. Paraplegia is caused by injury or disease involving the spinal cord. Below the level of the lesion there is locomotor paralysis and sensory loss, and bladder and bowel functions can be affected. About half the people whose paraplegia is the result of an accident have a complete lesion, meaning that paralysis is symmetrical and complete below the level of the injury. For the other half, the lesion is incomplete and paralysis is uneven, so that, for example, one leg may be more severely affected than the other.

Classification of paraplegia
In clinical settings paraplegics say that they are, for example, a C6 or a T4. A C6 is a person who has a lesion at the sixth cervical vertebra, and a T4 a lesion at the fourth thoracic vertebra. Counting is done from the neck; there are 7 cervical, 12 thoracic and 5 lumbar vertebra.

---

[22] Bib 93210, p220

As a rough guide a lesion in the lumbar region means that the rehabilitated person may be able to walk with the aid of calipers and sticks or crutches; where it is in the thoracic or cervical region he will need to use a wheelchair.

Incidence of paraplegia
Reliable data on the incidence of traumatic paraplegia are difficult to obtain. Evidence from DHSS and hospital units treating spinal injuries indicates that in England and Wales the number of new cases each year is about 750, representing about 1½ per cent of the total number of people to whom wheelchairs are issued [23]. The main cause is road accidents, followed by industrial and sports accidents. With the relative decrease of mining accidents the proportion of tetraplegics is rising. Of the total wheelchair population, traumatic paraplegics may account for some 2 per cent, equivalent to about 1 person in about 16 000 of the total population.

Standing exercise
To maintain health and assist circulation, particularly in respect of kidney function, paraplegics are encouraged by medical advisers to take regular standing exercise. With the support of calipers the paraplegic housewife may be able to work in a standing position at the kitchen sink (51560). In practice many paraplegics find that the business of putting on and taking off calipers is such a chore that they prefer to remain seated in their wheelchairs.

Design factors
Architectural provision should be on the basis that paraplegics are chairbound and not able to stand. For relevant notes see also Tetraplegia, 9190; Sensation (loss of), 9180; Incontinence, 9152.

9170   Parkinson's disease

A chronic disease of the brain principally affecting old people, also known as shaking palsy or paralysis agitans. It is characterized by tremors and muscle rigidity causing slowness of movement, shuffling gait and impaired speech. Mental faculties are not impaired.

For design factors see Incoordination, 9153.

9171   Peroneal muscular atrophy

A hereditary disease causing nerve damage with resulting muscle weakness involving the legs and hands. Life span is often normal. Calipers may be needed to counter foot drop and improve walking.

9172   Poliomyelitis

A virus disease affecting the anterior nerve cells of the spinal cord and brain stem, causing paralysis of the muscles. Polio virus does not strike in any regular pattern and in some cases recovery may be complete. In others the residual effects may involve complete or partial muscular paralysis, for example in one leg or arm, or in specific areas unevenly distributed throughout the body. In severe cases paralysis of all four limbs may be virtually complete.

Incidence
Polio vaccine was developed during the 1950s and its use is now universal. As a consequence polio, apart from outbreaks in tropical countries, has been virtually obliterated, and there is no possibility that it will ever recur in Britain on any major scale. In the epidemic years of 1947 to 1958 52 514 cases were noted in England and Wales[24]. In 1972 five cases were reported and in 1973 two[25]. There have been no deaths since 1971[26].

Respiratory polio
Where the lungs and breathing system are affected dependence on a mechanical breathing aid may be necessary. The most usual remedy is a tracheostomy whereby positive pressure air is pumped through the windpipe by a battery or mains electricity operated machine. Some people who have this aid use it constantly, others during the night for topping up their energy. There are now (1976) probably fewer than 100 people in Britain who use a breathing machine constantly, and for whom failure of the machine will lead almost immediately to suffocation and death. To enable such people to go out and about a special wheelchair, known as the Cavendish chair, has been designed which carries a battery capable of operating for some hours when the machine is not connected to mains electricity. If there is a failure the machine can be manually pumped.

As an alternative to the tracheostomy device a few people, perhaps some 20 or 30 in Britain, use at night time a respirator tank, of the kind once known as an iron lung, which forces air in and out of the chest by means of negative pressure. A few people instead of using a respirator tank have a cuirass which fits like an upturned saucer over the chest and operates similarly by vacuum action; these people have to adopt a more prone position than those having a tracheostomy device and lie constantly on a semi-reclining bed.

Privileged condition
As discussed in the commentary (1305) polio is the most privileged of disability conditions. Architects should be cautious about attaching significance to advice given to them by people with polio who generalize about the needs of all disabled people from the viewpoint of their own unrepresentative experiences.

The residual effects of polio vary widely among affected individuals, and no general design recommendations can be made.

[23] Undocumented evidence communicated by DHSS and spinal injuries unit.
[24] Bib 93236, p7
[25] Bib 93274, p42
[26] Bib 93781, p23

9173 Polyneuritis

General inflammation of the nerves of the peripheral nervous system, extending from the spinal cord and brain to the skin, muscles and other parts of the body. The condition can cause general paralysis.

9174 Prosthesis

Replacement of an absent natural part by an artificial one, for example a leg, arm, tooth or eye. It most commonly refers to artificial limbs.

9175 Quadraplegia

Synonymous with Tetraplegia, see 9190.

9176 Rheumatism

A lay term, generally applied to diseases involving inflammation or degeneration of the joints or muscles. It should not be confused with rheumatoid arthritis (9107).

9177 Rickets

A vitamin deficiency of infancy causing a delay in the hardening of bones and, if neglected, extensive deformity. It was once common and is now extremely rare.

9178 Rubella

Rubella, or German measles, causes little discomfort to adults. If contracted by a woman during the first three months of pregnancy the baby born subsequently can be massively handicapped. Disabilities can include blindness, deafness, total mental incapacity and associated physical defects of incontinence and complete lack of mobility.

9179 Scoliosis

A lateral or sideways curvature and twisting of the spine.

9180 Sensation (loss of)

In the case of certain disability conditions, for example multiple sclerosis and traumatic paraplegia, the nerve cells controlling tactile sensation are affected. This can mean an inability to sense hot and cold in the affected areas, with susceptibility to burns and scalds. There may also be a loss of feedback information regarding balance.

In private housing it is desirable that the hot water supply is thermostatically controlled (4110) and that radiator panels have a low surface temperature (4241). The underside of sinks and exposed hot pipes may be insulated (51501).

The blood circulation of people with sensory impairment may be restricted where temperature levels are inadequate. Whole house space heating is recommended.

9181 Slipped disc

See Low back pain, 9157.

9182 Spastic cerebral palsy

The most common form of cerebral palsy (9121). It may involve impairment of the lower limbs, of all four limbs, or predominant impairment of arm and leg on one side with milder impairment on the other.

Many spastic people need to use wheelchairs. Reaching can be difficult and walking often laborious. See also Incoordination, 9153.

9183 Spina bifida

A congenital disability resulting from deformity of the spine and spinal cord of the unborn child. Spina bifida can cause paralysis of the lower limbs, incontinence, and, in many cases, brain damage.

The developing spinal canal fails to close completely; as a result, part of the spinal cord can herniate through, damaging the nerves emerging from it. This causes paralysis of the legs, underdevelopment of bones and, owing to lack of nervous control of bladder and rectum, incontinence.

Hydrocephalus
Spina bifida is commonly accompanied by hydrocephalus (9149). The fluid secreted in the brain is unable to drain in the normal way and accumulates under pressure, causing compressing of the brain and making the whole skull enlarged, sometimes to enormous proportions. Unless the fluid is drawn off, brain damage occurs. In general therefore it is the spina bifida which causes physical handicap, and hydrocephalus which causes mental handicap.

Surgical intervention
In the 1950s surgical techniques were evolved for drawing away the fluid on the brain, an operation which to avoid further damage has to be performed immediately after birth. The problem is that, except in the worst cases where the situation is irreparable, it is not possible to predict with confidence what the final physical and intellectual state will be. So it is difficult to choose suitable cases for treatment, and in any event the possibility of technical success ought not to be the sole criterion. What is more important is whether the family has the resources, social, financial and psychological, to cope with a grossly handicapped child. Many families do not, and if on medical advice the decision to operate is made, the eventual outcome may be rejection by the parents, fostering by the local authority and a lifetime spent in institutions.

Incidence

About 1500 spina bifida babies are born each year in England and Wales, representing 2·8 per 1000 live births. The incidence varies from over 4 per 1000 births in South Wales to less than 1·5 per 1000 in East Anglia[27]. About 600 spina bifida children each year reach the age of five [28].

Design factors

In cases where there is no brain damage and where the child receives good social and economic support the prognosis can be reasonable. Design factors are similar to those for paraplegia (9169). Spina bifida children with short legs may need support by extending the seat of the wheelchair horizontally forwards, so increasing the overall length of the chair. Special sanitary units may be helpful, see 54106.

9184   Still's disease

A disease occurring in children, similar to rheumatoid arthritis in adults; see 9107.

9185   Spondylitis

A form of arthritis of the spine. Ankylosing spondylitis (the most common form) is most prevalent among men aged between 20 and 40. In some cases complete fixation of the spine may occur.

9186   Stroke

Cerebral haemorrhage, thrombosis or embolism. See Hemiplegia, 9147.

9187   Synovitis

A disease or injury causing inflammation of the membrane lining a joint.

9188   Syringomyelia

A rare and slowly progressive disease of the nervous system affecting adults. A cavity forms in the spinal cord, causing loss of sensation to heat, cold and pain. The sense of touch is not affected. As the disease progresses the legs may become spastic and extensive deformity and paralysis develop. In some cases the disease spontaneously stops worsening and the person affected is left with a moderate or severe physical disability. Mental faculties are not affected.

9189   Tabes dorsalis

See Locomotor ataxia, 9156.

9190   Tetraplegia

Paralysis of all four limbs, caused by an injury or disease to the nervous cells in the neck (see Paraplegia, 9169). The most common injuries are diving accidents, falls, and traffic accidents where the head is thrown forward following deceleration of the body.

The ability of tetraplegics to manage independently varies considerably. Where the lesion is complete at level C4-5 or above, the individual cannot control a self-propelled wheelchair and has to use an electric wheelchair. Where the lesion is not complete some residual function may be retained in the upper limbs and independent management may be achieveable.

Design criteria are as for paraplegics. For tetraplegics with complete lesions, provision may need to be made in the bathroom and bedroom for an overhead track to carry a manually or electrically operated hoist (261). To move about inside and around the home an electric wheelchair will be used, such as the E and J Powerdrive (2344); generous circulation spaces will be necessary.

9191   Thalidomide

A sedative drug prescribed in Britain in 1959 and 1960, withdrawn in 1961. A side effect was severe physical deformity among some babies born to mothers who used it, deficiencies including shortened or twisted legs, flipper limbs, vestigial fingers and toes, additional fingers or toes, no external ears, defective eyesight, deformities of the inner ear causing deafness and a variety of internal deformities. Mental faculties were not affected by the drug.

It is estimated that there are some 410 young people in Britain with disabilities attributable to the taking of Thalidomide[29]. Nearly all were born in the years 1960, 1961 and 1962. Owing to the circumstances under which the drug was used, for example middle class women affected by insomnia associated with emotional stress, many thalidomide children are intelligent.

The variability of disablement among thalidomide children means that no general guidance can be given on design considerations.

9192   Thrombosis

The formation of a clot in a blood vessel. The clot is in situ, as distinct from embolism where it travels. Thrombosis in the brain can cause hemiplegia.

---

[27] Bib 93282, p59
[28] Bib 93275, p121
[29] Bib 93294

9193   Tuberculosis

A general name for the group of diseases caused by the tubercle bacillus of which pulmonary tuberculosis is the most important.

The incidence of all forms of tuberculosis is decreasing steadily in England and Wales; the number of deaths assigned to the disease in 1973 at 1240 was the lowest ever recorded[30].

Pulmonary tuberculosis
Pulmonary tuberculosis causes damage to the lungs if not treated. Due to the high risk of infection by contact it was formerly common for those with pulmonary tuberculosis (other than hospital cases) to live and work in sheltered colonies. Because of the reduced incidence of the disease and the effectiveness of early diagnosis and treatment there is no longer a need for such provision.

Excessive dust circulation is harmful to people with pulmonary tuberculosis and some heating systems may be unsuitable (4204). Good ventilation is important.

Tuberculosis of the joints
Tuberculosis of a joint causes swelling and pain in the joint and wasting of adjacent muscles. Where the individual does not respond to treatment, fixation of the joint may be necessary and occasionally amputation.

---

[30] Bib 93273, p44

920 Functions of the bibliography

9200 The bibliography in section 93 has two functions. It serves first to identify the sources of evidence drawn on in the main text of the book, and second, to give a comprehensive list of references on the variety of topics discussed.

9201 The fact that more than four in five of the 660 or so references listed were not in the bibliography of the 1967 edition of this book is a measure of the proliferation in recent years of documentation relating to the environment of disabled people. It is disappointing that the quality of many of these publications is mediocre, and there are few which can be recommended without qualification to the researcher or practician looking for material beyond that set down in this book. The review which follows selects some of the more significant items.

921 Buildings for disabled people: General architectural guidance

9210 In respect of public building design, the basic reference is the British Standard Code of Practice CP96 *Access for the disabled to buildings* (93000); its shortcomings are discussed in 612. The comparable American code (93020) has remained unchanged since originally published in 1961 despite new evidence; its ethics and inadequacies are referred to in the commentary (1320). Among codes based on the American model are those from West Germany (93063), Switzerland (93064), Australia (93070), New Zealand (93071) and Canada (93072).

9211 The most valuable textbooks giving architectural guidance on designing for disabled people are the two German reports *Bauen für Behinderte und Betagte* (93061) and *Planen und Bauen für Behinderte* (93062). Both are exceptionally well produced and illustrated, and both contain a mass of useful information, in some respects more comprehensive than that given in this book. Neither has a summary translation. Of the two, the second is perhaps the more useful for practising architects.

9212 There are a number of shorter reports giving practical guidance on building design for disabled people, for example from Sweden (93040), Norway (93056), Finland (93054, 93055) and Holland (93058). These are generally of a straightforward factual character and are of limited value to the student or researcher. From Italy the Edilizia Popolare special issue *Le barriere architettoniche* (93066) is worth noting.

9213 Regarding buildings and facilities for handicapped people other than the physically disabled, Kenneth Bayes and Sandra Francklin's *Designing for the handicapped* (93350) is useful.

922 The urban environment, landscaping

9220 The most instructive study of the urban environment of disabled people is Henrik Muller's examination of the Stockholm suburb of Hogdalen (93046). The Edinburgh University study *Planning for disabled people in the urban environment* (93006) is of limited merit but is attractively presented.

9221 On signposting the report *A symbol for disabled people* (93082) is the most thorough study, with practical relevance notwithstanding the obsolescence of the symbol which it reports.

9222 Of the variety of town guides which have been published Freda Bruce Lockhart's *London for the disabled* (93091) is, despite the selectivity of its information, the most appealing.

9223 On the landscaping of facilities in relation to the needs of disabled people the official US report *Barrier free site design* (93997) contains useful practical information.

923 Housing and institutions

9230 The Department of the Environment's reports *Mobility housing* (93111) and *Wheelchair housing* (93120) should be referred to for practical guidance. For practising architects a valuable feature of both reports is the inclusion of a series of examples of house plans with comments on suitability and shortcomings. Felix Walter's *An introduction to domestic design for the disabled* (93106) and the Scottish report *Housing for special needs* (93113) are sketchy. On kitchens for disabled people, P M Howie's study of disabled housewives (93920) is unsophisticated. On house adaptations the Cheshire report *Made to measure* (93108) is useful. Anne Acland's MHLG design bulletin *Safety in the home* (93770) gives practical commonsense advice.

9231 The Swedish report *Principles of the Fokus housing units for the severely disabled* (93170) contains carefully documented practical guidance. Accounts of various European housing programmes for handicapped people are given in Derek Lancaster-Gaye's edited reports *Personal relationships* (93310).

9232 On institutions for handicapped people the most valuable study is Eric Miller and Geraldine Gwynne's *A life apart* (93131). Jean Symons' report *Residential accommodation for disabled people* (93130) exposes the shortcomings of hospital provision.

9233 On housing for mentally handicapped people Sandra Francklin's report (93361) is entertaining and informative.

9234 For practical guidance on old people's housing the MHLG bulletin *Some aspects of designing for old people* (93610) is helpful but outdated. Archie McNab's report *The environmental needs of the elderly* (93611) is diligent.

9235 For architects and others concerned with the building of sheltered housing for old people the *Anchor housing association design guide* (93639) contains extensive practical advice; its distribution is normally limited to consultants employed by the association.

9236 For architectural guidance on house planning the MHLG bulletin *Space in the home* (93723) is concise, practical and informative. The bulletins on kitchens (93900) and bathrooms (93950) give more detailed guidance. On bathrooms, Alexander Kira's report *The bathroom, criteria for design* (93951) is immensely valuable.

9237 The most thorough, detailed and authoritative studies of the planning and equipping of domestic spaces for disabled people are those undertaken by the Department of Handicap Research at Gothenburg University. The text of the reports on kitchens (93930, 93931) and on sanitary rooms (93965) is in Swedish.

9238 From North America the Canadian report *Housing the handicapped* (93197) gives straightforward design guidance.

9239 On institutions for old people Peter Townsend's massive sociological study *The last refuge* (93640) is of lasting value.

924 **Disabled populations**

9240 Despite the criticisms raised in the commentary (1104–1106) the OPCS study *Handicapped and impaired in Great Britain* (93210) is very valuable. Of the local surveys carried out following the passing of the Chronically Sick Act, the most impressive report is that from Canterbury (93221). Ian Earnshaw's report on disabled housewives (93237) is a model of its kind.

9241 The Open University set book *The handicapped person in the community* (93207) is a substantial collection of essays from a variety of sources, covering both physical and mental handicap.

925 **Psychology, sociology**

9250 Beatrice Wright's *Physical disability – a psychological approach* (93300) is essential reading on the psychology of disability, and has been drawn on extensively in section 13 of the commentary. In Britain no general primer on disability psychology has yet been published; Rosemary Shakespeare's *The psychology of handicap* (93309) deals exclusively with handicapped children.

9251 Paul Hunt's edited volume of 12 autobiographical essays *Stigma* (93320) is valuable; the essay he wrote himself is exceptionally provocative. *Despite disability* (93321) is also a collection of essays, on the 'How I overcame obstacles' theme.

9252 Regarding the psychology of deviancy, Erving Goffman's *Stigma* (93751) is required reading; so also, in respect of institutions, is his *Asylums* (93750).

926 **Education, special facilities**

9260 Regarding the administration of higher education buildings for disabled people, the report from the North-east London Polytechnic (93372) is valuable. On education for disabled children, Elizabeth Anderson's two reports (93380, 93381) are informative and very readable.

9261 On museums, theatres, community centres, universities, schools and related buildings, the American report *Arts and the handicapped* (93035) is a thorough analysis of access problems. On school design, the Department of Education design note on ESN special schools (93394) is a model of good architectural guidance. On sports centres and swimming pools Felix Walter's report (93580) is helpful. On employment buildings for disabled people there are no useful references.

927 **Rehabilitation services**

9270 For guidance on rehabilitation for daily living the most valuable reports are those by Rita Goble and Philip Nichols (93430, 93431). Also on daily living, Peggy Jay's *Coping with disablement* (93421) is discursive. The *Equipment for the disabled* catalogues of aids (for example 93450–93453) are a useful source of reference.

928   **Ergonomics, wheelchairs**

9280   The most valuable ergonomic study of wheelchair users remains that by W F Floyd and others (93500). The worth of Felix Walter's *Four architectural movement studies for the wheelchair and ambulant disabled* (93501) is compromised by its poor methodology. Of the two housing studies from the Loughborough Institute for Consumer Ergonomics, that on doorways and corridors (93506) is sounder than that on bathrooms (93960).

9281   On wheelchairs and wheelchair population the OPCS report *Wheelchairs and their users* (93512) will, when it is published, be unquestionably the most valuable source. Elizabeth Platts' Leicestershire study (93232) is drawn on extensively in section 22. The Bath study (93513) is unhelpful.

929   **Architects' Journal building studies, CEH**

9290   For practising architects the most useful references are the series of building studies published in the Architects' Journal. Among these are reports on housing for disabled people (93102, 93114, 93125), housing for old people (93652, 93632, 93633, 93634, 93636, 93638), residential homes for handicapped or elderly people (93141, 93653, 93335), schools for handicapped children (93390, 93391, 93395) and day centres for handicapped people (93470, 93471).

9291   The Centre on Environment for the Handicapped (see 940) issues regularly updated bibiliographies of references on environmental facilities and services for handicapped people. The reports of CEH seminars on specific topics are helpful supplementary references.

Contents

Bibliography items in the pages which follow are grouped under subject headings. These headings are listed here to facilitate the checking of references on specific topics.

930   Buildings and disabled people: General

9300   Buildings and disabled people: Sources in Britain to 1969

93000   Access for the disabled to buildings, Part 1, General recommendations
British Standard Code of Practice CP96
British Standards Institution, London, 1967

93001   Access to public buildings for the disabled
Attachment to joint circular from the Ministry of Housing and Local Government (71/65) and the Ministry of Health (21/65)
HMSO, London, 1965

93002   Designing for the Disabled (2nd edition)
S Goldsmith
Royal Institute of British Architects, London, 1967

93003   The disabled – a mistaken policy?
S Goldsmith
RIBA Journal, September 1967, p387

93004   Further thoughts on design for the disabled: (1) The American code and the Norwich project; (2) The draft British Standard Code of Practice
S Goldsmith
Architects' Journal: (1) 13 October 1965, p867; (2) 27 October 1965, p971

93005   Designing for the Disabled, design details
Official Architecture and Planning, May 1968, p647

93006   Planning for disabled people in the urban environment
Planning research unit, Department of Design and Regional Planning, Edinburgh University
Central Council for the Disabled, London, 1969

93007   Disabled people and the use of buildings – a psychological problem
S Goldsmith
Rehabilitation, April-June 1969, p67

9301   Buildings and disabled people: Sources in Britain from 1970

93010   The physical environment: Housing, outdoor mobility and access Unit 13 (Block 3 Part 3) A post-experience course, The handicapped person in the community, Providing supportive services
P Large
The Open University, Milton Keynes, 1975

93011   Planning for disabled people in the urban environment
Report of proceedings of study conference, March 1970
Central Council for the Disabled, London, 1970

93012   Planning for the disabled, the elderly, and mothers with young children
Report of proceedings of one day study conference, Cardiff, November 1971
Cardiff City Council, 1972

93013   Facilities for disabled persons
Working party report to the office accommodation standards committee of the Property Services Agency
Department of the Environment, London, 1975

93014   Architecture for the handicapped
L Hellman
The Architect, March 1975, p24

93015   Including the excluded
J Schwerdt
The Architect: (1) February 1971, p29; (2) March 1971, p51

93016   Building for Disablement
J Penton & others
Era (journal of the Eastern region of the Royal Institute of British Architects) November/December 1972.

93017   Services, planning and hardware for the disadvantaged
A McNab
Architectural Design, May 1973, p294

93018   Accessibility for disabled people – A personal viewpoint
O A Denly
Physiotherapy, September 1974, p267

93019   Buildings for people who are handicapped or disabled; pilot survey of the Greater London Area
J Symons and R Gardner
Centre on Environment for the Handicapped, London, 1975

9302   Buildings and disabled people: Sources in the United States to 1966

93020   American national standard specifications for making buildings and facilities accessible to, and usable by, the physically handicapped (USA standard A117.1 – 1961)
American National Standards Institute (formerly American Standards Association), New York, 1961.

93021   Design of buildings to permit their use by the physically handicapped
T J Nugent
New Building Research, Fall 1960, p51

93022   Proceedings of the national institute on making buildings and facilities accessible to and usable by the physically handicapped
National Society for Crippled Children and Adults, Chicago, 1966

93023   Time-saver standards: Building and facility standards for physically handicapped
H P Vermilya
Architectural Record, December 1962, p129

93024   Banning those barriers
Journal of American Insurance, Chicago, September 1964

93025   Architectural barriers – A personal problem
C E Caniff
Rehabilitation Literature, Chicago, January 1962, p13

93026   Accent on access
Rehabilitation Record, Vocational Rehabilitation Administration, Washington DC, November 1966, p11

93027   Architectural barriers – a blueprint for action
L Chatelain
National Institute on Architectural Barriers, Chicago, 1965

9303 Buildings and disabled people: Sources in the United States from 1967

93030 Design for all Americans, a report of the national commission on architectural barriers to rehabilitation of the handicapped
Rehabilitation service administration, Department of Health, Education and Welfare, Washington DC, 1967

93031 A barrier-free environment for the elderly and the handicapped
Hearings before the special committee on aging, United States Senate, October 1971 (3 parts)
US Government Printing Office, Washington DC, 1972

93032 Architectural barriers for the handicapped, A survey of the law in the United States
R Dantona, B Tessler
Rehabilitation Literature, Chicago, February 1967, p34

93033 State and local efforts to eliminate architectural barriers to the handicapped
Department of Urban Studies, National League of Cities
National League of Cities, Washington DC, 1967

93034 Making facilities accessible to the physically handicapped
State University Construction Fund, Albany, New York, 1967

93035 Arts and the handicapped: An issue of access
Report from Educational Facilities Laboratories and National Endowment for the Arts
Educational Facilities Laboratories, New York, 1975

93036 Barrier-free design: Accessibility for the handicapped
P L Tica, J A Shaw
Institute for Research and Development in Occupational Education, City University of New York, New York, 1974

93037 Barrier free architecture
J F Hilleary
American Institute of Architects Journal, March 1969, p41

93038 Barrier free design
Report of a United Nations expert group meeting
Rehabilitation International, New York, 1975

93039 Into the mainstream, A syllabus for a barrier-free environment
S A Kliment
American Institute of Architects: Rehabilitation Services Administration of the Department of Health, Education and Welfare, Washington DC, 1975

9304 Buildings and disabled people: Sources in Sweden

93040 Architectural facilities for the disabled
International Commission on Technical Aids/Netherlands Society for Rehabilitation
ICTA, Bromma, Sweden/NVR, the Hague, Holland, 1973

93041 Handikappbyggnormer (regulation for access for the disabled to buildings)
Publication 24
National Swedish Board of Urban Planning, Stockholm, 1969

93042 Accessible towns-workable homes
Document D9: 1972
National Swedish Institute for Building Research, Stockholm, 1972

93043 Town planning for the disabled, outdoor mobility
T Olsson
National Swedish Building Research Institute, Stockholm, 1969

93044 Survey of Swedish recommendations of building measures according to persons in wheelchairs or with walking aids
E Andren, S-O Brattgard, B Petersson
Department of Handicap Research, Gothenburg University, Gothenburg, 1974

93045 Rörelsehindrade barns utemiljö (outdoor environment of physically disabled children)
I Tengvall
National Swedish Institute for Building Research, Stockholm, 1973.

93046 Rörelshindrades stadsbygdsmiljö - en studie från Högdalen (A study of the accessibility to wheelchair users of buildings in the Stockholm suburb of Högdalen)
H Müller
Statens råd för byggnadsforskning, Stockholm, 1961

93047 The physically disabled and their environment
Report of ISRD conferences, Stockholm, 1961
SVCK (now the Swedish Handicap Institute), Bromma, 1962

93048 Accessibility of buildings to handicapped persons; Guidelines for Nordic building regulations
NKB-publication no 19
Nordiska Kommitten för Byggbestamelser, Stockholm, 1974

9305 Buildings and disabled people: Sources in Denmark, Finland, Norway and Holland

93050 Circular on the layout of building and construction work having regard to the needs of persons handicapped by limitations in their movements
Ministry of Housing Circular 49
Housing Committee for the Handicapped, Copenhagen, Denmark, 1972

93051 FIMITIC 2nd International Conference on Architectural Barriers
Report of conference held in Copenhagen and Malmo, May 1969
Landsforeningen af Vanføre, Copenhagen, Denmark, 1970

93052 Boligbebyggelser for alle
SBI – anvisning 98
F Vedel-Petersen, K Ranten
Statens Byggeforskningsinstitut, Hørsholm, Denmark, 1974

93053 Geboden toegang
Nederlandse Vereniging voor Revalidatie, Stichting Aanpassingen voor Gehandicapten
NVR, the Hague, Holland, 1973

93054 Eliminating the obstacles of the disabled: General aspects; town planning aspects; general design considerations
SAFA Planning and Building Standards Institute, Helsinki, Finland, 1969

93055 Ohjeita liikuntaesteiden poistamiseksi
Yhdyskuntasuunnittelutoimikunta Helsinki, Finland, 1965
(English summary 'How to abolish ambulatory barriers' available from Finnish association of disabled civilians and servicemen, Helsinki)

93056 Bygging tilpasset
funksjonshemmede
B Halmrast
Norges Vanførelag, Oslo, Norway,
1973

93057 Building regulations and the
handicapped
C Boysen, T Lange
Norwegian Institute of Building
Research, Oslo, Norway, 1972

93058 Voorzieningen Openbare
Gebouwen Lichamelijk
Gehandicapten
(Report on the working party on
accessibility of public buildings to
the disabled)
Stichting Technische Voorlichting
ten Behoeve van Lichamelijk
Gehandicapten, the Hague,
Holland, 1964

93059 Planning for the disabled
F Carlsson and others
Build International, Rotterdam,
Holland, January 1971, p6

9306 Buildings and disabled people:
Other sources in Europe

93060 Easier access to public buildings for
the physically handicapped,
Appendix to Council of Europe
resolution AP (72)5.
Council of Europe, Strasbourg,
France, 1972.

93061 Bauen für Behinderte und Betagte.
A Stemshorn
Verlagsanstalt Alexander Koch,
Stuttgart, West Germany, 1974

93062 Planen und bauen für Behinderte
H Kuldschun, E Rossmann
Deutsche Verlags-Anstalt,
Stuttgart, West Germany, 1974

93063 Bauliche Massnahmen für
Behinderte und alte Menschen im
Offentlichen Bereich
Planungsgrundlagen: Strassen,
Plätze und Wege (Blatt 1)
Planungsgrundlagen: Öffentlich
zugängige Gebäude (Blatt 2)
Construction measures for disabled
persons and old human beings in
the public field; design principles;
public accessible buildings
DIN 18 024
Deutscher Normenausschuss,
Berlin, West Germany, 1973

93064 Bauliche Massnahmen für
Gehbehinderte
Norm 521/500
Schweizerische Zentralstelle für
Baurationalisierng, Zurich,
Switzerland, 1974

93065 Architecture et accessibilité
Association Nationale pour le
Logement des Handicapés,
Brussels, Belgium, 1972

93066 Le barriere architettoniche
A Ornati and others
Edilizia Popolare, Rome, Italy,
September–October 1975, p5–77

93067 Gli invalidi e le barriere
architettoniche
Proceedings of FIMITIC
conference, Stresa, June 1965
Edizioni ANMIL, Rome, Italy, 1966

93068 Logement et handicapes physiques
Special number of Les cahiers de la
vie quotidienne (April – June 1973)
Comité National Français de
Liaison pour la Réadaptation des
Handicapés, Paris, France, 1973

93069 The accessibility of public life:
The case of the handicapped
articles by J Frederiksen; J F van
Leer; S Goldsmith; V I van der Does-
Enthoven
International Federation for
Housing and Planning Bulletin 1975
(4), p10

9307 Buildings and disabled people:
Sources outside Europe and the
United States

93070 Design for access by handicapped
persons
Part 1, Public buildings and
facilities
Standards Association of Australia,
Sydney, 1968

93071 Code of practice for design for
access by handicapped persons
Part 1, Public buildings and
facilities
NZS 4121, Part 1: 1971
Standards Association of New
Zealand, Wellington, 1971

93072 Building standards for the
handicapped 1970
Supplement No 5 to the National
Building Code of Canada
National Research Council,
Ottawa, 1970

93073 Architectural barriers to the
physically handicapped
S A Kirkland
Edmonton, Canada, 1971
(thesis reprinted for use of Building
Standards of the Associate
Committee on the National
Building Code of Canada, 1971)

93074 The needs of the physically
handicapped in respect to housing
and the design of public buildings:
(1) Committee on buildings and
housing; (2) A guide on building for
the handicapped
Community Chest and Councils of
the Greater Vancouver Area,
Vancouver BC, Canada, 1960

93075 Communication breakdown
D J DePape and others
Canadian Paraplegic Association,
Winnipeg, 1971

9308 Signposting

93080 Symbol of accessibility
K Montan, chairman ICTA
International Commission
on Technical Aids, Bromma,
Sweden, 1969

93081 Traffic signs: General
Department of the Environment
Circular Roads 59/71
Department of the Environment,
London, 1971

93082 A symbol for disabled people:
Symbol application manual
S Goldsmith, P Rea
Royal Institute of British
Architects, London, 1969

93083 A symbol for the disabled
S Goldsmith
New Society, 21 November 1968,
p760

93084 Accessibility for the disabled:
A pilot scheme on signposting
(unpublished)
Edinburgh Committee for the
Coordination of Services for the
Disabled, 1969

93085 International symbol of access for
the handicapped:
Use and application in Winnipeg
D J DePape and others
Canadian Paraplegic Association,
Winnipeg, 1971

93086 Code of practice for design for
access by handicapped persons
Part 2, Symbols and signposting.
(NZS 4121, Part 2: 1975)
Standards Association of New
Zealand, Wellington, 1975

9309   Guides for disabled people

93090   Directions for the preparation of a guide for disabled persons in towns and other built-up areas
International Commission on Technical Aids, Bromma, Sweden, 1966

93091   London for the disabled
F Bruce Lockhart
Ward Lock, London, 1967

For information on the availability of other local access guides enquiry should be made to the Central Council for the Disabled, see 940

93092   Access to public conveniences: A handbook for the disabled person
Central Council for the Disabled, London, 1973

93093   AA Services, Guide for the disabled
Automobile Association, London, 1972

93094   A guide to British Rail: A handbook for the disabled person
Central Council for the Disabled, London, 1975

931   Housing and institutions for disabled people

9310   Housing for disabled people: Britain: Sources to 1973

93100   Housing to fit the handicapped
A Shearer
The Guardian, London, 26 June 1973, p16

93101   Designing special accommodation – the disabled
S Goldsmith
Housing Review, London, May – June 1973, p106

93102   Integrated housing in Haringey: Building study
D Sharp (appraisal)
Architects Journal, 5 September 1973, p539

93103   Housing for the disabled, planning digest
P H Stringer
Scottish Local Authorities Special Housing Group, Edinburgh, 1972

93104   Housing the handicapped
M Whitaker
(private circulation) West Midlands Regional Housing and Planning Office of the Department of the Environment, 1972

93105   Housing for old people, with design standards for the disabled
New Scottish Housing Handbook Bulletin 3
Scottish Development Department
HMSO, Edinburgh, 1970

93106   An introduction to domestic design for the disabled
F Walter
Disabled Living Activities Group, Central Council for the Disabled, London, 1969

93107   Housing for the disabled
S Goldsmith
Official Architecture and Planning, May 1968, p635

93108   Made to measure: Domestic extensions and adaptions for handicapped persons
Cheshire county architect's department
Cheshire County Council, Chester, 1973

9311   Housing for disabled people: Britain: Sources 1974–5

93110   Housing for people who are physically handicapped
Department of the Environment Circular 74/74
HMSO, London, 1974

93111   Mobility housing
S Goldsmith
Housing Development Directorate Occasional Paper 2/74
Department of the Environment, London, 1974
(reprinted from Architects' Journal, 3 July 1974, p43)

93112   More able to manage
S Goldsmith
New Society, 27 June 1974, p764

93113   Housing for special needs
Part I, The physically handicapped
Scottish Local Authorities Special Housing Group, Edinburgh, 1974

93114   Housing for the disabled, Coventry: Building study
J Penton (appraisal)
Architect's Journal, 23 October 1974, p977

93115   Why Merton is top of the league
M Manning
Community Care, 8 May 1974, p12

93116   Designing for the handicapped: Houses before homes
M Hanson
Municipal and Public Services Journal, 20 September 1974, p1161

93117   Planning to house the disabled
M Manning
Community Care, 22 October 1975, p16

93118   House development manual: Housing for disabled and physically handicapped persons (second draft)
Greater London Council Housing Department Development Branch, 1975

93119   Criteria for rehousing on medical grounds
S Hodgson
Public Health, London, November 1975, p15

9312   Housing for disabled people: Britain: Sources 1975–6

93120   Wheelchair housing
S Goldsmith, J Morton
Housing Development Directorate
Occasional Paper 2/75
Department of the Environment,
London, 1975
(reprinted from Architects' Journal,
25 June 1975, p1319)

93121   Wheelchair and mobility housing:
Standards and costs
Department of the Environment
Circular 92/75
HMSO, London, 1975

93122   Survey of purpose-designed
wheelchair housing
J Morton
(unpublished) Department of the
Environment, London, 1976

93123   Housing for disabled people
C R Sharp
Eric Cole Design Group,
Cirencester, 1975

93124   Interim report of the working party
on housing for disabled people
J Ribbens (secretary)
Central Council for the Disabled,
London, 1975

93125   Housing for the disabled,
Friendship House:
J Penton (appraisal)
Architects' Journal, 29 January
1975, p240

93126   Disabled tenants and the older
housing stock
Research Unit of Scottish Local
Authorities Special Housing Group
Scottish Local Authorities Special
Housing Group, Edinburgh, 1976

93127   Housing for disabled people in
Greater London
Interim report of a pilot study
prepared for the Greater London
Association for the Disabled
S Tester
Greater London Association for the
Disabled, London, 1976

93128   Towards a housing policy for
disabled people
Report of the working party on
housing of the Central Council for
the Disabled (draft)
Central Council for the Disabled,
London, 1975

93129   Housing for the disabled in
Hillingdon
London Borough of Hillingdon
Social Services Research,
Hillingdon, 1975

9313   Residential accommodation for disabled people: General

93130   Residential accommodation for
disabled people
J Symons
Centre on Environment for the
Handicapped, London, 1974

93131   A life apart: A pilot study of
residential institutions for the
physically handicapped and the
young chronic sick
E J Miller, G V Gwynne
Tavistock Publications, London,
1972

93132   Parasite people
(review of Bib 93131)
P Hunt
Cheshire Smile, Autumn 1972, p15

93133   Disabled homes and the world
S Goldsmith
New Society, 20 June 1968, p909

93134   Report of the first survey of the
Cheshire Foundation Homes in the
United Kingdom
M M Clark
(unpublished) Cheshire
Foundation, London, 1972

93135   Communities for the handicapped
R Gaylord
Built Environment Research
Group, Polytechnic of Central
London, 1974

93136   Residential needs of severely
physically handicapped non-
retarded children and young adults
in New York State
J Fenton
New York University Medical
Center, New York, 1972

9314   Residential accommodation for disabled people: Buildings

93140   Residential accommodation for
physically handicapped people
Local Authority Social Services
Circular LASSL (75)19
Department of Health and Social
Security, London, 1975

93141   Residential centre for spastics
(building study of Drummonds
Centre at Feering, Essex)
Architects' Journal, 5 March 1969,
p635

93142   Observations on planning a home
for spastics
(comments on appraisal in Bib
93141)
L Gardner and others
Architects' Journal, 27 May 1970,
p1313

93143   Comment: Single rooms
P Hunt
Cheshire Smile, Winter 1968/69, p18

93144   A home for the disabled: Bishop
Herbert House, Norwich
S Goldsmith
Architects' Journal, 19 October
1966, p993

93145   Residential accommodation for the
physically handicapped
Appendix to MoH Circular 22/65
Ministry of Health, London, 1965

9315   Hospital accommodation for disabled people: General

93150   National Health Service, care of
younger chronic sick patients in
hospitals
Ministry of Health memorandum
HM (68) 41
Ministry of Health, London, 1968

93151   1967 survey of the younger chronic
sick in hospitals, enclosure to
HM(68)41
Ministry of Health, London, 1968

93152   Chronically Sick and Disabled
Persons Act 1970
Department of Health and Social
Security memorandum HM(70)52
DHSS, London, 1970

93153   Provision for the young chronic
sick
Report of meeting, 30 January 1970
Scottish Hospital Centre,
Edinburgh, 1970

93154   The care of the chronic sick
W A R Thomson and others
Proceedings of the Royal Society of
Medicine, Volume 65, February
1972, p201

93155   The younger disabled in hospital
D M Prinsley
Supplement to Health and Social
Services Journal on Aids for the
Disabled, London, 1973, p8

93156   The social needs of people in long-
term care
J R Elliott
King Edward's Hospital Fund for
London, London, 1975

9316 Hospital accommodation for disabled people: Buildings

93160 Younger chronic sick hospital care: Suggestions for the design of units, and model plan
Ministry of Health, London, 1968

93161 Provision for the young chronic sick in the South East Metropolitan Region
O A Denly
Hospital and Health Services Review, April 1972, p118

93162 Twyford House, a specially designed unit for the care of the younger disabled person
R O F Hardwick
Journal of the Royal Society of Health, January 1974, p30

9317 Housing for disabled people: Scandinavia

93170 Principles of the Fokus housing units for the severely disabled
Fokus Society Research Group
Fokus Society, Gothenburg, Sweden, 1968

93171 Housing and service for the handicapped in Sweden
S–O Brattgard, F Carlsson, A Sandin
Fokus Society, Gothenburg, Sweden, 1972

93172 Bostäder för vanföra (Homes for the disabled)
H. Müller
SVCK (now Swedish Handicap Institute), Bromma, Sweden, 1959

93173 The Danish appraoch to residential care and community integration
J Frederiksen
(contribution to Bib 93310, p41)

93174 General lines in designs of dwellings for handicapped confined to wheelchairs
V Leschly, I and J Exner
Polio Institute, Hellerup, Denmark, 1959

93175 Etageboliger for bevaegelseshaemmede (Competition for wheelchair housing)
Arkitekten (Copenhagen) 4 1974, 26 February 1974, p70

93176 Northern Europe, Housing for severely disabled people
S Goldsmith
(unpublished) Department of the Environment, London, 1973

93177 Bostadsanpassning: Grundlaggande atgarder för nagra grupper handikappade
S-O Brattgard, J Paulsson
Avdelningen for Handikappforskning, Gothenburg, Sweden, 1976

93178 Disabilities and housing needs
A Gustavii
International Commission on Technical Aids, Stockholm, Sweden, 1975

9318 Housing for disabled people: Holland and Belgium

93180 Het dorp: Village for the handicapped in Holland
S Goldsmith
Architectural Review, April 1971, p227

93181 Holland's approach to residential care
A Klapwijk, W P Bijleveld
(contribution to Bin 93310, p52)

93182 A village for the handicapped
J Barr
New Society, 25 May 1967

93183 Cité de l'amitié
Association Nationale pour le Logement des Handicapés
The Association, Brussels, 1972

93184 Rapport technique: Etude de logements adaptés aux besoins spéciaux des handicapés physiques, paraplégiques, poliomyelitiques et amputés
Institut National du Logement Section VI, Brussels, 1961

9319 Housing for disabled people: Other countries

93190 Wohnungen fur Schwerbehinderte Planungsgrundlagen
Dwellings for seriously disabled persons; design principles; dwellings for wheelchair users (sheet 1); for blind persons and those having essential difficulty in seeing (sheet 2)
DIN 18 025
Deutscher Normenausschuss, Berlin, 1972

93191 Küche, bad, wc, hausarbeitsraum
Kitchen, bathroom, wc, housework-room: Planning principles for housing
DIN 18 022
Deutscher Normenausschuss, Berlin, 1972

93192 Handicapés moteurs, logement
Association Française de Normalisation, Paris, 1966

93193 Housing for the physically impaired: A guide for planning and design
US Department for Housing and Urban Development
US Government Printing Office, Washington DC, 1967

93194 The functional home for easier living
Institute of Physical Medicine and Rehabilitation, New York, 1961

93195 Wheelchair houses
Paralyzed Veterans of America, New York, 1961

93196 Housing considering the disabled and aged
Housing research branch
Housing note 1
R Tonkin, D Saunders
Australian Department of Housing and Construction, Melbourne, Australia, 1976

93197 Housing the handicapped
Central Mortgage and Housing Corporation, Ottawa, Canada, 1974

93198 Die stadt: Wohnen körperbehinderten
G G Dittrich
Deutsche Verlags-Anstalt, Stuttgart, 1972

93199 Handicapés et réadaptation l'éducation ménagère, January – April 1966, Paris

932 Disabled people: Populations, health and welfare services

9320 Disabled people: Services: General

93200 The Chronically Sick and Disabled Persons' Act 1970
Joint circular from the Department of Health and Social Security (12/70), Department of Education and Science (13/70), Ministry of Housing and Local Government (65/70) and Ministry of Transport (Roads 20/70)
HMSO, London, 1970

93201 No feet to drag: Report on the disabled
A Morris, A Butler
Sidgwick and Jackson, London, 1972

93202 Care of disabled people in Britain
Reference division, Central Office of Information
Central Office of Information, London, 1975

93203 Help for handicapped people
Department of Health and Social Security
HMSO, London, 1972

93204 Proceedings of a symposium on the disabled young adult
ed W H Bradley
National Fund for Research into Crippling Diseases, London, 1967

93205 Physical disability: The challenge and the response
Report of College of General Practice meeting 7 June 1972
Proceedings of Royal Society of Medicine, February 1973, p131

93206 The disabled in society
P Townsend
Greater London Association for the Disabled, London, 1967

93207 The handicapped person in the community
(Open University setbook)
ed D M Boswell, J M Wingrove
Tavistock Publications, London, 1974

93208 Aspects of social policy: Provision for the disabled
E Topliss
Blackwell, Oxford, 1975

9321 Disabled people: Populations: General

93210 Handicapped and impaired in Great Britain: Part I
A I Harris (Office of Population Censuses and Surveys, Social Survey Division)
HMSO, London, 1971

93211 Handicapped and impaired in Great Britain: Part II Work and housing of impaired in Great Britain
J R Buckle (Office of Population Censuses and Surveys, Social Survey Division)
HMSO, London, 1971

93212 The physically handicapped in Denmark: 1 Technique and methods
B R Andersen
Social Research Institute, Copenhagen, 1964

93213 The physically handicapped in Denmark: 2 Major results of the study
B R Andersen
Social Research Institute, Copenhagen, 1964

93214 The physically handicapped in Denmark: 3 Housing conditions and transport problems
G V Mogensen
Social Research Institute, Copenhagen, 1965

93215 Registered as disabled
Occasional papers on social administration no 35
S Sainsbury
G Bell, London, 1970

9322 Disabled people: Local populations

93220 Physical disability and community care: A study of the prevalence and nature of disability in relation to environmental characteristics and social services in a London borough
ed F W Skinner
National Council of Social Service, London, 1969

93221 The Canterbury survey of handicapped people
Canterbury social services department
Social services committee, Canterbury, 1974

93222 Report on the survey of chronically sick and disabled people resident in Newcastle upon Tyne, 1972
Social Services Department, Newcastle upon Tyne, with Institute of Local Government Studies, University of Birmingham, 1972

93223 Survey of handicapped and impaired persons and persons aged 75 or over and living alone
J Buckle, P Baldwin
Social Services Department, Royal Borough of Kensington and Chelsea, 1972

93224 Report on the survey of chronically sick and disabled persons resident on the Isle of Wight, 1971
M J Brown, N M Thomas, A Smith
Institute of Local Government Studies/Department of Social Administration, University of Birmingham, 1972

Bib 93221–4 are four of the surveys of handicapped people undertaken by local social services authorities in Britain in response to section 1 of the Chronically Sick and Disabled Persons Act 1970. Similar surveys have been made by many other authorities.

9323 Surveys of specific handicapped populations

93230 Planning for the disabled: A survey of wheelchair users in Norwich
S Goldsmith
(unpublished) 1968

93231 Disabled drivers in Norwich
S Goldsmith
(unpublished) 1968

93232 Characteristics and requirements of wheelchair users: A survey carried out by postal questionnaire and interview questionnaire in the county of Leicestershire between 1966 and 1968.
E Platts
Department of Ergonomics and Cybernetics, Loughborough University of Technology, Loughborough, 1971

93233 Survey of wheelchair users in Taunton
(unpublished) Somerset County Welfare Department, 1966

93234 Survey of wheelchair users in Hull
P Gregory
(unpublished) Department of social
administration, Hull University,
1966

93235 Report of enquiry into the incidence
and problems of people with small
stature
National Council of Social Service
(unpublished) National Council of
Social Service, London, 1969

93236 The residue of poliomyelitis
M Lee
Office of Health Economics,
London, 1973

93237 Disabled housewives on Merseyside
(fourteen case-studies)
I Earnshaw
Disablement Income Group,
London, 1973

**9324 Disabled people: Welfare
services**

93240 Services for handicapped people
living in the community, the
Chronically Sick and Disabled
Persons Act 1970
Department of Health and Social
Security Circular 45/71
HMSO, London, 1971

93241 Report of the committee on local
authority and allied personal social
services: (Seebohm report)
Command 3703
HMSO, London, 1968

93242 Local authority social services
departments aids to households
Department of Health and Social
Security, London, 1973

93243 Caring for people: staffing
residential homes
Report of the committee of enquiry
set up by the National Council of
Social Service: (the Williams report)
Allen and Unwin, London, 1967

93244 Local authority social services
departments: Statistics of the
registered blind and partially
sighted persons during the 12
months ending 31 March 1974,
England
Department of Health and Social
Security, London, 1974

**9325 Disabled people: Financial
services**

93250 Handicapped and impaired in Great
Britain: Part III Income and
entitlement to supplementary
benefit of impaired people in Great
Britain
A I Harris, C R W Smith, E Head
(Office of Population Censuses and
Surveys, Social Survey Division)
HMSO, London, 1972

93251 Care with dignity: An analysis of
costs of care for the disabled
Economist Intelligence Unit
National Fund for Research Into
Crippling Diseases, Horsham, 1973

93252 The Housing Finance Act 1972 and
the payment of welfare grants to
housing associations
National Federation of Housing
Societies, London, 1973

93253 The disability trap
ed J Harrison
Disablement Income Group,
London, 1973

9326 Handicapped children

93260 The health of the schoolchild:
Report of the chief medical officer of
the Department of Education and
Science for the years 1969–1970
HMSO, London, 1972

93261 The health of the schoolchild
1966–68: Report of the chief medical
officer of the
Department of Education and
Science
HMSO, London, 1969

93262 Living with handicap: The report of
a working party on children with
special needs
ed E Younghusband
National Bureau for Cooperation in
Child Care, London, 1970

93263 Handicap: A study of physically
handicapped children and their
families
J K McMichael
Staples Press, London, 1971

93264 The family and the handicapped
child: A study of cerebral palsied
children in their homes
S Hewett
George Allen and Unwin, London,
1970

93265 Handicapped children
J D Kershaw
Heinemann, London, 1966

93266 Blind and partially sighted children
DES Education Survey 4
S R Fine
HMSO, London, 1968

93267 Children with cerebral palsy
DES Education Survey 7
HMSO, London, 1970

93268 Integration of handicapped
children in society
ed J Loring, G Burn
Routledge and Kegan Paul,
London, 1975

9327 Health services: General

93270 St Thomas's health survey in
Lambeth
(unpublished) St Thomas's Hospital
Medical School, 4 reports, 1966–8

93271 Services for chronic renal failure
Health Service Circular (Interim
series) 11
Department of Health and Social
Security, London, 1974

93272 Department of Health and Social
Security annual report 1973
Command 5700
HMSO, London, 1974

93273 On the state of the public health
The annual report of the chief
medical officer of the Department of
Health and Social Security for the
year 1973
HMSO, London, 1974

93274 On the state of the public health
The annual report of the chief
medical officer of the Department of
Health and Social Security for the
year 1972
HMSO, London, 1973

93275 On the state of the public health
The annual report of the chief
medical officer of the Department of
Health and Social Security for the
year 1971
HMSO, London, 1972

93276 Health and personal social services
statistics for England 1973
Department of Health and Social
Security
HMSO, London, 1973

93277 Priorities for health and personal
social services in England: A
consultative document
Department of Health and Social
Security
HMSO, London, 1976

9328 Studies of specific disabling
      conditions

93280 Collaboration between health and
       social services: A study of the care
       of responauts
       K Dunnell and others
       Community Medicine, London,
       22 September 1972, p503

93281 Management of incontinence in the
       home: A survey
       P Dobson
       Disabled Living Foundation,
       London, 1974

93282 The changing problem of spina
       bifida
       K M Laurence
       Nuffield Provincial Hospitals Trust
       (reprinted from Patient, Doctor
       Society) 1972

93283 Spina bifida: The need for
       community support
       B Spain
       Greater London Council
       Intelligence Unit Quarterly
       Bulletin, June 1973, p66

93284 So you're paralysed
       B Fallon
       Spinal Injuries Association,
       London, 1975

93285 At home with multiple sclerosis
       Multiple Sclerosis Society, London,
       1970

93286 Still at home with multiple sclerosis
       Multiple Sclerosis Society, London,
       1972

93287 Help yourselves: A handbook for
       hemiplegics and their families
       P E Jay, E Walker, A Ellison
       Butterworths, London, 2nd edition,
       1972

93288 Multiple sclerosis: Transcript of
       talk, London, 2 November 1974
       D J Donnelly
       Multiple Sclerosis Action Group,
       London, 1975

93289 Multiple sclerosis
       Office of Health Economics,
       London, 1975

9329 Glossary references

93290 Family health guide
       ed Readers Digest Association
       Hodder and Stoughton, London,
       1972

93291 Textbook of rheumatic diseases
       ed W S C Copeman
       E and S Livingstone, London, 1968

93292 Pear's medical encyclopaedia
       J A C Brown
       Pelham, London, 1963

93293 Black's medical dictionary
       W A R Thomson
       A and C Black, London, 1965

93294 Our thalidomide children: Three
       years on, the gloom lifts
       P Knightley
       Sunday Times, London,
       16 November 1975, p5

933 Disabled, blind and mentally
     handicapped people: Social
     studies, educational services

9330 Disabled people: Psychology,
      sociology

93300 Physical disability: A psychological
       approach
       B A Wright
       Harper and Row, New York, 1960

93301 The measurement of attitudes
       toward disabled persons
       H E Yuker, J R Block, J H Younng
       Human Resrouces Center,
       Albertson New York, 1966

93302 Proceedings of a symposium on the
       motivation of the physically
       disabled
       ed P J R Nichols, W H Bradley
       National Fund for Research into
       Crippling Diseases, London, 1968

93303 Uncle Tom and Tiny Tim: Some
       reflections on the cripple as Negro
       L Kriegel
       American Scholar, Summer 1969,
       p412

93304 Passage through crisis
       F Davis
       Bobbs-Merill, Indianapolis, 1963

93305 Physical disability and human
       behavior
       J W McDaniel
       Pergamon, New York, 1969

93306 Social and psychological aspects of
       rehabilitation of the disabled in the
       United Kingdom
       J K Wing
       Rehabilitation, April–June 1965,
       p11

93307 The social biology of disabling
       illness and rehabilitation
       D J Feldman
       (unpublished) Stanford University
       School of Medicine, Stanford, USA,
       1968

93308 Impairment, disability and
       handicap; a multi-disciplinary view
       ed D Lees, S Shaw
       Heinemann, London, 1974

93309 The psychology of handicap
       R Shakespeare
       Methuen, London, 1975

9331 Disabled people: Personal relationships

93310 Personal relationships, the handicapped and the community, some European thoughts and solutions
ed D Lancaster-Gaye
Routledge and Kegan Paul, London, 1972

93311 A right to love? A report on public and professional attitudes towards the sexual and emotional needs of handicapped people
A Shearer
Spastics Society, London, 1972

93312 Life together
I Nordqvist
Swedish Central Committee for Rehabilitation, Bromma, Sweden, 1972

93313 The Raging Moon
P Marshall
Hutchinson, London, 1964

93314 Phase 2: Discovering the person in 'disability' and 'rehabilitation'
V Finkelstein
Magic Carpet (Disabled Drivers' Association), New Year 1975, p31

9332 Handicapped people: Autobiographical reports

93320 Stigma: The experience of disability
ed P Hunt
Geoffrey Chapman, London, 1966

93321 Despite disability: Career achievements by handicapped people
ed R Bleackley
Educational Explorers, Reading, 1974

93322 Face to Face
V Mehta
Collins, London, 1958

93323 The childhood story of Christy Brown
C Brown
Pan, London, 1972

93324 Journey into silence
J Ashley
Bodley Head, London, 1973

93325 Mermaid on wheels
J Epstein
Ure Smith, Sydney, Australia, 1967

93326 Blind man's buff
H Minter
Elek, London, 1973

9333 Blind people: General

93330 Mobility and reading habits of the blind
P G Gray, J E Todd
(Government Social Survey)
HMSO, London, 1968

93331 Mobility: Report of a survey of the mobility of blind people in the external environment
D Liddle
New Beacon, Royal National Institute for the Blind: (1) May 1965, p115; (2) June 1965, p142; (3) July 1965, p170

93332 Studies in blind mobility
J A Leonard
Applied Ergonomics (IPC Science and Technology Press), March 1972, p37

93333 Report of the working party on workshops for the blind
Ministry of Labour
HMSO, London, 1962

93334 The physical environment and the visually impaired
P G Braf
ICTA Information Centre, Bromma, Sweden, 1974

93335 Residential accommodation for the blind: Building study of Pocklington Place, Birmingham
J Penton (appraisal)
Architects Journal, 12 September 1973, p599

9334 Mentally handicapped and mentally ill people: Services

93340 Better services for the mentally handicapped
Department of Health and Social Security, Command 4683
HMSO, London, 1971

93341 Even better services for the mentally handicapped
Campaign for the Mentally Handicapped Central Action Group
Campaign for the Mentally Handicapped, London, 1972

93342 Learning to live: The mentally handicapped and their needs
King's Fund Hospital Centre exhibition handbook
King Edward's Hospital Fund, London, 1971

93343 Adult training centres
Department of Health and Social Security Local Authority Building Note 5
HMSO, London, 1972

93344 Better services for the mentally ill
Department of Health and Social Security, Command 6233
HMSO, London, 1975

9335 The environment of mentally handicapped and mentally ill people

93350 Designing for the handicapped
ed K Bayes, S Francklin
George Godwin, London, 1971

93351 The therapeutic effect of environment on emotionally disturbed and mentally subnormal children
K Bayes
Kenneth Bayes, London, 1967

93352 The physical environment for multi-handicapped mentally retarded children and young people (English summary of National Swedish Building Research report R28:1972)
B Abramson, S Fridell
National Swedish Council for Building Research, Stockholm, 1972

93353 Mental handicap and physical environment
H C Gunzburg, A L Gunzburg
Bailliere Tindall, London, 1973

9336 Mentally handicapped and mentally ill people: Accommodation

93360 Residential accommodation for mentally handicapped adults
Department of Health and Social Security Local Authority Building Note 8
HMSO, London, 1973

93361 Mentally handicapped people living in ordinary houses and flats, some useful information for architects
S Francklin
Centre on Environment for the Handicapped, London, 1973

93362 Room for improvement: A better environment for the mentally handicapped
J Elliott, K Bayes
King Edward's Hospital Fund London, 1972

93363 The Wessex experiment: Comprehensive care for the mentally subnormal
A Kushlick
British Hospital Journal and Social Service Review, 6 October 1967, p688

93364 Ward units for physically and
mentally handicapped
A M Anderson and others
Scottish Hospital Centre,
Edinburgh, 1972

93365 Bristol Industrial Therapy Housing
Association: A contribution to
domestic resettlement
D F Early
British Medical Journal,
1 September 1973, p491

93366 Integrated living for the mentally
retarded in the adult age groups
M Beckman
National Swedish Institute for
Building Research, Stockholm, 1974

93367 Integration of minority groups:
Proceedings of a symposium held at
Design Research Unit, 19 March
1975
K Bayes, J Turner, A Shearer
Design Research Unit, London,
1975

93368 A normal log village: Report on
Westoning Manor community for
the mentally handicapped
P Davey
Architects' Journal, 27 August
1975, p399

93369 A real home life for the mentally
handicapped
Welsh Health Technical Services
Organisation, Cardiff, 1975

9337 Handicapped people: Higher and
further education services

93370 Access to university and
polytechnic buildings: A handbook
for disabled students
A A M Wells
Central Council for the Disabled,
London, 1972

93371 Disabled students in higher
education
National Innovations Centre
National Innovations Centre,
London, 1974

93372 Report of the academic board
working party on facilities for
disabled students
North-east London Polytechnic,
1973

93373 University of Sussex: Unit for
severely physically disabled
students
G Dight
Association of Disabled
Professionals Newsletter 9 (British
Council for Rehabilitation of the
Disabled), 1974, p2

93374 Centre for disabled use: Star centre,
Cheltenham
J Penton
Architects Journal, 29 May 1974,
p1192

93375 Preparing higher education
facilities for handicapped students
J F McGowan, T Gust
University of Missouri, Columbia,
1968

93376 Libraries for the handicapped
M J Lewis
Library Association, London, 1969

93377 The handicapped school leaver:
Report of a working party
commissioned by the British
Council for Rehabilitation of the
Disabled
British Council for Rehabilitation
of the Disabled, London, 1964

93378 Provision for the disabled at
universities: Notes on
implementation of the Chronically
Sick and Disabled Act 1970
University Grants Committee,
London, 1972

93379 The disabled student in higher
education: Proceedings of
conference, November 1973
North-east London Polytechnic,
London, 1974

9338 Schools and educational
services for handicapped
children

93380 The disabled schoolchild: A study of
integration in primary schools
E M Anderson
Methuen, London, 1973

93381 Making ordinary schools special:
A report on the integration of
physically handicapped children in
Scandinavian schools
E M Anderson
College of Special Education,
London, 1971

93382 Units for partially hearing children
DES Education Survey 1
HMSO, London, 1967

93383 Physical education for the
physically handicapped
Department of Education and
Science
HMSO, London, 1971

93384 The modification of educational
equipment and curriculum for
maximum utilization by physically
disabled persons: Design of a school
for physically disabled students
H E Yuker, J Revenson, J F
Fracchia
Human Resources Center,
Albertson, USA, 1968

93385 Special education: A fresh look
Report on Education no 77
Department of Education and
Science, London, 1973

93386 Special schools: Should we stop
building them?
S H Haskell
Rathbone Quarterly, October 1974,
p13

93387 Play, play equipment and play areas
with special reference to the
handicapped; publications and
addresses
R Hughes, P Pacey
St Albans School of Art, St Albans,
1974

9339 Schools for handicapped
children: Buildings

93390 Special schools for the physically
handicapped: Study of Richard
Cloudesley School, Islington and
Lonsdale School, Stevenage
J Penton
Architects' Journal, 12 June 1974,
p1323

93391 Bromley Hall School for the
physically handicapped: Building
study
Architects' Journal, 27 August
1969, p505

93392 Full marks for teamwork: Report on
Richard Cloudesley School for
Handicapped Children by Inner
London Education Authority
C McCall
The Architect, April 1973, p44

93393 Environmental design: New
relevance for special education
A Abeson, J Blacklow
Council for Exceptional Children,
Arlington, Va, USA, 1971

93394 ESN Special schools: Designing for the severely handicapped
Department of Education and Science, Architects and Building Branch, Design note 10
Department of Education and Science, London, 1972

93395 School for slow learners: Building study of Ravenswood school, Nailsea
E Pearson (appraisal)
Architects' Journal, 18 November, p1189

93396 Special school environments for handicapped children
J S Sandhu, H Hendriks-Jansen
Built Environment Research Group, Polytechnic of Central London, 1974

93397 Schools for handicapped
C A Urry
Build International, Rotterdam, Holland, January 1971, p16

93398 Lessons in schooling the handicapped: Report on special care unit at Hackney
S Goldsmith
Design magazine, July 1973, p30

93399 Planning buildings for handicapped children
I Nellist
Crosby Lockwood, London, 1970

934   Disabled people: Rehabilitation services, employment

9340   Rehabilitation services: General

93400 Rehabilitation: Report of a sub-committee of the standing medical advisory committee (the Tunbridge report)
HMSO, London, 1972

93401 Medical rehabilitation: The pattern for the future: Report of a sub-committee of the standing medical advisory committee of the Scottish Home and Health Department and Scottish Health Services Council (the Mair report)
HMSO, Edinburgh, 1972

93402 Aspects of rehabilitation
N Capener and others
National Fund for Research into Crippling Diseases, London, 1971

93403 Principles of rehabilitation
W R Grant
E and S Livingstone, Edinburgh, 1963

9341   Rehabilitation procedures

93410 The assessment of disability
P J R Nichols
Proceedings of the Royal Society of Medicine, February 1973, p141
(Section of General Practice, p11)

93411 Measuring disability: Occasional papers on social administration
No 54
S Sainsbury
George Bell, London, 1973

93412 Rehabilitation of the elderly lower-limb amputee
E A Hamilton, P J R Nichols
British Medical Journal, 8 April 1972, p95

93413 The design of a pre-school 'learning laboratory' in a rehabilitation center
R Gordon
New York University Medical Center, New York, 1969

9342   Disabled living: General

93420 Living with a handicap
P Nichols
Priory Press, London, 1973

93421 Coping with disablement
P Jay
Consumers' Association, London, 1974

93422 Independent living for the handicapped and the elderly
E E May, N R Waggoner, E B Hotte
Houghton Mifflin, Boston, USA, 1974

93423 Homemaking for the handicapped
E E May, N R Waggoner, E M Boettke
Dodd Mead, New York, 1966

93424 The physically handicapped housewife
SVCK (now the Swedish Handicap Institute), Bromma, Sweden, 1959

93425 Living with a disability
H A Rusk, E J Taylor
Blakiston, New York, 1953

93426 Kitchen sense for elderly or disabled people
S Foott, M Lane, J Mara
Disabled Living Foundation/ Heinemann, London, 1975

93427 Wheelchair to independence
E M and C R Gutman
C C Thomas, Springfield, Illinois, USA, 1968

9343   Rehabilitation for daily living

93430 Rehabilitation of the severely disabled: 1 Evaluation of a disabled living unit
R E A Goble, P J R Nichols
Butterworths, London, 1971

93431 Rehabilitation of the severely disabled: 2 Management
P J R Nichols
Butterworths, London, 1971

93432 The home economist in rehabilitation
L O Schwab
Rehabilitation Literature, Chicago, May 1968, p130

93433 Training in activities of daily living
P M Wood
Occupational Therapy, July 1965, p11

93434 Activities of daily living for physical rehabilitation
E B Lawton
McGraw-Hill Book Co, New York, 1963

93435 A manual for training the disabled homemaker
H A Rusk and others
Institute of Physical Medicine and Rehabilitation, New York, 1961

93436 Handling the handicapped: A guide
to the lifting and movement of
disabled people
Chartered Society of Pysiotherapy
Woodhead-Faulkner, Cambridge,
1975

93437 Managing the disabled at home
W R Grant
The Practitioner, January 1972,
p140

9344 Aids: General

*The Disabled Living Foundation
(see 940) issues regularly up-dated
lists of disablement aids and
equipment to subscribers to its
information service. These include
lists on communication aids, hoists
and lifting equipment, personal
toilet aids, transport aids and
household equipment.*

93440 Aids for the disabled: (Loose-leaf
index continually under revision)
International Commission
on Technical Aids, Bromma,
Sweden

93441 Aids for children: Technical aids for
physically handicapped children
except defects of vision, hard of
hearing, orthosis and prosthesis
International Commission
on Technical Aids, Bromma,
Sweden, 1972

93442 Aids for the disabled
BMA planning unit report no 2
British Medical Association,
London, 1972

93443 Some studies of mechanical aids for
the disabled
M W Thring
Journal of the Royal Society of
Arts, January 1973, p56

93444 Rehabilitation engineering
International Commission on
Technical Aids,
Bromma, Sweden, 1969

93445 Les cahiers de la vie quotidienne
Comité National Français de
Liaison pour la Réadaptation des
handicapés, Paris, updated
regularly

93446 Aids for the handicapped
N D B Elwes
Spastics Society, London, 1973

93447 Aids for the severely handicapped
ed K Copeland
Sector Publishing, London, 1974

93448 Equipment for the disabled;
8 Hoists, walking aids
ed E R Wilshere, E M Hollings,
P J R Nichols
National Fund for Research into
Crippling Diseases, Horsham, 1974

93449 Aiding the disabled
ed S Goldsmith
Design magazine (special issue)
November 1969

9345 Household aids

93450 Equipment for the disabled:
3 Home management
ed E R Wilshere, E M Hollings,
P J R Nichols
National Fund for Research into
Crippling Diseases, Horsham, 1973

93451 Equipment for the disabled:
4 Disabled mother
ed E R Wilshere, E M Hollings,
P J R Nichols
National Fund for Research into
Crippling Diseases, Horsham, 1973

93452 Equipment for the disabled:
5 Personal care
ed E R Wilshere, E M Hollings,
P J R Nichols
National Fund for Research into
Crippling Diseases, Horsham, 1974

93453 Equipment for the disabled:
7 Housing and furniture
ed E R Wilshere, E M Hollings,
P J R Nichols
National Fund for Research into
Crippling Diseases, Horsham, 1974

93454 The needs of the disabled: A guide
to the selection of household
furniture and equipment
S B Jones
British Hospital Journal and Social
Service Review, 26 January 1968,
p155

93455 The household needs of the
disabled: A guide to the selection of
furniture and equipment
S B Jones
British Hospital Journal and Social
Service Review, 11 April 1969, p679

93456 The household needs of the
disabled: A guide to the selection of
furniture and equipment
S B Jones
British Hospital Journal and Social
Service Review, 6 March 1970, p436

9346 Hydrotherapy facilities

93460 Hospital Centre Symposium:
Planning of Hydrotherapy
departments
G D Kersley, M J McMain,
P H P Bennett
Hospital Management Planning
and Equipment, December 1965,
p927

93461 Planning physiotherapy
departments: 2 hydrotherapy
P H Y
Physiotherapy, February 1968, p66

9347 Day centres

93470 Shieldfield health and social
services centre: Building study
J Penton (appraisal)
Architects' Journal, 9 January
1974, p74

93471 Social centre for old and
handicapped at Aberdare: Building
study
A Lipman (appraisal)
Architects' Journal, 25 February
1970, p485

93472 A report on day-care centres and
residential units
Multiple Sclerosis Society of Great
Britain and Northern Ireland
Multiple Sclerosis Society, London,
1967

93473 Architect's brief: Day centre for
physically handicapped adults
Cheshire Social Services
Department
Cheshire County Council, Chester,
1975

9348 Employment

93480 Sheltered employment for disabled
people: A consultative document
Department of Employment,
London, 1973

93481 The quota scheme for disabled
people: A consultative document
Department of Employment,
London, 1973

93482 Resettlement policy and services for
disabled people
Department of Employment
discussion paper for the National
Advisory Council for the
Employment of the Disabled
Department of Employment,
London, 1972

93483 Some aspects of the employment of disabled persons in Great Britain
M Greaves
British Council for Rehabilitation of the Disabled, London, 1969

93484 A place at work: The working environment of the disabled
R W C Rogerson, P H Spence
Scottish Red Cross Society, Glasgow, 1969

93485 Workshops for the handicapped in the United States: An historical and developmental perspective
N Nelson
C Thomas, Springfield, Illinois, USA, 1971

93486 Sheltered workshops: An architectural guide
F C Salmon, C F Salmon
Oklahoma State University Press, Stillwater, USA, 1966

9349 Rehabilitation buildings: General

93490 Family help unit: Bury St Edmunds
Roman Halter Associates
ERA (journal of the Eastern region of the RIBA), November-December 1972, p16

93491 Selected rehabilitation facilities in the United States: An architect's analysis
T K FitzPatrick
US Department of Health, Education and Welfare, Washington DC, USA, 1971

93492 Rehabilitation programs and facilities
T K FitzPatrick
US Department of Health, Education and Welfare, Vocational Rehabilitation Administration, Washington DC, USA, 1963

93493 Rehabilitation Center planning: An architectural guide
F C Salmon, C F Salmon
Pennsylvania State University Press, USA, 1959

93494 Planning and operating facilities for crippled children
W B Schoenbohm
C Thomas, Springfield, Illinois, USA, 1962

93495 Department of rehabilitation: A design guide
Department of Health and Social Security, London, 1974

935 Disabled people: Ergonomics, wheelchairs, mobility, special buildings

9350 Disabled people: Ergonomics, anthropometrics

93500 A study of the space requirements of wheelchair users
W F Floyd and others
Paraplegia, E and S Livingstone, Edinburgh, May 1966, p24

93501 Four architectural movement studies for the wheelchair and ambulant disabled
F Walter
Disabled Living Foundation, London, 1971

93502 Space and design for the wheelchair disabled
C W Noble
(unpublished) 1967

93503 Ergonomics and the disabled
P A Isherwood
International Rehabilitation Review, 1st quarter 1970, p9

93504 Wheelchair users: A study in variation of disability
P J R Nichols, R W Morgan, R E A Goble
Ergonomics, Vol 9 no 2 1966, p131

93505 A study of the functional anthropometry of two groups of wheelchair users, and a description of a method of measuring the upper limb strength of one of these groups
K L Knight
(unpublished) Loughborough College of Technology, 1965

93506 Housing for the disabled: Part 1 An ergonomic study of the space requirements of wheelchair users for doorways and corridors
R J Feeney, A Ownsworth
Institute for Consumer Ergonomics, Loughborough, 1973

9351 Wheelchairs: Sources in Britain

93510 Handbook of wheel chairs and hand propelled tricycles (MHM 408)
DHSS Supply Division
Department of Health and Social Security, Blackpool (under constant revision)

93511 Notes for doctors concerned with recommending supply of invalid chairs, powered vehicles and car allowances
Appendix 3 to Circular 822/69
Ministry of Health, London, 1969

93512 Wheelchairs and their users
Social Survey Division, Office of Population Censuses and Surveys
to be published 1976 or 1977 by HMSO, London

93513 Wheelchair survey
P Holt, N Tuft
Bath Institute of Medical Engineering, Bath, 1974

93514 Equipment for the disabled: Wheelchairs and outdoor transport
ed E R Wilshere, E M Hollings, P J R Nichols
National Fund for Research into Crippling Diseases, Horsham, 1971

93515 A symposium on the wheelchair
Report of Polio Research Fund conference, November 1963
Paraplegia, E and S Livingstone, Edinburgh, May 1964, p20

93516 Powered chairs
P Driver, N Whiteley
Cheshire Smile, Summer 1972, supplement

93517 Wheelchairs
M B Hawker
Modern Geriatrics, December 1974, p503

9352 Wheelchairs: Sources outside Britain

93520 The wheelchair book
H L Kamenetz
C Thomas, Springfield, Illinois, USA, 1969

93521 Samhällsplanering för rörelsehindrade: Inventering av rullstolar
G Zackrisson
Byggforskningen, Stockholm, Sweden, 1966

93522 Wheelchairs
Communications no 17
K V Lauridsen, T Lund
Polio Institute, Hellerup, Denmark, 1964

9353 Wheelchair design

93530 Wheelchair design: Part 1 An examination of factors influencing the requirements and design of short range mobility appliances for the disabled; Part 2 2nd draft specification of adult users' requirements
School of Industrial Design, Royal College of Art
Royal College of Art, London, 1968

93531 Proceedings of a symposium on wheelchair design: Report of a symposium held in London, April 1969
National Fund for Research into Crippling Diseases, London, 1969

93532 Post graduate wheelchair projects
A Isherwood, B Archer
Design magazine, November 1969, p28

93533 Wheelchairs
Designer (Society of Industrial Artists and Designers Ltd), London, May 1974, p9

9354 Disabled people: Mobility services

93540 Mobility of physically disabled people
Lady Sharp
HMSO, London, 1974

93541 Mobility for the disabled
Sir R Tunbridge and others
Proceedings of the Royal Society of Medicine, May 1974, p399

93542 Orange badge scheme: Parking for disabled persons
Chronically Sick and Disabled Persons Act 1970 – Section 21
Department of the Environment Circular 23/75
HMSO, London, 1975

93543 Conveyance of the disabled: Report of ad hoc committee to Joint Committee on Mobility for the Disabled Spastics Society, London, 1968

9355 Disabled people: Personal transport

93550 Vehicles for the disabled
Which?, Consumers' Association, March 1972, p94

93551 What kind of tricycle or car?
M Hall
Design magazine, November 1969, p34

93552 Conversion of cars for disabled drivers
International Commission on Technical Aids, Bromma, Sweden, 1966

93553 Der versehrte und sein fahrzeug
F Hörber
Joh Jüngling KG, Buch und Offsetdruck, Munich, West Germany, 1965

93554 Vehicles for the severely disabled
P Bray, D M Cunningham
Rehabilitation Literature, Chicago, USA, April 1967, p98

9356 Disabled people: Public transport

93560 The disabled traveller on public transport
Department of the Environment Circular 102/73
HMSO, London, 1973

93561 Entrance examination
K Moses
Commercial Motor, 4 November 1966, p70

93562 Taking the right steps?: A re-examination of bus entrance design
D and K Moses
Commercial Motor, 8 November 1968, p45

93563 An investigation of factors affecting the use of buses by both elderly and ambulant disabled persons
B M Brooks, H P Ruffell-Smith, J S Ward
British Leyland UK Ltd (Truck and Bus Division), Preston, 1974

93564 Travel barriers
US Department of Transportation, Washington DC, USA, 1970

93565 Adapting public transport for the handicapped
Summary of report SOU 1975:68
HAKO-utredningen, Stockholm, Sweden, 1975

9357 Disabled people: Public lavatories

93570 Design of public conveniences with facilities for the disabled
Ministry of Housing and Local Government Circular 33/68
HMSO, London, 1968

93571 Designing a public convenience for the disabled
S Goldsmith, P J R Nichols, B Rostance, J Angell, L Angell
Annals of Physical Medicine, Vol VIII no 8, 1966, p307

93572 Public convenience design for the disabled
J and L Angell
(unpublished) Birmingham School of Architecture, 1966

9358 Disabled people: Sports buildings and services

93580 Sports centres and swimming pools
F Walter
Thistle Foundation, Edinburgh, 1971

93581 Sports and open-air facilities
A Nygren, S Perryd, S Söderström
International Information Centre on Technical Aids, Bromma, Sweden, 1969

93582 Paraplegic centre
G Perrin
Architects' Journal, 10 September 1969, p606

93583 Sport for the disabled
Sports Development Bulletin special issue, July 1972
Sports Council, London, 1972

9359 Disabled people: Other provisions

93590 Vending machines for the disabled
I Roberts
British Hospital Journal and Social Service Review, 7 October 1972, p2234

93591 Environment of machinery-dependent people
J Prestwich
Responaut, July 1974, p21

936   Old people

9360   Old people's accommodation: Reports, surveys

93600   Services for old people: Co-operation between housing, local health and welfare authorities and voluntary organisations
Joint circular from Ministry of Housing and Local Government (10/61) and Ministry of Health (12/61)
HMSO, London, 1961

93601   Old people: Study of living patterns
K J Haynes, J Raven
Architects' Journal, 26 October 1966, p1051

93602   New housing for the elderly: A study of housing schemes for the elderly provided by the Hanover Housing Association
D Page, T Muir
National Council of Social Services, London, 1971

93603   Accommodation for the elderly: Comments on the adequacy of accommodation for the elderly and suggestions for further development
Age Concern, Mitcham, 1974

93604   Housing for the elderly
National Federation of Housing Societies and National Old People's Welfare Council, London, 1962

93605   Sans everything: A case to answer
B Robb
Nelson, London, 1967

93606   Housing in retirement: Some pointers for social policy
H W Mellor and others
National Corporation for the Care of Old People, London, 1973

93607   Retirement communities
C Collins
Built Environment, September 1974, p478

93608   Assessing the need for domiciliary services for the elderly
Q Thompson
Greater London Intelligence Quarterly, September 1974, p35

93609   New deal for the elderly: Fabian tract 435
N Bosanquet
Fabian Society, London, 1975

9361   Old people's accommodation: Buildings

93610   Some aspects of designing for old people
Ministry of Housing and Local Government Design Bulletin 1 (metric edition)
HMSO, London, 1968

93611   The environmental needs of the elderly
A McNab
Reabilities Trust, London, 1967

93612   Designing for the elderly: Environmental needs
A McNab
Official Architecture and Planning, May 1968, p641

93613   Housing for old people: Siting
M Empson, N J Sheppard
Architects' Journal, 19 July 1967, p177

93614   Design and equipment of dwellings for old people
M Empson
Housing Review, March-April 1961, p44

93615   Some aspects of housing for old persons
V Hole
Architects' Journal: (1) 20 April 1961, p583; (2) 27 April 1961, p605

93616   Rehousing old people
V Hole, P G Allen
Architect's Journal, 8 January 1964, p75

93617   Dwellings for old people
V Hole, P G Allen
Architects' Journal, 9 May 1962, p1017

93618   Framework for care: De drie hoven old people's centre, Amsterdam
S Lyall (criticism)
Architectural Review, February 1976, p71

9362   Sheltered housing for old people: Reports, surveys

93620   Grouped flatlets for old people: A sociological study
Ministry of Housing and Local Government Design Bulletin 2 (metric edition)
HMSO, London, 1968

93621   Wardens and old people's dwellings
National Old People's Welfare Council
National Council of Social Service, London, 1966

93622   Grouped dwellings for the elderly
Institute of Housing Managers
Institute of Housing Managers, London, 1967

93623   Preliminary report of an inquiry into the effectiveness of sheltered housing schemes and their bearing on the need for residential care
E Perrett
(unpublished) University of Keele, 1969

93624   Role of the warden in grouped housing
A J Willcocks (chairman, Age Concern working party)
Age Concern, London, 1972

93625   The role of sheltered housing in the care of the elderly: A re-appraisal
Report of Nottingham University seminar, April 1975
A J Willcocks and others
Institute of Social Welfare, Stafford, 1975

93626   Abbeyfield extra care for those elderly who cannot look after themselves
Geoffrey Salmon Speed Associates
Abbeyfield Society Ltd, Potters Bar, 1976

9363   Sheltered housing for old people: Buildings

93630   Housing standards and costs: Accommodation specially designed for old people
Ministry of Housing and Local Government Circular 82/69
HMSO, London, 1969

93631   Old people's flatlets at Stevenage
Ministry of Housing and Local Government Design Bulletin 11
HMSO, London, 1966

93632   Old people's housing at Tonyrefail, Glamorgan: Building study
J B Lowe (appraisal)
Architects' Journal, 26 May 1971, p1179

93633   Old people's housing at Newark: Building study
T D Muir, D Page (appraisal)
Architects' Journal, 31 May 1972, p1199

93634   Sheltered housing for old people at Nuneaton and Faversham: Building study
J Penton (appraisal)
Architects' Journal, 3 October 1973, p787

93635 Trust sheltered housing: Report on housing association scheme at Elm Park, London
S Bone
Built Environment, September 1973, p504

93636 Old people's housing at Tenterden, Kent: Building study
J Penton (appraisal)
Architects Journal, 28 May 1975, p1127

93637 Housing for the elderly: The size of grouped schemes
Department of the Environment
Design Bulletin 31
HMSO, London, 1975

93638 Old people's housing at Norwich: Building study
J Penton (appraisal)
Architects' Journal, 4 June 1975, p1181

93639 Help the Aged housing associations design guide (loose-leaf volume of information sheets)
Anchor Housing Association, Oxford, 1974

9364 Residential accommodation for old people: Reports, surveys

93640 The last refuge: A survey of residential homes and institutions for the aged in England and Wales
P Townsend
Routledge and Kegan Paul, London, 1962

93641 Sociology – what do old people want?
M Willis
Architects' Journal, 13 June 1957, p897

93642 Designing for old people: The role of residential homes
S Korte
Architects' Journal, 19 October 1966, p987

93643 Care of the elderly in hospitals and residential homes
Memorandum attached to Ministry of Health Circular 18/65
HMSO, London, 1965

93644 Old people's homes: Siting and neighbourhood integration
A Lipman
Sociological Review, November 1967, p323

93645 Building design and social interaction: A preliminary study in three old people's homes
A Lipman
Architects' Journal, 3 January 1968, p23

93646 A social research inquiry into the specification of old age homes: Report of preliminary findings for Cheshire County Council
Conrad Jameson Associates, London, 1972

93647 Home and homes
A Shearer
Design magazine, January 1974, p46

9365 Residential accommodation for old people: Buildings

93650 Residential accommodation for elderly people
Department of Health and Social Security Local Authority Building Note 2
HMSO, London, 1973

93651 Fire precautions in old persons' homes
Home Office Fire Prevention Note 2/1964
HMSO, London, 1964

93652 Accommodation for old people: Two schemes in Norwich
S. Goldsmith
Architects' Journal, 28 January 1970, p221

93653 Old people's home at Bury St Edmunds: Building study
S Goldsmith (appraisal)
Architects' Journal, 29 September 1971, p701

93654 From the cradle to the grave: Report on children's reception centre and old people's home in Peckham
L Hellman
Architects' Journal, 10 October 1973, p847

93655 An update on the workhouse
M Kemp
Built Environment, September 1973, p496

93656 Old age serene and bright?: Report on old people's homes at Crawley and Southbourne, Sussex
Architects' Journal, 29 May 1974, p1197

9366 Accommodation for old people: Sources in Europe

93660 Housing the aged in western countries
G H Beyer, F H J Nierstrasz
Elsevier, Amsterdam, Holland, 1967

93661 Building for the aged
ed F H J Nierstrasz
Bouwcentrum, Rotterdam, Holland, 1961

9367 Accommodation for old people: Sources outside Europe

93670 Better buildings for the aged
J D Weiss
Hopkinson and Blake, New York, USA, 1969

93671 Housing needs of the aged
A Kira
Rehabilitation Literature, Chicago, USA, December 1960, p370

93672 Buildings for the elderly
N Musson, H Hensinkveld
Reinhold, New York, USA, 1963

93673 Planning homes for the aged
G Mathiasen, E H Noakes
F W Dodge, New York, USA, 1959

93674 The design of pensioner housing
Architectural section, New Zealand Department of Health
New Zealand Department of Health, 1972

93675 Housing the elderly (2nd edition)
N Larsson
Central Mortgage and Housing Corporation, Ottawa, Canada, 1972

93676 Housing for the elderly: The development and design process
I Green and others
Van Nostrand Reinhold Company, New York, USA, 1975

9368 Old people: General: Reports, surveys

93680 The aged in the welfare state: Occasional papers on social administration no 14
P Townsend, D Wedderburn
Bell, London, 1965

93681 Old and alone
J Tunstall
Routledge and Kegan Paul, London, 1966

93682 Old age: A register of social
research 1972 onwards
ed M R F Simson
National Corporation for the care
of old people, London, 1973

93683 Telephones for the elderly:
Occasional papers on social
administration no 53
P Gregory
Bell, London, 1973

93684 Lifeline telephone service for the
elderly: An account of a pilot
project in Hull
P Gregory, M Young
National Innovations Centre,
London, 1972

93685 Day care and leisure provision for
the elderly
D Morley
Age Concern (National Old
People's Welfare Council), London,
1974

93686 Social medicine in old age
J H Sheldon
Oxford University Press, London,
1948

93687 Accidental hypothermia in the
elderly
A M Exton-Smith
Journal of the Royal Society of
Health, 1 1970, p11

93688 Body temperatures in the elderly.
A national study of physiological,
social and environmental
conditions
R H Fox and others
British Medical Journal,
27 January 1973, p200

**9369   Old people: Ergonomics and
anthropometrics**

93690 Anthropometric and ergonomic
recommendations in designing for
the elderly
BS4467:1969
British Standards Institution,
London, 1969

93691 Functional anthropometry of
elderly women
D F Roberts
Ergonomics, October 1960, p321

93692 Ergonomic data for evaluation and
specification of operating devices
on components for use by the
elderly
D Thompson
Institute for Consumer Ergonomics,
Loughborough, 1975

937   Ancillary references

9370   Buildings: General

93700 Specification 1975
ed D Harrison
Architectural Press, London, 1975

93701 AJ metric handbook (3rd edition)
L Fairweather, J A Sliwa
Architectural Press, London, 1969

93702 Architect's data
E Neufert
Crosby Lockwood, London, 1970

93703 Time-saver standards for
architectural design data (5th
edition)
ed J H Callender
McGraw-Hill, New York, USA, 1974

93704 Time-saver standards for building
types
ed J de Chiara, J H Callender
McGraw-Hill, New York, USA, 1973

93705 Planning volume 1 (9th edition)
ed E D Mills
Iliffe, London, 1972

**9371   Housing: General: Government
circulars**

93710 Housing standards: Costs and
subsidies
Ministry of Housing and Local
Government Circular 36/67
HMSO, London, 1967

93711 Metric housing cost yardsticks
Ministry of Housing and Local
Government Circular 56/69
HMSO, London, 1969

93712 Metrication of housebuilding:
Progress
Ministry of Housing and Local
Government Circular 27/70
HMSO, London, 1970

93713 Public sector construction work:
Contracting procedures
Department of the Environment
Circular 158/73
HMSO, London, 1973

93714 Homelessness
Joint circular from Department of
the Environment (18/74) and
Department of Health and Social
Security (4/74)
HMSO, London, 1974

93715 Housing Finance Act: Housing
subsidies
Department of the Environment
Circular 59/74
HMSO, London, 1974

93716 The housing cost yardstick
Department of the Environment
Circular 61/75
HMSO, London, 1975

93717 Housing: Needs and action
Department of the Environment
Circular 24/75
HMSO, London, 1975

93718 Housing Act 1974: House
renovation grants
Department of the Environment
Circular 13/76
HMSO, London, 1976

**9372   Housing: General: Government
reports and bulletins**

93720 Homes for today and tomorrow:
(report of the subcommittee of the
Central Housing Advisory
Committee under the chairmanship
of Sir Parker Morris)
Ministry of Housing and Local
Government
HMSO, London, 1961

93721 Council housing: Purposes,
procedures and priorities: (the
Cullingworth report)
Ministry of Housing and Local
Government
HMSO, London, 1969

93722 Widening the choice: The next steps
in housing
Department of the Environment
white paper, Command 5280
HMSO, London, 1973

93723 Space in the home
Ministry of Housing and Local
Government Design Bulletin 6
(metric edition)
HMSO, London, 1968

93724 House planning: A guide to user
needs with a check list
Ministry of Housing and Local
Government Design Bulletin 14
HMSO, London, 1968

93725 Co-ordination of components in
housing: Metric dimensional
framework
Ministry of Housing and Local
Government Design Bulletin 16
HMSO, London, 1968

93726 Housing single people: 1 How they
live at present
Department of the Environment
Design Bulletin 23
HMSO, London, 1971

93727 Housing single people: 2 A design guide with a description of a scheme at Leicester
Department of the Environment
Design Bulletin 29
HMSO, London, 1974

93728 Residential access roads and footpaths
Department of the Environment
Design Bulletin to be published by HMSO, London, 1976 or 1977

9373 Housing: Other references

93730 The housing situation in 1960:
P G Gray, R Russell
(Government Social Survey)
Central Office of Information, London, 1962

93731 Houses and people
W V Hole, J J Attenburrow
Ministry of Technology Building Research Station
HMSO, London, 1966

93732 Housing (Woningbouw):
Functional principles of housing
Bouwcentrum, Rotterdam, Holland, 1961

93733 Metric house shells: Two storey plans
National Building Agency architectural division
National Building Agency, London, 1969

93734 Single storey housing: Design guide
National Building Agency architectural division
National Building Agency, London, 1971

9374 Building types

93740 Community homes design guide
Department of Health and Social Security Advisory Council on Child Care
HMSO, London, 1971

93741 Boarding schools for maladjusted children
Department of Education and Science Building Bulletin 27
HMSO, London, 1965

93742 Public indoor swimming pools
Sports Council Technical Unit for Sport Bulletin 1
HMSO, London, 1973

93743 Bletchley leisure centre: Building study
G Perrin (appraisal)
Architects' Journal, 11 July 1973, p79

93744 Cheetham Crumpsall Abraham Moss Centre, Manchester
Department of Education and Science Building Bulletin 49
HMSO, London, 1973

93745 Hostels for young people
Department of Health and Social Security Development Group, Social Work Service
HMSO, London, 1975

9375 Psychology, sociology

93750 Asylums: Essays on the social situation of mental patients and other inmates
E Goffman
Penguin, Harmondsworth, 1968

93751 Stigma: Notes on the management of spoiled identity
E Goffman
Penguin, Harmondsworth, 1968

93752 Psychology and architectural determinism
T Lee
Architects' Journal: (1) 4 August 1971, p253; (2) 1 September 1971, p475; (3) 22 September 1971, p651

93753 The social minority
P Townsend
Allen Lane, London, 1973

93754 The sociological tradition
R A Nisbet
Heinemann, London, 1967

9376 Ergonomics and anthropometrics: General

93760 The measure of man: Human factors in design
H Dreyfuss
Whitney Library of Design, New York, USA, 1959

93761 A guide to user activity measurement in health buildings
Department of Health and Social Security Health Service Design Note 3
HMSO, London, 1969

93762 Anthropometrics for designers
J Croney
Batsford, London, 1971

93763 Anatomical, physiological and anthropometric principles in the design of office chairs and tables
W F Floyd, D F Roberts
BS3044:1958
British Standards Institution, London, 1958

93764 Anthropometry of British women
D Thompson and others
Institute for Consumer Ergonomics, Loughborough, 1973

93765 Ergonomic techniques in the determination of optimum work surface heights
J S Ward
Applied Ergonomics (Ergonomics Research Society), 3 September 1971, p171

93766 Behaviour and the physical environment: Case studies in psychology and ergonomics
H C W Stockbridge
Batsford, London, 1975

9377 Accidents in the home

93770 Safety in the home
A S Acland
Ministry of Housing and Local Government Design Bulletin 13
HMSO, London, 1967

93771 Falls on stairs: An epidemiological study of accidents (English translation circulated privately)
L Svanström
Lund University, Sweden, 1973

93772 Accidents in the home: A BMA report including a survey on non-fatal domestic accidents
British Medical Association, London, 1964

93773 A study of home accidents in Aberdeen
I A G MacQueen
E and S Livingstone, Edinburgh, 1960

93774 On the natural history of falls in old age
J H Sheldon
British Medical Journal, 10 December 1960, p1685

93775 Accidental coal gas poisoning
H D Chalke, J R Dewhurst
British Medical Journal, 19 October 1957, p915

93776 Safety in domestic buildings
Building Research Station Digests 43, 44
HMSO, London, 1964

9378 Demography

93780 Population projections No 2
1971–2011
Office of Population Census and
Surveys (Government Actuary)
HMSO, London, 1974

93781 The Registrar General's Quarterly
Return for England and Wales:
Quarter ended 31 March 1974
Office of Population Censuses and
Surveys
HMSO, London, 1974

93782 Census 1971: England and Wales:
County report: Essex: Part 1
Office of Population Censuses and
Surveys
HMSO, London, 1972

93783 Census 1971: England and Wales:
County report: Hampshire: Part 1
Office of Population Censuses and
Surveys
HMSO, London, 1972

93784 Registrar General's Statistical
Review of England and Wales for
the year 1963
Part III, Commentary
HMSO, London, 1966

93785 Variant population projections
1974–2011
Office of Population Censuses and
Surveys
HMSO, London, 1975

9379 Extraneous references

93790 Care and treatment in a planned
environment: A report on the
community homes project
Home Office Advisory Council on
Child Care
HMSO, London, 1970

93791 Education: A framework for
expansion
Department of Education and
Science
HMSO, London, 1973

93792 Rate fund expenditure and rate
calls in 1974–75
Joint circular from the Department
of the Environment (19/74), Home
Office, Department of Health and
Social Security, Department of
Education and Science, and Welsh
Office
HMSO, London, 1974

93793 The traffic signs regulations and
general directions 1975
Statutory Instruments 1975 no 1536
HMSO, London, 1975

93794 Road casualties in Great Britain
1974
Department of the Environment
HMSO, London, 1976

93795 Local authority expenditure in
1976–77: Forward planning
Joint circular from the Department
of the Environment (88/75), Home
Office, Department of Health and
Social Security, Department of
Education and Science, and Welsh
Office
HMSO, London, 1975

**938 Building regulations, building
elements, services installations**

9380 Building regulations

93800 The Building Regulations 1972
Statutory Instruments 1972 no 317
HMSO, London, 1972

93801 The Building (First Amendment)
Regulations 1973
Statutory Instruments 1973 no 1276
HMSO, London 1973

93802 The Building (Third Amendment)
Regulations 1975
Statutory Instruments 1975 no 1370
HMSO, London, 1975

93803 Encyclopedia of the law of town and
country planning
ed D Heap
Sweet and Maxwell, London, 1959
with subsequent insertions

93804 Constructional by-laws
London Building Acts 1930–39,
London Building (Constructional)
By-laws 1972
Greater London Council, London,
1973

93805 Places of public entertainment:
Technical regulations
Publication 378
Greater London Council, London,
1972

93806 GLC Code of practice means of
escape in case of fire
Publication 572
Greater London Council, London,
1974

9381 Regulations relating to fire

93810 Guide to the Fire Precautions Act
1971, 1 Hotels and boarding houses
Home Office/Scottish Home and
Health Department
HMSO, London, 1972

93811 The Fire Precautions (Hotels and
Boarding Houses) Order 1972
Statutory Instruments 1972 No 238
Home Office, London, 1972

93812 Precautions against fire: Flats and
maisonettes (in blocks over two
storeys)
British Standard Code of Practice
CP3: Chapter IV: Part I: 1971
British Standards Institution,
London, 1971

93813 Precautions against fire: Shops and departmental stores
British Standard Code of Practice
CP3: Chapter IV: Part 2 (1968)
British Standards Institution, London, 1968

93814 Precautions against fire: Office buildings
British Standard Code of Practice
CP3: Chapter IV: Part 3 (1968)
British Standards Institution, London, 1968

93815 How the Fire Precautions Act affects the architect
A C Parnell, W J Smith, A E Anderson
Architects' Journal: (1) 14 June 1972, p1339; (2) 21 June 1972, p1393; (3) 28 June 1972, p1453; (4) 5 July 1972, p37

93816 Fire safety and the disabled
S Simpson
Central Council for the Disabled, London, 1975

93817 Fire safety for the handicapped
Report of Edinburgh University seminar, 21 March 1975
ed E W Marchant
University of Edinburgh Centre for Industrial Consultancy and Liaison, Edinburgh, 1975

9382 Stairs, ramps

93820 Optimum dimensions for domestic stairways: A preliminary study
J Ward, P Randall
Architects' Journal, 5 July 1967, p29

93821 Optimum dimensions for domestic staircases
J Ward, B Beadling
Architects' Journal, 25 February 1970, p513

93822 Steps and lifts
S Alenmark
Build International, Rotterdam, Holland, January 1971, p22

93823 Association for rationalisation: Man and work booklet no 2
E A Muller, H Spitzer
Oldenburg, Munich, 1952

93824 A study to determine the specifications of wheelchair ramps
C D Elmer
(unpublished) University of Iowa, 1957

9383 Windows, doors

93830 The lighting of dwellings for old people: Report of the joint committee of the Medical Research Council and the Building Research Board on lighting and vision
The Medical Officer, 13 October 1961, p230

93831 Specification for internal and external wood doorsets, doorleaves and frames
BS4787: Part 1: 1972
British Standards Institution, London, 1972

93832 Door handles for the disabled: An assessment of their suitability
P J R Nichols
Annals of Physical Medicine, February 1966, p180

93833 AJ handbook ironmongery
G Underwood, J Planck
Architects' Journal, instalments commencing 28 May 1975, p1147

9384 Internal walls, floor finishes

93840 Performance requirements for partitions
Interdepartmental sub-committee for component co-ordination technical note 3
Department of the Environment, London, 1970

93841 Floors
AJ building enclosure handbook
Architects' Journal, 4 October 1967, p875

93842 Some thermal characteristics of enclosing surfaces
J K Page
Architects' Journal, 19 June 1963, p1311

9385 Heating services

93850 The disabled user: Gas fires
RICA comparative test report no 7
National Fund for Research into Crippling Diseases, Horsham, 1970

93851 Heating for old people: Some conclusions based on their experience of floor warming
F W Black
Building Research Station current papers series 19
HMSO, London, 1966

93852 Human factors in heating
F A Chrenko
Design magazine: (1) September 1962, p63; (2) October 1962, p50

93853 The effects of the temperature of the floor surface and of the air on thermal sensations and on the skin temperature of the feet
F A Chrenko
British Journal of Industrial Medicine, January 1957, p13

93854 A British unit for severely retarded defectives
J V Morris, G Aldis
American Journal for Mental Deficiency, vol 60 1955, p265

93855 Heated ceilings and comfort
F A Chrenko
Institution of Heating and Ventilating Engineers Journal, vol 29 1953, p365

93856 Human thermal comfort
J K Page
Architects' Journal, 19 June 1963, p1301

93857 Heating and air conditioning of buildings (4th edition)
O Faber, J R Kell
Architectural Press, London, 1966

93858 A guide to current practice 1959
Institution of Heating and Ventilating Engineers, London, 1959

9386 Electrical services, lighting

93860 Electric socket heights
Which? Consumers' Association, September 1971, p273

93861 Socket heights
Which?, Consumers' Association, November 1972, p328

93862 Socket outlets in public authority housing: Building Research Station report on tenant requirements
J Crisp, K J Noble
Electrical Times, 12 November 1959

93863 The IES code: Recommendations for good interior lighting
Illuminating Engineering Society, London, 1961

93864 Architectural physics: Lighting
R G Hopkinson
HMSO, London, 1963

93865 Artificial lighting
P Jay and others
Architects' Journal, 4 January
1967, p13

93866 Lighting
D Phillips
Macdonald/Council of Industrial
Design, London, 1966

9387 Sanitary services

93870 Services for housing: Sanitary
plumbing and drainage
D Cassels
Department of the Environment
Design Bulletin 30
HMSO, London, 1974

9388 Communications services

93880 Equipment for the disabled:
1 Communication
ed E R Wilshere, E M Hollings,
P J R Nichols
National Fund for Research into
Crippling Diseases, London, 1971

93881 Evaluation of alarm systems for the
elderly and handicapped: Interim
report
Institute for Consumer Ergonomics,
Loughborough, 1973

93882 Alarm systems for elderly and
disabled people
R J Feeney, M D Galer,
M M Gallagher
Institute for Consumer Ergonomics,
Loughborough, 1975

93883 Internal communications in old
people's housing
Local Government Chronicle,
23 May 1970, p1043

93884 Alarm systems in sheltered housing
R Carver
Voluntary Housing, Winter 1972,
p26

9389 Lifts

93890 A specification for lifts, escalators,
passenger conveyors and
paternosters: Part 3 Arrangement
of standard electric lifts
BS2655: Part 3: 1971
British Standards Institution,
London, 1971

93891 Lift operation and computers
H Parlow
Architects' Journal, 23 March 1960,
p747

93892 The development and effects of an
inexpensive elevator for
eliminating architectural barriers
in public buildings
H E Yuker, A Cohn, M A Feldman
Hofstra University, Hempstead,
New York, USA, 1966

93893 Mechanical circulation: People
AJ information sheet circulation 6
Architects' Journal, 25 March 1970,
p767

93894 Draft British Standard
Specification for passenger lift
installations: Part 1 Residential
buildings. Definitions, functional
dimensions and modulor
co-ordination dimensions (ISO/DIS
357/1)
(unplublished) British Standards
Institution, London, 1975

939 General spaces

9390 Kitchens: General: Sources in
Britain

93900 Spaces in the home: Kitchens and
laundering spaces
Department of the Environment
Design Bulletin 24 Part 2
HMSO, London, 1972

93901 Recommendations for provision of
space for domestic kitchen
equipment
BS3705:1972
HMSO, London, 1972

93902 Kitchen fitments and equipment
BS1195:1972
British Standards Institution,
London, 1972

93903 British standard specification for
kitchen equipment
ISO/DIS 3055
(draft) British Standards
Institution, 1973

93904 Kitchen worktop heights
N Sheppard, C Mahaddie
Architects' Journal, 30 September
1970, p787

93905 The determination of optimum
working surface heights by
electromyographic and other
psycho-physiological techniques
with particular reference to interior
domestic design
B Saville
(unpublished pieces) Loughborough
University of Technology,
Department of Ergonomics and
Cybernetics, 1969

93906 Contents of the kitchen: Report of
working party of Council of
Scientific Management in the Home
Architects' Journal, 8 September
1965, p545

93907 The kitchen
J E Walley
Constable, London, 1960

93908 Kitchen storage: What the
housewife needs and what she
thinks she wants
J E Walley
Housing Review, July-August 1961,
p102

93909 Kitchens (2nd edition)
J Prizeman
Macdonald/Council of Industrial
Design, London, 1970

9391 Kitchens: General: Sources outside Britain

93910 Kök-planering, inredning
Konsumentinstitutet, Stockholm, Sweden, 1972

93911 Kitchen layouts: Draft for equipment dimensions and plan types (Swedish text, English summary)
A Thiberg
National Swedish Institute for Building Research, Stockholm, 1968

93912 Functional studies of kitchens (Swedish text, English summary)
National Swedish Institute for Consumer Information, Stockholm, 1969

93913 The kitchen: Function and layout
F A Bosma
MV Philips Gloeilampenfabrieken, Eindhoven, Holland, 1965

9392 Kitchens for disabled people: Sources in Britain

93920 A pilot study of disabled housewives in their kitchens
P M Howie
Disabled Living Activities Group, London, 1968

93921 Disabled housewives in their kitchens: A series of one-day conferences, June 1969
Disabled Living Foundation, London, 1969

93922 The disabled user: Refrigerators
RICA comparative test report no 1
National Fund for Research into Crippling Diseases, Horsham, 1969

93923 The disabled user: Cookers
RICA comparative test report no 5
National Fund for Research into Crippling Diseases, Horsham, 1970

93924 List of kitchen equipment: A guide towards choosing equipment for the physically handicapped
Disabled Living Foundation, London, 1967

9393 Kitchens for disabled people: Sources outside Britain

93930 Normalkôket och de rörelsehinderade: 1 Köksstudier med rörelsehinderade personer
B Brax, J Paulsson, L Sperling
Gothenburg University, Sweden, 1973

93931 Normalköket och de rorelsehinderade: 2 Planeringsanvisningar och tillämpningsexempel
J Paulsson
Gothenburg University, Sweden 1973

93932 Köks och inredningsenheter, typ: SVCR för special och normalbostäder
Bröderna Granberg Snickeri AB, Norrköping, Sweden, 1973

93933 Küchen für Verfehrte (Kitchens for disabled persons – summary in English)
H Pauleit
Die moderne küche, Darmstadt, West Germany, September–October 1971, p9

93934 General lines in designs of dwellings for handicapped confined to wheelchairs: Part 2
V Leschly, A and B Kjaer
Polio Institute, Hellerup, Denmark, 1960

93935 Kitchens for women in wheelchairs
H E McCullough, M B Farnham
University of Illinois, Champaign-Urbana, USA, 1961

93936 Space and design requirements for wheelchair kitchens
H E McCullough, M B Farnham
University of Illinois, Champaign-Urbana, USA, 1960

93937 Planning kitchens for handicapped homemakers
V H Wheeler
Institute of Physical Medicine and Rehabilitation, New York, USA, 1966

93938 Kök även för handikappade
Informationsbladet B4:1975
J Paulsson
Svensk Byggtjänst, Stockholm, 1976

9394 Living rooms

93940 Furniture design for the elderly
B Laging
Rehabilitation Literature, Chicago, USA, May 1966, p130

93941 Sitting at table
D Meade
Design magazine, February 1962, p60

9395 Bathrooms, wcs: General

93950 Spaces in the home: Bathrooms and wcs
Department of the Environment
Design Bulletin 24 Part 1
HMSO, London, 1972

93951 The bathroom, criteria for design
A Kira
Cornell University, Ithaca, New York, USA, 1966

93952 Code of practice for sanitary appliances: Part 1 Selection, installation and special requirements
CP305:1974
British Standards Institution, London, 1974

93953 The ergonomics of wc pans
I L McClelland
Institute for Consumer Ergonomics, Loughborough, 1973

93954 Cast iron baths for domestic purposes
BS1189:1971
British Standards Institution, London, 1971

93955 Bath and bedroom
R Dumas
Build International, Rotterdam, Holland, January 1971, p24

93956 Sanitary fittings
M Withers
RIBA Journal, September 1974, p24

9396 Bathrooms, wcs: Disabled people

93960 Housing for the disabled: Part 2 An ergonomic study of the space requirements of wheelchair users for bathrooms
A Ownsworth, M Galer, R J Feeney
Institute for Consumer Ergonomics, Loughborough, 1974

93961 The disabled user, bath aids
RICA comparative test report no 13
National Fund for Research into Crippling Diseases, Horsham, 1973

93962 Bath aids for the disabled
I L McClelland
Institute for Consumer Ergonomics, Loughborough, 1972

93963 An investigation into the optimum position of hand rails around the bath for the disabled and debilitated subject
P M Bretten
(unpublished report) Loughborough University of Technology, 1971

93964 Sluices and their environment in
centres for severely disabled people
Design Guide No 1
Spastics Society, London, 1972

93965 Hygienutrymmen, Planering med
hänsyn till rörelsehindrade
(Sanitary rooms, Planning with
respect to the needs of the
handicapped)
E Andrén, B Petersson
Department of Handicap Research,
Gothenburg University, Sweden,
Part 1, 1974: Part 2, 1975

9397   Storage

93970 Clothes storage for the disabled
J Barden
British Hospital Journal and Social
Service Review, 12 June 1970

93971 An ergonomic evaluation of
domestic storage facilities
D Thompson
Institute for Consumer Ergonomics,
Loughborough, 1973

93972 Human energy expenditures as
criteria for the design of household
storage facilities
J L Pound
Architects' Journal, 16 October
1963, p817

93973 Skåp (Domestic storage furniture –
Swedish text)
E Berglund
Svenska Slöjdföreningen,
Stockholm, Sweden, 1960

9398   Garaging

93980 Cars in housing 2
Ministry of Housing and Local
Government Design Bulletin 12
HMSO, London, 1967

93981 Automatic garage doors
O A Denly
The Magic Carpet (Disabled
Drivers' Association): (1) Autumn
1964, p74; (2) Winter 1964, p7

9399   Gardens, external spaces

93990 The easy path to gardening
A S White and others
Readers Digest
Association/Disabled Living
Foundation, London, 1972

93991 Gardening for the elderly and
handicapped
L Snook
Pan, London, 1968

93992 Gardening for the handicapped
B Massingham
Shire Publications, Aylesbury, 1972

93993 Outdoor recreation planning for the
handicapped
Bureau of Outdoor Recreation
Technical Assistants' Bulletin
US Government Printing Office,
Washington DC, USA, 1967

93994 Guide book on the design of
exterior site facilities in order to
make them usable by the
handicapped
J Jorgensen
Department of Housing and Urban
Development, Washington DC,
USA, 1973

93995 Design and detail of the space
between buildings
E Beazley
Architectural Press, London, 1960

93996 Equipment for the disabled:
6 Leisure and gardening
ed E R Wilshere, E M Hollings,
P J R Nichols
National Fund for Research into
Crippling Diseases, Horsham, 1973

93997 Barrier free site design
US Department of Housing and
Urban Development
Office of Policy Development and
Research, Washington DC, USA,
1975

93998 Trends for the handicapped
Division of Federal State and
Private Liaison
Trends, National Park Service,
Washington DC, USA, July-
September 1974

This section lists agencies who may usefully be able to advise on environmental and related services for disabled people. Addresses and telephone numbers have been checked in April 1976; where there are doubts about their continued reliability enquirers are advised to check with the information officer of the Disabled Living Foundation.

940 Britain: Voluntary and professional agencies

Action for Research into Multiple Sclerosis
71 Grays Inn Road, London WC1X 8TR
01–568 2255 (counselling service)

Age Concern
Bernard Sunley House, 60 Pitcairn Road, Mitcham, Surrey CR4 3LL
01–640 5431

Association for Research into Restricted Growth
4 Laburnum Avenue, Wickford, Essex
037 44 3132

Association for Spina Bifida and Hydrocephalus
30 Devonshire Street, London W1N 2EB
01–486 6100

Association of Disabled Professionals
c/o British Council for Rehabilitation of the Disabled; see Central Council for the Disabled.

British Association of Occupational Therapists
20 Rede Place, London W2 4TU
01 229 9738

British Epilepsy Association
3–6 Alfred Place, London WC1E 7ED
01–580 2704

British Polio Fellowship
Bell Close, West End Road, Ruislip, Middlesex
089 56 75515

British Red Cross Society
9 Grosvenor Crescent, London SW1X 7EJ
01–235 5454

British Rheumatism and Arthritis Association
1 Devonshire Place, London W1N 2BD
01–935 9905

British Sports Association for the Disabled
Stoke Mandeville Stadium, Harvey Road, Aylesbury, Bucks
0296 84848

Brittle Bone Society
63 Byron Crescent, Dundee DD3 6SS
0382 87130

Campaign for the Mentally Handicapped
96 Portland Place, London W1N 4EX
01–636 5020

Central Council for the Disabled
34 Eccleston Square, London SW1V 1PE
01–821 1871
(a move is anticipated during 1976 to 23—25 Mortimer Street, London W1A 4QW, subsequent to a merger with the British Council for Rehabilitation of the Disabled)

Centre on Environment for the Handicapped
120–126 Albert Street, London NW1 7NE
01–267 6112

Chartered Society of Physiotherapy
14 Bedford Row, London WC1R 4ED
01–242 1941

Chest and Heart Association
Tavistock House (North), Tavistock Square, London WC1H 9JE
01–387 3012

Disabled Living Foundation
346 Kensington High Street, London W14 8NS
01–602 2491

Dr Barnardo's
Tanners Lane, Barkingside, Ilford, Essex IG6 1QG
01–550 8822

Handicapped Adventure Playground Association
3 Oakley Gardens, London SW3
01-352 2321

Help the Aged
8–10 Denman Street, London W1A 2AP
01–437 2554

Invalid Childrens Aid Association
126 Buckingham Palace Road, London SW1W 9SB
01–730 9891

Joint Committee on Mobility for the Disabled
14 Birch Way, Warlingham, Surrey
088 32 3801

Kings Fund Centre
120–126 Albert Street, London NW1 7NE
01–267 6112

Leonard Cheshire Foundation
7 Market Mews, London W1Y 8HD
01–499 2665

Multiple Sclerosis Society of Great Britain and Northern Ireland
4 Tachbrook Street, London SW1V 1SJ
01–834 8231

Muscular Dystrophy Group of Great Britain
Nattrass House, 35 Macaulay Road, London SW4 0QP
01–720 8055

National Association for Mental Health (Mind)
22 Harley Street, London W1N 2ED
01–637 0741

National Corporation for the Care of Old People
Nuffield Lodge, Regent's Park, London NW1 4RS
01–722 8871

National Fund for Research into Crippling Diseases (Action Research for the Crippled Child)
Vincent House, 1a Springfield Road, Horsham, West Sussex RH12 2PN
0403 64101

National Society for Mentallly Handicapped Children
Pembridge Hall, 17 Pembridge Square, London W2 4EP
01–229 8941

Parkinson's Disease Society of the United Kingdom
81 Queen's Road, Wimbledon, London SW19 8LR
01–946 2500

Partially Sighted Society
3 Charles Close, Hove, Sussex

Royal National Institute for the Blind
224 Great Portland Street, London W1N 6AA
01–388 1266

Royal National Institute for the Deaf
105 Gower Street, London WC1E 6AH
01–387 8033

Scottish Council on Disability
18 Claremont Crescent, Edinburgh EH7 4QD
031 556 3882

Spastics Society
12 Park Crescent, London W1N 4EQ
01–636 5020

Spinal Injuries Association
120–126 Albert Street, London NW1 7NE
01–267 6112

Wales Council for the Disabled
Crescent Road, Caerphilly, Mid Glamorgan CF8 1XL
0222 869224

941 Britain: Governmental agencies

Department of Education and Science
Elizabeth House, York Road,
London SE1 7PH
01–928 9222

Department of Employment
(Disabled Persons Branch)
168 Regent Street, London W1R 5TB
01–214 6000

Department of the Environment
(Policy divisions)
2 Marsham Street, London SW1P 3EB
01–212 3434

Department of the Environment
(Housing Development Directorate,
Building Regulations Directorate)
Becket House, Lambeth Palace Road,
London SE1 7ER
01–928 7855

Department of the Environment
(Property Services Agency)
Lunar House, 40 Wellesley Road,
Croydon CR9 2EL
01–686 3499

Department of Health and Social Security
(Policy divisions)
Alexander Fleming House, Elephant and
Castle, London SE1 6BY
01–407 5522

Department of Health and Social Security
(Architect's department)
Euston Tower, 286 Euston Road,
London NW1 3DN
01–388 1188

Home office
(Fire Department)
Horseferry House, Dean Ryle Street,
London SW1 2AW
01–211 3000

Housing Corporation
Sloane Square House, London SW1W 8NT
01–730 9991

Scottish Office
(Health department)
Scottish Home and Health Department,
St Andrew's House, Edinburgh EH1 3DD
031 556 8501

Scottish Office
(Housing department)
Scottish Development Department,
80–83 Princes Street,
Edinburgh EH2 2HH
031 226 3781

Scottish Office
(Social Work Services Group)
Scottish Education Department,
St Andrew's House,
Edinburgh EH1 3DD
031 556 8501

Welsh Office
(Housing administration, Architect's
department)
Oxford House, Hills Road,
Cardiff CF1 2SY
0222 44171

Welsh Office
(Local authority social services)
Pearl Assurance House, Greyfriars Road,
Cardiff CF1 3RT
0222 44151

942 International agencies

International Commission on
Technical Aids
Fack – 161 03, Bromma 3, Sweden
08– 87 01 70

Rehabilitation International
20 West 40th Street, New York,
NY 10018, USA
(212) 869.9907

The conversion tables in this section list the Imperial equivalents of metric measures noted in sections 11–90.

950 Length

Conversion factors: 1·000m = 39·37in; 1in = 25·4mm
Equivalents of measures below 0·100 are rounded to the nearest $\frac{1}{8}$in; between 0·100 and 2·000 to the nearest $\frac{1}{4}$in, and above 2·000 to the nearest 1in.

m	in
0·005	$\frac{1}{4}$
0·0075	$\frac{1}{4}$
0·010	$\frac{3}{8}$
0·012	$\frac{1}{2}$
0·013	$\frac{1}{2}$
0·015	$\frac{5}{8}$
0·019	$\frac{3}{4}$
0·020	$\frac{3}{4}$
0·024	1
0·025	1
0·030	$1\frac{1}{8}$
0·032	$1\frac{1}{4}$
0·035	$1\frac{3}{8}$
0·038	$1\frac{1}{2}$
0·040	$1\frac{5}{8}$
0·044	$1\frac{3}{4}$
0·045	$1\frac{3}{4}$
0·050	2
0·052	2
0·055	$2\frac{1}{8}$
0·060	$2\frac{3}{8}$
0·065	$2\frac{1}{2}$
0·070	$2\frac{3}{4}$
0·075	3
0·076	3
0·080	$3\frac{1}{8}$
0·085	$3\frac{3}{8}$
0·090	$3\frac{1}{2}$
0·095	$3\frac{3}{4}$
0·100	4
0·110	$4\frac{1}{4}$
0·113	$4\frac{1}{2}$
0·114	$4\frac{1}{2}$
0·115	$4\frac{1}{2}$
0·120	$4\frac{3}{4}$
0·121	$4\frac{3}{4}$
0·125	5
0·127	5
0·130	5
0·135	$5\frac{1}{4}$
0·138	$5\frac{1}{2}$
0·140	$5\frac{1}{2}$
0·145	$5\frac{3}{4}$
0·149	$5\frac{3}{4}$
0·150	6
0·155	6

m	ft	in
0·160		$6\frac{1}{4}$
0·163		$6\frac{1}{2}$
0·165		$6\frac{1}{2}$
0·170		$6\frac{3}{4}$
0·175		7
0·180		7
0·185		$7\frac{1}{4}$
0·186		$7\frac{1}{4}$
0·190		$7\frac{1}{2}$
0·200		$7\frac{3}{4}$
0·205		8
0·210		$8\frac{1}{4}$
0·215		$8\frac{1}{2}$
0·217		$8\frac{1}{2}$
0·220		$8\frac{3}{4}$
0·225		9
0·230		9
0·240		$9\frac{1}{2}$
0·245		$9\frac{3}{4}$
0·250		$9\frac{3}{4}$
0·255		10
0·258		$10\frac{1}{4}$
0·260		$10\frac{1}{4}$
0·265		$10\frac{1}{2}$
0·270		$10\frac{3}{4}$
0·275		$10\frac{3}{4}$
0·280		11
0·290		$11\frac{1}{2}$
0·292		$11\frac{1}{2}$
0·300		$11\frac{3}{4}$
0·305	1	0
0·310	1	$0\frac{1}{4}$
0·320	1	$0\frac{1}{2}$
0·330	1	1
0·335	1	$1\frac{1}{4}$
0·340	1	$1\frac{1}{2}$
0·350	1	$1\frac{3}{4}$
0·355	1	2
0·360	1	$2\frac{1}{4}$
0·370	1	$2\frac{1}{2}$
0·375	1	$2\frac{3}{4}$
0·378	1	3

m	ft	in
0·380	1	3
0·381	1	3
0·390	1	$3\frac{1}{4}$
0·394	1	$3\frac{1}{2}$
0·400	1	$3\frac{3}{4}$
0·405	1	4
0·406	1	4
0·410	1	$4\frac{1}{4}$
0·420	1	$4\frac{1}{2}$
0·425	1	$4\frac{3}{4}$
0·430	1	5
0·435	1	$5\frac{1}{4}$
0·440	1	$5\frac{1}{4}$
0·445	1	$5\frac{1}{2}$
0·450	1	$5\frac{3}{4}$
0·455	1	6
0·457	1	6
0·460	1	6
0·465	1	$6\frac{1}{4}$
0·470	1	$6\frac{1}{2}$
0·475	1	$6\frac{3}{4}$
0·476	1	$6\frac{3}{4}$
0·480	1	7
0·483	1	7
0·485	1	7
0·490	1	$7\frac{1}{4}$
0·495	1	$7\frac{1}{2}$
0·497	1	$7\frac{1}{2}$
0·500	1	$7\frac{3}{4}$
0·508	1	8
0·510	1	8
0·520	1	$8\frac{1}{2}$
0·530	1	$8\frac{3}{4}$
0·533	1	9
0·535	1	9
0·540	1	$9\frac{1}{4}$
0·545	1	$9\frac{1}{2}$
0·550	1	$9\frac{3}{4}$
0·555	1	$9\frac{3}{4}$
0·557	1	10
0·560	1	10
0·565	1	$10\frac{1}{4}$
0·570	1	$10\frac{1}{2}$
0·575	1	$10\frac{3}{4}$
0·579	1	$10\frac{3}{4}$
0·580	1	$10\frac{3}{4}$
0·584	1	11
0·590	1	$11\frac{1}{4}$
0·595	1	$11\frac{1}{2}$
0·600	1	$11\frac{1}{2}$
0·605	1	$11\frac{3}{4}$
0·606	1	$11\frac{3}{4}$

m	ft	in
0·610	2	0
0·615	2	$0\frac{1}{4}$
0·620	2	$0\frac{1}{2}$
0·625	2	$0\frac{1}{2}$
0·630	2	$0\frac{3}{4}$
0·635	2	1
0·640	2	$1\frac{1}{4}$
0·645	2	$1\frac{1}{2}$
0·650	2	$1\frac{1}{2}$
0·655	2	$1\frac{3}{4}$
0·660	2	2
0·670	2	$2\frac{1}{2}$
0·675	2	$2\frac{1}{2}$
0·678	2	$2\frac{3}{4}$
0·680	2	$2\frac{3}{4}$
0·685	2	3
0·686	2	3
0·690	2	$3\frac{1}{4}$
0·693	2	$3\frac{1}{4}$
0·700	2	$3\frac{1}{2}$
0·705	2	$3\frac{3}{4}$
0·706	2	$3\frac{3}{4}$
0·710	2	4
0·711	2	4
0·714	2	4
0·715	2	$4\frac{1}{4}$
0·720	2	$4\frac{1}{4}$
0·721	2	$4\frac{1}{2}$
0·725	2	$4\frac{1}{2}$
0·726	2	$4\frac{1}{2}$
0·730	2	$4\frac{3}{4}$
0·733	2	5
0·735	2	5
0·740	2	$5\frac{1}{4}$
0·745	2	$5\frac{1}{4}$
0·750	2	$5\frac{1}{2}$
0·751	2	$5\frac{1}{2}$
0·755	2	$5\frac{3}{4}$
0·756	2	$5\frac{3}{4}$
0·760	2	6
0·762	2	6
0·766	2	$6\frac{1}{4}$
0·770	2	$6\frac{1}{4}$
0·775	2	$6\frac{1}{2}$
0·780	2	$6\frac{3}{4}$
0·787	2	7
0·790	2	7
0·795	2	$7\frac{1}{4}$
0·800	2	$7\frac{1}{2}$
0·805	2	$7\frac{3}{4}$
0·810	2	8
0·815	2	8

m	ft	in
0·820	2	$8\frac{1}{4}$
0·825	2	$8\frac{1}{2}$
0·826	2	$8\frac{1}{2}$
0·830	2	$8\frac{3}{4}$
0·835	2	$8\frac{3}{4}$
0·837	2	9
0·838	2	9
0·840	2	9
0·845	2	$9\frac{1}{4}$
0·850	2	$9\frac{1}{2}$
0·855	2	$9\frac{3}{4}$
0·860	2	$9\frac{3}{4}$
0·864	2	10
0·870	2	$10\frac{1}{4}$
0·880	2	$10\frac{3}{4}$
0·883	2	$10\frac{3}{4}$
0·885	2	$10\frac{3}{4}$
0·890	2	11
0·895	2	$11\frac{1}{4}$
0·900	2	$11\frac{1}{2}$
0·910	2	$11\frac{3}{4}$
0·914	3	0
0·915	3	0
0·920	3	$0\frac{1}{4}$
0·923	3	$0\frac{1}{4}$
0·925	3	$0\frac{1}{2}$
0·926	3	$0\frac{1}{2}$
0·930	3	$0\frac{1}{2}$
0·935	3	$0\frac{3}{4}$
0·940	3	1
0·945	3	$1\frac{1}{4}$
0·947	3	$1\frac{1}{4}$
0·950	3	$1\frac{1}{2}$
0·955	3	$1\frac{1}{2}$
0·960	3	$1\frac{3}{4}$
0·965	3	2
0·967	3	2
0·970	3	$2\frac{1}{4}$
0·973	3	$2\frac{1}{4}$
0·975	3	$2\frac{1}{2}$
0·980	3	$2\frac{1}{2}$
0·985	3	$2\frac{3}{4}$
0·990	3	3
0·995	3	$3\frac{1}{4}$
0·998	3	$3\frac{1}{4}$
1·000	3	$3\frac{1}{4}$
1·010	3	$3\frac{3}{4}$
1·013	3	4
1·014	3	4
1·015	3	4
1·020	3	$4\frac{1}{4}$
1·025	3	$4\frac{1}{4}$
1·030	3	$4\frac{1}{2}$
1·035	3	$4\frac{3}{4}$
1·036	3	$4\frac{3}{4}$
1·040	3	5
1·050	3	$5\frac{1}{4}$
1·060	3	$5\frac{3}{4}$
1·065	3	6
1·067	3	6
1·070	3	$6\frac{1}{4}$
1·073	3	$6\frac{1}{4}$
1·075	3	$6\frac{1}{4}$
1·080	3	$6\frac{1}{2}$
1·085	3	$6\frac{3}{4}$
1·090	3	7
1·099	3	$7\frac{1}{4}$
1·100	3	$7\frac{1}{4}$
1·110	3	$7\frac{3}{4}$
1·115	3	8
1·120	3	8
1·125	3	$8\frac{1}{4}$
1·130	3	$8\frac{1}{2}$
1·140	3	9
1·150	3	$9\frac{1}{4}$
1·153	3	$9\frac{1}{2}$
1·155	3	$9\frac{1}{2}$
1·156	3	$9\frac{1}{2}$
1·160	3	$9\frac{3}{4}$
1·165	3	$9\frac{3}{4}$
1·170	3	10
1·175	3	$10\frac{1}{4}$
1·189	3	$10\frac{3}{4}$
1·190	3	$10\frac{3}{4}$
1·192	3	11
1·195	3	11
1·200	3	$11\frac{1}{4}$
1·205	3	$11\frac{1}{2}$
1·210	3	$11\frac{3}{4}$
1·214	3	$11\frac{3}{4}$
1·215	3	$11\frac{3}{4}$
1·220	4	0
1·225	4	$0\frac{1}{4}$
1·230	4	$0\frac{1}{2}$
1·235	4	$0\frac{1}{2}$
1·240	4	$0\frac{3}{4}$
1·245	4	1
1·247	4	1
1·250	4	$1\frac{1}{4}$
1·255	4	$1\frac{1}{2}$
1·257	4	$1\frac{1}{2}$
1·270	4	2
1·272	4	2
1·275	4	$2\frac{1}{4}$
1·280	4	$2\frac{1}{2}$
1·285	4	$2\frac{1}{2}$
1·293	4	3
1·300	4	$3\frac{1}{4}$
1·312	4	$3\frac{3}{4}$
1·320	4	4
1·325	4	$4\frac{1}{4}$
1·330	4	$4\frac{1}{4}$
1·331	4	$4\frac{1}{2}$
1·335	4	$4\frac{1}{2}$
1·337	4	$4\frac{3}{4}$
1·340	4	$4\frac{3}{4}$
1·344	4	5
1·350	4	$5\frac{1}{4}$
1·355	4	$5\frac{1}{4}$
1·365	4	$5\frac{3}{4}$
1·368	4	$5\frac{3}{4}$
1·370	4	6
1·375	4	$6\frac{1}{4}$
1·385	4	$6\frac{1}{2}$
1·400	4	7
1·410	4	$7\frac{1}{2}$
1·415	4	$7\frac{3}{4}$
1·420	4	8
1·425	4	8
1·430	4	$8\frac{1}{4}$
1·435	4	$8\frac{1}{2}$
1·440	4	$8\frac{3}{4}$
1·445	4	9
1·450	4	9
1·458	4	$9\frac{1}{2}$
1·465	4	$9\frac{3}{4}$
1·475	4	10
1·478	4	$10\frac{1}{4}$
1·479	4	$10\frac{1}{4}$
1·500	4	11
1·509	4	$11\frac{1}{2}$
1·510	4	$11\frac{1}{2}$
1·520	4	$11\frac{3}{4}$
1·521	5	0
1·530	5	$0\frac{1}{4}$
1·540	5	$0\frac{3}{4}$
1·545	5	$0\frac{3}{4}$
1·550	5	1
1·555	5	$1\frac{1}{4}$
1·569	5	$1\frac{3}{4}$
1·570	5	$1\frac{3}{4}$
1·575	5	2
1·585	5	$2\frac{1}{2}$
1·588	5	$2\frac{1}{2}$
1·590	5	$2\frac{1}{2}$
1·595	5	$2\frac{3}{4}$
1·600	5	3
1·604	5	$3\frac{1}{4}$
1·605	5	$3\frac{1}{4}$
1·610	5	$3\frac{1}{2}$
1·612	5	$3\frac{1}{2}$
1·615	5	$3\frac{1}{2}$
1·617	5	$3\frac{3}{4}$
1·630	5	$4\frac{1}{4}$
1·635	5	$4\frac{1}{4}$
1·640	5	$4\frac{1}{2}$
1·645	5	$4\frac{3}{4}$
1·650	5	5
1·655	5	$5\frac{1}{4}$
1·660	5	$5\frac{1}{4}$
1·661	5	$5\frac{1}{2}$
1·690	5	$6\frac{1}{2}$
1·697	5	$6\frac{3}{4}$
1·700	5	7
1·710	5	$7\frac{1}{4}$
1·715	5	$7\frac{1}{2}$
1·725	5	8
1·730	5	8
1·740	5	$8\frac{1}{2}$
1·750	5	9
1·753	5	9
1·755	5	9
1·765	5	$9\frac{1}{2}$
1·770	5	$9\frac{3}{4}$
1·780	5	10
1·790	5	$10\frac{1}{2}$
1·795	5	$10\frac{3}{4}$
1·800	5	$10\frac{3}{4}$
1·810	5	$11\frac{1}{4}$
1·830	6	0
1·840	6	$0\frac{1}{2}$
1·855	6	1
1·860	6	$1\frac{1}{4}$
1·900	6	$2\frac{3}{4}$
1·910	6	$3\frac{1}{4}$
1·930	6	4
1·940	6	$4\frac{1}{2}$
1·945	6	$4\frac{1}{2}$
1·950	6	$4\frac{3}{4}$
1·965	6	$5\frac{1}{4}$
1·980	6	6

950 Length *continued*

m	ft in	m	ft in
2·000	6 6¾	4·200	13 9
2·010	6 7	4·215	13 10
2·040	6 8	4·220	13 10
2·050	6 9	4·260	14 0
		4·300	14 1
2·100	6 11	4·395	14 5
2·110	6 11		
2·130	7 0	4·420	14 6
2·200	7 3	4·500	14 9
2·240	7 4	4·525	14 10
		4·570	15 0
2·300	7 7	4·650	15 3
2·310	7 7		
2·400	7 10	4·750	15 7
2·430	8 0	4·780	15 8
2·440	8 0	4·800	15 9
		4·845	15 11
2·500	8 2	4·880	16 0
2·510	8 3	4·900	16 1
2·550	8 4		
2·600	8 6	5·000	16 5
2·670	8 9	5·100	16 9
		5·200	17 1
2·700	8 10	5·800	19 0
2·720	8 11		
2·770	9 1	6·000	19 8
2·800	9 2	6·200	20 4
2·850	9 4	7·010	23 0
2·900	9 6	7·520	24 8
2·970	9 9	7·670	25 2
3·000	9 10	8·000	26 3
3·055	10 0	9·000	29 6
3·060	10 0	9·100	29 10
3·100	10 2		
3·200	10 6	10·000	32 10
3·300	10 10	11·000	36 1
		12·000	39 4
3·400	11 2	12·200	40 0
3·500	11 6	12·500	41 0
3·600	11 10		
3·700	12 2	13·000	42 8
		14·000	45 11
3·840	12 7		
3·850	12 8	20·000	65 7
3·875	12 9	30·500	100 1
3·900	12 10	36·600	120 1
3·975	13 0	60·000	196 10
		300·000	984 3
4·000	13 1		
4·040	13 3		
4·075	13 4		
4·100	13 5		
4·120	13 6		

951 Area

Conversion factors: $1\text{m}^2 = 10\cdot764\text{ft}^2$; $1\text{ft}^2 = 0\cdot0929\text{m}^2$.

Equivalents are rounded to the nearest 1ft^2.

m²	ft²	m²	ft²
0·8	9	12·0	129
0·85	9	12·21	131
0·95	10	12·24	132
		13·0	140
1·2	13		
1·3	14	14·0	151
1·5	16	14·04	151
1·6	17	15·0	161
1·7	18	16·0	172
1·9	20	16·5	178
2·0	22	18·0	194
2·38	26	18·6	200
2·40	26	19·38	209
2·5	27		
		20·0	215
3·0	32	20·5	221
3·57	38	30·5	328
3·7	40	33·5	361
		35·0	377
4·0	43		
4·41	47	42·0	452
4·5	48	44·5	479
		46·0	495
5·1	55		
6·21	67	50·5	544
7·28	78	59·0	635
7·35	79	64·5	694
7·5	81	71·0	764
8·0	86	100·0	1076
8·5	91	500·0	5382
9·0	97	1000·0	10764
10·0	108		
10·56	114		
11·0	118		
11·5	124		
11·52	124		

952 Volume

Conversion factors: $1\text{m}^3 = 35\cdot31\text{ft}^3$; $1\text{ft}^3 = 0\cdot0283\text{m}^3$.

m³	ft³
0·07	2·5
1·7	60·0
2·3	81·2
2·5	88·3

953 Mass

Conversion factors: $1kg = 2.205lb$; $1lb = 0.454kg$.

kg	lb	kg	lb
1·7	3·7	300	661
2·4	5·3	400	882
4·0	8·8	450	992
50	110	600	1323
100	220	630	1389
110	243	750	1653
140	309	900	1984
150	331	1000	2205
159	350	1200	2646
160	353	1500	3307
180	397		

954 Mass per unit area

Conversion factors: $1kg/m^2 = 0.205lb/ft^2$;
$1lb/ft^2 = 4.882kg/m^2$.

kg/m²	lb/ft²
1·4	0·29

955 Pressure

Conversion factors: 1 kilonewton/m² = 0·145lb force/in²;
$1lbf/in^2 = 6.895kN/m^2$.

kN/m²	lbf/in²
140	20·3

956 Resistance

Conversion factors: 1 newton metre = 0·737lb force ft;
$1lbf\ ft = 1.356Nm$.

Nm	lbf ft
8·0	5·90
12·0	8·85
13·77	10·15
19·45	14·34
21·80	16·08

957 Temperature

Conversion factors: $1°C = 1.8°F$; $1°F = 0.556°C$.

°C	°F	°C	°F
−1	30	32	90
		34	93
4	39	35	95
13	55	37	99
15·6	60		
16	61	40	104
17	63	43	110
18	64	45	113
19	66	48	118
		49	120
21	70	50	122
22	72		
24	75		
26	79		
27·2	81		
28	82		
29	84		